The Tragedy of
Cambodian History

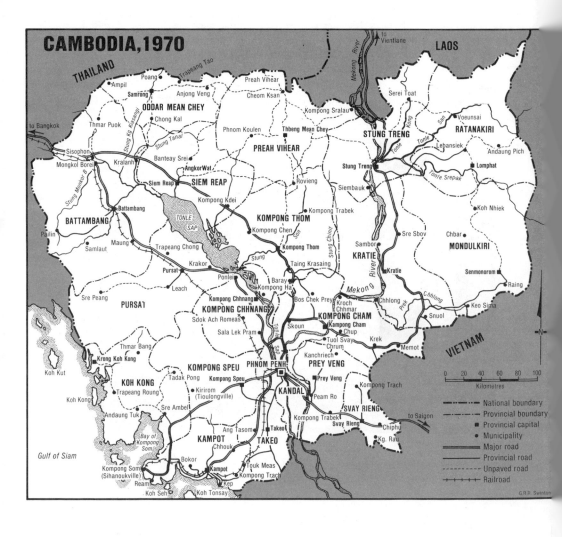

The Tragedy of Cambodian History

Politics, War, and Revolution since 1945

David P. Chandler

Yale University Press   New Haven and London

Published with assistance from the Kingsley Trust Association Publication Fund established by the Scroll and Key Society of Yale College.

Designed by James J. Johnson. Set in Iridium Roman and Icone types by The Composing Room of Michigan, Inc. Grand Rapids, Mich.

Printed in the United States of America by Vail-Ballou Press. Binghamton, N.Y.

Library of Congress Cataloging-in-Publication Data

Chandler, David P.
   The tragedy of Cambodian history: politics, war, and revolution since 1945 / David P. Chandler.
      p.   cm.
   Includes bibliographical references and index.
   ISBN 0-300-04919-6
   1. Cambodia—Politics and government.   I. Title.
DS554.7.C46   1991
959.604—dc20   91-17074
                                       CIP

10   9   8   7   6   5   4   3

Contents

Illustrations

Maps

Figures

Preface

Writing this book has been a happy and rewarding experience. I began work on it inadvertently at the end of 1960 when I arrived in Phnom Penh, my first overseas post in the U.S. Foreign Service, and was asked to prepare economic and political reports. Some of these jejune documents aged into primary sources and were released to me under the Freedom of Information Act. Fortunately I have also had access to other materials.

In 1985, I decided to write a sequel to *A History of Cambodia* (1983), which ended with Cambodia gaining its independence. Soon afterward, I received a generous grant from the Social Science Research Council (SSRC) in New York that enabled me to travel overseas in search of primary materials and participants in Cambodia's recent past. I was later awarded a similar grant from the Australian Research Council (ARC). I am grateful to these institutions for their support. I am also grateful to Yale University, California State University (Long Beach), the Institute of International Strategic Studies (London), and the Outside Studies Program of Monash University, which at various times defrayed my travel costs.

The time frame of the book (1945–79) was dictated by two considerations. After completing *A History of Cambodia,* I became aware of newly opened archival sources dealing with the aftermath of World War II. Because of these materials, I decided to cover the period 1945–53 again in more detail.

I chose to end my study with 1979 because of the difficulties I faced in organizing a coherent narrative about the 1980s. I was unable to obtain a visa to Cambodia until the book was substantially complete. More important, after the Vietnamese invasion in 1979, Cambodia became difficult to define, for it included not only the people and territory controlled by the government in Phnom Penh but also another three hundred thousand Khmer strung out in camps along the Thai-Cambodia border, a so-called government in exile, and perhaps three hundred thousand other Cambodians living overseas. At another level, the Vietnamese invasion and the collapse of the Pol Pot regime seemed an appropriate place to stop.

My work has depended heavily on archival sources and library holdings outside Australia. It was made easier by the cooperation of authorities in the Archives d'Outremer in Aix-en-Provence, the Service Historique des Armées de Terre in Vincennes, the Public Records Office in London, and the National Archives in Washington, D.C. I am also grateful for help received from the librarians of the Institute of Southeast Asian Studies (Singapore), the Indo-China Archive of the University of California (Berkeley), and the Echols Collection of the Cornell University Library. By mail, I have received several hundred documents from the Lyndon Baines Johnson Library in Austin, Texas, and the John F. Kennedy Library in Boston, Massachusetts. Finally, several officials of the Information and Privacy Staff of the U.S. Department of State were helpful in releasing voluminous material that originated in the U.S. embassy in Phnom Penh in 1955–64 and 1969–75.

Closer to home, Helen Soemardjo of the Monash Library and George Miller of the Menzies Library of the Australian National University hunted down references and answered many queries. Gary Swinton of the Monash Geography Department prepared the maps. Students in my seminar on Cambodia in 1990 sharpened my thoughts as the book was nearing completion.

My colleagues John Legge and John Rickard read parts of the book in draft form, and so did my students Justin Corfield and Kate Frieson. The four of them made many helpful comments. Serge Thion gave a close reading to the book's two final chapters, while Michael Vickery reviewed the manuscript carefully and suggested many improvements. Along with Timothy Carney, Justin Corfield, Kate Frieson, David Hawk, Stephen Heder, and Ben Kiernan, Michael and Serge were generous with materials from their personal archives. My wife, Susan, gave a critical reading to two versions of the text, and our children, Elizabeth, Margaret, and Tom, with cheerful exhortations of "How's the book, Dad?" have encouraged me to push along. The book would be poorer without these people's help.

While I was working on the project, more than a hundred men and women were generous with their hospitality, documents, photographs, conversation, correspondence, and introductions. Some of them helped in all these ways, and my gratitude to several stretches back more than twenty years.

In Australia, I am grateful to Anne Blair, David Bourchier, Wall Burgess, Frances Collingwood, Justin Corfield, Ian Cummins, Noel St. C.

Deschamps, Maurice Eisenbruch, Grant Evans, Herbert Feith, Kate Frieson, David Garrioch, James Gerrand, Michael Godley, Bruce and Joan Grant, Geoffrey Gunn, Ron Hatley, Im Nath, Emma James, Somsak Jeamteeraskul, Julio Jeldres, John Legge and Jane Drakard, Hong and Bopha Lim, Greg Lockhart, Angus McIntyre, David Marr, Milton Osborne, Pham van Luu, Craig Reynolds, Kelvin Rowley, Richard Tanter, Carlyle Thayer, Thong Thel, John Tully, Bunheang and Pinni Ung, Esta Ungar, Walter Veit and Irmline Veit-Brause, and Ken Young.

Those in France who helped me include Elizabeth Becker, Georges Boudarel, Pierre Brocheux, Philippe Devillers, Ananda Guruge, Bernard Hamel, Claude Jacques, Khing Hoc Dy, Pierre Lamant, Lim Kim Ya, Marie-Aléxandrine Martin, Charles Meyer, Jacques Nepote and Fanny Nepote-Desmarres, Nhiem Sothean, Panh Meng Heang, Eveline Porée-Maspéro and the late Guy Porée, Sokho Suon Kaset, Serge Thion, Lionel Vairon and Nicole Vairon-Khao.

Anne Fortin, Mika Levesque, and Tom Sakara made my visit to Montreal in 1989 immensely fruitful, while trips to the United Kingdom benefited from the friendship and assistance of Anthony Barnett and Judith Herrin, Stephen Heder, Michael Leifer, Andrew Mackay-Johnstone, Robert Taylor, and William Shawcross.

In Thailand and Malaysia I profited from the time I spent with Steven Erlanger, Murray and Linda Hiebert, Otome Hutheesing, James and Mealea Pringle, Sulak Sivaraksa, Phuwadol Songprasert, Michael Vickery, and Somkiat Wantana.

Finally, in the United States the following people were generous in many ways: Benedict Anderson, Lyall and Claire Breckon, Timothy Carney, Richard Cima, Nayan Chanda, Stuart and Doris Eagleson, May Ebihara and Marvin Gelfand, Edward Friedman, William Harben, Roy Haverkamp, David Hawk, Hin Sithan, Tom and Hana Hirschfield, Vora Huy Kanthoul, Mary Jackson, William Joseph, Peter Judd, George Kahin, Paul Kattenburg, Charles and Jane Keyes, Ben Kiernan, Judy Ledgerwood, John Marston, Carol Mortland, Leonard Overton, Douglas Pike, Gareth Porter, James Scott, Frank Smith, Hann So, Soth Polin, Frank Tatu, Keith Taylor, Michael Train, William Turley, Charles Twining, Khatarya Um, and John Westland.

I am also grateful to more than a hundred other men and women for their patience while I interviewed them under a variety of conditions.

My editors at Yale University Press, Charles Grench and Lawrence Kenney, have been helpful, assiduous, and supportive.

All of these people have made my work pleasurable, interesting, and easy. They also corroborate an adage of my former teacher the late Paul Mus that "Chacun se construit de ce que lui apporte l'ami." Without the friends I have mentioned, as well as those I made in Cambodia in 1960–62, what follows could never have been written.

Abbreviations

AKP	Agence Khmere de Presse
ASEAN	Association of Southeast Asian Nations
CGDK	Coalition Government of Democratic Kampuchea
CIA	Central Intelligence Agency
CINCPAC	Commander in Chief, (U.S. Forces) Pacific
COSVN	Central Office, South Vietnam
CPF	Communist Party of France
CPK	Communist Party of Kampuchea
CPT	Communist Party of Thailand
DK	Democratic Kampuchea
FBIS	Foreign Broadcast Information Service
FOIA	Freedom of Information Act
ICP	Indo-China Communist Party
ICSC	International Commission for Security and Control
JSRK	Jeunesse Socialiste Royale Khmere
KPRP	Khmer People's Revolutionary Party
KWP	Khmer Workers' Party
MET	Military Equipment Team
NLF	National Liberation Front
NUFK	National United Front of Kampuchea
PRC	People's Republic of China
PRG	Provisional Revolutionary Government (of Vietnam)
PRK	People's Republic of Kampuchea
SEATO	Southeast Asia Treaty Organization
STV	Standard Total Version
UEK	Union des Etudiants Khmers
UIF	United Issarak Front
UNEK	Union Nationale des Etudiants Khmers
UNESCO	United Nations Educational, Scientific and Cultural Organization
VWP	Vietnam Workers' Party

The Tragedy of
Cambodian History

Introduction

The prairie fire of revolution that swept through Cambodia between 1975 and the beginning of 1979 was one of the fiercest and most consuming in this century of revolutions. Under the regime of Democratic Kampuchea (DK), a million Cambodians, or one in eight, died from warfare, starvation, overwork, misdiagnosed diseases, and executions. Most of these deaths, however, were never intended by DK. Instead, one Cambodian in eight fell victim to the government's utopian program of total and rapid social transformation, which its leaders had expected would succeed at far less cost. This does nothing to alleviate the horror or their responsibility for it. When their program failed, the leaders were confused but unrepentant.

The number of casualties and their enormity are almost impossible to understand. So is the thoroughness of the attempted transformation. The DK regime abolished money, evacuated cities and towns, prohibited religious practices, suspended formal education, newspapers, and postal services, collectivized eating after 1977, and made everyone wear peasant costumes. Its economic plan called for average national yields of rice that were more than twice as high as those in the most productive areas of Cambodia. The regime proposed to wage a class war and to turn the economy around by abolishing class distinctions, destroying prerevolutionary institutions, and transforming the population into unpaid agricultural workers. In May 1975 a government spokesman proudly announced that "more than two thousand years" of Cambodian history had ended.

The Communist Party of Kampuchea (CPK) shared

a Marxist-Leninist ideology with Vietnam and other Communist countries. Cambodia's revolution, however, differed sharply from Vietnam's in the level of violence and utopianism involved, its rapidity, and the absence of discussion of policies inside the party. The CPK disavowed its socialist precedents, played down its documentary basis, and concealed its existence from outsiders until 1977, referring to itself only as the revolutionary organization (*angkar padevat*) or the higher organization (*angkar loeu*). The party's clandestine style was so encompassing that the secretary general of its central committee, Saloth Sar (b. 1928?), assumed a revolutionary name, Pol Pot, when he took office as prime minister of DK in 1976, just when an admission of his identity, rather than its concealment, might have been expected.

The following year, DK troops began a series of raids into southern Vietnam. By the end of 1977 the Vietnamese had responded in force, and throughout 1978 DK was engaged in a war that it had neither the manpower nor the equipment to win. The CPK was also wracked with purges of its so-called enemies: by the end of 1978, just before the regime collapsed, these had claimed two deputy prime ministers, several cabinet-level officials, and dozens of highly placed cadre. In the process, thousands of their relatives and acquaintances were also put to death.

In early 1979 DK was toppled by an invading Vietnamese army. Tens of thousands of Cambodians sought refuge soon afterward in Thailand. Pol Pot, the remnants of his army, and perhaps one hundred thousand people fled or were driven into the northwest. They reached the Thai border in the middle of the year. It was at that point that Cambodia swam into focus in the West as a metaphor for suffering and as a problem that needed attention. Money, medicine, and food collected in Western countries piled up for refugees along the border. Most of the medicine and food were consumed then and there, but some trickled through to the Vietnamese-backed government in Phnom Penh and flowed on to Cambodia's rural poor. Food and medicine were also diverted by Thai authorities to feed and heal Pol Pot's exhausted army so that it could fight another day.

For some observers, the melancholy occasion was conducive to the utterance of ideological statements. To those in the West engaged in the Cold War Pol Pot provided another proof of the iniquity of Marxism-Leninism. Others saw the Vietnamese invasion as an example of Communist disregard for international law. Still others interpreted the events as a by-product of the U.S. withdrawal from Southeast Asia or as an aspect of the Sino-Soviet split. Observers on the left dismissed DK as an un-

Marxian, fascist aberration. They saw its nationalism as chauvinist, spoke of genocide, praised the Vietnamese, and compared Pol Pot egregiously with Hitler.

These positions held grains of truth but little explanatory power. Few writers tried to examine what had happened from a Cambodian perspective, although the number of deaths and the fact that Cambodians themselves had done almost all the killing were startling to scholars, to most Cambodians, and to others who had thought of Cambodia as a happy place. The chaos of the 1970s and the perceived sufferings of 1979–80 have lent an urgency to the need to understand what took place. Why did the Cambodian revolution happen? Why did it take the course it took? Who was responsible for it? Had it been foreshadowed by earlier events?

I embarked on this study in 1986, hoping to deal with these questions from a historian's perspective, and a largely Cambodian one, through a narrative political history that examines a range of themes. Three of these that impinge on the narrative arise from Cambodia's location and accessibility, its style of leadership, and its people's perceptions of their past.

For several hundred years Cambodia has been wedged between the nation-states of Thailand and Vietnam. Phnom Penh and the Mekong River basin are within hours by road of Ho Chi Minh City and Bangkok. Although poor in mineral wealth, Cambodia's small population, its rich alluvial soil, and the Tonle Sap, or Great Lake, the richest freshwater fishing ground in the world, have made the country susceptible to outside influences and tempting to immigrants and invaders.

In the nineteenth century the Thai fought with Vietnam for Cambodia's territory, population, and allegiance. Had the French not arrived to impose their protectorate on Cambodia in 1863, those parts of the kingdom east of the Mekong might well have come under Vietnamese control and the area to the west might have been dominated by the Thai. As the French pushed Cambodia's neighbors back, modern Cambodia was born. When the French withdrew in 1954 the ambitions of Cambodia's neighbors reemerged. Thailand and South Vietnam were allied with the United States, and Cambodia's leader, Norodom Sihanouk, fearing their ambitions and spurning an alliance with the United States, chose a neutralist set of policies. Angered by his neutralism, the Thai and Vietnamese orchestrated plots to overthrow him. With some justification, Sihanouk believed that Cambodia was surrounded by hostile states.

Like many other countries of the region, Cambodia had no tradition of leaders sharing power, of a loyal opposition, or of national elections. In precolonial times, kings had in theory been absolute. Under the French, contentious politics were forbidden. With the arrival of independence, Sihanouk retained this aspect of French policy and took up where his ancestors had left off, capitalizing on the deference that characterized Cambodian attitudes toward royalty and toward anyone firmly in command.

Between 1947 and 1958, as I show in chapters 1 and 2, there was a possibility that the Democratic party based among Cambodia's educated elite and drawing its inspiration from parliamentary traditions in France might have taken Cambodia toward a constitutional monarchy and perhaps toward multiparty politics. The attempt was doomed when the French encouraged Sihanouk to move against this party and dissolve its government.

When Cambodia gained independence in 1953, internal politics were perceived by Sihanouk as his personal domain. He formed a "national movement" that had the desired effect of obliterating political parties. In the elections of 1958 and 1962, discussed in chapter 3, he picked unopposed candidates for the National Assembly.

A tradition of absolute command persisted under the governments of Lon Nol and Pol Pot. Like Sihanouk, they felt they deserved widespread acquiescence. In the Sihanouk era, few Cambodians were willing to desert their fields to engage in rebellion or other political activity. It was imprudent for them to do so, for most of them survived from year to year only by growing and gathering their own food. In the years 1945–79, some four-fifths of the population were farmers and their families, people who took their low status for granted and thought social change unlikely or impossible. Toward superiors they were deferential. They constructed arrangements with those they perceived as being above them, resented exploitation, and hoped for the best.

Rural Cambodians often thought of their leaders as meritorious. According to popular belief, merit accumulated in previous lives went a long way toward explaining a person's social position. This belief affected the way the leaders saw themselves. Those in power, it was widely thought, belonged in power; those at other levels of society had been born to take orders. Radical social action, like ideas of a just society, was less prestigious and widespread in Cambodia than in Vietnam or China because aside from the importance given such celebrations as Buddhist festivals and harvests little value was placed on communal activity and because political affairs were seen not as the people's business but as royal business (*reachkar*) that occupied the time of those in charge.

Some of the assurances of hierarchy broke down after World War II. In 1946–47, an increase in rural banditry and violence, a lapse in police protection, and the revolution in neighboring Vietnam encouraged Cambodian peasant resistance to the French and exposed many Cambodians to revolutionary ideas. Those most affected by these ideas were born in the 1920s and early 1930s. Several men and women of this generation later commanded the CPK. Thousands more joined the anti-French resistance, which was dominated by the Vietnamese Communists between 1946 and 1954, and became dedicated members of the Communist movement. Thousands enrolled in the French-sponsored militia. The activities of these men and women dominate much of what follows, but it is important to remember that hundreds of thousands of other Khmers took no sustained political action then or later, preferring to grow their food, raise their families, and hope for better times.

In the 1950s, Sihanouk's style of rule represented for many a reversion to traditional patterns. His narcissism made him enemies, but there is no doubt that he was the most gifted and popular politician to take command of Cambodia at any point between 1945 and 1979. Part of his success can be traced to his elimination of rivals but most is due to his genuine patriotism, his capacity for hard work, and his rapport with the aspirations of Cambodia's rural poor. By the 1980s, his virtues and flaws had become so entangled as to make him a tragic figure brought down by this entanglement, by real enemies, and by events beyond his control.

Lon Nol, who succeeded Sihanouk, was mediocre as far as executive ability was concerned. He based his legitimacy on inchoate patriotic feelings, Buddhist beliefs, and the loyalty of his subordinates. In power, he made much of the way his phlegmatic personal style contrasted with Sihanouk's hyperactivity. Like Sihanouk, he saw himself at the pinnacle of Cambodian society. He also believed that it was his destiny to overthrow the wicked king (*sdach piel*) of Cambodian prophetic literature. The military and personal disasters that overtook him in 1971 and 1972 convinced him that he had misread the prophecies and that he should never have betrayed the king. A stroke he suffered in 1971 was seen as an omen and reduced his capacities even more. Lon Nol's attempt to lead his country in a twentieth-century war against people he considered *thmil*, or unbelievers, led his army to defeat. He clung to office for four years as Cambodia collapsed around him.

Pol Pot, in turn, believed in collective leadership and abjured the cult of personality, but in what he took to be Marxist-Leninist style he stood alone at the pinnacle of the party and the state. By 1978, he had come to be known as Brother (or Uncle) Number One. In this position, he all but monopolized political authority. Like Sihanouk and Lon Nol, he drew on traditions of command that made it hard for him to distinguish between disagreements and treason. Like his predecessors, he ignored the lessons that previous leaders might have taught. All three men can be seen as dynastic founders whose one-reign dynasties collapsed.

A final theme in recent Cambodian history springs from Cambodian perceptions of the past. Between the tenth and fourteenth centuries, a kingdom now known as Angkor in northwestern Cambodia had dominated the Southeast Asian mainland, extending its influence over much of Thailand, Vietnam, and Laos. In the fifteenth century, a Thai Buddhist kingdom, Ayudhya, replaced Angkor as the paramount power in the region, and the area occupied today by Cambodia faded in importance. When the French extended their protectorate, there were fewer than a million people who owed allegiance to the Cambodian king, and although Angkor Wat was a place of pilgrimage for Cambodian Buddhists, no one in the country knew the names of Angkorean kings or could decipher Angkorean inscriptions.

French scholars busied themselves with Cambodia's early history, listing its kings, translating its inscriptions, and describing its greatness. At the same time French administrators froze Cambodia's institutions in place and protected it from the perils of autonomy. As they created something known as *Cambodia*, the French bequeathed to the Khmer the unmanageable notion that their ancestors had been for a time the most powerful and most gifted people of mainland Southeast Asia. They also decreed that Cambodia's subsequent attempts to live within its means represented a decline. Cambodians responded to these contradictory signals by using the grandeur of their past as a framework for the present and identifying themselves with Angkor. Since independence, an image of Angkor Wat, the most famous of its temples, has appeared on all Cambodian flags.

Sihanouk, Lon Nol, and Pol Pot shared this vision of Cambodia's past. Sihanouk's worldliness and his sense of realpolitik made him less certain of the efficacy of Angkor than his successors were, although in his visits to the countryside he identified Cambodia's "little people" favorably with the men and women who had built Cambodia's medieval temples. Lon Nol made similar grandiose comparisons, and in 1977, in the course of listing the accomplishments of the CPK, Pol Pot was optimistic about Cambodia's future, declaring, "If we can build Angkor, we can do anything."

A corollary of the idea of Angkor was that anything that went wrong in Cambodia could be blamed on foreigners. The Rousseauean notion of the essential *innocence* of the Cambodian people colored the thinking of all three leaders.

The People's Republic of Kampuchea (PRK) abandoned these readings of history, but the regime did its best to restore the ruins themselves and to emphasize the importance of Angkor in school texts that dealt with Cambodian history.

These themes—Cambodia's location, its traditions of leadership, and its perceptions of the past—are useful for students of recent Cambodian history, which can also be characterized as a series of sharp turns and slower transformations when events outside Cambodia, notably the Vietnam War, impinged on everyday life. More gradual changes can be traced to the expansion of literacy and mass education in the 1950s and 1960s, the decline of Buddhist practices among the urban middle class, the pressure of population on resources, and the effects of faraway events like the Cultural Revolution in China and the student uprisings of May 1968 in Paris. Several turning points have been used to frame the chapters that follow.

The first occurred in March 1945, when the Japanese forces who had been occupying Indochina with French permission interned French officials throughout the colony and informed the rulers of Laos, Vietnam, and Cambodia that their countries were independent. The Kingdom of Kampuchea, created in this way, lasted until October 1945, turned many Cambodians into patriots, and made it difficult for the French, when they returned in force in 1946, to take up the reins of power.

The ways in which the French and the Cambodians responded to these realities are dealt with in chapter 1. The chapter closes with 1950, soon after the French had granted Cambodia what Sihanouk later called 50 percent independence; at this time Sihanouk dissolved the National Assembly, which was dominated by the Democratic party. French concessions to Cambodia raised the young king's self-confidence, and his colonial patrons who still occupied powerful positions were as glad as he was to see the meddlesome Democrats, who wanted total independence, removed from the scene (the removal, however, proved to be temporary).

In 1951, the forerunner of the CPK, together with a similar party in Laos, was founded with Vietnamese guidance and advice. From then on, most resistance to the French inside Cambodia was dominated or led by local Communists and their colleagues from Vietnam. It was in this period, analyzed in chapter 2, that a generation of Cambodian students in France, including Saloth Sar, Hou Youn, Khieu Samphan, Ieng Sary, Son Sen, and many others, entered the French Communist party and envisaged radical solutions to Cambodia's problems. Many Cambodians in France, including Saloth Sar, were swept along by this revolutionary wave. Sihanouk's rough handling of the Democrat-led assembly, which he dissolved in June 1952, probably accelerated the radicalization of these students and other young intellectuals who remained at home.

Although the achievement of independence in November 1953 and the convening of the Geneva conference the following year were both important for Cambodia, a more significant set of turning points occurred two years later, when Sihanouk abdicated the throne and founded a national political movement that swept all the seats in national elections. These events are treated at the close of chapter 2. The disappearance of a significant opposition boosted Sihanouk's sense that he was the father of Cambodia's independence. The elections moved him onto center stage, where he remained for fifteen years.

The high tide of Sihanouk's rule (1955–62) is considered in chapter 3. During these years, Sihanouk dominated Cambodian political life. Infuriated by his "pro-Communist" policies, the pro-American regimes in Bangkok and Saigon plotted against him, with the knowledge of the United States. The most serious of these plots, involving the anti-Communist governor of Siem Reap, Dap Chhuon, seriously damaged U.S.-Cambodian relations. In the meantime, particularly after 1960, the clandestine Communist party began gathering adherents.

The year 1963, which began with serious anti-Sihanouk riots in Siem Reap and closed with Sihanouk terminating U.S. military and economic aid, ushered in a period of uncertainty in Cambodian politics that lasted until Sihanouk was overthrown in a bloodless coup in 1970. The first part of this period, lasting from 1963 to 1966, is discussed in chapter 4.

Soon after President John F. Kennedy's assassination Sihanouk broke off economic relations with the United States. He also nationalized the import-export sector of the Cambodian economy. He had probably been planning these moves for some time. They sprang from his increasing pessimism about the fortunes of non-Communist armed forces in Vietnam. Continuing military aid from the United States, he felt, might pull Cambodia into the Vietnam War. The break with the United States was also related to secret negotiations he was carrying on with the North Vietnamese and their surrogates in South Vietnam, the National Liberation Front. In exchange for allowing them to station troops on Cambodian soil, he hoped that they would allow Cambodia to remain independent when they won the war. The nationalization of exports and imports proved to be an economic disaster but had the effect, desired by Sihanouk, of reducing the economic power of the Chinese and Sino-Cambodian commercial elite.

Over the next three years opposition to Sihanouk developed among these very people and among anti-Communist politicians in the assembly. The prince responded by abandoning his practice of choosing the candidates himself and throwing open the assembly elections of 1966 to anyone who wanted to run. The results reflected local interests in many electorates. Most of the winners were conservative, but three Communist deputies who had questioned some of Sihanouk's policies were reelected with increased majorities. The commander of the Cambodian army, Lon Nol, for many years a faithful spear-carrier for the prince, was named prime minister, to the distress of the Communists and intellectuals on the left. It is fair to say that the assembly, heretofore a powerless political body, had drifted out of Sihanouk's control.

In 1967–68, resistance to Sihanouk from the assembly and the Communist movement posed serious threats to his control. These crises are discussed in chapter 5. The Communist-led insurgency in Samlaut in the northwest, followed by the decision of the CPK, whose leaders remained in hiding, to embark on a campaign of armed struggle against the prince meant that by the middle of 1968 Sihanouk's balancing act was in serious danger of toppling.

The prince believed that the North Vietnamese would win the Vietnam War and that the CPK was a creature of North Vietnam. In 1969, the analysis proved to be correct: Vietnamese forces and those raised by the CPK cooperated closely in the armed resistance to Sihanouk and to Lon Nol's army, which had begun attacking their supply routes and hiding places.

We also know, although Sihanouk did not, that by 1968–69 tensions had begun to build within the Cambodian Communist movement between those who had left Cambodia in 1955 and taken refuge in North Vietnam and the CPK central committee, who were hiding in the Cambodian forest. The Communists in Vietnam urged a policy of caution in dealing with the prince, whose support of the Vietnamese Communists was crucial to their war effort. The leaders of the CPK, on the other hand, argued that Sihanouk was the real enemy and that they should wage their own revolution rather than waiting for the Vietnamese one to succeed. To complicate matters, there were Cambodians in Hanoi who longed for independence from Vietnamese directives and others in Cambodia who felt loyal to Vietnam in view of its comradeship in the earlier Indochina war. These tensions did not break the surface, however, or split the alliance between Vietnam and the CPK for several years.

By 1969, pressures on Sihanouk from conservatives in Phnom Penh and radicals in the countryside had destabilized his authority and weakened his control. To recapture some initiative, he renewed diplomatic relations with the United States, but military aid on the scale he hoped for was not forthcoming. At the same time, clashes between Lon Nol's forces and those of the Vietnamese and the CPK on Cambodian soil became more frequent.

Sihanouk's response was to step up his attacks on those who, in his words, were betraying the country and also to retreat to the comfort of his entourage. Starting in 1967 much of his energy was channeled into receiving state visitors and making feature films. It is almost as if he despaired of governing the country. By then, many young people, particularly those in urban areas, had grown restive under his style of governing. Some drifted into the Communist resistance; others became depressed and pessimistic about the future.

The coup of March 1970, which I discuss in chapter 6, is such a major turning point in recent Cambodian history—especially in terms of its revolutionary dénouement—that it is tempting to organize one's interpretation of the 1960s in terms of an inevitable crisis. In fact, there were many variables in Sihanouk's demise.

He was out of the country when riots in Phnom Penh against the Vietnamese, which he had authorized from abroad, got out of hand and revealed how much many Cambodians resented their country's being used as a base by foreign troops. Lon Nol's support for the coup was uncertain until the night before it happened and was reluctantly given even then. Had someone else been put in charge of the Khmer Republic, as it came to be called after October 1970, what happened during the next five years might have been different. As it was, these years marked the high tide of factionalism and fragmentation in Cambodian politics. This period is dealt with in chapter 6. Similarly, there was nothing inevitable about Lon Nol's stroke in 1971, Nixon's abdication in 1974, or the American bombing of the Cambodian countryside in 1973. Had these variables been different, Sihanouk might have remained in power or returned to take it up. The successes of DK would have been harder to achieve.

The main effect of the coup was to draw Cambodia into the Vietnam War. This served the interests of the United States, the South Vietnamese government, and many in Cambodia who resented the Vietnamese Communist presence on Cambodian soil. Unfortunately, the Cambodian army lacked the equipment, training, and leadership to win. In a series of campaigns in 1970–71, its units were cut to pieces by Vietnamese troops that had been in combat for many years.

Another consequence of the coup was that the North Vietnamese began to send many of the Cambodians whom they had sheltered since 1955 back to Cambodia to assist in the revolution. The leaders of the CPK suspected that these men and women were loyal to Hanoi and began to purge them secretly in 1972.

United States officials and Sihanouk, however, persisted until 1975 in viewing the CPK as a creature of Hanoi. When a tentative cease-fire was signed in Vietnam at the end of 1972, most Vietnamese forces withdrew from Cambodia, leaving Cambodians to fight among themselves. Received wisdom still saw the CPK as a creation of the Vietnamese. Massive U.S. bombing in the first half of 1973 postponed a Communist victory, but Lon Nol's inept, exhausted government was unable to capitalize on this development or on the casualties suffered by the resistance. The war dragged on until April 1975, when Phnom Penh was captured by rebel forces.

There were several turning points over the next three years. These are treated in chapters 7 and 8. The first occurred in early 1976 when the party emerged from behind the united front it had joined with Sihanouk in 1970 and established its own regime. Soon afterward, sweeping economic reforms were put in motion, reforms that involved the forced communalization of hundreds of thousands of people, who were set to work to produce unrealistically high quotas of rice and other crops. The human costs were enormous. By September, if not before, rifts had appeared inside the party between Pol Pot's faction and others accused of preferring to continue the CPK's alliance with Vietnam.

Another turning point occurred in 1977, when the regime inaugurated its military raids into Vietnam, beginning a war it was unable to win and foreshadowing its own demise. As soon as the Vietnamese retaliated, raids engendered reprisals, and large-scale combat followed. By early

1978, a Vietnamese invasion showed Pol Pot how vulnerable eastern Cambodia was to attack and how far superior Vietnamese forces were to those of DK. His response was to declare the Vietnamese withdrawal that followed a Cambodian victory and to purge the Cambodian military leaders who had been defeated.

In 1978, DK spiraled toward collapse. The agricultural plans of 1976–77 had led to hundreds of thousands of deaths, which the leaders blamed on treachery rather than on themselves. The party devoted most of its energy to rooting out enemies from its ranks. Chinese military aid poured in to help Cambodia fight Vietnam, a Soviet ally, but Pol Pot's troops were poorly trained, and the Chinese equipment was mishandled and broke down. By mid-1978, the regime offered a general amnesty to its inhabitants (it went unnoticed in most of the countryside) and opened up Cambodia to a handful of sympathetic journalists. Some of their reports are discussed in chapter 8.

It was a case of too little, too late. By early January 1979, Vietnamese armies had captured Phnom Penh, thereby closing another phase of Cambodia's history as well as the narrative framework of this book.

In the 1980s, a new kind of isolation was imposed on Cambodia, along with a new protectorate. But the PRK was less hermetic than earlier governments had been; its isolation stemmed largely from the refusal of most foreign powers to grant it diplomatic recognition. When the Vietnamese withdrew their troops ten years later, the Cambodian government opened its frontiers to trade and exploitation, and its leaders abandoned their ideologies to an extent that some felt was opportunistic and even an abrogation of Cambodia's autonomy—but the boycott by powers who were friendly to China and the United States and who thus supported resistance to the PRK continued.

As Marxist-Leninist regimes relaxed their grip in many parts of the world at the end of the 1980s Cambodia opened up informally to extensive foreign trade, which brought tens of thousands of men and women back into a larger, more hospitable Southeast Asia, thereby eroding Cambodia's isolation and threatening its identity. At the same time its leaders maintained their friendship with Vietnam, the Communists remained powerful, and the Vietnamese maintained their advisory role. The process of change made thousands of Cambodians wealthy and thousands more impatient. As Cambodia opened up, the persistence of factions, corruption, the ambitions of neighboring powers, and the possibility of a prolonged civil war remained serious issues.

After 1979, it is possible to interpret Cambodia in terms of the fragmentation or devaluation of Cambodia as an imagined community, to use Benedict Anderson's phrase, or as a nation-state. Whether they like it or not, most Cambodians in 1990 inhabit a global village. This fragmentation and dependence contrast with the unattainable wish and violent efforts of DK in the late 1970s to seal itself off from the rest of Southeast Asia, from capitalism, and from other revolutions. In the 1990s, Cambodia is in the process of joining or being pulled into the wider region. It is difficult to predict the effects of this development on its sovereignty, its culture, and the well-being of its people. And it is impossible to say what uses Cambodians in the twenty-first century will make of their history since 1945.

one

In Search of Independence, 1945–1950

At 9:30 P.M. on March 9, 1945, in a bold, coordinated gesture, Japanese military forces throughout Indochina moved to disarm French units, to intern French officials, and to assume control of the peninsula. Nearly everywhere the French and local people were taken by surprise. Resistance was sporadic and casualties, in Cambodia at least, were relatively light: a report prepared later estimated that forty-one people, nineteen of them civilians, had lost their lives throughout the protectorate on March 9 and 10. The total probably included four or five Cambodian militiamen who had been guarding the French *résidence supérieure* in Phnom Penh. A Khmer policeman saw their bodies beside the road on the morning of the tenth as he bicycled to work.[1]

The *coup de force,* as it came to be called, was noted in the kingdom's *Journal officiel* on March 10. Two days later, Cambodia's twenty-two-year-old king, Norodom Sihanouk, proclaimed that the French protectorate established in 1863 had ended. Sihanouk expressed his support for the Japanese and added that the kingdom would now be known in French as *Kampuchea* rather than *Cambodge*—a decision repeated thirty years later when the Cambodian Communists came to power.

Sihanouk had never expected to be king. The only child of Prince Norodom Suramarit, who was a grandson of King Norodom (r. 1860–1904), and Princess Sisowath Kossamak, the daughter of King Sisowath Monivong (r. 1927–41), Sihanouk had led a cosseted childhood, first in Phnom Penh and later at a French lycée in Saigon, where he excelled in classical literature, music, and dramatics. When his mother's father died in

1941, Sihanouk was still a student, preparing for his *baccalauréat* examinations.

In choosing Sihanouk, the French passed over the likeliest candidate for the throne, Monivong's oldest son, Prince Sisowath Monireth, thirteen years older than Sihanouk and a serving officer in the French army. They hoped, it seems, to find in Sihanouk someone who could serve their interests as they tried to outlast the Japanese and retain control of their prosperous possessions in Indochina.

For the first four years of his reign, Sihanouk was a pliant monarch and a willing pupil. He was kept under a tight rein by the French, who allowed him to initiate some modest legislative and ceremonial reforms and encouraged him to tour the countryside, a habit that remained with him for the rest of his career. The French were not interested in training Sihanouk or his people for independence, and when it came as a Japanese gift, the king and his advisers were uncertain about how to behave.

Nonetheless, with the French removed from the scene, Sihanouk acted quickly on two issues that had angered Cambodia's powerful *sangha*, or Buddhist monastic order. On March 14, even before a new cabinet had taken office, he abrogated two French laws dating from 1943 and 1944: one had made the romanization of the Khmer alphabet compulsory in official correspondence and the other had shifted Cambodia's calendar from a Buddhist system of reckoning to a Gregorian one. The two laws, perceived by the French as self-evident modernizing gestures, had come under attack from the sangha, whose members regarded themselves as the curators of Cambodian culture, embodied in Cambodia's Indian-style alphabet and Buddhist reckonings of time. Discussing his decision to rescind the laws, Sihanouk said later, "We are a people known for honoring old laws, and customs from ancient times. The French laws would deprive us of customs, and of history."[2]

The Kingdom of Kampuchea

Eight days after the coup, a seven-man cabinet took office. None of its members had ever opposed the French; indeed, most of them had occupied high positions in the colonial regime. At the end of the month, in a related gesture, a dozen Cambodian political prisoners held on the French penal island of Pulo Condore off the coast of Vietnam were released by the Japanese. These men were not given government positions when they came home.

The new cabinet was headed by the minister of finance, Ung Hy, described in a contemporary French report as an "old [opium] smoker—sly, slack, without much character." In the same report one of his colleagues earned the accolade of being "a good boy: fond of France." The cabinet retained the advisory status it had enjoyed under the French. Whereas previously the cabinet had reported its decisions to a French *résident supérieur* who filled the role of premier, the new grouping reported to a Japanese adviser.[3]

French military personnel, executive officials, and members of the police had been disarmed and incarcerated on March 9–10, but for several days most other French civilians in Phnom Penh were allowed to remain at home. On March 22, soon after the Japanese posted spurious notices that "more than eight thousand" Vietnamese residents of France had been massacred by the French, Vietnamese residents of Phnom Penh turned against French civilians, wounding several with sticks and knives. After removing the notices, the Japanese gathered the French into compounds in the northern part of the city, where they remained until the end of the war.[4]

This action by the Japanese removed European observers from the Cambodian scene for the first time since the 1860s. Their unexpected departure probably convinced many Cambodians that something dramatic and open-ended was going on. Students in the capital, infected with what the French later called the virus of independence, included such future Cambodian radicals as Keng Vannsak, Rath Samoeun, and Ieng Sary as well as more conservative figures like Douc Rasy, Norodom Kantol, and Long Boret. In spite of his Francophilia before and after 1945, Sihanouk, like his parents, seems to have greeted independence with enthusiasm. For all of these men and women and for thousands of others the last nine months of 1945 were a psychological boundary between two political generations.[5]

The effects of these months on people in the countryside are impossible to determine. It seems likely that the removal of French authority and the French police led to a rise in banditry, tax delinquency, and autarchy at the village level. Lek Samoeun, then a lycée student, recalled that in the summer of 1945 many young men in the provincial capital of Svay Rieng began drilling with clubs and machetes in an ill-defined militia. Over the summer, communications lapsed between Phnom Penh and the provincial centers, between the centers and the countryside, and between Cambodia and the other components of French Indochina. At the same time, informal contacts increased among anti-French guerrillas operating in Thailand, Laos, and Vietnam. Information from 1945 is so sparse, however, that it would be as hazardous to assert, as a French official did at the time, that more than half the population was "indifferent" to politics as it would be to claim, as have more recent Cambodian historians, that the people rose up in 1945 to defeat the Japanese. Whatever ordinary Cambodians thought about the Japanese and the French, violent actions against either of them in 1945 were rare.

Between March and December 1945, Cambodian authorities promulgated 155 laws (*kram*) and 390 administrative decrees (*kret*). When the French returned to power, they allowed three-quarters of the laws and nearly 90 percent of the decrees to stand. Those they rescinded included the one that had proclaimed Cambodia's independence and others that had set up offices for a prime minister and a minister of foreign affairs. The French also rescinded those that had given Cambodian names to streets and institutions in Phnom Penh; and they replaced two holidays that celebrated independence—March 12 and July 20, the anniversary of an anti-French demonstration in 1942—with holidays from metropolitan France. Finally, the French canceled two laws enacted in October that may well have struck them as impertinent. These decreed that income and property taxes should be collected, for the first time, from Europeans as well as from Asian residents. Most of the kram and kret, of course, had little to do with independence. Ung Hy and his colleagues had learned how to "tick over" under the French. The regulations and laws from 1945 that the French found harmless, or even useful, ironed out anomalies, adjusted jurisdictions, and created faintly innovative, inexpensive administrative procedures.[6]

What else could such a cabinet do? The ministers were constrained by their temperaments and training. They were operating in wartime under the Japanese. In economic terms, their principal task was to commandeer food and raw materials to supply the occupying forces. Cabinet ministers also were expected to recruit labor to repair roads and to construct landing strips for Japanese planes. Politically, they were expected to maintain order and to free Japanese soldiers for more important tasks.

At the same time, the inertia of the government may be deceptive, for sources outside the *Journal officiel,* including some survivors of the period, convey something of the excitement and promise of the closing months of 1945.

On July 20 several thousand Cambodians paraded past the king, celebrating the anniversary of the demonstration of 1942. Sihanouk was joined on the reviewing stand by Prince Monireth, "ministers large and small," Japanese officials, and the newly installed foreign minister, Son Ngoc Thanh, who had participated in the earlier demonstration and had just come back from three years of self-imposed exile in Japan. Thanh was to play a major role in Cambodian politics, on and off, until his death in 1976.[7]

Son Ngoc Thanh

Like many Cambodian political figures, including Son Sann, Son Ngoc Minh, Tou Samouth, Son Sen, Sieu Heng, and Ieng Sary, Son Ngoc Thanh was born into the Cambodian minority population of southern Vietnam, known as Cochinchina by the French and as lower Cambodia, or Kampuchea Krom, by the Khmer. In fact, these seven men were born within ten miles of each other in the province of Tra Vinh. Thanh's parents were prosperous landowners. His father was ethnically Khmer, his mother Sino-Vietnamese. His birth in Cochinchina and his parents' prosperity gave Thanh access to an education in France; many southern Vietnamese, but only a handful of ethnic Khmer, enjoyed such a privilege. He pursued secondary and tertiary studies in Montpellier and in Paris, returning to Indochina in 1933 before completing his law degree. Soon afterward he joined the colonial civil service and while working in Cochinchina came to the attention of Suzanne Karpelès, a French scholar-administrator in charge of the Buddhist Institute in Phnom Penh. Karpelès brought him to Cambodia to work with her.

The institute had been founded in 1930 to lessen the influence of Thai Buddhism (and Thai politics) on the Cambodian sangha and to substitute more Indo-Chinese loyalties between the Lao sangha and their Cambodian counterparts. For more than forty years, the institute provided a focus and a meeting place for Cambodian writers and intellectuals, many of whom were monks or former monks who owed the French little gratitude or respect. Thanh became secretary of the institute in 1935.

Thanh also became associated with the Khmer language newspaper *Nagara Vatta* (*Angkor Wat*), edited by two young Cambodians, Pach Chhoeun and Sim Var. Unlike almost all of the kingdom's minuscule bourgeoisie, neither man held a government position. Although Thanh claimed when he was imprisoned by the French in 1945 that the paper had sought to "propagate the ideas of independence," its early issues were not particularly militant. Editorials urged Cambodians to awake and to compete with the Chinese and Vietnamese minorities in commercial life. The paper also reported on the activities of Cambodia's educated elite, which comprised its readership. *Nagara Vatta's* influence is hard to estimate, but its weekly circulation of five thousand copies suggests that it was widely read. Fifty years later, many elderly Khmer remembered reading it with pleasure. It was not particularly anti-French, but after French defeats in Europe in 1940 and at the hands of the Thai in Cambodia in 1941, several of its editorials were censored, and Thanh and his colleagues were emboldened to question the status quo when Japanese troops arrived in Cambodia, with French permission, at the end of May 1941. But their printed attacks on the French were infrequent and discreet. The paper appeared regularly until the end of July 1942, when Pach Chhoeun and several others associated with it were arrested for participating in an anti-French demonstration.[8]

The demonstration was a watershed in the history of Cambodian resistance to France. It took the form of a march on the résidence supérieure and involved some five hundred Buddhist monks and perhaps two hundred civilians. A few days before, the French police had arrested two Cambodian monks, accusing them of preaching anti-French sermons to the Cambodian militia and plotting a coup d'état. In their haste the police had failed to defrock the monks, which made the arrests sacrilegious as well as politically offensive. A French ethnologist in Phnom Penh, Eveline Porée-Maspéro, noted in her journal that the arresting of the monks had been a "monstrous gaffe," although French charges against them may have been well founded: Japanese agents had been encouraging members of the sangha to express anti-French ideas, and rumors circulated in Phnom Penh that the demonstration protesting the arrests would be followed by a Japanese-supported coup d'état. Chhoeun, Thanh, and their colleagues miscalculated the support that the Japanese would provide as well as the firmness of the French police. Chhoeun was arrested inside the résidence while presenting a petition. Thanh went into hiding in Phnom Penh. He soon fled to the Thai-occupied Cambodian province of Battambang and later to Bangkok, where he petitioned Japanese authorities, including Emperor Hirohito, to invite him to Japan "to interest the Japanese in Cambodian independence." After several months he received permission to go.[9]

In his petition Thanh called himself "the representative of the Khmer Nationalist Party," whose members, he said, included the entire peasant population of Cambodia, all Cambodians who were not functionaries, the "entire populations of the territories ceded [to Thailand by the French in 1941] as well as the Khmer portions of Thailand, the Khmer population of Cochin-China, and all the Cambodians living in Bangkok. In Cambodia itself, only the king and his close associates, the royal family, and those functionaries loyal to France are ineligible to participate in our movement." The "movement" was probably the product of Thanh's imagination.[10]

In Tokyo, he told a Japanese official that Cambodia's destiny should be separated from those of "the Siamese and the Annamites," a persistent theme of Cambodian nationalism in the years that followed. The official advised him to study Japanese. Thanh lodged with a Japanese businessman for three years, received a stipend of one hundred yen per month, and assumed a "Burmese nationality."

Five of his letters home, written in French in 1943, have survived. In them, Thanh struggled to lighten his isolation and to clarify his political ideas, which at this stage contained elements of racism, homesickness, anger at the French, admiration for Japan, and hopefulness that the Japanese notion of "familyism" might catch on among the Khmer. Looking for something to attack, Thanh noted that "Jewish occidentalism [sic] with scientific progress has spilled over into Asia." He also blamed French "materialism" for Cambodia's plight.[11]

Thanh's correspondence from 1944 and 1945 has not survived, so it is impossible to trace the evolution of his political ideas. Nonetheless, his reputation as a nationalist hero had grown inside Cambodia in his absence and spread by word of mouth, particularly by the sangha, whose leaders had been friendly with him for a decade. The monks were infuriated by the humiliation of 1942 and by the death in captivity of one of the arrested monks. By April 1945, Sihanouk himself was pleading with the Japanese for Thanh's return. Pressure on the king may have come from his father, a close friend of Thanh's before the war, but the idea of bringing back such a pro-Japanese patriot fitted with Japanese plans to enhance Cambodia's independence. Soon after Thanh came home, in May 1945, he was named Cambodia's foreign minister. At the same time, Sihanouk's uncle, Prince Monireth, became a special counselor to the throne.[12]

The Japanese saw Cambodian foreign relations largely in terms of conducting liaison with themselves, but in the middle of June they allowed the new minister to travel to Saigon, where he argued with the newly installed Vietnamese authorities, under Emperor Bao Dai, in favor of Cambodia's claims to parts of Cochinchina, including the area where he had been born and raised. The Vietnamese procrastinated, probably because they themselves were hoping for Cambodian political support.

During the summer of 1945, as Japanese military fortunes deteriorated, French military and civil authorities, no longer at war with Germany, were poised to return to Indochina, France's most profitable and prestigious overseas possession. In Vietnam, nationalists dominated by the Indochina Communist party (ICP) under the leadership of Ho Chi Minh, took advantage of the power vacuum to expand the areas under their control, particularly in the north, where a catastrophic famine had broken out.

The Coup d'Etat of August 9

Cambodia was relatively untouched by these upheavals, but the Japanese, fearing an Allied landing in Indochina, had increased their efforts to recruit Cambodians and Vietnamese into the militia. By the end of July, some seven thousand young Khmer had been mobilized into paramilitary groups. About five hundred of these formed an elite corps of volunteers known as the Green Shirts and led by a thirty-year-old Khmer named Thioun Moung, who had fled to Thailand with Son Ngoc Thanh in 1942. Members of the corps were drawn from Cambodian secondary schools and included many who became generals in the Cambodian army after independence; among the latter were Pok Saman, Oum Mannorine, and Sak Suksakhan. Celebrating the formation of the group, Thioun declared on July 18, "I am convinced that my compatriots and myself are the best Cambodian troops because we have been chosen from among the intellectuals. Our sole aim is to become strong to serve our independent nation."[13]

Several Khmer who were later active in the anti-French resistance, including Mey Pho, Prince Norodom Chantaraingsey, and Savang Vong, also joined the volunteers. Alongside the future Cambodian generals they underwent rudimentary military training and political indoctrination. No records of the indoctrination have survived, but it seems likely that while the Japanese would have encouraged political discussions that emphasized the importance of Asia, physical courage, and male bonding, Khmer teachers would probably have stressed the continuities they perceived between Cambodia's medieval grandeur and the volunteers' potential for

military success. The war ended too soon for the volunteers to prove themselves in battle. The abortive coup of August 9, in which some of them
participated, was their only significant act.

Three days before, Sihanouk's chronicle relates, a crowd of thirty thousand had assembled outside the royal palace. The militia had paraded
past the king, shouting slogans. It is possible that the coup was planned in
the aftermath of these celebrations, for "on the night of August 9," the
chronicle continues, "a group of Cambodians disobeyed the law and entered the royal palace." The intruders were members of the volunteer
corps. Two of them, according to a French source, had recently asked to be
trained as kamikaze pilots. The young men were dissatisfied with the Ung
Hy cabinet and came to demand that the king dismiss these men from
office. At 3:00 A.M., they rounded up the entire cabinet, except for Thanh
and Prince Monireth, and locked them up. When Thanh heard of this, he
fetched Prince Monireth, and the two of them ordered the prisoners
released.[14]

By that point, using one of Ung Hy's ministers, Var Kamel, as a hostage, the group burst into the royal palace, looking for the king. One of
them fired several shots, lightly wounding Sihanouk's private secretary,
Nong Kimny, who in the 1950s and 1960s was to be Cambodia's ambassador to the United States. They may have wanted to depose Sihanouk
himself, but he had been sent out of the palace earlier by his mother and
was hiding in a nearby *wat* (temple). In any case, according to Sihanouk (in
a speech given in 1952), his parents and Prince Monireth parleyed with
the intruders. Prince Monireth disarmed them and ordered their arrest.
Four days later, however, perhaps under pressure from the Japanese, the
king accepted the cabinet's resignation and announced that Son Ngoc
Thanh would be Cambodia's first prime minister.

No explanation of the events of August 9 was forthcoming either at the
time or later on. Those Cambodians who heard about it—like the students
at the Lycée Sisowath, near the palace—interpreted it as a coup intended
to benefit Thanh, as a blow for nationalism, and as a weakening of the
king's authority.[15]

The intruders thought they were acting in the national interest. Years
later, two of them in separate conversations denied that the Japanese or
Son Ngoc Thanh had put them up to it. At his trial in 1946, Thanh and the
Japanese witnesses agreed with this assessment. Rumors in the French
community at the time suggested that Pach Chhoeun, always more antimonarchic than Son Ngoc Thanh, might have incited the young men to act

and that the plotters may have felt that Monireth was a stronger bastion against the resumption of French control than Sihanouk. The involvement of other members of the royal family and of Japanese officials acting without authority cannot be ruled out. In the 1950s Thanh suggested that an "extranationalist group" styling itself a "revolutionary committee" had organized the coup, a view corroborated by unpublished French reports.[16]

Son Ngoc Thanh's Ministry, August–October 1945

The delay between the coup and Thanh's investiture suggests that the Japanese in Phnom Penh needed time to obtain approval from their superiors in Saigon before allowing him to take office. Thanh was certainly favored by the Japanese, and the date of his accession coincided with the installation of a pro-Japanese National Unity Front in Saigon. On the following day, however, Emperor Hirohito agreed to open negotiations for a surrender to the Allies. Cambodian nationalists, even those who were aware of this turn of events, like Thanh, would probably have seen the surrender as a stroke of good fortune, liberating them from Japanese control.[17]

Son Ngoc Thanh served as prime minister for two months. The laws and decrees enacted under his leadership reveal no systematic political agenda. Domestically, his program involved supporting the king, the royal family, and the monastic order. Some steps were taken to replace French with Khmer as the language of instruction in the schools, where several Cambodian students from the University of Hanoi, including Thiounn Mumm and Ea Sichau, had temporarily taken up positions formerly occupied by French teachers. For Thiounn Mumm, who became a Communist in France in the 1950s, the summer of 1945 offered a unique opportunity to indoctrinate students with his ideas of Cambodian nationalism.[18]

Thanh was worried about a French return to power. He placed his hopes for survival in securing military and political alliances with Republican China, Thailand, and Vietnam. He sent emissaries to China and Thailand and visited Vietnam himself. Unlike many Cambodian nationalists then and later, Thanh was not particularly anti-Vietnamese and tried to associate Cambodia with Vietnam's independence movement. By early September he extended diplomatic recognition to the Communist-dominated Viet Minh. The internationalization of Cambodian independence and Thanh's alliance with Communist insurrectionaries were crucial elements in the French decision, in October, to remove him from office.[19]

Thanh's three emissaries traveled to Hanoi by car but were turned back at the Chinese border, for by the time they reached it Thanh's government had been disbanded, Thanh was in jail, and events inside Vietnam were moving too fast for most observers to understand. The delegates returned to Phnom Penh with advice from the Viet Minh government in Hanoi to prepare for protracted armed struggle. The pro-French government in Phnom Penh that had replaced Son Ngoc Thanh's by then was impervious to this advice.[20]

While his emissaries were en route to China, Thanh traveled to southern Vietnam. He visited his native province of Tra Vinh, where he met with Viet Minh authorities. In 1960, a Vietnamese source claimed that Thanh had sought to propagate a "pro-Japanese" policy among the Cambodians in Tra Vinh. Twenty years later, however, another Vietnamese claimed that Thanh had sought Viet Minh cooperation for his regime. The allegations are not necessarily contradictory, and soon after the visit, the Viet Minh established a consular office in Phnom Penh. Thanh's efforts to form a durable alliance ran out of time and foundered on poor communications between Cambodia and the components of Vietnam as well as mutual distrust. According to the official interviewed in 1980, relations got off on a poor footing when Thanh insisted that the Vietnamese acknowledge Cambodia's residual claims to large tracts of Cochinchina.[21]

In September 1945 Thanh dispatched a retired provincial governor, Pann Yung, to Bangkok to seek support for his regime from the anticolonial government of Pridi Phanomyong. Thanh followed this up with a letter to Pridi that praised Thai–Cambodian friendship in general terms. Thanh hoped to gain Pridi's cooperation partly because in 1944 a Khmer resident of Thailand, Poc Khun (coincidentally the uncle of Prince Monireth's wife), had founded a movement called the Independent Khmer, or Khmer Issarak, which received support from Pridi's government. Its immediate purpose was to conduct anti-French propaganda in the Thai-controlled Cambodian provinces of Battambang and Siem Reap. On a larger scale, the Issarak movement and a similar one in Laos sought to remove the French entirely from Indochina. When Pann Yung visited him, however, Pridi was uncertain about his political future and was unwilling to become entangled with Thanh's regime.[22]

While these overtures were being made, French military officers representing Gen. Charles de Gaulle's provisional government in Paris had begun filtering back into Indochina by parachute and on foot. Those who parachuted into southwestern Cambodia in mid-September were brought into Phnom Penh and politely received by Cambodian authorities.[23]

To lend legitimacy to his regime before the French arrived in force, Thanh organized a national referendum, posing several questions to all Cambodian men between eighteen and sixty, who had never voted for anything before. One of these asked if they wanted the French to return or preferred to "remain as free as they were under [King] Jayavarman [VII, r. 1178–1220], with the temples of Angkor Wat." There is no evidence that any voting took place. Instead, it seems that the questionnaire was sent to provincial governors, who transmitted positive answers to the capital consisting of the number of eligible males under their jurisdiction. Over 540,000 such "ballots" approved Thanh's government. One ballot was found to be blank, and another gave a negative response.[24]

There is something dreamlike about the referendum and about Thanh's surviving writings from this period. His plans to fight the French alongside the Vietnamese unnerved his new minister of defense, Khim Tit, as well as Prince Monireth and other members of the royal family. As for Thanh himself, he may have thought that merely by being prime minister and by going through the motions of governing the country he could forestall the French return. He may have hoped that his rigged referendum would frighten the French away. In 1953, Sihanouk mentioned that Thanh had "very vaguely" proposed plans for a national resistance in the event of a French return, but it is impossible to reconstruct Thanh's thinking at this distance.

In the meantime, British and Indian forces under Gen. Douglas Gracey, sent in to disarm the Japanese under the provisions of the Potsdam agreement, had run into difficulty with the Viet Minh. Street fighting between Viet Minh guerrillas and British forces had broken out in Saigon. Over a hundred French residents had been massacred in a residential district, and the Viet Minh had imposed a blockade around the city. Food supplies from Cambodia, especially meat and rice, were crucial to the Western presence.

Gracey's original instinct as far as Cambodia was concerned was to cooperate with Thanh's regime, much as British forces were to cooperate with Aung San in Burma. He changed his mind when he received reports from his emissary in Phnom Penh, Lt. Col. E. D. Murray, who had arrived on October 8 with the imposing title of supreme Allied commander and a small detachment of Gurkhas. In 1982, Murray told an interviewer that he had worked closely with Khim Tit, who visited Saigon with a Major Gallois soon after Murray's arrival to discuss the crisis in Cambodia with the French military commander, Gen. Jacques Philippe Leclerc. On his return to Phnom Penh, Khim Tit published a disingenuous report denying that he had been negotiating with the French, but this is what he had been doing.[25]

On October 11, Murray flew to Saigon to suggest to Gracey and Leclerc that Thanh be placed under arrest. Two days later Leclerc sent birthday greetings to Sihanouk, whose French mechanic informed the French on the same day that the king, by accident or design, was leaving for a Buddhist pilgrimage on the fourteenth a day's journey from Phnom Penh.[26]

General Leclerc himself flew to Phnom Penh on October 15 accompanied by a bodyguard. Colonel Murray, who had not met Thanh until then, summoned him to his office, ostensibly to greet Leclerc. Thanh waited for an hour, making small talk until Leclerc and the bodyguard burst in. In 1982, Murray recalled the scene: "Poor little Prime Minister thought Leclerc was welcoming him and got up sort of to say, 'How lovely!' He was taken by the scruff of the neck by this gunman [Leclerc's bodyguard] bundled into a car and off."[27]

Son Ngoc Thanh, who had presided over ceremonies at the Lycée Sisowath that morning, arrived at the Saigon central prison in time for lunch. In early 1947, after a lengthy trial, he was condemned to twenty years' imprisonment, later commuted to "administrative surveillance" in France, where he completed a law degree. For the rest of his life, if his behavior and personal papers are to be believed, he felt that he retained the legitimacy he had enjoyed in his exhilarating months of power.

The French Return

Murray delayed announcing Thanh's arrest until a detachment of Allied troops could reach the king and escort him back to Phnom Penh. The official report about this period by Gracey's superior, Lord Mountbatten, states that Sihanouk's "neutrality in the *coup d'etat* had been preserved, for a day had been chosen when he was away on pilgrimage." Whether or not the French had encouraged Sihanouk to be absent from Phnom Penh, his neutrality was sufficiently in doubt to require Allied soldiers rather than his own entourage to bring him back.

Murray announced on October 17 that Thanh had been detained because his "intrigues were hurtful to the security of Allied troops and detrimental to the interests of Cambodia." On the same day, Prince Monireth, who had probably been instrumental in Thanh's downfall and whose military training made him relatively acceptable to the French, took office as prime minister in his place.[28]

Monireth and his colleagues realized that Cambodia was in no position to fight for its independence, but they sought something better for their country than the reimposition of a French protectorate. At a secret cabinet meeting Monireth proposed transforming the cabinet into a committee that would welcome the French and negotiate with them about Cambodia's future. Such a committee was formed the following month. In the meantime, the cabinet continued to administer the "kingdom of Kampuchea," even though on October 23, in a poignant display of what Paul Mus has called the "monologue of colonialism," Monireth's nephew, King Sihanouk, officially welcomed the acting French commissioner to Cambodia by reading a message composed for the occasion by the former résident supérieur.[29]

For the next eighteen months or so, the French in Cambodia were busy repatriating fellow citizens, reinstalling their administration, and reopening commercial enterprises such as the rubber plantations in the eastern portion of the kingdom, where valuable harvests had been stockpiled for several years. At the political level they engaged in discussions with Monireth and his cabinet about the future. The discussions culminated in a formal document known as a modus vivendi, which was signed in January 1946. The text acknowledged the king's autonomy in matters of internal administration and stressed the need for continuing conversations, while providing for a French high commissioner, French advisers at the provincial and ministerial levels, and continuing French control over minority populations, defense, and foreign affairs. Cambodia's autonomy, mentioned in the text, was constrained by its membership in the newly formed French Union, whose statutes were still to be defined. The modus vivendi was not particularly generous, but the word *autonomy* and provision for continuing discussions were probably all that Monireth wanted for the moment and certainly the most he could obtain without resorting to violence.

Soon after this, Philippe Devillers, a young French soldier who later became a distinguished scholar of Indochina, toured southern and central Cambodia with a propaganda film unit. In his unpublished report of these tours, Devillers provided valuable insights into conditions in rural Cambodia at this time. In the provinces of Kampot and Takeo, bordering

Cochinchina, Devillers recorded that the population was already subjected to propaganda from the Free Cambodia Movement led from
Cochinchina by Pach Chhoeun. A tract distributed by the movement
stated that "the French, whom we had thought had been chased out
forever, have begun to return, and as in the past are growing rich on the
labor of the peasants." Although the partisans are "not numerous," Devillers noted, "their presence in the region makes for a heavy atmosphere." Takeo and Kampot were Viet Minh strongholds throughout the
first Indochina war, a training ground for Cambodian Communists in the
1960s, and an important source for Communist cadre under DK.[30]

In northern Cambodia Devillers found the "general atmosphere much
more cordial" than in the southwest. He was impressed by the friendliness
of local people and the competence of Cambodian authorities. In economic terms, however, the region was "on the point of death." Transportation and public works were at a standstill, provincial treasuries were
almost empty, crops were not reaching the markets, and taxes were not
being collected. His conversations with Buddhist monks at monasteries he
visited convinced Devillers that Japanese propaganda among the sangha,
though intensive, had been inept.

Drafting a Constitution

Meanwhile, in the capital the Franco-Cambodian commission faced
two important tasks. One was to draft a constitution, as called for by the
modus vivendi. The other was to regain the provinces ceded to Thailand in
1941, following the Franco-Thai hostilities, arbitrated by Japan. The second task proved easier than the first, in spite of Thai intransigence and
their support for Issarak guerrillas, who attacked the city of Siem Reap
from Thai territory in August 1946. Several French soldiers were killed in
the attack, and Issarak forces occupied the medieval temples of Angkor
Wat and Angkor Thom for six days before retreating. Negotiations between the Thai and a Franco-Cambodian team in Washington continued
throughout 1946. Diplomatic pressure from the United States and Thai
eagerness to be admitted to the United Nations led Thailand to return the
provinces to Cambodia in November 1946. Thai support for the Issaraks,
however, continued through 1948.[31]

In drafting a constitution, the Franco-Cambodian commission faced
the intractable problem of meshing French and Cambodian perceptions
of national interest. The commission's first draft, written by the French,

was modeled on certain Middle Eastern texts. The document emphasized the allegedly absolute powers of the king and provided for an advisory national assembly, chosen under a two-tiered electoral system that gave limited suffrage to male members of the elite. The draft reflected French paternalism and also, Sihanouk later noted, Prince Monireth's authoritarian point of view.[32]

The king proposed two procedural amendments. The first was that the assembly should be elected by universal male suffrage. He also refused to promulgate the constitution without further consultation with an assembly elected for the purpose. This second amendment cleared the way for an unprecedented set of decrees that guaranteed freedom of speech, freedom of assembly, and the establishment of political parties, whose candidates could then compete for election, again by universal male suffrage, to the consultative body.

The amendments had other consequences too. Permitting universal male suffrage implied that the king, who possessed supposedly absolute powers, in some sense shared these with an electorate. At the same time, members of an elected consultative assembly might feel more obligations to the people who had put them there than to the king or to the foreign experts whose constitution they were later expected to approve. Furthermore, it was unlikely that such a group would be content to play the limited role envisaged for it by Sihanouk and his French advisers.

No one in power in Cambodia in 1946 expected such an unseemly confrontation. The French and high-ranking Cambodian officials shared the view that Cambodia's "little people" were not ready for self-government or for civil rights and that politics could proceed along the lines of "father knows best." Unprepared or not, thousands of Cambodians were being asked for the first time to exercise their rights. Almost imperceptibly, the power balance in Cambodia was beginning to shift away from the king and his protectors toward a larger, more unpredictable segment of the population. The consequences of that shift and the tensions it engendered preoccupied Cambodian politicians for another twenty-five years, until Sihanouk was overthrown.

Cambodia's Political Parties

The modus vivendi of 1946 had foreshadowed the possibility of political parties. The earliest to take shape, the Liberals (Kanaq Sereipheap, or Liberty party, in Khmer), was funded clandestinely by the French. Its founder, Prince Norodom Norindeth, was a prosperous landowner. There is some evidence that his ambitions to accede to the throne were encouraged by the French, who were nonplussed by Sihanouk's supposedly "pro-Japanese" activities in 1945. The party's platform sought to increase Franco-Cambodian "understanding and friendship." Its followers came from members and clients of the royal family, the Sino-Cambodian business community, and the bureaucracy.

The Democratic party, founded in April 1946, had a more impressive and varied array of founding members. They included Sim Var, a former editor of *Nagara Vatta*, Ieu Koeuss, a widely admired intellectual from Battambang, and several members of the educated Cambodian elite. Many of these men had been educated at the Collège (later Lycée) Sisowath in Phnom Penh. The party's motto, "Use the Elite to Serve the King and the People," encapsulated its original aims. The party also drew some of its adherents from the monastic order.[33]

The impetus for the Democratic party came in large measure from Prince Sisowath Yuthevong, a minor member of the royal family who had just returned home after having spent almost half his life in France. Only thirty-three in 1946, Yuthevong had a doctorate in mathematics and a reputation in French government circles for intellectual integrity. An admirer of the French Socialist party, he had attracted the attention of reform-minded French officials toward the end of the war when he joined the Senegalese poet and administrator Leopold Senghor to write a book about the future of French possessions overseas. He attended the Hot Springs economic conference in 1945 as a member of the French delegation. According to several of his associates, Prince Yuthevong was honest, inspiring, and hardworking. He had observed France's humiliations in World War II, but he had married a Frenchwoman and was by no means anti-French. He had many friends in official circles in Paris, and he had been away too long to have patrons or clients in Cambodia. To many young Khmer he offered an alternative to the colonial regime, its puppet rulers, and the family-oriented sluggishness of the elite.

A third party, the Progressive Democrats, was also formed at this time under Prince Norodom Montana, but it had few adherents. Its members consisted of people with close ties to the prince and senior bureaucrats uncomfortable with the other parties.[34]

Of the three, only the Democrats had clear links to the events of 1945. It was the only party with a national policy, a declared set of ideas, and a national organization. The Democrats made a serious effort to organize regional and provincial branches, taking advantage of traditional patronage and communications networks in Buddhist monasteries, schools, ministries, and government services. These communications were largely by word of mouth, among people who trusted each other. The party also took care to nominate candidates who commanded widespread local support, often choosing former monks, or *achar,* whereas its leaders were drawn from Cambodia's elite.

The party's political skills, its popularity, and its subdued nationalist message upset the French, who had treated Cambodia's constitutional development up to then as a charade. To make things worse, the party enjoyed the patronage of Sihanouk's father, Prince Suramarit, who had befriended many of the *Nagara Vatta* circle in the 1930s. Sim Var has recalled that at that time Monireth had expressed his disdain toward the possibility of educated Cambodians taking command of their lives. He found the idea of an educated elite subversive of good order, and his brusque paternalism drove Sim Var and his friends to choose Suramarit as their patron instead.[35]

Before the 1946 elections, Monireth was suspicious of the Democrats and joined the French in placing obstacles in their way. These included prohibiting civil servants from joining any political party (this provision was soon rescinded) and supplying newsprint and gasoline to Liberal and spurious "independent" candidates. French police and their Cambodian agents monitored the Democrats' political meetings, while Monireth saw its leaders as "demagogues wanting to grow rich at the expense of the people."

Detailed reports of the campaign itself have not survived, but the Democrats' organizational skills, the idealism of their leaders, and their links with 1945 worked strongly in their favor. In the elections, Democrats won fifty of the sixty-seven seats. Liberal candidates won fourteen, and independents three. In the process, long-standing hierarchies were dismantled. Many conservative Cambodians were disturbed by the way minor officials, elected to the assembly, had scurried up the political ladder. Some recalled the prophecy, or *tumneay* (cited again when the Communists came to power), that depicted a world turned upside down:

> Shrimps have laid their eggs on the summit of the mountain.
> Elderly people wring their hands and weep.[36]

During much of the campaign Monireth was out of the country negotiating for the return of Battambang and Siem Reap. When he came home, he refused for a time to step down as prime minister, on the dubious pretext, as V. M. Reddi has written, that a "suitable person to head the government had yet to be found." Sihanouk asked Monireth to form another government in early December, defying the Democrats' mandate, but his uncle was unable to do so. As a token of French displeasure, the Democrats' newspaper was proscribed for two months following the election. According to a close colleague of Prince Yuthevong, Thonn Ouk, these obstructions were lifted only when Sihanouk lectured his uncle on the mechanics of constitutional government and encouraged him to resign in favor of Prince Yuthevong, his constitutional successor.[37]

Inspired by their victory, Democrats in the consultative body, which convened in January 1947, began acting like a legislature by offering amnesty to Issarak forces willing to rally to the government. These offers, from the French point of view, usurped French authority. They involved Cambodians making contact with rebels and confirmed French suspicions that the assembly was a treasonous institution.[38]

In March 1947, French military police arrested seventeen members of the party, including the vice president of the consultative assembly, Sim Var, accusing them of belonging to a pro-Japanese secret society, the so-called Black Stars, with links to the Issarak movement. According to a French intelligence report prepared in 1952, long after the accused had been released without ever coming to trial, the Black Stars provided the "occult leadership" of the Democratic party. Members allegedly sported tattoos "either of the Buddha, or a black star" and recruited followers among railway workers, who shipped freight to the Issarak forces in Battambang. Thirty of these men were detained as members of the society. According to a prominent Democrat, Chhean Vam, the French obtained several spurious confessions under torture; he was told as much by a policeman, who had been released after confessing that Democrats at party meetings passed motions in favor of killing the French. French officials may have feared that statements like this would not stand up in court, and to avoid political embarrassment the prisoners were shifted to Saigon, where they were held for the remainder of the year without any charges being brought. Sim Var recalled that he was not physically abused but that other prisoners were routinely tortured.[39]

The Black Stars never existed. In 1987, Sim Var vigorously denied that it did, and no evidence for it has survived outside of French reports. The affair seems to have been concocted by the French security services in order to frighten the Democrats and to intimidate and sidetrack the consultative assembly.

Issarak Resistance, 1947–1948

Rural violence against the French increased during 1947 without coherent guidance from the Issarak movement in Bangkok. A joint Khmer Issarak–Viet Minh command, largely ceremonial in nature, was established in Bangkok in February. Its commander was a former member of the Cambodian militia, Dap (Sergeant) Chhuon, who had deserted in 1943 and with Thai support had organized anti-French guerrilla bands in the ceded provinces. Chhuon was thought to possess magical powers and had built up a following in the Kulen Mountains, north of Siem Reap, where a fanciful report of his strength cited his forces as consisting of "some 200 Germans, 300 Japanese who call themselves 'new Chinese', 200 Cambodian girls, and many partisans." The partisans were real enough and so were the girls, but the Axis deserters seem to have been thrown in to make Chhuon sound much more formidable than he really was. By early 1948, Chhuon was president of the Viet Minh–affiliated Khmer People's Liberation Committee and became its military commander, stationed on "the Kulen front."[40]

Two Issaraks more closely allied with the Viet Minh than Dap Chhuon were Sieu Heng, a Sino-Khmer from Battambang born in Cochinchina, and his wife's nephew, a Sino-Khmer named Long Bunruot, in 1946 a student at Thammasat University in Bangkok, where he joined the Thai Communist party. Sieu Heng told an interviewer in the 1970s, long after he had left the Communist movement, that he had become a Communist in 1945 because he was convinced by the movement's "perfect arguments." He played an important role in Communist-led resistance to the French in the 1950s but dropped out of politics afterward. Long Bunruot, on the other hand, remained a revolutionary, and by the 1970s, known as Nuon Chea, he had become the second most important member of the CPK. In 1975, when the CPK took power, one of Nuon Chea's first actions was to see that his cousin, by then half-paralyzed, was enticed from his home with promises of rewards as a "father of the revolution" and put to death.[41]

Two important bands of insurgents were operating in central Cambodia in 1947–48. These were led by Prince Norodom Chantaraingsey and Puth Chhay. Chantaraingsey had developed a taste for military life as a member of the Japanese-sponsored volunteers. His band operated in northern Kompong Speu, near the former royal capital of Udong, where patronage networks could easily be activated, and sometimes northward into Kompong Thom, in the district of Baray. Puth Chhay, in contrast, was a nearly illiterate rural Cambodian who had become an Issarak after serving time in prison for robbery and assault. He hated the French; "they have been in Cambodia too long," he said, and he fitted the accepted image of a bandit, being a heavy drinker, a womanizer, fond of magic, cruel to prisoners, and protective of his entourage. Like Dap Chhuon, he was thought by many to have supernatural powers. His personal courage and his brutality were legendary near his stronghold of S'aang, a riverside community south of the capital. By the end of 1948 he commanded some one thousand men.[42]

In the provinces bordering Vietnam, Vietnamese units, ideas, and organization played important roles in the development of resistance. Guerrillas in these areas were often commanded by Vietnamese, and Cambodians recruited into them often attended ICP political schools, where they were taught about Marxism-Leninism and the virtues of cooperation with Vietnam. However, some Issarak literature in the east in 1947 still stressed grandiose ideas about Cambodia's past. A tract captured along the Vietnamese border, for example, declared that "the Cambodian race, Cambodian blood, and Cambodian nationality are all the children of his majesty Jayavarman, the builder of Angkor Thom and Angkor Wat. Rise up, open your eyes, get back onto the proper path!" Another leaflet urged its readers to "come to the aid of the Khmer Issarak because the Buddha has need of you," adding, "Long live the pirates of religion, the modern Cambodians, descendants of Angkor Wat!"[43]

Khmer revolutionaries have faced two problems in trying to integrate such perceptions of Cambodian history into twentieth-century behavior. One was the difficulty of separating the grandeur of the kings of Angkor from the feudalism and Francophilia of the royal family. In the 1940s, in any case, most Cambodians were not ready to relinquish kingship as a component of their culture. Revolutionaries faced the additional difficulty, later on, of meshing the autonomy of Cambodia's past and Cambodia's national interests with the internationalist orientation of Marxism-Leninism, embodied in the guidance proffered to Cambodians by the Viet Minh.[44]

Two Khmer who were drawn closer to communism at this time were achar named Sok and Mean. Both of them had joined the ICP in 1945. Achar Mean, born in TraVinh around 1920 of a Cambodian father and a Vietnamese mother, had studied at Wat Unnalom in Phnom Penh during World War II and had left the capital following the monks' demonstration in 1942. At some point in 1946, he took the nom de guerre Son Ngoc Minh to capitalize on Son Ngoc Thanh's heroic reputation and to link himself in people's minds with Ho Chi Minh. After rising to command the political arm of Cambodia's Communist resistance in the first Indochina war, he chose to live in northern Vietnam after 1955 and died there in 1972. In the 1980s, he was honored as the father of Cambodian communism in Vietnam, Laos, and the PRK.

Achar Sok had worked as a monk with Son Ngoc Thanh and Suzanne Karpelès in the 1930s. Like Son Ngoc Minh, he had been born in southern Vietnam. According to an acquaintance who worked with him in the resistance, Sok was an outstanding Buddhist scholar and preacher. This popularity worked in his favor when he decided to join the ICP and was asked to proselytize among Cambodians in the eastern part of the country. By 1948, he had taken the revolutionary name of Tou Samouth and was known to the French as the interior minister of the Committee of Liberation of the Southeast. He remained in Cambodia as an active Communist until his assassination, probably at the hands of Sihanouk's police, in 1962. At the time of his death he was the secretary of the CPK's central committee. The religious backgrounds of both men and their reputation as achar gave them access to wats throughout Cambodia. Their nationalist credentials from 1942 placed them at odds with the French and the Cambodian monarchy and served them well throughout their political careers.[45]

In the meantime, the Democrats hoped for independence and concentrated on redrafting the constitution. Forty years later Thonn Ouk recalled sessions in the palace during which he and Prince Yuthevong went over clauses in the draft with Sihanouk and his principal adviser, a former résident supérieur named Jean de Lens. According to Thonn Ouk, the two men "listened carefully and accepted all of our proposals." Charles Meyer, a close adviser of Sihanouk for fifteen years, has written that the king was filled with a "juvenile ardor" for democratic reforms at this time. His involvement in the process, however, was neither deep or systematic. His passivity about the constitution and de Lens's admonitory presence are ironic in view of his tendency in later years to treat the document as his personal gift to the Cambodian people.[46]

The text that the Democrats were preparing was modeled on the French Constitution of 1946, which accorded more power to an elected assembly than to the chief of state. The choice to impose a republican constitution was deliberately made by the Democrats, who rejected the commission's draft of 1946 as conservative and authoritarian. Their success at the polls in 1946 convinced them that they could lead Cambodia toward independence and democracy. Although several articles in the text paid lip service to the absolute powers of the king (and were later used by Sihanouk when he sponsored amendments), it seems likely that the Democrats misread Sihanouk's good manners and timidity as wholehearted support for constitutional democracy and for a reduction in his privileges and rights.[47]

Two features of the constitution of 1947 caused difficulties later on. One was the stipulation that the prime minister and his cabinet did not need to be drawn from the assembly, although they had to gain and keep its confidence. The consequence of this provision was that Cambodian governments came and went at bewildering speed, with no effect on the lifetime of the assembly.

The second problematic feature was the wording that dealt with the succession to the throne. Those eligible for the throne included all "male descendants of King Ang Duang." There were over a hundred of these in 1947. Interestingly, Yuthevong and his brother, Prince Entraravong, were descended on their father's side from Ang Duang's brother, Ang Em, and may not have been eligible under these provisions. On the other hand, through their mother, the princes were great-grandsons of King Sisowath (just as Sihanouk was) and thus descended from Ang Duang. They were not, however, active contenders for the throne. This did not prevent Monireth and Sihanouk from claiming that Yuthevong had royal pretensions, perhaps the only kind of ambition they could understand.[48]

The Death of Prince Yuthevong

Prince Yuthevong had been in poor health since the closing months of World War II, and he died in Phnom Penh in July 1947, probably from complications arising from overwork, a recent attack of malaria, and a chronic tubercular condition. He was only thirty-four. A rumor swiftly spread that the French had killed him, but Thonn Ouk, who visited him in the hospital daily and "slept in the corridor" outside his room, thought this unlikely in 1986. He said, however, that Yuthevong delayed going to the hospital because he feared foul play at the hands of the French, and this delay may have accelerated his death. Coming so soon after the Black Star affair, Yuthevong's demise understandably raised Cambodian suspicions.[49]

Sihanouk and others in the royal family did not regret Yuthevong's death. In his memoirs, Sihanouk referred to his cousin sarcastically as Alexander of Macedon, and in 1952, when he heard that a collège in Battambang still bore the dead prince's name, he ordered the Ministry of Education to rename it.[50]

After Yuthevong's death the French and the royal family intensified their efforts to diminish the power of the Democrats, especially since a National Assembly was due to be elected at the end of 1947. To replace Yuthevong's cabinet an interim group was sworn in, led by an elderly member of the royal family with no political affiliations. Democrats were replaced as minister of the interior and chief of police, to assure independent scrutiny of the election. In August, two new political parties took shape. One, the Khmer Renovation party, was led by Nhiek Tioulong, Prince Sisowath Sirik Matak, and Lon Nol, all provincial civil servants who had been educated, like Sihanouk, at the Lycée Chasseloup Laubat in Saigon. The other, led by Khim Tit, took the title of National Union. In 1987, Tioulong recalled that the founders of the Renovation party had included "several personalities, of whom some were dissidents from the Democratic Party who thought the Democrats a little too progressive." The new parties proposed a national consensus, an idea later dear to Sihanouk, in place of the Democrats' concept of majority rule. The Renovation party specifically supported the monarchy. They were supported in turn by Prince Monireth, who was still angry at having been upstaged by the Democrats in 1946.[51]

A meeting of the Democrats in Phnom Penh before the election urged the French to release political prisoners "who had not taken up arms"—a reference to those being held in the Black Star affair. The meeting also voted to ask that a Cambodian battalion, which had been fighting under French command in southern Vietnam since 1946, be returned for duty in Cambodia, so as to "avoid friction with Vietnam, which will always be a neighboring country." Both motions were ignored, but the Democrats' unwillingness to confront Vietnam is interesting in view of the anti-Vietnamese coloration of so much of Cambodian nationalism later on.[52]

When the electoral campaign opened in October, the French commissioner, Léon Pignon, summoned the leaders of all parties and told them that the French would remain "absolutely neutral" in the elections. He admonished the politicians to conduct their campaigns with "the utmost prudence" so that the elections could take place in "the greatest possible calm." Candidates, he said, were not to discuss "royalty, [French] authority, and taxes," which "formed the bases of the Cambodian state." He closed by warning that Cambodia's neighbors, against whose "voraciousness" the French protected the Khmer, were "infinitely stronger and more dynamic." In official correspondence at this time, Pignon expressed his fears about open political discussion, claiming that the French would inevitably pay the price for the nationalist "overbidding" that would ensue.[53]

Very few primary sources from this period have survived, but when the votes were counted the Democrats had won 73 percent of the total and fifty-four seats in an expanded assembly. Liberal candidates won the other twenty seats; the Progressive Democrats and the two new parties failed to gain any. The Liberals ran well in Kompong Speu and in two provinces bordering Vietnam, but Liberal candidates won only two out of twelve seats in Kandal and one out of twelve in Kompong Cham. In Phnom Penh, where the candidates were Thonn Ouk and Ieu Koeuss, the Democrats won with ratios of more than five to one. In the first voting district, a Khmer quarter where many residents were government employees, Thonn Ouk won by 1,000 votes to 185.[54]

Several factors aided in the Democrats' victory. One was their linkage, via monks, activists, and achar, with Son Ngoc Thanh and the events of 1945. Another was their commitment to independence. Because the party's supporters extended from Phnom Penh to the village level and were joined by their literacy, shared excitements, and the notion of a new, imagined community the party was better organized and far more popular than its rivals, which relied on time-honored paternalistic connections between patrons and clients, the one providing protection (and cash), the other delivering loyalty (and votes). The Democrats may have overestimated the political sophistication of Cambodian voters. But many voters found this attitude preferable to those of the other parties, whose leaders held the idea of voting in contempt.

The Democrats' attacks on nepotism and corruption were also widely praised. Their role in writing the constitution and their confrontations with the French—in short, their national standing—were not matched by the other parties. All the same, they were not above bestowing favors on their supporters. In Phnom Penh, a nineteen-year-old technical student named Saloth Sar (known to the world since 1976 as Pol Pot) worked in the Democrats' campaign alongside a friend from the Lycée Sisowath, Ieng Sary. Sar's efforts probably helped him to obtain a scholarship two years later for tertiary study in France, awarded by a Democrat-controlled Ministry of Education.

The campaign gave many Cambodians their first taste of political action; those who worked to elect Democrat candidates were often younger and more idealistic than those working for the other parties, none of whose candidates mentioned independence or risked being imprisoned by the French.[55]

The new assembly convened in January 1948 under the presidency of Ieu Koeuss, while Chhean Vam, a respected associate of Prince Yuthevong, was named prime minister. Chhean Vam had spent World War II studying in France before resuming his duties as a teacher at the Lycée Sisowath. He was not a member of the assembly. With no financial support to speak of from the French, Chhean Vam faced almost insurmountable problems of inflation, shortage of revenue, growing insurgency, and lawlessness, all exacerbated by foot-dragging from the colonial administration.[56]

In May 1948, Vam accompanied Sihanouk to France, where the king enrolled for courses in equitation and tactics in the French army's cavalry school at Saumur. Chhean Vam, in the meantime, conducted fruitless discussions about independence with the French. He also attempted to reopen the question of the border between Cambodia and Cochinchina, which had been arbitrarily drawn by the French and which they were reluctant to discuss, for fear of antagonizing the Vietnamese.

On Vam's return to Phnom Penh, he faced a political crisis. A scandal had arisen in the assembly involving the illicit sale of rationed cotton thread. Several Democratic deputies were implicated. One was the vice president of the assembly, Sam Nhean, who was forced to resign from the party. Chhean Vam sought full powers to investigate the affair and to have the deputies' parliamentary immunity lifted pending the investigation. Ieu Koeuss was reluctant to set this precedent, which he thought would weaken the assembly, and the Democrats rejected Vam's proposal by twenty-three votes to twenty-one. At that point, Yem Sambaur, the commissioner of the police, destroyed the dossiers that implicated the assemblymen. Informed of this, Chhean Vam tried to dismiss Sambaur but failed to get his cabinet's support. Warning Koeuss that he was "nourishing a baby crocodile," Vam resigned in August 1948. Orderly constitutional government, already challenged by the Black Star affair, had failed to withstand the pressures of expediency. It was perhaps too fragile to last.

The ephemeral triumph of a particular faction, however, meant that from then on in Cambodia power belonged, as it had in precolonial times, to those who were strong enough to keep it.[57]

Yem Sambaur in Power

An editorial in a French-financed Phnom Penh newspaper in July 1948 declared that "a massive dose of democratic medicine has produced convulsions in the population." In fact, it is unlikely that the dose or the convulsions in the assembly affected many Cambodians outside Phnom Penh. For the months following Chhean Vam's resignation, Yem Sambaur and his associates in the assembly maintained pressure on the Penn Nouth cabinet that had replaced Chhean Vam's. In November, Sambaur and eleven deputies defected from the Democratic party, forming a loose coalition with the Liberal deputies.[58]

This infighting took place in the context of a deepening financial crisis, felt most severely by the Cambodian elite and the Chinese and Sino-Cambodian commercial sector. Tax revenues were down because of insecurity in the countryside, the destruction of tax rolls by Issaraks and Viet Minh, and the unwillingness of Khmer authorities to press as hard for taxes as the French had done. Insecurity also impeded the growth and movement of agricultural exports, and this affected government revenue because of the decrease in export taxes. The country's valuable pepper crop, for example, had come under Viet Minh and Issarak control by 1948, depriving the government of revenue and providing the insurgents with funds to purchase arms and ammunition from Thailand. While revenues fell, government expenditures rose. A French devaluation of the franc and the devaluation of the Indochinese piaster that had followed automatically led to high inflation and a shortage of imported goods. The Cambodians were too proud to ask for new injections of French aid. The French would have been hard-pressed to find the money.

In the meantime, Sihanouk and his parents had come to enjoy Yem Sambaur's problem-solving, contentious political style. Sambaur's exuberance offered a pleasant contrast for the king to the schoolmasterish manner of his French tutors and of many Democrats who had offered him political advice. Sambaur and his followers were less educated than many of the founders of the Democratic party. They probably would not have referred to themselves as intellectuals or as forming part of an elite. In early 1949 Sambaur told a reporter, "I am a child of the people, I have lived amidst the people, I know what every poor Cambodian wants."

In January 1949, Sambaur and his colleagues brought down the Penn Nouth government in the wake of a scandal involving fishing licenses for the Tonle Sap. The president of the assembly, Ieu Koeuss, proposed various names to the king as possible prime ministers, but the king rejected them all, insisting that Yem Sambaur be appointed because he had led the successful attack against Penn Nouth.

Yem Sambaur became prime minister of a "government of national unity" that included ministers from several parties, including some with no representation in the National Assembly. The Democrats refused to serve under him, and the new government soon faced its own financial crisis. Its budget called for expenditures of 375 million piasters, double the level of 1948 and nearly ten times the amount that had been budgeted in 1946. Receipts were lower than 200 million piasters. To make up the shortfall, Sambaur opened a dance hall and a gambling casino in Phnom Penh. The casino made huge profits—according to one report, it turned over half a million piasters every day—but was unpopular with those Cambodians who thought gambling immoral as well as with those who went bankrupt at its tables.

In April the French Union Assembly in Versailles voted 76–72 in favor of a new statute governing Franco-Cambodian relations; it was to replace the modus vivendi of 1946. Overseas members of the assembly joined Socialists and Communists to form the majority, which overrode a call for "further conversations." Yem Sambaur and the king were quick to capitalize on this development, pressing for more concessions from France while opening secret negotiations with Dap Chhuon in the northwest and extending the deadline for an amnesty to other Issaraks. The amnesty was complicated because the French had begun clandestinely supporting some of the Issaraks, such as Prince Chantaraingsey, who were willing to fight the Viet Minh. In areas where Viet Minh influence was strong, insurgents rejected amnesties offered by a puppet government like Yem Sambaur's.

Outside assessments of Cambodia in this period are so rare that the bleak report filed in June 1949 by a correspondent of *The Scotsman* is of interest. He noted that "because the French have officially gone (*sic*), most of the peasants believe they need pay no more taxes. Roads are seldom repaired and bridges off the main road are beginning to sag. The government cannot impose its authority. The capital, once as clean and swept as a French housewife's kitchen, is now sinking into dusty Oriental squalor." The report went on to say that Cambodia's economy was "dying like a hot house flower left out in the cold" and predicted that "the future of this strange, slow kingdom is unlikely to be a happy one."[59]

Yem Sambaur's attempt to rule through an assembly that opposed him was bound to fail. Jealous of their prerogatives, of Sambaur's support from the king, and of the headway Sambaur was making with the French, the Democrats in the assembly repeatedly threatened to bring down his government and bring on an election. These pressures suited neither Sihanouk, Sambaur, nor the French. Sambaur responded by asking the king to dissolve the assembly, as the constitution empowered him to do.

Sihanouk dissolved the assembly in September 1949 and selected a new cabinet, with ministers drawn from several parties. The action enabled him to rule by decree. The new French commissioner, Jean de Raymond, praised the move as "nonpolitical" and welcomed the friendship of the newly installed cabinet. On several other occasions, de Raymond was careful to point out the contrast between Sihanouk's patriotism and the immaturity of Cambodia's elected representatives. Flattered by such judgments, the king began to share them.[60]

Under the provisions of the constitution, however, national elections had to take place within two months. The king and Yem Sambaur perceived two obstacles in the way of fulfilling this requirement. An unstated one was probably their fear that the Democrats would win; the one they spoke of openly was insecurity. At a meeting convened to discuss the issue, Sambaur declared that conditions in the countryside would not permit elections. Ieu Koeuss argued in favor of elections and for an expanded assembly as well. The king, who was at the meeting, remarked that in the view of "public opinion"—not otherwise defined—the assembly had too many members already. An inquiry sent out soon afterward to provincial authorities revealed that in their view valid elections were possible only in Phnom Penh, Stung Treng, and scattered rural districts. For most other areas the "electorate would be at the mercy of important rebel forces." These responses probably represented the officials' perceptions of what the central government wanted them to say, for two years later, with insecurity even greater than before, a national election was successfully carried out. In any case, elections were indefinitely postponed, Yem Sambaur governed by decree, and the assembly continued to exist in an administrative limbo.

Toward the end of 1949, pro-Democrat students at the Lycée Sisowath, led by Ieng Sary and Rath Samoeun, went on strike to protest the dissolution of the assembly. Another Sisowath student, Lek Samoeun, has recalled that the strike involved wearing red neckties in defiance of school uniform regulations. The boyish gesture convinced the trigger-happy French authorities that the event was Communist-inspired.[61]

In the meantime, in Paris, a Franco-Cambodian delegation was slowly drafting a treaty that would provide Cambodia with a measure of autonomy. At this point the Issarak leader Dap Chhuon emerged from his forest headquarters on Phnom Kulen with four hundred armed men and rallied to Sihanouk in an impressively staged ceremony in the parklands of Angkor Thom. Negotiations with Chhuon had been under way for a year. They were carried out by Sihanouk's cousin Sisowath Sirik Matak, who was to be active twenty-one years later in deposing Sihanouk, and by a classmate of Sihanouk's at Saumur, Capt. (later Maj. Gen.) Pok Saman. Because the military sectors of Siem Reap and Kompong Thom had recently been transferred to the Cambodians as a good will gesture by the French, Dap Chhuon rallied to the king in liberated territory. In exchange for his submission, Chhuon received administrative and military carte blanche over Siem Reap, which soon became his personal fief.[62]

Ten days afterward, Sihanouk, Yem Sambaur, and Ieu Koeuss traveled to France to sign the newly drafted agreements, which Sihanouk said much later provided Cambodia with "50 percent independence." At the time, he proclaimed that the treaty marked a genuine liberation, for the only limits it placed on Cambodia's independence were, as France's President Vincent Auriol stated in a letter earlier in the year, "those brought to it by its membership in the French Union." These, in turn, were defined to fit with French interests, rather than with Cambodian ideas of independence. The French retained control over Cambodia's economy and its defense. The treaty granted little real autonomy to the Khmer. One exception was in the area of foreign affairs. As of 1950 Cambodia could receive diplomatic missions, accredited simultaneously to Cambodia and France and, with French approval, could send emissaries abroad. The United States and Great Britain promptly recognized Cambodia and the so-called Associated States of Laos and Vietnam (France's new name for Indochina), and American economic and military aid soon began to flow to these regimes. Indeed, it seems likely that American insistence on aiding the former colonies themselves, rather than the French, influenced

France's granting of token independence to the components of Indochina. Cambodia's application for UN membership was vetoed by the Soviet Union, but the kingdom soon joined several UN-affiliated bodies, such as the United Nations Educational, Scientific and Cultural Organization (UNESCO) and the World Health Organization.[63]

Sensing that time was on their side, Sihanouk and Yem Sambaur increased their pressure on the French authorities. Like most Cambodians, the two men were reluctant to be tied to Indochina or even to the Associated States, a French concoction dominated by Vietnam. They also hoped to gain French recognition of what they saw as Cambodia's residual rights over those parts of Cochinchina. For all these reasons, they did not want to finalize the frontiers between Cambodia and Vietnam. The French found this attitude unrealistic. Sharing this view, a British diplomat wrote at the time that "Cambodians are at one and the same time ambitious and indolent; more evolved than the Laotians, they lack their sense of reality and are a classic case of a people who are trying to run before they can walk."[64]

The Assassination of Ieu Koeuss

On the night of January 14, 1950, tragedy struck the Democrats again. An assailant rolled a grenade through the doorway of the party's headquarters and fatally wounded Ieu Koeuss, the president of the National Assembly, who was inside the building correcting proofs. Chhean Vam, at the nearby Cercle Sportif, recalled hearing the explosion but did not know what had happened. Taken by *cyclopousse* to the hospital, Koeuss died soon afterward of his wounds. A neighbor who had witnessed the attack ran after the assassin, collared him, and took him to the police.[65]

Koeuss's funeral cortege attracted more than fifty thousand people, the largest political procession in Cambodian history to date and the most spontaneous. Students, Democrats, government officials, monks, and ordinary Cambodians paraded, many wearing white tropical suits (or white shirts and trousers) and black armbands to demonstrate their grief. The banner most frequently seen was "Ieu Koeuss gave his life for the Party"—a devotion that may have struck Sihanouk and his associates as treacherous, foolish, or both. Sihanouk joined the mourners but does not mention the assassination or the funeral in his memoirs.[66]

The prisoner turned over to the authorities was an illiterate Khmer who first admitted and later denied being a member of the Liberal party. Fearing reprisals, Prince Norindeth, the head of the Liberals, hurried off to France before an inquiry convened under the guidance of the chief of the national police, Lon Nol. Norindeth's departure was not impeded and may even have been eased by Lon Nol and the colonial authorities. The French blamed the Issaraks who allegedly wanted to kill Ieu Koeuss before the assembly reconvened. They also hinted at Koeuss's republican tendencies. Other sources have blamed the French themselves, Sihanouk, or Yem Sambaur. It is possible that both men as well as the French police knew about plans for the assassination and did nothing to prevent it. For the Democrats, the loss of Ieu Koeuss was a serious blow.[67]

In the next few months, Sihanouk toyed with constitutional reforms that would have lessened the power of the assembly, but he received little support from the Democrats or Liberals, who wanted the assembly reconvened. At a meeting of political leaders in early March, Lon Nol complained that even after the assembly had been dissolved for five months it was still a dictatorship, while Prince Norodom Montana, whose party had made no showing in the elections, suggested that all political parties should be represented in the cabinet whether they had won seats in the assembly or not.

The minor parties also insisted on the augmentation of royal prerogatives, a strategy that suited commissioner de Raymond and the king, who told a correspondent in early 1950 that he considered himself to be "at the same time the father and the first citizen of the Khmer nation"—a view he retained for the rest of his career. He went on to say that although the established parties would support a national union government, provided that Yem Sambaur was excluded from it, he himself favored continuing to work with Sambaur. In early 1950, however, Sambaur began to grant special privileges to soldiers loyal to Dap Chhuon, and a month after founding his own political party he resigned. His cabinet was replaced by a nonpolitical one led by Prince Sisowath Monipong, Monireth's affable younger brother.[68]

The new cabinet was sworn in almost five years to the day after Son Ngoc Thanh, returning from Japan, had become Cambodia's first foreign minister. The position had recently been reinstated but had little meaning, for Cambodia's foreign relations remained under French control. As conditions in the countryside deteriorated, a satirical editorial noted wryly, "It is said that Patagonia and Tierra del Fuego are prepared to recognize the Associated States of Indo-China, and that the Eskimos are thinking seriously of proceeding along the same lines. All these recognitions, however, don't prevent the Khmer Issarak from blowing up all the bridges in Cambodia."[69]

two

Political Warfare, 1950–1955

Cambodia's political history experienced several important turning points in the early 1950s. The first of these was the eclipse of the Democratic party in 1952. This was followed soon afterward by Sihanouk's so-called Crusade for Independence. By the end of 1953, France had granted nearly all of Cambodia's political demands, and the country celebrated its independence. The Viet Minh and their Cambodian supporters contested the legitimacy of this, but by the end of 1954 armed resistance to the Phnom Penh government had come to an end. The final turning point occurred in 1955, when Sihanouk assumed personal command of Cambodian political life. Following elections that were dominated by his "nonpolitical" national movement, political parties effectively disappeared.

Most of the themes I discuss in this chapter lingered for the remainder of the 1950s. Certainly the major actors and the rivalries among them remained unchanged. What made the period 1950–55 different were the radicalization and increasing ineffectiveness of opposition to Sihanouk, the collapse of political parties, and the emergence of Cambodia and Sihanouk onto the international arena.

The radicalization of the opposition must be seen in light of both the final phases of the first Indochina war (1946–54) and the radicalization of many Cambodian students, particularly those in France, who were to play leading parts in the revolution of 1975–78. The collapse of political parties after 1955 occurred because of Sihanouk's aggressiveness, his developing skills, and the timidity and fragmentation of the parties themselves. The emergence of Cambodia onto the world stage had little impact on the history of larger powers, but Cambodia bordered on countries thought to be important by participants in the Cold War, and it soon became the plaything of these powers and the victim of its location.

Two new themes emerged in this period. The first was the conversion of a small group of Cambodians born in the 1920s and early 1930s to Marxism-Leninism. In the 1960s, these men and women—among them Saloth Sar, Ieng Sary, Son Sen, Khieu Samphan, and several others— came to form the leadership of Cambodia's Communist party. Nearly all of them studied together in France in the early 1950s. The second theme was Sihanouk's assumption of command over Cambodian political life. He had been edging in this direction ever since 1949. In 1952–53 he gained freedom of maneuver by skillful use of his political position and by playing on the reverence accorded a Cambodian king by nearly all Khmer.[1]

The Viet Minh and the Khmer Issarak

In 1950, the war in Indochina entered its fourth year, and the components of Indochina attracted hundreds of millions of dollars of military and economic aid from the United States. By 1954, Washington was providing 80 percent of the funds the French needed to prosecute the war. Similarly, Chinese aid in the form of weapons, ammunition, sanctuary, and training helped to turn the Communist Viet Minh forces in Vietnam into an effective military force. So did their experience in combat. In 1946 the ICP officially dissolved itself but secretly stepped up its efforts to recruit political cadre and logistical support as well as to gain control of the resistance movements in Cambodia and Laos. These were expected to provide sanctuary and supplies for the struggle inside Vietnam. By the middle of 1950 the ICP's leaders perceived the war in Indo-Chinese terms. Viet Minh efforts to guide the Khmer and Lao resistance, in turn, were facilitated by the fact that after 1949 Thai support for the two movements fell off sharply.[2]

The intensification of the war encouraged the Vietnamese to think about the rest of Indochina. In March 1950, Le Duc Tho, dubbed by French intelligence at the time the "delegate of the pseudo-government of Ho Chi Minh," and Nguyen Thanh Son, the chief of the Viet Minh's committee for foreign affairs in southern Vietnam (Nam Bo), met at Hatien, near the Cambodian border, with Vietnamese and Cambodian subordinates and cadre to determine how to accelerate the Cambodian revolution. On the Cambodian side, the meeting was attended by Son Ngoc Minh, Sieu Heng, Tou Samouth, and Chan Samay, among others. Nguyen Thanh Son delivered a speech analyzing Cambodian society as he saw it and estimating its prospects for revolution.[3]

After noting that Cambodia's Liberals were feudal and that the Democrats enjoyed wide support, Son came to grips with a major contradiction confronting revolutionary thinkers and practitioners in Cambodia, then and later. Looking for preconditions for a revolution, he noted that the country was "agricultural with scattered settlements and an autarchic, family-oriented mode of production. A small number of properties are in the hands of Chinese proprietors." In other words, the customary spurs for revolutionary mobilization—an exploitative class of landlords, a bourgeoisie, and a shortage of land—were absent or poorly developed. Cambodian peasants were autarchic and resistant to outside pressure, but they were "the most unhappy and numerous class, in the regions furthest from cities and bodies of water. This social class lives in the blackest of misery. They awake slowly but surely. They constitute the principal force of the Khmer revolution." The "principal force" of the revolution, in other words, was still *asleep,* and Son noted regretfully that "a powerful peasant organization" and a "revolutionary nationalist party" were lacking to give the peasants any guidance. So was a proletariat, although he failed to say so.

In other words, the people who constituted the principal force of the revolution were diffuse, autarchic, and asleep. They lacked leadership, ideology, and organization. The revolution could not proceed without them, but how could they be mobilized? Interestingly, Son makes no reference to the fact that Cambodian peasants might be mobilized to fight for Cambodia's independence more readily than they could be summoned to serve socialism or the clandestine ICP. Nguyen Thanh Son and Le Duc Tho would have preferred peasant leaders in Cambodia to be members of a Marxist-Leninist party, yet Son noted that the "Proletarian party," as he called the ICP, "has [up to now] been able to guide the movement, [but] it is composed for the most part of Vietnamese, and still has no deep roots among the Khmer people."[4]

Indeed, French intelligence estimated that at the time of the Hatien meeting only forty ethnic Khmer (and over a thousand resident Vietnamese) belonged to the ICP inside Cambodia. In the absence of a deeply rooted party, Son went on, Marxism-Leninism "must be dispensed, first of all, among the most evolved elements in Cambodia, whose own cultural, social and economic worth are still not developed."

These "elements" included Cambodia's small intellectual class, at this stage largely loyal to the Democrats. Son's plans for the peasants and his optimism about them mingled contradictions and astute observations with wishful thinking. Without meaning to do so, Son forecast the disastrous trajectory that Cambodian Communism was to follow for the next three decades, whereby a small intellectual elite pulled the poorest peasants not only into class warfare directed against the remainder of Cambodian society, but also toward an autarchic set of policies that led to a full-scale confrontation with Vietnam that was impossible to win. This trajectory was invisible in 1950, but prospects for a successful revolution were also difficult to discern. Cambodia's revolution began, at Vietnamese insistence, without an indigenous proletariat or any communally organized grouping, aside from the Buddhist sangha. There was also a shortage of trained and dedicated cadre. That shortage combined in a volatile manner with the perceived necessity of "awakening" Cambodian peasants to revolutionary violence. In the 1970s, when the inflammable mixture became a national policy, one in eight Cambodians died as a result.

In 1950, Son was buoyantly optimistic. He failed to see that the social ingredients for a Cambodian revolution were fraught with danger. He also took for granted that it would be subordinate to the revolution in Vietnam. The liberation of Indochina and its subsequent domination by Vietnam was what he had in mind. Relatively advanced Cambodians, he thought, would absorb enough Marxism-Leninism to lead their compatriots along a path illuminated by Vietnam's more sophisticated struggle.

Soon afterward, the "first national congress of the Khmer resistance" convened inside Cambodia. Those attending included many who had not been present at the meeting in Hatien and others who were not affiliated with the ICP. The congress ratified the formation of a Khmer Issarak Association, with a committee drawn from the southwest (Chan Samay and Son Ngoc Minh), the northwest (Sieu Heng), and the southeast (Tou Samouth and Chandara). According to Chandara's recollections, five of the eleven executives had been born in southern Vietnam. The meeting adopted an Issarak flag featuring a yellow, five-towered image of Angkor Wat on a red background, a symbol to be resurrected twenty-nine years later as the flag of the PRK. At the same meeting a temporary People's Liberation Central Committee was formed. Composed entirely of ICP members, it was led (as was the larger, open committee) by President Son Ngoc Minh. Ben Kiernan has aptly styled the committee a protogovernment. Two months later, on the grounds that the Issarak forces controlled one-third of Cambodian territory, Minh declared Cambodia's independence. His government was immediately recognized by the Viet Minh and by the Lao resistance movement, while the Viet Minh's military commander, Vo Nguyen Giap, was quoted as saying, "The Cambodian and Laotian revolutionary movements have thus surmounted all the difficulties which had prevented them from closely following the Vietnamese movement."[5]

In November 1950, the organization of the Khmer resistance was refined further at a meeting held in northern Vietnam and attended by several Indo-Chinese representatives. The attendees decided to form a Joint United Front of Indo-China. The Cambodian representative at the meeting was Sieu Heng, who also attended the Second National (sic) Congress of the ICP, held in February 1951, when the ICP in Vietnam was revived as the Vietnam Workers' Party (VWP). A resolution passed at the congress stated, "Because of new conditions in Indo-China and the world, Vietnam will establish a VWP with a political program and a constitution suited to Vietnam's conditions. Laos and Cambodia will also found their respective revolutionary organizations suited to the conditions of their respective countries."

These decisions were not made public. Instead, Viet Minh radio noted that a Cambodian Buddhist conference chaired by Son Ngoc Minh had recently taken place, and in April broadcast the communiqués issued by yet another meeting of United Front representatives that called on the Lao, Vietnamese, Cambodians to unite "even more closely." These broadcasts may have been veiled descriptions of the clandestine meetings, for Sieu Heng is listed in one of these as the "leader of the Cambodian Liberation Army."[6]

The decision to found the Khmer People's Revolutionary Party (KPRP) was taken in connection with the VWP congress. The foundation ceremony itself, if there was one, may have occurred at some point between the United Front meeting in March and the end of June 1951, which was the date celebrated later by the PRK as the founding date of the party.

The new grouping, like its predecessor, was subject to Vietnamese guidance. According to Bernard Fall, the KPRP's statutes were drafted in Vietnamese and then translated into Khmer. They were probably brought back to Cambodia by Sieu Heng, who stayed in Vietnam until August

1951. The final draft of the statutes, dated February 1952, consisted of a "simplified version" of the VWP statutes, with the references to Marx, Engels, Stalin, and Mao Zedong excised.[7]

Cambodian Radicals in France, 1949–1953

At the end of August 1949, a twenty-one-year-old student from the Ecole Technique in Phnom Penh, Saloth Sar, joined twenty other young Cambodians aboard the s/s *Jamaique* in Saigon to sail to France. Before their departure the students had been feted by the Democrats, whose officials in the Ministry of Education had been instrumental in obtaining scholarships for them. A month later the ship arrived in Marseilles, where the group dispersed for tertiary studies at various sites. Sar lacked a baccalauréat and had probably gained the scholarship in recognition of his work for the Democrats in 1947. Born into a family of wealthy landowners near the provincial capital of Kompong Thom in 1928 he had left home as a young boy to pursue studies in Phnom Penh and Kompong Cham. He had connections in the royal palace, where his brother held a minor administrative post and where an aunt, a leading dancer in the Royal Ballet, had borne a child to King Monivong. People who knew Sar as a secondary student have commented on his ingratiating manner, his fondness for sports, and his apparent lack of ambition.[8]

When he left for France he was not particularly radical, but he belonged to what soon became a radical generation of Cambodians. Of those aboard the *Jamaique,* five would have their scholarships rescinded for radical activities in France in 1952–53, and two others—Saloth Sar and Chau Seng—were to rise inside the Cambodian Communist movement without having been singled out for opprobrium while abroad.

On their long voyage through the Indian Ocean, the Red Sea, and the Mediterranean, many of these young Cambodians formed lasting friendships. They had all come to maturity in the late 1940s, the time of Asia's wars of decolonization, and China's civil war. Their arrival in Europe coincided almost exactly with the proclamation of the People's Republic of China.

When this group landed in France, approximately one hundred Cambodians were pursuing tertiary studies there. The number rose steadily in the 1950s. Most of these men and women were politically neutral and became bureaucrats or technicians when they returned to Cambodia. A few, exhilarated by their encounters in France with personal freedom, radical politics, and anticolonial ideas, joined the Communist Party of France (CPF) or became its *compagnons de route.* A handful in turn formed political beliefs, bonds, and alliances in Paris that endured through the DK era into the 1980s, when they still held high positions in the CPK. This group included Saloth Sar, Son Sen, Ieng Sary, Khieu Samphan, Thiounn Prasith, Mey Man, and the sisters Khieu Thirith and Khieu Ponnary. Others close to them also rose in the party but were purged in 1976–78. This group included Touch Phoeun, Hou Youn, Yun Soeurn, Hu Nim, and Sien An.[9]

It would be wrong to exaggerate the French ingredients of the thought-worlds of these Cambodians, but their shared experiences in the early 1950s—the era of Stalinism, the first Indochina war, the war in Korea, and the heyday of the CPF in French intellectual circles—were crucial in bonding them together and in giving them ideas about the transformation of Cambodian politics and society. Their experiences in France set them apart from Cambodians at home who collaborated with the French, confronted them as Democrats, or fought them as Khmer Issarak and Viet Minh.

Most Cambodian students in France saw themselves as intellectuals. It was a small step for them to see themselves as a vanguard, ahead and above the rest of their compatriots. Most of them first encountered communism and socialist ideas in the heady days between the triumph of communism in China and the death of Stalin four years later. Jacques Vergès, active in student circles and the CPF in these years, has called this period "the springtime of peoples," but to many Khmers in Europe at the time, communism seemed the wave of the future.[10]

To be sure, this period of Communist history was marked by bitter conflicts and distressing revelations. In France, as elsewhere, party discipline was strict and punishments for deviation severe. Arthur Koestler was stigmatized by the CPF for writing *Darkness at Noon*, and the party was at pains to deny or play down reports of purges, concentration camps, and forced labor in the USSR. Maurice Merleau-Ponty's disingenuous, influential book *Humanism and Terror,* in part an apologia for the show-trials in the USSR in the 1930s, was published at this time. For many young Khmer exposure to Communist thinking and Communist colleagues intensified their feelings of Cambodian nationalism. Communism for some of these young people was an international faith; for others, a mechanism for gaining self-assurance and political power; for most, it was the organizational, military, and political tool that they believed would liberate Cambodia from French colonialism and from its own retrograde sociology.[11]

The bloodless purges in the CPF at the time attracted the interest of party members and sympathizers from Indochina. Pierre Brocheux has recalled visiting his friend and fellow Communist Rath Samoeun in the hospital and listening to Samoeun speak approvingly of the possibility of some day conducting similar purges in the ranks of the ICP.[12]

Keng Vannsak, a student of Cambodian philology, was three years older than Saloth Sar. Having arrived in Paris in 1946, fresh from his baccalauréat, he was to play a key role among Cambodian students. Like Cambodia's only *polytechnicien,* Thiounn Mumm, who had preceded him to France by several months, Vannsak acted as an older brother for students from Cambodia, many of whom he had known in the 1940s at the Lycée Sisowath. As a linguist and scholar of Cambodian literature, he gained an intellectual reputation similar to the one Thiounn Mumm enjoyed among scientists, mathematicians, and engineers. In his philological work, Vannsak tried to uncover pre-Buddhist, pre-Sanskrit layers of Cambodian vocabulary and culture. The idea that Cambodia could and should be cut off from other cultures persisted in many Cambodian regimes and resurfaced not only in the Khmer Republic, but also among some of Vannsak's disciples in DK.[13]

During their first few years in France neither Vannsak nor Mumm was politically active, although they followed overseas developments and were eager to create some space between Cambodian students and Indo-Chinese ones, dominated by Vietnam. The pace of radicalization among Cambodians in France quickened when two students from the Lycée Sisowath, Rath Samoeun and Ieng Sary, arrived in October 1950. Both had been active in the strike of the preceding year, and both of them had already absorbed a smattering of Marxist teaching.

Soon after Samoeun and Sary arrived, they began to participate in an informal Marxist studies circle that met at Vannsak's apartment in the Fifteenth *arrondissement.* When Vannsak returned to Cambodia in 1952, the group moved to Ieng Sary's hotel room in the rue St André des Arts. The circle and others like it were associated with the *groupes des langues* set up in 1949 by the CPF among foreign students and workers. For organizational purposes, it seems, Indo-Chinese members of the CPF formed a single group, although Indo-Chinese people spoke three national languages. Vannsak's discussion group had no formal links with the party, but some of those who attended it were party members, and the group's readings reflected Communist concerns. The readings included Lenin's "On Imperialism," Stalin's "On the National Question" and "Dialectical Materialism," and the *Communist Manifesto*. The works were read in French; the discussions were held in a mixture of Cambodian and French, for many political terms had no Khmer equivalents.[14]

After the study circle was established, Ieng Sary introduced Vannsak to Saloth Sar. In 1951, Vannsak found Sar a room across the street from his own apartment. Sar was by then enrolled in a course of electronics but showed little interest in it, and according to Vannsak "spent most of his time reading." Mey Mann, who had come to France with Sar aboard the *Jamaique* and soon became a member of the CPF, recalled Sar years later as "a good man, just like you and me, with an interest in going to the movies." A contrary report, unfortunately unsourced, states that Saloth Sar was "the most intelligent, the most active, the most convinced" of all the Cambodian students in France and quotes him as predicting his own success, years later, as secretary of the CPK central committee: "I will direct the revolutionary organization," he said. "I will hold the dossiers." To Keng Vannsak, recalling him in 1987, he seemed unassuming, skilled in argument, and drawn to the organizational side of politics. Saloth Sar, unlike Sary or Vannsak, was not a university student, and some better-educated Khmer probably looked down on him. None of them singled him out as a potential leader.

Saloth Sar's relationship with the CPF is problematic. Before joining Vannsak's discussion group, he spent a month (August 1950) in an international work brigade in Yugoslavia alongside seventeen other Cambodian students and several hundred youths of other nationalities, all recruited in France. Together, they helped construct student housing at the University of Zagreb. At the time, the confrontation between Stalin and Tito was so intense that visiting Yugoslavia was grounds for expulsion from the CPF. Students were recruited for the summer by anti-Stalinist French radicals estranged from the party. As Michael Vickery has pointed out, Yugoslavian praxis at the time, which emphasized the collectivization of agriculture, self-reliance, voluntarism, and mass mobilization for public works, may have stuck in Saloth Sar's mind as an exhilarating model for Cambodia; in 1953 and again in 1978 he recalled his time in Yugoslavia with pleasure. Indeed, a letter sent to the Yugoslav authorities by another Cambodian student, Ieu Yang, thanking them for their hospitality contained phraseology eerily foreshadowing DK a quarter of a century later: "Everywhere the Peoples' Federated Republic of Yugoslavia resembles an enormous work site," he declared, "where factories, roads, railways, and hydraulic power stations are being built. This effort is even more estimable because the force and the faith of the people, united around their leaders, allow them to win successive victories, aware that this is a question of national independence."[15]

Almost a year after this, in July 1951, several Cambodian students in Paris attended a festival sponsored by the International Federation of Democratic Youth in East Berlin. They had been invited by Jacques Vergès, then in Prague coordinating Communist youth policy throughout Europe. Those who attended included Thiounn Mumm, his brother Thiounn Prasith, Sien An, Rath Samoeun, Hou Youn, and Ieng Sary. At the congress they learned from Viet Minh delegates about Cambodian participation in the struggle against France. They returned excitedly to Paris with brochures that included photographs of Son Ngoc Minh and a sample of the Issarak five-towered flag.[16]

Soon afterward, left-wing students were voted into control of the Union des Etudiants Khmers (UEK) in Paris, and discussions about the future of their country became heated. Those who had been to East Berlin were impressed by the militant cooperation between the Vietnamese and the Khmer in the struggle to liberate Indochina. They wanted to return to Cambodia as volunteers. Others, like Ea Sichau, Thiounn Mumm's fellow student in Hanoi, saw the liberation of their country in more Titoist terms, that is, as independent of Vietnamese supervision. Still others wanted Son Ngoc Thanh to take command of the Democrats and lead a parliamentary struggle. In September 1951, Thiounn Mumm and Ieng Sary visited Thanh in Poitiers to tell him about the Berlin conference. They urged him to endorse armed struggle in Cambodia. He failed to do so, for by then he was planning to return to Cambodia at Sihanouk's invitation.[17]

In the meantime, another electoral campaign was in full swing in Cambodia. Most Cambodians in Paris wanted the Democrats to win. Thiounn Mumm, however, argued that it would be better to lose some seats and build up a homogenous minority in the assembly that would not be obliged to govern the country and could support armed struggle in rural areas. He has recalled saying that "organizing the party is more important than winning elections." His line did not prevail: in the elections of 1951 the Democrats retained their majority. Soon afterward, Thanh flew back to

Cambodia, hoping to reach a compromise with Sihanouk. His departure left many Cambodian students in France disillusioned and without an indigenous political leader to respect.

Politics in Phnom Penh, 1950–1951

In the buildup to the assembly elections, the confrontation among Sihanouk, the French, and Cambodia's conservative politicians on the one hand and the Democrats and the armed resistance on the other continued. With the assembly suspended, there was little substantive debate among these factions. To lay the groundwork for elections, Prince Monipong's government drafted a new electoral law, but the Liberals and the Democrats urged him to reconvene the assembly to which their candidates had been elected in 1947. The minor parties, which had won no seats in 1947, wanted new elections. One politician, looking for precedents, cited Charles II of England's reopening of Parliament in 1661, but did not cast Cambodian actors for the roles of Cromwell and Charles I. Sihanouk asked the factional leaders to reach a compromise. Unable to break the deadlock, Monipong and his cabinet resigned in February 1951. An interim, nonpolitical cabinet took their place.[18]

The Democrats refused to join the new cabinet, and soon afterward Sihanouk told the U.S. minister to the Associated States, Donald Heath, that the people were "clamoring for an assembly and the maintenance of the constitution." Sihanouk was telling Heath what he presumed he wanted to hear. A few days later he told Commissioner de Raymond that elections were undesirable. Sihanouk's habit of trying to please his listeners by telling them what he thought they wanted to hear persisted throughout his career. It seems likely that he wanted new elections, so as to be seen as upholding the constitution. He also wanted the Democrats to lose. In his tours of the countryside he emphasized that people should be loyal to the constitution—about which they knew almost nothing—and also to Democracy, which he failed to explain. There is only one word for *Democrat* and for *Democracy* in Khmer—*pracheathipodei*—and years later Sihanouk claimed that the people had misinterpreted his advice as royal sponsorship of the Democratic party, which he failed to mention. In his memoirs, the Democrat leader Huy Kanthoul has admitted that these verbal interventions probably helped his party. On a larger scale, however, a feature of Cambodian politics between 1945 and 1955 was the way in which the Democrats could capitalize on voters' longings for independence and social change, which Sihanouk was fitfully beginning to address. The Liberals, on the other hand, pocketed French subventions, served their clientele, and had no national program.[19]

In the run-up to the elections, a new party calling itself the Victorious Northeast made its appearance. The force behind it was Dap Chhuon, the overlord of Siem Reap, and the new party was expected to serve his interests. Support for it came from his relatives, renegade Democrats, and local clients. French money may also have been involved, for as Vickery has noted, the appearance of the party meant that "a large piece of Cambodian territory would not . . . be under the effective control of a Democrat government"—a situation pleasing to Sihanouk and the French who were tactically united against the Democrats.[20]

The elections were relatively calm. There were 496 candidates from several political parties as well as 62 independents contending for 78 seats in the assembly. Because of insecurity, some 300 voting booths failed to open. This may explain why 117,000 fewer people voted in 1951 than in 1947, although absenteeism in secure areas, including Phnom Penh, was also high, suggesting that the issues posed by the election were unclear to many. Booths did not open in the areas under Viet Minh and Issarak control, but outside of these regions insurgent leaders were unable to enforce their policy of boycotting the election and had to be content with broadcasting that "700,000 French puppets"—in visual terms, a startling image—had participated in it.

For opponents of the Democrats the results were disappointing. The Democrats won 54 seats, the Liberals 18, the Victorious Northeast 4, and Khmer Renovation 2. The leaders of three minor parties—Sam Nhean, Lon Nol, and Yem Sambaur—failed to be elected and became bitter opponents of the assembly from then on. The Democrats, on the other hand, had gained less than 45 percent of the votes cast and the support of less than 25 percent of the registered voters. This falling-off may have been related to the party's failure to deliver independence, but Sihanouk and his colleagues in the poorly performing parties viewed the elections as a rebuff, tinted with lèse-majesté. Their impatience with elections sprang from their losing so many. They preferred to gain and hold power by other means.[21]

The Return of Son Ngoc Thanh

For several years, under pressure from his father and his father's friends in the Democratic party, Sihanouk had tried to persuade the French to reduce Son Ngoc Thanh's administrative detention and allow him to return home. The king may have hoped that Thanh's gratitude to him could be exploited to split the Democrats and that he could exploit Thanh's popularity to lever concessions from the French. According to a close associate of Son Ngoc Thanh, Sihanouk was also grateful that Thanh had intervened on his behalf with the Japanese in 1945, when they had wanted to replace him with a more militant member of the royal family. The French were not bothered by Thanh's return. They probably saw him as a spent force.[22]

They were mistaken. Thanh arrived in Phnom Penh by air on the afternoon of October 29 and was welcomed by Democrat officials. The six-mile trip into the city in an open car took more than an hour. The roadside was crowded with some one hundred thousand supporters carrying banners that read "Son Ngoc Thanh Our Hope" and "Son Ngoc Thanh, National Hero." Sihanouk felt insulted and made it a point, exactly two years later, to travel the same route on the last leg of a cortege that started in Siem Reap and be applauded by a larger crowd.[23]

Earlier in the afternoon of the twenty-ninth, almost certainly by coincidence, a Vietnamese houseboy employed by Commissioner de Raymond surprised him during his siesta, stabbed and hammered him to death, and managed to escape. Several days later, having found refuge in Vietnam, the assassin was declared a national hero by the Viet Minh. It seems likely that the Viet Minh had planted him in de Raymond's household, where the commissioner's allegedly bizarre sexual tastes made him an easy target. To replace him temporarily, the French named their military commander in Cambodia, Brig. Jean Dio, a bluff war hero who was expected to develop political skills while continuing to prosecute the war.[24]

A new Democratic cabinet headed by one of the party's founders, Huy Kanthoul, had been sworn in before Son Ngoc Thanh's arrival. Pach Chhoeun, recently released from detention in France, became minister of information, but Son Ngoc Thanh, pleading that he lacked ambition, refused the post of minister of foreign affairs. According to Prince Monireth, writing in the 1960s, Thanh had expected the Kanthoul government to resign en masse, so that he could form a government himself. This is not corroborated in other sources. In mid-December, Thanh explained to an American diplomat that "he had been outside Cambodia for a time and wished to continue his conversations with all elements" before accepting a cabinet position. Thanh struck the American as a "vigorous, voluble political leader" but "somewhat idealistic."[25]

In early 1952, while Huy Kanthoul was in France on an official mission,

Pach Chhoeun made a series of provincial tours in the course of which he praised local Democratic officials and the national achievements of the party. On these occasions, his old friend Son Ngoc Thanh trailed along as a "private citizen." Thanh's presence pleased antimonarchic elements in the party and the Buddhist sangha, but the French dispatched agents to attend the rallies. They became annoyed by Thanh's popularity and angered that the U.S. cultural attaché went along on some of the trips, allegedly to monitor public address systems provided by U.S. aid. The French were distressed that the Americans were supporting Cambodia's elected government. To complicate the picture, at some provincial receptions photographs of Ieu Koeuss and Yuthevong—but not of the king—were displayed.

The Democrats' energy and the slow progress of the war exasperated General Dio, who complained to his superior in Saigon, Gen. Raoul Salan, that a "fever of demagoguery [was] paralyzing the government." Following the appearance in a French-financed newspaper of an article that attacked the Democrats (it was entitled "The Infantile Malady of Nationalism"), Democratic candidates won three by-elections in regions where balloting had been postponed.[26]

The French insisted that Thanh and the Democrats were closely allied, and when Thanh's inflammatory newspaper *Khmer Krauk!* (Khmers awake!) appeared in January 1952 the French assumed that its calls for independence represented Democratic policy. In the meantime, as it later developed, Thanh had amassed some three hundred thousand piasters (approximately $40,000 at 1952 rates of exchange) in back pay, covering the salary he would have earned in the Indochinese civil service between his arrest in October 1945 and his return to Phnom Penh.[27]

On March 9, 1952, the seventh anniversary of the Japanese coup de force, Thanh, Ea Sichau, at this stage a customs official, and a handful of others drove out of Phnom Penh in official cars, ostensibly to inspect customs facilities on the Thai border. By nightfall, the convoy had failed to arrive. For several days the press, the police, and diplomatic missions were under the impression that the men had been kidnapped by Issarak guerrillas. In fact, an eyewitness later reported that the cars were met by armed men on horseback led by a well-known Issarak, Kao Tak, near Kralanh in northern Siem Reap. Tak then led Thanh and his colleagues peaceably into the forest. Joining the Issaraks had been Thanh's intention all along.[28]

Thanh's choice of Siem Reap, an autonomous zone that contained no

French combat forces, suggests that he did not expect to take on the French militarily. He may have expected some aid from Thailand, which was quietly supporting Kao Tak. More important, he hoped that his gesture would galvanize Cambodia's anticolonial movement. Unfortunately, only three hundred people, most of them students, rallied to his side.[29]

In Phnom Penh, the Democrats took no punitive action against what a British diplomat referred to as "Thanh and his merry men." Their opponents and the French were quick to accuse the party of condoning treason—a word the French had first used about Thanh in 1945. According to Thonn Ouk, Sihanouk's final alienation from the Democrats dated from their refusal to send security forces after Son Ngoc Thanh. A prominent Democrat, Sonn Voeunsai, said at the time that Thanh, by his departure, had "dug the grave of the Democratic party."[30]

Two weeks after setting up camp, Thanh's agents made contact across the Thai border with local authorities, seeking food and medicine. The deputy chief of police in the Surin border area, Capt. (eventually Maj. Gen.) Channa Samudvanija, who was to play a major role in Thai-Cambodian relations for the next thirty years or more, met Thanh soon after his defection and befriended him. He has said that his decision to help Thanh was a personal one, but it seems likely that his gesture was approved from authorities higher up. Certainly Thanh moved freely back and forth over the border during the next few years.

Of Thanh's new allies, Kao Tak was pro-Thai and anti-Vietnamese; his adopted sister, Muon, was also a combatant and urged limited cooperation with the Viet Minh, while Leo Keo Moni, also commanding Issarak forces in the northwest, was openly pro–Viet Minh. Thanh himself sought to distance himself from the Viet Minh and to seek allies among such non-Communist Issaraks as Puth Chhay, Prince Chantaraingsey, and Savang Vong. Small groups of potential followers were sent along to his camp by Chantaraingsey and Saloth Chhay, Saloth Sar's older brother, who had Issarak connections in Kompong Thom, while a dozen lycée students from Phnom Penh, including such future luminaries as Ieu Yang, Han Tun Hak, Um Sim, and Lek Samoeun, walked away from their studies to join Thanh in the maquis.[31]

In addition, "eighty to a hundred" boys and girls from the Thai-Cambodia border area were recruited at this time. One of them was Tak's nephew Sim Kin, who spent the next twenty years working and fighting on Son Ngoc Thanh's behalf. Kin has recalled that the Viet Minh sent emissaries to Thanh in 1952, asking him to send followers to fight inside Vietnam and proposing that he allow Vietnamese troops to fight alongside his followers in the northwest. According to Kin, Thanh rejected the proposals, fearing a Vietnamese takeover.[32]

Twenty years later, Michael Vickery interviewed Dom Thal, who had been an Issarak at this time and was familiar with Thanh's operations. According to Thal, Ea Sichau was the intellectual leader of Thanh's movement. Sichau, he said, "refused to take a drink, and never gambled, or danced." He was widely read and considered himself a Marxist but had no party affiliations. In 1988, Sim Kin remembered him as a "very decent man, who taught us politics. All the young people loved him," while Lek Samoeun has described his ideas as being "strong, nationalistic, and interesting." Discipline in Thanh's camp was strict, and recruits were taught to respect local people, to study local conditions, and to "persuade the peasants by example." In 1952, according to Dom Thal, Sichau was dispatched to Chantaraingsey's base area to supervise political training. A year later, when Thanh's movement was becalmed, Sichau became disillusioned with it, feuded with Thanh, and retired to a monastery in Bangkok. He returned to Cambodia eventually and died in 1959.[33]

Thanh's failure to unite the resistance probably surprised him. For the rest of the 1950s, he badgered world leaders with mimeographed letters, memoranda, and manifestos claiming that he had a large following inside Cambodia. He did not. By cutting himself off from Phnom Penh and by failing to come to terms with pro-Communist insurrectionaries, Thanh closed off his political career.

Sihanouk and General Dio, meanwhile, used Thanh's flight to castigate the Democrats and what Sihanouk now called the party's "policy of insecurity and treason." General Dio went further, remarking that he "found the Cambodians unworthy, their government corrupt and the king incapable of either self-assertion or sustained attention to affairs of state." In a report to Saigon, he complained of the "thousand proofs . . . of treason inside the government, although these are not the kind that can be exploited in a court of law."[34]

In this overheated atmosphere, the French toyed with the idea of setting up a government headed by Nhiek Tioulong or Prince Monireth. The French political councilor noted that whatever course was chosen, "we must move rapidly, for all Cambodians want true independence."[35]

Sihanouk's Coup d'Etat

In May and June 1952, the crisis over Thanh's flight came to a head. In early May, high school students on parade in Phnom Penh substituted anti-French banners for milder ones celebrating Cambodia's constitution. Rumors spread that troops involved in a French attack on Thanh's head- quarters had committed atrocities against civilians. In Battambang stu- dents paraded for "total independence"; others in Kompong Cham dem- onstrated "against the king." Radical Cambodian students in France cabled the government demanding that it push for independence. The telegram praised the constitution but failed to mention the king. Toward the end of the month, there were strikes and anti-French parades in Bat- tambang, Kompong Cham, and Phnom Penh; at the parade in Phnom Penh a banner read, "The French have sucked the Cambodians' blood for eighty years." Demonstrators in Battambang were fired on and wounded by police. What the Democrats saw as a tide running in their favor was perceived by the French and Sihanouk as impending chaos. Unfortunately for the Democrats, the French were armed and they were not.[36]

At the beginning of June, the Democrats convened a party congress in Phnom Penh. After pledging its loyalty to the king, "who has always deigned to lead the nation in . . . the direction of independence," the congress named a respected economist, Son Sann, as the party's presi- dent. The party appeared ready to cooperate with the king, but Sihanouk was still on the offensive. Two days after the congress he presided at the investiture of the Democrat-dominated Council of the Kingdom, or upper house, warning its members, in Khmer, of the dangers inherent in "the dictatorship of a single party." For ten days, Pach Chhoeun's Ministry of Information failed to publish a French translation of Sihanouk's remarks. This angered Sihanouk, and on June 7 tracts demanding that the assem- bly be dissolved and that Huy Kanthoul be dismissed from office circu- lated in Phnom Penh. Leaflets supporting the Renovation party were tossed from a passing army truck. The minor parties clearly hoped to goad the Democrats into an unconstitutional response.[37]

After 1955 gestures like these would have led to prison terms and executions. The Democrats responded cautiously by sending police with proper documentation to search the homes of the leaders of the minor parties. They detained Lon Nol, Sam Nhean, Mao Say, and Yem Sambaur. In his memoirs, Huy Kanthoul wrote that Sambaur's arrest—the only one that led to overnight custody—sprang from his alleged involvement two years earlier in the assassination of Ieu Koeuss. A case of grenades was found in his house, and three machine guns in Lon Nol's. Lon Nol was infuriated by his brief detention. Ironically, in view of his subsequent years as the force behind Cambodia's political police, he complained that his rights had been abused by his being held in custody for four hours.[38]

On June 9, the French joined Sihanouk in a pincer movement against the Democrats. Sihanouk conferred with Huy Kanthoul and the new French commissioner, Jean Risterucci, who left the meeting to request French authorities in Saigon to send a battalion of Moroccan infantry and an armored squadron to Phnom Penh "for ten days";[39] Huy Kanthoul had no knowledge of these communications. The requests were processed on June 11, and the troops and equipment were dispatched from Saigon three days later. In the aftermath of what followed, Risterucci told a British diplomat that it was purely coincidental that Sihanouk's coup d'état on June 15 took place on the same day as Risterucci, expecting "disorderly demonstrations" in Phnom Penh, ordered in the additional troops. According to Huy Kanthoul, Sihanouk and his parents were infuriated by Yem Sambaur's arrest. Before moving against the Democrats, they were assured of success by the court astrologer and by the promise of additional French troops.[40]

French support for a move to cripple the Democrats is not surprising, but the Democrats were not prepared for it. On Sunday morning, June 15, as the newly arrived Moroccan troops took up positions at several points around Phnom Penh, Sihanouk brusquely dismissed Huy Kanthoul and his cabinet from office. He named a new, non-Democrat cabinet and took over as prime minister, citing residual powers granted him in the constitution. His cousin Sirik Matak was put in charge of defense, and Suramarit's old friend Sim Var became minister of information.

The king promised to clean up corruption by 1954 and to gain independence from France by 1955. In the meantime, French Union troops surrounded the National Assembly, and French "tanks rumbled up and down Phnom Penh's principal streets." Two days later they were back in Saigon, and a royal decree banned political meetings and the diffusion of propaganda. Sihanouk's so-called Royal Crusade for Independence—a political carte blanche that Sihanouk issued to himself—was under way.

Sihanouk summoned the U.S. chargé d'affaires, Thomas Corcoran, and his Thai counterpart to the palace to explain what he had done. His reasons for dismissing Kanthoul, he said, were the Democrats' spoils system, the party's failure to take a forthright stand on Son Ngoc Thanh, and Democrats' "dictatorial policy toward minority parties." His real objection was that the elected government had been attempting to govern the country. The king was no longer willing to play the role of a constitutional monarch or to be an instrument of French colonial policy. Instead, he was edging toward ruling the country on his own. According to the U.S. embassy, Sirik Matak remarked soon thereafter that "democracy modelled on French parties in Cambodia had failed, and [that] democracy was fine under an absolute monarchy." In the wake of these veiled threats, Son Sann resigned as head of the Democrats and Huy Kanthoul left for a prolonged holiday in France.[41]

Sihanouk remained in the palace for several days. The U.S. chargé in Saigon, James Guillion, visited him there and found him in "an exalted state." Sihanouk told Guillion that he was "not only the giver of the constitution, but the giver of elections." He admitted that he needed French help with Cambodia's economy and to fight the insurgents, but he was also mapping out a strategy for himself. The French probably thought that after they had helped him sweep the Democrats aside, he would abide by their glacial timetable for relinquishing control. This was a serious miscalculation.

Cambodian radicals in France had sided with the Democrats in the coup d'état. A special issue of their student magazine, *Khemera Nisut* (Khmer student), was hurriedly pulled together by Keng Vannsak. Writing pseudonymously, Vannsak and Hou Youn were joined by Saloth Sar, writing as "Khmer daom" (Original Khmer). Sar's essays attacked royalty vigorously and noted that "royal edicts will not affect the solidarity of students, which is growing daily." He went on to say, "Democracy is a regime which all peoples of the world are adopting nowadays; it is as precious as a diamond and cannot be compared to any other form of government" and noted that the Buddha, like Prince Yuthevong, had been antimonarchic. The tone of his essay was Thanhist-Democrat rather than Marxian, but the eclipse of the Democrats led many Cambodian students to reconsider their political positions; in Thonn Ouk's view, the coup drove several of them into the arms of the CPF.[42]

Over the next few months, Sihanouk's self-confidence and his impatience with French delays increased, and at one point he remarked, "I carry on my shoulders the overwhelming responsibilities of sixteen centuries of royalty, which has given grandeur to the country and peace to the people."[43] What is curious about this sentence is that Sihanouk ascribed a role to all Cambodian kings similar to the one he believed had been played by the kings at Angkor. In fact, most of Cambodia's monarchs since the seventeenth century had been weak, unpopular, and dominated by neighboring powers. Had kingship been more efficient, powerful, and autonomous, the French would have never been able to establish their Protectorate, which was requested by the Cambodian king to relieve pressure from Bangkok. Had kingship been a strong institution in precolonial Cambodia or in colonial times, Sihanouk would have encouraged Cambodian schoolchildren to study post-Angkorean history. He never did. Instead, he used his own version of kingship stemming from Angkorean times to legitimize his rule.[44]

Like King Chulalongkorn in Thailand in the late nineteenth century (although there are serious differences), Norodom Sihanouk became an absolute ruler almost by accident, using modern techniques to institutionalize an absolutism that had previously been ceremonial, decrepit, and taken for granted. The regimes that followed him intensified the process. Absolutism was always easy to maintain. Cambodian kingship (and later, the leadership of Lon Nol or the CPK central committee) insisted on its unique legitimacy and allowed no plurality of views. Unlike these subsequent rulers, however, Sihanouk could draw on a fund of belief, widespread among rural Cambodians well into the 1960s, that he enjoyed access to beneficial supernatural forces and could assure the country's physical prosperity.[45]

Seen in this way, Sihanouk's coup of June 1952 allowed him to walk into the political arena unopposed. The coup nipped the prospect of pluralism in Cambodia in the bud and marked a major turning point in the kingdom's political history.

The Coup d'Etat: Stage Two

In January 1953, the National Assembly reconvened, and its Democratic leaders decided to confront the king. After Son Sann's resignation, the party's president was Svay So, who was less inclined than Sann to be conciliatory. Svay So's supporters saw the Democrats as having been elected to govern the country, even with their cabinet dissolved. On January 11, Sihanouk addressed the assembly and asked it to grant him special powers, on the grounds that the kingdom was in danger. He cited strikes at high schools in Phnom Penh and Kompong Cham and the assassination of a provincial governor by the Viet Minh. He traced these incidents erroneously to Son Ngoc Thanh and Ea Sichau and blamed the Democrats for supporting them. Sihanouk expected the Democrats either to collapse or to refuse his request, so he could brush them aside. They chose the second course. He then surrounded the assembly with Cambodian troops, dissolved it, and suspended a variety of civil rights.

Was Cambodia really in danger or was Sihanouk acting to expand the powers he had wrested from Huy Kanthoul? In his memoirs, Prince

Monireth suggests that several Democrats, enraged at Sihanouk's conduct in 1952, had planned to declare Cambodia a republic when the assembly reconvened. News of the plot reached Sihanouk's mother, Monireth asserts, via one of the deputies' disgruntled wives. Infuriated, Princess Kossamak ordered the royal printer to prepare a decree for Sihanouk's signature dissolving the assembly and, when it was ready, to thrust it at her son to sign. The story rings true; there is no reason for Monireth to have invented it for his privately circulated memoirs. At the same time, the plot probably never got further than idle conversation among men grown angry at repeated humiliations. Under his emergency decree, Sihanouk imprisoned seventeen Democrats, nine of them former deputies, for "plotting against the state." They were held for eight months but never brought to trial. Soon afterward, an editorial alleged that Cambodians had been accustomed to centuries of "paternalistic, authoritarian" government. The lack of a public response to the king's action, the paper went on, was proof of popular approval. At this point, Sihanouk departed for France, ostensibly on holiday, but in fact to attempt to wrest more concessions from the French.[46]

As the crisis was working itself out Saloth Sar returned home, once more aboard the *Jamaique*. He had passed no examinations while in France; his scholarship had been suspended. In Phnom Penh, he spoke warmly to his brother of his time in Yugoslavia and praised the Soviet Union. According to Keng Vannsak, who had returned before him, Sar soon left the capital to join the Issarak forces of Prince Chantaraingsey in nearby Kompong Speu. By August 1953, according to Vietnamese and Cambodian sources speaking after DK had collapsed, Sar presented himself to Viet Minh forces in eastern Cambodia, claiming to be a member of the CPF. The versions probably represent a sequence of events rather than a contradiction.

By the middle of 1953, several other Cambodians had returned from France to join the struggle. They included Mey Phat, Rath Samoeun, Sien An, Mey Man, and Chi Kim An. In 1981, Ieng Thirith told Elizabeth Becker that Sar had been given humiliating tasks by the Vietnamese, such as carrying excrement from latrines.

Whether Thirith's story is true or not, Sar's months with the Viet Minh were valuable to him, and it seems likely that the Viet Minh cadre considered him, with his French education, palace connections, and affable, bourgeois manner, an excellent recruit. Saloth Sar also came to Tou Samouth's attention at this time. Until his assassination in 1962, Samouth was Sar's patron in the party, and for several years Sar acted as his secretary. Sar's rise to power owes much to this relationship, while his time with the Viet Minh gave him an advantage over radicals who stayed in France.[47]

Sihanouk's Crusade for Independence

When Sihanouk himself went to France in early 1953, no one expected anything dramatic. French officials in Cambodia had looked on approvingly as he had dismantled parliamentary government, and they were willing for him to be an absolute monarch, provided that their own economic and military interests were preserved. The king's Francophilia seemed to guarantee that he would not make inordinate demands.[48]

In fact, Sihanouk's transformation into a strong political leader was gathering momentum. He felt that French power in Indochina was waning. This perception coincided with the disappearance of political competition. The Democrats had been the only group arguing within a constitutional framework for independence. Sihanouk now took up their cause, without sharing any credit. His subsequent writings suggest that his Crusade for Independence was the first pressure placed on the French by anyone in Cambodia since 1945. Once again historiographical highhandedness accompanied a finely developed sense of timing. As always, Sihanouk played to win.

Between February and November 1953, the king waged a courageous, astute, and rewarding campaign to regain Cambodia's independence. The crusade was his finest hour, but his independence-mindedness, coming so late and encased in Francophilia, struck the French people he spoke to as insane. They were surprised when he turned his holiday in France into a state visit and nonplussed by the closely reasoned letter he addressed to President Auriol after his arrival. The letter, which declared that the Cambodian people "are unanimous in wishing violently for independence," went unanswered for two weeks; Sihanouk wrote Auriol again and the French president—with a Gallic shrug, perhaps—invited him to lunch.[49]

Rebuffed on this occasion, Sihanouk learned from Jean Letourneau, the French commissioner for the Associated States, that the French considered his initiatives inopportune. Sihanouk became defiant as he traveled home via Canada, the United States, and Japan. In Washington, he was warned by Secretary of State John Foster Dulles that independence for Cambodia was meaningless. Without French protection, Dulles said, Cambodia would be "swallowed" by the Communists. "Profoundly disillusioned" by this interview, Sihanouk arranged for another with the *New York Times*, of which he wrote later that it "had the effect of a bomb on American and world opinion." In the interview he proposed that France grant commonwealth status to the components of Indochina and threatened that if independence were postponed the Cambodian people might "rise up against the present regime and join the Viet Minh." The interview had one desired effect: soon after it appeared, the French agreed to reopen talks with Sihanouk's negotiating team, which he had left behind in Paris. At the end of April 1953 Sihanouk proceeded to Japan, where he received a message from Dulles urging him to cooperate with the French.[50]

During his visit to the United States, Sihanouk's dislike of the Americans hardened into a conviction that the United States and its policies were inimical to him. He found Dulles's political sermons offensive, as he had a State Department proposal made during his visit that he fill in some of his free time by going to the circus. He was upset by President Dwight Eisenhower's failure to offer him a state dinner. By contrast, after 1955 and indeed well into the 1980s, the French and Chinese, his principal patrons, took care to place him in the foreground of their relations with his country. His estrangement from the United States had important effects on Cambodian history, none of them beneficial to the Cambodian people or to U.S. policy objectives in Southeast Asia.[51]

In Paris, meanwhile, continuing negotiations led to French promises to study Cambodia's proposals. The French were still unwilling to cede military control over the Viet Minh–dominated areas along the Cambodia-Vietnam border or to uncouple Cambodia's export economy from that of Cochinchina, where they had extensive interests. Sihanouk felt frustrated but found himself buoyed by waves of popular support when he returned to Cambodia in May 1953.[52]

To remove himself from the purview of French advice, Sihanouk set up his headquarters in Siem Reap, close to the Angkor temples. From there, he fired off demands to the French and welcomed armed Issaraks rallying to his cause. The French military commander in Cambodia, Gen. Pierre de Langlade, responded to this conduct by saying that Sihanouk was "a madman, but a madman of genius" (Il est un fou, mais un fou génial)—a remark that Sihanouk savored for years. General de Langlade wrote to his superiors at this time that in his view the situation in Cambodia was hopeless. A military victory, he argued, would require an additional fifteen French Union battalions; abandoning the country would lead to anarchy. Perhaps, he mused, granting the country independence would serve French interests best. "After all," he wrote, "the King has expressly stated, 'Give me complete independence, and I will lease Cambodia to you for ninety-nine years.'" He closed his letter by saying, "The Cambodian"—he probably had Sihanouk in mind—"is vain, susceptible, unintelligent, and extremely stubborn. It is useless to slap him in the face. On the contrary, by giving in at the point of vanity we can attach the country to us for many years."[53]

Sihanouk in the meantime was isolated in Angkor from the foreign press and foreign diplomatic missions. His royal crusade was stalled. According to Sim Var, who accompanied him there, he thought of entering the maquis, like Son Ngoc Thanh, but the idea was vetoed by his parents. In the middle of June, acting so impulsively that even his closest aides were taken by surprise, he decided instead to visit Bangkok to publicize his crusade. The Thai government was not notified in advance, and the British embassy in Bangkok reported that "the appearance of His Majesty and his entourage of some thirty people at the border caught the Siamese government wholly unawares. The cavalcade was stopped at the frontier, and as the occupants had no entry papers, hectic telephoning to Bangkok ensued."[54]

Thai officials drove out to meet Sihanouk, who had broken his journey at Prachinburi. When he reached Bangkok the next morning, "His Majesty's spokesmen . . . showered diplomatic missions and the local press with explanatory statements" denying that he was an exile and reasserting Cambodia's claims to independence. Sihanouk in fact hoped to enjoy the safety of exile without the restrictions which the protocol of a state visit might impose. He was playing a game whose rules he invented as he went along. The Thai greeted him, the British embassy reported, "with a display of inactivity at which they are so adept." After several days of accomplishing nothing Sihanouk returned in a bad temper to Siem Reap. One effect of his lunge into exile was to convince the French that he was mentally unbalanced or, as Malcolm MacDonald wrote from Singapore, "under at least partial influence of the extreme anti-French and pro–Viet Minh leaders."

In hindsight, these interpretations seem obtuse. It is hard to believe that French and British observers had so much trouble accepting Sihanouk's demands for independence at face value. To most of them, of course, the menace of communism loomed much larger than the idea of Cambodia's independence, Cambodia's interests, or the value of keeping Sihanouk as a friend. At another level, a colonialist perspective was difficult to alter. The French men and women who considered themselves experts on Indochina, especially those over fifty, had spent their careers savoring the colonial experience and, as they thought, nurturing (rather than exploiting) the Lao, Vietnamese, and Khmer. French and British reports about Cambodia in the early 1950s, written by such people, were often consciously parental. Those who wrote them took Sihanouk's nationalism as a passing fancy. The Americans, on the other hand, while more susceptible to Asian nationalist aspirations, were reluctant to entrust Cambodia's future to a man they regarded as unstable and despotic.

At the end of June, the U.S. chargé in Phnom Penh, Joseph Montllor, called on Commissioner Risterucci, who told him that he feared "the king has excited people to such an extent that it may be difficult to keep control." Three days later, Risterucci changed his tune, remarking that "history is on Cambodia's side." Other sources confirm that Cambodian public opinion was falling into step with Sihanouk's crusade. To most Cambodians it was time for the French to leave. As a British diplomat reported, "Immediate independence [was] more important than long-term survival." In the same tone, French military intelligence reported, "For the king, independence is an end in itself, and it matters little if Cambodia is unbalanced, internally, by a demagogic policy."

Another ingredient of Sihanouk's success was that the Laniel government in Paris had decided in early July to wind up the "dirty war" in Indochina. Negotiations with Cambodia responded to French government initiatives and to pressures on the French elsewhere as well as to Sihanouk's crusade. Sihanouk, however, was reluctant to share the credit for what happened or to connect Cambodia's destiny with those of Laos and Vietnam. He saw the French as responding unilaterally to his crusade and opening negotiations with him.

To strengthen his hand Sihanouk began to mobilize "popular forces" throughout Cambodia "to defend the country against insecurity, the Viet Minh, and eventually against all foreign aggression"—the last phrase a warning to the French. Over 130,000 poorly armed but enthusiastic men and women assembled throughout the kingdom by the end of August. Cambodian requests to the French for arms for these units went unanswered, but the open-ended mobilization spurred the French to accelerate negotiations. As they did so, one of their officers noted sourly that the king, technically a major general in the French army, had awarded himself another star.[55]

As his crusade gathered momentum, Sihanouk's relations with his former mentors cooled, and in June 1953 he told an American visitor that as far as he was concerned France was now "Cambodia's enemy number one."[56]

By October, the French had turned over control of the police, the judiciary, and many aspects of military operations to Cambodian authorities. Operational control of French units east of the Mekong remained in French hands, and several thousand French Union troops stayed on Cambodian territory under French command. Otherwise, Cambodia was independent. This does not mean that it was militarily secure. Perhaps one subdistrict in six was under guerrilla control, and more than half the country, at night at least, was subject to pressure from Viet Minh or Issarak bands. By the end of 1953, two years after its foundation, the KPRP had perhaps a thousand members. In addition, perhaps five thousand Khmers, including Saloth Sar, were enrolled with the Viet Minh in military units.[57]

After the independence documents had been signed, Sihanouk traveled from Siem Reap to Phnom Penh, cheered along the way by thousands of his subjects. "Along the 300 kilometers of his route," according to an official report, "the Khmer people, completely delirious, gave him an unprecedented triumph." A week later, two days before the country officially celebrated its independence, a quasi-legislative body made up of former members of the dissolved assembly declared Sihanouk a national hero. The document was countersigned by Sihanouk himself.[58]

Over the next six months, France, Vietnam, and larger powers edged toward negotiations at Geneva. During this time, Sihanouk sought to demonstrate that Cambodia could hold its own militarily. Operation Sammaki (Solidarity), with Sihanouk nominally in command, took units of the Khmer army into a rebel zone in the northwest. The ten-day episode was an exercise in public relations. Sihanouk told Jean Lacouture in 1971 that his troops suffered only one casualty and that the rebels had evacuated the area before his troops arrived. The unctuous official report on the campaign, prepared by Lon Nol, stressed the prince's military skills.[59]

Despite Sihanouk's political successes and the advent of independence, a good deal of sympathy still existed for Son Ngoc Thanh and the Democrats among young people in Phnom Penh and in intellectual circles. According to Montllor, Thanh continued to capture people's imaginations "not because they agree with his republicanism and political philosophy but because he stands for something, anything. This is more than [the] weak leadership of the constantly changing royal government has given them."[60]

Montllor's comments were astute. Having won independence, Sihanouk was uncertain how to proceed. Was the game over? Was another game being prepared? He had no program for governing Cambodia—no foreign policy, no priorities, no economic plans. Nonetheless, he had managed to lead his people and obtain their independence. He had succeeded where other politicians had failed. In June 1954, he told the French commander in Indochina, Gen. Paul Ely, that "those favoring democracy in Cambodia are either bourgeois or princes. . . . The Cambodian people are children. They know nothing about politics, and they care less."[61]

These brutal views were those of Sihanouk's cronies and of his French advisers, who since 1947 had helped him deconstruct the possibility of pluralistic, representative government in Cambodia and had led him to believe that people fighting for Cambodia's independence were bandits, traitors, Communists, or all three. The idea that most Cambodians were children, inherited from the French, was one that Sihanouk never abandoned. In 1953 he does not seem to have thought that governing the country might involve making adjustments to the style of rule he had recently discovered. Instead, he believed that the best government for Cambodia was an authoritarian, conservative, paternalistic one, while the best foreign policy would involve retaining close cultural ties to France. After ninety years of protecting Cambodians from their neighbors, from autonomy, and from enlightenment, the French had every reason to be proud of this particular pupil.

The Geneva Conference and Its Aftermath

Except in the eyes of the Cambodian delegation at Geneva, led by Sihanouk's foreign minister, Tep Phan, and Gen. Nhiek Tioulong, Cambodia's fate was not high on the agenda of the Geneva conference, convened by the Soviet Union and Great Britain in May 1954 to extricate France politically from Indochina. Vietnam was represented by a southern, non-Communist state set up by the French and by the Viet Minh, who, without gaining control of any major cities in Vietnam, had won the war psychologically by inflicting a stunning defeat a month before on the French garrison at Dienbienphu. Other nations attending included Laos, China, and the United States.[62]

As a supposedly independent nation, Cambodia enjoyed advantages at the conference that were not available to the non-Communist states of Vietnam and Laos. The Cambodians' position was strengthened by the fact that the Viet Minh case for governing Cambodia, or permanently occupying territory there, was weaker than it was for the other states in Indochina.

Nonetheless, the KPRP strenuously denied Cambodia's independence. By the summer of 1954, perhaps two thousand men and women belonged to the KPRP and had received political and military training. It would be incorrect to dismiss those who joined the party as puppets of Vietnam, as Sihanouk was soon to do, or as less Khmer than Puth Chhay, Dap Chhuon, or Sihanouk himself, but they differed from these figures in that some of them saw Cambodia's liberation from France as part of a larger process involving people throughout the world who were struggling against capitalism and imperialism. Accepting Vietnamese guidance in the meantime was as natural to them as accepting guidance from the Soviet Union was for members of many European Communist parties.[63]

The Viet Minh delegation to the Geneva conference included two Cambodian representatives of the United Issarak Front (UIF), Keo Moni and Mey Pho, and a Lao, but these "ghost government" representatives, as the Americans called them, were not recognized as belligerents, awarded official status, or allowed to make public statements. The Cambodian rebels, unlike the Lao, were allowed no territorial stake in their country after the conference.

The Communist delegates to Geneva played down their alliances with each other and their internationalist obligations so as to highlight the nationalist aspects of the resistance struggles in Indochina. This tactic ran counter to Vietnamese strategies for the region and played into the hands of Sihanouk's delegation. The head of the Vietnamese delegation, Pham Van Dong, argued that the Cambodian resistance movement was a native growth. To counter these arguments (and while Pham's two Cambodian representatives remained incommunicado) Sihanouk's delegation brought Dap Chhuon, Puth Chhay, and Savang Vong to Geneva and paraded them as genuine local guerrillas who had rallied to Sihanouk's government.

Zhou Enlai, the head of the Chinese delegation, took a soft line at the conference, and as far as Cambodia was concerned he did less than he might have to help the Vietnamese. He was unwilling, for example, to favor seating the UIF Cambodian delegates or to recognize them as belligerents. Perhaps he saw a united Indochina as undesirable in terms of

Chinese national interests. More likely he was reluctant to antagonize the United States to the point that they would station troops in Cambodia or Vietnam.

The Soviet delegate, Molotov, supported the Cambodian resistance, but the Viet Minh were unwilling in the end to take risks for their Cambodian colleagues. Cambodia was their weakest link in Indochina. In the interests of Vietnam, therefore, the Viet Minh abandoned their younger brothers. Signing the military portion of the accords, the Viet Minh delegate reportedly told Gen. Nhiek Tioulong, "We are leaving your country, but we are confiding our revolutionary friends to you. Treat them well."[64]

Throughout the conference the Cambodian delegation worked hard to frustrate the Vietnamese. Their hostility to the Viet Minh pleased the United States. Aided by telephone conversations with the king, Cambodian delegates wore down other delegations in all-night sessions. The Viet Minh were not allowed regroupment areas in Cambodia, as they were in Laos. Cambodia, unlike the rest of Indochina, was allowed by the conference to invite foreign soldiers onto its soil. Frightened by the Viet Minh, the Cambodians flirted with forming an alliance with the United States. Cambodia's policies reflected conditions on the ground. As far as Cambodia itself was concerned, it was difficult for the Vietnamese to claim that Mey Pho and Keo Moni had done more to liberate Cambodia than Sihanouk, even though the king had ridden to victory in the wake of the Viet Minh and had begun to struggle only when the French began to stop.[65]

Politics in Cambodia, 1954–1955

Sihanouk was euphoric about the outcome at Geneva. Cambodian Communists who remained in Cambodia were not. They faced the alternatives of going underground, participating in confrontational politics, expatriating themselves to Vietnam, or allying themselves with Sihanouk's feudal style of rule. Any of these moves was a betrayal of the goals they had been struggling for and postponed the real liberation of their country. Their Viet Minh colleagues suggested that some of them stay in Cambodia underground—Saloth Sar seems to have taken this advice— but that most retire to Vietnam, leaving a rear guard to organize a People's Group (Krom Pracheachon) under the protection of the International Commission for Supervision and Control (ICSC), a peacekeeping mechanism set in place at Geneva to oversee the transfer of power between the French and successor regimes in Indochina. In Cambodia, stipulations for the transfer included national elections, to be held in 1955.

The Vietnamese members of the KPRP interim executive committee hurried off to Vietnam, and so did six hundred Cambodian party members and a similar number of combatants. Several KPRP figures, including Sieu Heng, Sao Phim, and Nuon Chea, went along for a time but returned to Cambodia later. Over a thousand others, like Rath Samoeun and Son Ngoc Minh, stayed in Vietnam for many years. Those who remained in Cambodia or were sent back there to work on united front tactics with the Democrats may have felt betrayed. They were certainly in full view of Sihanouk's police.[66]

Like the Communists, the Democrats faced some difficult decisions. They had no forum from which to operate, and their efforts to gain Cambodia's independence had been overshadowed by Sihanouk's crusade.

Son Ngoc Thanh tried to rally to the government in September 1954, but Sihanouk refused to receive him and never saw him again. Thanh soon retired to the Thai-Cambodian border and came under Thai protection. With the formation of the pro-U.S. Southeast Asia Treaty Organization (SEATO) in late 1954, and Sihanouk's refusal to join it, Thanh became a willing instrument of the Thai, the South Vietnamese, and the United States.[67]

By February 1955, indeed, some two thousand Khmer Serei (Free Khmer) aligned with Thanh were installed in a semimilitary camp supported by the Thai just inside the Cambodian border. The camp was visited by a U.S. official from Bangkok who was chastised by his ambassador for reporting its existence. In hindsight, U.S. acquiescence to Thai and Vietnamese support for Thanh and other plotters in the 1950s probably drove Sihanouk more quickly to the left than he might naturally have gone. His uncle Prince Monireth was basically pro-Western but found U.S. officials and their policies in Cambodia intrusive and naive. In his figure of speech, the United States came to Cambodia following the Geneva conference with "many winning cards," including the anticommunism of the Cambodian elite, only to throw them away and turn up a succession of losing ones in the years that followed.[68]

Sihanouk still saw the Democrats as an obstacle to his ambitions. In 1953–54 young members of the party, including Keng Vannsak, had pushed it toward an antiroyalist, anti-American position. Taking advantage of the presence of the ICSC in Cambodia, former supporters of Son Ngoc Thanh also began agitating along republican lines. In July 1954, immediately after Geneva, Thiounn Mumm returned to Cambodia to take up political action. Shortly before his return, he told his friend Thonn Ouk that he intended to infiltrate the Democrats, in preparation for the national elections. He found allies in Keng Vannsak and his old schoolmate Ea Sichau. Mumm also encountered Saloth Sar, then living under a false identity in a Phnom Penh suburb. Vannsak and Mumm have both claimed that they worked with Sar at this time. So has a former Thanhist, Chhay Yat. There is something ambiguous about these recollections—and about Saloth Sar's silence about the period—and it is unclear what each of the four knew about the others' intentions. All three observers were struck by Saloth Sar's political skills and by his capacity for leadership, especially in small groups. Others noticed his fondness for subterfuge. A Pracheachon activist, Non Suon, purged in 1976, frequently saw Brother Number One (Saloth Sar) in 1955. He recalled his austere clothing and his appearance but was unable to learn his name even from associates in the movement.[69]

In the meantime, Sihanouk's friends in the smaller parties had formed a United Party (Sahapak). In November 1954, they established a weekly newspaper with the slogan "State, Religion, Monarchy," which was identical to Thai royalist phrasing; the newspaper was clearly intended to boost Sihanouk's standing among the electorate, but it was short-lived.

Sahapak intended to form a united front to defeat the Democrats. Its members quickly earned Sihanouk's support—those responsible for it (Lon Nol, Nhiek Tioulong, Sam Nhean, and Yem Sambaur) had been among his closest advisers for some time. They were looking for a strategy that would keep the Democrats out of office and would allow them to rule the country. Sihanouk counted on their organizational skills; they counted on his popularity. The alliance they formed endured throughout Sihanouk's years in power.[70]

In early 1955, Sihanouk decided that the Cambodian people should judge his crusade by means of a referendum. Shortly before the vote, the Democrats elected a new central committee composed of Thanhists, leftists, and a few moderates. Keng Vannsak and his colleagues had outmaneuvered the older members of the party and stacked its committee with younger figures, including Prince Norodom Phurissara, Thiounn Mumm, and Svay So. The new committee, angered by the prospect of a Cambodian-U.S. alliance, adopted a platform of neutrality. The U.S. embassy then reported that the committee was composed of a "left-wing republican element, strongly permeated by [a] Communist taint."[71]

Soon afterward the U.S. ambassador, Robert McClintock, while playing tennis in Phnom Penh, picked up a leaflet that fell onto the court, dropped with hundreds of others from a low-flying plane. It referred to the referendum: "This is how you should vote," it read. "If you love the King [use a] white ballot; if you don't love the King [use a] black ballot. You must believe this. Don't believe anyone who says differently."[72]

Nearly a million people voted in the referendum. A Canadian member of the ICSC wrote later that it was "orderly, but completely unsecret." At the polling stations he visited, "police asked voters whether they wanted a white or a black ballot, gave them both, and demanded that one be destroyed on the spot." The final vote was registered as 925,667 in favor of the king and 1,834 against. Over a hundred negative ballots came from a village near the Vietnamese border, "where a column of Khmer Viet Minh crossed the frontier, voted against the king, and then marched back into Vietnam."[73]

When the results were in, the king ordered the arrest of the editors of several Khmer language newspapers, including Saloth Sar's brother, Saloth Chhay, the editor of *Sammaki* (Solidarity), as well as those of two Thanhist papers and a pro-Democrat one. These papers had taken issue with Sihanouk's claim that he had won Cambodia's independence single-handedly, by dating independence from 1954 (the Geneva conference) rather than 1953.

With opposition silenced, Sihanouk and his advisers set about rewriting the constitution. The reforms they proposed gave women the right to vote, increased the king's executive powers, and allowed electorates to remove "unsatisfactory" representatives. The British legation noted that "the proposals are well-intentioned and are in fact far more suitable for application in Cambodia than was the 1947 Constitution. They are, however, considerably further removed from western ideas of liberal democracy, and may thus be regarded as a retrograde step, designed purely to protect the position of the king."[74]

The British opposed the reforms because they seemed to block stipulations calling for national elections. Sihanouk balked at the idea that his reforms had to meet with the assembly's approval, and he noted that the constitution had "emanated" from him, so he could change it when he wished. His proposals sprang from a mixture of idealism about Cambodia's "little people," his lingering anger at the Democrats, and the advice he was receiving from such antiparliamentarians as Sam Sary, Lon Nol, and Sim Var to depoliticize Cambodian politics.[75]

This second referendum never took place, and the British legation urged Sihanouk to proceed with national elections. On February 27 the king, surprised by the objections he was receiving to his proposals, suddenly abandoned them. Five days later, in order to take command of Cambodian politics and cease being merely a ceremonial ruler, he abdicated the throne he had held for fourteen years. In his memoirs, he calls his abdication, which he fails to explain, his "atomic bomb."

Sihanouk Takes Command

Sihanouk's abdication took even his parents by surprise. He had confided in no one, and as he wrote later, "Everyone was stupefied." His memoirs are reticent about his motivations, and an American report prepared at the time suggests that the abdication was not so much a tactical move, as it later came to appear, as an example of Sihanouk walking away from a situation that was too difficult to face. He had discovered, apparently, that the popular demonstrations in favor of his reforms had not been spontaneous but staged by his advisers and palace officials. Distraught that his popularity might be manufactured, Sihanouk was frightened of being cast aside by the political parties in the unavoidable elections. He also decided to attack his enemies head on.[76]

The abdication opened up a new political game. The elections were immediately postponed until September 1955. Sihanouk's parents took on the royal responsibilities that he had abandoned. The private citizen swiftly reemerged as a full-time politician and used his new status to reduce the distance that separated him from the people. He took the title *samdech upayuvareach* (the prince who has left the throne), and in a speech defending his action soon thereafter he attacked "politicians, the rich, the educated, who are accustomed to using their knowledge to deceive others and to place innumerable obstacles in the path on which I must lead the people."[77]

An English-language tourist brochure put out by the government at this time asserted, "This abdication was justified by [Sihanouk's] fervent desire to serve better his people by whom he is worshipped as a God. In short, he wanted to give his people the necessary strength to fight favoritism and oppression . . . and lead them back to the tradition of a glorious past."[78]

The scenario called for Sihanouk to turn the throne over to his father, Prince Suramarit, an experienced civil servant with no political ambitions. According to one report, Sihanouk forced the kingship onto him by

with his perceptions of Cambodia's national interest, themselves in tune with public opinion. Pro-Americans in Cambodia were few, and the kingdom could not be expected to make much of a contribution militarily if open warfare involving the United States developed in Southeast Asia.

One effect of Sihanouk's choice of neutralism was to encourage U.S. special services, including the Central Intelligence Agency (CIA), to support any anti-Communist Khmers they could find. Like the French in an earlier era, U.S. operatives in Southeast Asia and Washington found it hard to accept that Cambodia might have interests of its own, separable from those of the Free World. Thus, Ambassador McClintock argued that Sihanouk's unhappiness with U.S. pressure sprang from his "continued inner need to justify himself," rather than from genuine fears. To the radicals, Sihanouk's conversion to neutralism seemed tardy and insincere; the real problem, according to them, was American military aid, which they feared would turn the Cambodian army into an anti-Communist force. Their thunder had been stolen by Sihanouk's adroit volte-face. He adopted their policy as his own while holding on to U.S. military aid, which, by paying and equipping the army, served to balance his budget for the next eight years.[85]

The Elections of 1955

During the first half of 1955, Sihanouk tried hard to extirpate political parties from Cambodian life. As late as April, however, most observers still predicted that the Democrats would win the oft-postponed elections. After all, as Huy Kanthoul told an American diplomat, "The Prince [was] thoroughly hated, particularly by young people." Some observers at the time and others looking back at the campaign from the 1980s noted that the police and the special militia organized by Dap Chhuon were brutal and intimidating. Sim Var complained to the U.S. embassy that two Sangkum workers had been assassinated in the countryside, but casualties among Democrat workers and Pracheachon agents, never made public, were much heavier. Several independent newspapers were closed and their editors imprisoned. A pro-Democrat achar named Chung, the son of a famous vernacular poet, was arrested during the campaign for reciting poems that were interpreted by some to be insulting to the prince: he died in prison. In the countryside, Communists and their supporters were imprisoned without trial. News of the terror spread and was magnified by word of mouth. The effect was to cow people into inaction, for as the

British legation commented, "The Cambodians are not brave when faced with firmness on the part of the authorities."[86]

During the campaign, security forces intimidated candidates, beat up campaign workers, tore down posters, broke up meetings, and threatened Democrats and their supporters. On one occasion they forced local people to swear before groups of monks on the grounds of Buddhist monasteries that they would vote for the Sangkum. In some districts, Sangkum workers told officials that "their future depended on obtaining at least an 80 percent vote" for the movement, and in Siem Reap a U.S. embassy officer called on a Democrat candidate and reported that "conversation with him was . . . unprofitable as he was obviously scared. He did not even give me his name."[87]

The Liberals were easier to deal with. In June 1955 the party's founder, Prince Norodom Norindeth, resigned the leadership and threw his support behind the Sangkum. After the elections, he was named Cambodia's first ambassador to UNESCO, in Paris, and lingered there until 1960, when he was appointed ambassador to Belgrade.[88]

Although earlier campaigns had been hard-fought and had contained abuses, the campaign of 1955 was different. For the first time the combined weight of the state's security apparatus, the royal family, and the media was mobilized in defense of a slate of candidates. Even so, some Democrats were predicting as late as August that the Pracheachon would win seven seats of the thirty-five they were contesting and that the Democrats, gaining perhaps twenty seats, would be able to ally themselves with the Pracheachon to forestall Sihanouk's constitutional reforms and his alliance with the United States. By then, however, nearly all the Democratic candidates, fearing for their lives, had taken refuge in Phnom Penh.[89]

The quality of many Sangkum candidates was low. In Battambang, Huy Kanthoul encountered "a Sino-Khmer who could barely read a word of Cambodian," while in Svay Rieng, one Sangkum candidate was a nineteen-year-old popular singer who had somehow come to Sihanouk's attention. Other recruits included former Renovation party members who had been defeated in 1947 or 1951.[90]

The mixture of favoritism, propaganda, terror, and contempt for the elite that was to continue under Sihanouk for many years was heavily documented in 1955. The Democrats still felt free to talk with foreigners and with each other about Cambodia's fate and the possibility of pluralism in politics. After 1955, dissent was muffled, and dissenters were often put in prison. Sihanouk saw Cambodia's educated elite as his enemies.

Similarly, although becoming a member of the Sangkum usually meant papering over rather than dissolving political tensions and factions, being a member came to mean supporting Sihanouk against all comers.[91]

Thirty-one years later, Keng Vannsak, the Democrats' most tireless campaigner, recalled the campaign with zest. He had enjoyed taking risks in his speeches, he said. These attacked absolutism, underdevelopment, and exploitation so vigorously that Sihanouk began calling him King Vannsak (*sdach* Vannsak) in private. He drew large crowds. One person who heard many of his speeches was Khieu Ponnary, Khieu Thirith's older sister, who was to marry Saloth Sar the following year.

To counter Vannsak's arguments, a new Sangkum newspaper argued against notions of social unrest, claiming benignly that "those who are poor owe their poverty to previous lives," while the rich "are happy now, because of the previous good deeds."[92]

Three days before the elections, Sihanouk decided to neutralize Keng Vannsak. As he was addressing a rally in Phnom Penh, a Buick sedan bearing Sam Sary, heavily armed policemen, and a loudspeaker drove slowly into the crowd backed up by a truckload of Sangkum supporters. Shots rang out, and a Democrat chauffeur was killed. Vannsak was hustled from the rally, taken into custody, and, although unarmed, was blamed for inciting the violence. Vannsak was in prison for the next two months without being charged. He was released only after the Sangkum had won the elections, and he had apologized abjectly to the prince.[93]

When the elections took place, the U.S. embassy reported that in spite of the intimidation of candidates and campaign workers and Vannsak's incarceration they could not be "labelled unfree." Despite or because of the intimidation, indeed, a great majority of voters probably sensed a change in the political atmosphere and voted for the Sangkum. The British legation commented astutely that most Cambodians probably saw the elections as a "repetition of the referendum of February 1955."

On election day the results were never in doubt, but the margin—Sangkum candidates were credited with capturing 83 percent of the vote and all the seats—was obviously cooked and surprised many observers. Huy Kanthoul pointed to seats where the Sangkum, after its candidate was defeated, destroyed the ballot box and declared that its candidate had won.

The Pracheachon officially received 30,000 votes and over a quarter of those cast in several districts. It is likely that many of the 25 percent of registered voters who failed to vote would have chosen Democrat or Pracheachon candidates, but probably not in sufficient numbers to keep the Sangkum from winning a majority. The presence of some 309 candidates competing for 91 seats indicated that many would-be politicians did not expect the landslide that occurred. Bitterly summing up the event, Huy Kanthoul told a U.S. embassy officer soon after the elections that "in one constituency . . . the Democrats obtained zero votes because they were not allowed to provide Democratic ballots. In most other cases, the Sangkum ballot was so heavily printed that it showed through, which meant that anyone discarding it . . . was known to have voted against the Sangkum. In one case the [armed militiaman] standing with his eyes glued to the discard box whistled when he saw a Sangkum ballot being put there, whereupon the voter was beaten to the ground after leaving the polling place." Over thirty years later, Huy Kanthoul was still angry enough to write, "And what elections they were! Great gods!"[94]

There is no way of telling what results Sihanouk might have obtained with less intimidation, although Sangkum candidates would probably have attained a comfortable majority. Thus Sihanouk would have confronted a partially hostile assembly. The idea of an opposition, however impotent, was anathema to him, and he foreclosed the possibility.

Exhilarated by his victory, Sihanouk assembled a national congress of the Sangkum in Phnom Penh. Several thousand ordinary members of the movement voted with a show of hands in favor of the constitutional reforms that the prince had attempted to push through earlier in the year. These included the enfranchisement of women, the creation of provincial assemblies, and the establishing of the right of voters to recall unsatisfactory assemblymen. The vote prevented the newly elected assembly from discussing or amending the reforms. To Sihanouk, the congress followed the "ancient Greek pattern of democracy," and such meetings became prominent features of his years in power.

A new kind of democracy, then, had replaced the parliamentary variety that had been in place for nine years but had not flourished. Emerging from almost a century of French protection and nearly a decade of parliamentary wrangling, most Cambodians were willing to give their agile and talented father, then only thirty-three, the opportunity to take charge of his domain. It seemed appropriate that Sihanouk, who told them repeatedly that he had won Cambodia's independence single-handedly, should now be allowed to rule without the inconvenience of potentially hostile political parties. In October 1955 Sihanouk commanded the loyalties of most Cambodian people. A nine-year-old political game was over; a new game, one that was to draw on millennia of royal authority and a new sense of public relations, had begun.

three

Sihanouk Unopposed, 1955–1962

In the aftermath of the elections of 1955, many Democrats, fearful of Sihanouk's vengeful style and of the effects that not joining might have on their careers, joined the Sangkum. Yet some of the executive committee and many members of the party held back, thinking that the party might still play a constructive role outside the National Assembly. Nonetheless, the violence of the campaign and the imprisonment of several Democrats without trial dissuaded the executive committee from convening a meeting to discuss the party's future.

In early 1956, the Democrats were in limbo. Desultory talks about joining forces with the Pracheachon proceeded, for as Huy Kanthoul remarked to an American acquaintance, "When one is interested in politics, one either sides with the strongest, or the most radical." The Pracheachon, however, had little interest in lumbering itself with the Democrats. Indeed, members of the group seem to have benefited indirectly from the Sangkum victory. Their newspapers, unlike the Democrat-sponsored ones, continued to appear, and they were unanimous in praising the prince's foreign policy initiatives and his state visits to China, Poland, Czechoslovakia, and the USSR in 1956.

After his victory, however, the prince seemed more excited about the Sangkum idea than about eliminating the Democrats. At first, he does not seem even to have wanted to serve as prime minister. He preferred to be swept along by the "genuine democracy" of the Sangkum, buoyed up by waves of approval, domestically and overseas.[1]

Factions and cliques soon reappeared in the assembly, but party interests as such were no longer an impediment to legislation, and during the first few months of the Sangkum government the absence of opposition to government initiatives led to greater efficiency than in the past. By the beginning of 1956 the government had prepared a two-year economic plan. Even if, as the American embassy reported, this was "essentially an inventory of the economic aid projects already scheduled, plus a shopping list of additional projects . . . which [the government] hopes to sell to friendly countries," it represented a plausible beginning. The plan included such projects as a new Phnom Penh airport to be financed by the French, a U.S.–financed road connecting Phnom Penh to the sea, and increased expenditures for education.[2]

Sihanouk always enjoyed state visits. In early 1956, these took him to the Philippines and China. In Manila, he had his arm twisted by the Filipino government and the media, which assumed that his visit would "end in Cambodia's signing for SEATO," something he had consistently refused to do. On this occasion, he refused again, claiming later that it had been easy to outmaneuver the Filipinos, who were citizens of a "nation that had fallen under the domination of a foreign power." His own strategy assumed that he would receive more assistance, flattery, and patronage from Beijing—which he visited next—than from the Philippines and its pro-American allies.[3]

The prince's visit to China was most rewarding. He admired the way that China, unlike the Philippines, "stood on its own feet." He was impressed by its social mobilization, its sense of purpose, and the apparent absence of hierarchies and corruption. He renewed his friendship with Zhou Enlai and made friends, or so it seemed, with Mao Zedong. He was served superb food and was made to feel important. The Chinese also promised him about U.S. $40 million in economic aid. Unlike American aid, this came with "no strings attached." Later in the year, Sihanouk was given similar treatment and promises of aid in Prague and Warsaw.

On his return from China, he had to face the animosity of the regimes in Saigon and Bangkok, whose newspapers blustered that he was a red prince who had made an alliance with the devil. The Diem regime in South Vietnam imposed a brief economic blockade. These hostile reactions, ironically, convinced Sihanouk that he was on the right track.[4]

Given his preference for seeing politics in terms of personalities, it was unfortunate that the first U.S. ambassador to Cambodia, Robert McClintock, struck him as dogmatic, imperious, and gauche. McClintock attended at least one official reception accompanied by a dog; he moved around the capital in shorts and occasionally affected a baton. His lectures

to Sihanouk about the dangers of Communism resembled those about
constitutional democracy that the Democrats had given him years before.
They grated on Sihanouk's nerves. In contrast, the French ambassador,
Pierre Gorce, made a point of assuming that diplomatic relations with
Cambodia depended on maintaining cordial personal relations with the
prince.[5]

In March 1956, Sihanouk embarked on a program of Khmer socialism
for his country. While genuine socialism backed up by extensive reading
had motivated such diverse Cambodians as Prince Yuthevong, Ea Sichau,
and Thiounn Mumm, Sihanouk seemed entranced by the word itself and
by the fact that so many world leaders, including his new friends Sukarno,
Nehru, and Zhou Enlai, espoused it. Becoming a Socialist was a way of
keeping up to date. In later years, Khmer socialism modulated into Buddhist socialism, allegedly the consensus between rulers and ruled that had
allowed Angkor to flourish. Either doctrine, Sihanouk asserted, took what
was best in communism, and nothing from Karl Marx, so as "to *prevent*
the triumph of communism in Cambodia" (emphasis added).[6]

A society mobilized to perpetuate the status quo was what he had in
mind. His Khmer or Buddhist socialism was based on an idealistic reading of Cambodia's social relations. To make it work, Sihanouk counted on
the deference of ordinary people and the good will of more fortunate
Khmers. The system involved state intervention in many areas of life,
while agriculture and commerce remained in private hands. As far as
Sihanouk was concerned, socialism was a matter of keeping things as they
were, expanding educational facilities, and hoping for the best.

Visiting Beijing in the early 1960s, the prince sought to explain Cambodia's style of socialism to Mao Zedong. "In our country, we practice our
own brand of socialism," he said. "This involves the rich giving their
money to the poor." When Sihanouk's explanation had been translated,
Mao is alleged to have paused and then murmured, "Socialism is very
complicated" before changing the subject.

Two ironies underlay Sihanouk's socialist agenda. The first was that
with its rejection of foreign models and its emphasis on past glories it
foreshadowed policies espoused by the Khmer Republic and DK. "Our
socialism is national," Sihanouk declared in 1956, adding, "We Cambodians will never accept the tearing down of the barrier which preserves the
originality of our race, of our traditions, of our religious faith, and which
safeguards our independence vis-à-vis certain of our neighbors (particularly Vietnamese)."[7]

The second irony was that by making Khmer socialism consonant with Angkorean social practices, as he perceived them, he agreed unwittingly with local Communists and Democrats like Keng Vannsak that Cambodia had always been governed (some would say unjustly) in the same way. But whereas Communists and Democrats saw Angkorean grandeur in terms of slavery, feudalism, and exploitation, Sihanouk chose to interpret the past in terms of a harmony between rulers and ruled that socialism was attempting to revive. For Cambodian Communists, history was a series of struggles; for Sihanouk, it was embedded in its grandeur and embodied in its kings.

To understand Cambodian politics in the 1950s, we need to accept the social context of the time. Sihanouk's optimism about Cambodia's potentialities was genuine and widely shared. Between 1955 and 1963 (arguably until around 1966), he delivered much of what he promised, and an affectionate rapport existed between him and nearly all his subjects. To be sure, after 1952, or even earlier, some of the intellectual elite, many Buddhist monks, and most Cambodian Communists wanted him out of office. Yet by the late 1950s, their views had not spread very far. The masses during these years formed a deferential, silent, often smiling audience to the theatrical enactments of the government, personified by the prince, who often literally descended among them, a deus ex machina, in a helicopter. When he flew off, his children's lives resumed. When these grown men and women thought about politics they accepted their low status and Sihanouk's exalted position. By and large, they believed that the government was out there. In spite or because of this widespread diffidence, a shared warmth and loyalty can be perceived between Sihanouk and most Cambodians in the late 1950s, the midmorning of his long political career.[8]

He was certainly closer to the people than any Cambodian monarch had ever been before. Indefatigably he crisscrossed his kingdom, inaugurating schools, dams, parks, factories, and hospitals. Sometimes it seemed that he was prepared to inaugurate anything that had a fresh coat of paint. On such occasions, he would deliver speeches for hours to crowds of local officials, monks, schoolchildren, and their mature, less fortunate relatives, the so-called little people, who crouched in the sunlight, facing his pavilion. In these speeches, Sihanouk berated his enemies, joked about his love life, insulted foreigners, praised the people listening to him, and invoked the glories of Angkor. He told everyone to work hard for the nation and spoke of Cambodia's prestige. He inflated Cambodia's importance by making jokes at the expense of heads of state. Nearly everyone who listened to Sihanouk in these years loved every word he said.

The speeches were rebroadcast several times, but the summaries printed in the French-language press glossed over spicy or offensive passages. This meant that Sihanouk made one speech in Khmer for his children and another for the historical record. Unfortunately for him, his speeches were monitored and translated by the local Chinese-language press, the BBC, the U.S. embassy, and the U.S. Foreign Broadcast Information Service. On one occasion, in 1962, having told his audience that as far as he was concerned, "Americans are shit," Sihanouk added, "but I will deny having said so if they come and ask me about it," drawing laughter from the crowd and from a U.S. embassy officer assigned to monitor the speech.

By 1960, Sihanouk's popularity had reached its peak. He was not yet absolutely powerful, and power had not corrupted him. Moreover, he was not yet chief of state. Until his father's death in 1960, both of his parents exercised a moderating influence, as did some of his other relations. In any case, opposition to his leadership was disorganized and mute.

In material terms Cambodia was probably a happier place in those days than it was to become after 1965, when heavy fighting broke out in Vietnam. Nearly everyone in Cambodia had enough to eat. Nearly all the farmers owned their own land. There was plenty of cultivable land in most of the country, and there were still opportunities for employment in the towns. Exports of primary products such as rice, rubber, and pepper earned foreign exchange sufficient for Cambodia's needs. Foreign aid from France, the United States, and the Sino-Soviet bloc provided hospitals, schools, a deep-water port, and a highway linking the capital to the coast. Salaries for the army and the costs of military equipment were paid by the United States. Health care and sanitation, still rudimentary by Western standards, improved dramatically. The incidence of malaria and infant mortality decreased. Hundreds of thousands of men and women who had been illiterate a decade before learned to read, thanks to government programs. Hundreds of thousands of their children and grandchildren flocked into newly constructed schools. For the first time since 1945, the kingdom was at peace. Compared with what came later and what had gone before, the years 1955–65 constituted a kind of golden age.

For many Cambodians, these conditions in the country were traceable to their ruler. As a pedicab driver put it in 1956, "He speaks well, he loves the people, he judges more fairly than judges do, he rides a bicycle [a soon to be abandoned democratic gesture], he wants foreigners to build houses for us, and to give us money."[9]

Even when he moved among his people, Sihanouk remained, in their eyes, above or to one side of corrupt and incompetent government officials. He personally was honest—Carpentier remarked in 1955 that he was probably the only honest member of the Sangkum—but he did little to discourage corruption. He was not interested in far-reaching structural change. More important, although he was vengeful to people who attacked him and cruel to powerless opponents, he disliked violence and was unwilling to punish subordinates or members of his family for corruption or incompetence. Cambodia was his family. He wanted its people to be loyal, entertaining, and polite. Aside from a few trusted, overworked elder statesmen like Son Sann and Penn Nouth and advisers like Charles Meyer and Donald Lancaster, his entourage consisted of relatives, cronies, and hangers-on. Sihanouk was reluctant to expel these people, who amused him, into a world where some of them would barely have survived for half an hour. People who worked with him have recalled the experience with fondness and exasperation, even when they later came to see his personality as obsessive and his politics as harmful to the country.[10]

In 1956, inspired by what he had seen in China, Sihanouk set out to transform the surface of Cambodian society; but he was unwilling to make structural changes or to alter his own behavior. When he was in power, most of his favorite heads of state—de Gaulle, Kim Il Sung, Tito, and Ceauçescu—were authoritarians who enjoyed, as he did, all the trappings of power. Cambodian kings, democratic or not, had always been like that. Moreover, most people believed that he was Cambodia's tutelary spirit, a royal creature who lived by different rules. In 1970, after he had been deposed, the Lon Nol government accused him of having sold Cambodia to the Vietnamese. An old lady from a suburb of Phnom Penh rejected this accusation: "It's his country, isn't it?" she said. "He can sell it if he likes."[11]

The Demise of the Democrats

In March 1956 the Democrats' newspaper, which had been closed several months earlier, was allowed to reappear, but in April the party was refused permission to sponsor a parade in support of Cambodia's foreign policy. Some Democrats, however, joined Pracheachon members Hou Youn, just back from France, and Saloth Sar's brother, Chhay, recently released from prison, to form a Committee to Defend the Prince's Neutrality Policy. Then and later, Sihanouk made a distinction between Communist regimes with whom he was friendly and leftist "subversion" and party politics.[12]

Political discussion in Phnom Penh in the late 1950s was cautious, infrequent, and confined largely to polemics printed in the city's newspapers. Newspapers were allowed a relatively free rein, and by the end of 1956, there were twenty-six of them in circulation, in French, Khmer, Chinese, and Vietnamese. Several were openly left wing. The papers reached an audience of seventy thousand—a tenfold increase since 1946. These four- to six-page journals gave a political education of sorts to tens of thousands of Cambodians, particularly in the larger towns. Unfortunately for historians, however, the copies held in Cambodia's National Library were pulped and recycled in 1979.[13]

In October 1956, a Sangkum government took office under an experienced bureaucrat, fifty-one-year-old San Yun. Sihanouk hoped that Yun would be able to govern for a reasonable length of time. After all, as the press reported, "He is not a politician. He will follow the program and the examples given by the Prince, and will administer the kingdom like the father of a family [bon père de famille]."

The assembly, true to form, began attacking San Yun. Some parliamentarians who had recently visited France were impressed by the power of French representatives. This independence-mindedness was balanced by the body's dependence on Sihanouk and by its members' fear that Sihanouk would dissolve the assembly. As a conservative opponent of Sihanouk has pointed out, this residual power amounted to a "permanent sword of Damocles" hanging over the legislators, who were "relatively insignificant men who were picked . . . to ride to victory on Sihanouk's coat-tails, usually over Democratic opponents of superior caliber." Their mood was often impatient and resentful. They were seldom consulted or made to feel important; cabinet members rarely attended assembly debates; there were no assemblymen in San Yun's cabinet.[14]

Sihanouk had no respect for the assembly, but he wanted to avoid a crisis. When he passed the idea along to the assembly that San Yun was expendable, the vote to dismiss his cabinet was 72–2. At this point, Sihanouk became prime minister again, for the fourth time since 1955.

A series of crises and Sihanouk's fatigue led him to submit his resignation seven times. On six occasions King Suramarit refused to accept it, urging his son to take a rest and carry on. In July 1957, however, the king finally acceded; but Sihanouk, instead of taking a rest, decided to stay in

Phnom Penh as a private citizen to preside over the Sangkum's semiannual national congress. The candidate Sihanouk selected to succeed him as prime minister, Phlek Phoeun, began negotiating at the congress itself to name his cabinet. Angered by this effrontery, Sihanouk torpedoed Phoeun's candidacy then and there, turning the government of Cambodia over to the people within reach of his voice. The prince also attacked the Democrats as threats to his regime. After the congress he left Phnom Penh to rest in a monastery near Angkor. In his absence, the king appointed Sim Var prime minister.[15]

As these crises came to a head, the Democrats continued to exist as a party. In March 1957, Huy Kanthoul and Norodom Phurissara told American friends that they would probably not put up any candidates for the next elections but complained about corruption, adding that they hoped to "bring some influence to bear on Sihanouk so that he [might] run the country better." Sam Sary, favored by the prince, remained hostile to the Democrats. In June 1957, he had two members of the Democrats' committee arrested and charged with treason simply for asking in an editorial why political prisoners with charges pending against them since 1955 had not yet been pardoned "by the king." A few days later, the editor of the leftist journal *Ekapheap* (Independence) was also placed under arrest.[16]

Sihanouk's conduct at the national congress reflected his fatigue. He was, then and later, a prodigious worker, often putting in eighteen hours at a stretch with dossiers presented to him; but the work of so many ministries overwhelmed him, and before going to Siem Reap he distributed an open letter which complained that "at present I do nothing but receive criticisms from the public which has condemned me without respite." The Democrats were the targets of his abuse. At the national congress, he had said, "When I die, the Democrats will come to power. They are deviating very seriously. They receive money from the Americans and the Americans allow them to write articles in the newspapers attacking me, the Sangkum, and the throne."[17]

Over the years, one of Sihanouk's favorite tactics was to bequeath Cambodia to his opponents. These bequests were almost always followed by popular demonstrations arranged by government officials begging him to change his mind. These, in turn, appealed to his vanity, pushed him back into harness, and intensified his fatigue. Like the overworked parent he thought himself to be, he often projected his discomfort onto his children, accusing them of ingratitude or disrespect.[18]

People who found his tantrums comic or unbalanced did so at their peril, not only because Sihanouk always insisted on being taken seriously but also because the outbursts were built up out of irritating grains of truth. His charge of American support of the Democrats, for example, was based on the fact that throughout the late 1950s the U.S. embassy, under instructions from Washington, sought to find forces and personalities who could act as counterweights to Sihanouk's "pro-Communist" policies. A secret U.S. policy directive of April 1958 noted frankly that "in order to maintain Cambodia's independence and to reverse the drift toward pro-Communist neutrality [the U.S. government should] encourage individuals and groups in Cambodia who oppose dealing with the Communist bloc and would serve to broaden the political power base in Cambodia." By providing sub-rosa backing to people bold enough to oppose a popular, impatient, and absolute ruler the United States was embarking on a perilous course.[19]

From Siem Reap, Sihanouk announced his resignation from the Sangkum and from Cambodian public life. Two weeks later, however, he returned to the capital, forgot his resignations, and resumed his attack on the Democrats, inviting them to debate with him on national issues. The party's leaders asked for a private audience, but Sihanouk demanded that the press, members of the sangha, and the public attend a massive public debate. Police agents visited Democratic leaders in their homes and suggested that it would be treasonous to refuse the prince's offer. Five Democrats agreed to attend.[20]

The debate took place on August 11 on the grounds of the royal palace. It was broadcast in full, and thousands of people gathered outside the enclosure to listen to the proceedings over loudspeakers. Sihanouk did nearly all the talking. He demanded that the Democrats provide specific evidence, at once and in public, of any malfeasance by his regime. Cowed by the setting and by Sihanouk's belligerence, the Democrats murmured that preparing accusations would take time; but they said they were loyal to him and had not intended to cause any trouble. Sihanouk told them they were insincere and demanded that they join the Sangkum on the spot. Their hesitation, overheard by thousands of people, was made to seem tantamount to treason. After nearly three hours, Sihanouk adjourned the meeting, turned away, and wished the Democrats bon appétit.[21]

As the Democrats were leaving the palace, they were pulled from their cars, set upon by soldiers from the Palace Guard, and beaten to the ground with fists and rifle butts. Svay So was punched in the face and lost a tooth; his chauffeur required hospitalization.

Over the next three days more than thirty instances of violence occurred in Phnom Penh, with soldiers in uniform beating up anyone suspected of Democratic leanings. Orders for the violence may have come
from the palace, for many of the offending soldiers were in the Palace
Guard, but it was probably traceable to the army commander, Lon Nol.
Lon later declared that if the prince wanted the Democratic party dissolved, the army was prepared to perform the task. No apology for the
beatings came from Sihanouk or anyone else; none of the soldiers involved was ever punished. Indeed, according to Monireth's memoirs,
some of the offenders were rewarded by the prince. Following demonstrations held in his honor, Sihanouk departed for a holiday in France.[22]

The debate and its aftermath killed off the Democratic party. It was a
sad demise for an organization founded with such high hopes, such a
large following, and so many talented leaders. Political opposition to
Sihanouk among Cambodia's elite went underground, emerging ten years
later with more intensity from radicals and conservatives alike. The
Khmer Republic and the CPK were in a sense both children of the Democratic party and products of this repression. A more ominous legacy of the
confrontation was that elements of Sihanouk's behavior on display that
afternoon—violent rhetoric before a mass audience and the public humiliation of defenseless opponents followed by surreptitious physical
brutality—became increasingly characteristic of his treatment of
opponents.[23]

The Elections of 1958

After so much melodrama, Cambodian bureaucrats were relieved that
Sihanouk was out of the country and that the cabinet was guided by Sim
Var, who announced that his government had no specific program of
action: "We will limit ourselves to following the one already outlined by the
Prince."[24]

The assembly, however, soon reverted to its habits of influence ped-
dling and teaming up with importers and entrepreneurs. Such behavior
had grown rampant following the failure of several clean-up campaigns in
1956. The deputies also chafed under Sim Var's aloof, authoritarian leadership, and anonymous letters were soon reaching Sihanouk in France
condemning Sim Var, the assembly, and particular importers. Because
Suramarit was reluctant to intervene, Sihanouk's absence created a power
vacuum in Phnom Penh. By November 1957, Sim Var's newspaper began

printing editorials noting the people's longing for Sihanouk's return. Sim Var was ready to resign. At this point yet another financial scandal galvanized the deputies' opposition to him. Government business came to a halt.[25]

When Sihanouk returned from France, he did not want to be prime minister again and hoped that the new crisis would blow over. His optimism was misplaced because Sim Var was ready to resign and his enemies in the assembly wanted to throw him out. Assured of the prince's support, Sim Var suggested dissolving the assembly, but Sihanouk hesitated and took the matter to the national congress in January 1958.[26]

He may have hoped that a debate would clear the air, but the differences between Sim Var and the assembly were too deep. After two days of debate, the cabinet asked the king to dissolve the assembly. Suramarit's decree was read out, and the assemblymen elected in 1955 went home.[27] The dissolution moved elections forward by several months. Sihanouk was happy about this, for he was eager to improve the caliber of the assembly and to preside over a Sangkum government whose candidates could be elected unopposed.

Choosing these men and women augmented Sihanouk's political power. In February, the prince and a few advisers, including a leftist intellectual named Chau Seng who had recently returned from France, worked through the names of more than seven hundred people who had nominated themselves for the assembly. Those selected were unopposed, except in five districts where the Pracheachon proposed to field candidates. The new candidates were younger and better qualified than the members of the assembly of 1955, all but five of whom either declined to run or were not allowed to. Half of the new candidates were young. Nine (including the last prime minister of the Khmer Republic, Long Boret, then only twenty-five) were in their twenties, twenty-two in their thirties. Sihanouk was reaching into his own generation and into younger ones to form the new assembly. He made a point of choosing a handful of candidates who were known to be leftists, like Chau Seng, Hou Youn, So Nem, and Hu Nim. The only segments of the Cambodian elite not favored as candidates were women, recalcitrant Democrats, and members of the outgoing assembly.[28]

In making his choices, Sihanouk ignored the advice of Sangkum officials. New components of the movement, such as the Royal Socialist Youth (whose French acronym was JSRK), played a more important part in the campaign than the central committee did. Sihanouk had become impa-

tient with his movement and with the people he had chosen to run it. Two
secretaries general were removed from office in 1957. By the beginning of
1958, the leadership of the Sangkum was drawn from Sihanouk's entourage, and the movement's identity blended more thoroughly than ever
with Sihanouk himself, who was too impatient to allow it to grow slowly or
in unpredictable ways. As the years went on, the word *sangkum* itself—
drawn from the Pali word for "coming together" and meaning
"society"—became synonymous with whatever Sihanouk had in mind.
When he was speaking French, he referred to his creation as "Sangkum
society," a meaningless tautology.[29]

The Pracheachon was now in an invidious position. To survive as a
party, it had to remain in sight; being visible, it had to support the prince.
In an election, it had to run against the Sangkum without opposing it. To
win votes, it had to offer its own version of the prince's program and hope
that some of its proposals might persuade people to vote for candidates
who were under surveillance by the police.

In spite of Sihanouk's rewarding visits to Communist countries, and in
spite of or perhaps because of the insignificance of leftist opposition to his
rule, he became preoccupied with suppressing communism in Cambodia,
and the elections of 1958 were fought on anti-Communist lines. At the
national congress in January, Sihanouk accused the Pracheachon of stir-
ring up resentment among ordinary people. If the Pracheachon intended
to field candidates, he said, he felt obliged to warn his fellow citizens about
them. Just before the election, he published three articles on communism
in Cambodia. They traced the history of the Cambodian Communist
movement as he perceived it, stressed its dependence on Vietnam, and
said that communism was unfeasible for Khmer society. During the campaign the leftist press was closely monitored, and Pracheachon candidates and campaign workers were kept under surveillance. In Svay Rieng
more than two hundred police officials and Royal Socialist Youth were
assigned to follow the Pracheachon candidate around. Sihanouk visited
the districts where his opponents were running and attacked the candidates so vigorously that all but one of them, Keo Meas in Phnom Penh,
withdrew before election day.[30]

In some respects, the Pracheachon program in 1958 foreshadowed
some of the programs set in motion by the Communists when they came to
power, but most of the group's published material blurred the
Pracheachon's differences with the Sangkum. Indeed, the Pracheachon

candidate in Battambang, Achar Pres, a former Issarak–Viet Minh, claimed during his short campaign to be running both as a Communist and as a member of the Sangkum with Sihanouk's full support![31]

The Pracheachon's positions were occasionally contorted. In *Ekapheap* on March 8, for instance, an editorial urged people to "give their support without reserve to the candidates who have no connections with the imperialists" but took pains to assert that such advice "must not be interpreted as a refusal on our part to accord complete confidence" in Sihanouk. The message was probably too ambiguous for voters.[32]

The campaign itself was lackluster. Most Sangkum candidates, assured of victory, made token visits to their electorates, although Long Boret, in a pattern he repeated in 1962 and 1966, traveled hundreds of miles by elephant through his remote constituency of Stung Treng. Sangkum propaganda initially depicted a yellow-robed monk enjoining people to vote but became anti-Pracheachon in March, when photographs of a train destroyed by the Viet Minh and their Cambodian colleagues in 1954 went on display in provincial centers.[33]

When the votes were counted, the sole Pracheachon candidate in Phnom Penh, Keo Meas, had gained 396 votes, and another, "by mistake," as the official tally contended, picked up a dozen votes in Kampot. Nearly 700,000 other men and women voted for Sangkum candidates, but absenteeism was high, running to over 55 percent in Phnom Penh. It seems likely that many voters saw no relationship between the National Assembly and their daily lives.[34]

There were two by-products of the elections: since the assembly now comprised younger, better-trained representatives, cabinets could be formed more readily than in the past from inside the assembly; and Keo Meas, fearing arrest, took refuge for a time in the eastern part of Cambodia, bordering Vietnam. In his hurried departure, he left the urban branch of the KPRP in the hands of Saloth Sar, then thirty years old, and his colleague Vorn Vet. When he was purged in 1978, Vorn Vet, by then DK's deputy prime minister and a member of the CPK's central committee, stated, "In [the elections of 1958] the Pracheachon group put forward the names of a certain number of candidates. I could not see the possibility of a single candidate's winning the election, particularly after the experiences of '56 (*sic*) when all the candidates had been arrested and forced to confess by the enemy. I opposed these [1958] elections, and did nothing to agitate among the masses to support them, and this was against the will of the party. The campaign itself went off without the violence that had characterized 1956 (sic), the people were indifferent, and the revolutionary group made no great propaganda efforts."[35]

In 1977, a year before Vorn Vet's assessment, Pol Pot wrote that "in the elections of 1958, the enemy made use of its guns, laws, courts, prisons, and every other repressive tool to prevent the people voting for the revolutionaries, the patriots and the progressives."[36]

In the aftermath of the elections the prince addressed the new assembly, using a theatrical image: "I believe that my role is to advise you in a general manner. I would not be able to do this if I were President of the Council: in the theatre one cannot be at the same time actor, director and spectator." He went on to say that he need not be prime minister because "it is not I, but the Sangkum that is the basis of everything," yet added, "If you do not help me . . . Cambodia like other countries will have a revolution."[37]

The assembly named Sim Var prime minister again but soon quarreled with him over economic issues, and he resigned. When San Yun failed to gain the confidence of the assembly, Sihanouk assumed the office himself after demonstrations throughout the country had suggested that he do so. He appointed Hou Youn and Hu Nim to his cabinet.[38]

In the meantime, Cambodia's relations with South Vietnam and Thailand had worsened. In June, Vietnamese troops, allegedly pursuing escaped political prisoners and after moving the border markers several kilometers deeper inside the country, invaded northeastern Cambodia in battalion strength. Sihanouk complained to the American embassy about the incursion and threatened to bring the matter before the UN, but U.S. Ambassador Carl Strom warned him that U.S. military aid might be suspended if the Cambodian army used U.S.–supplied equipment to engage a friendly power. Within a short time Sihanouk informed Beijing that he was willing to extend diplomatic recognition to the People's Republic of China (PRC). This move was condemned in Western diplomatic circles as impulsive, but it had probably been in the planning stages for some time. It dismayed Cambodia's pro-Western neighbors and encouraged U.S. intelligence services to seek alternatives to the prince.[39]

Sihanouk may have been stung into recognizing Beijing by an incident earlier in the year in which Thai military forces took possession of the tenth-century Khmer temple of Preah Vihear (Khao Prah Viharn in Thai), which stood atop a cliff that straddled the Khmer–Thai border. The occupation threatened to erupt into open conflict. In 1959, Sihanouk brought the dispute to the attention of the World Court in The Hague. Three years later, to the Thais' chagrin, the court decided the case in Cambodia's favor.[40]

Sihanouk was not yet prepared to take on the United States or to forfeit its assistance. He made a visit to Washington in October 1958, his first since independence, and was again lectured, though less dogmatically than usual, by Eisenhower and Dulles. He was also interviewed by a journalist, Amelia Young, who remarked, "If Cambodia were a larger country this prince might be a great Asian leader." Sihanouk replied, "'The Prince' is less myself than our nation and its policy, *of which I am the incarnation* [emphasis added]. If we were 20 million, we would surely play an even more brilliant role on the international scene."[41]

On his return to Cambodia, Sihanouk faced the first serious opposition he had encountered since 1952. This took the form of two plots against him that were quickly foiled but that showed, in one, clear evidence of Thai, U.S., and Vietnamese involvement and in the other evidence of coordinated support by the same powers. The plots would never have occurred had U.S. policy in 1958 not tilted toward dissidents in Cambodia. They raised the stakes in Cambodia's relations with its neighbors, unnerved the prince, and permanently damaged U.S.-Cambodian relations.

The Sam Sary and Dap Chhuon Plots

Sam Sary, one of Sihanouk's most strong-minded advisers, was forty-two years old in 1958. After studying in Paris in the early 1950s, where he had avoided left-wing circles, he was frequently called on by Sihanouk to perform important tasks. He ironed out the details of Cambodia's negotiations with France; he was a skillful member of the delegation at Geneva and a driving force behind the foundation of the Sangkum and the electoral campaign of 1955. His hauteur, his involvement in financial scandals, and what one observer called his "sulfurous and vindictive personality," however, earned him many enemies. By the middle of 1957, his pro-Western views had cooled his intimacy with the prince. Sary had by then earned the dubious distinction of being, in the words of the U.S. Department of State, "the staunchest friend of the United States in Cambodia." His pro–U.S. position sprang in part from a three-month visit to America in 1956. Although evidence is lacking, he probably became acquainted with U.S. intelligence officers at this time. Toward the end of 1957, he became Cambodia's ambassador to London.[42]

Six months later, a Cambodian woman employed by the embassy as a governess to Sary's children complained to British police that Sary had beaten her so violently that she needed medical attention. The ambassador told the press that such conduct as his was normal in Cambodian culture; he did not disclose that the woman was an ex-mistress who had recently borne him a child. When the news of the scandal reached Cambodia, Sary was immediately recalled.

As soon as Sary got to Phnom Penh, Queen Kossamak warned him against engaging in political activity, but he soon began attacking Sihanouk for having him recalled. The prince was abroad at the time, but his government mounted a campaign against Sary, whose wife attempted to deflect criticism by telling the queen that she, rather than her husband, had beaten the governess. Unfortunately, no one seemed interested in Sam Sary, and no journal would publish his polemics. It was at this stage that he may have sought help from abroad to finance an opposition party.[43]

Sary's newspaper, *Reastrthipodei* (Democratic people), appeared in November 1958. Its title and timing were inept. He must have known that the word *thipodei* (democratic) was anathema to Sihanouk, and so was his appropriation of the word *reastr* (people or subjects) from its place in the full name of the Sangkum. His editorial attacks on China were also poorly timed. Because Sary had no visible patron, it was widely assumed that he was paid by the United States.[44]

When Sihanouk returned to Cambodia, he ignored the paper at first and then condemned it at the national congress. Obstinately, Sary asked his permission to found an opposition party. Sihanouk failed to reply. On January 13, 1959, in a speech in Kompong Cham, however, the prince referred to a "Bangkok plot" against his government, allegedly set in motion by the new Thai premier, Marshal Sarit Thanarat, and involving Sam Sary. He did not go into detail. Before long, Sary disappeared, and the National Assembly, knowing he was gone, demanded his arrest. When his house was searched, government sources claimed to have found documentary proof of his collusion with the Thai. This was never made public, but his property was confiscated, his wife was imprisoned, and several of his associates were rounded up and jailed. Sary had fled to Thailand, where he came under the protection of Maj. Channa Samudvanija, Son Ngoc Thanh's contact in the Thai government, who provided him with a house in Bangkok next door to his own.

Channa's superiors probably expected more from Sary than he was able to deliver. What the Americans expected of him is unclear. An alliance of sorts was stitched together in Bangkok between Son Ngoc Thanh and Sary, but the two men were never close, and support inside Cambodia for both of them was negligible. For the next few years Sary shuttled among Bangkok, Vientiane, and Saigon without making any political headway. He disappeared in 1962, probably assassinated by one of his foreign patrons.[45]

The Dap Chhuon affair, which came to light in February 1959, posed a more serious threat to Sihanouk's regime, although many elements of the plot (in both senses of the word) are difficult to explain. Dap Chhuon—or Chhuon Mchhulpich (Chhuon Diamond Needle), as he called himself, even though no one knew him by that name—had enjoyed close links with Thai authorities since the 1940s and had been an active Issarak before rallying to Sihanouk in 1949. Ten years later, as the governor of Siem Reap and military commander of the northwest, he commanded a well-equipped, ostensibly progovernment force. Cadaverously thin, with unblinking, deep-set eyes, Chhuon had a daunting personal appearance. Like Lon Nol, he was drawn to amulets and supernaturalism and managed to convince many people that he was invulnerable to bullets, knives, and fire.[46] He ruled Siem Reap as a personal fief. Because his punishments were prompt and severe, petty crime in the province was almost nonexistent, and foreign tourists visiting Angkor had their safety guaranteed. Tax revenues were higher than anywhere else in the country. People feared and respected Chhuon, but he was not beloved.[47]

Throughout his career, Chhuon was friendly with the authorities in Bangkok. By 1956, his outspoken anticommunism had also drawn favorable comment from Saigon, where Ngo Dinh Diem suggested to an American visitor that it might be feasible to conduct joint operations against Communist insurgents along the border, using Chhuon's forces. Diem said that this would be like America "co-operating with Mexico in dealing with bandits." The State Department backed away from the proposal not because it interfered with Cambodian sovereignty but because it "might lead to hopeless compromise or alienation of Dap Chhuon, who seems at present to represent [a] pro-U.S, anti-Communist element."[48]

When Chhuon was minister of the interior in 1957, he summoned members of the assembly to his Phnom Penh residence to say that he disapproved of Sihanouk's "pro-Communist" foreign policy. Over the next year or so, after returning to Siem Reap, he continued to complain along these lines to anyone who would listen. By then, he was under pressure from Bangkok to support Gen. Sarit Thanarat's impending bid for power and to refrain from sending Cambodian troops to attack the Thai garrison occupying Preah Vihear. Perhaps disturbed by reports of Chhuon's disaffection, Sihanouk appointed Puth Chhay as military commander of Kompong Thom, supposedly part of Chhuon's jurisdiction. At this point Chhuon may have reached his decision to take action against the prince.[49]

By then, Chhuon knew he could count on South Vietnamese support. The South Vietnamese, after enraging Sihanouk with their military excursion into Cambodia's northeast, were still anxious to undermine what they saw as his procommunist regime. In December 1958, according to Diem's director of political intelligence, Tran Kim Tuyen (writing in 1970), Diem's brother and close adviser Ngo Dinh Nhu ordered the South Vietnamese diplomatic representative in Phnom Penh, Ngo Trong Hieu, "to persuade Sihanouk to change his views" toward North Vietnam. According to Tuyen, Hieu suggested instead that "they should organize a *coup d'état* to get rid of Sihanouk. Both President Diem and Nhu agreed." Dap Chhuon was the instrument they chose.[50]

By that time Chhuon's activities had come to the attention of President Eisenhower, who learned from a daily intelligence summary on New Year's Day that Chhuon was "seeking U.S. support to overthrow Sihanouk." By then, Chhuon's plans to remove Siem Reap from Cambodia—the long-term goal being to destabilize Sihanouk's regime—were well advanced.[51]

In February, Chhuon failed to come to Phnom Penh to attend the wedding of Sihanouk's daughter Bopha Devi. He was the only provincial governor not to attend. By this time Sam Sary was in exile in Thailand and in touch with Son Ngoc Thanh. Whether or not Dap Chhuon was also involved in the so-called Bangkok Plot, Sihanouk interpreted Chhuon's absence as a personal rebuff.

Less than a month later, Chhuon's plot had come apart, and he was dead. The imbroglio is worth discussing because of the shadows it cast on U.S.-Cambodian relations and because new material about the plot as well as a persuasive explanation for its failure have recently come to light.

In late 1958, an American schoolteacher, Richard Cima, arrived to teach English in Siem Reap. He was the only American teacher at the school. He later recalled, "I came to believe that Dap Chhuon interpreted my assignment as some sort of signal from the Americans, largely because the official treatment that I received was far different from that given to

[French and Cambodian] teachers. I was invited to visit Chhuon in his office, while other teachers never met him at all."[52]

From time to time, Chhuon would summon Cima "ostensibly to chat," but Cima found the conversations "awkward, even bizarre, consisting of platitudes with an occasional oblique or not so oblique political note." One evening, Chhuon asked Cima to telephone Ambassador Strom for him and invite him to Siem Reap for conversations. As Cima recalls, "I was very naive at the time but I could see that such a call would be awkward if not downright dangerous"; calls from Siem Reap had to pass through an operator and were monitored by government agents.

Cima spoke to the embassy in a roundabout way and made sure that Chhuon's message reached the ambassador, who never responded to it. About this time, however, a CIA agent attached to the embassy, an American of Japanese parentage named Victor Matsui, paid a brief visit to Siem Reap to meet with Chhuon's brother Slat Peou. Slat Peou was the Siem Reap representative in the National Assembly. Like Sam Sary, he had been awarded a leader grant to the United States in 1956 and had probably been approached informally by CIA agents at that time. Matsui was observed by agents working for Lon Nol and by an army lieutenant assigned to keep an eye on Dap Chhuon.[53]

In early February Slat Peou was also visited in Siem Reap by Ngo Trong Hieu. In all likelihood this trip was the one on which Hieu transported a hundred kilograms of gold from the South Vietnamese treasury to equip and pay Chhuon's forces. Thel Thong, then an employee of the meteorological service at Siem Reap, recalls several flights coming in to the Siem Reap airport from the direction of Thailand also. In view of later developments, these probably carried arms and ammunition for Chhuon's men.[54]

Two days after Dap Chhuon failed to attend Bopha Devi's wedding, the Vietnamese provided him with powerful radio transmitters. These were to be used for making propaganda broadcasts and for maintaining contact with intelligence services attached to Diem's office. Chhuon was apparently so confident his plans would succeed that he invited some of his officials to the Siem Reap airport to witness the arrival of the transmitters. This behavior, bizarre to say the least, has another explanation, as we shall see: by going public Chhuon was attempting to save his own skin and set a trap for the Vietnamese. In any case, Sieu Chheng Y, at that time an employee of the provincial ministry of justice, has vividly recalled what happened next:[55]

We saw a big plane coming in to land. There were only two people on board, Vietnamese in civilian clothes—wearing short-sleeved shirts, and there we were, told to assemble with long-sleeved shirts, and ties! Just then, we saw Dap Chhuon's purple Mercedes drive onto the runway. When Dap Chhuon got out of the car, he called out to us: "Today we're really happy!" and he walked up to the Vietnamese and shook hands. We didn't know what to think. We didn't dare say anything. We heard Dap Chhuon talking with them—he knew some Vietnamese—and then after a few moments we saw a small airplane circling the field. When it landed, its pilot climbed out—he was alone in the plane, the only passenger. He was an American. It was a small, clean plane, very pretty, I'd never seen one like it. Dap Chhuon went over to the American and they shook hands. I didn't know what opinion to have, I was so confused by all this: first the two Vietnamese and then the American; they spoke with each other for a moment, and then the American climbed back into his plane and flew off. As soon as he had gone, we saw three General Motors trucks belonging to Dap Chhuon coming onto the runway. Dap Chhuon's soldiers were in the trucks. There were about fifteen of them. In groups of four, they unloaded wooden crates from the airplane, onto the trucks, and then drove off—not in the direction of Siem Reap, but towards Angkor. This was confusing, too. We didn't know what was in the crates—later we heard that perhaps they were radio transmitters. When the plane was unloaded, it took off again, and we were left on the runway, wondering what had happened. Dap Chhuon called out to us, "Thanks for coming, gentlemen!" climbed back into his Mercedes, and drove off.[56]

Four days later, according to Slat Peou's confession, Matsui provided him with another transmitter, which he was to use to keep in touch with the U.S. embassy regarding the progress of the affair. The only message sent from the embassy over the transmitter urged Chhuon not to use force against the government—a sentiment that hardly required such an expensive piece of equipment. About the same time, Chhuon told his brother that the Vietnamese had provided 270 kilograms of gold (valued in 1959 at approximately $165,000) in small ingots to use to pay guerrilla forces and to bribe Cambodian government officials. Sieu Chheng Y claims to have seen the ingots in Chhuon's house, where carpenters were preparing special storage space for them.[57]

News of Chhuon's activities reached Phnom Penh by several channels, including the French and Chinese ambassadors, as well as via French residents of Siem Reap. Like Sam Sary, Chhuon seems to have been supremely confident at first. However, a source who wishes to remain anonymous has recalled that Dap Chhuon became nervous as the plot thickened and, hoping to save his skin, informed Lon Nol and Queen Kossamak of the plot. In this account, Lon Nol informed Sihanouk of Chhuon's message. Sihanouk told him to negotiate with Chhuon, obtain the gold, and see to it that Chhuon and his close associates were shot.[58]

This explanation fits many available facts that are otherwise difficult to explain. These include Dap Chhuon's lax security while supposedly in revolt, Sihanouk's insouciance when the plot was uncovered (and Dap Chhuon was out of the way), U.S. embarrassment (for the embassy does not seem to have been aware that Chhuon had given Lon Nol details of the plot), and Sihanouk's suddenly enhanced appreciation of Lon Nol.[59]

By February 21, Sihanouk decided to move against Dap Chhuon, probably to forestall news of the plot reaching the public before it had been snuffed out. On the twenty-second, Lon Nol and the commander of the Cambodian air force, Ngo Hou, flew to Siem Reap, ostensibly to arrest Dap Chhuon but probably to parley with him. Had he been threatening a genuine armed revolt, the two men would never have traveled to Siem Reap in this fashion, for their lives would have been endangered. Similarly, had they been involved in the plot themselves—another possibility—it is unlikely that they would have flown to Siem Reap so openly and so late.

Backing them up, two battalions of infantry along with tanks and armored personnel carriers were dispatched by road to secure the town. As they traveled northward, soldiers cut the telephone wires connecting Siem Reap and Phnom Penh. They occupied Siem Reap later on the same day without firing a shot. Chhuon's soldiers were rounded up and disarmed but not mistreated. Several of his officers, on the other hand, disappeared soon afterward and were presumed to have been shot.[60]

At first Dap Chhuon felt himself in no real danger. He was surprised by two government soldiers while he was doing calisthenics. Sensing that something was wrong, he escaped on foot toward Phnom Kulen, where he was caught some days later by an army lieutenant whose niece he had abducted in 1958. Shot in the foot, he was taken on a litter to the main road, where he was assassinated, probably on Lon Nol's orders, without making a detailed confession.[61]

Three days after Siem Reap had been secured, but before Chhuon had been caught, Sihanouk gave a press conference there and excitedly displayed evidence seized in Chhuon's villa—including the transmitters, the ingots, two Vietnamese prisoners, and some documents implicating Ngo Trong Hieu.

The Americans had not yet been linked to the plot, and Ambassador Strom reported to Washington at first that the case against the Vietnamese was weak. Five days later he wrote that Ngo Trong Hieu "is believed to have told Dap Chhuon that American Embassy Saigon had given tacit assurance that American support would be forthcoming after coup action initiated. This is probably the most damaging statement Dap Chhuon could have included in his dying revelations but he may have said things to embarrass U.S. Embassy in other ways."[62]

Slat Peou's connections with the U.S. embassy had not yet surfaced, and before they did Matsui was transferred to another post. Because Dap Chhuon was dead, Ngo Trong Hieu sent home, the South Vietnamese humiliated, and Siem Reap secure, Sihanouk turned his attention to other issues, and the interrogation of Slat Peou and the Vietnamese prisoners proceeded at a leisurely pace. The U.S. government was able to maintain a lofty tone with the prince, who had written a passionate letter to President Eisenhower protesting against the complicity of America's allies, but not of the United States itself, in Chhuon's plot.[63]

By September, when U.S. involvement was revealed, Strom's replacement, William Trimble, had the unenviable task of dealing with the allegations against Matsui and the CIA as they emerged.

In an ironic footnote, Ambassador Trimble proposed a set of talking points for the State Department in conversation with the Cambodian ambassador to Washington, Nong Kimny, relative to the affair. Trimble suggested that one such point might be, "We have consistently felt it in the national interest to give [Sihanouk] our full support." In the copy of the telegram now housed in the U.S. National Archives, someone in the department penciled in a question mark beside the ambassador's suggestion.[64]

In the aftermath of the Dap Chhuon plot, but before the highlights of Slat Peou's confessions were made public, another attack against Sihanouk was hatched in Saigon, again with the approval of Ngo Dinh Nhu. Happily for the prince, it literally misfired.

On August 31, a pair of suitcases allegedly containing gifts for Sihanouk and the director of protocol in the royal palace, Prince Vakravan, were delivered anonymously to the palace, with the calling card of an

American engineer who had made Sihanouk's acquaintance when working in Cambodia. While the queen and Sihanouk were in an adjoining
room, Prince Vakravan opened one of the suitcases, which exploded and
killed him instantly. Another member of the palace staff was also killed by
the blast, and two were wounded.[65]

At the time, many people assumed (correctly, as things turned out) that
the gift was a clumsy attempt by the South Vietnamese to reassert themselves after the Dap Chhuon affair; some thought it a demented gesture
on the part of Sam Sary. American involvement was also alleged, and the
three plots—Sam Sary, Dap Chhuon, August 31—soon blended in
Sihanouk's speeches and in many people's minds to form a continuous
conspiracy.

Ngo Dinh Nhu had been infuriated by the Dap Chhuon fiasco. He
apparently hoped, with Sihanouk dead, to install Son Ngoc Thanh in
power in Phnom Penh. Thanh was by then receiving a three-hundred-
thousand-piaster monthly retainer from the Vietnamese, paid out of
Diem's "black budget." Tran Kim Tuyen's book asserts that the two suitcases had been packed in Saigon. A harmless suitcase containing presents
from Hong Kong was addressed to Vakravan. The plotters assumed he
would pass the other case, unopened, along to Sihanouk, but the director
of protocol opened both cases and was blown to bits.

After these disasters, the United States' search for an anti-Communist
ally inside Cambodia lost momentum, but Sihanouk became permanently
distrustful of American intentions. His suspiciousness played into the
hands of the Vietnamese Communists seeking to overthrow the Diem
regime.

Although Sihanouk was aware that several thousand Vietnamese
Communist troops were more or less permanently stationed in remote
border areas in Kompong Cham, Svay Rieng, and Prey Veng—and he
said as much to Ambassador Trimble—the prince was reluctant to attack
these troops and unwilling after the events of 1959 to lower his guard vis-
à-vis Ngo Dinh Diem. Instead, following the adage that one's enemy's
friend is one's enemy and heeding the suggestions of some of his advisers,
Sihanouk became increasingly estranged from the United States.[66]

Communism in Cambodia, 1955–1963

The early stages of communism in Cambodia are of interest because
the party came to power in the 1970s. Although in DK pronouncements

this process was made to seem inevitable, it is hard to study the 1950s without sensing that the party's success was due almost entirely to accidents, outside help, and external pressures. Throughout this period its leaders were suspicious of one another, inactive, and out of touch with Cambodian conditions. Their success, which came slowly, was contingent on events in South Vietnam, on Vietnamese Communist guidance, on the disastrous policies followed by the United States, and on blunders made by successive Cambodian governments.[67]

In fact, it is hard to say what the KPRP was doing in the late 1950s. After the withdrawal of over one thousand cadre to Vietnam in 1954 and the Pracheachon defeat in the elections of 1955, Cambodian radicals at home felt they had been cut adrift by their patrons in Vietnam. Instructed to carry on political struggle, they faced a difficult task.

In some ways, the KPRP's mission was simpler than ever. In others it had become impossible. In ideological terms, the enemy, made up of exploiting classes, merchants, moneylenders, corrupt officials, the royal family, pro–U.S. elements, and so on, were as easy to locate as they were anywhere in Indochina, but Sihanouk posed an almost insuperable problem, and the peasantry posed another.

Cambodian radicals could hardly assert, as their colleagues in South Vietnam did about Ngo Dinh Diem, that Sihanouk had been placed in power by the United States. Instead, the prince was seen by many as having brought about Cambodian independence. Since 1955, moreover, he had skillfully taken up leftist positions in foreign policy, including an anti-American stance. He had attracted patronage and aid from the Communist bloc. He had co-opted prominent Cambodian leftists into the Sangkum and some of them into cabinet positions. Domestically, he denied that exploitation existed in Cambodian society and allowed the Pracheachon to function as a political group—a privilege difficult for its members to refuse—while exposing it to obloquy, keeping its members under surveillance, and resorting to terror when they seemed to be stepping out of line.[68]

The Cambodian peasantry posed other problems for the KPRP. By and large, these men and women were reluctant to become involved in rebellious politics after Cambodia's independence had been won. Their individualism, conservatism, Buddhist ethics, and the fact that nearly all of them owned their land made them unlikely candidates for Communist recruitment. In most rural areas in the late 1950s, preconditions for revolutionary action were difficult to discern.

How then was the KPRP expected to carry on political struggle? The Pracheachon Group was unable to capitalize openly on elite and student discontent with Sihanouk. They were also unable to persuade former Democrats to support them. Radicals operating in clandestinity, on the other hand, could not hope to accomplish much either, in the absence of instability or widespread discontent.

In the 1950s, while awaiting developments, many Cambodian radicals embarked on teaching careers. In the long term, they affected and inspired many young Cambodians, some of whom joined them in the ranks of the Communist resistance later on. Others who had been students of radical teachers were pleased by Sihanouk's demise when it occurred in 1970.

Radicals began drifting into the schools as teachers after the Geneva conference, while the Democrats and the Pracheachon were jointly opposing a U.S. alliance and Sihanouk's dictatorship. In this period, several Communists began their careers as teachers in private schools in Phnom Penh. Two of these schools, Kambuj'bot and Chamraon Vichea, were especially important.[69]

Kambuj'bot (or Kambubot, in French transliteration) took its name from the pseudonym ("child of Cambodia") that Prince Yuthevong had used in Democratic journals in 1946–47. The school, financed by Democrat contributions, was founded in June 1952 in the wake of Sihanouk's coup. For several years, it was known informally as the Thonn Ouk school because most of the funds had come from this disaffected politician; by the late 1950s, its informal name had become Hou Youn, in honor of its most effective teacher. Throughout the 1950s and 1960s, it earned a reputation for harboring radicals. It was the only school visited by Zhou Enlai when he came to Phnom Penh in 1956; and two years later a U.S. embassy officer encountered a former student from the school who told him that at Kambuj'bot she and her friends "talked about nothing but politics." Students whose parents were Democrats tended to gravitate toward Kambuj'bot when the time came for them to study at a collège. Other loci of dissent included the Ecole Normale, where Son Sen was director of studies in the late 1950s, and the Lycée Sisowath, where teachers Khieu Ponnary and her sister Khieu Thirith (married by then to Saloth Sar and Ieng Sary, respectively) were remembered as being strict but adored by their many student disciples.[70]

A radical reputation also clung to the Chamraon Vichea (Progressive study) school, although the initial funding for it came from Prince Norodom Chantaraingsey and Lon Nol. Saloth Sar taught geography, history, civics, and French literature there between 1956 and 1963. Two of his former students remember him with affection. One, the novelist and editor Soth Polin, who studied French literature briefly under Sar in 1958–59, noted that Sar's teaching manner was genteel, almost unctuous, and that his favorite poets were the nineteenth-century romantics Alfred de Vigny and Paul Verlaine. "He spoke in bursts, without notes," Polin has recalled, "looking for the right word sometimes, but he was never caught short, carried along by his own lyricism." In a perceptive article published in 1981 Polin related Saloth Sar's speaking manner to the "diabolic gentleness" of DK pronouncements in the 1970s, and his ingratiating style to his palace connections. Another student, who prefers not to be named, studied history with Sar in 1960 and recalled that he was "very popular with the students and very correct in his ways. The French he spoke was easy for us to understand. He taught Cambodian history, stressing Sihanouk's Crusade for Independence. Had he taught history any other way, he would have gotten into trouble and the students would have failed their examination."[71]

You Sambo, then a student at another school, met Saloth Sar in the late 1950s. He has recalled him as being "extremely clean" (s'aat s'om), as "the kind of person whom you knew it would be easy to make friends with." Sambo noted that Sar was fastidious in his personal habits and spoke gently to people—as did his wife, Khieu Ponnary. His smooth face, genial manners, and smooth language blended in many people's memories, forming a confusing undertone to their knowledge of his behavior in the 1970s.[72]

In Cambodian culture the role of the teacher (Khmer kru: compare Sanskrit guru) and the student-teacher relationship have always been important in ethical, social, and intellectual terms. Before the 1950s, nearly all Cambodian boys learned to read under the guidance of a Buddhist monk; these men, emerging from monastic life into the community at large, were known as achar, or teachers, and continued to perform ceremonial roles. As we have seen, Son Ngoc Minh and Tou Samouth came to the Communist movement in the 1940s as achar with reputations for monastic learning. After independence, the knowledge imparted by secular teachers and the bonds that developed between teachers and students often shaped the students' political attitudes. The roles played by teachers at Kambuj'bot and Chamraon Vichea are crucial to the development of Cambodian radicalism. As one Cambodian told me, "Even mathematics teachers had the duty to impart morality." By the late 1960s, when a Communist-led rebellion had broken out in much of Cambodia, many guerrilla bands were made up in part of former teachers and their students who had followed them into the forest. In 1980, one such CPK cadre told Stephen Heder, "I went into the forest [in 1968] because of the influence of my teachers. The essence of their teachings was the sufferings of the poor and the ease of the rich, which made me angry."[73]

In Sihanouk's heyday, radical teachers had to express their political views with care, although their attacks on U.S. imperialism and on corruption could be tailored to echo Sihanouk's own. In the late 1950s and early 1960s, these teachers occasionally staged informal, after-hours seminars at the Lycée Sisowath and elsewhere to discuss civics, nationalism, and imperialism. These discussion groups, for those who persistently attended them, formed the basis of clandestine party cells that were organized later.

The teachers also provided role models by their dedication to teaching, their fairness, and their incorruptibility. Khieu Ponnary, for example, who taught Khmer literature, is remembered as being fair, inspired, and severe and as having a reputation for personal austerity. She was punctual, disciplined, and emotionally restrained. Similar reputations clung to Khek Pen, Tiv Ol, and Khieu Samphan.

At the party level, the leaders of the KPRP were divided. Sieu Heng defected to the government in 1959 and began feeding information about radicals to Lon Nol, whom he had met in the early 1950s. According to Ros Nhim, who had joined the Issaraks with Heng in 1946, Heng at this stage "no longer wanted to live secretly; he even said that making revolution was impossible." Some of Heng's information may have helped Lon Nol to disrupt rural networks of the KPRP, as Pol Pot was to claim in 1977, but Sieu Heng led government agents nowhere near his wife's nephew, Nuon Chea, or those who were busy in 1959–60 conducting clandestine party business in Phnom Penh.

The principal effect of Heng's defection was that the city-based members of the party lost touch with their colleagues in the countryside and gained a preponderant voice in party circles. As Kiernan has written, "The committee in charge of the urban movement slowly became the de facto central committee, despite the overwhelming preponderance of rural membership within the Party."

Most evidence points to a small, powerless, clandestine KPRP in this period, but Saloth Sar chose to paint a more heroic picture when he outlined the history of the CPK in 1977. "In 1956," he said, "the enemy continued to crack down and in 1957 the repression intensified. In 1958 . . . these attacks became even more severe, especially in the countryside, and many people were arrested. The arrests continued and multiplied in 1959 and 1960, both in the countryside and the cities. About 90 percent of our revolutionary forces in the countryside were destroyed in 1959, due to assassinations, arrests, recantations and surrender to the enemy."

Pol Pot's analysis echoes one made in the late 1960s in a "Summary of an Annotated Party History": "During [1957–59] . . . we did not understand Marxist-Leninist doctrine very well. We did not have firm control of the struggle between the social classes, nor did we understand political and organizational questions."[74]

What made life difficult for radicals in Cambodia at this time was not the thoroughness of government repression, although this was always a factor—the editor of *Pracheachon,* Nop Bophan, for example, was shot down outside his office, presumably by the police, in October 1959—but that there were so few of them and that their radical ideas enjoyed so little support. Sihanouk's popularity and his anti-imperialist policies made it hard for the party to work out a program that highlighted contradictions in Cambodian society or in Sihanouk's behavior. A by-product of the government's perception that the party posed no real threat was that most of its members were undisturbed. Repression never reached the same intensity it did in South Vietnam, where it pushed thousands of men and women into the resistance. In fact, as Pol Pot admitted in the *Black Book* (1978), conditions were so secure in Cambodia in this period that several high-ranking Vietnamese Communists, including Le Duan, found temporary sanctuary there. Interestingly, hardly any prominent Cambodian Communists (with the notable exceptions of Chou Chet, Khieu Samphan, and Non Suon) had spent even a night in jail before the CPK came to power.[75]

Throughout the late fifties, the formal leadership of the KPRP remained in the hands of Son Ngoc Minh in faraway Hanoi, but the KPRP in Phnom Penh was granted considerable autonomy. There is no evidence that KPRP cadre in Cambodia took advantage of this distance to formulate and spread an anti-Vietnamese party line. To be sure, by 1958, the eclipse of the Pracheachon must have made some local radicals impatient, and Pol Pot later claimed that by 1957 he was studying ways of improving the party's line. Vorn Vet, in his confession in 1978, referred to frequent study sessions among party members in Phnom Penh in 1958–59. Neither activity was in defiance of party discipline as laid down by Hanoi and by the temporary central committee inside Cambodia, consisting at this stage of Tou Samouth and another ICP veteran with links to the eastern part of the country, Sao Phim.[76]

The pro-Vietnamese alignment of the KPRP in the 1950s needs to be stressed because it was a crisis in Vietnam in 1960, not conditions inside Cambodia, that led to the formation of a more autonomous Cambodian party in September 1960.

Throughout 1959, pressure had been building inside the VWP to inaugurate armed struggle in South Vietnam, where party workers, sympathizers, and former Viet Minh were being imprisoned, tortured, and assassinated by Diem's army and his American-trained police. Limited armed struggle in South Vietnam broke out toward the end of 1959. In September 1960, the VWP convened its Third National Congress in Hanoi and approved plans for southerners to liberate South Vietnam. It seems likely that a decision was also taken at this time to organize a more autonomous but still subordinate Cambodian party.[77]

VWP strategy called for the establishing of closer ties between the governments of Cambodia and (North) Vietnam and between the two Communist parties. The eastern region of Cambodia, along with the northeast, was to be reconstituted as a base area through which Vietnamese forces and supplies could be funneled into the south. The KPRP was to play a supportive role in Vietnam's heroic drama. To play it properly it had to be brought to life.

Two weeks after the VWP congress twenty-one Cambodian radicals assembled secretly on the grounds of the railway station in Phnom Penh. Twenty-one years later, the PRK explained that this meeting was convened because "the revolution inside and outside the country was in confusion, which required a new political line." The PRK's hostility to the CPK notwithstanding, this is an accurate description. A major event "inside the country" (discussed below) had been King Suramarit's death in April 1960, and Sihanouk's becoming chief of state. Sihanouk's repression of local leftists was another cause for concern. At the end of August, several left-wing newspapers in Phnom Penh had been closed down and fifteen alleged Communists had been arrested by the police, as had Khieu Samphan, the editor of another left-wing newspaper, *l'Observateur.* The phrase "outside the country" undoubtedly referred to decisions taken at the VWP congress in Hanoi to renew armed struggle in South Vietnam.[78]

The KPRP meeting was not reported by the U.S. embassy and probably was not known to Sihanouk's security apparatus. It was not mentioned in party documents before 1972, when the September 30 date was celebrated as the twenty-first anniversary of the party. Evidence for the meeting in 1960 comes from several sources.

The congress has received considerable scholarly attention. Much about it remains uncertain, but three facts emerge. One is that Saloth Sar was appointed at the congress to the number three position on a newly constituted central committee, just below Tou Samouth and Nuon Chea. The second is that the KPRP changed its name on this occasion to the Khmer Workers' Party (*pak pul'kor khmer,* or KWP), placing it semantically on a level with the VWP. We also know that Son Ngoc Minh, in absentia, earned a place on the central committee.[79]

Ieng Sary and Koy Thuon were the only intellectuals besides Saloth Sar to be brought onto the committee, and although Pol Pot would later mark September 30, 1960, as "the day on which the Communist party of Kampuchea was definitively born," the decisions taken at the meeting, insofar as they have become known, were not controversial, and the definitive birth to which Pol Pot refers is probably his elevation to the central committee. By 1977, Saloth Sar, Ieng Sary, and Nuon Chea were the only survivors from 1960 still serving on the committee: the others had died or been purged.[80]

In 1960, however, the composition of the committee still favored those who had ties with the ICP. Saloth Sar probably owed his elevation to his years of party work, to the patronage of Tou Samouth, and to the importance of the urban wing of the party. In other words, the party leadership, put together with Vietnamese advice, was probably pleasing to VWP officials in Hanoi.[81]

At the same time, it must have been humiliating for young members of the KWP like Sar and Ieng Sary to receive guidance from Hanoi that imposed so much caution on them and paid so little attention to the injustices of Cambodian life and to Cambodia's own need for revolution. To these young men, their wives, and their associates, decisions taken at the meeting must have seemed like a replay of colonial times, when Cambodians seeking independence were enjoined by the French to wait politely for benefits that would accrue to them in due time. Whereas Vietnam, ironically, could approach its liberation in terms of Vietnamese nationalism, xenophobia, and the flow of Vietnamese history, the revolution in Cambodia had to follow a less precise, more international model, with no emphasis on local issues, Cambodia's history, or armed struggle. This subsidiary role for Cambodia in an Indochinese revolution made sense to the Vietnamese but may have looked like hegemony to the Khmer.

There was nothing they could do but accept such guidance. Moreover, in view of the Communists' activities in Cambodia over the next six years or so, there is no possibility that resolutions passed at the meeting in 1960 espoused a truly independent line. Nonetheless, in hindsight the participants were clearly breaking into factions. One of these, the eventual victor, was Pol Pot's own. Another, with links to the ICP and roots in the eastern part of the country, was personified by Sao Phim. Yet another easterner, Tou Samouth, presided over the party.[82]

At the 1960 meeting, then, a Marxist-Leninist party—with statutes, a central committee, a politburo, and so forth—came into being in Cambodia. Organizationally, this was a step forward from 1951. To DK spokesmen, it was the beginning of the party's march to victory. For PRK spokesmen after 1979, it marked the point at which communism in Cambodia went off the rails.[83]

Sihanouk Triumphant

In early April 1960 King Suramarit died after a long illness. The constitutional crisis that ensued, stage-managed by Sihanouk, came to a climax in a referendum in June that chose him as Cambodia's first nonmonarchic chief of state.[84]

Immediately after his father's death, knowing that the succession crisis would not be resolved within the three days demanded by palace tradition, Sihanouk persuaded Prince Monireth to preside over a regency council that could stand in for the deceased monarch until more permanent arrangements were made. Sihanouk himself had sworn never to return to the throne and had wanted no one more decisive or less reliable than his father to be king. His eldest son, Prince Rannaridh, was still a minor, and had he been appointed king, residual powers would have fallen to a regent, perhaps Prince Monireth, and after the king reached his majority he might become a focus for opposition. Another possibility, favored by Monireth, was to name Kossamak as queen in her own right after amending the constitution to permit a female monarch. In 1960 she was only fifty-three and was healthy, alert, and politically astute. In his memoirs Monireth declared, "It's a shame She is not a man. What a King we would have in Her! Certainly with Her, a great many disagreements, and a great deal of foolishness *[beaucoup de bêtises]* could have been avoided."[85]

Sihanouk, however, was fearful of abdicating to his mother, who acted, in Monireth's words, as "a painful brake" on him. In a rambling speech given soon after his father's death, Sihanouk rejected the possibility of her becoming queen: "Only God understands the reasons why I do not want my mother to ascend the throne," he said. Sihanouk may well have wished to lessen or escape from her powerful influence—and, incidentally, from her disapproval of his long-standing liaison with Monique Izzi—rather than to intensify it by allowing her to assume the throne.[86]

Monireth was always at pains to deny that he had royal ambitions, but Sihanouk suspected that he did, and relations between the two were never warm. Sihanouk, certain of his loyalty, called on his uncle in crises like this one, but he never allowed him any real power. No doubt Monireth, who had been trained in France for a military career, would have been a more competent leader of the Cambodian army than Sirik Matak or Lon Nol—but he was never given this command. Instead, as he wrote, he was used like "a water buffalo which people climb onto to cross a watery field." In the Cambodian royal hierarchy, Monireth, a king's son, ranked higher than Sihanouk, who was the grandson of a king on his mother's side and the great-grandson on his father's. Thirteen years older than the prince, Monireth was not daunted by him. In public his conduct was impeccable, but in private his relationship with Sihanouk was often uncomfortable because of what he saw as the childishness of so much of Sihanouk's behavior, including his obsession with victory and his craving for approval.[87]

Sihanouk packed the regency council with people sympathetic to him and undermined its work. When Monireth sought to review Cambodia's defense establishment, using the council as a forum, he failed to make headway. Sihanouk, for his part, refused to become prime minister again. Instead, he proposed in sequence five different associates (including Lon Nol and Nhiek Tioulong), who, one by one, refused the honor. The prince then named the head of the National Assembly, Chuop Hell, who agreed to serve as chief of state pro tem while Sihanouk, who wanted to assume the constitutional powers of a monarch without the ceremonial responsiblities, campaigned to be chosen in the referendum he called.

This referendum in effect dismantled Cambodia's thousand-year-old monarchy. The political repercussions are impossible to determine. Motivated by a mixture of patriotism, gamesmanship, and self-concern, Sihanouk acted as if the monarchy were his to foreclose, deconstruct, and disarrange. Here he parted company from Prince Monireth, who was embittered by his nephew's moves. Queen Kossamak's views are difficult to unravel, but she seems on balance to have sided with her son.

The referendum was a charade. Cambodia's voters were asked to choose between a ballot with Sihanouk's picture on it, one with Son Ngoc Thanh's (Thanh had already been condemned to death in absentia), a plain red one, indicating allegiance to the Communists, and one inscribed with a question mark, expressing confusion. The voters had to hand in the ballots they were rejecting to poll attendants, all Sangkum *fonctionnaires,* before depositing the one they preferred in a box. To vote against Sihanouk meant discarding his picture in public view, which in itself was grounds for imprisonment. As the government daily, *Réalités Cambodgiennes*, put it, somewhat dreamily, "The wind blew, and bore away along the streams and gutters [all the] ballots for Son Ngoc Thanh, for Communists, and those with question marks." Sihanouk received nearly 2 million votes; Son Ngoc Thanh and the Communists gained 133 apiece.[88]

Looking back at the referendum, we may well ask why it occurred at all. At the time, to those who saw the country as a kind of oriental Toyland unresponsive to the twentieth century, the referendum seemed appropriate enough. The childlike peasants, after all, were unprepared for anything more sophisticated. In this view, which Sihanouk shared, unanimous expressions of loyalty to the throne were more genuinely Khmer than the elections of 1946, 1947, and 1951 had been. In any case, for the next few years Sihanouk was able to govern Cambodia without looking over his shoulder for a potential rival on the throne, exigent advisers, his parents, or a coherent opposition. In Charles Meyer's words, the referendum "confirmed a state of affairs which no one had dreamed of calling into question."[89]

His mother stayed on in the royal palace as a symbol of the monarchy; in her company were the court regalia, the Brahmins, the astrologers, and the corps de ballet, two of whose leading teachers, ironically, were relatives of Saloth Sar. People close to Sihanouk have suggested that when he cut his ties with the palace by changing his residence he became freer, less responsible, and increasingly under the influence of Monique Izzi and her family. Others have seen the move as a bad omen, weakening the supernatural forces associated with the palace and with a reigning monarch. Certainly after 1960 the prince paid much less attention than before to royal ritual and to his mother's political advice.[90]

For the next three years Sihanouk ruled Cambodia with confidence and brio. Until the end of 1963, no major political crises complicated his work, and the Sanghum's institutions seemed responsive enough to Cambodian conditions. These included the national congresses that gathered twice a year beside the royal palace in Phnom Penh; the JSRK; manual labor, whereby civil servants lackadaisically devoted two weeks a year to public works; Buddhist socialism, which allowed leftists and rightists some freedom of maneuver; and tours of the countryside by Sihanouk, during which he would explain his policies to the people and toss bolts of cotton cloth to them from his helicopter or from a speeding car.

His opponents kept out of sight. Some on the left, like Khieu Samphan, Hou Youn, and Hu Nim, were co-opted into the Sangkum apparatus; others, like Tou Samouth, Nuon Chea, and Saloth Sar, remained in hiding. Former Democrats like Thonn Ouk and Chhean Vam sought livings outside politics, while supporters of Son Ngoc Thanh found safety and remuneration overseas.[91]

To be sure, the early 1960s brought many problems that remained unresolved and became significant later. They included the continuing eminence of Lon Nol as commander of Cambodia's army and minister of defense, financial extravagance on the part of Cambodia's elite, and mismanagement and corruption at all levels of the bureaucracy. Sihanouk did little serious thinking about long-range economic planning, particularly about improving agricultural yields, reducing rural indebtedness, or making use of an increasingly educated work force. Another problem, shrugged off by many at the time, was the monopoly on information and public opinion held by Sihanouk.

The absence of debate was probably the most pernicious aspect of Sihanouk's Cambodia. The National Assembly had nothing significant to do, and the national congress, with Sihanouk vetting the agenda, soon ceased dealing with issues like poverty and corruption. When an anticorruption campaign was launched in 1961, in fact, a left-wing newspaper that expressed hope that it would succeed was immediately shut down and its editor arrested.[92]

By contrast, hyperboles in Sihanouk's speeches went unchallenged. In January 1962, for example, he claimed that Cambodia had reached a level of "democratization . . . never attained by any other country." On the other hand, only a month before he had decreed that civil servants should no longer address him from a crouch because the practice might lead to "disagreeable interpretations" among diplomats and journalists. "Our socialism," he went on, "suffers from these showy expressions of respect." All of his contradictory statements and many that were false received full coverage and approval in the media he edited, manipulated, and controlled.

Some observers were overwhelmed—or pretended to be—by Sihanouk's personal charm. Those who wrote anything unfavorable were condemned as ungrateful; those who called Cambodia a paradise or compared Sihanouk to the great rulers of the past, like Jayavarman VII, were praised for their objective accounts. Sim Var, who fell out with the prince in the late 1960s, claimed that Sihanouk's personality was altered for the worse by the praise he received from French-speaking writers who shared his anti-Americanism, enjoyed his Francophilia and the luxury of his company, and found themselves coasting along on a journalistic inside track.[93]

Although Sihanouk saw Cambodian society in terms of consensus, his edgy, combative personality led him to do battle repeatedly against real and imaginary enemies, often chosen because they were defenseless. In 1961–62, as another election for the assembly approached, it was the Pracheachon's turn.

Sihanouk treated election campaigns as ways of obtaining 100 percent approval. Beginning in late 1961, he belabored what was left of the Pracheachon, humiliating its spokesman, Non Suon, at a special session of the national congress. The prince refused to respond to questions the Pracheachon wished to raise about corruption, rising prices, and unemployment, asserting that they had "arrived too late" to be considered. He followed the scenario of his confrontation with the Democrats in 1957—surrounding Non Suon with several thousand jeering supporters of the Sangkum but giving him police protection after people in the crowd threatened to assault him.[94]

Sihanouk's campaign accelerated in 1962, when several supposed members of the Pracheachon were arrested in Kompong Cham and charged with treason. Documents allegedly in their possession but never published were said to provide a blueprint for Communist surveillance of Cambodian politics on behalf of foreign powers. Non Suon was taken into custody a few days later, and by the end of the month the editor of *Pracheachon*, Chou Chet, was also put in jail. The leftist newspaper *Pancha Shila* continued to appear for a few weeks, until its editor was imprisoned for printing extracts from an eighteenth-century Cambodian poem that urged court functionaries not to mistreat the people.[95]

In speeches made at the time, Sihanouk remarked that the prisoners would probably be found guilty and condemned to death; the arrest of the newspaper editors was never publicized, but the prince declared, "There is no question here of arbitrary measures aimed at depriving [the] Pracheachon of any chances during the forthcoming elections." Sihanouk was being disingenuous, but there were indeed serious disagreements about the election inside the KWP. In their confessions Non Suon and Keo Meas said they had backed Pracheachon participation; they were probably opposed by Saloth Sar and his colleagues, who saw no point in running valuable cadre as candidates for the assembly when there was no hope of them winning and a good chance of their being imprisoned or killed by Sihanouk's police.[96]

In May 1962, shortly before the elections, Tou Samouth disappeared. In the words of a party history captured in 1973, "On 20/7/62 . . . Comrade TSM, secretary of the Party, was kidnapped by the enemy, leaving no trace. This was great grief for the Party, which had just been reorganized."

It seems likely that Samouth was assassinated by Sihanouk's security police, perhaps in the course of a raid. The Americans were apparently unaware of the event, for the U.S. embassy asserted in 1971 that he had disappeared "after 1955," and Lon Nol himself was still referring to him in 1969 as though he were still alive. It is also possible that Saloth Sar was involved in eliminating his patron and superior. Evidence from several sources points obliquely in this direction or toward connivance between elements in the KWP and Lon Nol, via Sieu Heng.[97]

Samouth's disappearance, in any case, advanced the fortunes of Saloth Sar, who later claimed to have "assumed the function of acting secretary" at some point in 1962. This does not mean that the party's independent policies, which developed after 1967, went into effect at this time. Even before Samouth's disappearance, however, Sar's faction had won a small victory when no Pracheachon candidates presented themselves in the elections of 1962. By the middle of the year, the Pracheachon had ceased to exist. Put another way, the KWP now entered a clandestine phase with which Saloth Sar and his colleagues were perfectly at ease.[98]

With the opposition terrorized, inert, or in prison, Sihanouk proceeded to fine-tune arrangements for the election by setting new requirements for candidates. Over five thousand names had been submitted to him, he said, indicating that the assembly was still perceived by many as a lucrative place to work. In April, Sihanouk and a committee of conservative advisers weeded out candidates who were over sixty years old, had no collège degree, or had joined the Sangkum since 1960. The electoral list was boiled down to 314 candidates, and then to a full complement of 75. In contrast with the elections of 1958, more than half of the incumbents were asked to run again. New candidates included Yem Sambaur, Douc Rasy, and Khieu Samphan. Summarizing the choices available to the voters, Sihanouk told an audience, "If you want to reject your mother the queen, that's your privilege; and it's your privilege if you want to reject prince papa [*samdech euv*]"—a title that the U.S. embassy noted was gaining "increasing currency" in Cambodia in 1962. For Cambodians unwilling to be arrested such "privileges" were unthinkable.[99]

The elections themselves brought few surprises, although absenteeism was even higher than in 1958. Just before the elections Non Suon and the prisoners from Kompong Cham were condemned to death, but the evidence against them was never published, and a few months later their sentences were commuted to life imprisonment. In July Sihanouk cited documents that he said emanated from Tou Samouth and had guided Pracheachon members in their voting, or abstentions. Interestingly, the PRK's date for Tou Samouth's disappearance (May 27, 1962) is only a little over a month before the date of Sihanouk's speech. The documents, if genuine, may have been recovered when Tou Samouth was killed.[100]

four

Cambodia Clouds Over, 1963–1966

The period beginning with the anti-Sangkum student demonstration in Siem Reap in February 1963 and ending with the elections for the National Assembly in October 1966 can be perceived as the first act of the nightmare that terrorized Cambodia after 1970.

During these years, Sihanouk's ability to control Cambodia's politics diminished, but it is hard to say whether this was a cause or an effect of his dwindling popularity among the elite. In part, it may have sprung from his own melancholy assessment of the future of Cambodia, colored by the intensifying conflict in Vietnam; but the Vietnam war aside, Cambodia changed in many ways between 1963 and 1966. Whether Sihanouk noticed the changes around him one cannot say. Some of them were demographic. Cambodia's population grew from 3.8 million when Sihanouk reached the throne in 1941 to nearly 7 million when he was removed from office in 1970. Others are more elusive. They include the impact of the fighting in Vietnam on Cambodia's budget, on radical activists in the country, and on its export-oriented economy. By 1966, more than a quarter of Cambodia's rice crop was being sold more or less openly to the Vietnamese insurgents. Since export taxes on rice traditionally provided a large percentage of government revenue, the effect of these sales was to unbalance the national budget. At the same time, radical analyses of society were increasingly frequent among Cambodian students and teachers, many of whom were anti-American as well as impressed by the Chinese revolution and disgusted by injustice and corruption close to home. As hundreds of thousands of

Cambodians learned to read, their horizons widened. So did explanations for injustice and opportunities for dissent.

The dramatic expansion of educational facilities (by 1969, more than eleven thousand Khmers were attending Cambodian universities, and at least two million were enrolled in primary and secondary schools) also affected people's attitudes and produced examples of social mobility and social frustration that would have been unimaginable in earlier times.

Problems arose because as segments of Cambodian society woke up, Sihanouk continued to use the machinery of absolutist rule to keep himself in power. His so-called children became more alert and better informed, but he allowed them no more freedom. The advice he received was often indistinguishable from flattery and reinforced his self-assurance.

The four years from 1963 through 1966 are hard to analyze because of the contraction of primary sources. During this period, to be sure, Cambodia was frequently the subject of purported analyses by pro-Western, neutral, and pro-Communist visitors. This expanded interest and the shallowness of what was written were functions of the Vietnam war and the fact that war correspondents vacationed in Cambodia. Partly it can be traced to the "Sihanouk phenomenon," which was often all that journalists took the time to write about.

In Robert Shaplen's phrase, Sihanouk was editor in chief for Cambodia in this period, and journalists who wanted to be allowed to return wrote stories that pleased him. The strands for such a story (for example, prince on a tightrope . . . island of peace . . . French villas slumbering behind immaculate lawns . . . mysterious ruins lost in the jungle . . . Sihanouk's charisma, and so on) were woven and unraveled as often as Penelope's web. Men and women who wrote such stories had their entry visas renewed. Those who mentioned one-man rule, repression, or dissent or pointed out that rice yields per hectare and per capita income remained throughout the 1960s among the lowest in Southeast Asia were usually barred from coming back. There was no export license for bad news.[1]

There are several other problems related to documentary sources of this period. One is that library files of Cambodian-language newspapers from the 1960s have disappeared while more or less official French- and English-language print media, to a large extent written and edited by Sihanouk, have survived. This means that material documenting Sihanouk's popularity has outlasted his disappearance from the scene, while texts that might have been used to trace the growth of dissatisfaction have disappeared. It is impossible to reconstruct the social history of Cambodia in the 1960s, for the Cambodian-language papers, in addition to following official policy and publishing the prince's activities in full, covered local events and human interest stories.[2]

Another problem is that the prince's own writings, speeches, and conversations covered such a wide range of topics and made excellent copy. Over the years, he adjusted his style and content to fit his listeners or the occasion, providing some observers with evidence of charming forthrightness, others with evidence of inconsistency or worse, and still others with evidence of his overwhelming desire to please. Having so many firsthand, "exclusive" interviews, few visitors looked any further; it was often hard to avoid quoting Sihanouk in the course of explaining what was going on.[3]

A third problem is that after the economic break with the United States in December 1963, political reporting from the U.S. embassy diminished. All reports ceased in mid-1965, when Cambodia broke off diplomatic relations with the United States.

Finally, very few critical studies of Cambodia were undertaken in the 1960s. Sihanouk's stranglehold on the media accounts for this. Cambodia's oncoming misfortunes, moreover, were perceptible to very few people in the 1960s. To foreigners working there, Cambodia seemed destined to go on forever. Empirical studies of Cambodian society by foreign residents were rare; Cambodian university teachers and their students, attuned to the risks of critical thinking, were even more constrained.[4]

With these limitations in mind, one can distinguish three themes emerging in the 1960s. The first is Sihanouk's gradual dispossession. Another is the consolidation of leftist opposition under the guidance of the Communist Party of Kampuchea (CPK), as the KWP renamed itself in 1966. The third has to do with the emergence in 1966 of anti-Communist, more or less pro-American segments of the Cambodian elite who were impatient with Sihanouk and angered by his alliance with the Communists in Vietnam. These men and women, as we shall see, were the main beneficiaries of the elections of 1966.[5]

This period can be examined in terms of the three factions Sihanouk, left, and elite—the same groups comprised in the Coalition Government of Democratic Kampuchea (CGDK) in the 1980s. None of them commanded the loyalties of many Cambodian people. In the 1960s, most Cambodians paid little attention to politics in Phnom Penh or to Communist exhortations. This is not to say that they had no moral views or were unaware of government corruption and malfeasance. In fact, in the early 1960s many peasants regarded the word *government* (*reachkar*) as being synonymous with *corruption* (*puk roluy*). Weapons to deal with injustice, however, had not yet been imagined or come to hand, and national politics seemed irrelevant to people's daily lives. Before 1967, factional conflicts among Sihanoukists, leftists, and the elite were centered in the cities and towns; they were low-key and remained unresolved. Lost opportunities for pluralism and consensus formed a major theme of Cambodian politics between 1945 and 1963. In the years that followed, the struggle among Cambodia's competing groups grew more intense and more vindictive. The transformation of politics from a ramshackle social contract into an obsessive search by inimical factions for a single answer—a fight to the death among paradigms—will be a theme of this chapter and of the remainder of the book.

The Left Takes Cover

Toward the end of February 1963, while Sihanouk was visiting China, a conflict broke out in Siem Reap between high school students and the police; hostility between the two groups had been simmering for months. On this occasion, a student had been killed, and demonstrators accused a policeman of corruption and brutality. When authorities refused to investigate, the students became violent. Over a thousand of them stormed the police headquarters and were beaten back with rifle butts. In the course of the melee, photographs of Sihanouk were torn down from public buildings and placards appeared declaring the Sangkum rotten and unjust. Several students were killed, and others, including a sympathetic teacher, were seriously hurt. The police were unable to restore order, and soldiers had to be brought in.[6]

When he heard of the events Sihanouk cabled from China that he had no intention of resigning as chief of state. The cabinet resigned instead, accepting responsibility for the disorder. In the meantime, sympathy demonstrations had occurred in Battambang and Phnom Penh.

The events had taken the government by surprise, although Lon Nol was quick to provide Sihanouk, on his return, with dossiers implicating "certain elements" among the students who were supposedly allied with Son Ngoc Thanh. The U.S. embassy suspected Communists of being involved. A demonstration at the Lycée Sisowath earlier in the month had led the Americans to speculate whether the school's "Communist connection" might be brought to Sihanouk's attention to gain some mileage for the United States.[7]

After being feted in China, Sihanouk was reluctant to blame the disturbances on Communists and turned instead on his old antagonist Keng Vannsak, then at the Pedagogical Institute and retired from politics. Vannsak had lectured in Siem Reap earlier in the year but could hardly be blamed for the violence of the police. Sihanouk also singled out Vannsak's former colleague Son Sen, who had resigned his post in 1962 after being accused of antimonarchical activities. There is no evidence that Son Sen had been active in Siem Reap.

Soon after these events, the WPK's urban committee, perhaps fearful of Sihanouk, convened a general assembly (some documents refer to it as a congress). Its main decision was to confirm Saloth Sar as the secretary of the WPK's central committee, replacing Tou Samouth, who was now presumed to have been killed. Two of the twelve positions on the enlarged committee were taken by intellectuals who had studied in France: Number Three, Ieng Sary, and Number Eleven, Son Sen. Son Ngoc Minh in Vietnam was again elected in absentia, and Vorn Vet joined the committee for the first time.[8]

Ieng Sary and Saloth Sar must have been rattled a few days later when Sihanouk announced the names of "thirty-four subversives" who, he claimed, had recently united in an unspecified way in an attempt to bring down the government. The list included Keng Vannsak, fellow-traveling journalist Tep Chhieu Keng, five members of the National Assembly, Son Sen, a few other intellectuals recently returned from France as well as Ieng Sary and Saloth Sar, who had not been identified as Communists before. The list, in other words, included the three intellectuals on the KWP central committee but none of the other members.[9]

The dossiers were prepared by Lon Nol and sprang from the ongoing surveillance of people known to be leftists, in particular journalists and teachers in the private schools. Important party figures such as Vorn Vet, Ta Mok, Sao Phim, and Nuon Chea did not appear on the list. As Stephen Heder has written, Saloth Sar and Ieng Sary "knew that . . . their anonymity had been seriously compromised, even if Sihanouk's intelligence services did not know exactly who they were."

Sihanouk soon challenged the people he had named to form a cabinet and govern the country. Those he named first—Keng Vannsak, Khieu Samphan, Tep Chhieu Keng, Hou Youn, and Chau Seng, among others—

knew enough about his personality and his security police to refuse the offer. Certain of winning, Sihanouk raised the stakes. He summoned thirty-two of the thirty-four men to his residence and offered them every portfolio except prime minister and minister of defense. Those assembled could probably hear policemen murmuring outside and realized that at least some of them would be killed, then or later, if they chose to oppose the prince. They refused his offer and urged him to take up the reins of government himself. As in 1957, the prince was free to turn on his heel and say goodbye before his audience was roughed up. To his credit, however, no one was arrested after the convocation, and in the second half of the year most of those accused continued in the jobs they had held in March.[10]

In May 1963, Saloth Sar and Ieng Sary vanished from Phnom Penh. They soon turned up, protected by Vietnamese insurgents, in the forest in eastern Cambodia, near the village of Ampil in Kompong Cham.

According to Keng Vannsak, the idea of leaving the city had been in Saloth Sar's mind for at least a year, ever since Sar had complained that he didn't know what to do about Sihanouk and that he (meaning presumably the KWP) lacked "allies overseas." Vannsak suggested "jokingly" that he should spend some time in the forest, banking up wisdom like a classical Khmer hero; he told Sar about a cousin of his who ran a lumber mill in Krauchhmar and who was in touch with former Khmer Viet Minh in the forest. Vannsak claims to have traveled by riverboat soon afterward to Kompong Cham and beyond with Saloth Sar and to have introduced him to his cousin. His story is uncorroborated, but when Saloth Sar and Ieng Sary left Phnom Penh their first base of operations was in this area. Son Sen joined them there shortly. Their wives remained in Phnom Penh until 1965 without being molested in any way.[11]

At this stage the KWP was closely allied with its counterpart in Vietnam, the VWP. One of Saloth Sar's young protégés, Bu Phat, wrote in his confession (made in 1978), that in 1962, before going into the maquis himself, Saloth Sar sent him off to work with the insurgents in South Vietnam, where, he says, he "helped with the work of the Khmer language radio department . . . when their announcer was ill." Phat also worked with dissident Cambodians on both sides of the border. He confessed that in the "middle of 1963," while staying with a Vietnamese propaganda officer, he "suddenly met Brother Number One [Saloth Sar], who took [him] back from the Vietnamese." He "went to live with our Organization [*Angkar*, the word used for the Communist party throughout its years of clandestinity], which at that time consisted of Brother Number One, Brother Vann [Ieng Sary], and Brother Khieu [Son Sen]."[12]

Two points emerge from this passage. The first is that Saloth Sar, Ieng Sary, and Son Sen, companions in Paris, and perhaps Sao Phim, a former ICP member from the eastern zone, now constituted the "Organization." They also comprised four-fifths of the top members of the party's central committee—the other being Nuon Chea, who remained in hiding in Phnom Penh. Pol Pot corroborated the point in 1977 when he asserted that 90 percent (rather than 80 percent) of the central committee had reached the countryside by 1963.[13]

The second point of interest is that the Cambodians relied for their security at this stage on the Vietnamese and on ICP cadre like Sao Phim, who was based near enough to be able to act as a witness at Bu Phat's wedding in 1964. The four party leaders were under Vietnamese protection in Office 100, as it was called, until the end of 1966 and were to remain close to Vietnamese bases elsewhere in Cambodia until 1972.

It is difficult to square the anti-Vietnamese stands of Pol Pot and Ieng Sary later on with their conduct in the 1960s. Had they been fearful of the Vietnamese in the earlier period, there were other secure places in Cambodia they could have gone to, particularly in the northwest. Seeking refuge under Vietnamese protection was a natural move for Sar and his colleagues in 1963, but by 1978, when Cambodia was at war with Vietnam, history was readjusted, and Pol Pot asserted that "in 1964 Vietnamese unleashed themselves against the Communist party of Kampuchea. They accused it of being adventurist and leftist. In fact, they were frightened by the success of the Kampuchean revolutionary movement. [At this time] they lost control of the revolutionary movement."

Whether or not the Vietnamese "lost control" of the KWP at this time (and there is no corroboration of their attacks) the leaders of the Cambodian Communist party took Vietnamese advice and stayed under Vietnamese protection for eight more years.

In Phnom Penh, Sihanouk's vendetta against the left gathered momentum. Soon after Saloth Sar and Ieng Sary's departure, Khieu Samphan and Hou Youn left their ministerial posts. Youn was dismissed for unconstitutional and antimonarchical policies. Samphan remained in office a week after a censure motion against him failed to gain a majority but then resigned, probably because he faced an uphill battle in the assembly getting support for his economic reforms.

The two were not punished further. They remained in the assembly and soon returned to teaching part-time at Kambuj'bot. The man Sihanouk named to replace Samphan in the ministry of commerce, Nin Nirom, was chosen because he had foolhardily agreed to take the position after criticizing Samphan at a national congress. Nirom had no administrative experience and was soon embroiled in a scandal of monumental proportions. He resigned a month after taking office, and as he left the assembly building he was met by a crowd of students, supporters of Khieu Samphan, who threw stones at him.[14]

Over the years, Khieu Samphan had earned a reputation for austere living, high principles, and personal integrity. These qualities were rare in the National Assembly and at the ministerial level of the government. A family acquaintance has remarked that although his conduct was admirable and his standards high, he had no "talent for being happy" (*ot cheh sobaay*); another Cambodian who knew him has recalled, "I never saw him laugh." Samphan lived with his widowed mother and spent his evenings reading books. His editorials in *l'Observateur* reveal a dry, intolerant personality softened somewhat by a sympathy for poor Khmer. During his editorship, Samphan was hauled before the police for questioning on one occasion and on another was beaten up in the street, stripped, and photographed by plainclothes policemen. After his election to the assembly, his celibacy, aloofness, and intolerance of his colleagues' way of life led fellow deputies to spread the rumor—or to genuinely assume—that he was either sexually impotent or homosexual. Solitude, bookishness, and an unswerving dedication to an ideal—communism, in Samphan's case—were so rare in Cambodia in the 1960s that Samphan was vilified by some and beatified by others.[15]

At the beginning of 1964, the KWP's importance in Cambodian politics was negligible. It seemed unlikely that radicalism could ever recover the following it had enjoyed in the 1950s, and aside from hiding in the forest, it is hard to say what the party's leadership was doing.

In 1977, Pol Pot explained this fallow period by saying that the party had decided to take illegal and clandestine forms of revolution as "the basis, because the enemy would not allow us to make revolution." In Phnom Penh, what remained of the left-wing press was closely monitored and periodically shut down. Schoolteachers and their students were routinely spied on.

Over the next few years, government-sponsored terror against these radicals increased, while the party was unprepared, unauthorized, and probably unable to respond with violence itself. Sihanouk's terror helped create resentment and fear in student circles and distress among politicized members of the monastic order. Repression of activists and the suppression of debate led many young people to join the ranks of the Communist movement.[16]

A further indication of the eclipse of Cambodian radicalism was the extended visit that Saloth Sar and several party colleagues made to North Vietnam, China, and North Korea in 1965–66. Their absence for several months suggests that the party at this time had few members and was neither active nor important. Indeed, Pol Pot himself asserted in 1977 that the rejection of U.S. aid in 1963, not party activities per se, was "a great event in our struggle." It was, he said, "the result of the people's struggle, the struggle of the pupils, students, intellectuals, workers and peasants, aided by the struggle of our prominent people working in the Assembly and the government, and supported by the struggles in the countryside."[17]

The break with the United States was indeed an important event, but the person who made it, Prince Sihanouk, is never mentioned in Pol Pot's marathon speech.

Sihanouk Breaks with the United States

In the last two months of 1963, Sihanouk chose to fight the United States on several fronts. To start with, he requested the immediate suspension of U.S. military and economic aid and the curtailment of diplomatic relations. The confrontation had long-term repercussions that were not foreseen by Sihanouk or by most U.S. observers. American behavior in Southeast Asia and U.S. interference in Cambodia had angered Sihanouk for several years. In November 1963, two events convinced him that he should distance himself officially from the United States.[18]

The first was the assassination of Ngo Dinh Diem and his brother Nhu on November 1, in the aftermath of an American-sponsored coup d'état. The two men had never been friends of Sihanouk, but their deaths confirmed the prince's suspicion that America could never be trusted as an ally.

The second event was the arrest of two Khmer Serei agents in Takeo province; they were en route to Phnom Penh from their sanctuaries in South Vietnam. The men were under the misapprehension that they could travel to Phnom Penh to discuss Khmer Serei policies and Son Ngoc Thanh's political ambitions with Sihanouk at the national congress. Although the Khmer Serei movement posed no serious threat to Sihanouk's rule, he was infuriated by its existence and by its clandestine radio broadcasts emanating from Thailand and South Vietnam, which made scurrilous attacks on him and the royal family. The detention of two adherents presented him with an opportunity to attack Son Ngoc Thanh and the Americans.

Another factor weighing on Sihanouk's mind was Cambodia's economic malaise. Although exports of agricultural products remained high, yields per hectare were low, industrialization had hardly begun, taxes were hard to collect, and Cambodia's international trade was handled by a small commercial class that was potentially hostile to Sihanouk's socialist policies. In Sihanouk's mind, wealthy people in Phnom Penh had become dependent on the luxury products imported under the U.S.-sponsored commodity import program. Revenues from the program, known as counterpart funds, were used to pay in-country costs of the U.S. aid program—including salaries for Cambodia's armed forces—amounting to over $15 million per year. In 1960–62, U.S. aid had accounted for 14 percent of Cambodian government revenue and had balanced the budget. The Chinese and Sino-Cambodian commercial elite, moreover, enjoyed connections with colleagues and relations in Saigon and Bangkok whom Sihanouk distrusted. The prince believed that the nationalizing of Cambodia's foreign trade and private banks would solve these problems, while making Cambodia seem more socialist to its allies, thereby attracting further economic assistance with "no strings attached." Last, he probably believed that a bold, anti-American move attractive to the French might gain support from de Gaulle's anti-American government and open a new phase in his political career.[19]

Sihanouk had planned his moves for some time, but in November 1963 he accelerated the pace. By then the only two Americans he had ever trusted—Ambassador William Trimble and the head of the U.S. Military Aid mission to Cambodia, Brig. Gen. Edward "Pony" Scherer—had left the country. Both men had made an effort to treat Sihanouk as a friend. They had also argued with their colleagues in favor of Sihanouk's anti-Communist posture and had urged U.S. officials in Thailand and South Vietnam to desist from condoning Thai and Vietnamese backing for the Khmer Serei.

Scherer's replacement, Brig. Gen. Robert Taber, was not in Phnom Penh long enough to make a strong impression, but Trimble's successor, Philip Sprouse, whose promising Foreign Service career spent largely in

China had been blighted in the McCarthy era, seemed more eager than Trimble had been to keep his anti-Communist credentials on display. Sprouse, a fastidious bachelor, was hardly Sihanouk's type. Moreover, rising American stakes in Vietnam were rapidly making any other policy issues in the region of secondary importance. The rapport between Sihanouk and the U.S. embassy, painstakingly built up by Trimble and Scherer, was soon dissipated in an atmosphere of mutual mistrust.[20]

Sihanouk's behavior at this time was also affected by fatigue and hypertension. Bouts of depression linked to recurrent obesity and a congenital diabetic condition often occurred after months of trying to manage Cambodia single-handedly. The U.S. embassy tended to refer to these bouts and to Sihanouk's foreign policy decisions as neurotic. The embassy perceived the conduct of foreign affairs as proceeding rationally along American lines. U.S. officials also ignored the possibility that Sihanouk's neutralist policies might be less dangerous for Cambodia than a full-blown alliance with the United States.[21]

Following the assassination of Diem and Nhu, Sihanouk, frightened by the implications of their deaths but no longer having to fear their retaliation, began attacking the Khmer Serei, who had enjoyed the Diems' support. In a speech on November 5, he declared that if Khmer Serei broadcasts from Thailand and South Vietnam did not cease before the end of the year, he would "dispense with free world economic and military aid." He made the United States responsible for the broadcasts. He assumed that since the governments in Bangkok and Saigon were its puppets the United States could shut the radios down.[22]

The warning was ignored by U.S. officials, who were preoccupied with the turmoil in Vietnam that had followed the coup. When Sihanouk included Thanh and Sary in his list of subversives, memories of the Dap Chhuon plot, of Sam Sary's fulminations, and of the bomb incident of September 1959 may well have mingled in his mind.

Celebrating Cambodia's independence day a few days later, the prince unveiled some sweeping economic reforms. These included the nationalizing of Cambodia's import-export trade, private banks, and distilleries, a curb on the importation of luxury goods, and the renouncing of American aid. Ostensibly, the proposals would enable Cambodia to take charge of its own affairs. In fact, the state-controlled import-export business and related enterprises soon fell into the hands of officials loyal to the prince but lacking administrative experience. The so-called socialization of Cambodia's economy made Sihanouk's entourage wealthier than before.[23]

To many observers, the proposals appeared misguided and impulsive, although we know that Sihanouk had planned them for some time. Cambodia's gold reserves, for example, had been moved from the United States to France at the beginning of November, before the campaign got fully under way.[24]

From Sihanouk's perspective, the proposals served Cambodia's immediate interests. In the longer term, the lessening of U.S. influence in the army, the restricting of local capitalists, and the creation of a poorly equipped military force also served the ideological interests of China and North Vietnam and those of de Gaulle's regime, which was eager to de-Americanize Southeast Asia. Some pro-French elements in the South Vietnamese army may, after the coup, have shared de Gaulle's vision of a neutralized Southeast Asia in which Sihanouk might have an enhanced role to play. In any case, in 1963 the prince received substantial sub-rosa subsidies from France while he was attacking the United States. He probably hoped that China and France would pick up the cost of the economic and military aid provided by the Americans. If he did, he was mistaken. Both powers knew they could retain his loyalty—which he had never given the United States—at a far lower cost.

In demanding that Khmer Serei broadcasts cease at once Sihanouk placed the United States in a difficult position. The Khmer Serei transmitters, he knew, were in Thailand and Vietnam. He guessed that the Saigon and Bangkok authorities would resist U.S. requests to shut them down. To Sihanouk, U.S. unwillingness to comply with his demands was proof not of U.S. inability to manipulate its puppets, but of its complicity in their behavior. This failure by neighboring powers to do his bidding provided an excuse for him to make more humiliating demands.[25]

On November 19, at a special national congress, Sihanouk announced the arrest of the two Khmer Serei operatives, Saing San and Preap In, who had entered Cambodia under a *laisser passer* granted by the governor of Takeo, In Tam, and approved by Sihanouk's prime minister, Prince Norodom Kantol. Preap In was In Tam's nephew. According to Sim Kin, a fellow Khmer Serei, he had volunteered to go to Cambodia and negotiate with Sihanouk. After several conversations with officials in Takeo, In and Saing San had been arrested peremptorily, brought to Phnom Penh under guard, and put on display in cages at the national congress. Facing the prisoners and surrounded by thousands of supporters, Sihanouk denied making any special arrangements with them, and the congress soon became an impromptu judicial hearing. Sihanouk asked both men to admit that the Americans were aiding Son Ngoc Thanh and providing the Khmer Serei with radio transmitters. Saing San said yes to both questions and was immediately released. Preap In, apparently in shock, stared straight to the front, refusing to answer. Sihanouk then demanded that he be subjected to the "will of the congress." Hundreds of spectators stormed the cage where Preap In stood in silence, bombarding him with rubber sandals, debris, and abuse until he was hustled away to face trial at the hands of a military court.[26]

He was condemned to death on November 25 and executed by firing squad in early 1964. Very little evidence from the trial was ever published, but Sihanouk ordered that a film of Preap In's execution, prepared by the Ministry of Information, be shown at every screening in Cambodian cinemas for a month. The film lasted fifteen minutes and spared no details. Posters depicting the execution were distributed to Cambodian schools. Memories of these macabre decisions—and of the photos themselves—frequently surfaced in the 1980s when informants sought to date the beginning of Sihanouk's decline.[27]

The special congress that condemned Preap In also approved Sihanouk's decision to renounce American aid. In his memoirs, Sihanouk treats the event as deriving from a popular initiative, pointing to the show of hands at the congress as justification from the people for the new set of policies. In fairness to the prince, his decision was probably popular at first. Sihanouk's attacks on the unnamed ogres (*yeak*) who persecuted Cambodia always struck a responsive chord, and so did his freewheeling disparagement of Cambodia's capitalists, a reference to the Chinese and Sino-Khmers who controlled Cambodia's commercial life.

On November 20, U.S. president John Kennedy spent more than an hour trying to come to grips with the Cambodian crisis on the telephone with State Department officials and at a White House meeting. He found it hard to believe that Sihanouk could break off economic relations with the United States because of the activities of the Khmer Serei, about whom he knew nothing. Assistant Secretary of State Roger Hilsman told him that the United States had indeed "played footsie" with the Khmer Serei in the Eisenhower period and that "there was money involved"; he suggested that the president clear the air by denying any continuing U.S. complicity. Kennedy agreed to do so and proposed that Dean Acheson, who had acted as Cambodia's attorney at the World Court during the Preah Vihear confrontation with Thailand, be sent out to Cambodia to meet the prince and calm him down. Hilsman asked Kennedy to postpone taking action on the matter for a few days. The draft memorandum of their conversation closes poignantly with the sentence, "The President said OK and that we would wait until the weekend and see." Two days later Kennedy was killed.[28]

There is no way of telling what he might have decided to do about Cambodia had he returned from Dallas or whether his policies toward Southeast Asia would have followed the same trajectory as those of Lyndon Johnson. The evidence that he was planning to reduce U.S. involvement in Vietnam, rather than increase it, is contradictory. There is no evidence that he felt Cambodia to be important on its own.

Norodom Kantol attended Kennedy's funeral, and President Lyndon Johnson, interviewing him, took pains to deny U.S. involvement with the Khmer Serei. Kantol also called on Undersecretary of State Averell Harriman, who tried to clear the air by claiming, "We have no direct or indirect connection with Khmer Serei nor any association with any group which is trying to impinge on [the] sovereignty and independence of Cambodia."[29]

Harriman's statement fell short of admitting that the United States was aware of its allies' support for the Khmer Serei and knew about Khmer Serei policies that he failed to regret. From Sihanouk's point of view, Harriman's statement was probably unsatisfactory.

In the midst of this activity, Sihanouk had been busy trying to gain support for a fourteen-nation conference that would guarantee Cambodia's neutrality. As George Kahin has shown, Sihanouk chose to occupy center stage in Southeast Asia just when a particular faction in the U.S. foreign policy establishment was maneuvering to catch President Johnson's attention and push him in the direction of a more aggressive policy toward Vietnam. Sihanouk's proposal for a conference to deal with the region was a casualty of the cross fire generated by these maneuvers.

Soon after Kennedy's death, Ambassador Sprouse and officials in Washington greeted Sihanouk's proposal for a conference warmly. It was rebuffed by U.S. Ambassador Henry Cabot Lodge in Saigon, by the Thai government, by the South Vietnamese, and by some of President Johnson's close advisers, who feared that such a conference would be a curtain raiser for a larger one to decide on the neutralization of South Vietnam. They were correct, insofar as this was clearly what Sihanouk had in mind.[30]

In the midst of these responses, U.S. and Cambodian government officials struggled to regain some balance in their relations. Conversations continued along several tracks: some dealt with the termination of aid, others with Sihanouk's proposal for a conference, and still others with silencing the Khmer Serei transmitters. None of the conversations was decisive, and for the medium term Ambassador Sprouse suggested several possible outcomes. "There are signs," he wrote,

> that Sihanouk's actions are neither fully understood nor approved by educated class, which for the most part lives in Phnom Penh and is also found in armed forces and government service throughout the country. It is same group which individually will feel major economic impact of cessation US aid programs and Sihanouk's nationalization and other economic measures. They will witness first hand, consequences in armed forces, commerce, schools and development projects, as well as their own urbanized style of life and private fortunes. If, as seems reasonable . . . substantial portion of this group proceeds from an attitude of not fully understanding and not approving Sihanouk's behavior to one of positive disagreement, the result, in terms of domestic political structure, may be both unprecedented and at this point unpredictable.[31]

The group of pro-Western deputies associated with *Phnom Penh Presse* (Douc Rasy, Phlek Phoeun, Long Boret, and a dozen others) were the sorts of people mentioned in Sprouse's cable. Many of them believed that Sihanouk was mistaken to "face the Communists alone," as Douc Rasy put it at the time. Sprouse may have been misled by the embassy's outspoken Cambodian friends in placing more confidence in opposition to Sihanouk's decisions than was warranted.[32]

On December 8, Field Marshal Sarit Thanarat, the Thai premier, died in Bangkok. Sarit and Sihanouk had traded insults for years, and Sarit's government had been belligerently anti-Khmer. Sarit wanted Sihanouk overthrown, and he had supported Khmer Serei forays along the frontier as well as their scurrilous radio broadcasts.[33]

On December 9, Sihanouk spoke about Sarit's death in a Cambodian-language broadcast that had a profound effect on U.S.-Cambodian relations. "At two-week intervals," he said, "our enemies have departed one after the other. At first the one in the south [Diem], then the great boss [Kennedy], and now the one in the west [Sarit]. All three have always sought to violate our neutrality and make trouble for us, to seek our misfortune. Now they are all going to meet in hell where they will be able to build military bases for SEATO. Our other enemies will join them. The gods punish all the enemies of neutral and peaceful Cambodia. The spirits of our former kings protect us."[34]

Sihanouk went on to propose that Cambodia enter a period of rejoicing to celebrate the deaths of the three men. People were encouraged to wear red armbands and to assemble near the palace every evening to listen to musical performances laid on for them by the state.

The official translation of the speech failed to mention the death of the "great boss," but a Ministry of Information communiqué echoing Sihanouk's major points was broadcast in Khmer and monitored in Bangkok by the U.S. Foreign Broadcast Information Service (FBIS). This text referred to the death of the "great boss" of Diem and Sarit. The communiqué proposed a period of rejoicing to celebrate the "end of persons who mistreated us."[35]

The Department of State, certain that the communiqué had been issued with Sihanouk's approval, sent a "Flash" cable to Sprouse instructing him to lodge a protest with the Cambodian government and to return to the States for consultations unless Sihanouk disavowed the communiqué. The U.S. ambassador to the United Nations, Charles Yost, had already confronted the Cambodian ambassador to the United States, Nong Kimny, and had called the broadcast barbaric. Kimny warned Yost about his choice of words, and Sihanouk's response to this "contemptuous and gratuitous insult" was to recall Kimny and the entire Cambodian diplomatic mission.[36]

In the meantime, Sihanouk's economic initiatives were having a negative impact on the Cambodian elite. The nationalization of private banks led to the collapse in mid-December of the Bank of Phnom Penh, Cambodia's largest financial institution. Its director, a Sino-Thai named Songsakd Kitchpanich, fled to Saigon by private plane on December 22, allegedly carrying with him over $4 million of the bank's assets. Cambodian bureaucrats, businessmen, and members of the royal family had used Songsakd's bank for years to shelter funds and investments. When he arrived in Saigon, Kitchpanich cannily asked for political asylum.[37]

The national congress soon afterward was summoned to close the stable door in a production stage-managed by Sihanouk, who was amused by so much embarrassment among the rich. The U.S. embassy reported the proceedings in telegraphese:

> Tone set by Sihanouk in opening ceremonies when he interrupted Prime Minister Kantol's address after five minutes and told him to tape his remarks for later broadcast to save time for Congress. In course proceedings, highest Cambodian personalities . . . have come to podium to exculpate themselves of connection with Somsakd's ac-

tivities. Prince intermittently interrupts . . . and occasionally speaks simultaneously from one side of platform. Some speakers, such as Douc Rasy, have been cut off by Sihanouk ringing gong when their explanations annoy or anger him.[38]

Rasy's objections to Sihanouk's new policies and to the termination of U.S. aid were serious and well argued; and so was his contention that Songsakd was a criminal rather than a traitor. Rasy, elected to the assembly in 1962, was a conservative with legal training. He was unimpressed then and later with Sihanouk's charisma. Sihanouk, for his part, was reluctant to embarrass officials, relatives, and cronies who had parked large sums in Songsakd's bank. He preferred instead to call Songsakd an agent of the United States. He also proposed an investigation, but the committee assembled for the purpose met only once, and its findings were never made public.[39]

By the middle of December, the crises were beginning to tell on Sihanouk's nerves. On the twentieth, he complained that "attacks on his person" were intolerable. "All my countrymen," he said, "as the Anglo-Saxons know perfectly well, venerate me as a divinity and regard my character as sacred. The truth is that 5 million Khmers identify themselves totally with Sihanouk. To insult me, to wound me, to humiliate me, is to strike at the Cambodian nation."[40]

Sihanouk had expected his new policies to distress the rich, but he had no plans to turn Cambodia into an austere socialist state. His cronies and advisers were allowed to run the new state enterprises without any demonstrated expertise, while other enterprises were placed in the hands of relatively pro-Western technocrats like Chhet Chhoeur, Chak Saroeun, and Chhean Vam. The prince also hoped to lessen the power of the pro-Western elite, many of whom had links, in turn, with Chinese and Sino-Cambodian business interests already suspicious of Sihanouk's performance. By allowing the private sector to run down, he alienated these people for good.[41]

After his downfall in 1970, Sihanouk frequently discussed his decision to break with the United States, which he perceived as a turning point in his career. In 1973, he told the Australian journalist Wilfred Burchett that the decision had been correct. Fifteen years later he entertained a shadow of a doubt. To be sure, he wrote, he had never committed any "faults or errors as serious as those committed by the Lon Nols and Sirik Mataks, the Pol Pots, Ieng Sarys and Khieu Samphans, and the Heng Samrins and Hun Sens." However, he went on, there is perhaps one thing which I regret: this was to reject, in 1963, the conditional, humiliating and corrupting aid accorded by the United States to my army and my administration. This rejection had the effect of transforming the majority of figures in my government, my administration, and my army into "Republicans", for they needed these kinds of aid from the United States if they were to "prosper" (and not to make Cambodia, or its people prosper). If I had allowed these forms of American aid to continue to rot my government, my administration, and my senior officers and generals, perhaps Cambodia and its people could have avoided the fatal putsch of March 18, 1970 and, as a consequence, the war of 1970–1975.[42]

Sihanouk's remarks do not address his decision to restore diplomatic relations with the United States in 1969 or the effects of the withdrawal of aid on the effectiveness of Cambodia's armed forces. His idea that those who opposed him in 1970 would have remained loyal had they continued to be rich is suggestive of his views of human nature.

In the early 1960s, Sihanouk's style of rule was never called into question, and insofar as it was colorful, plausible, and entertaining it gave pleasure to Cambodians locked into poverty, ill health, and exhausting, repetitive work. To the peasantry, those more fortunate than they were often perceived as corrupt, but they were also "above" those in the countryside and thus in a sense entitled to act as they did. In the DK era, after 1975, Pol Pot and others stated that a deep and widespread hatred by country people of those in the cities had fueled the revolution. Hatred or suspiciousness at least was certainly apparent in remote areas in this period and probably became more intense in the early 1970s. But outside of intellectual circles, Sihanouk himself was probably immune from such suspicions. Like Prince Rama and the heroes of the escapist Indian films so popular in Cambodia at this time, the prince lived in another world, breathed different air, and played by different rules. Farmers and their families probably were flattered when he visited them and spoke to them about issues which they could barely understand. As far as American aid was concerned Sihanouk knew more than they did. He was still the king, and what he said should be believed.

Several short-term benefits flowed from Sihanouk's anti-American stance. For one, the U.S.-induced commodity import program came to an end. Luxury imports fell off sharply (a temporary drop, as it turned out). For another, Sihanouk was no longer subjected to lectures by American officials. A third benefit was that National Liberation Front (NLF) and

North Vietnamese forces, allowed from this point on to camp peacefully along Cambodia's eastern border, unobserved by U.S. diplomatic personnel inside Cambodia, posed no subversive or military threat for several years, as they came to be stationed in Cambodia in increasing numbers. Finally, Sihanouk presumed that by quarreling with the United States and using leftist rhetoric to do so, he could retain the support of Communist regimes while neutralizing leftist opposition at home. In 1965, discussing his balancing act, he said, "There are Khmer traitors among the Communists and they are living among us. Siding with the Chinese and the Vietnamese they leave us alone as long as we remain enemies of the Americans. . . . When we become pro-American, the Chinese and Vietnamese immediately become our enemies and bring us insecurity. It is for this reason I think that we have greater advantages in continuing to quarrel with the Americans."[43]

In early 1964, Sihanouk concluded a secret agreement with the Vietnamese Communists that entitled the Cambodian army to skim off 10 percent of Chinese military aid, primarily weapons and ammunition, delivered to the Vietnamese via the port of Sihanoukville. Additional levies were charged for transporting food and other goods to the frontier in Cambodian army trucks and private ones contracted for the purpose. These arrangements, bemoaned by the United States and officially denied by Sihanouk, enriched the army officer corps, while undermining their morale. Many officers who had become rich by trading with the Vietnamese Communists joined Lon Nol and Sirik Matak in 1970 in attempting to drive their former patrons back across the border into South Vietnam.[44]

On balance, however, the disadvantages of rejecting U.S. aid were greater. The first of these, noted by Douc Rasy, was that Sihanouk now faced the Communist world more or less alone. Another, in Elizabeth Becker's phrasing, was that "Sihanouk forfeited the money that had balanced his budget" in previous years. Yet a third involved American military equipment used by Sihanouk's army: as it became unserviceable and was not replaced, the army degenerated as a fighting force. Military equipment given to Cambodia in 1964–65 by China, the USSR, and Czechoslovakia was not interchangeable and was useful largely for parades. The army, in turn, devoted most of its energies during these years to public works. A related consequence, linked to Sihanouk's economic initiatives, was that he alienated the Sino-Cambodian commercial elite. Finally, when relations with the United States were broken off for good in 1965, Sihanouk also lost an avenue of communication through which he might have been able to exercise a tempering influence on U.S. activities in Vietnam. As it was, he chose the opportunity presented by the departure of the Americans to move momentarily to the left, hoping thereby to gain a firmer foothold with the intellectuals and greater credit from his allies overseas. In particular, he counted on France and China.

The Prince Turns Left

In 1964–65, U.S. military intervention in Vietnam confirmed Sihanouk's fear and distrust of U.S. policies and led him to intensify his search for international guarantees to safeguard Cambodia. These developments, in turn, encouraged Cambodia's visible leftists to urge the prince toward greater rapprochement with the NLF and the North Vietnamese and a deeper alliance with China.

At the same time, the popularity of his foreign policy posed dilemmas for Cambodia's small pro-Western elite, anti-Communist members of the officer corps, and the clandestine KWP. The pro-Westerners became increasingly isolated because of their reluctance to support Sihanouk's economic policies and his alliances with Communist regimes. Some of them also faced a problem when, toward the end of 1965, it became profitable for many to trade with the Communist Vietnamese. This trade, which reduced government revenue from export taxes, had the effect of undermining Sihanouk's authority. It also strengthened the Vietnamese Communists and led to their exercising undisputed control by 1969 over large tracts of eastern and northeastern Cambodia.

Sihanouk's policies also presented quandaries for the KWP, mainly whether the party should advocate armed struggle or bide its time. The Vietnamese urged the latter course, for they had profited from Sihanouk's fears of Communism and were using Cambodian territory to rest and resupply their forces. Saloth Sar and his colleagues had no choice but to cooperate with them, although they resented being tied down by Vietnamese objectives and advice. Others in the party, including many who were later purged, probably saw advantages in cooperation and risks in pursuing a xenophobic, independent policy. Because of repression at the hands of Sihanouk's army and police, party members in hiding in Phnom Penh had no opportunity to express their views. Upstaged by Sihanouk in the cities and kept on a leash by the Vietnamese in the forest, the KWP went through an identity crisis. Its leadership, however, remained unchallenged, hidden, and intact.[45]

Did the leaders of the KWP have any genuine authority? Who had the final say in 1965—the KWP central committee, Cambodians in Hanoi, or the Vietnamese? In the areas bordering Vietnam thousands of Cambodians were soon recruited to supply and work for the Vietnamese Communist forces. The leadership was in no position to object to this recruitment or to command their adherents to resist.[46]

Another problem for the KWP's leaders was that more than a thousand Cambodian radicals, including those KPRP cadre evacuated in 1954–55, were still in exile in North Vietnam. Among them were Son Ngoc Minh, Rath Samoeun, and Mey Pho, and others who enjoyed high status among the Vietnamese. The KWP's central committee had no assurances that these men would be willing to pursue Cambodian goals when the time came to do so, as opposed to Vietnamese ones or others related to Indochina.

Meanwhile, in Phnom Penh many young Cambodians were encouraged to become politically active by Sihanouk's anti-American, anticapitalist policies. In January 1964, hundreds of them took to the streets to demonstrate against the Cambodian "right" and against the United States. The demonstrators, who did not have a permit for their march, unintentionally blocked Sihanouk's Lincoln, which was taking him to the airport for a state visit to Malaya. This gaffe kept the demonstration from being reported in the government press, although Pol Pot noted it twelve years later as a milestone in the Cambodian revolution, suggesting that the CPK's urban branch had been involved in organizing it.[47]

When Sihanouk returned home in March more demonstrations were staged, this time with his approval, outside the British and American embassies. The demonstrators, many of them trucked into the capital in government vehicles, included Cambodian soldiers in civilian clothes, workers, and students let out of school for the day. In a festive mood, they marched to directions given over Ministry of Information loudspeakers. Signs carried by the demonstrators objected to the "Anglo-Saxon" nations' reluctance to accede to Sihanouk's request for a fourteen-nation conference, to South Vietnamese military incursions, and to U.S. support for the Khmer Serei. The event lasted for several hours, and although damage to the embassies and their vehicles was extensive, there were no casualties. Sihanouk interpreted the size and enthusiasm of the crowd as evidence of his popularity and the unpopularity of the United States.[48]

Nonetheless, the violence of the protest march and the enthusiasm of so many students may have surprised him, for soon thereafter Lon Nol took the student leaders at Lycée Sisowath aside and warned them firmly against taking independent political action.

Vorn Vet and his colleagues in the KWP also were amazed by the size and vigor of the demonstration. In his confession, Vorn Vet wrote, "I had not thought that such a movement was possible. Looking at the strength of revolutionary forces, I thought it was impossible. [Its success] came from the fact that Sihanouk was stronger than the revolution."[49]

Sihanouk had hoped that by allowing his children to express their rage, he would impress his countrymen with his skills, while his victims would be frightened and accede to his demands. He was probably right on the first count; on the second, he was wrong because U.S. policies in Southeast Asia had by now become dominated by an eagerness to escalate the war against the Communists in Vietnam. Sihanouk's voice, which had always been just one of many that American policymakers listened to, now went unheard.

The new U.S. priorities became clear at the end of March, when a South Vietnamese attack on a Cambodian village strained U.S.–Cambodian relations further. U.S. military advisers accompanied the Vietnamese forces and witnessed the casualties inflicted on Cambodian civilians—seventeen killed and some twenty wounded. The U.S. embassy in Saigon blamed Cambodia's "poorly defined border" for the incident, and the United States and South Vietnam apologized and offered compensation to the victims, but the U.S. embassy in Saigon resisted Washington's pressure for a strongly worded apology. For many Americans in South Vietnam, Cambodia, by sheltering Communist troops, had forfeited its neutral status.[50]

In August 1964, the United States tried to accredit a new ambassador, Randolph Kidder, to Phnom Penh. The Cambodian Foreign Ministry agreed, and Kidder flew out to Cambodia to begin work. But Sihanouk temporized about announcing the appointment, and as he did so further border incidents involving South Vietnamese troops and American advisers led to civilian casualties. Sihanouk used the incidents as an excuse to humiliate Kidder, whom he sent home without allowing him to present his credentials.

The prince spent the rest of the year trying to obtain guarantees from other countries that Cambodia's borders and its neutrality would be respected. One method he chose was to renew his demands for a multinational conference on Indochina. The fact that the powers whose support Sihanouk sought included North Vietnam and the NLF infuriated officials in Bangkok, Saigon, and Washington. At the same time, Sihanouk refused to allow journalists to visit the border zones. His idea for a conference soon foundered on Thai and Vietnamese reluctance to play into his hands.

Relations with China were easier for the prince. In September 1964, he reported on his return from a visit to Beijing that the Chinese had granted him sizable quantities of unconditional aid as well as assurances of political support. "I wish to make it plain," he said, "that even though we go and beseech People's China to accept us as her lackey, she will not agree. Our Khmer nation is lucky, and this luck is rare. For other countries, China watches for an opportunity to swallow them. She has refused to swallow our country, even at our request. Our country is comparable to a girl who winks at China; this wink has kept China from touching her and blemishing her virginity."[51]

In the same speech, Sihanouk contrasted Chinese largesse and his confidence in the Chinese with his coolness toward the North Vietnamese. He said that he had refused an offer of aid from the North Vietnamese prime minister, Pham Van Dong. "I told him," he said, "you can stay away, and respect us from afar."[52]

The presence of North Vietnamese and NLF units in Cambodia angered the United States, which was prevented by international law from swooping across the border to destroy the facilities they had frequently photographed from the air.

The Cambodian army was not strong enough to drive the Vietnamese away, and it did nothing to oppose them except when Cambodian soldiers were killed. The army provided reports to journalists of U.S. and South Vietnamese incursions into Cambodia or its airspace, but did not mention the presence of Communist troops. In the twenty-four or forty-eight hours before journalists or the vestigial ICSC were allowed to visit the sites of such incidents, the troops made themselves scarce, and evidence of their presence was removed or destroyed beforehand by Cambodian forces and local people.[53]

By denying that the Vietnamese were in Cambodia, Sihanouk was able to paint the Americans and South Vietnamese as invaders barging across international boundaries, inexcusably, so as to maim and kill innocent civilians. These projections were widely believed, for the image of Cambodia as what he called an "island of peace" had deep roots in Cambodians' explanations of themselves. Blaming events on ogres was easier for the prince than admitting the presence of Vietnamese Communist bases on Cambodian soil or raising and paying a Cambodian army that could be shredded by Vietnamese of any political persuasion. Besides, Cambodian civilian casualties in the U.S.-South Vietnamese incursions and bombing raids were real, and they angered him.[54]

As we have seen, the collusion between the Cambodian government and the Vietnamese Communists increased in 1964 as Chinese weapons and military supplies shipped overland from Sihanoukville began to contribute to the Communist war effort. Short-term economic gains for the middlemen in these transactions were considerable, but the effects on the national economy, later disastrous, were still mixed. Illicit sales of rice, cattle, and other foodstuffs to the insurgents made large profits for local Chinese and Sino-Cambodian merchants in the towns and smaller ones for Cambodian peasants. Those transporting food and weapons also made money, and so did the army officer corps. In the eastern part of the country, a busy trade developed between farmers and NLF forces willing to pay much more for rice and other crops than Sihanouk's government or local Chinese merchants could afford. On the other hand, by 1966–67, official rice exports plummeted, and the losses of revenue normally derived from taxing them had begun to affect the national budget, already strained by Sihanouk's insistence on such prestigious projects as an Olympic stadium for Phnom Penh and the construction of luxury hotels.

Before these effects were felt too sharply, the prince's anti-American policy seemed to pay dividends to him. In March 1965 he convened an Indochina People's Conference in Phnom Penh to condemn U.S. activities in Southeast Asia, in preparation for a larger conference to which non-Indochinese powers were to be invited. Those who attended, aside from Sangkum representatives, were all representatives of Communist guerrilla movements or of minorities in South Vietnam sympathetic to Communist efforts. Sihanouk failed to attract any of them to the notion of a cease-fire, and the conference accomplished nothing, since uninvited powers resisted his calls for a larger conference.[55]

In the meantime, diplomatic relations with the United States were winding down. In December 1964, a meeting in New Delhi between U.S. and Cambodian representatives came to nothing, largely because of Cambodian insistence that the Anglo-Saxons cease (and thereby admit) their aggression in Vietnam and also agree unilaterally to several other conditions that the Americans found unacceptable. One of these was that the United States stop accusing Cambodia falsely of allowing Vietnamese troops on its territory. For relations to improve, on the other hand, no conditions were imposed on the Khmer. It was a classic Sihanouk scenario, programed as a Cambodian triumph in the face of American misunderstanding and built around a proposition that both sides knew was false.[56]

The last straw for Sihanouk in his decade of dealing with the United States came in April 1965, when an article in *Newsweek* reported that he had "one to several concubines" and that Queen Kossamak, who was "said to be money mad," ran a "string of bordellos at the edge of the city." The tone of the article enraged Sihanouk and provided an excuse for another demonstration outside the U.S. embassy.[57]

A few days later, Sihanouk finally broke off relations with the United States. They were not renewed for four years. Chinese and North Vietnamese pressure to remove the Americans from Cambodia played a role in his decision, and so did his advisers, but it was easy to make and popular with most Cambodians at the time. The United States had been expecting the break and did nothing to avoid it.

In 1977, Pol Pot gave credit to Cambodian radicals, rather than to Sihanouk, for the cessation of relations, calling it the "culmination of the continued, powerful struggles of our people." In a narrow sense, his analysis was correct. Breaking relations with Cambodia's Number One Enemy had been a goal of Cambodian radicals since the Geneva conference ten years before. Although radicals continued to suffer from Sihanouk's police, the rupture allowed those working in the open more influence for a time, particularly in the area of foreign affairs.

All the same, Sihanouk remained wary of these people. At the national congress in July 1965, a hapless student from Kambuj'bot who had expressed disquiet in a letter to the prince about the becalmed Kitchpanich investigation was hauled before the meeting. Sihanouk berated him for his impudence and asked him if he wanted to be prime minister. The student replied courageously that he wanted Cambodia to make progress. Sihanouk threatened him with a jail sentence of five to twenty years and sent him home. Turning to the audience, he asked if the student's letter was sufficient cause for "the Sangkum to be dissolved." As Sihanouk expected, a sea of hands approved the status quo.[58]

Saloth Sar's Visit to Vietnam and China

In 1964–65, North Vietnam and China began to work more closely with the Cambodian Communists, who were split between those inside Cambodia in the KWP and those in training camps or performing other duties in North Vietnam. At the end of 1964, Vorn Vet attended a meeting of the central committee "in the forest in the eastern zone," and there he encountered Keo Meas, who had supposedly been displaced from the central committee in 1963. The meeting took place "near a Vietnamese camp." Several months later, Vorn Vet wrote, he learned that Brother Number One (Saloth Sar) had traveled to Vietnam and China with Keo Meas as head of the delegation and that in the interim Brother Number Two (Nuon Chea) had been in charge of Office 100. Pol Pot, in the *Black Book*, corroborates the Vietnamese leg of the journey but fails to mention Keo Meas, placing himself at the head of the delegation. The same year, a Vietnamese official claimed that "Pol Pot and some of his friends" had stayed for "a few months" in Vietnam.

In Vietnam, according to the *Black Book,* VWP officials led by Le Duan scolded the Cambodian delegates because "the [KWP] had its own politi-cal line, and thanks to that line, the revolutionary movement in Kam-puchea had taken giant steps. This disturbed the Vietnamese, for if the revolution in Kampuchea continued, that would affect [Vietnamese] col-laboration with the ruling classes in Phnom Penh. Even worse, if the revolution in Kampuchea developed and became strong independently, the Vietnamese would be unable to control it."[59]

There is bravado at work here and perhaps echoes of a real imbroglio, but there is no evidence that the Cambodian revolution took "giant steps" in 1965 or followed an independent line. The *Black Book* account is proba-bly correct insofar as the Vietnamese, anxious to preserve their alliance with Sihanouk, clearly asked (and perhaps even commanded) the Cambo-dians to be cautious about initiating armed struggle. In 1978, Nguyen Cao Thach, the Vietnamese foreign minister, recalled specifically that the Viet-namese had urged Saloth Sar to "support Sihanouk while criticizing him, and maintain a political but not a military struggle." From a Cambodian perspective, this was a recipe for political frustration or mass arrests.

For most Cambodian Communists, indeed, Sihanouk had always been an enemy on the same scale as the United States. This animosity meant little to the Vietnamese, who had summoned the Cambodians in order to work out a milder form of struggle and to fine-tune the KWP's support for Communist forces in Vietnam.

A second matter undoubtedly discussed at the meeting was the future of Cambodians undergoing training in North Vietnam. Most of these men and women had been there since 1954–55. Several hundred others had arrived more recently. In December 1964, for example, two hundred Khmer from South Vietnam and eastern Cambodia had marched up to Hanoi—taking two months to do so—to enroll at a politico-military training school.[60]

A third matter to be dealt with was the future of cooperation between the two parties and the tenor of their relationships to the developing antagonism between China and the Soviet Union. Unfortunately, the documents about Saloth Sar's trip composed amid Cambodian-Vietnamese hostilities in the late 1970s say nothing about this issue.

A PRK official who spoke to Serge Thion in 1981, however, asserted that Pol Pot had given several lectures in Hanoi in 1965, a fact indicative of his prestige and of his acceptance by Vietnamese authorities. Another piece of evidence, also from Thion, is that a Vietnamese editor stated in 1981 that when he had tried to discover the names of the Khmers traveling with Saloth Sar in 1965, he was denied the information on the grounds that he did not have a "need to know."[61]

Evidence that Saloth Sar visited China and North Korea following his time in Vietnam comes entirely from 1978 or later. Pol Pot has never mentioned the visits; neither have Chinese documents, and except for passing references to them by Vorn Vet and another confession from 1978, the sources for them are Vietnamese. By 1978, of course, it was in Vietnam's interest to make Pol Pot a fanatical Maoist from as early a date as possible. One Vietnamese source asserted, for example, that Sar stayed in China for several months and received extensive political training, which suggests that he eluded Vietnamese control and had been contaminated by a Chinese virus. The infection may well have occurred, but whatever Saloth Sar did in China was obviously known in Hanoi. The Vietnamese had encouraged him to go to China to demonstrate that they were being helped in their liberation struggle by a fraternal, pro-Chinese party. Chinese party officials may well have given Sar and his colleagues discreet support, and Mao Zedong may have shaken his hand, but Chinese figures still saw not Sar's quixotic party but their alliance with Sihanouk and their support for the North Vietnamese-NLF alliance as serving China's national interest.[62]

At the same time, Saloth Sar may have been encouraged and the Vietnamese alarmed by an article published in September 1965, while Sar was in China. Written by Lin Piao, it stressed that wars of national liberation should be autonomous and self-supporting. To Sar, this might have implied a lessening of Vietnamese guidance and control; to the Vietnamese, it seemed to threaten a lessening in Chinese military aid.

But these are speculations. Nothing is known of Saloth Sar's movements between his visit to Hanoi in 1965 and his return to Office 100 in September 1966, when the central committee decided to change the name of the KWP to the Communist Party of Kampuchea (CPK). It is unclear if the Vietnamese were informed of the decision or approved of it. Indeed, it is possible that the new title was a secret gift from the Chinese and that Saloth Sar supported the change to align his party more closely with the rapidly unfolding Chinese revolution, while keeping the development secret from his patrons in Vietnam. Such an explanation fits with Sar's obsessive interest in covering his tracks and concealing his intentions. It is also conceivable that Sar decided to change the name himself, never informed any foreign powers, and trusted his immediate colleagues to keep the secret.

In China and perhaps in North Korea (evidence for a visit there is very thin) Saloth Sar may have become aware of a way of being a Communist that differed from the way he had chosen since 1953. As a high-ranking Vietnamese official, Truong Chinh, asserted angrily in 1979, Chinese leaders may have complimented the Cambodian delegation in 1965, calling the CPK "the center of the revolution in Southeast Asia," in exchange for being told by Saloth Sar that "Mao Zedong's thought [was] present-day Marxist-Leninism." In the context of 1965, these exchanges, if they occurred, were harmless enough; by 1979 they represented treachery to Vietnam and betrayals of Marxism-Leninism.

Saloth Sar must also have drawn his own conclusions from the pace and style of events in China. While he was there, Lin Piao and others inaugurated the hegemony of "Mao Zedong thought," the early stages of the cultural revolution, and also the doctrine of people's wars. Looking back, it is appealing to suppose that the combination of national autarchy and tightened personal leadership at the top appealed to Sar, who inaugurated similar policies in Cambodia after 1975. In late 1965 and early 1966, however, the decimation of the world's leading Maoist party in Indonesia must also have made Saloth Sar pause before bringing the CPK into the open and become more dubious than ever about linking the party's fortunes to Sihanouk's, as the Communist Party of Indonesia (PKI) had allied itself with Sukarno.[63]

The trip, then, is hard to evaluate; it had no immediate effects on CPK policy or behavior. A year passed before the CPK central committee began sponsoring armed struggle inside Cambodia, six years before the party adopted an antagonistic posture toward Vietnam, and ten years before Pol Pot publicly acknowledged his intellectual debts to China. The change in the party's name, of course, which may have been inspired by his visit, was known to very few people. But perhaps Saloth Sar saw the virtues of ruling Cambodia in terms of his own thought and perceived advantages in following Mao's lead and blaming dissidence inside his party on bourgeois elements whose former comradeship, when weighed against personal loyalty, was insufficient to keep them from being purged.

Sihanouk on Display

The year 1966 saw several turning points in Cambodia's political history. The assembly elected in September, while still composed exclusively of Sangkum members, consisted for the first time of candidates who had neither sought nor received Sihanouk's endorsement. These men and women owed less to Sihanouk than any deputies since 1951. During 1966 also, a good deal of evidence suggests, Sihanouk began to stop caring about day-to-day Cambodian politics; as his grip loosened, potential opponents became alert.

In August 1966, he lost sight of the elections because he was preoccupied with preparing for General de Gaulle's four-day visit to Cambodia, which took place at the end of August and the beginning of September. For many years, the prince had idolized de Gaulle. He visited him in 1946, when the general was out of office, and years later, after the coup of 1970, he likened himself to de Gaulle in World War II, with Lon Nol cast as Marshal Pétain and the Americans as the Nazi army.

In terms of spectacle, grandeur, and stage management, the general's visit was the apogee of Sihanouk's years in power and a curtain call for a century of France's special relationship with Cambodia. The visit certainly provided Sihanouk with three days of the global recognition he craved and perhaps with a glimmer of hope that his neutralist policies might gain support from large powers.

The elaborate ceremonies for the general and his wife went smoothly, but in the midst of them an Australian cameraman, Neil Davis, caught sight of a fiasco not covered in other dispatches:

Prince Sihanouk told de Gaulle that he would now see an exhibition of rowing a royal barge. The boat crew were trying a bit too hard, and taking quite a lot of water on board. As they got right up to the official dais, they were all supposed to raise their paddles in salute . . . but the boat just sank. Suddenly there were all these guys in gold helmets, Cambodian silk stockings and traditional dress floundering around in the water.

All I could see through my view-finder was de Gaulle's huge nose, which had been inclined up to take the salute, come slowly down to take in what had happened, point across to look at Sihanouk, and then go back up into an elevated position. De Gaulle seemed unimpressed with Cambodia and Cambodian organization.[64]

De Gaulle's speech in Phnom Penh warmly supported the prince's policies and attacked the escalation of the conflict in Vietnam. The general was the heaviest weapon Sihanouk could call on to influence world events. As far as the Americans were concerned, the speech provided a minor irritation but had no effect on the fighting. Their war was unstoppable by then.

All through 1966 the prince continued his campaign to have Cambodia's frontiers and its neutrality recognized internationally, via a series of statements by foreign powers. He opened the campaign once his plans for an international conference to settle the Indochina war had come to nothing. As the months passed, foreign states paraded up to him, agreeing to his stipulations and offering their homage. The French, who had drawn the frontiers, pledged benignly to respect them. So did several states that did not border on Cambodia. Their so-called comprehension of Cambodia was featured prominently in Sihanouk's press. States that bordered on Cambodia were not prepared to enshrine Sihanouk's readings of the frontiers as definitive. The United States dragged its feet, unwilling to guarantee borders that its allies in Southeast Asia were reluctant to accept. Its disdain for Cambodia, as usual, played into Sihanouk's hands.[65]

Speaking in the 1980s, many Cambodians pointed out that in 1966–67 Sihanouk seemed to grow weary of political life. He sought refuge from his exhausting, repetitive work in hobbies and in the company of his entourage. Some informants have connected this withdrawal to the decline of Queen Kossamak's influence, others to the growing influence of his wife, Monique Izzi, and still others to the intractability of the political and economic problems he faced.

A former associate recalls a night when Sihanouk, among friends, cried out almost desperately, "I wish I could quit. I'm completely exhausted!" The cry was undoubtedly sincere, but Sihanouk was unwilling to allow anyone but himself the final word. To maintain his momentum, he continued his attacks on the Khmer Serei and local Communists. According to the prince, KWP documents accusing him of being a U.S. agent had recently been captured. If they are accurately described, these documents provide evidence that the party was shifting its propaganda in an anti-Sihanouk direction. The prince, in turn, noted that Hou Youn had supported Son Ngoc Thanh when the two were in France in the early 1950s and fantasized that this meant that the Khmer Reds were "Son Ngoc Thanh's partisans." If they were "genuine Communists," he continued, they would "be satisfied with us, as their masters are. The Khmer Reds should admire us." Unlike any Communist country, he added, Cambodia had the courage to break with the United States.

Faced with increasing evidence of economic decline, Sihanouk campaigned for austerity—but without conviction. As part of the campaign, he abolished the title Your Royal Highness, forbade genuflections, and ended the custom of being sheltered by an equerry carrying a tiered umbrella. He did nothing to alter his extravagant life-style, which he believed was expected of a chief of state. He saw these ceremonial moves as setting a democratic example and announced in May that the year would be spent "at work," with the nation taking "a new step toward socialism," otherwise unexplained. Three weeks later, he decreed that an additional five thousand copies per month of the gossipy, semipornographic magazine *Pseng Pseng* (Different things), which he edited, should be printed at government expense.[66]

In 1965, Sihanouk revived a hobby he had taken up in the 1940s: making feature films. He may have been pushed into it by his envy of the success of an American production of *Lord Jim* made in Cambodia in 1964. The French director Marcel Camus, who had made a film in Cambodia in 1962, also encouraged Sihanouk to move in this direction. Between 1965 and 1969 the prince wrote, cast, produced, and directed nine films. Because he had no formal cinematographic training, monopolized the stage, permitted no criticism, and listened to little advice, the films turned out to be amateurish and self-indulgent. None of the actors was paid, and budgets were not maintained. Some of the costs were recouped by encouraging government employees to pay to see the films, which projected Sihanouk's ideas about history, Cambodia, and himself. They reveal the hothouse character of the Phnom Penh elite. The first of them, *Apsara* (The goddess), was screened in May 1966 and starred Sihanouk, his wife, and Nhiek Tioulong cast as a philanderer. The last two, *Joie de vivre* and *Crépuscule* (Twilight), were screened in 1969.[67]

It is impossible to say if Sihanouk's mania was the result of or a symptom of his disenchantment with politics. Over the years, he had succumbed to a series of preoccupations—competitive horse-riding, musical composition, cooking, volleyball, basketball, theatrical performances—with similar enthusiasm, but filmmaking had always been a special favorite. Shortly before the Communist victory in 1975, he told a visitor in Beijing that he expected to return to Cambodia and make films while the revolution carried on without him; and a decade later, in exile in North Korea, he continued to busy himself with making films.

Sihanouk screened *Apsara* at a time he was telling the nation to tighten its belt and get to work. The scenes of the film, as noted by Milton Osborne, included "Scene 5: A Facel Vega, driven by a pretty young woman; Scene 6: General Ritthi and Rattana get out of his Jaguar; Scene 10: Along a fine asphalted road . . . drives a black Cadillac convertible," and so on. As Charles Meyer has written, "Official vehicles, planes, ships, infantry, youth, ministers, generals and officials . . . were all requisitioned for the needs of the production." *Apsara*, like *Joie de vivre* and *Crépuscule,* depicted the raffish behavior of Sihanouk's circle. None of the films, including the ostensible historical ones, had any footage of ordinary people.[68]

The Elections of 1966

The fourth assembly election since independence was scheduled for September 1966. Nominations closed on the last day of July. At that time, 425 candidates had nominated themselves for 82 electoral districts (the 1966 assembly had 5 new seats). Of the 77 outgoing representatives, 34 chose not to run. The six-week campaign stressed local issues, and in most districts Sihanouk honored his pledge not to interfere. Nonetheless, fearing the popularity of Hou Youn, Hu Nim, and Khieu Samphan, who were running for reelection, he published several polemics on Cambodian communism during the campaign, and pressure was unsuccessfully applied at his behest against these candidates and against the conservative, anti-Sihanouk assemblyman Douc Rasy.[69]

Sihanouk seems to have started out with a plan to select the candidates himself, as he had in 1958 and 1962. In June, however, he changed his mind, declaring, "I am not very satisfied with my selection for several reasons. For instance, there are certain people I do not wish to pick as candidates. But because of certain influences from prominent quarters, I was compelled to select them. . . . I am not satisfied with my personal choices [from 1962?]. They have aroused the dissatisfaction of their voters, either by their incompetence or the incomprehension of their constituents' problems, or by their attacks against the Sangkum."

The prince went on to say that thousands of candidates had put their names forward but that if any non-Sangkum candidates presented themselves, "we shall immediately withdraw all this muddle of candidates and will immediately present . . . our single candidate." His remarks suggest that he had begun to select a slate of candidates but had been unwilling or unable to to make his choices or rejections stick. According to Douc Rasy, he had been under pressure from those with an entree to his entourage to bestow seats on political incompetents. Unwilling to act against the interests of his cronies and convinced that the assembly was nothing for him to worry about, he walked away from the elections. His decision to do so had unforeseen, disastrous consequences.[70]

How he expected the elections to come out is impossible to say. Like all those since 1955, they were orderly, although defeated candidates raised objections in many districts, and corruption in the form of vote buying and bribes was apparently widespread. According to Milton Osborne, several candidates were bought off by rivals prior to the elections; in other districts, voters were paid off in advance. Absenteeism averaged around 35 percent of registered voters in most districts and over 80 percent in Phnom Penh.

It is hard to generalize about the results, for in the seventy-five electorates in which more than two candidates were running, only eleven winners earned an absolute majority. Several earned less than 25 percent of the vote, and most earned less than 40 percent. Four of the decisive winners— Hu Nim, Hou Youn, Douc Rasy, and Khieu Samphan—had been targeted by Sihanouk as enemies of the regime. Their pluralities were so high as to suggest that Sihanouk's animosity had acted in their favor. More generally, as Charles Meyer has pointed out, it was common knowledge at the time that candidates who campaigned as supporters of the prince were frequently defeated.[71]

The new parliamentarians, in other words, owed nothing to Sihanouk and little to anyone else.

Scattered evidence suggests that candidates who concentrated on local issues were victorious. Khieu Samphan, for example, had worked hard to endear himself to his electorate of S'aang, visiting it frequently in an unpretentious car and on one occasion lending money to local farmers to pay the costs of installing electric pumps. Hou Youn, similarly, had cultivated his Kompong Cham electorate, where he was recalled as being egalitarian and humane. In 1966 he earned 78 percent of the vote. In Siem Reap, a new candidate, Keuky Lim, whose father was a well-known fishing entrepreneur, capitalized on his knowledge of local conditions to win a seat.[72]

The refocusing of politics onto local issues and the redeployment of local patronage networks were reminiscent of pre-Sangkum campaigns, but there were differences as well. For one thing, whereas the Democrats' support for Cambodian independence had been the concealed reason for their popular support, in 1966 national issues were not discussed and party lines never suggested, since the candidates all claimed to be loyal members of the Sangkum and risked arrest if they declared their independence. In the elections themselves, the high rate of absenteeism in Phnom Penh suggests that people's apathy in rural districts, where local officials brought out the vote (and compiled the statistics), was probably more widespread than the statistics suggest. The apathy may have stemmed from Sihanouk's failure to whip up enthusiasm for the elections and from the reluctance of officials, who were receiving either mixed signals or none at all from Sihanouk and Phnom Penh, to push the voters or the statistics in one direction or another.

Douc Rasy has called the winners "people who were already well off, and knew how to please others." The assembly was a new body. Only twenty-eight of its members—roughly 35 percent—had been elected in 1962. Several left-wing deputies chose not to run again, but the winners were not recipients of Sangkum patronage. Indeed, as Vickery has written, "Six seats were won by Sangkum conservatives of 1955, who had been passed over in the elections of 1958 and 1962, while 13 others had last been seen in the 1951 elections, mostly as candidates of right-wing splinter parties." The new assembly included several people, such as Yem Sambaur, the "enemy" deputies, and the redoubtable Sim Var, who had grudges against the prince.[73]

The upshot of the elections was that Sihanouk was unable to prevent his antagonists from entering the assembly. In 1973, after he had been deposed, he told Jean Lacouture that the assembly of 1966 was the "most reactionary and corrupt" of any to which he had "submitted," an interesting word for him to choose. At the time, however, still exhausted by de Gaulle's visit three weeks earlier, Sihanouk reacted to the results in a comparatively subdued manner.[74]

Lon Nol Becomes Prime Minister

Before the assembly reconvened, Sihanouk was hospitalized for a complete rest. The assembly, when it met, voted that Gen. Lon Nol be made prime minister. Fifty-nine votes were cast in his favor, after bids by Sim Var and Norodom Kantol had been rejected.

Sihanouk had given the green light to Lon Nol, who had not been eager for the job. As soon as Lon Nol obtained it, however, the prince hastened to reassert himself, for the cabinet Lon Nol was assembling seemed composed of unsupportive people. Sihanouk announced that he had decided to form a countergovernment made up of leftists hostile to Lon Nol and some dependable cronies. The countergovernment, he said, was to monitor the assembly, "to point out what is right, what is wrong, and what is irregular," and to demonstrate to foreign powers that "Cambodia was not a dictatorship."[75]

The new formation demonstrated the reverse, for the purpose of the countergovernment was to reassert Sihanouk's control. To justify his decision, he claimed that Cambodia's young people had asked him to form the group. There is no evidence for this. Instead, he was trying to take command of opposition to his own prime minister, Lon Nol, so as to neutralize it and claim credit if Lon Nol faltered. Playing things even safer, he placed his close associate Nhiek Tioulong in charge of the army, replacing Lon Nol, at the end of October 1966.

By forming the countergovernment, Sihanouk encouraged the resurgence of factional politics. His motives for doing so may have been a mixture of theatricality and a desire to keep everyone off balance. Old rivalries soon surfaced. One was between Sim Var, by then estranged from Sihanouk's policies, and leftists like Chau Seng, who supported the prince for the time being, especially in the sphere of foreign relations.

The progovernment daily *La Dépêche* had recently come under the control of Sim Var. Sihanouk's reaction was to encourage Chau Seng to found a countergovernment newspaper, *La Nouvelle Dépêche.* For several months, the two papers engaged in attacks on each other that disguised but failed to hide the deep rifts that were developing between those who favored the CPK and those who had more conservative ideas.

Soon after the elections, pro-Sihanouk demonstrations were staged in

Phnom Penh by students from leftist schools, and Sihanouk referred in a speech to what he called the political crisis, for he felt uneasy about Lon Nol's government as well as about leftist opposition to it. He saw that some aspects of power had begun to slip away to people he was unable to control. The assembly had hardly been in session for a month when Sihanouk was quoted as saying, "The whole question comes down to this. Do I have the right to overthrow Lon Nol, chosen by the Assembly?"[76]

One must be wary of judging Sihanouk or Cambodian politics at the end of 1966 on the basis of knowing in what direction the elections would lead. The Communist-led uprisings of 1967 and 1968 (discussed in chapter 5) flowed from Lon Nol's assumption of power, from nervousness and impatience among the urban left, from rural discontent, and from increasing opposition to the prince in many segments of society. These consequences of the elections were imperceptible to most Cambodians in 1966, however, and Sihanouk seemed to be playing his customary game of keeping political factions grateful to him, frightened, and off balance.

By the end of the year, he had regained a measure of initiative and control. He continued to dominate the media and to outmaneuver his opponents. In the sphere of foreign relations he was still immensely popular. Through adroit diplomacy he kept Cambodia out of the Vietnam war and all but a few Cambodians from being killed.[77]

By allowing Lon Nol to become prime minister and to form a government of like-minded senior figures, however, Sihanouk permitted someone who had personal ambition and a clientele of his own to hold power. At the time, he did not think he was running a risk.

Lon Nol, after all, seemed an entirely safe bet. Over the years, he had not exhibited military talents or expressed controversial views. A devout Buddhist, he was popular with the officer corps but had made little impression on anyone else. He was a good listener, and one informant has explained his endurance as arising from his status as a "good cop" who painstakingly assembled dossiers for Sihanouk and for himself on potential enemies of public order. As a cofounder of the Renovation party, he had always resented the assembly, particularly after his brief detention in 1952. He had supported Sihanouk's Crusade for Independence by mobilizing a national militia and had helped to stage-manage Operation Samakki. Two years later Sirik Matak had recommended him to Sihanouk as minister of defense. In that portfolio, Lon Nol's incompetence over the years infuriated Prince Monireth, who wanted the job himself, but he consistently demonstrated loyalty to Sihanouk. His troops had set upon the Democrats in the palace meeting of 1957, and he had helped to defuse the Dap Chhuon plot. In the sixties, his agents and those of his colleague Kou Roun routinely arrested, tortured, and assassinated Communists, Khmer Serei, renegade students, and other enemies of the state.[78]

Throughout his career, Lon Nol had revered the prince. To many, his personality was an enigma. In private and at meetings he seemed impassive—"silent as a carp" in Charles Meyer's phrase—seldom venturing an opinion but always conscious of rivalries and weaknesses that he might exploit later on. These talents served him well and the national interest poorly when he held power in the 1970s. In 1965, Prince Monireth wrote that he had "unlimited ambition." Sihanouk, a cynical man, underestimated this trait and interpreted Lon Nol's silence as evidence of vacuity or devotion.

In 1988, however, Sihanouk claimed to have noted long before that Lon Nol was a man "capable, one day, of leading my government and my army," adding that his "lack of 'flamboyance', his popularity with the *sangha,* in the army, and among non-Communist youth also made him an attractive candidate for high office."[79]

By allowing him to head the government, Sihanouk may have hoped to placate the pro-Western Cambodian elite. Perhaps he thought that it was time to bring the army into power and to frighten dissidents on the left. If Lon Nol faltered or behaved rashly, other Sihanouk loyalists such as Nhiek Tioulong, Son Sann, and Penn Nouth could be called in. The countergovernment and Sihanouk's power of dissolving the assembly were other factors strengthening his hand. Sihanouk's choice of Lon Nol contained elements of expediency, cynicism, and flair but little perceptible risk.[80]

One problem with treating 1966–67 as a turning point in Cambodian history, as it now appears to have been, is that so few people noticed at the time that a crossroads had been reached. Most people seem to have thought that Sihanouk would continue directing *Cambodia* and acting the male lead for many years. In the seventies, to be sure, CPK documents claimed that the party had correctly predicted events in the sixties. Evidence of this clairvoyance is lacking. The central committee's decision at the end of 1966 to move its headquarters from Office 100 in northern Kompong Cham into the sparsely inhabited hills of Ratanakiri—a journey of several weeks on foot—does not suggest increasing self-confidence or eagerness to oversee an armed insurrection, but rather that the leaders believed they needed more time to think and be in hiding. The move may have been made on Vietnamese advice. In any case, the national revolution they hoped for and were dreaming of was several years away.

1. Norodom Sihanouk and Charles de Gaulle, Phnom Penh, 1966.

2. Crowd welcoming General de Gaulle, Phnom Penh, 1966.

3. Execution of Khmer Serei prisoner, 1964.

4. Prince Sihanouk deposed. Graffito in Phnom Penh, September 1970.

5. A Cambodian patriot attacks a Vietnamese who is trying to saw off Cambodian territory. Poster, Phnom Penh, 1971.

6. Norodom Sihanouk at Banteai Serei, 1973.

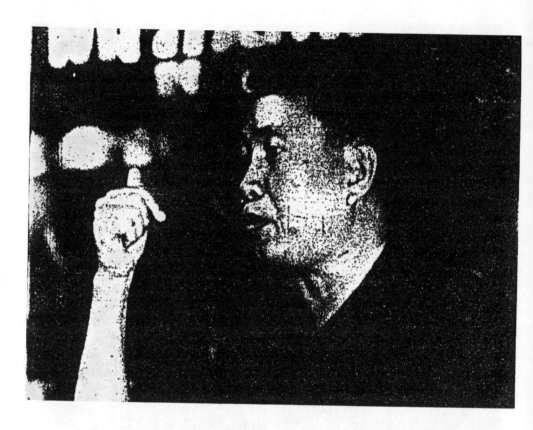

7. Saloth Sar (Pol Pot), 1978 (photographs of Saloth Sar are not readily available).

8. Norodom Sihanouk, Paris, 1979.

9. DK cadre in Thailand.

10. Excavated DK execution ground, Kompong Speu, 1979.

five

Changing the Rules,
1967–1969

Tensions among Cambodia's political factions broke into the open with the Samlaut rebellion in north-western Cambodia in early 1967. For the next three years Sihanouk, the urban elite, and the Cambodian left were engaged in mortal combat. Broadly, this period can be seen in terms of the left's ascendancy, the urban elite's increasing restlessness, and Sihanouk's decline.

Between 1967 and the beginning of 1970 the left and pro-Western segments of the Phnom Penh elite overran and usurped Sihanouk's political position and dissipated his hegemony. By 1969, if not before, educated people under thirty had deserted Sihanouk en masse, and many of them made a point of turning off their radios when he began to speak. More ominously, several thousand peasants, teachers, and students had left their homes by then to join the Communist-led resistance. To maintain control, Sihanouk called on a time-honored repertoire of tactics, but much of his magic had evaporated, and he found himself almost without support.[1]

Right up to the coup d'état the journals in Cambodia took a pro-Sihanouk, anti-American line, but spokesmen for a left-wing alliance with the prince against the United States and a united front against the right fell out of favor. By the middle of 1967, Hou Youn, Hu Nim, and Khieu Samphan had joined their superiors in the CPK in the maquis. When Sihanouk cracked down on allegedly Maoist opposition, hundreds of young people and intellectuals followed the three ghosts, as they were called, into the forest.

Gaps also opened up in this period between Cambodia's rich and poor and between the cities and the countryside. Government expenditures increased, but agricultural exports faltered. The population kept increasing, but rice yields stayed the same, and tens of thousands of people flocked to the cities to work for wages that may be regarded as derisory. In several districts bordering Vietnam, day-to-day administration by 1968 was often in the hands of North Vietnamese and NLF cadre, who extracted taxes from local people but balanced this by purchasing rice and other products at inflated prices. This process sapped the government's ability to rule. Between 1967 and 1969, indeed, Cambodia's economy as well as its political control showed signs of breaking down.[2]

In rural areas, hardships associated with economic mismanagement, chronic indebtedness, and unemployment were readily blamed by local Communists on Sihanouk's rule and on local members of the elite. By 1968, when armed struggle against his regime broke out, Sihanouk had become the CPK's Enemy Number 1. In the process, policy differences emerged between the CPK and the Vietnamese Communists, who had urged cooperation with the prince because of his support for their insurgency.[3]

In the towns, young men and women graduating from schools and universities were often unable to find appropriate jobs. Unwilling to return to rural life or to make a stab at commerce, they lingered in Phnom Penh and looked for scapegoats. The prince and his family came easily to mind. So did high-ranking, corrupt officials, who sat in "golden chairs" *(kau-ei meas)*. For positive role models, many young people turned to the three ghosts and occasionally to radical politics. This drift to the left, among Sino-Khmers especially, was inspired at a distance by the Cultural Revolution and perhaps by the student uprisings against de Gaulle's government in Paris in May 1968.[4]

In the meantime, Sihanouk's insistence on monopolizing political life alienated many Cambodians who felt themselves increasingly capable of articulating their own ideas. As they drew away from the prince, some came to admire Lon Nol and what they saw as his implacable opposition to the Vietnamese Communists, whose presence in Cambodia came to be seen as an unwarranted invasion. Part of this hostility sprang from the fact that most NLF in Cambodia units were replaced in mid-1968 following the Tet offensive by regular army units from North Vietnam. These men were more recognizably aliens on Cambodian soil and often behaved more abrasively toward local people.[5]

Chaotic conditions in China, the escalating Vietnam war, insurgency in Cambodia, and a financial crisis traceable in part to the absence of American aid led Sihanouk in 1968 to consider renewing diplomatic relations with the United States. The resumption of relations the following year was a reversal (many would say a betrayal) of his foreign policy and provided a tactical opening to supporters of Lon Nol, who had opposed breaking with America in the first place. Some of these men took up cabinet positions in 1969 and formed what Sihanouk despairingly called a Government of National Salvation. At that stage, if not before, Sihanouk had become merely a constitutional chief of state.

Later on, Sihanouk often interpreted the late 1960s in terms of pressures from outside Cambodia, treason, and betrayal. His assessment is correct insofar as he would probably never have been overthrown without the Vietnam war. For those who betrayed him, however, the period afforded unprecedented opportunities to seize the initiative, to destroy their opponents, and to reshape Cambodian society. Many Cambodian students in Paris, for example, guided by Thiounn Mumm and other longterm residents, watched Sihanouk's decline, the events of May 1968, and the apotheosis of Maoism in China approvingly or with fascination. To some of them a worldwide revolution in which they themselves were active performers seemed a real possibility. The world's future and Cambodia's potentialities seemed to be opening up before their eyes.

The Political Crisis, January–March 1967

By the end of 1966 Sihanouk had regained momentum. As usual, his tactics were eclectic. Using his countergovernment and his domination of the media, he appealed to the people over the heads of their elected representatives, informing them that they were neither right nor left but, like him, "socialists following the Buddha." As for himself, he told monks at a Buddhist congress convened at this time, "I am neither a Khmer Serei or a Khmer Red. I am pure Khmer."[6]

In mid-January 1967, the prince went to France, where he underwent medical treatment. He was gone for a month and a half. While he was away, *Phnom Penh Presse* featured wire service stories about the rise of General Suharto in Indonesia and the accompanying decline of Sukarno. The replacement of an erratic "father of independence" by a hardheaded, developmentally oriented military man was too good a story for this mildly anti-Sihanouk journal to miss. The parallels, although inexact, were not lost on Sihanouk, the Cambodian intelligentsia, the officer corps, or Lon Nol.

At the same time, the massacre of more than five hundred thousand suspected Communists in Java and Bali by enraged civilians and Indonesian armed forces in 1965–66 intensified pressures inside the CPK to abandon any pretense of collaboration with Sihanouk—who, like Sukarno vis-à-vis the Indonesian Communists, could offer them no real protection. Events in Indonesia encouraged prudence on the part of some members of the CPK and led others in the party to consider launching an armed struggle preemptively against the government.[7]

While Sihanouk was still in France, government agents fanned out into the countryside to explain a new policy of purchasing rice from farmers directly in order to avoid sales going to middlemen or to the insurgents in Vietnam. The scheme was part of the nationalization of exports that had taken effect in 1963 and reflected the government's nervousness about losses of revenue. In the campaign of 1967, soldiers entrusted with obtaining deliveries often acted brutally, molesting women, and stealing movable property. As if to countenance this behavior, Lon Nol's cabinet officers and the general himself toured the provinces to explain the policy. They drew large crowds—probably many of the same people who would have turned out for a Sihanouk tour—and made the point that the government was larger than Sihanouk, who was still abroad. In contrast, when Sihanouk was home, cabinet ministers seldom went on tour and got almost no coverage in the press.[8]

The expropriation policy was difficult to sell to people who were being offered lower prices for their harvests than they could earn on the black market, but Lon Nol's tours of Battambang probably encouraged his subordinates to be rapacious with local people. In February and March, opponents of the policy began distributing antigovernment tracts throughout the country. It was at this stage that a young monk in Phnom Penh, Hun Sen, left his monastery and joined the resistance. Thirteen years later he would be the prime minister of the PRK.[9]

By the beginning of March, government spokesmen claimed to have amassed over one hundred thousand tons of rice in the northwest. Soon afterward, antigovernment incidents (not yet of revolutionary dimensions, however) broke out, and Jacques Decornoy of *Le Monde* wrote that a peasant uprising (*jacquerie*) was occurring in the northwest. Before returning to Cambodia, Sihanouk fired off a letter to *Le Monde* stating that "the rebellion in Battambang is essentially political and is run by foreigners."[10]

In the meantime, while inspecting military installations in Koh Kong, Lon Nol's jeep overturned, and the general was taken to the hospital in Phnom Penh. The accident occurred shortly before the prince was scheduled to return. Soon after Sihanouk's arrival but without his blessing leftist students demonstrated in the capital against Lon Nol. Their tracts and banners demanded the dissolution of the government, reductions in prices, a new assembly election, and the withdrawal of government forces from "the vicinity of Pailin" in Battambang.

Sihanouk found the demands impossible to meet, although he declared that Cambodia "must evolve toward the left, from right to left" and that had he not been born a prince he would probably be "on the left" himself. Had he chosen the government, he said, he would have selected "an entirely different team." To calm the demonstrators, he placed their demands on the agenda of a special national congress. He invited them to come to the congress and put their case, presuming that they would be too frightened of the police to do so.[11]

The prince was correct. The special congress voted to keep the National Assembly in office, but Khieu Samphan used the occasion to complain that some of his constituents in S'aang were being forced to serve as militia on the Vietnamese frontier unless they paid bribes to local officials. Attacks on corruption were often coded attacks on Sihanouk's rule, and the prince interpreted Samphan's remarks in this fashion. His riposte was to offer to visit S'aang to verify the charges on the following day.[12]

In S'aang, he attacked Samphan's assembly colleague Hu Nim as a Red and offered the electorate a million riels (approximately US $18,000) as "a gift from the national bank" to repair a nearby road. He refused to arm local militia forces because his government was broke and because he did not want to antagonize the two million troops—Thai, South Vietnamese, insurgent, and U.S.—who were surrounding Cambodia. He also claimed that he was the Red Khmers' Enemy Number One. It was a bravura performance, but during Samphan's speech introducing him, Sihanouk noted that the deputy had raised his voice and addressed his monarch face to face. A few days later, Samphan told Charles Meyer that he feared for his life. Within a month, he left Phnom Penh for the maquis.[13]

The Samlaut Rebellion

Between March and May 1967, an antigovernment rebellion broke out and ran its course in the vicinity of Samlaut in western Battambang. By the end of the year the localized uprising had developed into a civil war in many parts of the country. The questions to ask about the rebellion have to do with the extent of centralized CPK control and whether a split between Maoist and pro-Vietnamese wings of the Cambodian radical movement, so evident later, was operative at this stage.[14]

The subdistrict of Samlaut lies less than fifteen miles southwest of Battambang city and ten miles from the Thai frontier. During the first Indochina war, the forested, inaccessible region had provided shelter for Viet Minh and Issarak bands. Sihanouk's Operation Sammaki had passed through it, and the region had attracted the prince's attention for its agricultural potential. After independence it was chosen as one area where landless peasants from the southwest and Cambodian refugees from South Vietnam could be resettled. Several hundred of these people had been brought into the area in 1965–66. The newcomers enjoyed small government subsidies and often incurred the resentment of local people. In the nearby district of Andoeuk Hep, where a cotton cultivation boom (linked to the opening of a textile factory in Battambang) led to a doubling of the population in 1964–66, many local proprietors were driven from the land as it was bought up by merchants and officials. The cotton crop of 1966 was poor, and farmers were heavily in debt.[15]

The government's campaign to buy up rice in Battambang at deflated prices also made local people angry. The historian Hin Sithan has cited the testimony of a former village clerk who witnessed the surrender of several so-called rebels in April 1967: "At that time, a group of people surrendering at Samlaut with a captured rifle stated that their group was not Red Khmer, but that they had run off into the forest because they were furious with provincial officials who, allied with local capitalists, had robbed local people of their land."[16]

The government's incursions had also included harassment of Issarak veterans. The mention of Pailin in the demonstration in Phnom Penh suggests that Lon Nol's activities had come to the CPK's attention. An operational link between Communists in Samlaut and Phnom Penh was provided by central committee member Nuon Chea, who had been born and raised in Battambang and had enjoyed ties with Issarak and Viet Minh forces in the region in the 1950s. In early 1967, he was in hiding in Phnom Penh but visited Battambang from time to time.[17]

On April 2, 1967, two hundred local inhabitants bearing antigovernment banners and armed with knives and homemade weapons attacked a JSRK camp at Stung Kranhung in the Samlaut region. The rebels killed two soldiers and captured their rifles. The campers, who had been clearing the area to plant crops, fled, and their camp was burned down. Later in the day, two other guard posts were attacked, additional rifles were captured, and a local official was killed. By nightfall, according to Sihanouk, the rebels had seized "thirteen rifles belonging to the nation." Skirmishing continued for two days until fresh troops arrived, restored order, and rounded up some local suspects. In the meantime, some two thousand men, women, and children had fled or been herded into the forest. Some found refuge in an old Issarak base area, more recently favored by the CPK, in Phnom Vay Chap. By the middle of May, eight battalions of regular soldiers had been dispatched to the area, and militia units of enthusiastic vigilantes had been recruited in Battambang, armed with staves, and told to go into the region to "hunt the Reds"—including the people who had fled from their villages for their lives.[18]

In a message to the nation Sihanouk correctly perceived the uprising as being leftist harassment of Lon Nol and local radicals' impatience with newcomers in their "Red Khmer land and fields." In his peroration, he lashed out at the "Khmer Viet Minh," who owed allegiance, as captives had suggested, to an unnamed great chief. "I do not know," Sihanouk said, "whether this great chief is a foreigner or a Khmer in Phnom Penh. [The captives] said they were acting on the orders of their great chief [in] the struggle against national forces. This means they can only stop when their great chief orders them to do so. If their big chief does not give the order, they will definitely not stop their attacks against us."

As he did the Khmer Serei, Sihanouk saw the Samlaut uprising primarily as a personal insult and cited captives who referred to him as "that fellow Sihanouk" (*a-Sihanouk*) rather than use his honorific form of address. In retaliation for this, he said, he had ordered the offenders' villages razed and renamed. The number of casualties, never announced, probably ran into the hundreds. Donald Lancaster has written of bounties paid to anyone who could produce a rebel's severed head.[19]

On April 7 Sihanouk declared that he might "treat the Khmer Reds as I have treated the Khmer Serei." He was referring not to the repression in Battambang, which was proceeding unchecked, but to the possible execution of such leftist personalities as Hou Youn, Hu Nim, and Khieu Samphan. To drive this point home, three Khmer Serei agents were publicly executed, and films of the executions were shown throughout the country.[20]

Charles Meyer has recalled pleading with Sihanouk at this time to delay repressive action against Samlaut until a thorough investigation of the uprising had been completed. Sihanouk preferred to barge ahead. In 1971, he remarked offhandedly, "I've *read somewhere* that these confrontations caused ten thousand deaths" (emphasis added). By 1987, however, his estimate of casualties had fallen to fewer than one hundred.

Sihanouk also threatened to hale Khieu Samphan and Hou Youn before a military tribunal to answer questions. Fearing for their lives, both men slipped away from the city before long, and when their disappearance was acknowledged it was widely assumed in Phnom Penh that they had been killed.[21]

In the backwash of these events, Lon Nol resigned as prime minister. He pleaded ill health and departed to seek medical treatment in France. He was to be gone for six months. Sihanouk took over as president of what he called an Exceptional Government, saying that he had to "grasp the helm to save the nation." In effect, this meant the dissolution of the government put into power by Lon Nol. The new cabinet Sihanouk appointed included three leftists, some cronies, and a few apolitical technicians like Kol Touch, who was named to the now-sensitive position of minister of agriculture. It contained no assembly deputies. According to the prince, the government had three tasks: "to end the political crisis and the rebellion in Battambang; to solve the disorders of administration; and to find a solution for the problem of the budgetary deficit." The second and third tasks, insoluble because of Sihanouk's style of rule, were hardly new.[22]

The Samlaut uprising sprang from local grievances against injustice and social change, corruption, and ham-fisted government behavior. Leftist teachers and students from Battambang city undoubtedly encouraged people to blame their troubles on feudalism, Lon Nol, and the United States and probably helped them prepare their banners for Stung Kranhung, but these criticisms, easy enough to make, did not respond to orders from the CPK central committee to attack Sihanouk's government directly.[23]

Pol Pot's history of the CPK, published ten years later, plays down the party's role in the affair while praising the revolutionary zeal of the participants:

In 1967, revolutionary violence reached a high level. It was in this ripening revolutionary situation that an armed uprising broke out in 1967 in Samlaut. . . . *This was set off by the people through their own movement. The Party Central Committee had not yet decided on general armed insurrection throughout the country.* In Battambang . . . the movement of peasants . . . had reached the boiling point. But the Party was there to give leadership to the movement and decided to suspend temporarily the armed struggle in Battambang until the whole country could complete its preparations [emphasis added].[24]

The decision to "suspend . . . armed struggle" was an admission of defeat. Whatever the CPK had in mind for Cambodia in 1967, the Samlaut uprising proved that armed struggle was not yet a viable option, although it provided a model and a precedent for later attacks, and the government's harsh response likely made it easier for the CPK to recruit adherents in the area at that time.[25]

Factional Politics, 1967–1968

When the uprising died down in late May, Sihanouk visited Samlaut, and in a speech there he lambasted the so-called Red Khmers and announced a massive program of government aid, resettlement, and rehabilitation. As he spoke, scattered fighting continued between government troops and supposed insurgents, many of whom were probably villagers who had fled into the forest.[26]

Pressure against Sihanouk from the pro-Western segments of the elite eased with Lon Nol's departure and the removal of his supporters Mau Say and Douc Rasy from the cabinet. With the right thus neutralized, Sihanouk wheeled against the urban left, particularly against radicalized high school students.[27]

In the province of Kandal, more than fifteen thousand students had reportedly gathered at various monasteries to mourn what they called the martyrdom of Hou Youn and Khieu Samphan. Similar demonstrations occurred in Kompong Cham. Angered by them, the prince requested the principals of Kambuj'bot and Chamraon Vichea to find some "red excellency" who could lead a homogenous government. Under pressure from the prince, Hu Nim contended at a national congress that he was loyal to Sihanouk and that anti-Sangkum tracts discovered in Samlaut and elsewhere had been planted by Lon Nol's agents. Sihanouk found these assertions cowardly and found the courage to attack Hu Nim at a moment when the deputy was outnumbered by several thousand to one.

Sihanouk's anti-Communist speeches formed a smoke screen for the secret negotiations that his new prime minister, Son Sann, was carrying out with representatives of North Vietnam and their South Vietnamese surrogates, the NLF. For several months Sihanouk had been pressing the

Viet Minh and the Viet Cong, as he labeled the two, for a formal, public recognition of Cambodia's existing frontiers, in exchange for formally allowing unspecified numbers of their troops to continue to take shelter in Cambodia; in addition, overland passage and landing rights for military supplies at Sihanoukville were to be granted. Sihanouk was not conceding anything by this proposal because for at least the past three years the Communists had been preemptively exercising these rights and privileges without his sanction, and Sihanouk sought recognition of Cambodia's frontiers as a quid pro quo. The Vietnamese delegates, for their part, had been unwilling to make any commitments about the frontiers, probably because they felt that the prince, hoping to tie their hands when the war was over, would publicize them. This was undoubtedly what Sihanouk had in mind. In May 1967, however, the Vietnamese softened their negotiating stance after a U.S.–South Vietnamese military exercise known as Operation Cedar Falls had driven the Central Office of South Vietnam (COSVN)—the party headquarters in the south—out of Vietnam and into Cambodia, where it remained until the early 1970s.[28]

The upshot of the negotiations was that in exchange for statements from the NLF that it would recognize and respect Cambodia's existing frontiers, the front received quasi-diplomatic recognition, which was important both to its war effort and to the image of political independence from North Vietnam that it promoted. The Soviet Union and North Vietnam soon produced similar statements about Cambodia's borders. These were followed by a declaration from China.[29]

In pushing for these arrangements, Sihanouk accepted the risk of further alienating the pro-Western elite, perhaps because he felt that the Communists would win in Vietnam. For the time being, he fell back on the hope that the Vietnamese, after so much favored treatment, would keep their promises to him and be courteous. "Concerning the Viet Cong [NLF] and the Viet Minh [North Vietnamese] who are struggling against the imperialists," he said, "we have helped them in all aspects. . . . Now they must show their gratitude."[30]

In the same speech, Sihanouk declared the Samlaut uprising officially over. He expected that his concessions to the Vietnamese would lead to their calling off the insurgents, whom he assumed that they controlled.[31]

Fresh from what he perceived as his diplomatic triumphs, Sihanouk faced a new outbreak of factionalism in Phnom Penh. Remnants of the intellectual left had rallied around Chau Seng—now back in the cabinet—and *La Nouvelle Dépêche.* Whereas the left had often been able to dominate the French-language media in Phnom Penh, by mid-1967 they found themselves criticized by Sim Var, whose Khmer-language paper *Khmer Ekkaraj* (Independent Khmer) took an antileftist line. Banking on Sihanouk's support, the left decided to strike back.

Hu Nim opened the campaign by writing in *La Nouvelle Dépêche* that Sihanouk presided over a "national front which responds exactly to the aspirations of the people." The phraseology may have alarmed the prince, but following further taunts from *Khmer Ekkaraj*, hundreds of young Cambodians stormed through the editorial offices of the paper and destroyed its printing plant. Damage was extensive, but there were no casualties and no arrests. Graffiti scrawled inside the building included "Sim Var is a Dog," "Sim Var is an American Dog," and (in Chinese) "Long Live Prince Papa." Interestingly, a photograph of Sihanouk hanging on the wall of the office was first reported torn and later undisturbed. The same report noted that many of the participants had been ethnic Chinese, reportedly angered by Sim Var's denigration of their devotion to Chairman Mao. The rampage served Sihanouk's purposes, and the cabinet's investigation of the incident produced a report that contained no expressions of regret.[32]

Nonetheless, the sight of rioting Sino-Khmers in Phnom Penh who were mesmerized by the Cultural Revolution and were declaring themselves loyal to Mao was distressing to Sihanouk, who based much of his foreign policy on his personal alliance with China. He was also worried that Khmer leftists openly supported the Khmer-Chinese Friendship Association, which was active in the Chinese-language schools in praising Mao Zedong. He was angered, finally, when journals in China reported to their readers that "all Cambodian workers" believed in Chairman Mao.[33]

Resorting to a well-worn tactic, Sihanouk threatened to turn over the government to "the pro-Chinese Reds." Speaking at the national congress, he said, "If I refuse to hand over to them, I shall agree to being beaten by them, even beheaded by them under that flagstaff which is in front of me. I will agree to do anything, and I will not resent transferring power to them."

No one stepped forward, but shortly thereafter Sihanouk sent his foreign minister, Prince Norodom Phurissara, to Beijing to sound out Chinese attitudes. Zhou Enlai made soothing remarks but noted that Chinese should "be permitted to display their pride of the cultural revolution and their love for Chairman Mao."[34]

Sihanouk stepped up his attacks on urban radicals in the second half of the year while trying to wean away potential rebels in the countryside with assistance. He poured money into public works projects in Khieu Samphan's electorate and into road building and housing in Samlaut, and he promised to pay 10,000 riels (about US $200) to every Red Khmer from the northwest who rallied to him. In August, two hundred ostensible ralliers from Samlaut were brought to Phnom Penh at his expense and given tours of Sihanoukville and Angkor at his expense before being returned home, but "when everything was settled," he noted later, "they went back to the Khmer Reds again."[35]

In early September, Sihanouk closed down the Khmer-Chinese Friendship Association along with all other binational friendship societies. When Chau Seng's *Nouvelle Dépêche*, three days later, tactlessly printed a telegram from Beijing sending the defunct organization "militant greetings" on its anniversary and praising its struggle against reactionaries, Sihanouk called the statement "the first attack by China" and decided to close Cambodia's private newspapers. He targeted the Chinese-language ones but also shut down several Khmer papers supportive of the Sangkum. This left the field to the four journals that he himself edited and to the daily report of the government news agency, Agence Khmere de Presse (AKP). He suggested that a subsequent referendum, to be held in early 1968, "when the people are no longer busy with farming," might legitimize his action. The referendum never took place, but the private newspapers were allowed to reopen at the end of the year.[36]

In a speech he gave at this time, Sihanouk blamed the crisis on events in China and went on to say, "This does not mean that we fear the communists, but if one wants Cambodia to become communist, the Khmer people must be able to do it themselves. I would have no objection. But if . . . Mao Zedong's thought is used to prepare Khmer communism, that is unacceptable. . . . Today people become national communists in each country. . . . How can Cambodia alone become a lackey of China? If we ever turned communist, we would prefer Khmer communism."[37]

By this point the prince was beginning to conceive of an authentically Khmer Communist movement, separable from foreign control and made up of men and women who were dedicated to bringing him down and to destroying his vision of Cambodian society. This partial realization must have unnerved him, and as he thought about it the silence of Khieu Samphan and Hou Youn was ominous. Where were they? he wondered. What were they doing?

Another target for his obsessions was Hu Nim, who lingered in the

National Assembly. When Nim submitted a petition from some constituents asking that the Khmer-Chinese Friendship Association be reinstated, Sihanouk, accompanied by Kou Roun, the chief of the political police, stormed down to his electorate in Kompong Cham. In Hu Nim's presence he threatened him with a trial by military tribunal. As Kou Roun looked on, Sihanouk told Hu Nim, "You are no longer a Cambodian. You have completely betrayed the people by using the people to oppose your state and nation. This is treason."[38]

Time had run out for Hu Nim. A couple of days later, he fled to a CPK base in the Cardamom Mountains. Several other urban intellectuals, feeling threatened by Sihanouk's belligerence, also left the city in 1966–67. They included Tiv Ol, Koy Thuon, Touch Rin, and Khek Pen. All of them went on to play active roles in DK before being purged by the party in 1977. Hu Nim's young colleague Phouk Chhay was arrested two days later and threatened with a death sentence before being jailed for life.[39]

Sihanouk's vendetta reduced his freedom of maneuver vis-à-vis the pro-Western segment of the elite. Deserted by the Communists, whose support had always been linked to his foreign policies rather than to his domestic behavior, Sihanouk now found himself alone, for his animosity toward the elite, dating from the heyday of the Democratic party, had never altered, and even though they were his only feasible allies he was too proud to apologize to them. Sensing his uneasiness, the elite made no conciliatory moves.

The ongoing turbulence in China combined with the use of Cambodia by Vietnamese Communist forces meant that the prince, surrounded by pro-Western regimes in Bangkok and Saigon, was now encircled by Communists as well. None of his strategies for earning their gratitude had been effective, but he distrusted those who wanted to distance themselves from the Communists and resume relations with the United States. To preempt this group he began to edge toward rapprochement with the United States on his own terms. These included playing host to an unofficial visit by Jacqueline Bouvier Kennedy in October 1967.[40]

The Bowles Mission and CPK Armed Struggle

Two events that occurred in January 1968—just before the Tet offensive in Vietnam—had important effects on the remaining years of Sihanouk's regime. One was the CPK's decision to embark on armed struggle. The other was the visit of Chester Bowles, the U.S. ambassador to New Delhi and the highest-ranking American to meet with Sihanouk for several years. The party's decision meant that until the beginning of 1970, Cambodia's armed forces were engaged simultaneously in providing support for the NLF and North Vietnamese and in fighting local Communist guerrillas, themselves supported, Sihanouk thought, by the Vietnamese Communists.

Bowles's visit laid the groundwork for the resumption of U.S.–Cambodian relations. From an American perspective, it was important because an off-the-cuff remark by Sihanouk to Bowles was later used by Henry Kissinger to justify the U.S. bombing of Cambodia, which began in 1969 and was kept concealed from the American people. From a Cambodian perspective, the visit was important because it forestalled U.S. military plans put together in 1967–68 to invade Vietnamese sanctuaries in Cambodia.[41]

Sihanouk had been toying for some time with the idea of revitalizing the ICSC, which had been set up following the Geneva conference and had remained in Cambodia ever since, with vestigial responsibilities. He hoped that inspections by ICSC teams composed of Indian, Canadian, and Polish members would reduce U.S.–South Vietnamese incursions and bombing raids. The United States supported Sihanouk's proposals because it felt that the teams could confirm and publicize the presence of Vietnamese bases on Cambodian soil. These had been recorded by aerial photographs and by clandestine U.S. intelligence teams. Toward the end of 1967, under a program entitled Operation Vesuvius, the United States had begun to transmit copies of this photographic evidence to Sihanouk via the Australian ambassador in Phnom Penh, Noel Deschamps. From a strategic point of view, U.S. military leaders were eager to neutralize South Vietnam's southwestern flank. To discuss these issues—as well as to benefit from the good will generated by Mrs. Kennedy's visit—Bowles came to Cambodia for four days in January 1968.[42]

The mission began with separate conversations Bowles had with Prime Minister Son Sann and Gen. Nhiek Tioulong. The prince was outside the capital when the delegation arrived, and Son Sann was reluctant to foreshadow anything Sihanouk might say on his return. Nhiek Tioulong told the delegation that the Vietnamese had no sanctuaries in Cambodia at all.[43]

The delegation saw Sihanouk the following day. They found him "undaunted and unresponsive," pleading merely for an invigorated ICSC until, as the delegation's report phrased it, "in one of his amazing reversals": "The Prince said that he would not object if the U.S. engaged in 'hot pursuit' in unpopulated areas. He could not say this publicly or officially, but if the U.S. followed this course it would help him solve his own problem. Of course, if the U.S. engaged VC/NVA forces on Cambodian territory, both sides would be guilty of violating Cambodian soil, but the VC/NVA 'would be more guilty' (sic). If we pursued VC forces into remote areas where the population would be unaffected he would 'shut his eyes.'"[44]

Nothing of this appeared in the communiqué released by Son Sann and Bowles at the end of the visit, but the passage has been cited to show that Sihanouk gave permission to the United States to bomb the border areas systematically with B-52s beginning in 1969.

The record fails to clarify what Sihanouk was allowing America to do. To Sihanouk, the issue of hot pursuit was less important than gaining the good graces of the United States, but it would be difficult to confuse his statement with permission to conduct a full-scale program of bombing.

Sihanouk's priorities were modest Cambodian ones, later cut to fit America's grand designs. Son Sann urged Bowles to argue in Washington for a resumption of diplomatic relations and for an American pledge to honor Cambodia's frontiers. Both moves were stalled for almost a year by Thai and Vietnamese reluctance to make similar pledges and by U.S. reluctance to displease them.[45]

Bowles's visit coincided with a Vietnamese Communist buildup in eastern Cambodia for the Tet offensive. Intelligence reports reaching the prince also told of renewed insurgency in the Samlaut region and of unrest in tribal areas in the northeast—two areas where the CPK, which inaugurated a policy of armed struggle about this time, were active.[46]

Soon after Bowles's departure but before the Tet offensive, Sihanouk announced that several young Communists had been arrested in Phnom Penh for distributing tracts attacking the Yugoslavian chief of state, Marshal Tito, soon to arrive on a state visit. Tito's independence inside the Communist movement had angered the Chinese. It is possible but unlikely that Chinese Communists plotted to assassinate him during his visit. Instead, Sihanouk's police probably invented the assassination plot so as to crack down on pro-Chinese students who might have demonstrated against Tito and embarrassed the prince. Sihanouk spoke of a "handful of individuals, excluded from the community, sabotaging national independence," adding that "they distributed cases of grenades to assassinate Tito and myself." Capital punishment awaited those who had distributed the tracts, he said. Tito's visit was uneventful, but those accused (later referred to dismissively as "four Chinese") had already been shot, and no evidence of their conspiracy was ever published.

Ominous reports were reaching the prince in early 1969 of fighting between insurgents and government troops in several parts of the country. This fighting was especially severe in Battambang. Nine years later, Pol Pot asserted that the CPK had "launched armed struggle" in Battambang at the beginning of 1968. There was no public announcement at the time. By the end of February, unaware of the CPK decision, if there was one, Sihanouk was already referring to the fighting as a civil war.

The insurgency was marked by sharp regional variations. The eastern zone of the country, where an insurgency might have impeded Vietnamese preparations for the Tet offensive, was slower to take up arms than elsewhere. This reluctance may reflect the continuing Vietnamese influence over the CPK in that region. The Vietnamese were unwilling to jeopardize their shelter areas by allowing the Cambodians to take on Lon Nol's armed forces and invite reprisals. The entire region, particularly north of Kompong Cham, was crowded in early 1968 with Red Khmers and Vietnamese Communist forces.[47]

In Battambang and Ratanakiri, forces affiliated with the CPK were more militant. In Battambang, Lon Nol's troops pursued remnants of the Samlaut rebels. In scattered clashes the rebels inflicted casualties and captured weapons. This led to increased repression and spiraling violence on both sides. In the northeast, complaints by minority people and military action against them also led to clashes.[48]

In February 1968, an uprising broke out in Ratanakiri among the Brao people; it was centered in a village that was close to the CPK headquarters at the time. The Brao resented government intrusions into their region: some of them had been forced off their lands by people resettled from the south, and others had been displaced by a government-owned rubber plantation. Their complaints and their response to pressure resembled those of people in Samlaut in 1967. In the course of the month, the Brao killed several ethnic Khmer, and with Sihanouk scheduled to visit the region soon, the reaction of government troops was vigorous and harsh.[49]

Some of these forces passed close to the central committee's hiding place. As Bu Phat, then a minor party official, stated in his confession in 1978, "Around February 1968 Brother Number One [Saloth Sar] convened the very first military branch [cell] training. I joined in this branch myself but Brother Number One had just presented the program of study when the soldiers of the contemptible Lon Nol came out on one of their rampages . . . capturing the guns of the couriers assigned to protect . . . the military school."

According to Pol Pot's speech of 1977, this near-disaster came a month after the party had launched armed struggle at Bay Domram in the north-west, an event later celebrated as the first engagement of the Cambodian revolutionary army. By the end of March 1968, he said, "it was the turn of the Northeast Zone for an uprising. *Four or five guns were captured.* Added to the three or four previously used to defend the headquarters of the Party's Central Committee, we had a total of *10 guns for the entire zone*" (emphasis added).[50]

In 1977, Pol Pot wanted to demonstrate how the CPK had come from capturing a few guns in 1968 to assuming state power just seven years later. In doing so he revealed how weak the party had been in 1968.

Fighting continued in the northwest for the rest of the year, but the CPK central committee remained far away in a province frequently tra-versed, as Battambang was not, by Vietnamese Communist troops. Viet-namese protection was probably a motive in choosing the region (or of the Vietnamese in choosing it for them) as a hiding place. The Vietnamese, for their part, wanted peaceable, sympathetic inhabitants—as well as laborers—along their trails leading into the south. As time went on, CPK cadre worked hard to recruit followers and raise the consciousness of tribal people in the northeast. These efforts were crucial in the evolving ideology of DK, for the CPK cadre, largely urban in background, were deeply impressed by the tribespeople's survival skills, their obedience to their leaders, and their prowess as warriors and hunters.[51]

Pol Pot and Ieng Sary also claimed later to have been inspired by the spirit of people who had no private property, no markets, and no money. Their way of life and their means of production corresponded to the primitive communist phase of social evolution in Marxist thinking. More-over, these men and women were, in Maoist terms, "poor and blank" receptacles for revolutionary doctrine. In 1968–70 hundreds of tribal peo-ple from Ratanakiri, especially ethnic Tapuon and Jarai, were recruited into CPK units. In 1971, when he arrived in Beijing after eight years in the forest, Ieng Sary said that these people "may be naked, but they have never been colonized." Lecturing in Phnom Penh in 1976, he remarked that tribal people were particularly "faithful to the revolution, not com-mercially oriented, and . . . had class hatred." After 1975, many of these people were employed as cadre, as messengers for party leaders, and as bodyguards.[52]

By the end of 1968, large areas of the northeast had passed out of government control. The development of these liberated zones inspired programs of Vietnamese political indoctrination. A Vietnamese document captured in 1969 gives details of cooperation between their forces and friendly Cambodians in the region, which suggests that Vietnamese Communist attitudes toward armed struggle in Cambodia varied in proportion to the pressure placed on the Vietnamese by Cambodian government forces. Where this was strong, as in the northeast, local guerrillas were encouraged to respond in kind, while the Vietnamese refrained from making direct attacks.[53]

Kiernan has argued that by embarking on armed struggle the CPK put itself at odds with Vietnamese policies of placating Sihanouk and encouraging the Cambodians to limit themselves to "political struggle" (known in Vietnamese as *doi tran*). It could also be argued, however, that the Vietnamese saw the decision as a means of tying down Cambodian government forces while the Vietnamese prepared for the Tet offensive. The fact that the places chosen for armed struggle, particularly in the northwest, were far removed from the zones from which the offensive was launched supports this argument.[54]

Unrest in Battambang caused Sihanouk special concern—perhaps because Vietnamese involvement there was so difficult to discern. At first, he praised the guerrillas for their skill and swore to improve his military response along guerrilla lines, adding, "I worked out our national defense years ago. I told our instructors . . . to prepare our army chiefly for guerrilla warfare, because the classical methods cannot be applied—and the experience of Battambang bears me out entirely."[55]

Shifting his attack onto French journalists like Jacques Decornoy of *Le Monde,* who had blamed "the Army's 'suppression of the people'" for the continuing unrest, Sihanouk demanded that "pro-Chinese" journalists be "intellectually honest" and refrain from blaming the Sangkum for anything that went wrong. Sihanouk himself was eager to deflect the blame for the civil war onto foreign shoulders. He spoke of a collaboration among the Americans, the Khmer Serei, the Thai, the South Vietnamese, the Viet Cong, and the CPK—a bizarre bouillabaisse that foreshadowed DK accusations of CIA-KGB collusion with Cambodian traitors later on. At the same time, he approved intensified repression, reporting after his return to Phnom Penh that "at least 20 of those we had arrested shot, but I ask you not to tell this to the press agencies or the papers. However, I announce it . . . because the communists have waged total war . . . I have liquidated them, I have liquidated them with pleasure, and I feel no remorse. . . . It is a total war."[56]

A week later, he said, "At present, there is no need to send [rebels] to a military court. Whenever we laid hands on them, we shot them immediately [applause]. In other words, we 'roasted' them pitilessly. . . . In Battambang and Koh Kong . . . our aircraft bomb and strafe the traitors hidden in the forest."[57]

The violence of Sihanouk's speeches encouraged the militia to commit further violence and provincial officials to stage demonstrations in the prince's favor. In March 1968, in Kompong Cham, "gallant demonstrators carrying arms declared they were determined to fight in order to eliminate the Khmer Reds and Viet Minh Khmers from Cambodian territory." In neighboring Kratie, demonstrators carried side arms, axes, clubs, bows, and rifles and marched to the office of the province chief, where one of the demonstrators read "a motion of support for the throne, *samdech euv* [Papa Prince], and the Buddhist Socialist regime. The motion also condemned the Khmer Reds and Blues in a variety of terms."

In this turbulent atmosphere, Sihanouk reshuffled his cabinet, changed governors in several provinces, and toured the trouble spots, blaming foreigners and intellectuals for the renewed insurgency. At the end of March, he declared the insurgency over, but fighting continued in Battambang and in the northeast for the remainder of the year.

By that time, Sihanouk's armed forces were receiving contradictory signals. On the one hand, Cambodian military trucks continued to funnel weapons and supplies to Vietnamese camps along the border, and the officer corps continued to enrich itself in the process. Cambodian farmers, for their part, often sold their crops to Vietnamese agents or to people working on their behalf. Sihanouk continued to support the NLF and the North Vietnamese struggle against imperialism while denying the existence of their bases on Cambodian soil.

On the other hand, the army and the population were now enjoined to use arms against local insurgents, supposedly the lackeys of the North Vietnamese and the NLF. While retaining his own alliance with the Vietnamese Communists and supporting their presence in Cambodia, Sihanouk was ordering their local supporters killed and was also slowly opening a door to the United States. Presumably, by limiting his vituperation to the Red Khmers, he hoped to keep his forces and those of the Vietnamese Communists from a full-scale confrontation. The game involved many variables—and enormous risks.

In setting the variables in motion the prince apparently felt that he could turn his people's violence on and off at will. At the same time, he now viewed the insurgents as a genuine threat. An indication of that view was his allowing Lon Nol, the Communists' main enemy, to resume his duties as minister of defense in 1968.[58]

Sihanouk Loses His Grip

Once the coup of March 1970 had removed Sihanouk from office many more people said that they had seen it coming than had predicted anything of the kind in 1968 or 1969. In fact, except to the plotters themselves, the coup came as a surprise. Most observers thought that the internal pressures on Sihanouk's rule, although strong and varied, were insufficient by themselves to overthrow him.

Nonetheless, it is easy to interpret Sihanouk's conduct in his last year and a half in office as that of a man whose confidence was badly shaken. The rise of conservative rivals, armed resistance from the left, and the return to power of Lon Nol all suggest that the prince was no longer able or willing to exercise the sort of control that had marked his earlier years in power. Whether this decline was a matter of choice or was imposed by outside forces is difficult to determine.

Armed resistance was still at an early stage. The leaders of the CPK were busy gathering strength, weapons, and recruits. They were unprepared for a full-scale civil war. By conducting armed struggle on a limited scale, the party hoped to gain experience, train its cadre, and improve its revolutionary credentials, while waiting for the opening that would allow them to proceed to victory.

Hindsight is at work here, of course. Looking in the 1960s for the roots of the Communist victory in 1975 may lead us to exaggerate the military menace that the CPK posed to Sihanouk in 1968–69, when fewer than five thousand poorly armed guerrillas were scattered across the Cambodian landscape, uncertain about their strategy, tactics, loyalty, and leaders. These men and women were unsettling to the prince and undermined his notion of consensus, but they were not a genuine military threat. In spite or perhaps because of his friendships with Communist leaders, the Red Khmers offered a sustained example of lèse majesté and also killed more people than the Khmer Serei, the Pracheachon, or the Democrats had ever done. In October 1968, for example, they were responsible for twenty-five attacks in eleven provinces that claimed thirty-two lives.[59]

Evidence from 1969–70 suggests the occurrence of a shift in the balance of power away from Sihanouk and toward the forces opposing him. The shift is hard to document, for it was not marked by any events as important as the break with the United States or the Samlaut rebellion.

Sihanouk's popularity had faded among young, urbanized Cambodians, but it had by no means disappeared. His efforts to maintain it, however, seem to have become more strident in 1969. As the Vietnam war thundered on, often within people's hearing in Cambodia, more and more Cambodian schools, clinics, monasteries, factories, and even consumer products were named after the prince and members of his family. What seems like desperation, however, may have merely been Sihanouk carrying on as usual, as the male lead in his production of "Cambodia" with the sound of artillery in the wings.[60]

During the late 1960s, Sihanouk retained his habit of finessing the discussion of serious issues, especially financial ones. By the middle of 1969, however, he realized that some of these had become insoluble. His response was to name a Government of Salvation under Lon Nol as the successor to what he had called his own Last Chance Government. This was an act of abdication.

In choosing to step aside, Sihanouk was aware of several economic indicators that had ominous implications. After several years of economic growth, Cambodia's gross national product was now expanding at a lower rate (2.3 percent) than its population. Agricultural credit provided by the government was insufficient to alleviate indebtedness in rural areas, where interest payments often ran higher than a family's annual income. The money allocated to agriculture in the annual budget paid the ministry's bureaucrats but had little effect on improving crop varieties, diversifying what was grown, or increasing yields, which in much of the country remained the lowest in Southeast Asia. Yields had not improved, on a national basis, on those from the 1940s.[61]

In the crowded, impoverished provinces bordering Phnom Penh landlessness had become a serious problem. One effect was a flow of people into the capital, where underemployment went hand in hand with increased demands for services that the government was unable to provide. In the countryside, meanwhile, low levels of mechanization, poorly conceived and underfunded irrigation schemes, and grandiose resettlement programs hampered the rational development of Cambodia's agriculture.

To make things worse, exports of rubber, Cambodia's most valuable product, fell as a result of declining world prices. Harvests were also affected by U.S. defoliation bombing on both sides of the frontier and increased insecurity in the plantations themselves, where the largely Vietnamese labor force had for many years provided recruits for the Communist resistance.[62]

The development of other crops for export—pepper, kapok, cotton, and tobacco, for example—was hampered by bureaucratic lethargy and by the state monopoly of exports inaugurated in 1963, which crimped initiative and added another layer of bureaucrats to the process of selling Cambodia's goods. The key impediment to progress, however, was probably Sihanouk's lack of sustained interest in economic affairs.

Industrialization had also proceeded slowly. Inexperience, mismanagement, poor equipment, isolation from foreign markets, and shortages of raw material kept heavy industry from developing. Since 1963, industrialization had also been impeded by an unwillingness of Sihanouk's government to welcome foreign investment or to encourage businessmen to borrow money overseas. By 1969, state-operated factories constructed with Chinese and Czechoslovakian aid and manufacturing plywood, cement, tires, cotton textiles, and phosphate employed about five thousand workers. Most of these factories were poorly managed, operated at a loss, and were propped up by government subsidies and tariffs against similar products entering the country.[63]

Light industry, on the other hand, which remained in private hands, had grown dramatically. Whereas there had been only 271 firms (largely rice mills) classified as agricultural and food-oriented in Cambodia in 1954, there were nearly 2,000 such enterprises in 1968. Similarly, only 93 companies provided building materials in 1954, compared with nearly 200 in 1968. Comparable advances had been noted in the number of enterprises making paper and cardboard and processing lumber.

Sihanouk insisted that Cambodian industry be a showcase for the Sangkum. Often this meant, as Laura Summers has pointed out, that state-owned enterprises founded to conserve foreign exchange ended up costing the state more than importing the products that the plants produced. Moreover, the boards of directors of manufacturing industries were stacked with government officials and cronies of Sihanouk who were often less interested in productivity than in extracting profits for themselves.[64]

Again, the pressure of subsequent events makes it tempting to seek an economic crisis to precede and catalyse the military and political ones that overtook Cambodia in 1970. In the years just before the coup, Cambodia's economy was suffering from the same problems that affected many developing nations. Unlike many of them, however, Cambodia was not in debt, and in fact, had its conservative financial establishment been willing, its foreign exchange holdings could have been used as collateral to obtain credits from abroad for development projects. Its technocratic elite, for a country of its size, was adequate to the demands of industry and finance, but all economic policies were subject to Sihanouk's whims, which, except for his emphasis on education, were mostly geared for short-term, prestigious results. In short, had Sihanouk conscientiously attacked Cambodia's economic problems, using the human and financial resources at his command, economic discontent among the elite might have lessened, and the coup of 1970 might have been postponed. But the shortage of hard currency earnings to pay for essential imports was acute. People in the private sector, watching a boom developing in northeastern Asia as well as in Thailand and South Vietnam, were becoming restless.

Another problem affecting economic performance was rooted in Cambodian sociology. Most members of the elite took Cambodian agriculture, forestry, and fisheries for granted. Most high school graduates felt that by virtue of their education, they had stepped up from agriculture or petty commerce and had become intellectuals, immune from manual labor and rural life. The University of Agricultural Science, which opened in 1965, had only 44 students in 1968, at a time when 650 students attended the University of Fine Arts. In a pattern shared with other countries of the region, male graduates sought bureaucratic positions while their female counterparts, by and large, sought husbands in the bureaucracy. Hundreds of other young Cambodians strung out their tertiary studies in France and elsewhere, unwilling to forsake the political excitement and personal freedoms of the 1960s for low-paying employment at home and, if they had radical political views, police surveillance.[65]

To many of these young men and women (nearly eleven thousand were attending tertiary courses in Cambodia in 1968) the countryside and the peasantry seemed remote. In coffee shops and seminars, radicals complained about the feudal attitudes of the peasantry, while many conservatives took their inferiority for granted. Sihanouk loved moving among them, but he seldom worried about their welfare. Instead, he measured progress in terms of the quantity of new Sangkum constructions such as clinics, dams, factories, and schools, which often outstripped the infrastructure needed to make them work.[66]

The gaps between city and countryside widened at this time. As divisions between Cambodia's rich and poor grew sharper, so did mutual resentment and disdain. In addition, endemic, unpunished corruption affected nearly all official decisions. For any kind of government service, money changed hands. In Cambodian slang, these transactions were called *bon jour*. People's contacts with the government were almost always

occasions for *bon jour*. By the mid-1960s, a membership card in the Sangkum, for example—needed for government employment of any kind—
cost 1,000 riels, or roughly a week's salary for a civil engineer.[67]

Sihanouk himself, writing for a French audience, declared that what
was happening economically in Cambodia in 1968 was a miracle. "I
should emphasize," he wrote, "that our nation has known how to pursue
the modernization of its territory without renouncing its traditions, without having recourse to constraint, while conserving that *'joie de vivre'*
which is so precious to us, and that smile which astonishes and charms
visitors coming here from other countries. If one needs to talk of a 'miracle,' perhaps this is where we can locate the Cambodian 'miracle.'"[68]

Sihanouk went on to say that 95 percent of the population supported
"Buddhist socialism," adding that "the only opposition comes from small
groups who dream of cultural revolution or the American way of life"—in
other words, from those he often labeled Reds and Blues.

Sihanouk's domestic policies and his tendency to drift had a negative
effect on Cambodian politics and encouraged his opponents, but his policy of keeping out of the Vietnam war, maintained against great pressures,
needs to be placed in the balance.

The war reached a crescendo in 1968 and 1969. Cambodia was the
only component of Indochina in which large-unit battles and aerial bom-
bardments were not a daily occurrence. The kingdom's survival for so
long certainly owes a great deal to Sihanouk, who made a series of choices,
disastrous in the long run, perhaps, but rational at the time and geared
to his perception of Cambodia's welfare in a way that American decisions
in Vietnam were seldom if ever geared to the welfare of the Vietnamese.

Had he refused to aid the Vietnamese insurgents, they would have set
up their bases in Cambodia without his permission and killed as many
Cambodians as they felt was necessary to achieve their larger aims. Had
he allied himself with South Vietnam, Cambodia would have been sucked
into the maelstrom of the war. Had he come out in support of any con-
tender in the conflict, the others would have opened fire. By 1969 he felt it
prudent to cultivate the North Vietnamese while improving his relations
with the United States. His contradictory policy of pursuing nonaligned
alignments enraged his opponents but made sense to him. The alternatives were worse. Unfortunately, however, his style also infuriated so many
Cambodians that those who overthrew him in 1970 disregarded this aspect of his rule, tried to confront Vietnam, and set Cambodia alight.

In examining the Sihanouk era, one must balance the prince's diplomatic skills, patriotism, and capacity for hard work against his tolerance of corruption and his self-centered, erratic style. Anyone trying to form a judgment about his years in power must also confront his disdain for educated people, his impatience with advice, his craving for approval, his fondness for revenge, his cynicism, and his flamboyance.

By 1968 or so many educated Cambodians deemed that the prince's virtues were overshadowed by his shortcomings. Instead of strengthening Cambodia's army, for example, he made films. Instead of curbing the financial depredations of his entourage, he allowed them to roam around the edges of the economy amassing personal fortunes. He also ignored the drought that brought much of the countryside near Phnom Penh close to starvation in 1968.[69]

In the meantime, his security police, commanded by Kou Roun and Sihanouk's wife's half-brother, Oum Mannorine, responded to his increasingly violent moods by becoming more repressive, particularly toward Sino-Khmers and high school students.[70]

Many survivors of the 1960s have recalled an atmosphere of terror that pervaded intellectual circles and smothered student politics in Phnom Penh. Douc Rasy, speaking in 1988, said the period was filled "with threats and shadows." As government-sponsored violence became widespread and remained unpunished, the fabric of Cambodian self-confidence, never tightly woven, began to unravel. A former schoolteacher has recalled that several of his colleagues were held without charges in the late 1960s, while others disappeared—either into the maquis or killed by the police. In some regions rewards were given for rebels' severed heads. In Kampot in 1969, several alleged dissidents were thrown alive off a high cliff; their heads were later displayed in the Kampot market.

Sihanouk did not object to these outbursts of cruelty committed on his behalf. Meanwhile, Lon Nol, in command of Cambodia's security apparatus and enjoying Sihanouk's confidence, stepped up the pressure on dissidents and bided his time. In July 1968, he was appointed deputy prime minister. Three months later, Cheng Heng, a colorless official, was elected president of the National Assembly. After the coup in 1970, he replaced Sihanouk for a time as Cambodia's chief of state.[71]

As Sihanouk's capacity to influence events diminished, so did his interest in governing the country. He took refuge in the company of his entourage, in feverish provincial tours, in making films, and occasionally in his passion for haute cuisine.[72]

Bombing, Politics, and Rebellion

In early 1969, soon after President Richard Nixon took office in the United States, Cambodia became embroiled directly in the Vietnam war. In February, the U.S. commander in Saigon, Gen. Creighton Abrams, asked Washington for permission to use B-52 bombers to destroy the COSVN, the Vietnamese party headquarters located just inside Cambodia. Abrams's request was approved in mid-March, but he was told to keep the bombing secret.

The exercise was code-named Operation Breakfast. The first raid occurred on March 18, and Radio Phnom Penh promptly objected to what it called "the intensification" of U.S. bombing. Over the next fourteen months, until a month after the coup d'état in Phnom Penh, over thirty-five hundred bombing sorties were carried out along the Cambodian side of the frontier. By November 1969, according to the U.S. Joint Chiefs of Staff, the Vietnamese had been forced "to disperse over a greater area than before"—presumably, into more heavily populated areas immune from U.S. bombing.

In response to the bombing or to "counterbalance" it, Sihanouk raised the NLF trade mission in Phnom Penh to the status of an embassy and intensified his diplomatic overtures to the United States. He also publicized the Vietnamese Communist presence in Cambodia for the first time. He still hoped to keep his country out of the war. In April 1969, soon after the secret bombing had begun, Sihanouk said that he would change policy toward Vietnam only when the Communists' pressure became too strong for Cambodia's own forces to resist. In that event, he said, "I will resign as chief of state, and turn the office over to Lon Nol"—which is more or less what happened.[73]

The economic situation facing Sihanouk by then was grim. The economy had failed to expand in 1968. Agricultural production was stagnant because of government pressures and a serious drought. The budget deficit amounted to nearly an eighth of the budget, and exports had fallen off. Some of Sihanouk's advisers suggested reduced expenditures, foreign loans, and, in Charles Meyer's words, "[putting] an end once and for all to improvisations, fantasies, and prestige spending"—a precise description of Sihanouk's modus operandi.[74]

Sihanouk rejected this advice and looked for a solution that would enable Cambodian life and the joie de vivre he associated with it to continue. Having noted how much money was being poured into illegal gambling in Phnom Penh, he proposed that the government open its own gambling casinos in Phnom Penh and Sihanoukville, farming out the operation to those who, with police connivance, had been running the illegal operations for several years. The prince had resisted others' proposals for introducing legalized gambling, but he was now convinced that by making such a move the government's shortage of cash could be alleviated in the short term, while foreign loans in hard currency were being negotiated. Moreover, members of his wife's family and several relatives of his own, including his cousins Sisowath Sirik Matak and Norodom Chantaraingsey, stood to profit from the enterprise.[75]

The casinos opened in early 1969. The state's take from the Phnom Penh casino alone amounted to 9 percent of budget revenue for 1969 (that is, 700 million riels, or approximately $10 million). The costs to individual gamblers were enormous. The casino was open twenty-four hours a day. Students, peasants, cyclo-drivers, merchants, soldiers, and officials mingled at the tables and lost their money. Several people, faced with bankruptcy, committed suicide. A fever gripped the city's population. No bad news about the casino was allowed to appear in the press, and Sihanouk was absorbed with making *Crépuscule*. After he was overthrown, many people in Phnom Penh cited the casino as a major catalyst of the coup d'état. It was closed in January 1970, while Sihanouk was overseas.[76]

Sihanouk also had to contend with renewed radical unrest. The insurgents amounted to only a few thousand men and women scattered in the corners of the country, but they were inflicting casualties and tying down much larger military forces. The fact that they were Cambodians angered the prince, who felt that the Vietnamese, in exchange for his protection, should have been able to control the Cambodian insurgents. His campaign went hand in hand with efforts to resume diplomatic relations with the United States. On receipt of a statement from the United States proclaiming its recognition of Cambodia's frontiers, relations resumed in June 1969. Disappointingly for Sihanouk and for many in Lon Nol's government who had expected massive infusions of aid, the American presence was low-key, and economic relief was nowhere in sight.[77]

The Communist guerrillas, for their part, lacked a coordinated plan. In 1977, Pol Pot admitted as much when he said, "The guerrillas were in 17 of Cambodia's 19 provinces. . . . No zone could come directly to the aid of another, since they were very far apart. Our leading body was . . . in the northwest, southwest, east, northeast and in Phnom Penh, places very far from each other. All contact involved at least a month."

Because of these delays, Pol Pot went on, "the Central Committee in

Ratanakiri" was in a position only to "state our general line, principles, and broad orientation," leaving other decisions to regional commanders. These zonal differences persisted into the 1970s.[78]

CPK forces behaved differently from one zone to the next. In those bordering Vietnam, Vietnamese guidance of the local forces was the most systematic, and in the long run had unfortunate effects on local people, who came to be perceived as traitors by the CPK. A Vietnamese document captured in October 1969 consists of political notes taken in the preceding month by a Vietnamese cadre in Cambodia. The document states that "in the past we did not respect the territorial integrity of Cambodia and looked down on the Cambodian people. For instance, our messing, billeting and movement have had adverse effects on the Cambodian people's standard of living." The Vietnamese were inclined to impress the Cambodian people with their weapons and thought they could bribe them with money.[79]

The text says nothing about indigenous resistance or cooperation. Its analysis of government policies and factions is accurate, however, and a line is drawn between Sihanouk, who is listed as progressive, and his armed forces, which consist "of people with narrow-minded nationalism"—the same accusation the Vietnamese were to level against Pol Pot after 1977.

The major area of fighting was in the northeast. Under Gen. Nhiek Tioulong, a new headquarters was established in Stung Treng at the end of 1968, following Sihanouk's admission that the Vietnamese had "occupied a third of the province"; but placing Cambodian troops astride major Vietnamese Communist supply routes running through the northeast invited disaster. A Vietnamese document captured at the end of the year noted that the Communists in this part of the country inflicted heavy casualties on government forces: between May and September "over 1,000 of them were killed or wounded."[80]

In Kompong Cham, Svay Rieng, and Kompong Speu smaller rebel bands managed to pin down government troops and local militia. François Ponchaud and Kol Touch, who lived in rural Kompong Cham in this period, remember hearing of dissident units moving through at night and collecting food and taxes. In general, the rebels behaved well with local people. When captured, they were often executed on the spot and left where they fell, as warnings to others.[81]

When Sihanouk extended diplomatic recognition to the Provisional Revolutionary Government (PRG) of South Vietnam, the PRG's president,

Huynh Tan Phat, visited Phnom Penh at the head of a sixteen-man delegation. His schedule was personally arranged by Sihanouk, who entertained Phat and his colleagues throughout their visit. One purpose of his attentiveness was to cajole Phat into promising that Vietnamese forces would leave Cambodia when the war was over; another was to arrange a formal trade agreement, so that Vietnamese payments for Cambodian food and other supplies could be made to the government rather than, as before, to individuals.[82]

The Beginning of the End

By this time, Sihanouk was under pressure from the financial crisis, the insurrection, the Vietnamese occupation of the border zones, and elite impatience with his rule. In July 1969 at the national congress, he resigned as chief of state and proposed a Government of Salvation, to be selected by a special congress composed of members of both houses of parliament, representatives of the Sangkum's youth movement, the countergovernment, and local newspaper editors. The special congress convened on August 4, and Sihanouk proclaimed that the failure of the outgoing government had been due to a lack of courage among the Cambodian elite, who, he said, were unwilling to face problems as squarely as he did. By refusing to take any responsibility for the economic condition of the country, he dared the delegates to do better.

The meeting was Sihanouk's last hurrah. The congress voted that Lon Nol, already acting as prime minister because of Penn Nouth's poor health, be named head of the new government. The second highest number of votes went to Prince Sisowath Sirik Matak, chosen by Lon Nol a few days later to serve as his deputy prime minister. Matak soon became the strongman of the regime. His unwillingness to submit to Sihanouk's control made the new cabinet offensive to the prince.[83]

The cabinet's sixteen members were chosen by Lon Nol and approved by the assembly. They included nine who had served in the outgoing cabinet but only four who could be labeled Sihanoukists. In 1971, Sihanouk wrote that this cabinet had "represented the local compradores, feudal elements and their foreign backers." At the time he said nothing of the kind. Pomonti and Thion, however, cite a witness's comment, made a few days after the cabinet was named, that the new government represented "a revolution that nobody noticed, for the bourgeoisie has just seized power, without violence or fuss." It could be argued that in all of

Sihanouk's governments, the bourgeoisie—whatever the term may mean in a Cambodian context—had always held nearly all the positions. The difference in 1969 lay in the economic activism, the pro-Western orientation, and the relative political independence of Sirik Matak himself.[84]

Sisowath Sirik Matak was nine years older than Sihanouk. Like him, he had been educated at the Lycée Chasseloup Laubat in Saigon, where he had befriended Lon Nol. The two of them had embarked on careers as provincial civil servants on the eve of World War II. Matak occupied military and cabinet posts in the early 1950s and important ambassadorships later on. He had close ties with Monique Izzi, whom he had sheltered as a young girl. Matak's branch of the royal family were not serious claimants to the throne. His disagreements with Sihanouk lay in the field of economic policy, and he disliked Sihanouk's tolerance for corruption. Matak was active in Sino-Cambodian capitalist circles in Phnom Penh. In 1963, he had opposed the nationalization of Cambodia's exports.[85]

Lon Nol, as we have seen, had different skills and virtues, but his appointment as prime minister raised serious questions about Sihanouk's judgment. Looking for ways to describe him, *Réalités Cambodgiennes* noted that he was "solid, serious, preferring action to verbiage, endowed with common sense." In 1988, Sihanouk defended his choice of Lon Nol by asserting, "Cambodia has never been rich in able and virtuous leaders"—a point echoed by many survivors of DK, who blame that deficiency on Sihanouk himself.[86]

Sihanouk knew that the general was detested by the left. Perhaps he hoped either that the left would bring him down or that the general could neutralize them, but there were elements of desperation in his retreat from power. Lon Nol seemed the least dangerous choice for a replacement. In Sihanouk's eyes, his loyalty and malleability made up for his defects.

For the remainder of the year, Sihanouk played a muted role in domestic affairs, and the politics of this period are hard to figure out. Everyone seemed to be waiting for something to happen. In September, the prince attended Ho Chi Minh's funeral in Hanoi, the only chief of state to do so. He hoped by his gesture to restrain or reduce the Vietnamese military presence in his country. Despite Sihanouk's effusions of grief at the funeral, Pham Van Dong used the occasion to complain that Lon Nol had recently accepted a substantial payment in dollars from the Chinese for Cambodian rice and medicine to be shipped to the NLF but had never handed over the rice. On Sihanouk's return to Phnom Penh, Lon Nol was evasive about the money, but when he traveled to Beijing himself later in the month and was questioned by Pham Van Dong, he allegedly refused to guarantee delivery or to return the money.[87]

At home, Sihanouk was slowly being pushed aside. Problems of his own making, and others that were not, were crowding in on him. Cambodia had become too complex and volatile for one-man rule. The amalgam of trust, fatalism, and laissez-faire that had held the kingdom together had dissolved. The prince was probably aware of this but avoided the issue by lavishly entertaining foreign visitors—Princess Margaret of Great Britain and, a week later, the president of Niger—and by pouring himself into his films.[88]

At the end of October, Lon Nol left Cambodia again to seek further medical treatment in France. The very next day, Sihanouk attacked the National Assembly, saying that it was "making traitors out of people loyal to the chief of state." He resented the fact that Sirik Matak had begun sending him only a selection of state papers and had encouraged ambassadors to write the prime minister directly.

Sirik Matak brushed Sihanouk's complaints aside, and over the next few weeks his government made several decisions that struck at the heart of Khmer socialism and at the financial interests of Sihanouk's entourage. These included allowing private banks to reopen in Cambodia, devaluing the riel by almost 70 percent, and returning several state monopolies to private hands. The moves were made to encourage foreign investment, to meet the requirements of international lending bodies, and to increase revenues from exports. They were moves that the prince had postponed making for years or considered unimportant.[89]

Sihanouk's own energies were taken up with producing and directing films. Recalling these in 1973, he remarked to Oriana Fallaci, "Oh, there were many people who said that my movies were worthless, in fact that they were awful, that I didn't know how to act or use the camera. But I love the movies and what do I care about what they said? I'd answer, 'If nothing else, it helps to educate the people.'"[90]

The climax of Sihanouk's filmmaking career came in November 1969 at an international film festival organized and held in Phnom Penh. His film *Crépuscule* was awarded the grand prize—a solid gold, two-kilogram Buddhist angel ordered from the National Bank. To avoid potentially embarrassing comparisons, *Crépuscule* had not been placed in competition against other entries, and the angel was presented to Sihanouk as a special prize by his long-time admirer, the Sino-Belgian writer Han Suyin.

A dozen smaller statues and some fifty additional awards were presented to other prizewinners from friendly countries (called "left-leaning" by the *New York Times*). When the ceremonies were over, the royal corps de ballet tossed handfuls of rose petals onto the audience. Sihanouk gallantly promised to restage the festival in 1970.[91]

The Twenty-Eighth National Congress, convened soon afterward, was Sihanouk's last performance as chief of state. During one discussion, he tried to discredit Matak's economic measures and managed to get a vote prohibiting the reintroduction of private banks (a vote later reversed by the National Assembly). To show Sihanouk's displeasure with Sirik Matak, the four Sihanoukist cabinet members—Ung Hong Sath, Chuon Saodi, Srey Pong, and Tep Chhieu Keng—had offered their resignations just before the congress convened. But the ploy backfired when Matak accepted their resignations and replaced them with technocrats and opponents of the prince. Now Sihanouk did not have a single spokesman in the cabinet. Melodramatically he demanded that the assembly gathered at the congress choose between him and Sim Var, whose paper continued to attack his policies. He did not take on Sarik Matak or Lon Nol. Sensing that Sihanouk was no longer in command, only eleven of the deputies pledged their unqualified approval; the others judiciously abstained. The prince then demanded that the deputies vote their confidence in him. All but one (Douc Rasy) agreed to this, but Sihanouk's amour propre had been bruised.[92]

For the first time since 1952, Sihanouk had encountered sustained and well-organized opposition. Sirik Matak was not afraid of him. The assembly elected in 1966 relished its augmented role. Sihanouk could take no credit for the economic reforms that were beginning to take effect or for the anti-Vietnamese mood that was beginning to spread in the elite.

The confrontation at the congress was relished by those who seemed to be winning, but it did nothing to alleviate the problems Cambodia faced. The military threat of the Vietnam war remained severe. So did the ongoing civil war. More ominously, the plans of the Americans inside Cambodia remained uncertain. Diplomatic relations had led neither to an economic bonanza, as many had hoped they would, nor to the resumption of military aid. In fact, officers in the low-key American diplomatic mission—which included several CIA operatives—were already renewing ties established in the early 1960s with sympathetic Cambodian officials, including Sirik Matak.

Worn out by his exertions and by the Vietnam war and dispirited by the buffeting he had received at the congress, Sihanouk booked himself into a hospital in early December 1969, suffering from exhaustion, wondering what to do next. Bruised by his encounters, he decided to leave the country and allow events to take their course.

On January 6, 1970, the prince flew out of Phnom Penh, ostensibly for his annual course of medical treatment in France. People who saw him off noted that his luggage was much more extensive than usual, and many who knew him have called his departure a flight. Sihanouk probably hoped that while abroad he could turn the tables on Sirik Matak, using his diplomatic skills with the Soviet Union and China, which he proposed to visit on the way home, to ease the pressure on Cambodia from the Vietnamese. Perhaps Lon Nol and Sirik Matak would stumble or quarrel in his absence, and Prince Papa could rescue the country from distress. The tactic had worked before. On this occasion he miscalculated the single-mindedness of his opponents.[93]

Following his overthrow, and for years thereafter, Sihanouk deplored the people whose policies for Cambodia ended its privileged international status, closed off his own career, and plunged its people into a destructive decade. Could these horrors have been avoided had he remained in power? There is no indication that he was willing to share the stage with anyone, and by the end of 1969 he lacked the allies to push Lon Nol and Sirik Matak aside. At the beginning of 1970, Cambodia, which was to an extent his own invention, had begun to separate from him. The country he had created, nurtured, and served was no longer responsive to his will. Its new identity, if it was to assume one, was unclear.

six

Sliding toward Chaos, 1970–1975

At the beginning of 1970, with Sihanouk and Lon Nol out of the country, Sirik Matak and his colleagues enjoyed an unprecedented opportunity to implement policies aimed at introducing rationality into Cambodia's economic affairs and at facing the implications of the Vietnamese occupation of the border area. Both policies were keyed to improved relations with the United States. Unfortunately, Matak sought an alliance with the Americans at a moment when the United States was beginning to reduce its commitments to Southeast Asia.

Sirik Matak was confident of his ability to introduce and manage change. The government hoped that progress would spring from a releasing of the productive energies of Cambodia's tiny entrepreneurial class and a streamlining of the government itself as it engaged in throwing off Sihanoukism and transforming Cambodia's army into an effective fighting force.

Sirik Matak's goals were commendable, and some people around him may have been honest and talented enough to achieve them had there been no Vietnam war or other international pressures. In setting out on the course they chose, however, they took four badly calculated risks: that Sihanouk would allow his hands to be tied and his policies overturned in exchange for being permitted to remain in power as a figurehead; that the North Vietnamese and NLF would acquiesce to Cambodia's priorities and cross back into Vietnam from their sanctuaries to face the fury of the United States and South Vietnam; that the South Vietnamese and the United States would stand aside from a genuinely nonaligned Cambodia and allow it to proceed as if the Vietnam war were not taking place; and that the CPK would give up its struggle to gain power.[1]

In combination, these miscalculations were colossal, but perhaps no more so than Sihanouk's wooing of the Communist bloc or his feeling that he could alienate Cambodia's educated men and women indefinitely and at will. Sirik Matak and his colleagues hardly foresaw the disaster of the 1970s. His faction entered the new year with confidence.

In January, the National Office of Mutual Aid, for several years a conduit for Sihanouk's largesse, was closed. Receipts were drawn from showings of Sihanouk's films, from the take of the casino, and from "voluntary contributions" from government employees. Expenditures included recompense to victims of U.S. bombing and Communist depredations, gifts to monasteries, and handouts of various kinds. Officially, receipts were deemed insufficient to justify the continuation of the bureau. In fact, the government's motive was to lessen Sihanouk's influence.[2]

Soon afterward Lon Nol returned from France, where he had consulted with Sihanouk about what tactics to follow vis-à-vis the Vietnamese. Lon Nol had traveled to Rome in January to meet Sihanouk on his arrival in Europe. News of this rendezvous convinced many in Phnom Penh that the two men had agreed on a coordinated anti-Vietnamese policy. According to the journalist Pierre Max, Lon Nol had also urged Sihanouk to return quickly to Cambodia, but Sihanouk was reluctant to do so.[3]

Lon Nol made a vigorous anti-Vietnamese move immediately after his return. He ordered in all outstanding 500-riel (c. $10) notes, ostensibly because counterfeit notes had begun to appear but in fact to deprive North Vietnamese and NLF agents of the notes they had been using to purchase supplies inside Cambodia. François Ponchaud, then a missionary in Kompong Cham, has recalled being approached by his Vietnamese sacristan to change a "few notes"; the sum turned out to be more than 500,000 riels ($10,000). The sacristan, it turned out, was the local treasurer for the NLF. Many of the notes that surfaced in Phnom Penh over the years had been bought up by the Chinese Communists via Hong Kong and were coming back into Cambodia through diplomatic channels. To prevent last-minute transactions, Lon Nol tailored the decree to call for the scrutiny of diplomatic pouches until the old notes were to be redeemed. Losses to the Communists were estimated at more than $70 million.[4]

Another aspect of Lon Nol's strategy, probably approved by Sihanouk, was to call for assistance from Son Ngoc Thanh. For several years, Thanh had been living in southern Vietnam, where he used his links with the Saigon regime, the subsidies provided him, and his popularity among ethnic Khmer to aid the Vietnamese and the CIA in recruiting and training Khmer batallions to fight in the Vietnam war.[5] In 1969, emissaries from Phnom Penh had approached him to seek his support in the event of a Vietnamese Communist attack on Phnom Penh. After "consulting with [his] American friends," as he later put it, Thanh agreed to help.[6]

Several hundred armed Khmer Serei partisans had already "defected" to the prince, who welcomed them into his army. Sihanouk hoped to pressure the Vietnamese Communists by increasing the military risks of their occupation. Thanh's well-trained, fully equipped batallions offered a perfect means of doing so. Sihanouk did not think the operation risky, for he knew that Lon Nol and Son Ngoc Thanh distrusted each other and thought them unlikely to form an alliance at his expense.

The overtures suited U.S. interests in Saigon, even though a widening of the war did not suit the fledgling U.S. mission in Phnom Penh or some factions in the Department of State. Over the next six months, however, President Nixon's perception of Cambodia as a key to the war overrode these objections. Nixon supported those who wanted the fighting to spread because broader hostilities would relieve pressure on the United States's withdrawal from Vietnam. America thus came to share the responsibility with Vietnam, Sihanouk, and the Lon Nol government for plunging Cambodia into a war that any anti-Communist government in Phnom Penh was bound to lose.[7]

In February 1970, Cambodian forces began shelling North Vietnamese and NLF installations inside Cambodia. A captured Vietnamese document understandably called these attacks "confusing to our people."[8]

The scene became melodramatic on March 11, when massive demonstrations were held outside the North Vietnamese and NLF diplomatic missions in Phnom Penh. The protest undoubtedly had Sihanouk's permission, for his brother-in-law, in command of Cambodia's police, did nothing to put it down. There were no casualties among the demonstrators, whose well-prepared banners were reminiscent of similar arranged occasions, but the demonstration soon got out of hand. Rioters got into the two buildings, sacked them, and burned their contents. The Vietnamese diplomats, though manhandled, escaped unharmed. At that point, according to *Realités Cambodgiennes*, the police closed the gates and "mounted guard on the smoking debris." That night scattered bands roamed the Vietnamese section of the city ransacking Catholic churches, looting shops, and harassing passersby.[9]

In Paris, Sihanouk said that the demonstrations sprang from a "plot to throw our country into the arms of a capitalist imperialist power." He

promised to return home immediately to allow the people to choose between him and these "personalities": "If they choose to follow these personalities on a path that will make Cambodia a second Laos," he said,
"then they will permit me to resign." Talking with the *New York Times,* he
said that the Communists could choose between respecting Cambodia's
neutrality or seeing a pro-American government in Phnom Penh. On
March 12, as the CIA in Washington was digesting a report from Phnom
Penh entitled "Indications of a Possible Coup in Phnom Penh." Sirik
Matak canceled the Cambodian–PRG trade agreement, and Lon Nol
demanded that all North Vietnamese and NLF troops leave Cambodia by
dawn on Sunday, March 15. Probably the most unrealistic order issued by
a Cambodian official since independence, the ultimatum expired without
any response from the Vietnamese.

By this time, Sihanouk had changed his mind about returning home,
but rather than hurry back via Prague, he chose a more time-consuming
route through Moscow and Beijing. Before leaving Paris, he told reporters
that the assemblymen were "patriots of the dollar." On the previous night,
in a conversation at the Cambodian embassy that was secretly recorded,
he threatened to have the Government of Salvation killed on his return.
The cassette reached Cambodia before the coup and according to several
sources terrified the cabinet, galvanized the National Assembly, and
catalyzed support for overthrowing the prince.[10]

Up to the last moment, Sihanouk's schedule remained uncertain. As
late as March 16, people in Cambodia expected him home by the twentieth. Pierre Max, who dined with him in Paris on the ninth, has quoted
him as saying that evening, "The situation in my country? Yes, it's serious.
Yes, the communists are invading it. The Vietnamese are hereditary enemies; as for the Viet Cong, I must smile broadly to their faces, and smack
them on the back. I'm going to tour the capitals—Moscow, Beijing, Hanoi.
It will suffice if I talk to them, they're all my friends. . . . The Russians and
the Chinese will oblige the Vietnamese to go no further, and remain in
their sanctuaries."[11]

The cassette from Paris and Sihanouk's altered plans meant that Sirik
Matak had to accelerate his plans. The assembly convened on March 16,
ostensibly to question Oum Mannorine, Sihanouk's brother-in-law, and
Gen. Sosthene Fernandez on a charge of smuggling textiles from Hong
Kong. An attack on a person so close to Sihanouk was unprecedented.
Those opposed to the prince obviously meant business.

Outside the assembly, hundreds of students with anti-Vietnamese placards and banners blocked off the building from Mannorine's police, isolating Mannorine inside. Lon Nol had placed several hundred paratroopers in civilian clothes at the edges of the crowd. Aware of this support, Sim Var, Douc Rasy, and others moved that the smuggling issues be postponed so that political issues raised by the students could be discussed. Four motions were received. Three endorsed the anti-Vietnamese demonstrations. The fourth, unsigned and in pencil, mentioned "certain Khmer high personages [who] have thought only of their personal and family interests, have supported the enemy of the nation by authorizing him to bring in supplies, arms and medicines, and have co-operated with the masters of the enemy."

In the debate that followed Douc Rasy urged that the army be expanded. "If we do not chase them from our territory before they win victory, our country will become Vietnamese. . . . We belong to the Khmer nation. We have our own dignity; we are not oxen or buffalo. We have our honor, and we want to live honorably, not like animals who can do nothing but pray they will not meet the hunters. We want to live in honor. Otherwise, it is better that we die [applause]."[12]

Sihanouk had hoped to use the demonstrations against the Vietnamese embassies to persuade China and the USSR to press the Vietnamese to reduce their activities in Cambodia. Douc Rasy and his colleagues, on the other hand, believed that the emotions released in the demonstrations could be deflected against the prince, who had endorsed the Vietnamese incursions in the first place.

Others were not so sure of Rasy's plan. Most people expected Sihanouk to be back at any moment. Welcoming banners and decorations had been strung up along the road between the airport and the city; the side road leading into his residence had been resurfaced to make the prince's ride more comfortable. Few could imagine Cambodia without him. Immediately after the demonstrations, indeed, the assembly had voted to send Yem Sambaur and Norodom Kantol to Moscow to apprise him of the situation in Cambodia and to invite him home. By telephone Sihanouk told Sirik Matak he would refuse to receive them. He later claimed to have had reason to fear for his safety. His behavior can also be explained in terms of his having decided to seek asylum in Beijing, France, or elsewhere. He remained in Moscow longer than planned and postponed his return to Cambodia for a week. This decision cost him his position as chief of state.[13]

The Coup d'Etat

When Sihanouk arrived in Moscow, Soviet president Nikolai Podgorny told him to hurry back to Phnom Penh "to ensure that Cambodia doesn't drift into an American takeover." Sihanouk replied, he wrote later, that he would "have to think things over very carefully. There was much to think about."

Sihanouk found the Soviet leaders unwilling to put pressure on their Vietnamese allies, although they offered him their support if he wanted to take up arms "against the extreme right." In Sihanouk's words, "[Premier Aleksei] Kosygin said to me: 'If you decide to fight, we can send you arms, equipment and trucks in six or seven months' time'—to which I replied that without equipment and trucks 'in some weeks' time', I would be shot, and that combat was possible only if massive military aid was sent at once."[14]

Were the Russians saying that Sihanouk should take up arms against Lon Nol? or that, using Lon Nol's army, he should attack the forces of South Vietnam and the United States? Either proposal was nonsensical, and Sihanouk's request for Soviet aid must have struck the Russian leaders as whimsical or unbalanced.[15]

In the limousine on the way to the airport on March 18, Kosygin informed Sihanouk that he had been voted out of office by the National Assembly. Sihanouk has written recently that he told Kosygin that the move was unconstitutional and immoral and then declared that he would fight imperialism with all his strength. These remarks are missing from his earlier books. Speaking at the airport, Sihanouk noted merely that he might consider setting up a government in exile. Official ceremonies then proceeded as planned, and the prince flew off toward an uncertain future.

Late that night, the Ilyushin 62 ("luxuriously fitted out," as Sihanouk has recalled) made a scheduled stop in Irkutsk, where the provincial governor was on hand to greet the prince and provide him with an enormous meal. Even though Sihanouk must have been almost suicidal at the time, Alain Daniel, then his private secretary, has recalled that he behaved with "exquisite courtesy" toward his hosts. In his memoirs, Sihanouk claims to have spent the flight composing a call to arms. This is unlikely, for one of the first things he did on landing in Beijing was to ask the French ambassador about the possibility of being granted political asylum in France.[16]

In Phnom Penh, meanwhile, an attempt by Oum Mannorine to arrest

Lon Nol on the night of March 16 had backfired, and Mannorine was arrested himself. On the following day, the assembly dismissed him from his position. He was replaced by Sirik Matak, who now controlled the police. Lon Nol was still in command of the army. Where did he stand? Before dawn on March 18 Sirik Matak and two army officers entered the general's house, woke him, and demanded that he sign a document approving the overthrow of the prince, to be proclaimed later in the day. Lon Nol hesitated, and Sirik Matak cried out, "Nol my friend, if you don't sign this paper, we'll shoot you!" Lon Nol burst into tears, pulled himself together, and signed the decree. His action brought the army in on the side of the coup. Troops were ordered to guard strategic points around Phnom Penh, and Cambodia's airports at Phnom Penh and Siem Reap were closed.[17]

Lon Nol was a mass of contradictions. Normally, he was reluctant to take risks and unwilling to betray the prince. On this occasion, he was frightened and eager to please Matak. Later on, when war engulfed Cambodia, Lon Nol blamed himself for it and told associates that he regretted what he had done. He even wrote President Nixon, whom he considered his personal friend (although the two never met), that the coup had taken him out over his depth. At the same time, he saw himself as a predestined Buddhist chief of state, leading his people in a religious war.[18]

When the assembly reconvened, it withdrew its confidence in Fernandez, who immediately resigned. The vote was 25–8, with 36 abstentions. His resumption of military responsibilities at a higher rank less than two months later suggests that he was helping the coup planners test the numbers in the assembly.

Several speakers then argued that article 15 of the constitution, declaring the nation in danger, should be invoked. The article gave the government the power to suspend a range of civil rights. The vote in favor was unanimous, and at 11:00 A.M. the assembly moved on to discuss "the case of Norodom Sihanouk." A series of speakers attacked the prince, his wife, and his in-laws and charged them with treason, corruption, and extravagance. The film festival of 1969 and the casino were cited as offenses, as was Sihanouk's charge that some politicians had wanted to "sell Cambodia to a foreign power." One speaker noted that "Sihanouk treats the members of the Assembly, the authorized representatives of the people, like animals." For nearly two hours, speakers attacked the prince and his associates by name. They were giving vent, as Charles Meyer has written, to "rancor that had been suppressed for too long."[19]

At 1:00 P.M., they voted to withdraw their confidence from the man whom some of them had named as chief of state ten years before. The vote was secret; the final count against the prince was 89–3, later altered to unanimity. The president of the National Assembly, Cheng Heng, in keeping with constitutional provisions, became the acting chief of state pending an election.[20]

Sihanouk's downfall was announced on the radio that afternoon; later, Lon Nol broadcast a short, supportive statement. The banal proceedings were in sharp contrast to Sihanouk's way of doing business and provided a muted ending to his flamboyant years in power.

As armored vehicles patrolled the city, the government delayed celebrations of the coup and broadcast the assembly debates only after dark. Not certain how to interpret events and with no guidance from Sihanouk or from anyone else, the population in Phnom Penh did nothing. To the U.S. legation, this reaction seemed "explainable in large measure to [sic] Buddhism and weariness and disappointment with Sihanouk." Other witnesses have suggested that inactivity concealed widespread anger and disbelief.[21]

Sihanouk Declares War

Sihanouk's two accounts of his arrival in Beijing are separated by eleven years and differ in detail. Both of them suggest that he was uncertain about what would happen and about how he should proceed. He was met at the airport by Zhou Enlai and an honor guard, but when he reached the embassy and was given Cheng Heng's letter dismissing him from office, the prince tore the letter into small pieces and strode around the room "like a wounded tiger," saying repeatedly, "I must return to Paris! I must return to Paris!" In response to a request by Sihanouk himself, the French ambassador, Etienne Mana'ch, offered him asylum in France. According to Sihanouk, writing in 1971, Zhou Enlai then suggested a more difficult choice: "He said more or less as follows: 'If you engage firmly in combat, we will help you to be victorious over imperialism. But you should not have any illusions: this will be your war, at first, and it will be long, hard, dangerous, sometimes even discouraging. . . . But if you are determined, we will be with you. . . . Are you ready for it? If you are, we shall win. Think it over. We will meet again in twenty-four hours.'"[22]

Eleven years later, Sihanouk wrote that the message had come from Mao Zedong, adding, "China didn't hesitate to support me, for they knew that by sustaining my fight they could offer the Red Khmers a unique chance to communize Cambodia." If this thought occurred to Sihanouk in 1970, it was soon overshadowed by what he calls his thirst for justice. Shawcross suggests that the attacks launched in Cambodia against Sihanouk and his wife on March 19–20 fueled his resolve. His admiration for the purity of the Communists was also genuine. When he was fired up and safely installed in Beijing, his rancor and his international status served the interests of the Chinese, the Vietnamese, and the invisible CPK.[23]

Within twenty-four hours of his arrival, the Chinese summoned Pham Van Dong to Beijing. Since Pol Pot later claimed to have participated in the negotiations that ensued and has admitted being in Hanoi beforehand, he probably came to Beijing with Pham Van Dong. There is no evidence that he was present at the negotiations.[24]

According to the Cambodian ambassador to China, Nay Valentin, later executed by the CPK, Pham Van Dong told Princess Monique that Vietnamese forces could help Sihanouk regain power within twenty-four hours. According to Sihanouk, Dong asked to see him on March 22; the prince recalled, "Since I'd passed the nights since March 18 without sleeping, I was prepared to see him at sunrise, if necessary." Pham Van Dong came for breakfast and afterward held a working meeting with Sihanouk, who claims to have set the terms for the alliance involving Chinese aid to the Khmer resistance, a "summit conference of Indo-Chinese peoples," and military training in Vietnam for his supporters.[25]

The arrangement suited everyone's interests at the time. In exchange for Sihanouk's taking command of a national front and calling for armed resistance by his royal government to Lon Nol the Vietnamese were relieved of pressure on their forces inside Cambodia and the CPK gained a heavily armed ally in its own ascent to power. Sihanouk saved face; the Vietnamese were allowed to expand the war; and the CPK began its relatively short ascent to political control.[26]

In 1978 Pol Pot took credit for suggesting to the Chinese that Sihanouk should "take the offensive" and claims that the Vietnamese were grateful to ally themselves with the CPK. The reverse is more likely. Eight years after the fact, Pol Pot restructured history out of wishful thinking. Like Lon Nol, but unlike Sihanouk, he believed by then that Cambodians could defeat the Vietnamese because they were inherently superior.

The fruit of Sihanouk's discussions in Beijing was the prince's broadcast on March 23. This was a declaration of war: "The liberty, democracy, prosperity, unity and national union which our people enjoyed not long ago," he said, "have all been destroyed, reduced to nothing." He proposed a National Union Government, a National Liberation Army, and a National United Front of Kampuchea (NUFK), which would govern Cambodia in accordance with *"social justice,* equality and fraternity among Khmers" (emphasis added). He called on Cambodians to disregard laws and decrees issued from Phnom Penh, asserted that "millions of Khmers at home and thousands of Khmers abroad will certainly . . . uphold the banner of revolt," and called on his "children . . . to engage in guerrilla warfare in the jungle against our enemies." He said nothing about his alliance with China and Vietnam.[27]

Sihanouk's declaration had little effect in Phnom Penh. The new government was too busy releasing political prisoners, reopening airports, welcoming foreign correspondents, and removing Sihanouk's picture from public buildings to react to his call to arms. The vernacular press continued its attacks on the prince and his entourage. Photographs of nude women with Monique's face added appeared alongside spurious accounts that members of Sihanouk's family had literally sold Cambodian land for cash to the Vietnamese. After years of subservience and repression, the press coverage was like a slaves' rebellion. For the first time in nearly twenty years, educated Cambodians were free to express their political opinions. Accounts of recent Cambodian history that included actors other than Sihanouk were no longer taboo. Books and articles praised the demonstrations of 1942, Democrats, and Issaraks. Thousands of students lined up to join the army to "drive out the Vietnamese." Poorly equipped and poorly led, thousands of them were maimed and killed. At the same time, thousands of other people were lining up in the countryside in response to the call from Prince Papa to drive out the Americans.[28]

The main effects of the coup and of Sihanouk's response to it were to free Vietnamese forces from the restraints imposed by their alliance with Sihanouk and to pull all of Cambodia into the Indochina war.

In rural areas, cassettes of Sihanouk's call to arms were played by Vietnamese and CPK cadre. On March 6, in their first public statement since 1967, Hou Youn, Khieu Samphan, and Hu Nim announced their support for the front and appealed to Cambodia's peasants to become guerrillas. A CPK activist remembered Sihanouk's speech ten years later: "We immediately stopped attacking Sihanouk," he said, "and started pointing out that he was Chairman of our Front."[29] In Kompong Cham, university students joined villagers and plantation workers to demonstrate against Lon Nol, sacking the governor's mansion, burning tax records, and plastering the town with portraits of the prince.

On the night of the twenty-sixth, via buses and trucks commandeered from the rubber plantations, several thousand Khmers—including some bewildered passengers detained aboard the buses—decided to drive to Phnom Penh, fifty miles to the southwest, to express their support for the prince. They were met at the approaches to the city by paramilitary army units that opened fire on them. Roughly a hundred bus riders were killed and wounded. Others sought refuge in Vietnamese villages bordering the Mekong, where they were hunted down and arrested over the next few days.

Demonstrations in Takeo and Kampot were brutally suppressed. Two assemblymen sent to Prey Veng to explain the coup returned quickly to Phnom Penh, fearing for their lives. In Kompong Cham, news of shootings led mobs to regroup. On the twenty-sixth, Lon Nol's brother, Lon Nil, who owned a rubber plantation in the area, was set upon and cut to pieces. On the twenty-seventh they burned down the local courthouse and hacked to death two national assemblymen who had been sent to negotiate with them. Two days later government forces regained control in Kompong Cham. In Tam, a former governor of the province, now a deputy, was made an army colonel and put in charge of restoring order.[30] At this stage many young Khmers decided to join the resistance. One of them said in 1980, "I was so angry at being shot at; I wanted to take to the forest and build a new country

The ferocity of these events embarrassed the government and probably delayed the declaration of a republic, but no more demonstrations of support for Sihanouk occurred for the remainder of the war. The demonstrations reveal that in several parts of the country ordinary people had been shocked by the coup, which had overturned their world, and had been drawn toward Sihanouk by his emotional appeal.[31]

Warfare and Politics, 1970

April 1970 proceeded in Phnom Penh as if Lon Nol and his government controlled events, even as the general withdrew six thousand troops from the northeast, where his army had been heavily engaged since 1968. The withdrawal left the region to be occupied by North Vietnamese and NLF forces for the remainder of the war.[32]

In Phnom Penh, most people paid little attention to these events. T. D.

Allman wrote that "most of Cambodia [that is, Phnom Penh] is on a psychedelic trip: the intoxicant is a potent mix of nationalism and dreams of economic gain." Thousands of young people were let out of school to demonstrate against the prince and the Viet Cong. They dressed in khaki, trained in military formations, and believed that they could drive the Vietnamese away with their righteousness and determination. As Allman noted, "Every day they could be seen setting out from the city, hanging on to the sides of Coca-Cola trucks or brightly painted busses, wearing shower clogs or sandals, shorts or blue jeans, parts of old French uniforms or oversized American fatigues, some emptyhanded, some carrying French, Russian, East German, American, Chinese weapons . . . laughing as they headed for the war."[33] Between April and June 1970, thousands of these volunteers were killed in battles near the capital. Battle-hardened after a quarter century of warfare, the Vietnamese found them easy targets.

As the volunteers were being killed and wounded, anti-Vietnamese feeling in Phnom Penh intensified. In May 1970, acting on orders from overwrought superiors and panicky themselves, army and police units rounded up and killed thousands of Vietnamese civilians in Phnom Penh and its environs. Grisly, corroborated stories circulated of women and children being gunned down by soldiers, wounded prisoners being left to bleed to death, strings of corpses floating down the Mekong, and Vietnamese civilians sent out against armed Vietnamese units bearing white flags and propaganda tracts. The massacres were widely reported in the international press. Although Lon Nol's government agreed with authorities in Saigon to allow perhaps half a million surviving Vietnamese to immigrate to South Vietnam, the massacres brutalized the conduct of South Vietnamese troops coming to the aid of his government in 1970–71 and eroded the small fund of good will that the regime had earned in other countries. At best the killings showed that Lon Nol was unable to control the violence of his subordinates; at worst they revealed that Lon Nol and his associates were willing to conduct a racially based religious war against unarmed civilians whose families had lived in Cambodia for generations.[34] Significantly, no Cambodians—not even those in the Buddhist sangha—condemned the killings, and when Lon Nol apologized to the South Vietnamese government, whose military aid he sought, he grumbled that "in many cases it was difficult to tell whether [the] Vietnamese were Viet Cong or peaceful citizens."[35]

Ambassador Emory C. Swank, who arrived in Cambodia several

months later, observed in 1987, "We should have taken these massacres as a very ominous sign of things to come." Lon Nol now began referring to the Communists as Thmil, a Buddhist term drawn from Sri Lanka that originally meant "Tamil," or nonbelievers.

In the U.S.-South Vietnamese invasion of Cambodia in April-June 1970 some thirty thousand U.S. troops and over forty thousand troops from South Vietnam plunged into eastern Cambodia, looking for the Vietnamese Communist COSVN, which had been moved westward to safety several weeks beforehand. Lon Nol was not informed of the incursion in advance. After the incursion had been going on for ten days, however, *Réalités Cambodgiennes* referred to it gallantly as indispensable. The principal effect of the operation—beyond the casualties incurred and the intensified U.S. alliance with Lon Nol—was to push mainforce Vietnamese Communist units deeper into Cambodia, where they soon began to take apart Lon Nol's poorly trained forces.[36]

The incursions also encouraged South Vietnamese troops to carry out operations in Cambodia for the rest of 1970 and for most of 1971. These forces often behaved like bandits and earned a fearsome reputation. In the meantime, the prospect of receiving massive American military aid boosted the morale of Lon Nol's government. Assistant Secretary of State Marshall Green, who visited Phnom Penh soon after the incursion, which he had opposed, has recalled the optimism in the U.S. mission and in the upper ranks of the Cambodian government. Lon Nol himself, Green found, was "completely upbeat . . . even over-confident" about his army's ability to defeat the Vietnamese.

Soon afterward, Sihanouk was tried in absentia in Phnom Penh by a military tribunal. No high-ranking witnesses were called and no revelations were forthcoming. Sihanouk was charged with "inciting the Communists to commit aggression" and "inciting Cambodian soldiers to join the enemy."

Both offenses had occurred after the coup, which meant that the court had no jurisdiction. Besides, since Sihanouk was chief of state his person under the constitution was inviolate. These objections were brushed aside. Sihanouk was stripped of his citizenship and condemned to death. The trial paved the way for the declaration of a republic and for the return of Son Ngoc Thanh, who was named a councilor to the president in August. At the same time, seventeen of Sihanouk's associates in the National Front were tried and condemned to death and eleven were sentenced to twenty years' imprisonment. Princess Monique, described by the court as "the very soul of treason," received a life sentence.

As the war cut Phnom Penh off from the countryside, Lon Nol's statements became more grandiose. As Vietnamese troops closed in on several provincial cities, he boasted of his friendship with President Nixon and urged people joining the army to learn the "occult sciences practiced by our ancestors, which permit us to escape the enemy's fire." These sciences included magical spells, inscribed vests, astrology, and techniques of unarmed combat that had intrigued Lon Nol since his lycée days in Saigon. His instructions for soldiers noted that the "Mon-Khmer race . . . has always had the magic key to victory in combat": based on obedience to Buddhist precepts while remaining aware of "actual scientific progress," it was defined as follows: "Out of stones and wood, we can make beefsteaks (*sic*), cloth, and other useful objects; we can travel through space to the stars, use an electronic brain, communicate across oceans, and go round the world in less than twenty-four hours."[37]

As far as Lon Nol was concerned, Buddhist teaching, racial virtues, and modern science made the Khmers invincible. He confided to CIA director William Colby that "the war had 'a spiritual basis' and derived from the glories of Angkor." By the end of the year, he was seeking military advice from a Buddhist monk named Mam Prum Mani, who claimed to be a reincarnation of Jayavarman VII, a twelfth-century Cambodian monarch.[38]

Many Cambodians believed these exhortations and hurried off to be tattooed with magical designs or to acquire scarves and amulets inscribed with spells and blessed by Buddhist monks.[39]

Others, more cynical, had backed the coup in the hope, as one officer put it, that a "faucet of dollars" would be permanently turned on.

The cynical officer was right. When the United States began paying Cambodia's military bills, many officers discovered ways of getting rich. One was by padding their payrolls with nonexistent soldiers; another was by not reporting deaths and desertions; a third was selling arms, gas, medicine, ammunition, and equipment to the enemy. In the meantime, the precoup army of thirty-five thousand had expanded to over one hundred thousand. Lon Nol hoped to put a quarter of a million Cambodians under arms. Recruits grew younger and poorer as the children of the elite arranged for noncombat postings, overseas scholarships, or exemptions from service and as rural manpower came under enemy control.[40]

The Cambodian army was no match for the Vietnamese units opposing them, but the breathing spell afforded by the American-South Vietnamese incursion led Lon Nol and his associates to think that he could go on the offensive. In early September, a military operation named Chenla 1 after a semilegendary Cambodian kingdom pushed off from the capital to relieve pressure on Kompong Thom, eighty-five miles to the north. Lon Nol assumed personal command. His tactics involved marching his main force along Route 6, the Phnom Penh-Kompong Thom highway. Because it was the rainy season, maneuvering off the roads was impossible. The forces, with dependents and equipment, were strung out along the road for several miles and moved at a snail's pace. Resistance was light, but at Taing Kauk Vietnamese forces delayed the column for a week. Elements of the column reached Kompong Thom on October 11, but most of the troops remained bogged down. U.S. fighter bombers were brought in to demolish the Vietnamese. By early November, the campaign was labeled a victory and called off. Misjudging its success, Lon Nol began planning a follow-up for 1971.[41]

The proclamation of the Khmer Republic on October 9 did nothing to alter Cambodian politics. Lon Nol and Sirik Matak were still relatively popular among intellectuals, students, the commercial elite, and the officer corps. They helped themselves to promotions (to full general and lieutenant general, respectively), and a new flag replaced the one designed in 1947 by Ieu Koeuss. For a time after Chenla 1, the fighting diminished, and the American presence remained low-key. The faucet of dollars had not yet opened up. Ambassador Swank and his politico-military aide, Jonathan Ladd, sought to provide modest U.S. support while trying to restrain the American presence and Cambodian military demands. In Beijing, Sihanouk's National Front also seemed becalmed and in late 1970 began to cede power inside Cambodia to CPK officials, designated as vice ministers of the national government. These officials included Saloth Sar, who was placed in control of the rebel army, and Nuon Chea, named political counselor.[42]

The Front, Vietnam, and the CPK

In April 1970, Thiounn Mumm, who had been in France since 1955, joined Sihanouk in Beijing. He was aware of the recent history of the CPK. Sihanouk, on the other hand, still assumed that the Cambodian party was synonymous with the Pracheachon and was run by the Vietnamese. For the next three years Mumm and his brother, Thiounn Prasith, provided intellectual ballast for Sihanouk's government in exile and valuable liaison with Cambodian intellectuals in France and elsewhere.

The prince was useful as a figurehead, but his activities and pronouncements were closely monitored. In Beijing, he lived in the former French embassy on Anti-Imperialism Street and went off from time to time on diplomatic junkets. He had no real power. In September 1970 he told a Western journalist that those carrying out the work of the front inside Cambodia were Red Khmers. Although he sometimes called himself a Marxist and referred to "my Communists," he knew that they despised him and that his luxurious life in Beijing set him apart from anyone waging war on his behalf.[43]

The political program of the front was drafted in May 1970 by Thiounn Mumm. It was a rousing, high-minded document that sought to unite all Cambodians behind the front, so as to defeat American imperialism and "the Lon Nol–Sirik Matak clique." It concealed its socialist inspiration, played down the front's alliance with the Vietnamese, and was vague about long-term political objectives, but it gave Sihanouk no role to play in postwar Cambodia and contained the germs of many DK policies, such as an emphasis on self-reliance, the preeminence of public values, and a respect for the "good traditions of the Angkor civilization."[44]

About this time Saloth Sar returned home along the Ho Chi Minh Trail. In his absence, according to the *Black Book,* the Vietnamese had been trying to negotiate with Son Sen and Ieng Sary for a joint military command, for Cambodian help in protecting COSVN, now transferred to Kratie, and for logistic support along the trails running through the region into South Vietnam. These proposals were sweetened with promises of military aid.[45]

Pol Pot claimed in 1978 that the CPK had brushed the proposals aside. He added that by September 1970 he had moved his headquarters southwestward into the Phnom Santhuk region of Kompong Thom. By then, COSVN had moved to rural Kratie, not far from Phnom Santhuk. Between June and September 1970, in other words, Saloth Sar and his associates moved *closer* to the Vietnamese, which suggests that a joint military command was already in operation. Corroboration of these arrangements comes from a Khmero-Vietnamese who told Ben Kiernan ten years later that by August 1970 "we were taken into the thick forest near Phnom Santhuk . . . [where] we trained in combat drill and tactics, and studied Vietnamese. Our group held daily meetings in which we discussed our ideas, in Vietnamese. I also taught some of the Vietnamese to speak Khmer."[46]

In other parts of the country, Cambodian and Vietnamese Communist troops were fighting side by side. In *dombon* (region) 25 southwest of

Phnom Penh Cambodians fought under Vietnamese orders until 1972. In battlefield conditions, errors were inevitable and frictions occurred, intimating more serious conflicts later.[47]

In October 1970, a North Vietnamese defector stated that a Vietnamese Advisory Organization had been set up in Cambodia soon after the coup "to provide key cadre and technical support." The rallier said that the organization's mission was to "aid in the development of a Communist infrastructure in Cambodia by providing experienced cadre to fill the key positions" in the National Front and to "organize and train Cambodian personnel."[48]

The same month, Vorn Vet attended a political training session for several days in Phnom Santhuk. A document captured in rural Kratie may well have emanated from this meeting; it foreshadows many DK policies not openly expressed before the Vietnamese Communist withdrawal from Cambodia in 1972. For example, ignoring the existence of the front, the text makes a strong plea for class warfare: "We should not tolerate the regime of the imperialists, feudalists, and capitalists, which causes endless suffering to the people. We should serve the interests of farmers and workers, the suppressed people."

The only reference to Vietnam in the document makes a case for Cambodian autonomy: "We have to co-ordinate with Vietnam in order to struggle against the American imperialists. However, we must protect our independence, our individual characteristics, shape the future of our people, preserve solidarity in our anti-American efforts, and be free from intervention in internal affairs."

Other passages exhibit an ambiguous, slightly menacing phraseology that resembles Pol Pot's speeches in the DK era. One passage asserts that the "immediate purpose" of the movement is to "destroy everything which is instrumental in suppressing our people." The text defines class as the "level of people with distinctive political tendencies," states that there are "two classes in rural Cambodian society" but does not identify them, and notes that "the revolutionaries are in the middle; the revolutionary organizations are behind the revolutionaries; and the masses surround the organizations"—a field placing that is hard to visualize. The text suggests that a major aim of the revolution was to protect the leadership, and a final passage describes the "conduct of a revolutionist" as follows: "A revolutionist should be kind and sympathetic to the people; a revolutionist should always use kind words when talking to the people. These words should cause no harm; make the listener sympathetic to the speaker; be easily understood by the listener; sound polite in all circumstances; be pleasing to everyone; and make the listeners happy."[49]

A related document entitled "Strategy and Rural Policy of the Party" noted, "Farmers are a source of endless strength. They can produce manpower and material power. The Revolution of our country cannot proceed without their strength. Farmers should be used to promote and maintain solidarity among the workers"—the "vanguard" whom they overwhelmingly outnumbered. Under "imperialism, feudalists, and reactionary capitalists," the text continued, "[farmers] are deprived of their right to vote, to study, and read progressive books, and of travelling freely to earn their living." Not one of these rights was reinstated when the Communists came to power.[50]

In the Eastern Zone, where manuals and procedures probably owed more to Vietnamese models, a pamphlet from 1971 entitled "Morality of Revolutionary Fighters" listed a "Twelve-Point Morality" drawn from Chinese Communist documents. The list admonished against molesting women and eating and drinking in a "nonrevolutionary" way, and stressed the need to maintain a "burning rage toward the enemy" and to help people with their daily tasks. By 1972, three new points had been added. The first urged cadre to "awaken in order to make the revolution by oneself; do not depend on others or foreigners. [You] must clearly understand that this revolution is the revolution of the people of Kampuchea and the people must make it themselves and seize the destiny of the nation themselves; do not sleep waiting for foreigners to do it." The second point stressed "mastery of the task at hand" and the third the necessity of believing in ultimate victory. The additions stressed revolutionary will at the expense of theory or practice.[51]

Most Vietnamese Communists, on the other hand, saw cooperation with their Cambodian counterparts both as a practical measure and in terms of solidarity and long-term mutual obligation. This does not mean that they were starry-eyed. A document of April 1970, for example, noted, "We should make [the Cambodian revolutionaries] realize that their existence depends on ours. Our helping them is one of our international obligations. On the other hand, Cambodia is our staging area. The Cambodian revolution is weak, and its organization loose."[52]

Soon after the coup, more than a thousand Cambodians who had been in Vietnam since 1954–55 and others recruited later began returning home to participate in the resistance. Most had been trained at the Vietnamese-Khmer Friendship School in Hanoi, where the curriculum included Vietnamese, political study, and periods of military training. After completing these courses, graduates of the school were better prepared for a Marxist-Leninist revolution and for military combat than were men and women already engaged in these activities in Cambodia—a further cause for the CPK to feel envious and alarmed.[53]

The returnees traveled south in groups of a hundred. The arduous trip took three months. Perhaps a third of them died along the way from bombing, accidents, and disease.

When they reached Cambodia, the newcomers were often greeted with distrust. One returnee with the rank of major claimed he "was advised . . . to declare that he had left the Vietnamese Communist party to be faithful toward the Red Khmers and the Cambodian people." Others said they had to abjure any connection with the KPRP and the Pracheachon Group. They were told to give up their military rank to conform with Khmer practice and because they had not yet performed any services for the revolution and the Cambodian people. They were all disarmed.[54]

The repatriated Cambodians were a mixed blessing for the CPK, whose forces, although more numerous in 1971 than in 1970 (some estimates ran as high as 125,000 men and women, with perhaps 10,000 under arms), were poorly trained, badly equipped, and often unresponsive to discipline. The newcomers were welcomed for their training and expertise but were suspected at higher levels of working for Hanoi. Over the next year or so, factions in agreement with the central committee's increasingly anti-Vietnamese stance gained power at the expense of those arguing for cooperation. The earliest victims were the returnees, who were secretly purged beginning at the end of 1971.[55]

Warfare and Politics in Phnom Penh, 1971–1972

By early 1971, two political parties had arisen in Phnom Penh. The U.S. embassy described one of them as "a rejuvenated Democratic Party, with significant support, particularly from Buddhists, for Son Ngoc Thanh." The other party, known as Republican, was made up of former opponents of the Democrats. By and large, Democrats followed In Tam and Republicans Sirik Matak. Lon Nol felt himself above political groupings, while his younger brother, Lon Non, sought to destabilize all of them so as to advance his brother's fortunes and his own.

Outside the National Assembly and intellectual circles, these alignments passed unnoticed. Cambodians in the countryside and those crowded into Phnom Penh were more concerned with the disruptions in their lives and the depredations committed by Republican, South Vietnamese, Khmer Krom, NLF, and Red Khmer troops who swept across the landscape in cycles of pursuit, destruction, and retreat.[56] In January 1971, Vietnamese Communist commandos attacked Pochentong airport, destroying the Cambodian air force, which consisted of ten planes and four helicopters. Casualties were forty killed and some two hundred wounded.

The morale of city dwellers was shaken, and so was Lon Nol's optimism. Two weeks later, after providing the National Assembly with a two-hour *tour d'horizon,* the general suffered a stroke that affected the left side of his body. He had been sleeping less than three hours a night for several weeks and was exhausted. After being diagnosed, he was evacuated to a U.S. military hospital in Honolulu.[57]

The stroke was mild, and Lon Nol recovered quickly. He was in serious condition for less than a week and away from Cambodia for only two months. His illness, however, coming so soon after the Pochentong disaster and Chenla 1, was taken as a portent and convinced many Cambodians that his leadership was doomed. Political maneuvering both to dethrone him and to prop him up began while he was away and continued for the next four years.

It was at this stage that U.S. military assistance to Cambodia grew from discreet support totaling less than $20 million to a congressionally funded package of over $180 million. The new program took effect in January 1971 and was initially under the direction of Brig. Gen. Theodore Mataxis, working out of Saigon. The program was supervised by Adm. John McCain, commander in chief of U.S. forces in the Pacific (CINCPAC) in Honolulu. This chain of command angered Mataxis's former superiors and also the U.S. embassy in Phnom Penh, where Ambassador Swank had favored the continuation of a low-profile policy with the Cambodian army. For several months, members of Mataxis's Military Equipment Team were not allowed by the embassy to stay overnight in Phnom Penh. The team's response was to transmit their cables to McCain from Saigon, without passing copies to Ambassador Swank.[58]

While Lon Nol recuperated in Honolulu, the first anniversary of the coup passed quietly in Phnom Penh. Public demonstrations were banned, and a French observer reported that "the streets were almost empty, the shops closed. Frightened citizens watched military patrols on the sidewalks, armored cars moving up and down the boulevards. The only official ceremony drew together a hundred people, in front of the National Assembly. An airplane dropped tracts which showed a Khmer with a pitch-fork, slinging a Vietnamese—recognizable by his conical hat—out of Cambodia."[59]

In Hawaii, Lon Nol was often visited in the hospital by Admiral Mc-Cain. William Shawcross has described the admiral as a "tiny, sprightly man with a straightforward view of the world." His world picture included briefing maps in which China, painted red, was equipped with claws or arrows reaching south, east, and west toward the rest of Asia. He got along well with Lon Nol; both men saw Communists as unbelievers. During his convalescence, Lon Nol told McCain that he wanted to convene a Buddhist conference in Phnom Penh, with delegates from Thailand, Laos, and Burma, to discuss the Communist menace.

In a cable to Sirik Matak, Lon Nol urged his deputy to "make every possible effort to increase the struggle of the Buddhist line against the Thmil line and, to this end, convene a conference in Phnom Penh." Sirik Matak referred the request to a committee and wished Lon Nol a speedy recovery. Two weeks later, Lon Nol proposed to McCain that the United States dam the Mekong north of Stung Treng to "stop the NVA [North Vietnamese Army] from using the river." He suggested that U.S. troops could guard the dam, to internationalize the war if the Vietnamese attacked. He said nothing about what might happen to the water. The admiral passed the unworkable idea along to his superiors without comment, closing his message by remarking cheerfully, "Lon Nol looks good."[60]

In April 1971, the general, using a cane, returned to Phnom Penh to take charge of a twentieth-century war. One of his first statements, made over Phnom Penh radio, was to remind his listeners that Buddhism would last five thousand years and that "the Thmil are not invulnerable."[61]

Lon Nol paid little attention to technology. Before his stroke, the *New York Times* reported, "He reads no newspapers, never listens to the radio or watches television, and never uses a telephone." Allowed by his doctors to spend only an hour a day on government business, he spent the rest of the time honing his political skills. He received a stream of visitors, particularly army personnel and Buddhist monks. His followers did not want him to relinquish control, and neither did the Americans, who considered him essential to the endgame being played in Vietnam.[62]

While convalescing Lon Nol resigned briefly as premier, setting off a political crisis that highlighted his increasing distrust of Sirik Matak and the assembly's distrust of both figures. As a temporary solution, Lon Nol named Matak to the anomalous position of premier-designate, telling

Matak to "act as if I'm overseas." In exchange for Lon Nol's graciousness in resigning, the assembly promoted him to the rank of marshal. The somnambulistic ballet continued for a month. Paralysis had replaced Sihanouk's volatile dictatorship, and public opinion, insofar as it could be gauged, began to drift in a pro-Sihanouk direction. Lon Nol's popularity, widespread in 1970, began to ebb.[63]

Ambassador Swank visited Lon Nol for two hours in July and found the marshal mentally alert. They spoke of continuing U.S. aid. When they turned to the domestic situation, Lon Nol became more animated. "He spoke of the historic superiority of the Khmer people to their western and eastern neighbors," Swank reported. He recounted the legend explaining this decline involving the capture by the Thai of a sacred buffalo impregnated with the creative soul of the Khmer nation, thereafter lost for centuries. The present task, he continued, "is to restore to the nation its soul." In 1987, Ambassador Swank remarked, without referring to this cable, that he had never encountered a "situation so fraught with ambiguity" in his career. He found that "it was often difficult to disguise the conviction that the Cambodians were doomed."

In August, while Sirik Matak was visiting the United States, Lon Nol inaugurated Chenla 2, a tactical replica of Chenla 1. Its aims were to reopen the road between Phnom Penh and Kompong Thom (closed soon after the success of Chenla 1) and to cut off supplies to Vietnamese Communists in Vietnam. The operation was a repetition, from the west, of the U.S. incursion of May 1970 and was geared to U.S. interests.[64]

In General Mataxis's mordant metaphor, the offensive was something to throw from the troika as the wolves closed in. Regular troops, including Cambodia's best units, were once again strung along Route 6, forming a "spearhead" into enemy territory, which included forested areas on either side of the road. Lon Nol expected American air power to neutralize the thmil. As his troops moved north, encountering light resistance, Chenla 2 was declared complete. Advance units continued toward Kompong Thom, reaching the city in mid-October. Their arrival prompted the government to proclaim a major victory. The proclamation was premature.[65]

The month before, Lon Nol had dismissed In Tam, the popular minister of the interior, whom he and Matak had always viewed as a potential rival. Meanwhile, the assembly's five-year mandate was running out. No one wanted to risk a general election. Moreover, Sirik Matak and Lon Nol were irritated by the assembly's intransigence and fragmentation. On October 16, Chief of State Cheng Heng by decree transformed the two-house chamber, whose mandate had expired, into a constituent assembly, whereupon Lon Nol formed a new government and referred in a speech to the need to end "the sterile game of outmoded liberal democracy." Surprisingly, two-thirds of both houses agreed to the transformation. The drafting of a new constitution was left to the ousted members of the legislative branch under In Tam's direction, setting the stage for further conflict.[66]

The military situation had deteriorated sharply. In late October, Communist forces launched attacks on roads supplying Phnom Penh, on the rubber plantations in the east, and on the Chenla 2 columns along Route 6. The Communist forces were estimated to number some fifty thousand, including several thousand guerrillas under CPK command. The attacks in the east were blunted by South Vietnamese troops, but pressure on the Chenla column intensified, and on December 1 Lon Nol ordered the column to retreat. A military spokesman in Phnom Penh called the situation "very serious but not alarming." The situation was a rout. More than three thousand of the marshal's best-trained troops were killed; thousands more were wounded. In the shambles that ensued, some fifteen thousand soldiers and civilians fled north, south, and west, abandoning their weapons and equipment, some of which had to be destroyed by American fighter bombers. Other troops, hitchhiking into Phnom Penh, reported that some of them had not been paid for two months. One positive aspect of the campaign, from the American point of view, was that the Seventh North Vietnamese division suffered heavy casualties and was in no position to play a role in the Communist offensives of March and April 1972. In private, Lon Nol blamed the debacle on insufficient American support.[67]

The defeat undermined American optimism in Lon Nol. Instead of leading to a reassessment of policy, however, negative reporting from the embassy was now discouraged. William Harben, then the political counsellor, has recalled that officers began to "sniff the wind in Washington" before they prepared reports relating to corruption, military defeats, or Lon Nol's somnolent, authoritarian rule. The embassy also became more cautious after several cables—including one in which Ambassador Swank called Lon Nol "a sick man, mentally and physically"—were leaked to hostile columnists in the United States. Chenla 2 was the last major offensive mounted by the Khmer Republic.

The lessons of the campaign were lost on the higher echelons of the U.S. command, at least as far as image making was concerned. The chairman of the U.S. Joint Chiefs of Staff, Admiral Thomas Moorer, chose the aftermath of the disaster to visit Phnom Penh, where he presented Lon Nol with "a cowboy pistol from heroic times, telling him that he should use it 'to celebrate his victory.'" A month later, President Nixon, with no intended irony, announced that "Cambodia is the Nixon doctrine in its purest form"—meaning that Cambodians, rather than Americans, were the ones who were being killed.[68]

With the new year, the military situation stabilized because of U.S. bombing of enemy supply lines and positions. Nonetheless, many Cambodians in Phnom Penh now came to believe the war was lost and that the Republican government should open negotiations with Sihanouk. The prince refused. The Cambodian officer corps also opposed negotiations, and the Vietnamese and Khmer Communists, for reasons of their own, delayed a frontal attack on Phnom Penh. The war dragged on for three more years. The effects on Cambodian society and on the psychology of survivors were far-reaching, but they are impossible to assess. Between 1970 and 1975, an estimated half-million Cambodians, most of them noncombatants, lost their lives. Certainly the period saw thousands of young Cambodians join the revolution and hundreds of thousands of others lose interest in the war.

Lon Nol was less adroit than Sihanouk, less conscientious, less popular, and in worse health. He concentrated his flagging energies on an effort to stay in power. This meant upstaging In Tam and Sirik Matak and keeping an eye on Son Ngoc Thanh. Corruption flourished. At one stage, Lon Nol appointed his personal physician as minister of commerce, while Lon Non manipulated, bought off, and brutalized his opponents. Many of those who might have honorably served the government became dispirited or drifted into the resistance. Hundreds of thousands of refugees came to settle in Phnom Penh, in extreme discomfort. For the next three years, Lon Nol seems to have been sustained by a vision of self-righteousness drawn from his contorted sense of history. Before he suffered his stroke, citing prophecies (*tumneay*) drawn from popular Buddhist culture, he saw himself as the predestined ruler of Cambodia and saw the republic as heralding a utopian age "where everyone is equal." He was supported throughout by the United States and by his belief that President Nixon was a personal friend. The marshal was a poignant, unconfident figure, out beyond his depth. On several occasions, contemplating what was happening to his country, he burst uncontrollably into tears.

The CPK, 1971–1972

In July 1971, the CPK convened a conference for cadre at its headquarters near Phnom Santhuk. In attendance were more than sixty representatives from the various combat zones as well as others from Hanoi. Vorn Vet later recalled that "studying was intense." A short time later a new central committee of some thirty members was elected. No one who had come down from Vietnam was chosen for the committee.[69]

The CPK made two important decisions at this time. One was to send Ieng Sary to Beijing, where he called himself "a delegate from the interior" whose mission it was to oversee Sihanouk and, in Elizabeth Becker's phrase, "[to make] sure that the hall of mirrors did not collapse." The other was to celebrate the September 30 anniversary of the congress of 1960. No record of the celebration has survived, but the date chosen for the Declaration of Patriotic Intellectuals issued in the Liberated Zone of Cambodia—September 30—was probably not fortuitous, and several members of the new committee, including Saloth Sar, Son Sen, and Khieu Samphan, signed the declaration.[70]

The second meeting produced several study documents. These probably included party statutes (the earliest known version of these was captured a month later) as well as documents dealing with foreign policy and the economy. Some informants have not only suggested that the texts voiced decisions to abolish markets and collectivize the economy, but also asserted that disagreements broke out between CPK members who adopted relatively lenient positions (and who were later purged) and more radical ones, such as Son Sen, who survived.[71]

The CPK leadership also used the meeting to discuss their policies toward Vietnam. Several issues were at stake, including the persistence of mixed commands in some areas and Cambodians fighting under Vietnamese command in others; the status of the returnees, militarily and inside the party; and differences in immediate and long-term politico-military goals. On the last point, it seems likely that the CPK leadership wanted to liberate Phnom Penh as soon as possible rather than wait for the liberation of Saigon. This view grew more attractive after Chenla 2. It was stymied, however, by Vietnamese unwillingness to provide arms and ammunition for a final push.

Many Cambodian Communists shared racially based ideas about Vietnam with their countrymen who had executed Vietnamese civilians in May 1970. In a serious incident at Baray in Kompong Thom, after Chenla

2, CPK forces assassinated several unarmed Khmer who had given shelter to Vietnamese Communist forces. Baray was close to CPK headquarters and probably subject to party discipline; it was also the home district of the CPK's local commander, Ke Pauk, who was close to Pol Pot throughout the DK period. The massacres were therefore probably messages from the CPK rather than blunders in the heat of battle. Other cases of friction in 1971 are cited in captured Vietnamese documents, one of which declared, "We fully agree with the Khmer cadre who said, 'The Vietnamese and Khmer people will embrace each other after beating each other black and blue.'"[72]

By the end of 1971, so-called Hanoi Khmer began to be purged from positions of responsibility. An informant in 1980 claimed that "by early 1972 the Khmer from Hanoi were completely cleaned out" from the district where he had been active, in the southwest. Another informant said in 1978 that "by the beginning of 1972 they began to dismiss us, and transfer us elsewhere."

The September conference probably also decided to play down Sihanouk's importance. A CPK circular distributed in the Eastern Zone several months earlier had stated, "With regard to Prince Sihanouk . . . it is not necessary to display his picture. All achievements have been gained by our people's armed forces, not by Sihanouk. We should not deny his contribution flatly, but should tactfully explain to the people that the success was not due to Sihanouk, but it is due to our Party. If the people ask why we do not display Sihanouk's picture during the celebration, we should explain that we have his picture at home."[73]

The revolution proceeded at different speeds in different parts of the country—probably with the greatest intensity in the southwest, under the leadership of Chhit Chhoeun, fighting under the revolutionary name of Ta (Old Man) Mok, and more subject to compromise in areas where Vietnamese troops were active or where former ICP members like Non Suon and Sao Phim retained responsible positions. In dombon 25, near Phnom Penh, for example, directives from party officials in early 1972 enjoined local Cambodians to "display a spirit of internationalism . . . observe discipline and revolutionary ethics . . . and avoid displaying such mannerisms as boasts, threats or vengeance" toward Vietnamese. In the northwest, also, the transformation to a purely national revolution was relatively slow. In March 1972, CPK cadre in the region were saying ambiguously, "Everyone must love Sihanouk. Everyone must study the revolutionary law."[74]

Three illuminating accounts of life in liberated zones were written by outsiders in 1972–73. One was by a French sociologist, Serge Thion, and others by Cambodian school inspectors Ith Sarin and Kuong Lumphon. Thion had taught at a high school in Phnom Penh in 1969 and coauthored a study of Cambodian politics in 1971. Considered persona non grata by the Khmer Republic, he walked into Cambodia from Thailand, hid in Phnom Penh for a week, and was driven into a liberated zone less than half an hour from the capital in early February 1972. For ten days, he lived among guerrilla forces in Kandal and Kompong Speu. His sympathetic account, published in *Le Monde,* strengthened the view that Vietnamese forces were playing a muted role in Cambodia, that Sihanouk remained popular, and that the front was a reality rather than a facade. Thion found what he was looking for, but he knew Cambodia well and asked good questions. His account reveals how little support Lon Nol's government enjoyed and also how a new language of revolutionary politics had entered many people's minds, producing for the first time a loyalty to the future that matched or exceeded a devotion to habitual social relations. At this stage of the revolution, party cadre were gaining control rather than exercising it. Change was in the wind, but the old ways of doing things had not yet been destroyed. Thion witnessed Cambodians at an exciting stage of social transformation. He was optimistic about what he saw.[75]

Two months later, a twenty-nine-year-old school inspector, Ith Sarin, left Phnom Penh to join the resistance. "I had lost hope with Phnom Penh," he recalled in 1988. "Everything was corrupt and dishonorable there." He was accompanied by a similarly disillusioned colleague named Kuong Lumphon. Their move had been cleared with CPK cadre hidden in Phnom Penh, and they spent nine months together as candidate members of the party in the so-called Special Zone traversed by Thion at the beginning of the year. Sarin wrote an account of the sojourn, in French, and this was followed by a short Cambodian book, *Sranoh prolung Khmer* (Regrets of the Khmer soul).[76]

These two texts and Kuong Lumphon's account reveal that the CPK was deeply rooted, well organized, and widely respected in the countryside near Phnom Penh. The accounts also set out the social program of the Red Khmers in detail. Many aspects of the program were widely admired. So was the personal conduct of cadre. As Thion had written, the cadre's exemplary behavior fitted more closely with Buddhist ideals of propriety and social justice than anything emanating from Phnom Penh. After years of neglect and desultory oppression, many local people were ready to abandon the old society and start afresh.

The two Khmers spent several weeks in a CPK political school, where students met for nine hours of reading and discussion every day, followed by self-criticism meetings. At the time, Hou Youn privately warned Sarin about the NLF and North Vietnamese. In Ith Sarin's paraphrase, Youn said, "In 1970–71 the Viet Cong and North Vietnamese (the Red Khmer call them Number 7 friends in the ranks of Communist nations. As for themselves, they boast that they are Number 3, after People's China and Albania) robbed and plundered property from rural people, exploited and robbed Red Khmers, and pressed down on genuine Red Khmer cadre at a time when the Red Khmer were weak, lacked weapons, and had no permanent forces."[77]

Youn went on to describe CPK-Vietnamese friction but claimed that by mid-1972 they could "boast of [their] independent stand. . . . The Vietnamese must respect the Khmer." In public Hou Youn was more discreet, and it was only in 1973, when nearly all the Vietnamese troops were gone, that CPK cadre began calling them the Number One Enemy. In 1988, Sarin recalled that Ta Mok had urged listeners to "destroy Friend Number Seven secretly where possible," and even Non Suon, in spite or perhaps because of his ICP experience, was anti-Vietnamese in private.[78]

Sarin and Lumphon worked as candidate members of the CPK in the office of information and culture in the Special Region. The office was staffed largely with former students from Phnom Penh. "We lived in a circle of comrades," Sarin wrote, "who had a socialist revolutionary philosophy that was strict and far to the left." The party's high-mindedness, rigor, and egalitarianism attracted Sarin, but he was frightened by the way the revolutionary process, as he saw it, turned people into "machines" and by "the unbounded authority of the Party over everything." In March 1973, he returned, discouraged, to Phnom Penh.

The two accounts reveal that many of the CPK's ideas and its modus operandi were perceptible and fully developed by the second half of 1972. Documents distributed to cadre dealt with such topics as the division of Khmer society into classes, class struggle, correct and incorrect pride, and building proletarian principles, to name only four. For reading, Lumphon recalled, they were given Mao's *Selected Works* (volume 2), Stalin's *The Principles of Leninism* ("a medium thick book, 249 pages"), and the CPK's monthly journal, *Tung Padevat* (Revolutionary flag).

On September 30, 1972, Sarin and Lumphon attended ceremonies celebrating the twenty-first anniversary of the CPK. Sarin was appalled when the party flag, with its gold hammer and sickle on a red field, was unfurled. He whispered to Lumphon, "It's as if I'd been stabbed in the chest with a knife. . . . I've got the feeling that I'm living in the Soviet Union." Few others at the meeting would have recognized the flag, but most would have remarked on the novelty of the ritual and the respect they had been asked to show—collars buttoned, their sleeves rolled down, assuming "a prayerful attitude with their right fists above their faces"—paying it more homage than any Cambodian flag had ever received.[79]

When Sarin's book appeared in 1973 foreign journalists paid little attention to it, focusing instead on the growing U.S. constitutional crisis as it spilled over into Indochina. Lon Nol was more perceptive. Sarin was placed under surveillance for a time, and his book was withdrawn from circulation, after it had sold several thousand copies.

Asked in 1988 if he would write his book differently, Ith Sarin said that he should not have entertained any hope that the CPK could run Cambodia fairly. Had he known about the violence that would characterize DK, he said, he would have lacked the courage to write as positively as he did. All the same, he added: "At the time, I believed some of the things they said. I loved the cleanness of their ideas."[80]

The Khmer Republic in Extremis

After Chenla 2 and the withdrawal of North Vietnamese troops from Cambodia in 1972 the CPK took more than two years to win a war that Lon Nol's army had lost. There are several reasons for the long delay. One is that Cambodian forces had needed Vietnamese assistance to smash Lon Nol's units and lacked the weapons, ammunition, and training to do so once the Vietnamese were gone. Another is that the CPK's control of the countryside was uneven. Cambodia east of the Mekong, except for a few large towns, was under Communist administration from the end of 1970 until 1975. Areas closer to Phnom Penh changed hands more than once during the war. Still others in the northwest remained under the Khmer Republic until 1975.[81]

On March 10, 1972, shortly before the Constituent Assembly was to approve the much-revised constitution, Lon Nol suspended the deliberations and announced that he would take Cheng Heng's place as chief of state.

The real target of the announcement was Sirik Matak. Demonstrations against him stirred up by Lon Nol's brother, Son Ngoc Thanh's adherents, and disaffected tertiary students had been occurring for several weeks. The demonstrators accused Matak of hauteur and royalist ambitions. Two days after the announcement, he retired from public life.

Lon Nol then set up a new constitutional commission, empowered to write a text that would reflect some of his bewildering ideas. On the second anniversary of the coup, he swore himself in as president, relinquishing the title of chief of state but remaining prime minister and minister of defense. For the position of his first minister, which was new and powerless, Lon Nol named Son Ngoc Thanh, who had last held the post in 1945. Thanh was the marshal's sixth choice; five others, including In Tam and Yem Sambaur, refused the dubious honor.[82]

In April, just as Sarin and Lumphon were leaving for the maquis, Lon Nol proclaimed a constitution that was modeled on those of France and South Vietnam and that gave him augmented powers. The text was then allegedly "endorsed by 96 percent of the electorate," although less than 40 percent of the voters lived under Republican control. Lon Nol also proposed a presidential election. To his chagrin, several rivals presented themselves, and two of them—In Tam and Keo An—refused to withdraw.[83]

In Tam enjoyed widespread support. In his years as a civil servant, he had never become rich or joined a political party, and his common touch had endeared him to many. When his candidacy was announced, small contributions flooded into his headquarters, until he had enough—some 3 million riels, or approximately $50,000—to rent a small plane and pay a pilot to fly him to provincial centers to campaign. In a private meeting, Ambassador Swank warned him "to do nothing that might weaken the non-Communists," and the embassy remained neutral in the contest, a stance that favored Lon Nol. In the campaign, the marshal claimed that if he lost the election, American aid would cease. The embassy made no effort to deny this spurious allegation. As for In Tam, he was unprepared for the fraud and violence perpetrated by Lon Nol's supporters as the elections drew near. Tam's representative in Pursat was assassinated. In other provinces, his ballot papers disappeared from polling stations, his relatives were expelled from their homes in Kompong Cham on election day, and so on. In Phnom Penh, where In Tam was victorious in most booths, several ballot boxes were sequestered and In Tam's ballots destroyed. By 11:00 P.M., before ballots had been counted in many provinces, Lon Nol was declared the victor. Provisional results, released the following day, asserted that the marshal had gained 55 percent of the votes, In Tam 24.4 percent, and Keo An, the rector of Phnom Penh University (who was popular with young people), the remaining 20 percent. Keo An traced his success to his espousing the return of Sihanouk as a private citizen, but his candidacy also reflected an effort by Lon Non to divide the opposition to his brother. Lon Non later boasted in private that he had inflated his brother's results by 20 percent. When the charade was over, In Tam has recalled, a U.S. diplomat asked him to "help Lon Nol, so that he won't make all the decisions by himself." Tam replied bitterly that Lon Nol "listens only to Americans" and asked the American to stew in Lon Nol's juice.[84]

Lon Nol had poignantly hoped to generate a Sihanouk-style 100 percent consensus. For the assembly elections, scheduled for September 1972, the marshal and his brother revised the electoral laws; the new laws were designed to devalue urban votes while favoring those from districts no longer in government hands, whose sharply reduced electorates could be found in refugee camps under military command. In addition, the assembly was expanded, in response to population growth since 1966 but without regard to the fact that many electorates were out of reach.

The assembly elections were open to political parties but only 10 of the 126 seats were contested. All were won by the Socio-Republican party, sponsored by Lon Non and backed at the polling stations by the military police. In the districts where Democrat candidates appeared to be gaining a majority, the ballots were destroyed, and some electoral officials were put in jail.[85]

Lon Nol then asked Son Ngoc Thanh to resign. The worn-out patriot, who had accomplished little in his months in office, returned to South Vietnam. In his place the marshal promoted one of Thanh's followers from the 1950s, Han Tun Hak, to serve as his first minister. The cabinet contained nine holdovers from the previous one. In political terms, the most significant aspect of the assembly elections and the new cabinet was that In Tam, Sirik Matak, and Cheng Heng had been deprived of power.[86]

The elections also meant that Phnom Penh was still a mailing address for American military aid. Because there was no installation of a neutral or anti-American candidate, the elections satisfied American priorities in Cambodia, which were based on protecting their withdrawal from Vietnam.[87]

The new government's priorities were more arcane. One was to discover a Khmer-Mon costume appropriate for everyday use by government officials. A five-man delegation led by Keng Vannsak traveled to Thailand, Burma, Malaysia, the Philippines, Hawaii, and New Zealand seeking examples of traditional costumes worn by "Khmer-Mon" people speaking "Austronesian" languages. According to William Harben, the delegation "returned with some sixty garments ranging from bark-cloth breach clouts to elaborate robes." A French resident of Phnom Penh has recalled that a Phnom Penh tailor was commissioned to consolidate the samples into a prototype. His sketches called for a floor-length white silk robe and a matching turban—but, Harben adds, "the national costume died . . . of too much material."[88]

With Lon Nol in power and American aid pouring into the country, politicians in Phnom Penh found it difficult to think of Cambodia or their careers in a wider context. Years of isolation, patronage, fatalism, and a hermetic point of view led the figures, in William Harben's phrase, into a pattern of behavior "almost ritualistic in its predictability." The behavior focused on individuals, families, feuds, tactics, and power rather than on institutions, strategies, and political ideas.

Government service was seen as being synonymous with getting rich. The governor of Kompong Chhnang, for example, sold hundreds of tons of petroleum and military equipment to the enemy and never considered himself a revolutionary or a traitor. So did the general commanding Lon Nol's forces in the eastern part of the country. The governor of Battambang, Sek Samiet, was notorious for his commercial dealings with enemy forces but claimed that only American money was involved. By the end of 1972, military spokesmen admitted that every month the pay of some one hundred thousand nonexistent men and women was pocketed by commanding officers. Confronted with the figures, Lon Nol is alleged to have replied, "Calm down! The Americans are killing a thousand of our enemies every week. Victory is ours." The marshal customarily erased enemy units from his tactical maps as soon as he had ordered them bombed by the United States.[89]

In mid-November 1972, Henry Kissinger flew in for three hours to brief Lon Nol on the latest round of Paris talks between the United States and competing Vietnamese factions that had been in progress since 1969. It is uncertain if the marshal registered that "peace was at hand." He hoped that U.S. military aid would continue and that a cultural consensus would lead people to lay down their arms.[90]

Three months later, U.S. Vice President Spiro Agnew also visited Phnom Penh for a few hours and asked Lon Nol not only to declare a unilateral cease-fire linked to the one then in effect in Vietnam but also to widen his political base by giving some responsibility back to In Tam, Sirik Matak, and Cheng Heng. Lon Nol succumbed to the pressure and began consultations with his rivals. As In Tam remembered one conversation, Sirik Matak said, "Well, Nol, why have you summoned us?" and Lon Nol replied, "Our foreign friends, who provide so much aid, have asked me to reconstitute the 1970 government"; he did not suggest why this should be done. He offered Sirik Matak the vice-presidency; the prince refused. In Tam was briefly made a counselor but soon resigned. In the meantime, a Cambodian paper wrote, "President Lon Nol has not been impressed by any event. . . . Amidst the storm, and despite the cries of anguish from his followers, the President sits and drifts calmly into the past." About this time, graffiti began to appear in Phnom Penh calling for his resignation.[91]

On the third anniversary of the coup, a "disaffected air force captain," Pech Kim Luon, coincidentally a friend of one of Sihanouk's daughters, stole a T-28 from a military base near Phnom Penh and dropped two bombs on Lon Nol's compound. The bombs hit a neighboring barracks and killed forty-three military dependents, mostly children, wounding many more. Lon Nol was unhurt. The pilot flew the plane to a rebel zone.[92] Earlier in the day, a teachers' strike had led to demonstrations against the government. They were broken up by a grenade attack, probably ordered by Lon Non.

The marshal's response to the events was uncharacteristically decisive. Within hours, he declared a state of siege, suspended civil liberties, closed down nongovernmental newspapers in Phnom Penh, and lengthened the curfew. In view of the pilot's pedigree, he also ordered the detention or house arrest of more than fifty members of the royal family, including Prince Monireth, and three hundred other suspects who, in Elizabeth Becker's phrase, had "little more in common than an ability to irk the administration." Sirik Matak's house was placed under surveillance and his telephone cut off. Four days later, he told a reporter, "I believe that this regime must not survive and will not last; it is not supported by the people."

Within days, under new American pressure, Lon Nol began serious negotiations with Sirik Matak, In Tam, and Cheng Heng to form a "special government" that would share power while the legislature was suspended. As part of the strategy, Lon Non resigned from the cabinet at the end of April 1973 and departed on a three-month mission overseas. The new High Political Council—which the *London Times* referred to as "a euphemism for a municipal council of Phnom Penh"—was to govern Cambodia by decree.[93] Before long, council members were quarreling among themselves; Lon Nol encouraged them to do so. "Unintentionally," Ros Chantrabot has written, "the new leaders set about destroying themselves." By the end of the year, the council was a rubber stamp.

In the meantime, American bombing of Cambodian targets—"the only game in town," as CIA director William Colby called it later—had turned much of Cambodia into a free-fire zone under Operation Freedom Deal. The campaign killed thousands of people not at war with the United States. It also had the effect of digging a fire trench around the capital, providing a breathing spell to the Cambodian army, and slowing down the advance of CPK forces. Some of the raids struck enemy positions less than a dozen miles from Phnom Penh. Until the bombing was halted at the insistence of the U.S. Congress in August 1973, U.S. planes, secretly and openly, dropped half a million tons of bombs on Cambodia. The tonnage was more than three times the amount dropped on Japan in the closing stages of World War II. Casualties, although certainly high, are impossible to estimate.[94]

In Washington, the bombing of Cambodia came to be seen less in terms of the harm (or the good) it was doing than as part of an ongoing contest of wills between the U.S. Congress and the beleaguered executive branch. A CIA report entitled "The Short Term Prospect for Cambodia," prepared in May 1973, expressed alarm at the determination of the U.S. Congress to stop the bombing. Continued bombing, the report suggested, might only keep Lon Nol in office for a few months. However, it went on, in terms of "overall implications . . . the installation of a Communist-leaning government in Phnom Penh would be of less significance than the circumstances which brought this about. If the President were forced to halt military action in Indo-china, this would . . . [forecast] the end of any significant US military role in this area."[95]

Lon Nol saw the bombing as he saw America itself: as a deus ex machina. In July, government newspapers expressed the hope that the bombing would continue indefinitely and that the U.S. would also resume the bombing of North Vietnam. These hopes were not realized. When the U.S. Congress ordered the bombing stopped, Gen. Alexander Haig said to President Nixon, "We've lost Southeast Asia," and Nixon replied, "Al, I'm afraid you're right."[96]

In March 1973, William Harben noted in his diary,

We have propped up the regime not against the Communists, but against the non-Communists. To say that there is no alternative to a chief of state who received only about 35 percent of the vote . . . eight months ago before his popularity began to decline really seriously seems to me to run counter to the whole raison d'etre of the United

States itself. The result will . . . be a shift of support to the enemy, which we have already begun to witness among the students. In short, U.S. policy has been unwittingly to increase the chance for a Communist victory by permitting the suppression of the non-Communist opposition and supporting a regime which is almost a caricature of the ideal opponent for Marxist-Leninists. . . . There is still a chance to win, but not with Lon Nol.[97]

Lon Nol's regime, like the war itself, had two more years to run.

The Red Khmers Take Command

In late 1972, three of the four North Vietnamese divisions fighting in Cambodia withdrew into Vietnam; the fourth occupied the border area in Kompong Cham. Freed at last from Vietnamese supervision and control, CPK forces in some areas organized demonstrations against the Vietnamese, dismantled guerrilla forces supporting Sihanouk's return to power, and purged returnees from North Vietnam. When the North Vietnamese queried Khieu Samphan about the purges, he replied that they were "possibly plots of the CIA." In southwestern Cambodia fighting broke out between Cambodian and Vietnamese Communist military units. In some areas, Cambodians sought to prevent Vietnamese from repatriating their equipment. The response of COSVN was conciliatory. In mid-1973, COSVN advised its forces, "If the Red Khmers violate our sanctuaries, to kill our troops, we must . . . react for self-defense; but we must not open fire first. We only need to threaten the [Cambodian] troops. Limit damages to the minimum."[98]

Shawcross has suggested that CPK military forces also pressed for victory with depleted equipment in 1973. Their advance on Phnom Penh was delayed or stopped by the American bombing. Pol Pot later denied that the bombing had much effect on his troops, who were "constantly moving," and Khieu Samphan was to assert, in 1976, that "even the B-52s could not destroy our administrative power." U.S. estimates suggest that the CPK army suffered heavy losses—perhaps as many as sixteen thousand men and women, or more than half of the CPK's frontline forces, killed in the final weeks of the bombing campaign. Many of them died in a foolhardy attempt to take Phnom Penh during the period between the announcement that the bombing would be discontinued and the actual date of the halt, August 15, 1973.[99]

In May 1973, the CPK promulgated decrees that sought to collectivize agriculture in certain liberated zones. The process was extensive in the southwest, and a CPK cadre speaking in 1980 noted, "In 1973 at the time of co-operativization in areas where there were a lot of poor people, we went immediately to higher-level co-operatives, whereas where there were fewer [poor], people stayed at lower-level co-ops. This was a Central Committee directive. . . . The line from above was correct but at the lower level the implementation was ultra left or right. The leftist errors and rightist errors [occurred] countrywide." The quotation suggests that Cambodians in liberated zones were often as unready to be collectivized as their compatriots were in 1975–78 and that attempts to collectivize them were often hasty and severe.[100]

About this time the CPK distributed a new history of the party. It seems to have been written to coincide with some anniversary (the date is blank in the text) of the party's foundation, which "subsequent to the 1966–1967 decision of the Central Committee" is given as September 30, 1951. On each of its anniversaries, apparently, the party's history was studied and revised. The history put out in 1973 stresses the 1950s, when the party had been led by Sieu Heng, Son Ngoc Minh, and Tou Samouth. As the document asserts, "Proletarian class Marxism-Leninism was injected into our revolutionary movement by the international communist movement and by the Vietnamese communists." It goes on to state that membership in 1951 included about forty people trained in the ICP in Cambodia, ten trained in the French Communist party, and three or four in the Thai party. Some of these are listed under easily decipherable initials, such as TSM for Tou Samouth and SH for Sieu Heng. Saloth Sar's name does not seem to be included. The text mentions Sieu Heng's defection, Tou Samouth's disappearance, and the split between urban and rural branches of the party. It closes with the party poised to exercise "a great influence" in 1964, that is, after the removal of "90 percent" of the central committee to its rural base.[101]

Between the end of February and early April 1973, Prince Sihanouk, his wife, and Ieng Sary slipped away from southern China to tour the liberated zones of Cambodia. The three-thousand-kilometer trip (made "on tiptoe," as one of Sihanouk's former aides later described it) was intended by the Vietnamese and Chinese to provide Sihanouk more legitimacy than the CPK was willing to bestow. The primary sources for the visit are a film prepared by the front, later edited in China, a photograph album of the trip released in Beijing in late 1973, and extracts from Princess Monique's private journal, published in 1987.[102]

In making the trip, Sihanouk had been asked to play a role for his patrons; he did so with much of his customary panache. This does not mean that he gained anyone's confidence or changed anyone's mind. For much of the time he spent in the liberated zone he must have been terrified of being killed.

His wife's artless narrative reveals the care the Vietnamese and the CPK took to keep her and Sihanouk comfortable and happy. For eight days, accompanied by an entourage of 150 Vietnamese, including a mobile surgery, the royal pair went down the Ho Chi Minh trail in Soviet jeeps, stopping each night at "very pretty little chalets" constructed for their visit. These were equipped with plumbing, and the royal couple received "French meals every day, with fresh bread and fresh vegetables."

At the Cambodian frontier, they were met by Hu Nim and Son Sen, and were joined two days further on by Khieu Samphan and Saloth Sar, "Chief of the Army," and two days later still by Hou Youn and Khieu Ponnary. The prince's convoy reached Phnom Koulen north of Angkor on the fifteenth day of the trip. Here they found a house, as Princess Monique wrote, "built specially for us": "It's our White House in the liberated zone! I love this Khmer-style construction. The inside is prettily decorated. There's a study, a little salon, and a curtain separating these from the 'bedroom'—there's even a carpet on the floor, and curtains in the windows, and a big silver bowl containing water. . . . Truly, we are spoilt by our brothers in the interior. . . . I would love to be able to stay here with Samdech until liberation!"[103]

For the next few days, Sihanouk and Monique attended ceremonies in their honor and presided over a meeting celebrating the third anniversary of the foundation of the front. In fresh guerrilla costumes, they also visited Angkor Wat and other temples. Then, retracing their steps, they reached Hanoi on April 5. Before leaving Cambodia, Sihanouk composed a song (*moderato*) entitled "Thank You, Ho Chi Minh Trail." In Beijing, Monique told the French ambassador that in the course of the trip she had lost ten pounds.[104]

Soon after returning to China, the prince embarked on an eleven-nation tour aimed at securing diplomatic support. As always, when he could, he spoke his mind and menaced the alliances that had formed around him. He noted his antipathy toward the Red Khmers and the ambiguity of his future. In May, in an interview with the Italian journalist Oriana Fallaci, Sihanouk said he was "100 percent with the Khmer

Rouge." He added, "I am useful to them because without me they wouldn't have the peasants, and you can't make a revolution in Cambodia without the peasants." He also noted that his "worst enemy" was Ieng Sary: "What's more, I find him antipathetic. But what does that matter? Even if one day, they want to assassinate me, what does that matter? Aren't they fighting against my enemies? What sort of a patriot would I be if I made everything revolve around my own person and my personal antipathies?"[105]

Foreign media coverage of Cambodia in these months focused on the termination of U.S. bombing. Cambodia was, briefly, news in the United States. Reporters crowded into Phnom Penh, expecting to tell the story of its collapse. When the U.S. bombing stopped and nothing happened, most of them drifted away.[106]

The U.S. Defense Department estimated at this point that the Lon Nol government controlled 60 percent of Cambodia's population but only a quarter of its territory. Over 750,000 refugees had streamed into Phnom Penh and other provincial capitals—a third of them since April 1973. While "ammunition costs" for the Republic were estimated in Washington at approximately $1 million per day, U.S. aid funds earmarked for these refugees amounted to less than $3 million per year. Embassy spokesmen said that the United States lacked personnel to administer a welfare program and that the Cambodians were incapable of doing so.[107]

In September 1973 Ambassador Swank ended his tour of duty and held his first press conference, noting that the war was "losing more and more of its point and [had] less and less meaning for any of the parties concerned."

Cambodia was still linked, in U.S. policy, to the destiny of South Vietnam. It retained President Nixon's interest even as his regime was coming apart. As the months dragged on, Lon Nol remained in command, hoping for a miracle and for continuing American help. Communist forces, in the meantime, intensified their military activity, and the U.S. embassy estimated that combat incidents involving government and Communist troops rose "to the highest level of the war" when the bombing ended.[108]

In late December, the Communists began rocket attacks on Phnom Penh. These killed and wounded hundreds of civilians as well as a few soldiers walking in the streets. By the beginning of 1974, the rockets were supplemented with shells from captured 105mm howitzers, firing at maximum range—seven miles—into the center of the city.

Endings and Beginnings, 1974–1975

As the Communists tightened their noose around Phnom Penh, over two million newcomers were crowded into the capital, and 250,000 others had found shelter in Battambang. For most of them social services soon broke down (or never existed). Hundreds of thousands of school-age children saw their education stop in the 1970s, and thousands died of malnutrition.

Corruption was widespread. In 1973, for example, several new provinces were created in order to create new governorships, themselves paid for by applicants who, given power over areas they never visited, could siphon off funds intended for these regions, funds emanating in the first instance from the United States intended for these regions. Governors sold arms and ammunition to rebels, and army units, in many cases manned by twelve-year-old boys, were at half-strength but paid in full. The degradation of Cambodia made it easier for the Communists to gain recruits and easier for those who watched their country coming apart to hope and even insist that the "forest Khmer" rather than the "old society" offered a viable future to the Cambodian people.[109]

The new American ambassador, John Gunther Dean, was more attuned than Ambassador Swank to Washington's priorities. He hoped to strengthen the Republic's military performance sufficiently to induce the Communists to negotiate an end to the war, perhaps one involving Prince Sihanouk, who had been ignored up to then by American planners. Dean's efforts to get negotiations started foundered on the CPK's stubbornness, Lon Nol's torpor, and Sihanouk's lack of autonomy and on fears among Republican leaders that negotiations might produce a bloodbath, and the destruction of what remained of privilege—and of democracy, for that matter—in Cambodia.[110]

In the meantime, artillery shells and rockets rained down on the capital. People were killed while eating noodles, selling fish, standing around, nursing their children, and bicycling to work. They were defenseless. The war, if it had ever made sense to ordinary Khmer, made none in early 1974, and the U.S. embassy reported primly that "the mood of the less advantaged segments of the . . . population seems to be predominantly one of weary resignation."

Attuned to this mood, Son Sann proposed that Lon Nol leave the country "for medical treatment" so as to allow negotiations to proceed. University students supported the proposal; Lon Nol refused to leave but did nothing to chastise Son Sann. Soon afterward, Son Sann visited Ambassador Dean and pleaded with him for American support in stopping the slaughter. To his chagrin, the ambassador urged him and his countrymen to "hang on" for a few more months—that is, to allow a few thousand more Cambodians to be killed—perhaps until Secretary Kissinger and other busy men in Washington could turn their attention to Cambodian affairs.[111]

In early 1974, Communist forces tried to deliver a knockout blow to Phnom Penh. Their plan involved isolating the capital to prevent food and munitions from reaching it, softening it up with artillery and rocket attacks, and finally launching a general assault. The CPK also hoped to recruit followers, by force if necessary, to enlarge their army. When their troops overran the former royal capital of Udong, north of Phnom Penh, in March 1974, some twenty thousand people were led off into the countryside, where the "class enemies" among them were executed and the others put to work. Meanwhile, in Phnom Penh, Lon Nol took advantage of a brief absence by Ambassador Dean to dismantle the council foisted on him in 1973 by the United States. He thus achieved his long-standing objective of removing In Tam from the political scene.[112]

By April 1974 plans for a "protracted resistance program" were disseminated from the CPK central committee to provincial cadre. The program had two phases. In the first, cadre were to "explain clearly to the Cambodian people under their control the meaning of socialism, as opposed to the conditions presently existing under the Lon Nol government. They are to make the people understand that they are to have a gun in one hand and a plough in the other."[113]

In the second phase, cadre were "to point out that [Communist] units are fighting for a single political ideal—socialism" and that other political groupings were to be "unmasked . . . as traitors and saboteurs who have deliberately created divisions . . . among the Cambodian people." As CPK strategies coalesced, the need for a united front evaporated, along with any role for Sihanouk or for those who hoped for his return to power. Men and women who had thought they formed part of a united resistance would be "arrested for trial and thus . . . subjected to the death penalty."

As government forces struggled to retake Udong, disillusionment and desperation swept through what was left of intellectual circles in Phnom Penh. To many students and their teachers, generously exempted from the draft, life in the liberated zones as described by Ith Sarin probably seemed like paradise, compared with what they saw around them. Interminable violence, foreign intervention, corruption, uncertainty, and a vacuum of leadership had become intolerable. The revolutionary alternative, supposedly fashioned out of justice, autonomy, honesty, and self-assurance, seemed preferable and for young people abandoning the past posed few real problems.[114]

Things came to a head in early June, when antigovernment demonstrations developed into running battles between students and the police. On the fifth, the minister of education, Kim Sangkim, and his deputy Thach Chea were taken hostage by demonstrating students and marched off to a Phnom Penh high school, which was soon besieged by military police. The hostages were held in a classroom opening onto a second-story terrace, accessible to stairs at either end. At 4:00 P.M., a single gunman got into the room where the two were being held (a few moments before, they had been seen "joking with students, and eating peanuts") and shot them both with a .45 automatic. The assassin, sighted by journalist Stephen Heder, escaped into the crowd. In the aftermath, over a hundred students were arrested, and three died from gunshot wounds.[115]

In July 1974 Lon Nol's forces reoccupied Udong. Rockets and artillery shells continued falling on Phnom Penh, but the CPK offensive never materialized and shelling tapered off toward the end of the year, as Republican forces expanded their defensive perimeter. Rice and other supplies arrived by convoys up the Mekong or by air. Ambassador Dean, for his part, kept pressing the government to make reforms and to prosecute the war, but bureaucrats prevaricated and solutions were elusive. Inside the city, people were running out of food and money. At Kompong Seila, seventy-eight miles southwest of the capital, a Republican garrison, besieged for nine months and starved of supplies, began eating human flesh, while refusing to surrender. Every day, three hundred Cambodians were killed or wounded. Under American pressure, Lon Nol offered to talk with the insurgents, without preconditions. Sihanouk rejected the offer, demanding instead the unconditional surrender of the regime. In November 1974, the Republic barely survived a credentials vote at the United Nations. With victory in sight, the CPK had no interest in talking; conversely, the United States and Lon Nol were now willing to negotiate to avoid a humiliating defeat. Time was not on the side of the Republic. Nor were its original patrons. In August 1974, President Nixon, the "Cambodian Desk Officer" of 1970–71, was driven from office.[116]

The Final Offensive

On New Year's Day 1975, the CPK opened its assault on Phnom Penh with a rocket and artillery barrage. Supplementary tactics involved choking off the Mekong supply line, through which rice, petroleum, and ammunition were reaching Phnom Penh, while tightening a noose around the city so as to close the airport. In the meantime the city was to be subjected to rocket and artillery attacks.

Several months before, Sihanouk's government in exile had "nationalized" Cambodia's rubber plantations and obtained credits from China in lieu of future sales. These went toward the purchase of Chinese-made floating mines, which came into Cambodia along the Ho Chi Minh Trail and appeared on the Mekong in early 1975. The mines were so effective that river convoys almost immediately stopped running; by the end of February, the United States was forced to airlift in supplies. The food brought in was insufficient. The city needed one thousand metric tons of rice a day but in February and March was receiving less than half that amount. Prices rose astronomically, and rice was unavailable to most of the population. Children were particularly hard-hit. Thousands of them starved to death in the waning days of the Republic.[117]

Having failed in his efforts to open talks, Lon Nol came under pressure from Ambassador Dean to leave the country, so that someone else could open negotiations that took Sihanouk into account. Dean stated that "a new Communist-oriented Cambodia [was] bound to emerge" and added that he assumed "we would prefer that the successor regime in Cambodia be oriented toward Peking rather than toward Hanoi. If this assumption is correct, and we consider Sihanouk to be Peking's man, the question arises whether anything can be done to strengthen Sihanouk's hand at this late stage so that he can return to Phnom Penh with some power, rather than abandon Cambodia to the *Hanoi-leaning Khmer Rouge*" (emphasis added).[118]

The marshal temporized. On March 9, he invited some foreign correspondents to his villa, where they watched him walk around the garden, leaning on a cane. He said, "Good morning" to them but nothing else. Three days later, he accepted Sosthène Fernandez's resignation as head of the armed forces; Fernandez then flew out to permanent residence in France. The fifth anniversary of the coup passed unnoticed in Phnom Penh. By then, electric power operated for only four hours every other night; fuel, charcoal, food, and medicine had run out in much of the city.

Lon Nol reshuffled his cabinet, moved with difficulty, and was driven to his appointments in his slate gray Rolls Royce. To the very end, he avoided hard decisions, such as ending deferments for university students or firing corrupt subordinates. By March 22 he had obtained passports for himself and his family. It is hard to determine if he understood what was going on.

The crisis in Cambodia had caught the attention of the new U.S. president, Gerald Ford, and the largely hostile U.S. Congress. The two wrangled about giving aid to Cambodia. Ford's emergency figure, largely for ammunition, was US $122 million. No one in the administration could suggest what the ammunition might obtain. What frightened the Americans was precisely what exhilarated the CPK forces, who were poised to liberate Phnom Penh and to impose what Ambassador Dean called an "uncontrolled solution" before the Vietnamese Communists succeeded in capturing Saigon. To the Americans, Sihanouk suddenly became a player. He was the last chance to salvage something pleasing to the United States.

In late March, Sihanouk wrote a letter to President Ford, asking him to to see if the U.S. embassy in Phnom Penh could locate prints of his films from the 1960s and convey them to him in Beijing. The letter praised Nixon for persuading Lon Nol to allow Sihanouk's mother to go into exile in 1973 and offered Ford "a collection of my modest musical compositions." As for the films themselves, Sihanouk went on, they were "self-styled as fiction [but] each one contains many sounds and images related to 'physical' Cambodia, artistic Cambodia, cultural Cambodia, archaeological Cambodia, social Cambodia, the Cambodia of peasants, the Cambodia of citizens, Cambodia of the past and modern Cambodia."[119]

It is uncertain if the letter meant more than it said, but the U.S. representative in Beijing, George Bush, offered to meet the prince through intermediaries, and Kissinger ordered Dean to locate the films in question. Sihanouk refused to meet Bush and resisted last-minute American proposals that he fly back to Cambodia and interpose himself before the fighting stopped. The upshot was that Sihanouk regained possession of some of his films, and Kissinger could later claim, mendaciously, that he had wanted Sihanouk in power in Cambodia "all along."[120]

At the beginning of April Lon Nol and his family left the country, allegedly for an informal visit to Indonesia and medical treatment in Hawaii. Everyone knew he would never return. To sweeten his departure, the government gave him a million dollars and named him a national hero. On the day he flew out of Cambodia, weeping at the airport, insurgents captured the military base of Neak Luong, south of Phnom Penh, which had been under siege for several months. The capture opened up other approaches to the capital, whose fate was thereby sealed.[121]

By this time, the Phnom Penh airport was being bombarded daily, and the American airlift was slowing down. Kissinger delayed Ambassador Dean's departure, hoping against hope for a "Sihanouk solution," but on April 10 most Americans, including the embassy staff, were lifted out by helicopter. The president pro tem of Cambodia, Saukham Khoy, climbed into one of the helicopters and left the country. The rest of the cabinet stayed behind. Sirik Matak refused to leave and wrote to Ambassador Dean, "I never believed for a moment that you [would abandon] a people who had chosen liberty. You have refused us your protection and we can do nothing about it."[122]

The prime minister, Long Boret, who had accompanied Lon Nol to Indonesia, flew back to Phnom Penh and certain death. On the night of April 15, he discussed the alternatives facing his government with a reporter, Jean-Jacques Cazeau, who suggested that he declare Phnom Penh an open city. Boret agreed; Cazeau, who had been talking with him—at his invitation—for three hours, excused himself. Four hours later, Boret telephoned him, saying, "My generals won't consider an unconditional surrender"—as if other options existed. Indeed, soon after this brave stand, several generals agreed to the proposal and fled the capital by helicopter. Hundreds of other well-to-do Cambodians had already left on spurious missions or seeking medical attention. As the insurgent forces reached the suburbs of Phnom Penh, two million others in the capital waited to see what would happen.

On April 17, as Red Khmer troops converged on the city from three directions, Mean Leang, an Associated Press reporter in Phnom Penh, transmitted the last message that the bureau was to receive from Phnom Penh for many years. Its broken, colloquial English located it in the American chapter of Cambodian history, which was also coming to an end. The message read, "I alone in post office. Losing contact with our guys. I have so numerous stories to cover. I feel rather trembling. Do not know how to file out stories. How quiet the streets. Every minute changes. At 1300 local my wife came and saying that [Red Khmer] threatened my family out of the house. . . . Appreciate instructions. I, with a small typewriter, shuttle between the post office and home. May be last cable today and forever."[123]

seven
Revolution in Cambodia, 1975–1979

The revolution that swept through Cambodia between 1975 and 1979 left over a million Cambodians dead and half a million more exiled in Thailand and elsewhere. Many of the survivors were scarred physically and psychologically by what they had gone through. To understand what happened and why, one must regard the revolution both in terms of its relations with Cambodia's past and in terms of its horrifying uniqueness; not only that, one must view it against the background of revolutions elsewhere in order to determine what may have been characteristically Cambodian about it.

Government spokesmen in DK frequently boasted that on April 17, 1975, more than two thousand years of Cambodian history came to an end. The final assault on Phnom Penh, which had begun on January 1, was timed to coincide with the Buddhist New Year in April to stress this new beginning.[1]

Characteristically, revolutions fracture continuity. At the same time, many continuities persist from prerevolutionary to revolutionary regimes. In the Cambodian case, continuities of context and behavior combined with external factors made the revolution itself by 1978 a failure for its leaders and a disaster for nearly everyone else. Partly, this was the fault of the harsh, erratic behavior of the revolutionaries themselves. After the end of 1976, failure sprang from the leadership's fixations with Vietnam and treachery within their ranks.[2]

The failure can also be traced to the refusal of millions of Cambodians to pay attention to revolutionary promises and ideas. If survivors are to be believed, very few people were willing to overturn their lives as com-

236

pletely as the CPK demanded or risk the consequences of revolutionary change. Others were appalled by the human costs involved. Hundreds of thousands took the risk of waging a revolution for a while and then drew back. Tens of thousands remained true to revolutionary ideals. But most of the people failed to catch fire.[3]

A third reason for the failure of the revolution was that the foreign models it followed without acknowledgment were ill-suited to Cambodian conditions. These models included the French Revolution, the collectivization of agriculture as practiced in the Soviet Union and Vietnam, the total mobilization of the population for collective purposes, as in China's Great Leap Forward of the 1950s, the postrevolutionary renewal of class warfare from the Chinese Cultural Revolution, and a pervasive notion of self-reliance resembling the *chuche* policies of North Korea. The literalness and speed with which these models were followed made them especially destructive.

The Cambodian revolution did not destroy so many people or fail because it was too Marxist-Leninist or because it was not Marxist-Leninist enough, although Marxism-Leninism in DK was a blunt instrument and a destructive weapon. Rather, the Cambodian revolution crashed to the ground because of the persistence of so many counterrevolutionary ideas among rulers and ruled, so much poor leadership, and so much counterrevolutionary behavior.

Between 1975 and 1979, the CPK wanted to exercise absolute control and hoped to preside over the destruction of Cambodia's past. After 1979, many survivors recalled the failure of this attempt. To explain it, they cited contradictions in revolutionary behavior, such as acts of kindness by Communists toward their own relatives and toward older people. They also recalled the greed, venality, and cynicism of many party members, which resembled the behavior of prerevolutionary officials. These recollections, however, probably represent an effort by survivors to fit the DK period into earlier times and earlier models of behavior, and so to hold on to their own frames of reference rather than to unacceptable revolutionary ones. In other words, if people in the 1980s could locate old humanity or old injustice in the 1970s they might also discount and dismantle what was different or startling about the revolutionary experience.[4]

As far as political ideology is concerned, three emphases persisted in the DK era from prerevolutionary times. These worked in some ways to accelerate and in others to undermine the revolution. In combination, they gave it a Cambodian flavor. These emphases were on Cambodia's glorious past, the uniqueness of the Cambodian "race," and, particularly after 1976, the Cambodian people's supposedly universal hatred of Vietnam. In terms of practice, a major continuity was that DK held it proper to concentrate power in the hands of a single person. Prince Papa and Marshal Lon Nol were followed by Comrade Secretary Pol Pot. In an attempt to destroy the personalism that, in their view, had corrupted previous regimes, the CPK stressed the collective nature of its leadership and kept most of its leaders hidden. Nonetheless, its style of operation, with its lack of accountability, its self-deification, its monopoly on information, and its single voice uttering unchallengeable commands, amounted to one-man rule, and by 1977 Brother Number One (Pol Pot) and Brother Number Two (Nuon Chea) had become synonymous with the Organization.

Another continuity that connected Sihanouk, Lon Nol, and the collective leadership around Pol Pot was that these men (and women, in the DK case) saw themselves as new types of rulers—a private citizen monarch, a nonmonarchic chief of state, a set of comrades wielding national power. They paid no homage to their teachers, to foreign models, or to previous chiefs of state.

In April 1975 Pol Pot and his colleagues seized the opportunity to refashion Cambodia. They did so with extraordinary speed and intensity: within a week, to quote François Ponchaud, the "foundations for an egalitarian, communitarian society had been dug into the living flesh of the people." Whether the speed reflected the leaders' overconfidence or their insecurity is difficult to determine. A novelty in 1975 was that the refashioning responded to a master plan, which the leaders of the CPK had worked out and purified in their years of close association. Unlike Sihanouk and probably unlike Lon Nol, Saloth Sar and others in the CPK believed that their victory and their assumption of power responded to laws of history rather than to chance, supernatural intervention, or personal skill. Because these laws had made their victories inevitable, their plan to collectivize and transform Cambodia as rapidly as possible, they thought, was also bound to succeed. For the time being, however, the word *socialist* was seldom mentioned, and the party's existence was hidden from outsiders.

In formulating policy, the leaders of DK ignored data that contradicted their preconceptions. For example, in his speech of 1977 celebrating the achievements of the CPK and announcing its existence to outsiders, Pol Pot blamed rural injustice in Cambodia on landlordism, a phenomenon that fitted his theories but in fact was relatively rare. To justify a national policy of collectivization, he cited the only provinces of the country, Svay Rieng and Battambang, where landlordism had been rife. That most Cambodian peasants, happy or not, were in debt to Chinese moneylenders but not yet dispossessed would have fitted neither the party's national analysis nor its utopian ideas. "Smashing the landlords" and taking their land fitted with the class war that the Communists wanted to wage across the country as well as with its unacknowledged Soviet, Chinese, and Vietnamese models. Taking away people's small-holdings, houses, and livestock without compensation, which is what the regime did next, alienated nearly all the people.[5]

It is hard to say if Pol Pot believed what he was saying about landlord-ism or said it merely to justify the party's national program, decided in advance. The second explanation seems more likely. Pol Pot and his col-leagues believed in the necessity of revolution. Some of them, by 1975, had spent over twenty years attempting to bring one to fruition. Being a revolu-tionary was a full-time, lifelong occupation. In describing Pol Pot, a former companion of his appropriated the celebrated remark made by Axelrod about Lenin: that he was "the only man who had no thoughts but thoughts about the revolution, and who in his sleep dreamt of revolution." Others, like Son Sen, Khieu Samphan, and Nuon Chea, had similarly incandes-cent views. They were not prepared to abandon them in the wake of their victory because they discovered that preconditions, social analyses, or human resources for a revolution in Cambodia were lacking or in short supply.[6]

Like Sihanouk's fashioning of Buddhist socialism or Lon Nol's enter-taining of ideas of Khmer-Mon hegemony, the CPK leadership's choosing to wage revolution everywhere in Cambodia did not spring from a study of Cambodian social conditions or from consultation with others but from a conviction on the part of the CPK's leaders that a recognizably Commu-nist revolution needed to be waged. If the right preconditions did not exist, that problem could be overcome by revolutionary fervor. The absence of a proletariat in Cambodia, for example, was not seen as an impediment to progress. An industrial labor force could be created from poor peasants and young children operating en masse. Cambodia soon became a gigan-tic prison farm.[7]

The CPK's correctness before April 1975 was demonstrated retroac-tively by its extraordinary victory. What use were precedents in view of the unprecedented events of April 17, 1975? The peasant armies that had defeated the Americans (two weeks before the fall of Saigon!) were descended from the laborers who had built Angkor. Why should they look elsewhere—or anywhere—for models or advice?[8]

The evacuation of the cities was a case in point. A confidential CPK document asserted that "the expulsion of the population from Phnom Penh is a measure one will not encounter in any other country's revolution." In a similar vein, Ieng Sary told a German correspondent in 1976, "It is still too early to announce what we are doing in our country. Since our action is not based on models, we are learning in the course of the experiment."

He returned to the point a year later, saying that "the Khmer revolution has no precedent. What we are trying to do has never been done before in history." In the DK era, statements of this kind occur too frequently to be dismissed as rhetoric. In terms of Cambodia's material wealth, small population, technological backwardness, and military potential the dithyrambic assertions of uniqueness made little sense, but they struck a responsive chord in ordinary Cambodians worn down by centuries of poverty, disdain from foreigners, and subservience to elites. Sihanouk, Lon Nol, and Pol Pot, in different ways, boasted about Cambodia's potential greatness and about how, under inspired leadership, Cambodia was at last assuming its place in the world. Of the three, only Pol Pot placed the blame for injustice on the Cambodians themselves.

For thousands of young, impoverished Khmer, Pol Pot's analyses and his triumphalism led to personal conversions. For the rest of the population, his actions and ideas and the consequences that flowed from them were incomprehensible and totally alien to people's concerns.[9]

In stressing these continuities, however, I do not want to lose sight of four major discontinuities engendered by DK. These were the priorities given to social transformation and control, the dismantling of a market based economy, the extent of terror and violence sanctioned by the regime, and the unacknowledged imitation of foreign models. None of these priorities had roots in earlier times, but they were made easier to accomplish by traditions of commandism in Cambodian government and apathetic responses of ordinary people to centuries of exploitation. The new priorities also responded to inchoate wishes on the part of a smaller number of Khmer for empowerment and social justice.[10]

For their social agendas, Sihanouk and Lon Nol adhered to the status quo. They assumed that what Cambodians wanted was more of the same. The DK regime differed profoundly from theirs. Its commitment was to the total transformation of Cambodia's economy and of people's ways of working, thinking, and behaving.

The short, unhappy history of DK can be seen, in Andrew Walder's phrase, in terms of the "tyrannization of practice at the hands of theory." One example of this process was the way in which the regime, in order to produce the symmetrical checkerboard depicted on the DK's coat of arms, insisted on realigning rice fields until they were precisely one hundred meters square, regardless of topographical peculiarities. Similarly, rice varieties developed locally to meet local conditions were often scrapped to impose uniformity throughout a given district.

A second set of discontinuities was the closing down of markets and salaried employment, the abandonment of money, and the abolition, in theory, of masters and servants. These changes were imposed nationally soon after April 17. Everyone except poor peasants, soldiers of the revolutionary army, and some industrial workers had their work-related identities and their social positions wiped out.

These policies sought to dissolve old modes of production, hierarchies, and ceremonies of deference and exploitation. They sought to enforce equality by abolishing jobs. They offered power to the poorest people in the country and to the young. Hierarchy soon reemerged under DK, but high positions were held by different categories of people from before and were no longer expressed in terms of money, possessions, or prerevolutionary titles. Instead, those with power and status in DK had access to three commodities that most of the population lacked: food, weapons, and information.

As for revolutionary violence, the third discontinuity, it would be misleading to say that the Cambodian people were intrinsically peaceable before the 1970s. Nor were they made violent by American bombing, Marxism-Leninism, or the provocations of the Vietnamese. The potential for violent behavior was always there, supported by abundant evidence from nineteenth-century wars, bandit depredations in colonial times, the Issaraks, and more recently the anti-Communist commandos mobilized in the 1960s. What was new about violence in the 1970s was the increase in its occurrence, on the one hand, and the absence or erosion of legal or community sanctions against it, on the other. As Khmer society tore itself apart, violent death became a national phenomenon. The war and the DK regime undermined or removed institutional and psychic restraints on violent behavior by people entitled to bear arms.

Between 1970 and 1975, both sides fought with desperation and brutality. Neither took any prisoners. After 1975, DK licensed violence in part by discrediting Buddhism, and by a process of moral inversion sanctified the use of terror, ostensibly as a temporary measure, in the name of the revolution. Violence became a virtue. Waging war became prestigious. So did smashing enemies of the party.

For revolutionaries in Cambodia the teamwork, aggression, and self-lessness that had gained the military victory were soon rechanneled into postwar tasks. Peace provided an opportunity to continue wartime solidarities, violence, and patriotism. It also allowed combatants (*yothea*) to launch new and repeated offensives (*vay samrok*) in agriculture and against enemies (*khmang*). Politics became the continuation of warfare by similar means.

Encouraged to launch offensives and to smash the enemies of Angkar, enraged young soldiers executed hundreds of new people and former Republican soldiers in the weeks following the end of the war. Taking the order literally, they often used hoes and shovels to smash their enemies' heads.

In 1975, the violence was widespread in Battambang, less frequent in other regions, and rare in the eastern part of the country, but everywhere individual rights and preferences were subordinated to revolutionary duties and to the class interests of poor peasants as perceived by the Organization. Before Angkar's priorities became known, many "April 17 people" were punished and executed for actions they considered harmless or beneficial, actions such as foraging for family members, concealing rations, telling the truth about their education, or complaining about work conditions.[11]

When Lon Nol took power, he released several hundred political prisoners. Those whom he imprisoned were similarly released in April 1975. In January 1979, however, when the Vietnamese and their Cambodian colleagues reached Phnom Penh, they discovered virtually no prisoners. Instead, thousands of people who had been detained had been systematically tortured, interrogated, and killed. There were regional detention centers too, where executions were less frequent, but, as survivors' stories were collected it became clear that execution had been the normal punishment for most crimes in much of the country.

Under Sihanouk and Lon Nol, the poor lived badly and had no inalienable rights. Between 1970 and 1975, thousands of them joined the CPK, which trained them to perceive their status as flowing from exploitation (the Cambodian words for exploitation, *chi cho'n,* mean "ride and kick"). Bitter memories and promises of empowerment hastened the process of conversion. Between 1970 and 1975, membership in the CPK expanded from about four thousand to more than fourteen thousand full and candidate members. Those chosen by the party to serve as village cadre were often, in the words of one refugee, "people who had been the poorest of the poor, without livestock or tools, who didn't even own a handful of earth." Another noted that they had been "very poor workers and lazy students." In Maoist terms, these men and women were "poor and blank" pages on which a revolution could be inscribed.[12]

Even before victory, Cambodians thirteen and fourteen years old were often taken from their homes in liberated areas and subjected to short indoctrination courses from which they emerged, according to a U.S. embassy study in early 1975, "fierce in their condemnation of the 'old ways', contemptuous of traditional customs, and ardently opposed to religion and parental authority." Freed from family obligations, they displayed a loyalty to the Organization that was often absolute. According to two such children interviewed in 1979, young people became Communists in some cases because this meant that "they didn't have to work, and could kill people." These boys and girls became the revolution's cutting edge.[13]

Many new people encountered two difficulties with the transformation of the poor and the empowerment of children. First, they often found it impossible to accept that they had become the servants of dark, uneducated people. The second difficulty was, in George Steiner's words, that the "impact of revolution had made of every man and woman a political animal, an inhabitant of history." The rural poor had emerged into the foreground. Politics had taken command of their lives before a similar process had occurred among the newcomers from the towns. The April 17 people were expected to transform this freedom from exploitation into increased agricultural production. They were "ridden and kicked" by those whom the revolution had empowered. Some revolutionary priorities, such as the renunciation of ties (*lea bang*) and the adoption of a twelve-point moral code, were ethical. Others drew their strength from class hatred; still others attacked prerevolutionary ways.[14]

The revolution was exhilarating for some but left millions of others humiliated and confused. For this majority, village Buddhism, shared experiences, leisure, patronage, and family loyalties had served for centuries to mediate violence and injustice and to explain suffering and disorder. Under DK, familyism (*kruosaniyum*), individualism, private property, personality, and vanity, and feudal religious practices were all renounced. In their place, people's biographies (*pravatt'rup*) were sought, not to uncover skills useful to DK but to determine class origins and affiliations, seen as keys to attitudes and behavior. In this, the CPK was following

Maoist practice, which made class an ideological rather than an economic category. Many new people learned quickly to lie about their past.[15]

As in the past, there was little if any conversation between rulers and ruled. Those at the top commanded, and everyone obeyed. Under DK, however, two new elements emerged: the top leaders stayed hidden and officials and cadre at the village level, so long as they obeyed directives from above, enjoyed more autonomy than ever before, including in many cases power to judge and execute offenders. At the same time, ordinary people were encouraged to talk to those in charge of them about the tasks that each unit needed to perform. This relative autonomy and the fact that cadre were not drawn from the previously ruling class were probably what the regime meant in calling itself democratic.

The commands from the Revolutionary Organization covered every aspect of people's lives. As in Thomas More's Utopia, strict rules for behavior were laid down. These governed clothing, haircuts, vocabulary, leisure, and sexual relations, to name only five. Commands emanated from power holders at the village level, and in some areas from illiterate, heavily armed children patrolling the villages at night. What these young people interpreted as disobedience was often punishable by death.[16]

DK gave local cadre greater autonomy, but absolute control was now exercised by radio-telephone and messengers (*nir'saa:* literally, "trusted persons") sent out from the center with instructions to the zones, from the zones to the districts, and so on. These young men and women, the subject of at least one revolutionary song, were handpicked by the regime and entrusted with commands that were to be explicitly obeyed.[17]

The final discontinuity between DK and earlier regimes was DK's imitation of foreign models. Sihanouk's approval of a French-style constitution in 1947, his Gaullism later on, and Lon Nol's choice of a republic in 1975 were imitations intended to please others. After 1975, DK eclectically followed Soviet, Chinese, North Korean, and Vietnamese precedents, models, and examples, while proclaiming that its decisions arose from objective data and were entirely Khmer. In fact, the CPK was a properly constituted Marxist-Leninist party and recognized as such by other parties. Its statutes resembled those of Communist parties elsewhere. As late as 1978 the revolutionary flag was the one associated everywhere with a Communist party. This means that the CPK placed itself within a foreign tradition. At the same time, it kept its existence secret from everyone except its members. Its rationale for doing so probably sprang from the fact that its leaders felt comfortable when hidden, and by denying the existence of the CPK they could deny their affiliation with an international movement.[18]

In the 1950s Vietnamese influence on the CPK was substantial, and many Cambodian Communists took up arms alongside the Vietnamese to fight the French. After 1975, at least as far as ends and means were concerned, the revolution drew on Russian and Chinese experiences, moving smoothly from something resembling Soviet war communism (1919–21 in the USSR, 1973–75 in Cambodia) to the collectivization (in 1976–77 in Cambodia) of the sort that had gripped the USSR after 1927 and China after 1949—skipping over, as the Chinese had done, the relatively pragmatic, unrevolutionary model provided by the USSR's New Economic Policy in the early 1920s. The DK's Four-Year Plan, set in motion in 1976, resembled Stalin's policies in the early 1930s and their offspring, the Great Leap Forward in China in the 1950s. Its principal aim was to increase agricultural production so as to raise revenues enough to enable the purchase of the machinery that would provide the bases first for light industry and later for heavy industry. Indeed, it referred to itself as a Super Great Leap Forward, going the Chinese one better. Cambodia's puritanical cultural policies had probably filtered through policies of the Chinese Cultural Revolution, themselves inherited in part from the Soviet movement of the same name.[19]

What the CPK lacked compared with Communist parties elsewhere was a documentary dimension and a sense of sharing experiences with former revolutionaries or with contemporaries in foreign countries.[20] And yet foreign models and experiences were important, even though their importance was hidden or denied. Whereas Sihanouk's Buddhist socialism and Lon Nol's Khmer-Monism had been uncoercive, intellectually mediocre efforts to mobilize the Cambodian people to greater autonomy and self-respect, the Cambodian revolution, which had these goals as well, was also waged so that Cambodia could achieve some of the same socialist results as China, the USSR, and North Korea. If Marxism-Leninism responded to laws of history and transcended national differences, what was contingent in a nation's history—in theory at least—was ephemeral. The Cambodian Communists were never able to resolve the contradiction between their revolution's being a genuine socialist one (and thus comparable to others) or uniquely Cambodian, without precedents or offspring. Indeed, some documents from the DK period suggest that the latter idea occasionally caught hold among the leaders of the CPK. Another element at work here was that although the regime claimed to have made great strides in eliminating illiteracy in Cambodia, there is no evidence that it gave people outside the party anything to read.[21]

The tensions between competing imperatives became sharper after 1976 and set off the waves of purges that swept through the party beginning in September of that year. Ironically, the regime's decision to adapt notions of total self-reliance from Chinese and North Korean thinking kept them from acknowledging such models because doing so would call Cambodia's own autonomy into question.[22]

The relationship between the Cambodian revolution and developments in China between 1960 and 1979 would reward further study, and so would the personal relationships between the leaders of the CPK and ideologues in China at this time, in particular the so-called Gang of Four. Many aspects of DK ideology and behavior, including the militarization of language, the preference for *Red* over *expert*, the theory that peasants are to be learned from rather than taught, the idea of class as an ideological rather than economic category, the notion of continuous revolution, and the emphasis on revolutionary will seem to have been borrowed from China, whereas others, like maintaining the secrecy of the leadership and the primacy of terror, perhaps owe more to Soviet models. The party-to-party relations between Cambodia and China and those between the parties of Cambodia and Vietnam between 1970 and 1978 are also important, and so is the training that Cambodian cadre underwent in China and Vietnam.[23]

By keeping itself hidden, its leadership unnamed, and its intentions ambiguous, the Upper Organization (*Angkar Loeu*), as the central committee came to be known, was as distant, mysterious, arbitrary, and impossible to question as any Cambodian monarch had been in precolonial times. But there were differences as well, for Pol Pot and his associates were stepping back from the cult of personality as practiced in China and North Korea, which in their view had been so harmful to Cambodia ever since the 1950s and perhaps throughout its history. They believed in collective leadership and collective action. Another difference between DK and precolonial monarchies was that the latter could not impose their will on regions more than a few days' walk from the capital and were seldom strong enough to do even that, whereas the Organization could enforce its will quickly and brutally over wide areas.

Emptying the Towns

In the week following April 17, 1975, Phnom Penh and those provincial towns still occupied by the Khmer Republic—Battambang was the largest of these—were emptied of their populations. Over the next two months, between two and three million people were moved into the countryside to become agricultural workers.

At first, CPK cadre explained the evacuations by saying that the Americans planned to bomb the cities. Later on, when the operation was over, high-ranking officials variously claimed that the towns had been emptied to forestall resistance organized by the CIA, to prevent epidemics, and because there was not enough food in the towns to feed the people. These explanations are partially plausible. Not one of them accounts for the totality of the operation, for the emptying of smaller towns, where food shortages, disease, and CIA agents were not a problem, or for the evacuation of all the patients, many of them Republican battle casualties, from at least one hospital in Phnom Penh.[24]

The decision to empty the towns was a calculated, political decision, part of a wider agenda, with an economic and ideological rationale. It was made by the CPK central committee in February 1975, along with decisions to abolish money, private property, and markets, to repatriate Cambodia's Vietnamese minority, and to execute high-ranking Republican officials and army officers. Taken together, the decisions were intended to topple and overturn prerevolutionary Cambodian society, to strike a deathblow to private property, and to allow the CPK to come to power. Subsequent decisions collectivizing Cambodian agriculture, dismantling Buddhism, and limiting family relations fitted into the same framework.[25]

The decision to evacuate the towns also sprang from the CPK's antiurban ideology. Since 1968, the party had waged an armed struggle from the countryside with a peasant army whose class enemies, in theory at least, lived in cities and large towns. These people had exploited the peasantry for millennia, consuming the fruits of peasant labor and giving nothing back.

As in Chinese revolutionary thinking, urban conglomerations themselves were seen as impediments to revolution. In their propaganda, the Red Khmers referred to Phnom Penh as "the great prostitute on the Mekong," while party leaders admired the primitive communism they had noted in hill tribes and isolated rural populations, among whom party cadre had worked and hidden for several years. More to the point, there are no examples of the Red Khmers administering cities during the war. Kratie, for example, occupied by the Vietnamese and some Red Khmer troops in 1970, was cleared of its population in 1973 when the CPK took over. As early as 1970, according to a survivor, "the schools were closed, and everyone was made to grow rice."[26]

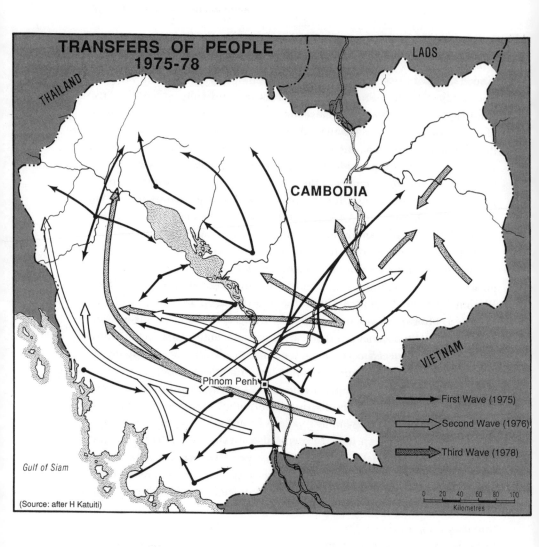

TRANSFERS OF PEOPLE
1975-78

THAILAND

LAOS

CAMBODIA

VIETNAM

Phnom Penh

Gulf of Siam

First Wave (1975)
Second Wave (1976)
Third Wave (1978)

(Source: after H Katuiti)

0   20   40   60   80   100
Kilometres

Saloth Sar and his colleagues had not spent years in the forest in order to become city councilors in Phnom Penh. Their time in hiding had convinced them of the correctness of an antiurban strategy that empowered poor peasants and turned urban dwellers into agricultural workers. By choosing to stay in the towns, these men and women had become enemies of the revolution. This made them new people, April 17 people, or depositees, as they came to be called, regardless of their social origins. If they were driven into the countryside just when rice and other crops needed to be planted to take advantage of the rains, they might conceivably become productive workers. If not, the revolution would proceed without them. In the chilling phrase used repeatedly by cadre and recalled by many survivors, "Keeping [urban dwellers] is no benefit; losing them is no loss."[27]

The Red Khmers stressed that Cambodia's revolution was pure, unprecedented, and autonomous. For this reason, soon after April 17 the government radio announced that humanitarian aid that had sustained Phnom Penh since the beginning of the year would no longer be sought or accepted. From then on, Cambodia would grow its own food. The emphasis on self-sufficiency persisted for the lifetime of the regime and into its years in exile, even though during the DK era tens of thousands of Cambodians died of malnutrition and of inadequate health care owing to the regime's refusal to import medicine and pesticides, including DDT. The lack of DDT meant that malaria reemerged as a major cause of death in rural areas in 1975–76.[28]

The leaders of the CPK knew that the country's agricultural base had been damaged and many of its marketing mechanisms destroyed in the war. At the same time, they considered it essential to embark at once on a full-scale national revolution based on the collectivization that they had introduced in liberated areas in 1973. Perhaps they were not convinced that they could persuade the new people to share their vision and decided to force them into the countryside, where they could be supervised and posed no threat to the party's leaders. They may have realized what a precarious political position they were in, but for economic reasons seldom explained to the evacuees emptying the cities made some sense. For the revolution to proceed and for Cambodia to survive everyone had to be put to work. Food had to be grown quickly or millions of people would starve. For the second half of 1975, raising food to feed the country became their major preoccupation.[29]

The decision to clear the towns was closely held. Some cadre leading the final assault on Phnom Penh had not heard of it even as late as April 15 and thus had little time to prepare base areas outside the city for the influx so many people. Others had heard about it ten days before the order took effect. Some cadre in the Eastern Zone disagreed with the decision, it seems, but everyone obeyed it. There is some evidence that Hou Youn's disappearance at the end of 1975 was connected to his opposition to the evacuation policy. Killing this popular, outspoken figure also fitted the interests of Saloth Sar and Nuon Chea, who wanted to stamp their own collective will onto the entire country.[30]

People in the cities were glad the war was over, but evacuation was the last thing they expected to happen. Most of them welcomed the solemn, heavily armed young soldiers dressed in black pajamas or olive-green, Vietnamese-style uniforms who began filtering into Phnom Penh and Battambang on the morning of April 17. The city dwellers were impressed by their seriousness, their discipline, and their youth. Many soldiers were weighted down with mortars, ammunition, and machine guns. Most of them seemed to be less than fifteen years old. They were "alert and distrustful, like soldiers on patrol," and stared at westerners as if they were "creatures from different planets." As city dwellers tried to welcome them and journalists sought interviews, they remained hostile and aloof.[31]

City dwellers wanted to see the young soldiers smile, to hear them suggest consensus. They wanted to shake hands. Defeated in the war, they wanted a rationale by which they could continue living. They were physically and emotionally wrung out. Friends or relatives had been among the half million Cambodians who had died in the civil war. For over a year, Phnom Penh had been subjected to shelling and rocket attacks, food shortages, overcrowding, and disease. Most refugees from the countryside had been cut off from their villages since 1972 or 1973. Many of them were out of work, homeless, and undernourished. Few retained any faith in prerevolutionary politics or social arrangements, and most wanted an end put to the corruption that had tainted the Khmer Republic. Better educated ones hoped to retain their positions and probably some privileges, but if the strange word *revolution* (*padevat*) was needed to reinvest Cambodian life with material welfare, honesty, and self-respect, most of them were prepared to help. The Red Khmer were Cambodians too. Something could be arranged.[32]

In the week that followed the Communist victory, most of these expectations were overturned. It is unwarranted to accept DK pronouncements that two thousand years of history had come to an end on the "glorious 17th of April," but for most of the people in Cambodia's towns what happened during those few days literally overturned their lives.

Many survivors have vivid memories of the day their world turned upside down. You Hon Chea, a civil engineer employed by the Department of Public Works in Phnom Penh, has recalled going off duty as usual on the evening of the sixteenth. When he returned to work early the next morning, he was told that the Red Khmers were coming. There seemed little point in standing guard at the ministry, as he was rostered to do, so he strolled over to the nearly deserted central market, hoping to find some noodle soup. For the first time in his memory, there was none for sale. "We were glad the fighting was over," he has said, echoing the views of many published accounts. He was tired and vaguely optimistic. He went home without waiting to welcome the liberating army.[33]

Of the twelve people in Chea's household on April 17, six were to die of disease and execution over the next four years, but for the moment the Red Khmer were not a daunting prospect. Like many other graduates of the Lycée Sisowath, Chea had admired the honesty and dedication of the three ghosts. He had studied English with Khieu Thirith and Khmer literature with her sister, Ponnary. After 1968 or so, in his last years at the lycée, he had become disillusioned with Sihanouk. Many of his contemporaries saw themselves as on the left, as far as the Khmer Republic was concerned. Some had disappeared into the maquis, and others, like his wife's supervisor, were known to be Red. Chea dismissed as propaganda the stories that had circulated about Red Khmer atrocities. Whatever had been going on in the countryside, he thought, could not have been worse than the disorder and corruption of the Khmer Republic.[34]

Kol Touch, who had served briefly as minister of agriculture in the 1960s, was even more hopeful on April 17 than You Hon Chea. He had spent several years running a rubber plantation in Kompong Cham and had made friends among the local population. He had encountered numerous Red Khmer and Vietnamese Communist soldiers. Unlike many of the Cambodian elite, Touch admired rural people and enjoyed their company. He had been used to hunting and camping in the countryside with his father since the 1930s. The friendships he had formed over the years and his knowledge of rural conditions probably saved his life.

Although nominally a Democrat, Touch was apolitical and estranged from Sihanouk "because of his corruption." By 1975, he said, conditions in Cambodia had become so appalling that he "wanted the Red Khmer to win." His son, Dorathy, an engineering student in France, had become a member of the CPF in the 1960s and later of a Maoist student organization. In 1973, the son had flown to Beijing with about thirty like-minded Cambodian students, hoping to take part in the Cambodian revolution.

He walked the length of the Ho Chi Minh Trail before presenting himself to CPK authorities. Touch was proud of his son's idealism but had not seen him for several years. With the Communist victory, he looked forward to becoming reunited with him and helping in the effort of national reconstruction.[35]

The Communists whom Touch met on April 17 were relatively polite, asking him and his family to leave their houses when they felt ready to do so. By nightfall, Kol Touch and eleven members of his family were moving slowly inside a sea of humanity eastward across the Monivong Bridge. Touch was buoyed up during his departure by the hope that he would encounter his son in the eastern part of the country.[36]

Compared with what happened to people evacuated from Phnom Penh, those who were cleared out of Battambang and other provincial towns traveled in most cases only a short distance before being put to work in liberated villages and newly established work sites. Because Battambang had always been Cambodia's most productive rice-growing province, the CPK hoped that under revolutionary conditions prewar harvests could be doubled or even tripled to reach yields of three metric tons per hectare on land that had previously produced much less. This was the essence of the Four-Year Plan drafted in 1976. The Communists believed the new yields would be possible because the collective energies of the people would be so much greater than profit-oriented individualism had been. In time, the utopian goals proved impossible to meet, particularly when the workforce was treated so harshly, fed so little, and given inadequate tools. The debacle did not make the leaders question their tactics or assumptions. Instead, they assumed that traitors in the party and resurgent capitalism were to blame.[37]

Battambang was not evacuated for a week. During this time, Red Khmer forces gradually phased out the use of money and rounded up those they suspected of having been officers in Lon Nol's army. Several hundred of these men were executed near the city in early May, after being told to put on their uniforms and come to "welcome Sihanouk" (who was still in Beijing). News of the massacre spread rapidly through the northwest and diminished many people's enthusiasm, tentative to begin with, for the revolution.[38]

Peang Sophi, a factory worker who escaped from Battambang to Thailand six months after the liberation, was not favorably impressed by the peasant soldiers who occupied the city. He recalled that they were "real country people, from very far away." Many of them had never seen a city or printed words. They held Cambodian texts upside down, pretending to puzzle them out. Most of them came from revolutionary bases in southern Battambang, near Samlaut. Over the years, they had been trained to hate "enemies of the Organization"—the Americans, who bombed the country, the traitors allied to the Americans, and the city dwellers, who had refused to join the revolution. They were taught to relish their resentments; a CPK cadre told Sophi, "We were so angry when we emerged from the forest that we didn't want to spare even a baby in its cradle."[39]

The evacuation of Phnom Penh began for most inhabitants on the afternoon of April 17, but the city was not emptied for several days; some residents remained in hiding for a week, but by then everyone had left.[40] The evacuation took place along three major highways leading east, north, and west from the capital. People proceeded at different speeds along these roads and encountered different levels of intimidation. Discipline was poorest and casualties most extensive along the northern route, particularly after it branched at Kompong Luong, where Route 6 led east toward Kompong Cham and Route 5 proceeded northward toward Kompong Chhnang, Pursat, and Battambang. Refugees were halted at this crossroads for several days and sorted out by CPK cadre who made them prepare biographical statements aimed at clarifying their class origins as well as their links with rural areas. Those with ties in eastern Cambodia were allowed to proceed in that direction. People with ties in the north and northwest and those without rural connections were sent along Route 5, the same one followed, two weeks later, by westerners evacuated from Phnom Penh.[41]

Because Route 5 led eventually to Thailand, it was the route followed by most of those who managed to escape from Cambodia in 1975 and 1976. Those in this first wave of refugees were nearly all urban dwellers. Many of them, being from the middle classes, felt insulted by the revolution and took a dim view of social change. In general, they reported greater hardships than did people who were evacuated in other directions. The latter group's stories of this period, collected after 1978, were affected by their memories of much worse experiences later on.

When the stories of the first refugees broke into print in the West, they confirmed many readers' stereotypical views of a Communist regime; some writers who were sympathetic to the revolution, however, tried to show that the stories were false or, if true, atypical and designed to create impressions useful to enemies of social change. Anecdotally, proponents of each side as well as skeptical observers were able to make a case. After all, there were millions of true stories.[42]

To say that conditions differed along the routes is not to say that the exodus along any of them was an excursion. Many of those who made the trek were old, infirm, or unfit. Several thousand people deprived of medical attention succumbed along the way. Food was scarce and of poor quality. April being the end of the dry season, potable water was hard to find. The countryside, especially near Phnom Penh, had been bombed, torn up, and fought over since 1970. Once prosperous towns like Kompong Speu had literally disappeared. In this inhospitable landscape hundreds of thousands of refugees waited for permission to return to their urban homes—but it never came.

The evacuees found themselves in a strange land. Everything they counted on to sustain them was abolished, forbidden, or broken up. Money, status, employment, education, possessions, and influence meant nothing. Few of them knew how to cope with rural life. The villages they moved through were often hostile to them. The young soldiers prodding them along were unfriendly and difficult to bribe. They said that everyone must obey the Organization, but not one of them was able to define what it was.

Nobody knew what would happen next. Some of the evacuees were allowed to rest for days at a time in villages and forage for themselves; others made to push along, regardless of hardship. Some voyages took a few days, others as long as two months. Some refugees settled in villages where they were known and had relatives; others were told by their relatives to move on; still others were parked in faraway villages where they knew no one. In remote, malarial areas of Pursat, for example, April 17 people were made to build new villages from scratch, using unfamiliar tools and local timber, thatching, and bamboo. Some remember cadre at this early stage—roughly through the remainder of 1975—as being cruel and doctrinaire. Others remember instances of kindness and understanding. Still others cite examples of austere, literal, and lunatic dedication to the revolutionary cause, random executions, sadism toward women and old people, and so on.

To the leadership, perhaps, these violent acts were understandable, as long as they accelerated the revolution and did not last too long. After all, as Khieu Samphan remarked in early 1977, revolutionaries were in the process of "turning their anger into a driving force, transforming their grief into strength for the struggle." In the early stages of the regime, it was said, "those who stand in the path of the revolution will be crushed beneath it." More important, there is no evidence that young soldiers who executed enemies during these months—usually at sunset, out of sight of other villagers, never with any public explanations—were punished or even chastised for their behavior.[43]

Testimony about this period collected from survivors after 1979 is colored by what happened to them after 1976. This makes prorevolutionary evidence from this period particularly valuable. Some refugees, like Peang Sophi in Battambang, were indeed welcomed in "base villages," particularly those with links established there through colleagues, relations, acquaintances, and even family servants. Others were treated with suspicion and contempt. Few new people older than fifteen welcomed the changes, but many younger people found the early stages of the revolution, which released them from obligations, almost exhilarating and often an adventure.[44]

The leaders of the CPK reached Phnom Penh soon after it had been cleared of its population. Some of them, including Pol Pot and Ieng Sary, had not been in the city for eight years. Ieng Sary told Elizabeth Becker in 1981 that the leaders had "expected to find a greater cache of military hardware" there. The two men picked their way gingerly through the debris, and Sary says he was "stunned by all that was not in Phnom Penh." The devastation, however, failed to discourage them. At a special congress convened on April 25, they set in motion several measures dealing specifically with the establishment of an "independent, peaceful, neutral, nonaligned, sovereign, democratic and prosperous Cambodia that had national integrity and a just and classless society, free of exploitation of man by man." In public announcements, the word *socialism* did not appear, and the CPK was never mentioned. And yet it is not hard to imagine the privately expressed enthusiasm of these men and women, some of whom had nurtured a vision of a Communist victory in Cambodia for over twenty years and had spent the last seven or eight engrossed in a costly and discouraging struggle waged against what they believed was the whole weight of imperialism itself. The ties that bound the leaders to one another and their conviction that they were right gave them extraordinary strength and made them unwilling to listen to dissent. Their victory encouraged them to inflict their utopian ideas on everyone else, at once.

Building and Defending the Country

For six months after the towns were emptied, the country's citizens were enjoined to build and defend (*kosang nung kapea*) Cambodia, constructing a new society on the ruins of the past and standing guard against widespread but poorly defined enemies who threatened the Organization and its revolution.

Building the country meant many things. It referred to increasing agricultural production and in particular the yields of rice. The process also involved building dams and irrigation works to permit double-cropping. Political education sessions also aimed at building new personalities that could serve the Revolutionary Organization. In some areas, the word *building* was used as a warning: people who resisted being built were cast aside. Finally, it meant installing CPK members or sympathizers in positions of authority at all levels of the administration.[45]

Defending the country meant maintaining the offensive spirit which had defeated "the American imperialists and Lon Nol." Such a spirit, it was thought, could withstand attacks by enemies inside the country and from abroad. The job was given to the combatants (*yothea*) who had won the war and to the CPK cadre (*kamaphibal*).[46]

The need to defend the country arose immediately after liberation when Cambodian troops were dispatched to the Thai and Vietnamese frontiers to guard against a (South) Vietnamese offensive or a Thai incursion. According to the DK's *Black Book*, published in 1978, the leadership also wanted to ensure that Vietnamese Communist troops on Cambodian soil, many of whom had been there for over a decade, were now returning to Vietnam.

Saigon did not fall to Communist forces until the last day of April. In the two previous weeks the CPK leadership sent Cambodian troops to occupy several islands in the Gulf of Siam, some known to be under Vietnamese jurisdiction and others disputed between Cambodia and Vietnam. Thach Sok, a former motorboat driver in the Khmer Republican navy, which was based at Ream, was conscripted soon after April 17 to transport Cambodian Communist troops to occupy one of these islands, nominally under South Vietnamese ("Thieu-Ky") control. He has recalled putting six boatloads of troops ashore. When he returned with supplies for them several days later, the South Vietnamese had recaptured the island, inflicting heavy Cambodian casualties. Sok also landed a smaller detachment of troops on another island, Koh Trol (Phu Quoc), claimed by Cambodia but never administered by the Khmer. Swimming ashore, the troops planted a plain red revolutionary flag on the beach (DK did not have a national flag until early 1976). The flag was strafed by Vietnamese helicopters and replaced many times by Cambodian soldiers, whose foolhardy courage impressed Thach Sok. Fighting continued on several islands after the Vietnamese Communist victory.[47]

On the surface, however, the two countries remained friendly after Pol Pot, on an unpublicized visit to Hanoi in June 1975, papered over some outstanding problems before proceeding to Beijing. According to Wilfred Burchett, Pol Pot told the Vietnamese that his forces had been "ignorant of geography," implying that the attacks were a mistake.

In May 1975, an American freighter, the *Mayaguez*, carrying unspecified military equipment from the United States to Thailand, strayed inside Cambodian territorial waters and was impounded with its crew by the Cambodians, who suspected it of espionage. The United States reacted swiftly and at the highest level: President Gerald Ford approved the landing of a detachment of two hundred Marines on a nearby island to rescue the crew of the ship, thought to be held hostage there. The Marines were pinned down under heavy fire, and eighteen of them were killed. Ironically, the *Mayaguez* crew was not on the island and in fact was released unharmed (less than a week after being impounded) before the Marines could be withdrawn. While the United States waited for them to be released, bombing missions launched from the USS *Coral Sea* destroyed most of Cambodia's naval facilities at Ream and its only oil refinery at Kompong Som. No estimate of Cambodian casualties was ever made.[48]

The incident displayed Cambodian pride and suspiciousness, poor communications between Phnom Penh and the outside world, and American bitterness in the backwash of the war. When the *Mayaguez* and its crew were released unharmed, both sides interpreted the incident as a victory. President Ford and U.S. military forces earned favorable publicity at a time when it was in short supply. In the wake of the incident Ford's popularity rose by a percentage point.[49]

From May 1975 until the first DK forays into Vietnam and Thailand in the spring of 1977, the phrase *defending the country* did not imply overt military action against Thailand or Vietnam. Instead, haphazard commercial relations soon developed along the Thai border, and "militant fellowship" between the Cambodians and the Vietnamese was openly celebrated soon after the Communist occupation of Saigon. All the same, the leaders of the CPK remained suspicious and alert. Cambodia's military forces, numbering some eighty thousand in April 1975, were not demobilized or disarmed. As the most thoroughly politicized and mobilized segment of society and the only one to bear arms, the yothea, *chhlop* (youthful guerrillas), and kamaphibal were the spearheads and inspirations for the rest of the population.[50]

The revolutionary army also provided security for the party leadership. In 1977, Pol Pot paid it special tribute: "Only the cadres of the revolutionary army, formed in the fire of combat, can acquire the necessary experience and forge a sound ideological, political and organizational position. Our revolutionary army correctly applied the military line of our party. That is what gave it its fighting spirit and its great effectiveness."

Politically, the last eight months of 1975 were confusing to most Cambodians and to analysts outside the country. Cambodia's government in exile, headed by Sihanouk, was ostensibly still in command, but all real decisions were made by an invisible body called the Revolutionary Organization (*angkar padevat*) or the Higher Organization (*angkar loeu*). Many survivors later recalled this period as a kind of golden age, compared to what happened later. Conditions were harsh and unfamiliar, but in most of the country family units stayed together, purges were rare, and everyone had enough to eat.

According to Peang Sophi, speakers at political meetings held during this period urged people to be self-reliant, humble, and hardworking. Two sentences he remembered in particular were "We have only ourselves; we must offer our work to Angkar" and "Robbery satisfies only one person." The most effective speaker was the leader of militia attached to the damsite where Sophy worked in the last months of 1975. One of his speeches went something like this:

> In the old days, the big people told us we had independence. What kind of independence was that? What had we built? Well, they had built an Independence Monument. Where did they build it? In the capital. Who saw the thing? The big people's children. Did country people see it? No, they only saw photos. The big people's children went in and out, to this country, that country, and then they came back, to control the poor. And now, what do we do, in contrast to this? We don't build Independence Monuments. Instead, by raising embankments, digging canals, and so on, the children of Cambodians can see what they have done, and country people can see that in the time of their grandfathers, the time of their fathers, and their uncles, they built their own independence.[51]

During this period the regime concentrated on getting people throughout the country to grow and harvest rice and other crops. Mobile production brigades (*chalat*), a species of agricultural shock troops, were set up in late 1975. Composed of young, unmarried men and women fifteen years of age and older, new people and old mixed together, these groups traveled from district to district inspiring citizens and building up, in many cases, an unprecedented esprit de corps. Many prerevolutionary industries were put back into production at this time as well.[52]

Several other DK practices were put in place. These included long working hours for everyone (known as "following the sun"), a rejection of Western-style medicine, an abolition of play, and the imposition of a new vocabulary that dismantled hierarchical pronouns, resurrected supposedly peasant language, and imposed an almost syrupy politeness on commands. People taken off to be killed, for example, were asked to "help us collect fruit" or to "come with us for further study." The ethical focus of the cadre and the chhlop, their literal-mindedness, and the infallibility of the Organization came as a surprise to many, accustomed as they were to prerevolutionary norms. Definitions of communally owned property, for example, in some places came to include wild berries and edible roots. People with glasses were assumed to be capitalists, as were those with pale skin and soft hands. Women were forbidden to wear their hair long, to put on jewelry, or have their shirts unbuttoned, even at the neck. Any behavior deemed (by intellectuals) not to coincide with that of poor peasants before the revolution was proscribed.[53]

Working hours exceeded those that most Cambodians had ever known, except in the busiest seasons of the agricultural year. In many areas, particularly the northwest, work in the fields began before sunrise and ended long after dark, with only short breaks in between. More arduous work, such as that on irrigation canals, occupied fewer hours per day but was so exhausting that one survivor has recalled coming home on all fours. The work was made easier, the party claimed, by the singing of revolutionary songs, intoned in unison by work crews while marching to work sites and performing agricultural tasks.[54]

Memories of the DK period flowed together in survivors' minds in the 1980s to such an extent that it is difficult to reconstruct conditions of 1975–76 and the reservoir of good will among many people that evaporated over the next few months. "In 1977, everything got worse," is a frequent recollection of survivors. One of them said, "If we'd been given enough to eat, the revolution would have succeeded." By 1977, the grinding, repetitive, unrewarded work, illness, shortages of food, family dispersion, executions, broken promises, and revolutionary rhetoric had blended in everyone's minds, congealing into the phrases *chiik prek loeuk tomnup*, "dig canals, raise earthworks," and *booboo ot bay*, "gruel without rice," often uttered with two or three fingers held up to indicate the number of grains of rice in a given bowl of gruel. As the country began to starve, the triumphalist rhetoric of political meetings and national radio broadcasts continued unabated, and when workers returned at night, bone-tired, to meager food, they were subjected to house-to-house surveillance carried out by vindictive boys and girls trying to keep anyone from complaining about the regime or using foreign words in conversation. Because everything they did seemed to be observed, people remarked in awe that "the Organization has a thousand eyes, like a pineapple." Cambodia was an enormous cage.

Constructive self-criticism was encouraged. At nighttime meetings, villagers were asked to share experiences in an effort to improve work practices, increase production, and root out enemies of the Organization. Verbal attacks on people who had criticized themselves occasionally became heated but seemed to many a safe way to proceed. Criticizing of the cadre, on the other hand, often led to the critic's disappearance.[55]

Many new people saw the point of working to feed themselves and increase agricultural production. This willingness faded after the 1975 crop was harvested and villagers saw most of it hauled away in government trucks to undisclosed destinations. In fact, in a contorted stab at self-reliance, the regime exported several thousand tons to China to pay for Chinese aid. The rice harvest of 1976 was exported also, but by then government demands on the population were even greater, and starvation occurred on a national scale.

In addition to backbreaking work and interminable meetings, everyone had to endure almost random terror and unexplained disappearances at the hands of cadre and chhlop. Villagers would come across the bodies of victims later, by chance, and the jingle *Angkar somlap, min dael prap* (Angkar kills but never explains) became current. The killings and rumors about them held people in place and forestalled most political conversions. In a strange way, Pol Pot's description of Cambodia as a country bedeviled by landlordism became accurate under DK. People who had been free, if not especially prosperous, became the unpaid serfs of an invisible feudal lord.

By the middle of 1976, most Cambodians had settled into a Spartan, oppressive routine. Accounts of the second evacuation—from the southwest to the northwest in late 1975 and early 1976—have a trancelike quality. The image of tens of thousands of people jammed upright into trucks and slow-moving freight cars, making their way through an empty landscape toward an uncertain but ominous future, hauntingly echoes the Jewish experience in World War II. There was an important difference, however: in Cambodia the oppressors had the same nationality and (until shortly before the evacuations) the same religion as the oppressed.[56]

The CPK Takes Command

On April 17, Sihanouk praised the Communists' victory warmly from Beijing, singling out Cambodia as the first country in the world to defeat the "most insolent imperialism of all time, namely, U.S. imperialism"; but he seemed in no hurry to return home and received no invitation from the Organization to do so. During the last two weeks of April he was preoccupied with his mother's health (she was suffering from an illness that proved to be fatal). As far as the CPK's leaders were concerned he had outlived his usefulness. They no longer needed a united front or a prince as their chief of state. At the same time, they were aware of Sihanouk's friendship with Zhou Enlai and Kim Il Sung as well as of his high standing in international forums.[57]

Pressure from China and North Korea, indeed, was needed to persuade them to allow the prince to return to Phnom Penh for nineteen days in September to prepare a speech for the United Nations and to be briefed for an international tour promoting the new regime. Despite his subsequent claims to have known about the iniquity of the CPK at the time, Sihanouk performed these tasks willingly, much as he had carried out public relations exercises for the French in the 1940s. His claim that his decision to return to Cambodia sprang from his "almost physical love" for the Cambodian people, however, is probably true, and his decision to come home was a courageous one. When he returned to Beijing briefly in October 1975, he told his entourage that they were free to follow him to Cambodia or to make other arrangements. Almost all of them sought asylum in the West.[58]

If Sihanouk had hoped to play a role in Cambodian foreign policy, his hopes were dashed in August 1975, when Ieng Sary traveled to Lima to represent Cambodia at the so-called Non-Aligned Nations Conference. Sihanouk's own trip to Romania and Yugoslavia soon afterward was less important. At the end of 1975, he returned to Phnom Penh, accompanied by his wife, Monique, her mother, and a few retainers. They were greeted at the airport by Khieu Samphan, Son Sen, and his faithful non-Communist minister Penn Nouth, while crowds with bouquets of flowers, urged on by cadre, shouted praise for Angkar and the revolutionary army. "The scene," Sihanouk wrote later, "had something unreal and Kafka-esque about it."[59]

The constitution of Democratic Kampuchea, promulgated a month later, was Cambodia's third. Khieu Samphan made a broadcast explaining the document two weeks before its promulgation. He said that the cabinet had decided to draft it soon after the liberation of Phnom Penh, on the advice of "300 workers' representatives, 500 farmers' representatives, and 300 representatives of the revolutionary army."[60]

The text said nothing about the CPK or the role it was expected to play in Democratic Kampuchea, as the country was to be named. The authorship of the constitution was said to be collective. Khieu Samphan noted that it was "not the result of any research on foreign documents, nor [was] it the fruit of any research by scholars. In fact, the people—workers, peasants, and revolutionary army—wrote the Constitution with their own hands."[61]

The operative portions of the constitution collectivized "all important means of production" in one sentence and stipulated that "Democratic Kampuchea applies the collective principle in leadership and in work." In his explanation, Khieu Samphan listed collectivized items as "fields, orchards, farmlands, factories, trains, automobiles, ships and motor boats," leaving only clothing, personal effects (but not jewelry), and tools in private hands. The so-called People's Representative Assembly (for which elections were held in March 1976) was composed of 250 members, of whom 150 represented the peasants and 50 each workers and the revolutionary army. The text failed to say how these representatives were to be chosen or who could vote for them. Above the assembly was a State Presidium, which it supposedly selected. The assembly also was to select judges, whose duty it was to "defend the democratic rights of the people"—not otherwise defined—and, more ominously, to "punish any act directed against the people's state or violating the laws." There is no evidence that any judges held office in DK or that there was a legal system in Cambodia between 1975 and 1979.

The main right of citizens bestowed by the text was the "right to work," although citizens were also "entitled to . . . a constantly improving material, spiritual, and cultural life." Other passages in the constitution described the national flag. It was to have Communist colors, that is, yellow on red, depicting a three-towered Angkor. The constitution also specified a national coat of arms showing factories, irrigation canals, and rice fields and, further, stated that DK's foreign policy would be based on its adherence to the "great family of nonaligned nations."

The text avoided any reference to socialism, Cambodia's monarchic traditions, Buddhism, or a chief of state. By stressing the value of labor, collectivization, and the role of class origins and the revolutionary army, the text mobilized people in unheralded ways but placed no limits or controls on the interventionary powers of the state.[62]

Over the next two months, the leaders of the CPK began wheeling the new government into position. During this period, hundreds of thousands of new people were resettled to the northwest, in preparation for the agricultural offensive planned for the growing season of 1976. Sihanouk was taken on a guided tour of the north in early 1976 to observe the accomplishments of the regime.

In March, national elections were held for the People's Representative Assembly. New people were not allowed to vote, and the candidates proposed by the CPK engaged in no electioneering. It seems likely that the elections proceeded most systematically in base areas; after 1979, several refugees could correctly recall the names of candidates but naturally knew nothing of their legislative careers, since the assembly met only once—for three days in April 1976—to set the DK government in place.[63]

Shortly before the elections, Phnom Penh Radio announced that 515 candidates had been nominated for 250 seats in the assembly. Representatives had no territorial constituencies but represented segments of the population at large—workers, peasants, and the revolutionary army. Candidates had to be over twenty-five and have a "good record of revolutionary struggle." Ironically, they were being selected just as the feudal assemblymen, including Khieu Samphan and Hu Nim, soon to be ministers in DK, had been chosen by Sihanouk in 1958 and 1962. Little is known about the backgrounds or experience of most of the winning candidates, and the names of the losers were never published. Pol Pot—using his nom de guerre officially for the first time, as far as we know—ran as a representative of the rubber workers in the eastern zone, slyly making reference perhaps to his days in the Viet Minh.[64]

The elections demonstrated DK's adherence to internationally accepted norms. They obscured the central roles of Saloth Sar and his colleagues in the CPK in governing the country. Ten days after the elections, a secret meeting of the CPK central committee noted, "The world has seen that the political situation in our country is good, for we have been able to prepare such good elections." Pol Pot perceived no substantive role for the assembly, and he said nothing about the elections when he traced the history of the CPK in September 1977. Indeed, a party document from 1978 insisted that state power had come to the party not through elections or documents but "by our violence."[65]

At the end of March 1976, the CPK central committee met to discuss a variety of questions. Typewritten notes from the meeting have survived. They contrast sharply with the high moral tone and occasional evasiveness of the Organization's public pronouncements. The notes record a series of decisions dealing with a dozen issues. The first delegated "the authority to smash [people] inside and outside the ranks [of the party] to Zone Standing Committees and the Staff of the Army." The text then sets a goal of "three tons per hectare" as the amount of *padi* that was to be harvested throughout the nation under socialist conditions.

The notes go on to suggest that historians of the CPK should "set the birth of the party at 1960. . . . Do not use 1951, so that we are not close to others—make a clean break." The decision cut the CPK off from its Vietnamese roots and set its beginning at the congress at which Pol Pot and Ieng Sary, among others, were first elected to the central committee.

In the next paragraph, it was decreed that the "Christian cathedral" built by the French in the 1950s should be demolished. The phrase translated as "Christian" (*ong ko*) is a colloquial Khmer expression for "Vietnamese," many of whom were Catholic. The two items suggest that an anti-Vietnamese policy was in place inside the CPK by early 1976.[66]

The notes also dealt with larger political issues. In January, Zhou Enlai died in Beijing. The CPK had been reluctant to move against Sihanouk as long as Zhou, his patron, retained influence in China. The DK leadership had mourned Zhou's death in official statements but at its meeting of March 1976 noted brusquely that Sihanouk "has run out of wind. He cannot go any further forward. Therefore we have decided to retire him, according to the wishes of others." The last sentence is obscure. Were the leaders admitting that they were accepting advice—perhaps from China or North Korea—not to execute Sihanouk? or were they taking advice to depose him instead of keeping him on as a figurehead? "Others" may also be an invention of a party leadership intent on sidestepping direct responsibility and on keeping their options open.[67]

In mid-April, Khieu Samphan announced that Sihanouk would be given an annual pension of US $8,000 and that a monument would be erected in his honor. Neither promise was kept. Samphan's announcements were for foreign consumption. From the CPK leadership's point of view, Sihanouk was lucky to be alive. Removed from the limelight for the first time since the early 1940s, he spent the next three years living in fear and luxury, forbidden to make public statements or to see visitors from abroad.[68]

The eclipse of Sihanouk coincided with the rise of Pol Pot. When Pech Kim Luon, a former Republican pilot who had bombed Lon Nol's compound and then joined the Red Khmers in 1973, defected to Thailand three years later, he insisted that Saloth Sar was the most important person in Cambodian politics. He correctly named Nuon Chea ("Mister Nhun") as Number Two, Ieng Sary as Number Three, and Son Sen as Number Four in the Communist hierarchy. He described Saloth Sar, whom he had flown around the country in a helicopter, as being fat and noted that he had delivered the principal speech at the April 17, 1976, anniversary ceremonies, although Khieu Samphan's was the only one broadcast over the radio. Luon had not yet learned of Sar's new name and said misleadingly that "Pol Pot [was] not important" compared with Saloth Sar.[69]

Regional and Temporal Variations

Democratic Kampuchea combined highly centralized control and what often appears to be an unchanging character with complex regional and temporal variations. In some ways the revolution was consistent and nationwide. Money was not in use anywhere, for example, and in national terms there was no education system, no freedom of movement, and no postal service. With rare exceptions, Buddhism, like all religious practices, was outlawed, and defrocked Buddhist monks were made to perform agricultural work. Gambling, sport, jewelry, and extramarital sex were forbidden. Throughout DK, "base people" (neaq mul'than), cadre, and soldiers enjoyed more privileges than the April 17 people resettled in the country, but it would be difficult to speak of these men and women as being privileged classes in the same way prerevolutionary elites were. Throughout the country, the patterns of organization laid down by the CPK—from family groups through work teams to village cooperatives and regions to geographical zones—were scrupulously followed. Similarly, at least in 1976 and 1977, the major aims of the government—to build and defend the country, to maintain the CPK's monopoly of power, to dismantle prerevolutionary society, and to increase agricultural yields—were generally agreed on and consistently enforced.[70]

This consistency served the interests of the party's leaders, who expected all Cambodians to join in waging a full-time national revolution. The idea that conditions were equally fearsome because equally Communist throughout Cambodia between April 1975 and January 1979 served the interests of anti-Communists outside Cambodia, who by 1976 had drawn up, largely on the basis of contradictory evidence from refugees fleeing into Thailand from Battambang, what Michael Vickery has called the Standard Total View (STV) of the Cambodian revolution.

This view, from Vickery's perspective, had elements of truth but was often oversimplified, skewed, and misleading. Since it was his research in 1980–81 that was the first to examine regional and temporal variations in DK in a systematic way, and since these variations undermine many of the assumptions of the STV, the latter needs to be examined before the variations are set forth.[71]

In general, writers adhering to the STV perceived a close fit of, on the one hand, reports about the evacuation of Phnom Penh and events in Battambang in 1975 and, on the other, what they expected from a wicked Communist regime. Given the perception of DK as an updated version of *Animal Farm*, what occurred there, insofar as it could be determined, was thought to reflect a totalizing, Stalinist official policy that was responding to centrally conceived and inhumane commands. This perspective ignores initiatives resulting from whimsy, regional differences, and genuine social ideas as well as the tumultuous conditions associated with mass movements of people in the aftermath of a civil war and with vengeance, victory, and defeat. The violence of CPK cadre and combatants in Battambang in 1975, for example, is now known to have been more extensive than anywhere else in the country and is thus a poor basis for generalizing. This does not exculpate those who committed the murders; but events in Battambang reported in 1975 and early 1976 provided an inaccurate blueprint.

Writers who favored the revolution in Cambodia, on the other hand, sometimes minimized the violence or sought non-Communist parallels for it, for instance in France in the aftermath of World War II. Anti-Communist writers found their analogies in what they believed were the botched performances of China, Eastern Europe, and the USSR. The difficulty of knowing what was going on, exacerbated by DK's decision to make Cambodia a hermit state, did not deter those anti-Communist writers—or anticapitalist ones for that matter—from discussing DK in detail. Harsh treatment of some intellectuals and doctors (or of people with glasses or an education) in 1975–76 was assumed by writers sympathetic to the revolution to be deserved and by critics of DK to be a national policy of extermination. The Battambang massacres in May 1975 led leftist writers to assume that such a settling of scores was inevitable, especially insofar as "fascists" were involved, and those on the right to assume that waves of assassination were occurring in other parts of the country. Critics pointed to the number of people who had died along the routes out of Phnom Penh; supporters of DK and skeptics cited people who had seen no corpses or pointed to the millions who survived.[72]

Some early critics of DK took the sufferings of the Cambodian bourgeoisie as emblematic but wrote little about the sufferings of those with less status, darker skins, and fewer possessions. In the polemical literature that developed, very few writers on either side were prepared to give either their opposites or contradictory data the benefit of the doubt. As these short-term polemics became part of the record, they made interpretation of events in 1975–76 much more difficult. For these reasons, a discussion of temporal and spatial variations is important.[73]

The geographically designated zones (*phumipeak*) into which Cambodia was divided after 1975 were military ones, inherited from the war of 1970–75. They did not reflect existing administrative areas. There were seven of them plus a special region in Kratie and an autonomous zone for the port of Kompong Som. Three zones bordered Vietnam: the Northeast, the East, and the Southwest, comprising roughly eastern Stung Treng, Ratanakiri, Mondulkiri, Prey Veng, Svay Rieng, eastern Kompong Cham, Kandal, southern Kompong Speu, and Kampot. The Western Zone was made up of Koh Kong, the remainder of Kompong Speu, and Kompong Chhnang. The Northwestern and Northern zones, bordering Thailand, included the provinces of Pursat, Battambang, Oddar Meanchey, Siem Reap, Preah Vihear, and western Stung Treng. The Central Zone was composed of Kompong Thom, western Kratie, and western Kompong Cham. Each zone was headed by a politico-military committee appointed by the CPK.[74]

The zones, in turn, were divided into twenty-nine administrative sectors (dombon) identified by numbers, a tradition dating from the war years, when some districts (*srok*) were numbered by the CPK for security reasons. The dombon in the northwest at least were made up of collections of prerevolutionary srok. The dombon numbers do not seem to have composed a single numbering system but rather the traces of several earlier ones, reflecting zonal differences in the wartime period. The boundaries

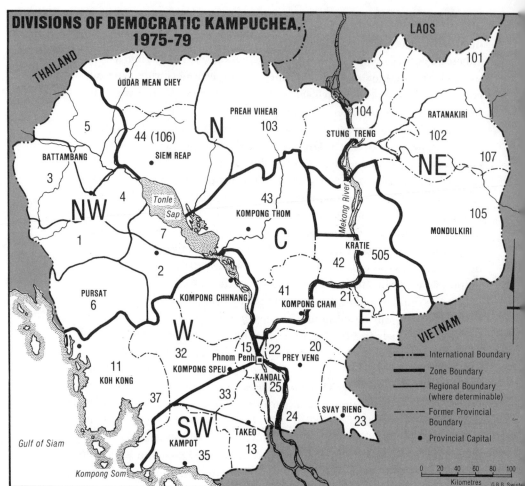

DIVISIONS OF DEMOCRATIC KAMPUCHEA, 1975-79

LAOS

THAILAND

ODDAR MEAN CHEY

PREAH VIHEAR
103

104

STUNG TRENG

RATANAKIRI
102

107

N

NE

5

44 (106)

SIEM REAP

BATTAMBANG

3

4

Tonle
Sap

43

KOMPONG THOM

C

105

MONDULKIRI

NW

1

7

KRATIE

42   505

2

41

PURSAT
6

KOMPONG CHHNANG

KOMPONG CHAM

21

E

VIETNAM

W

32

15

Phnom Penh

22

20

PREY VENG

11

KOH KONG

KOMPONG SPEU

KANDAL

25

37

33

24

SVAY RIENG
23

SW

TAKEO

Gulf of Siam

KAMPOT

35

13

Kompong Som

Mekong River

International Boundary

Zone Boundary

Regional Boundary
(where determinable)

Former Provincial
Boundary

Provincial Capital

0   20   40   60   80   100
Kilometres

G.R.R. Swint

from Chandler and Kiernan. (1983)

268

of the dombon are unknown, but they seem to correspond to those of srok or collections of srok in prerevolutionary times. Inside these boundaries, villages retained their prerevolutionary names, although some villages were abandoned, others were founded, and many were combined into cooperatives (*sahakor*), which became the administrative units of Cambodia in 1977.[75]

Living conditions in the zones varied, and inside the zones they varied from district to district and even from village to village. Conditions also changed over time. In general, the Northeast, East, and Southwest had the largest number of experienced cadre, the longest history of CPK indoctrination, and the greatest number of base people. These zones were thus relatively more benign, at least as far as newcomers were concerned, and for a time more reliable in the eyes of the CPK leadership. By and large, conditions in the Northeast and the East were more tolerable than in the Southwest, and easier in the Northeast than in the East, with the Kratie autonomous region being credited as a salubrious place to live, with few executions, sufficient food, and responsive cadre. Vickery has suggested that conditions were better in areas where new people could learn agricultural techniques from base people and there were no severe food shortages, worse where base people and new people were jumbled together in unproductive areas, and worst of all where new people were cast into forests to fend for themselves, before any crops could be planted.[76]

Conditions in the north and northwest, where more than a million new people were resettled in 1975–76, were the harshest in Cambodia, with the exception of dombon 3 in Battambang, which earned a good reputation, and occasional cooperatives where good harvests coincided with responsive cadre. Through much of the northwest, where production quotas set by the party were unrealistically high, cadre were often intolerant; a CPK member recalled of a visit to dombon 1: "Things were very strange. . . . People seemed to be very much afraid of the cadres and would sometimes shake in terror when the cadre came by as if the cadre were feudal lords."[77]

The worst conditions of all were probably in dombons 2 and 6 in Pursat, where new people were made to carve villages out of malarial forest. In these zones, deaths from starvation, disease, and overwork were frequent, while CPK cadre suffered from regional purges in 1976 and 1978. They were replaced, here and in the northwest, by cadre brought in from the Southwestern Zone, the area controlled by Ta Mok, who earned a fearful personal reputation in the DK era and after but whose cadre, while remembered as being strict, were often more disciplined and less corrupt than those who had been purged.[78]

Most survivors of DK agree that living conditions (that is, rations, working hours, disruptions to family life, and the use of terror) deteriorated sharply in 1977, even when compared to the trauma of being uprooted from urban life. A refugee from Battambang in 1978, a former engineer, stated, "In 1975, we thought next year would be better; each year has been the same. . . . We have lost faith in the Khmer Rouge promises, it has just gotten worse, the people are now desperate, and our desperation is confounded by the fear of death."[79]

There are three major reasons for this deterioration. The first was the regime's insistence on meeting impossible agricultural goals at a breakneck pace. The DK's Four-Year Plan minimized the problems associated with going too fast on the grounds that "we have [already] achieved a socialist state straight away." The plan called for a doubling of the production of rice between the beginning of 1977 and the end of 1980; specifically, it proposed more than doubling the average rice yield in prerevolutionary times throughout the nation and at once.[80]

The unintended effects of this policy, particularly in the northwest, where production quotas were higher than elsewhere, were administrative chaos and exhaustion from overwork and malnutrition. The only way for cadre to meet production quotas was to falsify their reports and to send rice intended for consumption along to the center for use elsewhere. After the collapse of the regime in 1979, a former CPK cadre told Stephen Heder that "the line of independent self-reliance was implemented too toughly. The people did not have enough to eat or to wear, and worked to death. At the same time there was too much subjectivism. The upper levels did not investigate the concrete situation but simply sat in their offices reading reports and believing them. Meanwhile at the lower level the cadres were [trying] to please the Center and hiding facts from it."[81]

The second cause of deteriorating conditions was that by the middle of 1976 Pol Pot and his colleagues believed that plots against them were being hatched, first in the north around Siem Reap and then in the northwest. Regional party secretaries were replaced, interrogated, and killed. So were regional military commanders. The plots and the suspicion they engendered broke down the remaining bonds of trust between the government and the people. By October 1976, the CPK's leaders believed, with some justice, that they were surrounded by enemies.[82]

In September, following the death of Mao Zedong, a factional fight broke out inside the CPK that resulted in the execution of several veteran

Communists associated with the Pracheachon Group, including Keo Meas and Non Suon. During this period, Radio Phnom Penh announced that Pol Pot had resigned "for reasons of health" and would be replaced temporarily by his deputy, Nuon Chea. Pol Pot resumed office in October, and since Nuon Chea was never purged or demoted, Pol Pot's retirement seems to have been tactical rather than imposed. He may indeed have been genuinely ill.[83]

If Pol Pot's retirement was a tactical move, it remains a mystery why it was announced over Radio Phnom Penh, known by the regime to be monitored overseas. Security precautions imposed in Phnom Penh in October 1976 included the placing of armed guards at factories around the clock and stricter curfews.

Pol Pot's paranoia intensified in 1977 and 1978. So did the purges and executions. These were directed first against party members and then against the population of the Eastern Zone. By that time, the Vietnamese had invaded Cambodia, captured hundreds of prisoners, and withdrawn. The people in the east who had failed to defeat them were thought to have "Cambodian bodies and Vietnamese minds." Tens of thousands of them were rounded up to be evacuated toward the northwest, but the evacuation degenerated into a massacre in many places. In others, Eastern Zone troops fought with troops sent from the capital to put them down. Perhaps a hundred thousand Eastern Zone people were killed, transforming the zone from one of the most humane in DK to one of the most brutal.

The third cause of deteriorating conditions was the war with Vietnam. After scattered encounters in 1975 and 1976, full-scale conflict, almost certainly instigated by DK, broke out in the middle of 1977. Fighting continued until the Vietnamese invasion in January 1979. Mopping up went on for several months after that, particularly in the northwest.

The war preoccupied the leaders of DK, intensified their fears, and dominated their thinking. As the purges of allegedly pro-Vietnamese traitors inside the CPK widened and came closer to the leadership itself, they consumed two deputy prime ministers and several members of the CPK central committee. By the end of 1978, the utopian goals of DK had been obscured by the party's struggle against its enemies, now perceived increasingly as Vietnamese. The struggle became the party's raison d'être. Talking to Jan Myrdal in August 1978, Pol Pot said that the "main achievement" of DK was that it had "put into pieces (*sic*) successively the schemes and activities of interferences, subversions, attempts at coup d'etat and aggressions perpetrated by enemies of all kinds."[84]

For nearly all of its history, the CPK has delighted in secrecy. For the first two years of DK, the party's leaders did not say that the Revolutionary Organization was a Communist party or that it envisaged a socialist future for Cambodia. The maintaining of secrecy enabled the party to strike more effectively at its enemies. In September 1977, just before visiting China, Pol Pot admitted the existence of the CPK and retroactively claimed that the party deserved credit for all the positive developments he could perceive in Cambodia's history since 1945. At the local level, however, party members concealed their membership from others, and most party policies were hidden.

In 1978, the CPK tried to juggle the priorities imposed by the Vietnam war, by its need to improve its image, and by what it perceived as enemies embedded at every level of the party. It was in the context of these contradictory campaigns that the American journalists Elizabeth Becker and Richard Dudman and a Scottish Marxist scholar, Malcolm Caldwell, visited DK for two weeks in December 1978, less than a month before the regime collapsed. All three were shot at—and Caldwell was killed—in an attack on the guest house in Phnom Penh where they were staying. Three days later Vietnamese forces invaded Cambodia. By January 7, 1979, they occupied Phnom Penh. Pol Pot's unseemly flight, by helicopter, echoed that of U.S. ambassador Dean in 1975. From then on, DK became a government in exile and its army a guerrilla force. It drastically altered its modus operandi, but those left unscathed in the final purges remained in power.

Within this temporal framework, several million life histories (*pravatt'ruup*) make up the living history of DK. Like the Nazi occupation of Western Europe, the Depression of the 1930s, or any overwhelming social crisis, the lineaments of 1975–78 in Cambodia are instantly recognizable among survivors, even when their zones and experiences differed. What had happened in DK was what they underwent together—and their half-miraculous survival. Outsiders can only glimpse the edges of these events, but as DK imposed its totalizing policies, it also imposed a consistency of experience on millions of Khmer.[85]

eight

Inside the Typhoon:
Testimonies

The testimonies discussed in this chapter were gathered in the course of my research. Each of them tells an unusual story. The witnesses include two former government ministers, a French citizen, a practitioner of traditional medicine, a former member of the Communist party of Thailand, a former civil engineer, and a leftist intellectual who returned to DK in 1976 from France. Only the Thai can be called a Communist. Everyone but he lost family members in the DK era. All of these people remember the time as one during which they suffered malnutrition, overwork, and victimization, but they are astute observers with interesting stories to tell beyond that. More important, all of them have had time to think about the DK era, not necessarily to relieve the distress of personal hardship and loss but to explain the episode and to clarify their ideas about Cambodian history.[1]

Chhean Vam and Kol Touch

Chhean Vam and Kol Touch, roughly contemporaries, had grown up in Cambodia in the colonial mid-afternoon that preceded World War II. Vam had been educated partly in France and became a teacher at the Lycée Sisowath; Touch trained and worked as a forester in Cambodia, building roads in the forests of Kompong Cham in the early 1940s. Unlike many others in the Cambodian elite, both men earned reputations for integrity, fairness, and tolerance. These qualities as well as their physical fitness and capacity for hard work probably saved their lives. Very few people of comparable rank survived.

Under any other regime Chhean Vam might have expected privileged treatment. As a founding member of the Democratic party and a prime minister of Cambodia in 1948, he had impeccable nationalist credentials. After abandoning politics he had become a businessman; he was untainted by close collaboration with either Sihanouk or Lon Nol. His wife, Thiounn Hol, was the sister of several high-ranking DK officials. During the civil war, Vam had remained in touch with his relatives in the resistance. These connections favored him slightly in 1978 and probably helped to keep him in dombon 15 near Phnom Penh, although for the first two and a half years of DK, when he was already in his sixties, he worked as an ordinary peasant. So did his wife and her elderly mother.

In the evacuation of Phnom Penh, Vam and his family took four days to cover the sixteen kilometers between the capital and Samrong, near Kompong Speu. After a few days there, they were located by CPK cadre and taken by truck "with pigs and other agricultural products" to a nearby village, where conditions were very hard. Vam had the advantage, however, of knowing the dombon chief, Cheng An, who with his wife, also a CPK member, had been jailed by Sihanouk in the 1960s. In 1976, Cheng An became the DK's minister of industry before being purged as pro-Vietnamese with his superior, Vorn Veth, two years later. An's wife was in charge of medical facilities in the dombon. She visited Vam at one stage and gave his family some sweet potatoes. Soon afterward, with her approval, the family was relocated in Udong but without much improvement in their material conditions. Indeed, in August 1978 Vam and his mother-in-law had both become sick, and his mother-in-law was evacuated to the April 17 Hospital in Phnom Penh, the only fully functioning Western-style facility in DK. Some days later Vam and the rest of his family were taken to the capital also and housed in a villa near the Olympic Stadium. Vam had apparently been brought in at the request of his former colleague at the Lycée Sisowath, Khieu Ponnary.[2]

Vam remembers hearing that Pol Pot addressed a massive meeting at the stadium around this time—perhaps to celebrate the party's anniversary on September 30, 1978. He learned from one of his brothers-in-law, who had attended the meeting, that a guard at the stadium had been executed when it was found that his carbine was loaded, undoubtedly by mistake. DK soldiers, apparently, were issued ammunition only when they went into combat—intriguing evidence of the distrust and suspicion among leaders of the party at that time.

In a neighboring villa, Vam recalls seeing a delegation of some twenty

English-speaking Africans (presumably from South Africa) who had come to Cambodia to study its revolution. Their study seemed to consist of unarmed military drill, feeding pigs, and planting vegetables, for the Africans knew almost no Khmer, and the DK cadre who gave them military drill (Vam remembers them calling out, "*Muoy pi, Muoy pi,* One two, one two") spoke no English. Vam was told that villas elsewhere in that part of Phnom Penh housed revolutionaries from other countries, including Thailand, but he never saw them.[3]

About this time, Vam was approached by a high-ranking party cadre and asked if he wanted to meet Pol Pot, who was known by the title *om lekha,* or Uncle Secretary. Vam replied gamely that since he was older than Pol Pot it would be improper to address him as Uncle and refused the invitation.[4]

Like Chhean Vam, Kol Touch had joined the Democrats in the 1940s and had become disillusioned with Sihanouk in the 1960s, retiring from a bureaucratic position in 1961 to manage a government-owned rubber plantation at Tapao in Kompong Cham. Touch became minister of agriculture in 1967. He soon resigned because of his impatience with official corruption and returned to Tapao. Evacuated back into the area in 1975, he was in an ideal position to watch developments in the Eastern Zone.

His life under DK was marked by a succession of fortunate events. In May 1975, after taking refuge in a village in Kompong Cham with over a thousand other new people, he was told to stay behind when the other refugees moved off. Some local people, who had been under CPK control for several years, had known Touch in earlier times. "You'll be better off here with us," one of them told him.

In fact, conditions were harsh. Touch and the remaining new people had to live for the first few months underneath houses in the village, customarily the location for animals in prerevolutionary times. The base people, who "believed what they had been told" by the Communists, treated new people poorly but gradually came to view some of them, particularly Kol Touch, as being helpful and friendly. By October 1975, locally grown rice had run out, and the village depended on what food it could obtain by bartering its bamboo with villages along the Mekong to the west. Conditions improved for Kol Touch in 1976, as people came to know him better and after a female member of his work team remembered that he had helped her parents with a loan of money many years before. By the middle of the year, he recalled, "they knew they had nothing to fear from me."

To gain the confidence of the young soldiers in the village, all children of local people, he planted tobacco beside his hut, so that the boys and girls could come and smoke with him when they were free. Already in the middle of 1976, there were reports of scattered fighting between the DK combatants and Vietnamese units across the border—surprisingly, for the village was a former Viet Minh zone, and the Cambodian soldiers had told Kol Touch the year before that the Vietnamese were their friends. In 1976, however, rice planted in some fields near the border had been uprooted and replanted by the Vietnamese with the roots in the air, as an insult or a warning. At the village level, nothing was explained; the skirmishes, like many in prerevolutionary times, may have arisen following cross-border raids for cattle or valuables by renegade units from either side. When fighting broke out in 1977, Kol Touch recalls that some Cambodians sought refuge in Vietnam, hoping for less severe conditions; but they were returned promptly and exchanged for cattle before being taken away and presumably killed as traitors.[5]

Like most of Cambodia, Touch's village was deprived of information about the outside world. In the best of times, the villagers knew little about the world beyond Kompong Cham, and some had never even gone to the nearest market town, less than fifteen miles away. Not surprisingly, they were susceptible to rumors. In early 1977, when the sound of artillery reached the village, some inhabitants thought that "Sihanouk's son" was leading an army to rescue them. Kol Touch, who was genuinely fond of the villagers, was saddened by the way the Communists and others before them had exploited their credulity. As fighting with the Vietnamese intensified in 1977, political meetings grew more frequent. Villagers were told that the Cambodian army could be in Saigon in seven days and that they had nothing to fear because the CPK had "beaten the Americans [in 1975] and cleared the road for the Vietnamese." There was "no need for new people who could read and write," the villagers were told. Kol Touch also recalls meetings at which Cambodia's revolution was favorably compared with North Korea's, which was called "as swift as a flying horse," incorporating North Korean imagery that was familiar to Cambodian peasants from their own folk tradition.

In December 1977, however, when the Vietnamese launched a serious attack, the Cambodian troops in Touch's region "fled, throwing away their sandals; hardly a shot was fired." By then, Kol Touch and his family had been moved to a village five miles from the previous one; earlier in the year he had narrowly missed being executed when a female cadre who had known him in prerevolutionary times defended him against her own husband's accusations; she called him "an important man, but good-natured" (*lok thom, pontae chet l'oo*).

The village was overrun by Vietnamese forces, and its inhabitants were rounded up and taken off in "eighty trucks" to Vietnam, leaving only a handful of people behind, including Kol Touch and his wife. A short time later, the central government, distressed by the army's conduct in battle, began purging political and military cadre throughout the Eastern Zone, calling them people with Cambodian bodies and Vietnamese minds. Locally recruited soldiers were replaced by teenaged boys and girls brought in from the Central Zone and the Southwest. The newcomers, Touch thought, were better equipped and more thoroughly trained than the local soldiers had been. After the Vietnamese retreated in early 1978, tens of thousands of civilians were rounded up in the Eastern Zone and evacuated west of the Mekong, in a poorly planned operation that soon became vicious and chaotic. Thousands of unarmed men and women were massacred by trigger-happy soldiers as enemies who had failed to resist the Vietnamese invasion. On one occasion, as people were being herded onto trucks, a young soldier whispered to Touch to keep walking; those in the trucks, he learned later, were all killed.

By the end of 1978, when the Vietnamese opened their final attack, Kol Touch had come full circle, almost like a pilgrim, and found himself on the outskirts of Phnom Penh. Unlike tens of thousands of others from the Eastern Zone and nearly everyone who had been a cabinet minister under Sihanouk or Lon Nol, he survived the DK era.[6]

Denise Affonço

Denise Affonço, a French citizen, is the daughter of a schoolteacher who was originally from Pondicherry and who had taught Sihanouk himself in primary school in Phnom Penh in the 1930s. Her mother, a Vietnamese, had sought refuge in Vietnam in early 1975. At that time, Affonço was married to a Sino-Khmer of Maoist leanings who had been in charge of the hotel facilities at Phnom Penh airport. His boisterous approval of revolutionary rhetoric—he told some chhlop after the evacuation that he spoke the same language as they did—soon landed him in trouble with the CPK. He disappeared in the middle of 1976, leaving Affonço, their twelve-year-old son, and five-year-old daughter to cope for themselves. The family until then had spoken French; Affonço knew hardly any Khmer.[7]

In September 1975, Affonço and her children were evacuated by truck and then by train to Phnom Leap in northern Pursat (probably in the dreaded dombon 2). In 1977, the cadre there were purged and replaced by cadre brought in from the southwest (*nir'dey*). The newcomers, she found, were fairer but severe and had had more political training. At one point, a cadre chatting with her asked what work she might do if she ever returned to France. Diplomatically, she replied, "I have learned a new trade. Thanks to angkar, I have learned to grow rice"—an apparently satisfactory response.

Affonço's recollections of details of her work and political meetings match those of many other survivors. She recalls, for example, being told at one meeting that new people were not "worth a bullet"; she remembers severe punishment being meted out for trivial crimes. During the dry season everyone in the cooperative was assigned to move earth for embankments: Affonço was required to dig a hole one meter square and three meters deep every day. Those who failed to meet the quota were not fed when they came home. She recalls returning from work on her hands and knees and harvesting corn and manioc by moonlight. Meanwhile, she saw that the CPK cadre in her village had plenty to eat, and while most women workers stopped menstruating under DK, the cadre's wives had normal pregnancies. From time to time, these women would appear in the fields and work for an hour or so, as if setting an example. In fact, without knowing it they were reenacting the habits of exploiters in the past and the farce of manual labor whereby Sihanouk invited diplomats and functionaries to engage in public works for an hour or so a month, exertions that were followed by a picnic with champagne. Affonço recalls working to survive and to save her family and because she wanted to live through DK to be able to discuss it later on when it collapsed, as she was certain it would.

Kru Khmer Chen

Kru Khmer Chen ("Chinese traditional doctor"), as he wishes to be called, is a Sino-Khmer trained in traditional medicine in China between 1955 and 1962. In late 1975, he and his family were evacuated from Poipet to dombon 3, in Battambang. His profession was favored under DK because of its supposedly indigenous origins and the reliance of traditional healers on local products instead of imported ones for medicine. Unfortunately, in their stampede toward revolutionary authenticity, some cadre refused to believe that traditional medicine required any training. Having no concept of hygiene, diagnosis, or sterile medical equipment, nurses throughout the country killed thousands of their compatriots with dirty needles, misdiagnoses, zealousness, and neglect.[8]

In the first village he lived in, Chen concealed his background, but when people noticed him caring for and curing his own child, they came for help. The cadre, sensing a threat, called a meeting to "build" him, arguing that "no doctors are allowed in the revolution." They relented in the end and allowed him to practice in the village and later in the srok and at the level of the dombon.

By the end of 1976, Chen was training nurses and paramedics for service throughout dombon 3. He was encouraged to choose the poorest children with the darkest skin as his students and had to teach them "according to revolutionary principles"—which is to say, without written texts—as best he could. The training course lasted a month. At first, he was aided by two other men with medical qualifications, but in the course of training both ran afoul of authorities. They were taken off to study and never reappeared. Chen's life too was fraught with danger; he was always in view, always suspected, and he possessed quasi-magical skills that soldiers and cadre thought might be turned against them at any time.[9]

When cadre from the southwest replaced local people in 1977, Chen was taken from his medical work and made to raise pigs and later on "seventy thousand chickens and ducks." At one point, however, he was recognized by a cadre who remembered his medical skill and was allowed to resume his practice. The dombon secretary, whose son he cured of an infection, favored him at first, but he soon got into trouble for making up a batch of Western-style medicines and refusing to follow instructions from cadre about how to treat his patients. For this refusal, he was called a traitor to Angkar. When some of his patients died or failed to get better, Chen was accused of trying to kill them. On one occasion, he was ordered to cure a particular patient or be killed himself. Ironically, two traditional doctors from China who were in Cambodia to care for Chinese aid personnel came to his defense and told local cadre that if there was no work for Chen in dombon 3, they would be happy to take him back with them to China. In an offhand anecdote typical of many who see their survival into the 1980s in terms of fate, Chen recalls being taken from the village one evening to be beaten up or killed, but the young soldiers escorting him turned back because it was raining too heavily for their comfort. By morning, they had forgotten him altogether.

Kasien Tejapira

Unlike the other witnesses, Kasien Tejapira was not a victim of the Cambodian revolution, but a participant. As a Thai citizen recently recruited by the Communist Party of Thailand (CPT), he was assigned to work as a propagandist in northeastern Thailand. In June 1977, fleeing from what he calls the Thai government's containment policy, he took up residence in a CPT base inside Cambodia named March 8 Village in honor of International Women's Day. Located south of Surin, the village was one of several Cambodian towns located along the Thai-Cambodian border where CPT cadre and evacuated Thai civilians lived under the protection of the CPK. Approximately two hundred Thai resided in the village. They were guarded by a Thai-Khmer militia unit of perhaps twenty men and women under Cambodian command. The village was isolated, but DK authorities provided it with abundant supplies of white rice and salt fish brought in by truck and ox-cart.[10]

Kasien and his colleagues were fascinated and chagrined by the Cambodian revolution. Unlike its counterpart in Thailand, the Cambodian revolution had succeeded, and the CPK had gained state power. This meant that its ideas and practices could not be ignored. The abolition of money, for example, seemed to some of the CPT an inspired stroke. On the other hand, the Thai were chagrined by the unquestioning loyalty, violence, and literal-mindedness of so many of the CPK's adherents. Some young soldiers assumed that people with wristwatches, glasses, or pale skin—like most of the CPT cadre, in fact—were capitalists (*nay tun*) who needed to be smashed. "Their understanding of Marxism, of socialism and class analysis was terrible," a colleague of Kasien wrote. "They could not understand Thai society at all." Such ignorance was owing partly to the fact that the revolution had fulfilled many of these poor peasants' dreams. What need was there to study from foreigners whose revolution had gotten nowhere? In Kasien's words,

> The Khmer Rouge conceived their revolution in an extremely puritanical sense, one of their favorite revolutionary songs . . . beginning with the memorable phrase, *"Padevat borisut l'oo l'aa"* [pure, proper, beautiful revolution]. The purity of their revolution seemed to consist in its purely lower-class character—it was the revolution of the downtrodden, pure and simple. Thus it did away with all oppression, exploitation, socioeconomic inequalities and class distinctions—in sum, the "old society"—altogether in a single absolute stroke.[11]

The victory of the Khmer revolutionaries in April 1975 contrasted sharply with the failure of the CPT to attract support from Thai peasants, most of them ethnically Khmer, across the border in Surin. In 1978, therefore, the CPT in March 8 Village decided to adapt the CPK tactic of "sweeping up the masses," hoping to gain converts by gathering people in Thailand against their will and herding them across the border into Cambodia for political training. They hoped to cooperate with CPK militia to achieve their ends. This change in tactics was contrary to CPT teaching, which held that the masses must participate in the revolution voluntarily. Kasien remembers approving the new policy at the time as a means of increasing populations in the CPT bases inside Cambodia and of depriving the Thai government of their services. The cross-border raids in 1978 soon degenerated into raiding parties. Civilian casualties were high; the political aims were forgotten by the Cambodians, who became overexcited by combat and loot. Many Thai families were broken up on the way back into Cambodia. When some three hundred peasants were finally brought into March 8 Village, nearly all of them were angry and wanted to go home. After several weeks of political training, only two of them joined the revolution. Others complained that conditions were too hard: "In our villages," they said, "we ate chicken. Here we eat salt fish." Within a few days, they had drifted back across the border.[12]

The CPT cadre allowed the Khmer to execute CPT soldiers accused of dereliction. From time to time, Kasien recalls, he came across corpses in the forest—those of local people who had disappeared or those from farther away who had been attempting to escape from Cambodia to Thailand. The bases closed down in early 1979.

Seng Kan

Seng Kan, a native of Takeo, was trained as an engineer in Phnom Penh in the 1950s. Over the next twenty years, he rose to become director of public works in Svay Rieng. As with Kol Touch, his rural contacts and his own good reputation worked in his favor after 1975.

For two or three months after the fall of Phnom Penh, he traveled around by foot and on a bicycle looking for a place to settle down. He first tried his own village near Phnom Chisor in Takeo but found conditions there too hard; he then moved to S'aang, where he had relatives, but found neither food nor shelter. Thinking that his skills might be welcome in Phnom Penh, he hitched a ride to the city. On the outskirts, in Ta Khmau, he found five fellow engineers housed with a CPK supervisor.

Taking him aside, one of them told him, "Don't come here; if things improve, perhaps they'll send for you." He left the next morning and learned later that all five had been executed soon afterward.

In June 1975 Kan decided to settle in Svay Prohout in Svay Rieng, where his former wife had relatives and where their children could be looked after. When he arrived, however, he was imprisoned in a wat for ten months along with more than a hundred former Republican soldiers and a handful of high-ranking civilians, like himself. Conditions were harsh and so was daily work, but rations were sufficient, and there were few deaths. The civilians were released toward the end of 1976, after having been transferred to a newly constructed prison building. Again, Kan's acquaintance with the prison cook from former times—the cook had been a policeman in Svay Rieng city—helped him, and so did the patronage of the political secretary, a former coolie who had known Kan by reputation in the 1960s. Later on, Kan's welfare was assured by his acquaintance with a cadre in the Eastern Zone whose wife had asked his help in Republican times.

The prison was closed by local authorities in April 1976. Two days later, Kan was at work with several thousand others a few miles away. At times over the next few months, he worked in a gang repairing the roads whose maintenance and construction he had supervised in the 1960s.[13]

Fighting with Vietnam broke out in 1977 to the north and south of Svay Rieng province. At the same time the CPK began purging its enemies in the Eastern Zone. Little by little, the Organization was falling apart. High-ranking military cadre sometimes came to Kan's village to rest between engagements. On one occasion, he recalls asking a regimental commander in private what would happen to him next—a severe breach of protocol in DK. Wearily the officer replied, using a metaphor of a banana tree to describe, it seems, the DK body politic: "I'll say one thing to you, and one thing only. I have ten hectares of bananas in Kompong Cham. In the first year [after liberation] we cut off the fronds; in the second, we cut off the fruit; in the third year [that is, 1977] we cut down the trees themselves."

"Is that true of all kinds of fruit?" Kan asked.

"Don't ask any more," the commander answered. "If it happened to me, it happens to everyone."

Ong Thong Hoeung

Ong Thong Hoeung, born in 1945, had earned a government scholarship for tertiary study in France when he was twenty. He lived in Paris for the next eleven years and was drawn into left-wing political circles after the student uprising in May 1968 and the coup d'etat in Cambodia two years later. Hoeung was an enthusiastic supporter of the NUFK, though motivated less by his fondness for Sihanouk than by his anger at the United States and his distaste for Lon Nol's regime. The front's political program seemed to Hoeung to be a refreshing departure from Cambodia's past.[14]

Hoeung was affiliated with the UEK rather than with the more extreme Union Nationale des Etudiants Khmers (UNEK), the Maoist organization to which Kol Touch's son belonged. Some thirty members of the UNEK, including Touch's son, were allowed back into Cambodia in 1973 after being vetted by Cambodians in Beijing. Students like Hoeung who were affiliated with the UEK were told to wait, and none returned home until after April 1975.[15]

In 1974, Hoeung and others in the movement went to Bucharest to meet Ieng Sary, who was traveling with Sihanouk. One evening, after Sihanouk and his supporters had left, Sary called in several students for a private meeting. He ostentatiously took down the photograph of Sihanouk and an NUFK flag that was hanging in the room. He told the students about the Revolutionary Organization—without mentioning the CPK— and lamented that it as yet had no flag of its own.[16]

In the second half of 1975, perhaps thirty Khmer expatriates were brought in to Cambodia from Europe, in particular from the Soviet bloc, via Beijing, but it was not until April 1976 that Hoeung and his wife received permission to travel in the fourth group of returnees, each of which numbered about forty men and women. Hoeung has written an eloquent account of the shock he received on arriving in Phnom Penh. There was no one to greet him. The city he had dreamed about for so many years was silent, empty, and oppressive. Expecting to use his tertiary training and his intellectual skills, he was pitchforked into the world of revolutionary praxis.[17]

For the rest of 1976, Hoeung worked in Phnom Penh in a factory making electric pumps and in an agricultural cooperative at Ta Khmau on the outskirts of the city. The workers at Houeng's factory slept and ate where they worked. They were not allowed to communicate with outsiders or to exchange information with anyone they met by chance. Working conditions were harsh, but food was adequate. Hoeung found, along with millions of other Cambodians, that "politics was everything. Political formation dominated every other activity." So-called livelihood meetings (*prachum chivapheap*) took place each day:

They attacked the individualist idea successively, in material terms, in terms of thought, and in terms of feelings. Materially, we had to denounce those who had more than the people. In terms of thought, each of us had to keep an eye on everyone else, to disclose any attitude that didn't conform to the line of the party. Everything was interpreted: words, gestures, attitudes. Sadness was a sign of spiritual confusion, joy a sign of individualism, [while] an indecisive point of view indicated a petty bourgeois intellectualism.

To expunge their individualism people were enjoined to "concentrate their memory" (*bantoum sati aram*) on their past behavior, their class origins, and their attitudes with an intensity that reminded Hoeung of Buddhist meditation techniques.[18]

At longer, more formal meetings the returnees were lectured by Khieu Samphan on such topics as the struggle of the Cambodian people and the cooperative as a basis for the future. Some were allowed to attend more restricted seminars dealing with the history of the CPK. Little by little, the returnees were being drawn toward the revolution. But their transformation was incomplete, for they were not yet trusted. Moreover, there may well have been disagreements among the CPK leadership about what roles they might eventually play.

In December 1976, in any case, Hoeung was moved with more than two hundred other returnees to a camp known as B-17 (the prefix *B* indicated that it was under the jurisdiction of the Ministry of Foreign Affairs) in Stung Trang in the red soil area of Kompong Cham.[19]

He remained there with his wife until the autumn of 1978, when all the returnees were brought back to Phnom Penh in a belated effort by DK to utilize their talents and training. In the meantime, many of those evacuated to this region had been executed or had died of misdiagnosed disease; food, however, was never as scarce as in the large cooperatives in the northwest, and housing seems to have been better. What stung the returnees was less the work itself, which they got used to, than that their intellectual skills and their devotion to the revolution were not acknowledged. All around them people were promoted because they *lacked* an education. To the intellectuals this was a severe blow. Moreover, as leftists they felt that they knew more about Marxism-Leninism than those who lectured them about politics. Yem Nolla, a former engineer who was in B-17 with Houeng, has recalled that one chief in the camp was an "illiterate Phnong" (a derogatory word for hill tribesmen) who "knew a hundred words of Marxism"—too few for any discussion and barely enough to decorate his commands.[20]

Voices from Tuol Sleng

Since the Vietnamese occupation of Phnom Penh in early 1979, the DK's interrogation center at Tuol Sleng—designated S-21—has come to symbolize the horrors of the regime. The center, which takes its name from the suburb in which it is located, is a former high school, the Lycée Chau Ponhea Yat. It began operations in late 1975. Under the PRK, the site was transformed into a "genocide museum." Visitors were encouraged to perceive parallels between Tuol Sleng and Nazi concentration camps.[21]

What happened at Tuol Sleng was horrible indeed, but the analogy to Nazi camps is imprecise. Analogies to the purges of the 1930s in the USSR—and the confessions these evoked—are closer, and in fact the purges may have provided the executioners and the people they worked for with a precedent and a model. Most of those whose executions at the site are recorded were members not of an ethnic or political minority but of the CPK.[22]

Regarding the DK's treatment of minorities the record is mixed. The party seems to have favored the Upper Khmer but discriminated against the Chams, a Muslim minority unsympathetic to the revolution. Nearly all the Vietnamese inhabitants of Cambodia who survived the civil war were repatriated in 1975, while Chinese and Sino-Khmers were treated poorly, not because they were Chinese but because they were thought of as capitalists. Arguably, they escaped worse treatment because of DK's alliance with China. By and large, the regime discriminated against enemies of the revolution rather than against specific ethnic or religious groups.[23]

What transpired at Tuol Sleng between early 1976 and the beginning of 1979 was also different from the killings, deaths, and disappearances that occurred elsewhere in Cambodia in terms of the documentation involved. The deaths inflicted there—perhaps twenty thousand in all—were decided on before the prisoners reached Tuol Sleng. Archival evidence suggests that with perhaps six exceptions, no one who entered S-21 came out alive.[24]

Some fourteen thousand names of prisoners in Tuol Sleng have survived, together with several thousand handwritten and typed confessions running to tens of thousands of pages. The texts are not useful for determining the guilt or innocence of those who made them, but they enable us to trace the CPK's collective paranoia and S-21's efficiency as a killing machine. In 1975, when it opened, fewer than 200 prisoners entered Tuol Sleng. The number rose to 2,250 in 1976, the great majority of whom were arrested between September and December. In all of 1977, 6,330 prisoners were brought in. The records for the second half of 1978 have disappeared, but in the first six months of the year some 5,765 prisoners were registered.[25]

Although several dozen confessions have come into private hands in the West since 1980, these texts have not yet been fully pooled. None of them has been published in Khmer, and only one, that of DK information minister Hu Nim, has so far been published in translation. The S-21 phenomenon warrants detailed attention because of the way it illuminates the thinking of the CPK leadership about their subordinates in the party and about the world and because the confessions themselves and other documents associated with S-21 form the most copious primary source for a political history of DK.[26]

This section will deal with eight confession dossiers. The earliest, from May 1976, is that of Chan Chakrei, an Eastern Zone military commander who was transferred to Phnom Penh at the end of 1975. Chakrey was accused of mounting a military coup against the government.

Keo Meas's confession, made four months later, reveals the CPK's capacity to devour one of its founding members. In early 1977, as hostility mounted against Vietnam, several ambassadors and lesser diplomats accused of pro-Vietnamese and pro-Soviet views were arrested. One Foreign Ministry official, Hak Sieng Lay Ny, arrested in late 1976, confessed to knowledge of a detailed Vietnamese plot against DK. The dossiers of Koy Thuon, Soeu Van Si (Doeun), Mao Khem Nuon, and Khek Pen date from February to May 1977, when cadre in the Northern and Northwestern zones were purged, along with intellectuals who had joined the CPK in the 1950s and 1960s. These four men were charged with conspiracy to plan a coup d'état. By the end of 1977, CPK members from the Eastern Zone, under suspicion because of the zone's proximity to Vietnam and because they recommended a military strategy unacceptable to Pol Pot, began to be purged in a systematic way. These purges continued through 1978. A good example of these confessions is that of the military commander Som Huy (Meas Tal), extracted in June 1978.

What emerges most strikingly from the confessions is that as far as the regime was concerned nothing was more criminal than differing with the party leadership and attracting its disapproval. For the leaders nothing was more important for themselves—and synonymously for the party, Cambodia, and the revolution—than that they remain in power. Their sacralized status emerges from the confessions, by implication. None of those I have seen contains any insulting phrases or derogatory material about Brother Number One or Brother Number Two, although some attack their policies and although all the prisoners confessed to plotting against them. Similarly, none of the prisoners took issue with the party or blamed its practice or ideology for anything that went wrong. S-21 saw itself as a watchdog for Pol Pot and his colleagues, protecting them not only from treacherous subordinates, but even from the charges leveled against them.

The idea that lèse-majesté (transformed into *lèse-parti)* was the worst Cambodian crime flowed from Sihanouk and earlier rulers to Brother Number One. So did the idea that the ruler had a special aura and should be revered. It would be unhelpful to press these resemblances too far and to argue that Pol Pot's personality, as a variable, was a major determinant of policy, as Sihanouk's had been. Brother Number One, unlike Sihanouk, presided over a genuine collectivity, a handful of men and women with whom he had been in close proximity in some cases for twenty years and with whom he had developed a political vision. These people preserved themselves while they conducted purges. It was their vision of party rather than of the ideas of Pol Pot that determined the fate of citizens in Tuol Sleng. The party was always correct. Its accusations were also correct in the historical context in which they were made. In other words, the revolution was, unlike majesté, a moving target. An acceptable revolutionary action or attitude one day could become counterrevolutionary the next. Counterrevolutionaries were always put to death. Once they reached S-21, it mattered very little whether what they confessed was objectively true or false, although the people they named under torture were usually rounded up, tortured, and killed. By entering S-21, people became counterrevolutionaries who had left the world already.

Since the party was all-seeing and secretive, it was difficult for interrogators to know what information the party required of a given prisoner. Sometimes interrogators' instructions were ambiguous. In his notes from a CPK study session in 1977 a young interrogator wrote, "The Party changes rapidly and frequently; [it] changes the prisoners we have to interrogate. The Party [changes the way] of making up documents, the methodology of interrogation . . . propaganda, torture. In all of the above, it is necessary that we have a lofty organizational discipline and thereby be untainted by complications. We must adjust to the situation in time. Leaping along with the movement for 3 tons per hectare."[27]

Another characteristic of the confessions is their tone of abnegation. Many begin by addressing the "beloved and respected party" and close with humble admissions of guilt, followed by expressions of gratitude to the party for having elicited the truth concerning their counterrevolutionary actions. The only direct evidence of torture is that in many confessions calligraphy deteriorates sharply in the course of a given day. In others, the documents for a single prisoner are written in several hands, suggesting that his confessions were rewritten by S-21 personnel.

The alleged military uprising led by Chan Chakrei, although snuffed out before many shots were fired, occurred in Phnom Penh in April 1976. Chakrei, a thirty-three-year-old military commander, was the son of middle peasants and had joined the revolution as a former monk in 1963. In 1968 he became a member of the CPK "in the forest, in Baray" (Kompong Thom). He served on the standing committee of the CPK in the Eastern Zone during the war and in 1976 was transferred to Phnom Penh to serve on the general staff. According to a CPK cadre interviewed by Stephen Heder in 1980, Chakrei antagonized a high-ranking CPK official in 1968, and this led to his being suspected of plotting against the regime eight years later. "Around April 1976," the witness continued, "artillery was set up on the outskirts of Phnom Penh to bombard Pol Pot's headquarters. The Center found out about the plan and suppressed it before it could be carried out."[28]

Chakrei was interrogated for over two months. Several hundred pages of documents springing from these interrogations have survived. At this stage of the party's history interrogators were looking for links with the United States rather than with the Vietnamese Communists or for plots inside the higher echelons of the party. Primarily, they were looking for the names of Chakrei's associates. His Eastern Zone connections were seen in terms of links with the Khmer Serei. Hun Sen, later the prime minister of the PRK, said in 1980 that Chakrei had admitted under torture to a plan to seize Phnom Penh while colleagues in the east seized Prey Veng and Svay Rieng. In August, Suas Nau (Chhuuk), the party secretary of dombon 24 in the Eastern Zone, was arrested, closing off this stage of purges in the east. They were to be renewed in 1977 and burned out of control in 1978.[29]

In September 1976, the CPK's youth magazine published an article to celebrate the party's twenty-fifth anniversary. Shortly thereafter, Keo

Meas, a veteran of the ICP and the Pracheachon who had served the revolution for nearly thirty years, was secretly arrested. From 1967 to 1975 Meas had lived in Hanoi and Beijing, and as a CPK bureaucrat he may have been involved with the publication of the youth journal. After his arrest, he was grilled for a week about the significance of the years 1951 and 1960 in relation to the history of the party. The degeneration of Keo Meas's calligraphy in the course of the week is suggestive of torture, but he was uncertain what crime he had committed or how his guilt could be connected with these two dates. Pol Pot and his colleagues, on the other hand, wanted to nail down 1960 as the date when the CPK had been founded to cut themselves off from the Vietnamese-influenced KPRP and from their post-1960 alliance with Vietnam. In this context, Keo Meas keeps missing the point, confesses to nothing, and relates party history in a clearheaded way. None of these tendencies saved his life.[30]

Meas's confession whetted the appetite of S-21 and its patrons for other important figures from the party's past. Non Suon, a prominent member of the Pracheachon Group, was arrested in early November 1976 when he returned from a trip overseas. He was interrogated for several months. The executions of Chan Chakrei, Keo Meas, and Non Suon seemed aimed at clearing the ground of people associated with the Pracheachon movement, who ostensibly were linked to 1951 and to the ICP. Before Non Suon's return, a special issue of the party's theoretical journal had published an article celebrating the *sixteenth* anniversary of the party's foundation. The article contained a statement by an anonymous writer, perhaps Pol Pot, that declared, "We must arrange the history of the Party into something clean and perfect"—that is, without a Vietnamese phase.[31]

At the end of 1976, then, factionalism within the CPK was breaking into the open. From the leaders' point of view, what was at stake was the consolidation of their power. At a meeting called in December 1976 to review the political achievements of the year, a CPK spokesman noted, "There is a sickness inside the party. . . . We cannot locate it precisely. The illness must emerge to be examined. Because the heat of the people's revolution [before 1970] and the heat of the democratic revolution [1970–75] were insufficient at the level . . . of class struggle, we search for the microbes within the Party without success. They are buried. . . . If we wait any longer, the microbes can do real damage."[32]

The 1976–77 purges appear to have focused on three types of victims: intellectuals and diplomats, including many who had recently returned from abroad; figures connected with the Pracheachon Group and the ICP; and people linked with the party secretary of the Commercial Branch, Koy Thuon, who had joined the central committee with Saloth Sar in 1960 and had served in 1970–76 as secretary of the Northern Zone. Koy Thuon's urban origins meant that those connected with him included many who had joined the CPK from Cambodia's lycées in the 1950s and 1960s.[33]

Suspicions also focused on anyone with Vietnamese or Soviet connections. On December 17, 1976, Hak Sieng Lay Ny, a Cambodian Foreign Ministry official who had served in Moscow and Beijing, was arrested. His confession asserted that the USSR and Vietnam were plotting to overthrow DK in order to place a pro-Vietnamese regime in power in Phnom Penh. He said that the conspiracy would involve "former political figures, members of the Pracheachon and of the [CPK]," who would soften up the CPK by urging it to have closer relations with Vietnam. Two Vietnamese diplomats in Phnom Penh ("the contemptible Minh and the contemptible Ba"), he said, were orchestrating the conspiracy. Vietnamese plans called for attacks on Cambodian islands in the Gulf of Siam in March and April 1977 because the seabed "is rich in oil." The seizure of the islands, Lay Ny went on, would alter the Cambodian-Vietnamese sea frontier to Vietnam's advantage. In addition, he said, Vietnamese forces would probe the frontier at Svay Rieng and elsewhere. The Vietnamese felt that they needed to strike quickly, he said, because DK was "already tough and sturdy." Difficulties foreseen included "how to mobilize the people in the cooperatives to fight the Organization" and the recognition that "there was no way of gathering increased support" inside Cambodia. These problems meant that Vietnamese strategy had to be worked out "from one day to the next."[34]

While Lay Ny was being interrogated, the ex-ambassador to Hanoi, Sien An, a former KPRP member who had studied in Paris in the 1950s, was arrested. He was presumably quizzed about the conspiracy and his own pro-Soviet stance.[35]

In early 1977 DK military forces began small-scale, unpublicized attacks across the Cambodian-Vietnamese border, particularly in areas where the frontier was in dispute and where the Cambodians felt justified in regaining Cambodian land. These attacks widened in March and April 1977—just when Vietnamese attacks had been forecast by Hak Sieng Lay Ny. The evidence, which is self-serving on both sides, suggests a coordinated DK strategy with attacks along points in the frontier as far apart as

Kratie in the northeast and Kirivong in the southwest. There is no evidence, even from DK sources, of Vietnamese attacks before mid-1977, although both sides engaged in artillery duels without crossing frontiers in 1976. Hun Sen told Ben Kiernan in 1980 that Eastern Zone troops had been ordered to cross into Vietnam in March 1977. Some attacks were also launched across the border in the southwest.[36]

The war lasted for eighteen months. Their troops also crossed the frontiers first, but DK accusations against the Vietnamese cannot be dismissed out of hand, given the possibility of Vietnamese involvement in the Chakrei affair in April 1976, the political confusion in September and October, and the politico-military planning described by Lay Ny. It is also possible that the CPK uncovered genuine details of such involvement as well as terrified, spurious admissions of allegiance to the CIA, Vietnam, the KGB, and so on.[37]

At the beginning of 1977, when Koy Thuon was arrested, open warfare had not yet broken out. If Hu Nim's confession of five months later is to be believed, Thuon had come to the unfavorable attention of Pol Pot in 1975 for sexual misdemeanors and was thought to be implicated in a series of bomb explosions in Siem Reap in early 1976. He had been taken from his Northern Zone position and brought to the capital. Separated from his power base, he was vulnerable to arrest.[38]

Thuon's arrest brought the strings (*ksae*) of traitors much closer to the leadership itself. After attending the Lycée Sisowath in the 1950s, he had worked as a journalist with Khieu Samphan in 1959–60 and had taken to the maquis soon after Saloth Sar and Ieng Sary. He had been close to Hu Nim in northern Kompong Cham in the 1960s. Under torture, he confessed to founding a rival Communist party and to being employed first by the Khmer Serei and later by the CIA. He claimed to have been recruited into the CIA by one of Lon Nol's colonels in 1960, just before fellow intellectual Tiv Ol, who was purged later in 1977 as a CIA agent, sponsored him for membership in the CPK. As secretary of the Northern Zone, he had been responsible for the preparations for Sihanouk's visit in 1973. Like Chan Chakrei, he seems to have attracted the disfavor of Ke Pauk, the Northern Zone military commander. This rivalry and Thuon's sexual behavior were probably enough to indicate treasonous intentions or to motivate others to lay charges against him.[39]

With Thuon's execution, the CPK began to devour intellectuals who had been drawn to the party in the 1950s and early 1960s. Like many others targeted for execution—and like those selecting the targets—

Thuon had been a schoolteacher before going into the maquis. Deputy Prime Minister Vorn Vet, arrested at the end of 1978, corroborated the sequence in his confession: "After the Chakrei affair . . . the Party decided to arrest the contemptible Touch [Koy Thuon] and the string of intellectuals."[40]

A set of instructions written for Koy Thuon after he had been interrogated for a month reveals how S-21 was often more interested in humiliating its prisoners than in determining the facts, which had usually been decided on beforehand. In the instructions the head of S-21, Duch, thanked Thuon for implicating Ney Sarann, the Northeastern Zone secretary purged in May 1976, and his own replacement, Soeu Van Si (Doeun), who had been arrested after him. Duch added, "But to continue, please explain truthfully and clearly why it was that you so fervently believed—in the CIA, with its rotten name, in Vietnam with its rotten name, in the People's Party of Cambodia [Thuon's spurious party] and the Khmer Serei with their rotten names. . . . This is the problem you have not explained clearly. This is the problem you have avoided."

Two weeks after Thuon's arrest, the man who had replaced him briefly at the Commerce Ministry, Soeu Van Si (Doeun), was sucked into the charnel house of S-21. Doeun was questioned for more than five months. Until taking up Koy Thuon's position he had been the administrative officer of the CPK's central committee. Enjoying greater freedom of movement than most officials in DK, he was ideally situated to plot a coup d'état and was accused of doing so by Koy Thuon and others arrested later. In his confession, he accused several high-ranking CPK members, nearly all of them already arrested, of plotting with him.

Doeun's dossier does not provide details of his early life. He was active in Kompong Cham in the Eastern Zone in the 1960s and had welcomed the Vietnamese when they came to help after the coup of 1970. Like Chan Chakrei and Koy Thuon, he had spent part of the war as a military cadre in the northern part of the Eastern Zone and had brought his troops to Phnom Penh soon after liberation. By early 1976, he said, he had begun plotting in the capital with Koy Thuon and Touch Phoeun, the secretary of the Ministry of Transport who was arrested in January 1977. Neither the details of the plot nor the reasons for the plotters' dissatisfaction with the CPK are spelled out.

In April 1977, Doeun confessed that the plot had also involved several former members of the ICP. By May, he confessed that he had been employed since the 1960s by the CIA. Questioning continued into July.

From the documents, it is impossible to judge Doeun's guilt or innocence, but the length of his interrogation suggests that officials in S-21 were convinced he could lead them to many guilty colleagues. Such an official, in early 1977, might have been disillusioned with DK and was seeking to overturn its leadership. Doeun's status within the party before his arrest and the crisis caused by his defection are reflected by the fact that his wife was second in command of the Foreign Ministry, after Ieng Sary, and that Doeun was replaced at the central committee office after his arrest by the ostensible chief of state, Khieu Samphan.[41]

By 1977, Pol Pot and Nuon Chea were suspicious of anyone who had come in contact with foreigners of any sort, whether abroad or in the restricted diplomatic community in Phnom Penh. Touch Kamdoeun, formerly a student in France and later a DK diplomat, confessed revealingly that "[Cambodian] students in France learned to be happy like Europeans, and *thus how to oppress ordinary people*" (emphasis added). The mingling with foreigners required of diplomats caused serious problems, for foreign affairs could not be conducted in terms of struggle, the diplomats' class background, and their revolutionary will. Impoverished peasants made poor diplomats, but the CPK's leaders were also swept along in their contempt for the Foreign Ministry (B-1) by their xenophobia and anti-intellectualism and by their preference for revolutionary practice over paperwork. These attitudes, of course, were echoed by the less-educated, heavily armed elements of the party. In 1977–78, repeated purges burned out B-1 and most of the Cambodian diplomatic corps.[42]

Regional purges in the north and northwest in early 1977 suggest that the CPK's leaders were dismayed by the slow progress of the revolution in these areas. They struck out against any traitors they thought they could identify. Traitors were often perceived as being people with urban backgrounds and intellectual skills who might have hoped to occupy the top positions in the party. Hu Nim, Tiv Ol, and Phouk Chhay, who belong in this category, were all purged before the year was out. So were hundreds of former schoolteachers and students returning from abroad. A typical target in this campaign was Mau Khem Noeun, arrested in April 1977 while serving as the administrator of the CPK's political training school in Phnom Penh.

Under torture, Noeun claimed to have been recruited into the CIA by a Khmer undercover policeman after participating in the anti-American demonstrations of 1964. The ceremony as he described it replicated that connected with joining the CPK, and Noeun undoubtedly drew on the

CPK initiation to describe another ceremony that had never taken place. In the late 1960s, he was active in radical circles in Phnom Penh; he mentions his friendships with intellectuals, also purged in 1977. In 1969, he went to the northeast as a combatant.[43]

Faithful service earned Noeun the gratitude of the CPK, and he was placed in charge of its party school in 1976. The later portions of his dossier describe an implausible plot supposedly initiated by Doeun in 1975–76 to take over the party school in 1977 and to mount an attack from there on the leaders of the party. The discussions reported by Noeun lament that the dissidents had no weapons, and the raid, if it ever really was contemplated, never got past the discussion stage. Interestingly, Noeun's confession contains a rare example of outright criticism of the CPK. Quoting Doeun, he asserts, "Those who are discontented with new methods amount to 60 or even 65 percent, more than half the population, a formidable force." Admitting that this majority was swollen with new people, Doeun suggested that an alliance with them was a necessity.[44]

In another dossier, Noeun claimed that the headquarters of the proposed coup ("We planned to fight the revolution everywhere, in the factories, the communes, and the army") would be in the Eastern Zone. He implicated the powerful secretary of the zone, Sao Phim, vice president of the State Presidium and a member of the central committee, as well as dombon secretaries throughout the east, nearly all of whom were to be purged in 1978. It is indicative of Phim's popularity and of his power base in the east that the leadership was unwilling or unable to move against him for twelve months after these allegations and those in other confessions were made.[45]

Reports reaching Phnom Penh about cadre excesses and target shortfalls in the northwest led to a purge of cadre there between February and June 1977 and later to the importation of cadre into the region from the southwest. By the middle of the year the secretaries of all the northwestern dombon and more than thirty other CPK members were brought into S-21, interrogated, and killed. A year later, this campaign was being referred to in party circles as the northwestern sweep or the second battlefield, to distinguish it from the first battlefield in the Northern Zone.[46]

There are suggestions that Pol Pot was personally involved in the purges in this area and in those affecting the Northern Zone as well, where cadre from the southwest were also brought in. According to Gareth Porter, who cites an interview with an unnamed U.S. official, Pol Pot traveled throughout DK in 1977 "investigating [the] loyalty and competence" of CPK officials, "ordering purges and personally lecturing re-education classes."[47]

Charges leveled against some of the cadre seem vague. Khek Pen, a former schoolteacher in charge of dombon 4, for example, admitted to joining the CIA in 1964 in the hopes of making Cambodia a capitalist country and to trading surreptitiously with Thailand since 1975; he confessed as well to plotting a coup in September 1976 that would have handed over Battambang and Pursat to Thai administration. At the time of his confession, he was serving on the CPK central committee. None of the admissions except trading seems plausible, but the number of new people in the northwest and the comparative leniency of some of the cadre there made the party leadership suspicious of him. His dossier is interesting because of the precise information it supplies about the geography and administration of the northwest and about the cadre staffing the region. Biographical details suggest that many of them were poor, illiterate peasants who were latecomers to the revolutionary cause. These facts are corroborated by the memories of survivors and may explain the harsh and doctrinaire attitudes that many cadre displayed toward new people in the northwest in 1975–76.[48]

In each confession, the act of joining the CIA seems to indicate a moment when—in the perception of S-21—someone decided to betray the party. No confession I have read specifies that the act involved being paid by Americans or reporting to U.S. agents. *Joining the CIA* was a code phrase for ex post facto high-level disapproval. It was crucial for interrogators to determine (or to assert) that their captives had taken the step before or soon after they joined the revolution. Tainted from the moment of conversion, or before, they had never served the party and should never have been trusted.[49]

Information about CIA recruitment is idiosyncratic. Koy Thuon, for example, identified one of Lon Nol's colonels as the head of the CIA, and Mau Khem Noeun spoke of being recruited into the agency by a Khmer in "a small room with an American flag on the wall and flowers arranged in front of the flag." Touch Kamdoeun claimed to have been enrolled at Lycée Sisowath by Cambodian officials and by American Evangelist missionaries. Men Tul, a doctor at the April 17 Hospital who had been regrouped from northern Vietnam in 1970, confessed eight years later that he had joined something called the Vietnamese CIA. He even claimed that an American CIA agent had visited Hanoi as a tourist in 1956 and recruited several Khmers!

It is tempting to treat such anecdotes as comic, until we remember that they were told in the hope of avoiding or postponing excruciating pain. They were extracted in the process of crushing people whose adult lives had been spent in loyally serving the CPK and who, in at least some cases, we can assume to have been innocent of the charges leveled against them. To avoid pain, the prisoners confessed to what they were told to, thereby fulfilling a quota of foreign agents who were "smashed to pieces" at S-21.[50]

By the end of 1977, after fighting had broken out with Vietnam, the party had admitted its existence under prodding from China, and the suspicions of the party leaders had shifted to the Eastern Zone, where Sao Phim still enjoyed widespread, threatening popularity. Here and there in the east people were allowed to wear their own clothes in place of the black peasant uniforms decreed by authorities elsewhere. People were allowed to forage to supplement their diets, and communal eating, the widely unpopular practice ordered on a national scale at the beginning of 1977, was slow to catch on, particularly in isolated districts, where, as one confession puts it, "visitors were few." By the middle of 1977, Sao Phim's name had surfaced in several confessions at S-21. Over the next twelve months, many of his military commanders, protégés, and former associates were purged.

In this context, the last confession to be discussed—that of Sam Huoy (Meas Tal)—which describes Tal's "traitorous activities" between July 1977 and his arrest in May 1978, is of interest. Tal, a military commander, confessed that Eastern Zone military cadre had begun plotting against DK in mid-1977 and planned an attack on the capital in September to coincide with the party's anniversary. Plans had been coordinated by Sao Phim, Tal said, aware as he spoke that Phim had committed suicide on June 3, 1978, to avoid being assassinated by troops sent by Pol Pot to fetch him to Phnom Penh. Phim was to be aided in the coup, Tal said, by Ros Nhim, the party secretary in the northwest, who was related to him by marriage and was Phim's colleague on the State Presidium. Like Phim, Ros Nhim had begun fighting the French in the late 1940s.[51]

According to Tal, Phim wanted to establish a rival political party. "We must work secretly, and with care," he said, "to establish a Party *whose line is the reverse* of that followed by the CPK. We plan to spend money again. There will be salaries, and badges of rank. There will be markets. These are our goals. We must build toward them" (emphasis added).

Phim's plans to use Eastern Zone troops in a coup d'etat in September

1977, Tal said, were preempted by a Vietnamese incursion that the Eastern Zone troops, buttressed by others from the Central and Northern zones, were expected to oppose. In October, Sao Phim therefore shifted his strategy from one of organizing a coup against Phnom Penh to one of allowing the Vietnamese forces to enter Cambodia at will. This policy was cited by the regime to explain the poor performance of DK troops against the Vietnamese invasion of the east that occurred in December 1977.

According to Tal's confession, plotting continued in the east in early 1978, after the Vietnamese withdrawal. By early April, Khmer-language broadcasts over Radio Hanoi had called on Cambodians to revolt against DK, and Cambodians were being trained in southern Vietnam to act as a vanguard for a Vietnamese invasion.[52]

In early May, the center reacted to the plots by sending loyal troops into the east. They purged the zone cadre and imposed CPK control after a series of bloody skirmishes, in the aftermath of which several hundred survivors, including the future president of the PRK, Heng Samrin, fled to Vietnam to seek asylum. By the beginning of June, Phim and all his trusted cadre had been arrested or killed or had fled the region. Later in the year, the center forcibly evacuated tens of thousands of people from the east toward the northwest, in anticipation of another sustained Vietnamese attack. The violence associated with this movement of people was as extensive as any in the DK period and ended only with the collapse of the regime. By the end of the month, Ieng Sary announced that a major coup attempt, concentrated in the Eastern Zone and involving the Vietnamese, had been foiled by the regime.[53]

Over the next few months, violence in the east had died down. Visiting journalists saw no evidence of a rebellion when they went on supervised tours of the region. Some of the rebel leaders had found shelter in Vietnam, and hundreds of Eastern Zone cadre and their relatives had been processed earlier in the year into S-21, about which the journalists knew nothing.[54]

Perhaps the failure of the Vietnamese to attack again in mid-1978 convinced Pol Pot that the war was over and encouraged him to project even more grandiose schemes for Cambodia's future. One of these had to do with the transformation of Cambodia from an agricultural into an industrial country. Industry in DK was controlled by the deputy prime minister, Vorn Vet.[55]

In mid-November Vorn Vet was arrested. His confession offers many insights into the history of the CPK. Vet claimed that he joined the CIA in

1956 and said, "While my appearance was revolutionary, my character was not." Over the next few years, he was active in the urban branch of the party. He helped the three ghosts to escape Phnom Penh in 1967, before fleeing himself in 1969 and joining a guerrilla band in the southwest. Like Non Suon and many old members of the party, Vet had spent much of the war in dombons 15 and 25, near Phnom Penh. In 1974, he confessed, the revolution "was proceeding so well that I couldn't implement the CIA plan." As deputy prime minister in charge of the economy, he weathered the storms of 1977. It is possible that he fell into disfavor when Pol Pot and his colleagues shifted their hopes for Cambodia from agriculture to industry in 1978. He was a victim of rivals in the upper echelons of the party. Judging from the confession alone, there is no way of reaching a judgment about his innocence or guilt, but Pol Pot seems to have believed that Vet had plotted with Phim to hand Cambodia over to the Vietnamese. DK cadre told Y Phandara in early 1979 that Pol Pot had been so angry at his old friend's treachery that he had beaten him himself and broken one of his legs.[56]

Had the Vietnamese not reached Phnom Penh in January 1979, there is no evidence to suggest that the CPK's purges would have stopped. They might have burned themselves out in the course of 1979, however, and the party might have edged toward a policy of liberalism to improve its reputation abroad, to attract foreign investment, and to gain foreign support for its fighting with Vietnam. Several moves in this direction were made in 1978.

Yet the moves did not alter the priorities of the party's leaders. The first priority was to retain power and control. The major threat to DK's survival, these men and women believed, came from the alliances which they perceived between all of their enemies and the Vietnamese. Poor harvests, factionalism inside the party, a slow pace of industrialization, the war itself, and declining welfare were blamed on foreigners, traitors, and subversion. The halcyon days of 1975–76 were over. In the words of the party journal, *Tung Padevat,* "There are enemies everywhere in our ranks, the Center, the general staff, the zones, the bases." The perception seems to have been correct.[57]

In this atmosphere, the torturers and interrogators of S-21 continued to serve their "respected and beloved party" fastidiously to the end. They may have hoped that the dossiers they were putting together would eventually connect all the confessions and tie all the strings together to form an immense, intricate, and self-referring circuit of betrayal, a final report on the "treason project" of which the leaders of the party, so many of them former teachers, could be proud. In July 1978, a document drafted in S-21—known in its English translation as "The Last Joint Plan"—listed nine major counterrevolutionary plots launched at different times and places. The text is a marvel of neatness, single-mindedness, and organization, with subheadings, parentheses, and intricate cross-references to a multitude of dossiers. Eastern Zone people were the most recent scapegoats. Others included intellectuals and people who had not been peasants before 1975. Soviets, Vietnamese, Americans, Thai, French, Germans, and overseas Chinese were also suspect. There were still some loose ends, however. Some of these connected Son Sen, a central committee member, with counterrevolutionary acts. The Vietnamese arrived before he could be arrested, or anything else could be tied together.[58]

Several problems spring from using the confessions to construct a history of opposition to DK. The most important is whether they can be treated as communicating historical events—and if so, in what sense. Generalizations are impeded further by the fact that so many confessions remain to be read.

Are the confessions true or false? Most of the ones I have studied contain information useful to historians of the period—including some fragile evidence (for example, in Hak Lay Ny's confession) to suggest that Vietnam may have been working to destabilize the DK regime earlier than the outbreak of war between the two countries in the middle of 1977—but the documents also abound in fantastic allegations, ephemera, and obvious untruths. Some confessions contain material that is not available anywhere else, such as the biographical data in Khek Pen's confession about cadre in the northwest; similarly, Vorn Vet's confession, like several others, provides useful information about the early history of the CPK and the biographies of people who joined the revolution in the 1950s and 1960s. Nearly all the confessions, on the other hand, contain bizarre passages about the prisoners' involvement with foreign powers. Some of the allegations about CIA recruitment and anti-DK alliances among Washington, Moscow, and Hanoi are primarily of psychological interest. So are the recurrent stories of rival Communist parties, sometimes composed of only two or three members, that prisoners confess to having founded or joined. Finally, the compulsion of the interrogators to cobble all the confessions into a series of master plots means that prisoners were often pushed to confess along lines that satisfied this obsessive sense of neatness: their confessions thus may not conform to anything they might have done. In fact, in many cases a prisoner's telling the truth about his or her activities might have derailed the interrogation. This range of contradictions—accurate factual data on the one hand, bizarre admissions on the other—calls the larger admissions contained in the documents into question. Which ones can we believe? Which ones are false?

For the psychological insights they afford into the leaders of DK and how their preoccupations altered between 1975 and 1978, the confessions are invaluable. They are of less use for a political history of the period, even though it seems likely that at least some of the prisoners were guilty of some of the charges leveled against them.

It would be difficult to imagine a regime like DK or a party like the CPK in which no one in a position to do so was plotting to overthrow them. Yet we must assume that the vast majority of prisoners were falsely charged. They may have been victims of vendettas within the party or of the leaders' whimsy; they may have been loosely associated with other prisoners or related to them by blood or marriage but not coconspirators or not cognizant of their conspiracies; they may have been arrested by mistake. Many of these prisoners (but which ones?) were innocent of everything they confessed.

If we assume that some of them were guilty as charged, however, we must ask two questions: First, were the CPK leaders justified in believing that the party was infested with people who wanted to overthrow them? Second, to what extent did Vietnam employ CPK members to destabilize DK in the two years before the outbreak of hostilities initiated by the Khmer in 1977? The second question is at the core of DK's political history and is crucial to reaching an understanding of its self-destruction and collapse. Both questions are impossible to answer, for the evidence pointing at Vietnamese collusion comes only from the confessions and from official DK statements. At the same time, there is no prima facie reason to accept Vietnamese denials of any interest in destabilizing DK before the middle of 1978. Throughout the 1960s, after all, they had sponsored a Cambodian Communist apparatus in North Vietnam; in the early 1970s, they had tried to control the pace of the Cambodian civil war; and after mid-1978, they showed no hesitation in building a "liberation movement" out of prisoners of war, hostages, and CPK cadre who had fled across the border, in most cases to save their lives.

Without exculpating the leaders of the CPK for the million or more deaths, including tens of thousands of murders for which their policies and party members are responsible, one can cite evidence from the confessions which points to the possibility that in the second half of 1976, if not before, party leaders discovered that some high-ranking cadre—especially those linked in the civil war to the Eastern Zone or before that to the Pracheachon Group—had begun to waver in their loyalty to the party center. Further, the confessions hint that the cadre had been encouraged to do so covertly by Vietnam. The question of 1951 vs. 1960 in this scenario is symptomatic.

The response of the regime to this information (which harmonized with what they wanted to believe) was bloodthirsty and excessive. At the same time, if the information was correct, the response was logical and in keeping with their appraisal that they had earned the right to govern Cambodia without the interference of foreign powers. Information about the plots and Vietnam's refusal to read the Vietnamese-Cambodian frontier as Cambodia demanded pushed the CPK leadership, never very trusting of Vietnam, over the edge into acts of overt aggression.[59]

These military offensives were sometimes explained to combatants by claims that they were to retake territories of lower Cambodia. Once the fighting began, the behavior of teenaged *yothea* toward Cambodia's so-called hereditary enemies was brutal in the extreme, just as it was toward fellow Cambodians and Thai. When savage, uncontrolled fighting began, the Vietnamese obviously had to strengthen their defenses, decide on counterattacks, and accelerate their efforts to destabilize DK. It would have been imprudent not to begin working with disaffected Cambodian cadre even before the outbreak of hostilities. Evidence of such activity may have surfaced in interrogations of Eastern Zone officials in 1976 and 1977 and in the confessions of diplomatic personnel who could have been approached by Vietnamese colleagues overseas. Until other evidence and more confessions become available, it is impossible either to dismiss these possibilities or to put the case more strongly.

The causes of conflict between Vietnam and Cambodia in 1976–77 are a mélange of the obvious, the compulsive, and the puzzling. The conflict was played out against a background of international tension and confusion involving shifting alliances and animosities among the United States, China, and the Soviet Union. These developments had an impact on Vietnam and Cambodia and helped to force them into a so-called proxy war in 1977. There is some intellectual neatness to choosing this global frame of reference, but it would be rash to ignore local causes and local perceptions in the equation. The Vietnamese and the Cambodians responded to the crisis in terms of their perceptions of national interest. In the Cambodian case, these were a mixture of prerevolutionary preoccupations, peasant millenarianism, and a sense that revolutionary consciousness preempted and surpassed the reality of power relations or material strength. In other words, both powers acted as if they were right and had sufficient power to enforce their interests.[60]

Ironically, the Cambodian position closely resembled the courageous, foolhardy opposition of the Vietnamese Communists, first to France between 1945 and 1954 and later to the United States. The differences were also important. The Vietnamese, unlike the French and the Americans, were not in a position to go away, and the Cambodians, unlike the Vietnamese, embarked on their national crusade after destroying almost every possibility of popular support. For these reasons, when the Vietnamese invaded in force at the end of 1978, Cambodia cracked open like an egg, and those on whose behalf the Cambodian revolution had ostensibly been waged—millions of poor peasants—did nothing to impede the occupation of their country by a foreign power. The regime, for one thing, had never trusted them with arms.

The Final Months

As with Sihanouk in 1969–70 or with the Khmer Republic in 1973–75, one is tempted to approach 1978 in terms of DK's "inevitable" decline. Certainly, refugees who escaped in the course of the year to Thailand or Vietnam were unanimous in their opinion that material welfare diminished almost everywhere in 1978. The rice harvest of 1977 was siphoned off to feed the army, to be stockpiled in forest hideouts, or to earn hard currency abroad. One refugee gave a thumbnail chronology of DK: "In 1975, we ate rice until October, and then only rice gruel [baba]. In 1976, we had rice until July, and in 1977, rice until February. In 1978, we had no rice at all, only gruel."[61]

Many refugees also cited renewed purges and witch-hunts in the east and the northwest. They spoke of having to prepare new autobiographies and of long, exhausting political meetings. In the northwest, malnutrition was endemic. As the revolution faltered, the regime grew more distrustful. Class warfare broke out in earnest, and purges of new people were renewed. A former engineer who escaped from Battambang in October 1978 reported, "Lately they started asking me what I owned: how many cars? How many houses? etc. I became terrified." At the same time, purges within the party fell off somewhat but by the end of 1978 had reached some of the highest ranking people in the party.[62]

The leaders of DK had every reason to be scared. The Vietnamese incursion of December 1977–January 1978 and other cross-border raids had demonstrated that their forces could enter Cambodia at will. Thousands of Cambodian civilians from the east and the southwest were taken into Vietnam as hostages, and thousands of others slipped voluntarily across the border. DK raiding parties also occasionally rounded up any Khmers they could find inside Vietnam. DK's response to the Vietnamese military offensive was ambiguous, as we have seen. On the one hand, the leaders proclaimed that the Vietnamese withdrawal was a major defeat inflicted by the DK armed forces. On the other, military leaders in the Eastern Zone were purged for failing to do better, troops from the center were sent in to put down subsequent disorder, and the area around Svay Rieng was fortified in expectation of a renewed attack. DK placed more than half of its troops in the so-called Parrot's Beak in Svay Rieng and the Fishhook in Kompong Cham, hoping for the Vietnamese to reenact the American invasion of 1970. Thus prepared, they decided on a two-pronged policy of accelerating the revolution and opening Cambodia up, very slightly, to the outside world.[63]

Evidence of the turmoil of DK's final months has come to us largely through refugee testimony after the collapse of the regime, from the Vietnamese, and through documents from Tuol Sleng and elsewhere.

Firsthand accounts of DK written by visitors in 1978, therefore, offer an interesting picture, even though the visitors were shown what the regime wanted them to see and were regaled with official statements disguised as interviews. Those sympathetic with DK, such as the delegates from Marxist-Leninist, anti-Soviet parties in Europe, Australia, and the United States and left-wing militants like Jan Myrdal and Malcolm Caldwell, were pleased by what they saw. Caldwell, for example, after touring the country for two weeks, remarked only half in jest, "I have seen the past, and it works!" Others, like a Yugoslavian journalist and television team, a Japanese friendship mission in October, and the Western journalists who traveled with Caldwell, present a more nuanced picture, part way between the paradise described by true believers and the hellish conditions, particularly in the northwest, which they were not allowed to observe.[64]

In March 1978 a Yugoslav team representing the state television network and three periodicals visited DK for two weeks. Their report is the most thoroughgoing to be written by any visitors to the regime because they were allowed greater access to the country than others and because as fellow socialists they were able to analyze DK inside a socialist framework.

Their criticisms of DK, however, were guarded and ironic. "The people do not go hungry," one of them reported. "But they are not very happy either. There was no singing to be heard, nor did we see any folk dancing."

The team traveled to the southwest and the northwest and was granted an interview with Pol Pot. Their television coverage of sites and cooperatives provided Western audiences with their first glimpse of the regimented life in rural DK. Laurence Picq, a Frenchwoman who spent 1976–78 working in the DK Foreign Ministry (she was married to a DK official), watched the Yugoslavian footage at a diplomatic reception in Phnom Penh and later wrote, "The terror which emerged from the scenes filmed in rural areas transmitted itself to the spectators." The spectators included the diplomatic corps, assembled by Ieng Sary to watch a more upbeat Chinese production. The projectionists who had shown the Yugoslavian footage, presumably by mistake, were arrested and taken off to S-21.[65]

Many who saw the Yugoslavian film have recalled that the only person in it who smiled was Pol Pot, who explained through interpreters, "We are building socialism without a model." Still smiling, he went on to say, "We do not wish to copy anyone; we shall use the experience gained in the liberation struggle. There are no schools, faculties or universities in the traditional sense, although they did exist in our country prior to liberation, because we wish to do away with all vestiges of the past."[66]

In most areas visited by the Yugoslav team, rations appeared to be sufficient. They saw communal dining halls where over a thousand families were served, "mountains of rice" stacked outside storage sheds in some areas, and several irrigation projects. The team estimated that only twenty thousand people inhabited Phnom Penh and that water and electricity were available only to a few ministries and the eight foreign embassies. Interestingly, seven of the latter were in one street, the Chinese embassy being the lone exception. The visitors saw children in factories so young that they had to stand on platforms to reach the machinery they were using. They saw twelve-year-old boys driving DK motorboats off Kompong Som. The grounds of the royal palace were neatly maintained, but wats everywhere else were used for storage. Son Sen's wife, Yun Yat, the minister of culture, told the visitors that "Buddhism is incompatible with revolution," although a former monk noted for their benefit that Buddhism and Communism in fact had "similar humanitarian aims."[67]

Touring the southwest, the team visited a model cooperative at Le Bo (so did the Japanese, Caldwell, and the other journalists). They were told that the DK forces had destroyed sixteen Vietnamese tanks in the Vietnamese incursion of 1978 but reported, "We saw no traces of [the tanks], and our hosts explained that because of the metal shortage the peasants had used every scrap of them to make ploughshares, hoes and shovels, and even cooking utensils. Interestingly enough, in some other regions we came across the wrecks of American tanks which had been standing by the roadside for three years already."[68]

The team noted that "not a single book belonging to the Marxist classics has been published" in DK, and in rural areas people were not told who the members of the CPK were: the party "keeps itself in complete secrecy, and operates behind the scenes." Similarly, no one they spoke to knew anything about Pol Pot (although Brother Number One later gave them a version of his biography, the first vouchsafed to anyone outside the party).

The Yugoslavs had mixed feelings about their visit. They found irrigation works in the northwest involving thousands of workers "a magnificent sight." They praised the élan of a particular mobile brigade, whose well-fed young men and women "showed a striking enthusiasm for their work while we were present." At the same time, their footage of work sites (some of it used to arrange crowd scenes in the film *The Killing Fields* in the 1980s) told another story, replete with regimentation, exhaustion, and unhappiness.[69]

Most other visitors to DK in 1978 were more sympathetic to the regime than the Yugoslavs were and dismissed negative reports as propaganda. These visitors acted as conduits for statements by the leaders of DK. Delegates from Belgian, Australian, French, Norwegian, and U.S. Marxist-Leninist parties were shown the same model sites, regaled with the Cambodian side of the conflict with Vietnam, and speeded on their way. Some delegations also enjoyed more private conversations at a party-to-party level.

One of these, between delegates of the Communist Workers' Party of Denmark and Nuon Chea, has been edited by Laura Summers.[70] The conversations took place in late July 1978. Several themes emerge from them, the most important being that Nuon Chea, the second-ranking person in the CPK, was eager to purvey charges of CIA-KGB-Vietnamese cooperation in plotting against DK. The Danish delegates requested clarification:

> Q. Is it cooperation between the CIA and KGB or is it rivalry for the control of Kampuchea?

A. Both. On the one hand they cooperate; on the other they are rivals. . . . They compete for control at the same time. This is an open form of cooperation [*sic*]. As for the secret one, some CIA agents joined up with the Vietnamese in order to come to Kampuchea. Because the US was unable to come, it had to rely upon Vietnam. The Vietnamese do not discriminate in choosing agents.[71]

The second theme of Nuon Chea's remarks was his close identification of the CPK and secrecy. Before liberation, he said, "our party chose two forms of struggle: political struggle and armed struggle. These are interrelated. The political struggle was promoted through legal struggle and illegal struggle, with the illegal being the basic form of struggle. Now we struggle openly and in secret with secret struggle as the basis of our struggle."[72]

Secrecy had served the CPK well in its years of illegal struggle, and the rationale for continuing to keep so many things secret, Nuon Chea went on to say, was to protect the leadership of the party. Ironically, in a regime that stressed life histories and obedience to the Organization so much, the identity of the Organization as well as the life histories of the party's leaders were kept secret. The prerevolutionary names of Pol Pot and Nuon Chea, for example, were not made public, and other leaders hid behind revolutionary names or numerical designations. In Nuon Chea's words, "The leadership apparatus must be defended at any price. If we lose members but retain the leadership, we can continue to win victories. . . . As long as the leadership is there, the party will not die. There can be no comparison between losing two or three leading cadres and 200–300 members. . . . It takes 10–20 years to build up good leading communists. If you lose one, you lose a lot. And party secrecy can be lost."[73]

Chea's rationale for secrecy explains many of the activities of S-21, preoccupied as it was with uncovering and smashing plotters against the leadership of the CPK. The leadership accepted no responsibility for conditions that led people to oppose it and shunned debate on strategic and tactical decisions. One effect of this was the wave of purges that swept the party in 1977–78. Another was that the leadership itself remained untouched and thus perhaps convinced of its correctness. On the other hand, with Nuon Chea himself locked into a society in which access to information was so strictly controlled, it is hard to assess the authenticity of his self-confidence.

In October 1978 a friendship delegation led by Kozo Sasaki, the former chairman of the Japanese Socialist Party, visited DK for two weeks. Like the Danes, the Japanese were received warmly. The English-language notes of Sei Ito, a journalist who accompanied the visitors, summarize the stories he prepared later on for the Kyodo News Service.

In talking with young cadre, Ito was impressed at how "frank and confident they were in responding to our questions. . . . We were given clear answers to every question as if we were talking to the top leaders of the country." Ito traced this frankness to the "flexible organization of the Party" rather than to the fact that the cadre attached to his party had the leadership's confidence and had been trained to give the proper answers.[74]

As for the evacuation of the cities in 1975, the Japanese were told that "most of the three million people in the cities were farmers" who suffered no hardships in being forced to resume agricultural tasks. Similarly, "under the revolutionary regime no one was allowed to claim privilege he had had before liberation. However, we were reminded that about ninety percent of Cambodian people were farmers who never had any privileges in the past."

The delegation did not visit the northwest, where the Yugoslavian footage had been shot, but on a visit to the same cooperative the Yugoslavs had in the southwest they were favorably impressed by what they saw, even though "we had no way to know the real thoughts of the farmers. Those who answered our questions were ones selected by the authorities. However, we were impressed by the cheerful welcomes we came across. . . . Our motorcade was often stopped by cattle and water buffaloes, and sometimes by cheering children to greet us. We were impressed by the adaptability of Cambodian farmers to the new situation."

The Japanese also visited schools, factories, and model villages, reporting what they saw as positively as they could. In the cooperative in the southwest, they noticed that people's "houses were nothing but a place for sleep." Ito's notes continued,

"Raised the question: is there any trouble between this kind of collective life and farmers' persistence [sic] on land and traditional family life?

"A senior official of the Foreign Ministry answered that the matter was dependent on revolutionary consciousness, and that they had already learned this was the best way."

Cambodian peasants had learned the virtues of collective labor, especially in cultivating rice, at least two thousand years before Karl Marx, but the iniquity of eating in family units, cooking their own food, and keeping families together was never adequately explained to them. The collectivization of eating throughout DK in 1977–78, which was universally unpopular, is another example of the leaders of the CPK trying to outdistance revolutionary accomplishments in other countries while tightening their day-to-day control over the very people on whose behalf the revolution was ostensibly being waged. Judging from the available sources, it is impossible to tell if policies like communal eating sprang from a genuine belief in the liberating character of collectivization, from hatred of uncontrolled behavior, or from a fascination on the part of the leaders of CPK, many of whom were former teachers, with the idea of total, continuous control.

The first non-Marxian journalists to visit DK arrived in early December. Elizabeth Becker and Richard Dudman were Americans who had covered the war in Cambodia for their newspapers in the early 1970s; they were accompanied by a Scottish academic, Malcolm Caldwell, who had supported the Cambodian revolution enthusiastically for several years. Caldwell had been invited to DK as a friend. Becker and Dudman had been invited in the hopes that their reports might balance the denunciatory accounts already blanketing the media in the West. In Becker's words, "Our guides were determined that we see nothing that would confirm these [negative] stories. Their solution was to keep us surrounded by cadre, imprisoned in guest-houses and automobiles, peering out at their revolution." Their reports, all the same, are of considerable interest. What makes them even more intriguing is the fact that Caldwell was assassinated on their last night in Cambodia and that DK collapsed less than two weeks after they left.

Shortly before their arrival on December 3, Radio Hanoi had announced the formation of a United Front for the National Salvation of Kampuchea, headed by a former DK military commander in the Eastern Zone, Heng Samrin. A month later, the front became the basis of the PRK. Between the formation of the front and the Vietnamese attack on Christmas Day, however, large-scale fighting subsided. Becker, Dudman, and Caldwell traveled through a lull before the storm.

Both the account Becker wrote at the time, published just before DK collapsed, and the book she published eight years later benefited from her memories of Cambodia as it had been in the early 1970s. These helped her notice such things as the disappearance of the Catholic cathedral, people's grim, unsmiling faces, the silence everywhere, the absence of children, and the absence of color in people's clothes. From time to time, Becker tried to penetrate the facades flung up before the group. In doing so, she antagonized their interpreter guide, Thiounn Prasith, later DK's ambassador to the UN. When the group reached Battambang, her insistence on interviewing new people led to Prasith's refusing to allow them onto any cooperatives in the zone.

On December 21 they toured the Le Bo cooperative in Takeo. Here and elsewhere, Becker was impressed by what she could observe of the economic achievements of the regime: "The lasting impression I came away with of rural life in Cambodia," she wrote, "was a tableau of scores of peasants, clad in black, tending abundant rice fields. . . . The economic system, I am forced to conclude, seems to be working." Becker questioned the methods used to achieve this self-sufficiency and the human cost. Nonetheless, she reported, as Dudman did, that some of the people they saw, particularly peasants in the southwest, seemed content with the regime and had benefited from the revolution. On balance, however, she came down in favor of refugee reports. After two weeks in Cambodia "that seemed like two years," she was unnerved by the anonymity of people, the omnipresent controls, the lies she was told, and the disappearance of the Cambodia she had known.[75]

On December 22, the day before their departure, Becker and Dudman were granted an interview with Pol Pot. They were driven to the meeting in a Mercedes that was even larger than the one in which they had toured the country. Pol Pot, who struck Becker as "elegant, with a pleasing face, not handsome but attractive," greeted them from a thronelike armchair in the reception hall of the former French Résidence Supérieure. Speaking in a soft, low voice, Pol Pot spent the hour "without a script, without a scrap of paper, slowly, painstakingly building up the case against Vietnam." He ended by suggesting that the USSR and the Warsaw Pact nations were in the process of taking over Southeast Asia and that Vietnam might call on European troops to help them. Behind the garbled ideas may have been an appeal for help from the United States, but this was not made clear. Reading Becker's account a decade later, one supposes that Pol Pot relied heavily on the intricate accusations contained in the Last Joint Plan, built up from confessions at S-21. The plan assumed that the Soviet Union, the CIA, and Vietnam were conspiring to destroy DK.[76]

Pol Pot put on an extraordinary performance. Later in the afternoon, he spoke privately with Malcolm Caldwell, who "returned delighted" from this interview in time for dinner with Dudman and Becker. The two men had spent their time, Caldwell said, discussing economic theory. Pol Pot had invited him to return in 1979 "to measure how the revolution had prospered." The three visitors separated around 11:00 P.M.[77]

Two hours later, the guest house where the three were staying was broken into by an unknown number of armed Khmer. Becker and Dudman were threatened, and Caldwell was shot down. One of the intruders was also killed. No one arrived to investigate the event for over an hour. A few days later, two middle-ranking CPK cadre were arrested and charged with the crime. In their confessions, they blamed Vorn Vet, already dead, and Son Sen as well as other high-ranking DK officials. None of these men was subsequently purged. Becker and Dudman attended a service for Caldwell the next day at which Ieng Sary delivered a brief oration. Later in the day, the journalists flew off, as scheduled, to Beijing. Caldwell's body accompanied them. Three days later, on December 25, the Vietnamese launched their final offensive.[78]

The assault involved over one hundred thousand troops as well as naval and air elements. It began at midnight on December 24 with columns crossing into Kratie from Ban Methuot. The commander of this column, General Hoang Cam, had led the Vietnamese forces during Chenla 1 and Chenla 2. Kratie fell on December 29 and Stung Treng two days later to a column of troops advancing from Laos. In the east and southwest, DK troop concentrations were bombarded from the air and with artillery. Poorly dug in and having few heavy weapons with which to counterattack, thousands of DK soldiers were killed before their positions were overrun. By January 4 the Vietnamese controlled Cambodia east of the Mekong and were poised to advance on the capital.[79]

On January 2, Sihanouk and his small entourage had been hurriedly evacuated from Phnom Penh and driven off to Battambang in what the prince called "a beautiful black Mercedes." Several diplomats from Phnom Penh, including the Yugoslavian ambassador, accompanied him. Three days later, he and his family as well as the diplomats were allowed back into Phnom Penh. It seems likely that this excursion was arranged after a Vietnamese commando team sent to Phnom Penh to kidnap Sihanouk had been captured on the outskirts of the city on New Year's Day.

Radio Phnom Penh continued to announce important military victories right up to January 6, and ministries in the capital continued to function as they had in peacetime, but several thousand Chinese experts were evacuated from the country after the New Year.[80]

Pol Pot, in a desperate gesture, invited Sihanouk to dinner on the evening of January 5. It was their first encounter since 1973. Pol Pot treated the prince respectfully, using the royal language he had learned in palace circles forty years before. He apologized for not having talked to Sihanouk in five years, pleading the press of business. The dinner was delicious and impeccably served, the two men maneuvering gracefully to avoid catching each other out. After dinner, Pol Pot took Sihanouk to an adjoining map room, where he showed him the strong position of the DK armies. Sihanouk was then driven home. His wife and mother-in-law, convinced that he had been called away to be killed, were relieved to see him.[81]

On January 7, Laurence Picq and her colleagues in the Foreign Ministry began work as usual, soon after sunrise. Many of the ministry personnel had been evacuated during the night. Picq spent the next two hours translating communiqués from the battlefronts. All of them announced impressive DK victories, but no one had told Picq why her fellow workers had been taken away. Once her translations were done, there was no one to mimeograph them. "I felt sadly alone," she wrote later, "in the midst of these people who made a state secret out of everything." Around noon she was evacuated with the others who were still working at the ministry, supposedly as a temporary measure. Picq and her daughters were part of a truckload of workers who drove out of Phnom Penh for Battambang. Pol Pot had left the city shortly beforehand by helicopter, like Ambassador Dean in 1975. Ieng Sary escaped by train, with the Vietnamese forces were less than five miles away.[82]

Elsewhere in Cambodia, the last phases of DK were less precisely marked. In some places, cadre disappeared overnight; in others, villagers, upon learning of Vietnamese victories, slaughtered local authorities; in still others, villagers had to wait for the arrival of Vietnamese troops before they were able to say that life under DK had ended. For hundreds of thousands of Cambodians who were herded up as porters and workers by the DK armed forces, the next eight months under Communist control and increasingly harsh conditions were the worst times since 1975. Because of their "Red Khmer associations" many of these forced laborers were refused refugee status in Thailand or overseas and remained under DK discipline for many years, in most cases probably against their will.

DK forces never reoccupied much Cambodian territory for long. Pol Pot and his colleagues had suffered a devastating defeat. The regime that had boasted of ending two thousand years of Cambodian history and of ushering in a longer period of social justice had held onto power, largely through terror and intimidation, for less than four years.[83]

Cambodia since 1979

The Vietnamese decision to occupy Cambodia west of the Mekong seems to have been hastily made. It sprang from the ease of their military victories to the east, from arguments in the Vietnamese army against protracted political warfare, and from a wish on the part of many Vietnamese leaders to solve the Cambodian problem. The political aspects of the decision involved putting a sympathetic Cambodian government in place, composed in part of those who had escaped or been taken off to Vietnam under DK and in part of any trustworthy Cambodians who could be found. Originally, the Vietnamese were to have installed this government in the eastern part of the country, much as in the 1840s they had tried to install a rival dynasty in that region while western Cambodia was under Siamese control. The proposal also echoed the installation of a supposedly independent state in eastern Cambodia in 1951.[84]

In light of the collapse of DK, the speed of the Vietnamese advance, the poor performance of the DK armies, and the uncanny absence of popular resistance, the Vietnamese rethought their plans. Only two days before their forces entered Phnom Penh the United Front for the National Salvation of Kampuchea, founded in December, convened a congress of the Kampuchean People's Revolutionary Party, which was to take over from the discredited CPK. This so-called third congress, while recognizing the congress of 1960 (and thus supporting the contention that it, too, had been convened with Vietnamese approval), ignored the congresses held by the CPK in 1975 and 1978. In effect, it closed the lacuna presented by Pol Pot's period as secretary of the party's central committee.[85]

The congress had several enduring political results. Less than a week after it adjourned, probably to demonstrate that Cambodian forces rather than Vietnamese ones had liberated Phnom Penh, the People's Republic of Kampuchea was proclaimed. There was no interim period during which the Vietnamese admitted that they were an army of occupation. Instead, the move suggested a smooth, legitimate transfer of power from DK (soon to be referred to officially as the "genocidal regime of the Pol Pot/Ieng Sary clique") to the PRK.

The PRK endured and flourished in Phnom Penh for longer than the governments of Lon Nol and Pol Pot put together. Despite harsh conditions in 1979–80 that could not be blamed on Pol Pot or the Vietnamese, the regime provided the time for many Cambodian wounds to heal, for hundreds of thousands of children to be born, and for nearly all Cambodians to resume some form of family life. These accomplishments occurred in an atmosphere of international disdain for the regime, except on the part of India and the Soviet bloc; as well, they occurred under conditions of extreme poverty, renewed outbreaks of disease, guerrilla attacks, and the ongoing crisis in the international Communist movement that had been brewing since the 1960s.

For those Cambodians who chose or were forced to leave the country, the inauguration of the PRK opened a new colonial era, a continuation of human rights abuses from earlier times, and a period of governments-in-exile. The PRK also renewed a commitment to socialism that many Khmer believed had been discredited or overtaken by events.

To the people who stayed behind, the demise of DK was greeted with relief. Over the next year or so, the Vietnamese and the PRK bureaucracy were cautious about imposing stringent political or economic controls. During this period, roads everywhere were crowded with people trying to return to their homes, to find missing relations, to make money, or to leave a country that had become unresponsive to their needs. The exodus was fanned by famine conditions that hit Cambodia in 1979–80—a "push" factor—and by the "pull factor" of relief agencies along the Thai-Cambodian border providing food and, after 1980, the opportunity (for some) to be resettled abroad. Famine conditions occurred because so many people "voted [against DK] with their feet" that rice was neither planted nor harvested in many districts in 1979.[86]

Over the next ten years, conditions slowly stabilized, the economy stumbled to its knees, and the Vietnamese loosened their control over many PRK ministries and the PRK's military forces. Little by little, the Vietnamese also withdrew their troops, promising in 1989 that they would all be gone before the end of the year. Nearly all the troops departed on schedule in September, but the State of Cambodia, as the PRK called itself by then, had to sustain its legitimacy by fighting other factions, including a DK army and groups loyal to Sihanouk and Son Sann, all of which sought to provide Cambodia with one sort of anti-Vietnamese government or another. Cambodia's prime minister, Hun Sen, a former DK military commander who had sought refuge in Vietnam in 1977, was less than forty years old. In this respect and in several others he offered a welcome contrast to many of his colleagues in the PRK and certainly to the leaders in exile arrayed against him.

In the 1980s, refugee camps along the border with Thailand held over three hundred thousand Cambodians who had left the country; the camps also served as recruiting grounds for dissident forces. After 1979, another two hundred thousand Cambodians sought residence overseas. Unfortunately for Cambodia, these included most of the skilled and educated men and women who had managed to survive DK. Those who stayed behind faced an uphill task in reconstructing Cambodia's communications network, its irrigation system, its hospitals, and its schools— to name only four components of the country that had been torn apart in the 1970s.

In 1981, the CPK announced that it had dissolved itself. All of its leaders remained in place, none was punished, and the dissolution probably never occurred. Conditions in camps in Thailand under CPK control remained harsh throughout the 1980s; discipline correspondingly was much lower in the anti-Communist camps, where anarchy often prevailed.

After 1981, Sihanouk became a player once again, under pressure from China and the Association of Southeast Asian Nations (ASEAN) states. Under his leadership, CGDK was formed. This body became the only government-in-exile officially recognized by the United Nations. It encapsulated the political rivals of the 1960s discussed in chapters 4 and 5 above in a time-warped replay of Cambodian politics. The factions included Sihanouk's, the DK, and a more amorphous group commanded by Son Sann. Chinese arms and supplies, delivered with Thai cooperation, kept the DK forces strong enough to destabilize the western parts of Cambodia and to require large military investments by the Vietnamese throughout the 1980s. This policy of punishing Vietnam was pursued with vigor by China and the United States and had the effect of postponing a political settlement in Cambodia. So did Vietnamese stubbornness. Largely fruitless negotiations, conducted in Europe and in various ASEAN cities, occupied much of the decade. In the meantime, hundreds of Cambodian civilians were killed or maimed every month by mines and guerrilla raids, and hundreds of Cambodians along the border perished from artillery fire and as combatants for the CGDK. A continuing war in Cambodia served outside powers' long-term interests, while the survival of Cambodia as a viable nation-state remained a low priority. In other words, the tragedy of Cambodian history, arguably enacted since the early 1950s, refused to end.

These developments, however, are outside the parameters of this book. By the end of the 1980s, Cambodia was still far from being as prosperous as it had been twenty years before. Its people had been literally decimated and metaphorically burnt. Nearly everyone who had survived had lost relatives or friends in what one historian has called the "howling wilderness" of the 1970s. Many had suffered permanent psychic damage. In some areas, widows outnumbered married women by three to one. The process of recovery was slow. While the flag of Democratic Kampuchea continued to fly at United Nations Plaza throughout the 1980s, the pre-1970 flag replaced it (but DK's participation in the UN continued) in 1990. Cambodia's economic recovery proceeded at a snail's pace. At the same time, the Vietnamese remained for much of the period obsessed with keeping the CPK, or any other Cambodian force, from taking power.

Little by little, all the same, many of the wounds inflicted in the 1970s, if by no means all of them, began to heal. Much of Cambodia came back to life. Some observers regarded the ten years of Vietnamese tutelage that ensued with horror or disdain; others saw them as a time when rationality as well as foreign patronage reentered Cambodian political life. Still others saw the years in terms of the resilience of the Cambodian people, who, especially in the capital and its environs, were able to reconstruct the sorts of lives that many of them had lived before the war. There were even signs, in the late 1980s, of the reemergence of a capitalist elite. Some visitors to Phnom Penh reported a resurgence of corruption among government officials. The PRK was more tolerant of dissent than DK had been, but it was hardly an open government. Its opposition to pluralism placed it squarely in line with every Cambodian government since 1955 and with several other governments of Southeast Asia. For nearly all Cambodians, its relative openness was a blessing, and the government's propaganda was based less on its performance than on the contrasts it offered to DK.

Whether from good sense or force majeure, the PRK and the State of Cambodia allowed most of its people to resume something that resembled their prerevolutionary lives, although in monetary terms nearly everyone was much poorer than they had been before the revolution. Overland communication was poor, there was little money for education, and public health was precarious. But on balance, as the tumultuous events of the 1970s faded in people's memories, those men and women who had lived through the civil war and under DK felt lucky to be alive, and so did their children, listening to stories about what their parents had endured. The beneficiaries of DK, an infinitesimal minority, wandered off into exile or, if they stayed behind, had to be content like everyone else with living in a postrevolutionary world.

The Tragedy of Cambodian History

Cambodia's political history between 1945 and 1979 may fall too neatly into a narrative format, with the rise and fall of the Democrats, Sihanouk slowly being overtaken by events, and the visitation of war and revolution in the 1970s. Such exigencies of narrative as the necessity of forward movement, excitement, and the narrator's privileged simplification of events (as well as his knowledge of the way that things turn out) reduce the value of contradictory witnesses, inexplicable happenings, and synchronic structural patterns. My own narrative has tended to focus on political events inside Cambodia, at the expense of foreign influences and other aspects of Cambodian life. The concentration on politics, in turn, has also privileged the testimony of male witnesses at the expense of those of women. It might be argued that allowing politics to take command of Cambodia in the 1970s led to a disempowerment of women in Cambodian society, where they had always dominated or at least had played a powerful role in the nonpolitical spheres of everyday life.

A narrative political history, however, has the virtue of staying close to the way that many people who experienced this portion of Cambodian history prefer to remember it and close to the unfolding, overlapping narratives of their lives. These narratives, in turn, are often used as explanations by survivors. A narrative treatment also has the advantage of exploring political and behavioral continuities among Cambodia's leaders and of discerning a kind of plot among successive regimes. Conceiving of recent Cambodian history as a continuing story helps us to locate places where its narrative broke off or changed direction. By and large, these points have coincided with the endings of individual chapters.

The regimes themselves broke with each other and with tradition. The five governments dealt with in this book—the French colonial one, Sihanouk's, Lon Nol's, Pol Pot's, and the Vietnamese protectorate of the 1980s—made conflicting demands of ordinary people, whose preoccupation with politics from above, as opposed to their devotion to their own concerns, was often intermittent.

And yet in Cambodia as elsewhere, political imperatives impinged often and persistently on people's lives. In less than half a century, Cambodian men and women were asked to alter and exert themselves to fit the interests of their leaders or the ephemeral concerns of other states. They were asked in the 1950s to be more democratic, in the 1960s to be more submissive, and in subsequent years, in a bewildering pattern, more republican, more socialist, and successively more suspicious and more tolerant of Vietnam. In most cases, they were asked to associate these demands not with their own interests but with those of their political leaders and with foreign threats. Few politicians after independence bothered with the day-to-day concerns or material welfare of the resilient, impoverished people on whose behalf they claimed to rule. Doing so might have implied sharing power with them, instead of knowing better.

Over the years, as ordinary Cambodians were forced to cope with these demands, with traumatic economic and social changes, and with intensifying, often random violence, they were also expected to raise their families, produce crops for sale and export, become wiser with age, and provide cannon fodder for one regime after another. They were seen as servants (in Khmer, *neaq bonmrao*, "those who are commanded") of those in power. Their concerns ran deeper and wider than politics but were subordinated to shallower, narrower causes by people who suffered less than they did, were often ignorant of Cambodian conditions, and had no commitment to Cambodia's survival.

If one keeps these ideas in mind, it is feasible to see the narrative of Cambodian history since 1945 as a tragedy and to perceive several major figures as tragic heroes, in the sense that they were caught up by their vanity and their abilities and by forces too elusive and gigantic for them to control. Sihanouk, Lon Nol, and Pol Pot can be studied in this way, and so can the men and women who encouraged them to exercise so much power. This is the history that I have tried to trace, without losing sight of the victims.

In 1979, this pattern was broken by a foreign invasion and a new protectorate. In the years that followed, a tragic approach to Cambodian political history, in the short and medium term, became less explanatory than it had been in earlier times. Leaders had less authority; countries had blurred their edges, the people were harder to reach, and no one tried to govern the country with the totalism that had characterized Sihanouk, the Americans in Indochina, or Pol Pot. When the Vietnamese withdrew their troops from Cambodia in 1989, the country seemed on the brink of joining the outside world as a small Southeast Asian nation, rejecting the grandiose anthems and slogans that had discolored the recent past. The process was delayed by foreign intransigence and by the insistence of some Cambodians, including Sihanouk and Pol Pot, on reinstating Cambodia's tragic social arrangements.

Lon Nol was no longer in the equation: he had died in Hawaii in 1987. Sihanouk and Pol Pot, however, were still receiving Chinese protection, seeking military support, and harboring hopes that they would return to power. Both men saw themselves as entitled by history to do so. Although they continued to perceive themselves as actors, the curtain had already fallen, many in the audience had gone home, and the two men had lost their tragic allure. Neither of them went through a real fifth act, in which glimmers of self-awareness traditionally come at the price of personal destruction. The times transformed these heroes, without their knowing it, into those left behind by the tragedy and therefore, in a sense, into clowns.

The fifth act of Cambodia's tragedy has been reserved for those Cambodians whose health and personalities have been broken by events of the 1970s and 1980s. Many of these men and women are now living thousands of miles from Cambodia, in Long Beach, Tacoma, Creteil, Toulouse, and Cabramatta. The older ones are besieged by memories, losses, and longings, aware that something has happened to them—probably history—which they are not in a position to explain. Their children, cut off from Cambodia, have become citizens of other countries. Over seven million Cambodians continue to live inside Cambodia and continue to lose their arms and legs to land mines and their children to malnutrition and disease. What is a game for outside powers entranced by their perceptions of the Cambodian problem is a continuing disaster for these Cambodians, who are trying to mesh their personal priorities, and their life histories, into a society in which politics as they have always considered the term—that is, as visitations from above—has lost its value, probably for good.

Notes

Chapter One. In Search of Independence, 1945–1950

1. France, Archives d'outremer, Aix-en-Provence (hereafter AOM), 7 F 29 (4), and Eveline Porée-Maspéro, manuscript journal, March 12, 1945.

2. *Brahrajbangsavatar norodom sihanouk* (Royal chronicle of Norodom Sihanouk) (hereafter RNS) (n.d. [1949?]), 507.

3. For cabinet, see V. M. Reddi, *A History of the Cambodian Independence Movement* (Tiruptai, 1971), 89; for comments, see AOM Cambodge 121/1101 ("Renseignements sur les gouvernements pro-japonais en Indochine"); on prisoners, see Bunchhan Mul, *Kuk niyobay* (Political prison) (Phnom Penh, 1971), 257.

4. Eveline Porée-Maspéro journal, MS, March 20, 1945; Porée-Maspéro letter to author, July 1982.

5. See Pol Pot, *Long Live the Seventeenth Anniversary of the Communist Party of Kampuchea* (New York, 1978), 18. Lek Samoeun interview, February 1989; Keng Vannsak interview, November 1986.

6. See AOM Cambodge 139, and France, Service Historique de l'Armée de Terre, Chateau de Vincennes (hereafter SHAT) 10 H 5585, "Documentation sur le Cambodge (1936–1953)."

7. Channa Samudvanija kindly provided an archive of papers relating to Son Ngoc Thanh's career (hereafter SNT papers).

8. On *Nagara Vatta,* see Bunchhan Mul, *Kuk Niyobay*, 18–22; Sim Var interview, November 1987, Thiounn Mumm interview, May 1988, and So Bun Hor interview, February 1989.

9. See Bunchhan Mul, "The Umbrella War of 1942," in *Peasants and Politics in Kampuchea, 1942–1981*, ed. Ben Kiernan and Chanthou Boua (London, 1982), 120–26, and Porée-Maspéro journal, July 20, 1942; Douc Rasy interview, May 1988. See also *Réalités cambodgiennes* (hereafter *RC*), July 11, 1959, for a denial of palace involvement, and Norodom Sihanouk, *Souvenirs doux et amers* (Paris, 1981), 75.

10. SNT papers, "Le Parti Nationaliste Khmer pour l'indépendance du Cambodge," undated typescript, corrected in Thanh's hand.

11. SNT papers and Thanh's interrogation, October 16, 1945 (France, Archives de la Justice Militaire) (hereafter AJM). Leonard Overton kindly shared with me his notes from this archive.

12. Testimony of Kanichiro Kubota, March 9, 1946 (AJM).

13. Reddi, *History of the Cambodian Independence Movement*, 94. According to *Cambodge,* July 17, 1945, the corps was drawn from "among 3,500 candidates." Michael Vickery, letter to author, November 1988. Pok Saman interview February 1989. According to Son Ngoc Thanh (AJM papers) the name Green Shirts was chosen because the minister of defense, Khim Tit, had obtained a large quantity of green cloth from a merchant in Kampot. See also AOM, Cambodge 128 (I), Police report, April 26, 1947, an interrogation of Khvan Theach, who joined the volunteers in April 1945 and later went into the resistance.

14. Sihanouk, *Souvenirs doux et amers*, 106–09, and Bunchhan Mul, *Charet khmer* (Khmer mores) (Phnom Penh, 1974), 19–20. In 1959, when Thanh was an opponent of his regime, Sihanouk wrote that "when Thanh became premier, he put the King's ministers in jail, shot Nong Kimny, and put a gun at the King's throat." *Neak cheat niyum* (The nationalist), September 19, 1959 (Michael Vickery's notes). In fact, Thanh became premier two days later; he released the ministers as soon as he learned they had been locked up; and Sihanouk was not present for the confrontation between the insurgents and his parents.

15. Porée-Maspéro journal, August 11, 1945; Pung Peng Cheng interview, May 1988. On Keng Vannsak, Ben Kiernan, *How Pol Pot Came to Power* (London, 1984) (hereafter *HPP*), 50. Thonn Ouk interview, May 1988.

16. Pung Peng Cheng interview, November 1987, Thanh interrogation, October 16, 1945 (AJM). Those involved in backing the intruders included Thach Sary, Neth Laingsay, Kiman Dore, Hem Savang, and Mom Koun; on Pach Chhoeun, see Norodom Sihanouk, "Le Cambodge, deviendra-t-il un république?" *RC*, August 22, 1959, and Sihanouk, *Souvenirs doux et amers*, 107.

17. Gareth Porter, "Vietnamese Communist Policy toward Kampuchea, 1930–1970," in *Revolution and Its Aftermath in Kampuchea*, ed. David P. Chandler and Ben Kiernan (New Haven, 1983), 57–98 at 64. The post of prime minister was created by Kram 88NS of August 14, 1945.

18. Thiounn Mumm interview, May 1988, and his letter to author, November 1988. Mumm's grandfather had been an immensely powerful palace minister for the first forty years of the twentieth century and amassed an enormous fortune. Mumm's father, Thiounn Hol, was the first nonroyal Cambodian to receive a high school education in France. Mumm and several of his brothers became active in the Cambodian Communist movement.

19. After Cambodia's independence, several members of Thanh's family came to consider themselves Vietnamese. One of his brothers served in the South Vietnamese Senate under Ngo Dinh Diem.

20. Sok Chhong testimony at Thanh's trial, January 3, 1946 (AJM); Thiounn Mumm interview, May 1988, and his letter to author, November 1988. En route to Hanoi, the delegates met with representatives of the fledgling government of Vietnam in Mytho and transmitted a memorandum to Thanh (found in his briefcase when he was arrested on October 15) that promised Vietnamese aid to Cambodian paramilitary units.

21. Kiernan, *HPP*, 51 ff. See also Khim Tit, *RC*, July 2, 1967. There was heavy fighting in Tra Vinh between ethnic Khmer and Vietnamese in the summer of 1945 (Pierre Brocheux interview, May 1987).

22. For the text of the letter, see U.S. Political Adviser, Bangkok (Charles Yost), U.S. Legation, Bangkok's 7, December 24, 1945. Khim Tit, *RC*, July 7, 1967. Sihanouk, *Souvenirs doux et amers*, 112.

23. Porée-Maspéro journal, October 17, 1945, and Thanh's interrogation, October 17–18, 1945 (AJM).

24. On the referendum, see RNS, p. 568, and *Cambodge*, September 6, 8, 1945 (Michael Vickery notes).

25. See Thanh's letter to Gracey (document found in his briefcase when arrested: AJM), and also Vice Admiral Earl Mountbatten of Burma, *Report to the Combined Chiefs of Staff by the Supreme Allied Commander Southeast Asia Section E: Post Surrender Tasks* (London, 1969), 288–89. See also Khim Tit's articles in *RC*, June 9, 16, 1967; Charles Meyer, *Derrière le sourire khmer* (Paris, 1971), 115–16; Norodom Sihanouk, *L'Indochine vue de Pékin* (Paris, 1972), 43.

26. See AOM, Cambodge 137/24, "Renseignements 1945," note by Loupy, royal mechanic, October 13, 1945, mentioning king's departure for three days on October 14, 1945.

27. The court had originally requested the death penalty. Murray interview with Anthony Barnett (1982); Barnett kindly provided a transcript. Sim Var interview, November 1987. Porée-Maspéro journal, October 7, 1945.

28. Murray interview with Barnett.

29. On October 20 cabinet meeting, see SHAT, 10 H 5585, "Relations franco-khmers 1950–1955, Séances plénières du Conseil de Ministres 1945"; Thonn Ouk interview, May 1987, and Porée-Maspéro journal, October 18, 1945.

30. Devillers kindly provided me with a copy of this manuscript. Reddi, *A History of the Cambodian Independence Movement,* 152n, claims that Pach Chhoeun told him that the Viet Minh had been "cool" to his request for aid to make an armed attack on Phnom Penh in December 1945.

31. On Siem Reap attack, Great Britain, Public Record Office (hereafter PRO) FO 371 75693, "Chronology 1946"; AOM, Cambodge 145/7, "Dossier sur Battambang et Cambodge."

32. Sihanouk, *Souvenirs doux et amers,* 135. See also Pierre Gentil, *Remous de Mekong* (Paris, 1949), 294 ff., which describes a state visit by Sihanouk and Monireth to Laos in 1948.

33. Material on the Democrats is based on interviews with several former members of the party, including Son Sann, Thonn Ouk, Douc Rasy, Chhean Vam, and Sim Var.

34. On the three parties, see Pierre Lamant, "Les partis politiques et les movements de résistance khmers vus par les services de renseignement français (1945–1952)," *Guerres mondiales,* no. 148 (October 1987): 79–96. Lamant's essay draws on AOM, 7 F 29 (4), "Etude sur l'évolution de la politique intérieure et les partis politiques khmers (1951)." A Khmer-language history of Cambodia published in 1987 dismisses the parties as creations of the French. Ministry of Education, *Pravattivichea kampuchea thnak ti 8* (History of Cambodia, level 8) (Phnom Penh, 1987), 65–67.

35. Interview with Sim Var, November 1987; *Le Démocrate,* August 5, 1946. Interestingly, graduates of the French lycée Chasseloup Laubat in Saigon tended to oppose the Democrats and to gravitate toward other political parties. See Soth Polin, *Bei thngai mun 18 mina* (Three days before 18 March), in the Cambodian newspaper *Sereipheap* (Long Beach, Ca.), September 18, 1988.

36. On preferential distribution of gasoline and newsprint, Thonn Ouk and Chhean Vam interviews. For Monireth's remark, AOM, Indochine 127, report from Saigon dated August 30, 1946. See also Sihanouk, "Le Cambodge, deviendra-t-il une république?" where he fails to mention the Democrats, saying that the French asked him to "offer his people a constitution." In fact, they allowed him to authorize the document. On the prophecy, Thel Thong (personal communication).

37. Thonn Ouk interview, May 1987. On the crisis in September-December, Michael Vickery (personal communication), citing 1946 issues of *Cambodge 38.* On the assembly's early phases, see Philippe Preschez, *Essai sur le démocratie au Cambodge* (Paris, 1961), 23 ff.

38. PRO FO 371/69657, "Saigon Military Intelligence Report 10 August 1948."

39. Interviews with Thonn Ouk, May 1987, Sim Var and Chhean Vam, November 1987. See AOM, Cambodge 7F 29 (7), *Etude sur les movements rebelles au*

Cambodge, 1942–1952. The Black Stars were not mentioned in press, but the arrests were widely known. Philippe Devillers has recalled that Pignon believed in its existence (personal communication). See also M. A. Martin, *Le mal cambodgien* (Paris, 1989), 64.

40. AOM, Indochine 128, report from February 12, 1947. *Germans* may refer to deserters from the French Foreign Legion. Dap Chhuon probably worked for the Thai after 1946: interviews Maj. Gen. Channa Samudvanija, August 1981 and May 1988; Kiernan, *HPP*, 54.

41. On Sieu Heng and Nuon Chea, interviews with Hin Sithan, December 1987; S. Suon Kaset, November 1986, May 1987, and February 1990; and Ty Sophen, February 1989.

42. On Kao Tak, see Kiernan, *HPP*, 22, 54, 58–59; interviews Sim Kin, November 1987, Ith Sarin, October 1988, and Channa Samudvanija, May 1988.

43. On Puth Chhay, interviews with Hol Kong, March 1987, and Ong Thong Hoeung, May 1988.

44. On historiography in the DK period, see David P. Chandler, "Seeing Red: Perceptions of Cambodian History in Democratic Kampuchea," in Chandler and Kiernan, *Revolution and Its Aftermath*, 34–56.

45. See Stephen Heder interview with Chea Soth, July 1981 (typescript). "For courtesy, modesty, and easy-goingness (*sic*)," Soth told Heder, Samouth was "comparable to Ho Chi Minh."

46. Interview with Thonn Ouk, May 1987; Meyer, *Derrière le sourire khmer,* 117.

47. Huy Kanthoul memoirs (untitled ms. 1988), 102–03; interview with Thonn Ouk, May 1987. Martin, *Le mal cambodgien,* 65–67; Sihanouk, *Souvenirs doux et amers,* 135 ff.

48. On Yuthevong, Michael Vickery letter to author, November 1988, and U.S. Embassy, Phnom Penh's 269, July 18, 1956, enclosure 1. The first draft of the constitution had reserved the succession to Sihanouk's sons.

49. Thonn Ouk interviews, November 1986, May 1988; Huy Kanthoul memoir, 102; Keng Vannsak interview, November 1986, recalled that a militant in the Communist Party of France (CPF) in the late 1940s tried to convince him in Paris that Yuthevong had been assassinated by the French. See also Stephen Heder interview with Thiounn Mumm, who was in France in 1947 and was convinced, thirty-three years later, that Yuthevong had died of "an injection" administered by the French. Yuthevong's niece, Sisowath Aryawady (interview June 1989), however, claimed that these suspicions were not harbored within Yuthevong's immediate family.

50. Sihanouk, *Souvenirs doux et amers,* 139 ff.

51. Preschez, *La démocratie au Cambodge,* 31 ff. Nhiek Tioulong letter to author, November 1987. Other figures active in the Renovation Party included Kou Roun, Measketh Caimerone, and Chuop Hell. See Phouk Chhay, "Le pouvoir politique au Cambodge" (Diss., Faculty of Law, Phnom Penh, 1966), 150.

52. *La Démocrate,* September 25, 1947; *Cambodge,* October 10, 1947.

53. On 1947 elections, see *La Démocrate,* December 25, 1947, *Cambodge,* December 22, 1947, interviews with Chhean Vam, Sim Var, and Thonn Ouk. Vickery, "Looking Back at Cambodia," 92. Lon Nol, running in Soung (Kompong Cham), came in third behind the Democratic victor, who earned 5,067 votes. Lon Nol gained only 444.

54. Preschez, *La démocratie au Cambodge,* 34–35. In later years opponents of

the Democrats often cited their organizational skills, rather than their ideas or their popularity, as the reason for their success. In fact, the party persuaded most voters by its hidden agenda to seek independence from France. This worried Sihanouk and attracted French hostility. See State of Cambodia, Ministry of Education, *Pravvati vichea,* 70–71.

55. Keng Vannsak interview, November 1986. Other students who were active in the 1947 campaign and were later important in the Communist movement included Rath Samoeun and Hou Youn. See Martin, *Le mal cambodgien,* 104 ff, and Keo Meas confession, September 1976, 5–7.

56. Interview with Chhean Vam, November 1987; Sihanouk, *Souvenirs doux et amers,* 140.

57. On Chhean Vam's discussion of the border issue, interview with Thiounn Mumm, June 1989; Sihanouk, *Souvenirs doux et amers,* 154–57. Chhean Vam interview, November 1987.

58. *La Liberté,* April 16, 1949; Preschez, *La démocratie au Cambodge,* 39.

59. Patrick O'Donovan, "Plunder and Persecution in 'Paradise' of Cambodia," *Scotsman,* June 16, 1949. The article continues, "No one can quite say what these Issaraks are or why. They are a symptom certainly of a disease. Now, for want of anything better they are coming under the influence of Annamite Communists. They at least know quite precisely what they want."

60. Preschez, "La démocratie au Cambodge," 39; *Cambodge,* September 29, 1949; Thiounn Mumm letter to author, November 1988.

61. U.S. Consulate Saigon's 199, October 15, 1949. Lek Samoeun interview, February 1989. *Pracheathipodei,* November 22, 1949 (Vickery notes). During the strike, more than a hundred students were arrested.

62. On Dap Chhuon's rendition, *La Liberté,* October 10, 1949; Reddi, *History of the Cambodian Independence Movement,* 162; on Chhuon at this time, see Norman Lewis, *A Dragon Apparent* (London, 1951), 204. Charles Meyer interview, May 1987. Pok Saman and Sisowath Olary (Sirik Matak's daughter) interviews, February 1989.

63. See especially Reddi, *History of the Cambodian Independence Movement,* 167 ff. In 1951, the Communist resistance movements declared their independence and were recognized by some members of the Sino-Soviet bloc.

64. See U.S. Consulate Saigon's 448, December 16, 1949. PRO, FO 371/ 73962, British Legation Saigon's unnumbered despatch, April 19, 1949.

65. For details of the assassination, So Bun Hor interview, February 1989, and interview with Chhean Vam, November 1987. On the following day, Keo Meas, until then a Democrat, decided to join the Indo-China Communist Party (Keo Meas confession, September 30, 1976).

66. See *La Liberté,* January 25, 1950, and the photos in Bunchhan Mul, *Charet Khmer,* 109–10. Koeuss's cremation volume was republished in Phnom Penh in 1990. A letter to *La Liberté,* January 28, 1950, noted that "90 percent of the mourners were [ethnic] Khmers."

67. See U.S. Consulate Saigon's 44, January 20, 1950; *La Démocrate,* May 11, 1950; *La Liberté,* January 17, 1950, carries Huy Kanthoul's statement that Ieu Koeuss was preparing a report proposing to reform Cambodian political parties. See also *Pracheathipodei,* May 18, 1950 (Vickery notes).

68. Preschez, *La démocratie au Cambodge,* 40.

69. *La Liberté,* April 22, 1950.

Chapter Two. Political Warfare, 1950–1955

1. Before the mid-1950s, Cambodians listened to the king from a crouched position and would have thought it offensive to applaud (Son Sann interview, November 1986).

2. Kiernan, *HPP*, 80–81. Stephen Heder has pointed out (personal communication) that this period was one in which the ICP resorted to a united front strategy that later proved useful, in a different context, to the Cambodian radicals and marked off a crucial stage in their political formation. On this period of Lao history, see Geoffrey C. Gunn, *The Struggle for Laos, 1930–1954* (Bangkok, 1988).

3. U.S. Legation Phnom Penh's A-165, November 8, 1971. See also Kiernan, *HPP*, 79. "Exposé relatif à la situation et à la mission de la Révolution Khmere présenté par le Camarade Thanh Son," SHAT, 10 H 284, "Divers Cambodge 1949–1950." As far as I know, this speech has not been cited elsewhere.

4. Nguyen Thanh Son, "Exposé." In Lenin's *What Is to be Done?* Karl Kautsky is quoted as suggesting that the leadership of the proletariat must fall into the hands of the "bourgeois intelligentsia"—which is what happened in Cambodia after 1975. See R. Service, ed., V. Lenin, *What Is to be Done?* (Harmondsworth, 1988), 106.

5. See Kiernan, *HPP*, 82–83, on Sieu Heng, and United States, Foreign Broadcast Information Service (hereafter FBIS), January 24, 1951. See also Porter, "Vietnamese Communist Policy toward Kampuchea," 57–98. Giap quotation is cited in SHAT, 10H 284.

6. See PRO, FF 1017/3 (BBC Monitoring Service, April 24, 1951). On Buddhist conference, Kiernan, *HPP*, 79.

7. Kiernan, *HPP*, 82–83; Bernard Fall, *Le Viet Minh* (Paris, 1959), 128–29; Porter, "Vietnamese Communist Policy toward Kampuchea," 68–69. On the 1951–60 controversy, see David P. Chandler, "Revising the Past in Democratic Kampuchea: When Was the Birthday of the Party?" *Pacific Affairs* (Summer 1983): 288–300.

8. On Democrat fete for students, see *La Démocrate*, August 18, 1949. On Pol Pot's early life, see Kiernan, *HPP*, 25 ff., and Elizabeth Becker, *When the War Was Over* (New York, 1986), 67 ff. Interview with Keng Vannsak, May 1987, and S. Suon Kaset, June 1989. On the other students, see Cambodge, Ministère de l'Education Nationale, *Controle des étudiants boursiers, Carnet No. 1* (manuscript, n.d. [c. 1960], Echols Collection, Cornell University).

9. See Kiernan, *HPP*, 119 ff. Interviews with Pierre Brocheux, May 1987; Douc Rasy, November 1987; Keng Vannsak, November 1986, May 1987; Panh Meng Heang and Yem Nolla, May 1988; and Sok Bunthan, July 1989.

10. The literature on communism in Paris in the early 1950s is vast. Two recent studies are Alain Besançon, *Une génération* (Paris, 1987), and Jeannine Verdes Leroux, *Au service du Parti: le parti communiste, les intellectuels, et le culture (1944–1956)* (Paris, 1985). See also Dominique Dessanti, *Les staliniens* (Paris, 1975). For English parallels in this period, see Edward Upward, *The Rotten Elements* (London, 1969), and Frank S. Meyer, *The Moulding of Communists* (New York, 1961). These paragraphs also draw on interviews with people who were close to the CPF in the early 1950s, including Pierre Brocheux, Keng Vannsak, Thiounn Mumm, Jacques Vergès, and Georges Boudarel. See also Milan Kundera, "Afterword," in *The Book of Laughter and Forgetting* (New York, 1981), 234, which refers to this period in terms of its "collective lyrical delirium."

11. For much of the period, the titular head of the CPF, Maurice Thorez, was absent from France. See Dessanti, *Les staliniens*, 283 ff.

12. Interviews with Pierre Brocheux, May 1987 and June 1989. See also Arthur Koestler, "On disbelieving atrocities," *The Yogi and the Commissar* (London, 1945).

13. Interviews with Keng Vannsak, Thiounn Mumm, and Douc Rasy. According to Vannsak, Ieng Sary had first read *The Communist Manifesto* in the home of Yuthevong's brother, Prince Entaravong, who had picked up a copy in France in the 1930s. Entaravong's daughter, Sisowath Aryawady (interview June 1989), confirmed that Ieng Sary boarded in Entaravong's house and tutored his children in the 1940s.

14. Interviews with Keng Vannsak, Pierre Brocheux; Thiounn Mumm letter to author, November 1988; François Debré, *Cambodge: La révolution dans la forêt* (Paris, 1976), 77–95. Debré wrote his book before Saloth Sar was identified as Pol Pot and speculated (78) that Pol Pot was Rath Samoeun. Talking to Yugoslav journalists in 1978, without admitting his previous name, Pol Pot said that he "was a fairly good student" in his first year in France—i.e., before the arrival of Ieng Sary.

15. Letter from Pierre Brocheux to author, June 1987; *La Démocrate*, August 31, 1950 (for number of students); Kiernan, *HPP*, 110; Becker, *When the War Was Over*, 74–75; Vickery, *Cambodia 1975–1982*, 275 ff; *Khemara Nisut*, January 11, 1951, p. 36; and see F. Fejto, *The French Communist Party and the Crisis of International Communism* (Cambridge, Mass., 1967), 20 ff. Keng Vannsak claimed in 1987 that Saloth Sar "never mentioned" the trip or his palace connections. To Yugoslav journalists in 1978, Pol Pot said he had spent "more than a month" in Yugoslavia, "working on a highway near Belgrade."

16. Interviews Thiounn Mumm, Keng Vannsak, Thonn Ouk. On Vergès, see F. Fejto, "A Maoist in France: Jacques Vergès and Revolution," *China Quarterly* 19 (September 1964): 120–28. The five towers may have stood for the components of Indochina. David Marr, *Vietnamese Anti-Colonialism* (Berkeley, 1972), 218, describes a five-starred Vietnamese flag from 1912 that included stars for Cambodia and Laos.

17. Interview Thiounn Mumm, May 1988. Mumm noticed, when he visited Thanh, that he had French editions of the works of Marx and Lenin, but "the pages were uncut."

18. On British precedent, *La Liberté,* January 28, 1951. Interestingly, in March 1951 the "second Khmer film," *Crime of a Spy*, was presented at the royal palace. One of its stars, Oum Manorine, cast as a traitor, was the half-brother of Sihanouk's wife-to-be, Monique Izzi, still a schoolgirl when the film was made and living under the protection of Sihanouk's cousin, Prince Sisowath Sirik Matak, whose brother married Monique's elder sister. Monique's mother, Mme Pomme, had been married in the 1930s to a Franco-Italian contractor who had returned to France in 1940 and never provided for their two daughters. Mme Pomme's sister, in turn, had married Prince Sisowath Entaravong, Yuthevong's elder brother. Monique became Sihanouk's consort in 1951 and his wife in 1955. Material on her early life is drawn from several interviews.

19. U.S. Legation Phnom Penh's 56, June 17, 1952; U.S. Legation Saigon's 2637, June 30, 1952; Preschez, *La démocratie au Cambodge*, 44–45; Huy Kanthoul untitled memoirs, 120; Sihanouk, *Souvenirs doux et amers*, 174.

20. Vickery, "Looking Back at Cambodia," 94; *Cambodge*, September 10, 1951. See also U.S. Legation Phnom Penh's 7, August 1, 1951.

21. *La Liberté,* September 12 and October 24, 1951; *Cambodge,* September 11, 1951. U.S. Legation Phnom Penh's 21, October 17, 1951; Huy Kanthoul memoirs, 118 ff. My discussion of this election and subsequent ones benefits from Justin Corfield's research in progress.

22. See Sihanouk, *Souvenirs doux et amers,* 170–73; Preschez, *La démocratie au Cambodge,* 47–48. Prince Monireth's unpublished memoir (185) states that Sihanouk paid the costs of Thanh's travel himself.

23. *Cambodge,* October 30, 1951. In his memoirs (127), Huy Kanthoul claims that Thanh's reception had been opposed by senior Democrats "for fear of upsetting the King, so susceptible in matters of popularity," but that their objections were overridden and "tens of thousands" of Cambodians went to welcome Son Ngoc Thanh. Lek Samoeun, a high school student in 1951, has recalled that when he and his classmates heard Thanh's airplane circling Phnom Penh, they fled their classrooms to go see him enter the city. Interview February 1989.

24. On de Raymond, Charles Meyer interview, May 1987, and Soth Polin's letter to author, December 1988. On his assassin, *Cambodge,* November 16, 1951. See also Khmer Peace Committee, *Khmer Armed Resistance* (n.p., October 1952), which claimed that a "Khmer patriot" had assassinated de Raymond (Vickery notes). On Dio, Thomas Corcoran interview, November 1987, and PRO, FO 371/10143, British Legation Saigon's 51, April 18, 1952: "The gallant general, who is known to be a sincere admirer of the British people, is unfortunately unfitted to handle the delicate Cambodian creature which is just emerging from its colonial chrysalis. He will undoubtedly have to be removed."

25. U.S. Legation Phnom Penh's unnumbered despatch December 19, 1951; Monireth memoir, 187.

26. *Cambodge,* November 29, 1951; SHAT, 10 H 284, letter from Dio to Salan, January 8, 1952; interview with Hoeung Hong Kim, February 1989. Kim, a Buddhist novice in 1953, has recalled antimonarchist sermons preached to large audiences at this time.

27. *La Liberté,* May 29, 1952; Huy Kanthoul memoirs, 128–29. Following civil service practice, Thanh had been promoted twice in absentia between 1945 and 1952 on the grounds of seniority. Twenty issues of *Khmer Krauk!* appeared between January 1952 and the end of March, two weeks after Thanh's disappearance. Articles, poems, and editorials stressed the need for independence, but the paper also carried serialized fiction and foreign news. The March 14 issue noted that a group of "forest people" had captured Thanh and Sichau on March 9. I'm grateful to Michael Vickery for photographs of these texts.

28. *La Liberté,* March 20, 1952; *Cambodge,* March 20, 1952; Hin Sithan, *No na kitt'kam* (Who are the murderers?) (Seattle, Wash., 1986), MS, 30. Sithan's book, drawing extensively on oral history, is a major contribution to Cambodian historiography.

29. U.S. Embassy Saigon's WEEKA March 15, 1952. Sim Kim interview, November 1987, and Lek Samoeun interview, February 1989.

30. Voeunsai remark in Huy Kanthoul memoirs, 128; Thonn Ouk interview, November 1986. U.S. Embassy Saigon's WEEKA 14, April 13, 1952; Phung Ton, "La crise cambodgienne" (Diss., University of Paris, 1954), 87.

31. Sim Kin and Lek Samoeun interviews. Among those who joined Thanh in 1952, Han Tun Hak became prime minister of the Khmer Republic in 1973, while Um Sim was the Khmer Republic's last ambassador to the United States.

32. Interview Channa Samudvanija, August 1981; Sim Kin interview, Novem-

ber 1987. On Tak's reputation, Ith Sarin interview, November 1988, and Lek Samoeun interview, February 1989. Tak, who has close links with Thai authorities, had survived a Viet Minh ambush in 1951 (Hin Sithan letter to author, June 1990).

33. Michael Vickery, letter to author, November 1988; Sim Kin interview, November 1987; Lek Samoeun interview, February 1989; Channa Samudvanija interview, September 1981.

34. British Legation Saigon's 51, April 18, 1952. General Dio also complained that the Americans had "a deplorable tendency to meddle in local politics."

35. Sihanouk, *Souvenirs doux et amers,* 175 ff.; U.S. Legation Saigon's 1892, March 28, 1952; SHAT, 10 H 284, undated 1952 memorandum from Troude.

36. On banners, Thonn Ouk interview, May 1987. See also U.S. Embassy Saigon's WEEKA 19, May 18, 1952; its 585 June 9, 1952; and its WEEKA 22, June 1, 1952.

37. Vickery, "Looking Back at Cambodia," 94–95; *Cambodge,* June 10 and 13, 1952. See U.S. Embassy Phnom Penh's 53, June 9, 1952; Corcoran interview, November 1987. An editorial in the Renovation party's newspaper, *Pannakar,* had compared the Democrat party to Hitler on May 22 (Vickery notes). The leaflets accused the Democrats of using a "dead man's picture (Yuthevong's or Ieu Koeuss's) to gain votes" (Vickery notes).

38. Corcoran interview, November 1987. U.S Embassy Saigon's WEEKA 23, June 7, 1952, notes that the Democrats had failed to notify the palace of their intention of arresting Yem Sambaur. Huy Kanthoul memoir, 130–32.

39. Monireth memoir, 196; Preschez, *La démocratie au Cambodge,* 47–49; U.S. Legation Phnom Penh's 55, June 16, 1952; Sihanouk, *Souvenirs doux et amers,* 176.

40. U.S. Embassy Saigon's WEEKA 28, July 15, 1952. Huy Kanthoul memoirs, 129 ff.

41. Later in the year, Sim Var told a British diplomat, "Independence costs money. Money means French support." See enclosure to British Legation Saigon's 145, October 22, 1952. See also Sam Sary and Mao Say, *Bilan de l'oeuvre de Norodom Sihanouk pendant le mandat royal de 1952 à 1955* (Phnom Penh, 1955), 6–7. See also *La Liberté,* July 3, 1952, letter from "Khmerobotha": "Blessed are the angels *(tevoda)* who have inspired the liquidation of such a regime."

42. Keng Vannsak interview, November 1986, and Kiernan, *HPP,* 121–22. For a French translation of Saloth Sar's article, see Serge Thion and Ben Kiernan, *Khmers rouges!* (Paris, 1981), 357–61. Thonn Ouk interview, May 1988. In January 1953, Sihanouk told a visitor that the "troublemakers following the Communist line" in Paris numbered "only six." U.S. Legation Phnom Penh's unnumbered despatch, January 30, 1953.

43. *La Liberté,* September 12, 1952.

44. See Chandler, "Seeing Red: Perceptions of Cambodian History in Democratic Kampuchea," in Chandler and Kiernan, *Revolution and Its Aftermath,* 34–56.

45. See Milton Osborne, *Politics and Power in Cambodia* (Hawthorn, Australia, 1973), 77 ff.

46. Monireth memoir, 197–98; *Cambodge,* February 10, 1953 (last quotation); Vickery, "Looking Back at Cambodia," 95–96. See also Bunchhan Mul, *Charet Khmaer,* 120–21.

47. From 1953 on, Saloth Sar's conduct was characterized in part by his love of

clandestinity and subterfuge. On his membership in the CPF, Nayan Chanda, *Brother Enemy* (New York, 1986), 58. Kiernan, *HPP*, 123; Elizabeth Becker, interview with Khieu Thirith, October 1980 (tape recording); Keng Vannsak interview, November 1986; letter from Thiounn Mumm to author, November 1988. Earlier evidence is in Non Suon's confession, XII, pp. 1–2, November 22, 1976, which mentions that Pol Pot "joined the armed struggle in the eastern zone" in 1953. Talking to Yugoslav journalists in 1978, Pol Pot claimed to have "entered the militant underground in Phnom Penh" and then to have joined "the [otherwise unspecified] guerrillas."

48. Sihanouk, *Souvenirs doux et amers*, 181–83.

49. Preschez, *La démocratie au Cambodge*, 53 ff; Sihanouk, *Souvenirs doux et amers*, 183–85.

50. Sihanouk, *Souvenirs doux et amers*, 184; see also Norodom Sihanouk, *La monarchie cambodgienne et la croisade royale pour l'indépendance* (Phnom Penh, 1955), 103. U.S. Embassy Saigon's WEEKA 17, April 26, 1953, reported that the French were shocked by the *New York Times* interview: "Up to now, [they] had considered him the only intelligent Cambodian; now they consider him a fool."

51. See Monireth memoir, 141. On the invitation to the circus, Paul Kattenburg (personal communication). On Sihanouk's anti-Americanism see Sihanouk, *Souvenirs doux et amers*, 200, and Martin, *Le mal cambodgien*, 138.

52. Sihanouk, *La croisade*, 107–08; *Cambodge*, May 19 and June 4, 1953; *Liberté*, May 9, 1953.

53. Sihanouk, *L'Indochine vue de Pékin*, 53. A copy of de Langlade's letter is enclosed in U.S. Embassy Saigon's 21, July 3, 1953.

54. See Sim Var, "Mémoire du Cambodge," *Moulkhmer* (Paris), no. 112 (November-December 1988): 6. Sim Var was a close friend of Sihanouk's parents at this time. British Legation Bangkok's 42, June 21, 1953.

55. See "Message royal à la nation," in *L'oeuvre de Norodom Sihanouk*, 163–64. On additional star, report from Chef de Batallion Raguet, August 11, 1953, SHAT, 10 H 5588. Sihanouk retained this rank up to the coup d'etat of 1970. Lon Nol rose to become Cambodia's first and probably its last field marshal.

56. *Cambodge*, August 14, 1953. *La Liberté*, August 5, 1953. The government later denied that Sihanouk had made the statement. By late September, de Langlade's replacement was writing that "Cambodia has drunk a full draft of the poison of independence, which has turned it into a hostile country, an enemy country, whose xenophobia exceeds that of India or Pakistan." SHAT, 10 H 5617 (GOBN: création-organisation); letter of September 20, 1953.

57. Kiernan, *HPP*, 125 ff.

58. Sihanouk, *Souvenirs doux et amers*, 201–02. Huy Kanthoul memoir, 133, refers to the French decision as "an extremely tardy gesture of good will." Sihanouk chose the date, exactly two years after Thanh's return to Phnom Penh, to show that he could attract even larger crowds.

59. See Sihanouk, *L'Indochine vue de Pékin*, 49–50, and *Souvenirs doux et amers*, 205–207; also Meyer, *Derrière le sourire khmer*, 124. Lon Nol's report is in SHAT, 10 H 5621, "Armeé Royale Khmere," which lists enemy casualties as six dead and no wounded, and friendly losses, largely to mines, as one dead and twenty-six wounded. The troops involved, totaling more than six thousand men and women, captured five prisoners and thirty grenades. According to Kiernan, *HPP*, 140, the Viet Minh hoped to secure a regroupment area in the northwest to use in bargaining at Geneva but were unable to do so before the conference opened.

60. U.S. Legation Phnom Penh's 136, May 13, 1954.

61. U.S. Embassy Phnom Penh's 86, June 18, 1954. Thiounn Mumm interview, May 1988; Becker, *When the War Was Over*, 92–96; Kiernan, *HPP*, 141 ff.

62. Kiernan, *HPP*, 140 ff; François Joyaux, *La Chine et le règlement du premier conflit d'Indochine* (Paris, 1979), esp. 213–36. Thiounn Mumm interview, May 1988.

63. Joyaux, *La Chine et le règlement*, 229; Kiernan, *HPP*, 142 ff.

64. Joyaux, *La Chine et le règlement*, 234–35; Sihanouk, *L'Indochine vue de Pékin*, 58. Nhiek Tioulong conversation with author, September 1981. See also Burchett, *The China-Cambodia-Vietnam Triangle*, 27–44.

65. On relations of delegation with United States, see Wilfred Burchett, *The China-Cambodia Vietnam Triangle* (London, 1981), 42: "Thus the Western powers, with China's connivance, dismembered Indochina."

66. Kiernan, *HPP*, 154–55; Becker, *When the War Was Over*, 152 ff.; and see U.S. Embassy Phnom Penh's A-5, January 13, 1972, "Khmer Rouge Rallier Keoum Kun." It seems that somewhere between one and two thousand "Khmer Viet Minh" were taken off to North Vietnam in 1954–55. See also DK document, *Ompi ksae songvat . . . reboh C.I.A. nung yuon lep tuk dei* (On the Vietnamese-CIA conspiracy to swallow the country), translated in Karl Jackson, ed., *Cambodia 1975–1978: Rendezvous with Death* (Berkeley, 1989), Appendix D, which asserts that Sao Phim was sent back to Cambodia by the Vietnamese, who had become distressed that Tou Samouth "had begun to favor those who had studied in France, and in particular Brother Number 1 [Saloth Sar]."

67. Sim Kin interview, November 1987, Lek Samoeun interview, February 1989.

68. Gen. Channa (interview, August 1981) dates U.S. involvement with Thanh to the period "after Geneva." For February 1955 visit, see U.S. Embassy Bangkok's 1995, February 17, 1955. Monireth memoir, 108.

69. Interviews with Thonn Ouk, November 1987; Thiounn Mumm, May 1988; and Chhay Yat, February 1990. See S. Ishikawa and T. Suzuki, "Interview with Pol Pot," *National Times*, December 11, 1979. Martin, *Le mal cambodgien*, 68, claims that Saloth Sar was teaching school in Phnom Penh in 1955, and Chheån Vam (interview November 1987) asserted that Sar visited him "once or twice" in 1955 to discuss election tactics. Sar's brother, Loth Suong, claimed that Sar had "changed greatly" once he returned from "working with the Viet Minh" (interview with Kate Frieson, February 1990).

70. On the alliance, see Vickery, "Looking Back at Cambodia," 97 ff., and Vickery, letter to author, November 1988, drawing on 1955 Cambodian newspapers. On the motto, see also RNS, 522, describing banners at a demonstration in Phnom Penh in August 1955. Much of what follows is based on Vickery's notes taken from these sources, which disappeared after 1979.

71. Interviews with Sim Var, Thonn Ouk, and Keng Vannsak. U.S. Embassy Phnom Penh's 572, February 3, 1955. British Legation's letter 1012/12 55 G refers to the commitee as "dominated by young fellow travellers with French University degrees." Sim Var's letter condemning the new committee is in *La Liberté*, February 5, 1955.

72. U.S. Embassy Phnom Penh's 579, February 4, 1955.

73. PRO, FO 371/117125 (Canadian 82, February 8, 1955, forwarded by British Legation); U.S. Embassy Phnom Penh's 597, February 10, 1955; *La Liberté*, February 9, 1955. Twenty-three black ballots were cast in Phnom Penh and ninety-one in Kompong Cham. It is possible that the results were lightly cooked, for

Sihanouk in 1971 recalled that negative votes numbered "some tens of thousands." Sihanouk, *L'Indochine vue de Pékin,* 61.

74. PRO, FO 371/117125, British Legation Phnom Penh's 109, March 20, 1955.

75. Vickery, "Looking Back at Cambodia," 96–97.

76. PRO, FO 371/117124, British Legation Phnom Penh's telegrams 86 and 87, February 26–27, 1955.

77. For background on the abdication, see British Legation Phnom Penh's 103, March 15, 1955, in which Minister Hempel notes, "I learn from a reliable source that [Sihanouk] insisted that if [his parents] did not occupy the throne, he . . . would leave the country." See also U.S. Embassy Phnom Penh's 709, March 7, 1955. It is possible that Sihanouk was maneuvered into the abdication by advisers like Sam Sary, who convinced him that the decision would consolidate his political power. See also British Legation Phnom Penh's 23, March 22, 1955.

78. *Tourists [sic] Notes Cambodia* (Phnom Penh, n.d. [1955]), 12.

79. See Sihanouk, *Souvenirs doux et amers,* 216 ff. Sim Var interview, November 1987.

80. PRO, FO 371/117125, British Legation Phnom Penh's 23, March 22, 1955.

81. See Preschez, *La démocratie au Cambodge,* 59–60; Vickery, "Looking Back at Cambodia," 95–96; Sihanouk, *Souvenirs doux et amers,* 218–19; for statute, PRO, FO 371/ 1012102/55G, letter from British Political Councillor, Littlejohn-Cook.

82. On recruitment, U.S. Embassy Phnom Penh's 397, May 3, 1955; British Legation's 82, February 8, 1955. On Kao Tak, see *Liberté,* March 2, 1955, Sim Kin interview, November 1987, and Lek Samoeun interview, February 1989.

83. Kiernan, *HPP,* 158 ff. U.S. Embassy Phnom Penh's 416, April 29, 1955. Phurissara had been dumped from his job with the National Railway the preceding month, presumably for his political affiliations. Later active in the Cambodian Communist movement, he was purged in 1977.

84. On Sihanouk at Bandung, see Roger M. Smith, *Cambodia's Foreign Policy* (Ithaca, N.Y., 1965), 65 ff. In his memoirs, Sihanouk places Bandung on the eve of the elections, and thus after the U.S. aid agreement, which was in fact concluded after his return. Sihanouk, *Souvenirs doux et amers,* 223.

85. Speaking to Kate Frieson in 1988, Tep Khannoul, of the DK delegation to the United Nations, claimed that left-wing Democrats, including Ea Sichau, had changed Sihanouk's mind and inspired his neutralist policy. It is more in keeping with Sihanouk's practice for him to have borrowed the ideas to outwit and neutralize those who proposed them. According to Sim Var (interview November 1987) Sihanouk had floated the idea of a neutralist foreign policy in 1954, on the Swiss model, but had been dissauded from it by his advisers, who pointed out the topographical, industrial, and economic differences between Cambodia and Switzerland.

86. See U.S. Embassy Phnom Penh's 1445, April 26, 1956. On abolition of U.S. aid in 1963, see chapter 4.

87. PRO, FO 117125, British Legation Phnom Penh's Telegram 1012, July 15, 1955; U.S. Embassy Phnom Penh's 37, July 29, 1955, for Huy Kanthoul's statement, not repeated in his memoirs, which gives an account of the campaign, 134. *Neak cheat niyum,* August 19, 1955—the Sangkum journal—claimed that Chung, arrested in Siem Reap, had died in prison of an illness contracted before his arrest

(Vickery notes). U.S. Embassy Phnom Penh's 47, August 23, 1955; Vickery, "Looking Back at Cambodia," 98–99; the description of the campaign draws on several interviews.

88. Department of State Instruction CA-6626, February 7, 1961, "Norodom Norindeth, New Cambodian Ambassador to Yugoslavia." The document reports intriguingly that Norindeth had joined the CPF while a student in France in the 1920s.

89. Vickery, "Looking Back at Cambodia," 98, reports that nongovernment newspapers in the summer of 1955 were filled with reports of intimidation of non-Sangkum candidates and workers.

90. Huy Kanthoul memoirs, 134; interview with Im Proum, November 1987.

91. The British political councillor in Phnom Penh reported, "We want Prince Sihanouk to win because he is staunchly anti-Communist, pro-Western, and in part pro-British." PRO, FO 371/117127.

92. *Sangkum Reastr Niyum*, July 29, 1955 (Vickery notes).

93. Keng Vannsak interviews, November 1986 and May 1987. U.S. Embassy Phnom Penh's 314, September 11, 1955, and 139, November 5, 1955.

94. U.S. Embassy Phnom Penh's 319, September 14, 1955; Huy Kanthoul memoir, 135. See also Kiernan, *HPP,* 159–61. Two Pracheachon candidates gained over 20 percent of the vote in their respective districts while imprisoned by the government. The election issue of *Cambodge*, containing preliminary results, had those from a Siem Reap electorate taped over in the National Archives copy (later microfilmed, and since destroyed), which suggests that the editors had not understood the signals for unanimity when they went to press. Justin Corfield kindly provided this information.

Chapter Three. Sihanouk Unopposed, 1955–1962

1. See Phouk Chhay, "Le pouvoir politique au Cambodge" (Diss., University of Phnom Penh, 1966), 185 ff.

2. See U.S. Embassy Phnom Penh's 241, January 17, 1956.

3. Sihanouk, *My Wars with the CIA* (Harmondsworth, 1973), 76 ff.

4. See U.S. Embassy Phnom Penh's 411, June 3, 1956, Sihanouk, *Souvenirs doux et amers*, 277 ff., and Meyer, *Derrière le sourire khmer*, 129–36.

5. Philippe Devillers, *Asie du Sud-Est* (Paris, 1969), 618 ff; Sihanouk, *My Wars with the CIA,* 84–85. *RC,* September 22, 1956, called McClintock "sometimes rude, sometimes picturesque." See also British Embassy Phnom Penh's 1013, August 24, 1956: "It must be admitted that McClintock does not always flatter the dignity of leading Cambodians, especially those whose ability he considers second-rate."

6. See U.S. Embassy Phnom Penh's 305, March 21, 1956, and J. Barré, "Le socialisme khmer n'est pas marxiste," *Liberté,* March 9, 1956. On Mao, Meyer interview, November 1987. See also *My Wars with the CIA*, 99, which asserts, "'Of the people, by the people, for the people' . . . had been the motto of my royal ancestors for centuries in their conduct of public affairs."

7. *Neak cheat niyum,* April 16, 1956.

8. The paragraph draws on my memories of such occasions. See also J.-C. Pomonti and Serge Thion, *Des courtesans aux partisans* (Paris, 1971), 70 ff., and Michael Field, *The Prevailing Wind* (London, 1964), 237–51.

9. P. Devillers and J. Lacouture, *Indochine: la fin d'une guerre* (Paris, 1957), 341, and Martin, *Le mal cambodgien*, 76–91.

10. This paragraph draws on interviews with several people who worked closely with Sihanouk.

11. The quotation is from an interview with S. Suon Kaset, November 1987.

12. Kiernan, *HPP,* 170; *RC,* April 8, 1956.

13. See U.S. Embassy Phnom Penh's 328, March 13, 1957, on pulping. Justin Corfield, personal communication. Corfield has interviewed a Cambodian hired by the Vietnamese in 1979 to assist with pulping.

14. Douc Rasy, "La crise du conscience khmere," MS, 1988, 2.

15. See U.S. Embassy Phnom Penh's 350, April 29, 1957, and *Angkor,* March 27, 1957.

16. Drawn largely from U.S. Embassy Phnom Penh's 41, August 4, 1957. Phlek Phoeun was a founding editor, in 1963, of the mildly anti-Sihanouk daily, *Phnom Penh Presse,* coedited by Douc Rasy.

17. U.S. Embassy Phnom Penh's 22, July 15, 1957, and 102, September 27, 1957. The former notes "Sihanouk's frustration at seeing this opposition party overtly inactive but knowing that they are talking among themselves and to anyone who will listen in derogatory terms about his Sangkum regime."

18. U.S. Embassy Phnom Penh's 70, July 19, 1957.

19. Martin Herz, the political counsellor of the U.S embassy in 1955–57, favored the Democrats, and did so in his book, *A Short History of Cambodia* (New York, 1958); Keng Vannsak interview, November 1986; Leonard Overton interview, May 1986. See also U.S. National Security Council Document NSC 5809, "U.S. Policy in Mainland Southeast Asia," April 2, 1958.

20. See U.S. Embassy Phnom Penh's 102, September 27, 1957. The British embassy reported that "in week preceding meeting there were vague reports of beatings of civilians by soldiers" in Phnom Penh. British Embassy Phnom Penh's 1015, August 24, 1957.

21. Vickery, "Looking Back at Cambodia," 99; U.S. Embassy Phnom Penh's 148 (August 12, 1957) and 102. See also Svay So's account in *Cambodge,* April 22, 1970; Monireth memoirs, 169, and Bunchhan Mul, *Charet Khmaer,* 123.

22. Monireth memoir, 170, and U.S. Embassy Phnom Penh's 115, October 14, 1957.

23. For a roundup, see U.S. Embassy Phnom Penh's 221, January 17, 1958.

24. Monireth memoir, 112–13. In 1974, Hou Youn addressed a meeting celebrating the anniversary of the foundation of the CPK. Tracing the party's history, he linked its beginnings with the hopes and failures of the Democrats between 1947 and 1953. Untitled handwritten report in Tuol Sleng archives photographed by Anthony Barnett in 1980 (Echols collection, Cornell University).

25. On an abortive anticorruption campaign led by Prince Monireth, see *RC,* September 22, 1956. Interview with Sim Var, November 1987.

26. U.S. Embassy Phnom Penh's 234, January 28, 1958. According to Sim Var (interview), Suramarit told him at one point, "This rotten Assembly must be dissolved."

27. Sim Var interview. On the National Congress, see *RC,* January 18, 1958, and U.S. Embassy Phnom Penh's 234, January 28, 1958.

28. *RC,* February 1, 1958. See also U.S. Embassy Phnom Penh's airgram 256, February 19, 1958. The one female candidate, Mme Pung Peng Cheng, was reelected in 1962 and 1966.

29. On the etymology of *Sangkum,* Michael Vickery, personal communication.

30. See Norodom Sihanouk, "Communisme au Cambodge," *RC,* March 8, 15,

and 22, 1958. In the second article Sihanouk stated that left-leaning newspapers in Cambodia had a circulation approaching ten thousand copies, roughly 20 percent of the known newspaper subscribers (Kiernan, *HPP*, 180). See *Angkor*, September 28, 1956, for an earlier estimate. On Svay Rieng, U.S. Embassy Phnom Penh's 989, March 22, 1958. By 1987, Sihanouk, anxious to prove that he had presided over a multiparty system, wrote that "several" Pracheachon candidates had presented themselves, and in a free election had been rejected by the voters. See his *Letter to the Editor of Indo-China Report*, March-April 1987, 14 ff.

31. Memorandum from Irving Kalin, U.S. Public Affairs Officer, Battambang, March 20, 1958. On Achar Pres's earlier career, see Kiernan, *HPP*, 44.

32. U.S. Embassy Phnom Penh's 288, March 14, 1958, encloses a translation of Pracheachon program. The cultural portion foreshadows the puritanism of DK and proposed to "forbid movies that make one forget one's conscience, particularly films dealing with cowboys, love, and war propaganda"—the very ones that tens of thousands of Cambodians flocked to see as often as they could.

33. For a detailed account of the electoral campaign, see U.S. Embassy Phnom Penh's 288, March 14, and 383, June 28, 1958.

34. On final results, see U.S. Embassy Phnom Penh's 135, October 17, 1958.

35. Vorn Vet confession, typed version, 8.

36. Pol Pot, "Long Live the Seventeenth Anniversary," 22.

37. U.S. Embassy Phnom Penh's 315, April 4, 1958.

38. See *RC*, August 2, 1958. Both men, colleagues in the clandestine KPRP, were executed by DK: Hou Youn in 1975 or 1976 (accounts differ) and Hu Nim in 1977.

39. Field, *The Prevailing Wind*, 209–10, and U.S. Embassy Phnom Penh's 156, July 29, 1958.

40. Sihanouk, *My Wars with the CIA*, 102; interviews Channa Samudvanija, August 1981 and May 1988.

41. *RC*, November 1, 1958, for a French translation of the interview. Ironically, in view of later events, Sihanouk felt that U.S.–Cambodian relations had improved in the course of his visit. See U.S. Embassy Phnom Penh's 460, October 10, 1958.

42. For biographical data, see Department of State Instruction CA-7011, February 13, 1958; for a negative assessment of Sam Sary, Monireth memoir, 196.

43. U.S. Embassy Phnom Penh's 144, October 23, 1958; Monireth memoir, 188 ff.

44. *RC*, January 17, 1959, pointed out that Sary's paper was distributed free and suggested that it had received foreign backing. Boy Scouts in mufti were recruited to distribute it (Oeur Hun Ly interview, January 1989). See U.S. Embassy Phnom Penh's 737, December 22, 1958. See also British Embassy Phnom Penh's 477, January 22, 1959.

45. Lacouture and Devillers, *La fin d'une guerre*, 348, asserts that foreign diplomats informed Sihanouk of U.S. support for Sary. This is corroborated by U.S. Embassy Phnom Penh's 835, January 19, 1959. Charles Meyer, at a press conference, connected Sary with the CIA operative Edward Lansdale (U.S. Embassy Phnom Penh's 259, January 21, 1959); Channa interviews, 1981 and 1988, and interview with Lek Samoeun, February 1989. In the countryside in 1959–60 people thought to have differences with the government were accused of "working for Sam Sary" (May Ebihara, personal communication).

46. For views of Chhuon in the late 1940s, see William Gedney, "A Gallery of Picturesque Personalities," in *Papers from a Conference on Thai Studies*, ed. R. J.

Bickner et al. (Ann Arbor, 1986), 1–18; Thonn Ouk interview, November 1986; Meyer interview, May 1987; on Chhuon's alleged invulnerability, Thong Thel interview, March 1988, and interview with Venerable Tep Vong, January 1989. U.S. Ambasador McClintock had found Chhuon "a man of vital energy, but bordering on the lunatic fringe." Phnom Penh's 535, January 26, 1955.

47. On taxes, see *Angkor,* August 6, 1956.

48. See U.S. Embassy Saigon's 504, August 10, 1958, and U.S. Department of State's 469 to Saigon, August 14, 1958. When U.S. Senator William Fulbright visited Siem Reap in 1958, Dap Chhuon said that Cambodia needed friendly relations with its immediate neighbors, rather than with China. Robert Barrett interview, September 1988.

49. On assemblymen, see U.S. Embassy Phnom Penh's 920, March 6, 1959, which reported that Chhuon had stated that "he considers himself to be working for Cambodia and not repeat not for the Prince." See also British Embassy Phnom Penh's 1012/7/57 G, January 23, 1957, which reported that Chhuon told a British interviewer, "Sihanouk's neutralism leaned toward Communism," and that he had already established friendly, sub rosa relations with Saigon and Bangkok. On Puth Chhay, Thong Thel interview, March 1988.

50. See Cao De Thuong, *Lam te . . . ton* (How to kill a president) (Saigon, 1970), 313. Pham van Luu kindly provided the reference and a translation. For corroboration, see British Embassy Phnom Penh's 20, March 3, 1959.

51. The intelligence summary presented to Eisenhower read in full, "Dap Chhuon, a powerful anti-Communist warlord, is seeking U.S. support to overthrow Sihanouk. His plan would involve support from Thailand and South Vietnam. Like other conservative Cambodians, Chhuon is alarmed by growing Communist influence." George Kahin kindly provided me with this reference. See U.S. Embassy Phnom Penh's 1091, February 24, 1959.

52. Richard Cima letter to author, January 1988.

53. On the Matsui visit, Cima cites the Lon Nol "spy," a personal friend. The embassy must have assumed that Matsui, as an Asian, would melt easily into the Cambodian population. In fact, he was probably the first Japanese sighted in Siem Reap since the war and presented an easy target for surveillance.

54. See Sihanouk, *My Wars with the CIA,* 106–07. Thel Thong interview, August 1987.

55. See U.S. Embassy Phnom Penh's 394, October 1, 1959, reporting Slat Peou's confession; *RC,* March 7, 1959; Sieu Chheng Y interview, December 1987; also interviews with Thong Thel, Charles Meyer, and Robert Barrett.

56. Sieu Chheng Y interview, December 1987. There is no direct corroboration for this extraordinary story, but many details in the interview, which lasted over an hour, are corroborated from other sources. One incorrect detail seems to be that the Vietnamese were the only passengers on the plane. See British Embassy Phnom Penh's 20, March 3, 1959.

57. U.S. Embassy Phnom Penh's 394, October 1, 1959; Sieu Chheng Y interview; Tran Kim Tuyen, *How to Kill a President,* claims that only one hundred kilograms were transferred to support the coup.

58. Sihanouk (*My Wars with the CIA,* 107) claimed that Lon Nol had been involved in the plot. Lon Nol's involvement seems to have been decided on to link the general, then heading a treasonous government, with the CIA in the 1950s. The French ambassador told an American that Chhuon had written the queen "announcing his intention to go into dissidence": U.S. Embassy Phnom Penh's 1151, March 2, 1959, and British Embassy Phnom Penh's 20, March 3, 1959.

59. U.S. National Archives, 751. H. 00 1-359, U.S. Army message from Phnom Penh, February 22, 1959.

60. Thong Thel interview, March 1987. See also U.S. Embassy Phnom Penh's 1217, March 14, 1959, which mentions "several executions" in Siem Reap following the exposure of the plot.

61. Thong Thel interview; Sieu Chheng Y interview, Charles Meyer interview, February 1990. U.S. Embassy Phnom Penh's 1177, March 6, 1959, reports that Chhuon had been interrogated en route to Siem Reap; three days later, Meyer said that Chhuon had been in a coma and had said nothing. On the possibility of Lon Nol's involvement, see Sihanouk, *My Wars with the CIA*, 108–09.

62. U.S. Embassy Phnom Penh's 1133, February 28, and 1175, March 5, 1959. William Colby, *Honorable Men* (New York, 1978), 48–51. I am grateful to Thomas Hirschfeld for this reference. Much of the correspondence between Washington and Phnom Penh about the affair in the U.S. National Archives is still inaccessible for research.

63. For Eisenhower's letter to Sihanouk, see U.S. Department of State's 844, March 28, 1959. In 1968, Sihanouk treated the incident in his film *Shadows over Angkor*, casting the villain as an American, Colonel Hillandale, with Sihanouk playing a Cambodian naval officer in love with a Filipina diplomat, played by Sihanouk's wife. In the film, the Sihanouk character graciously allowed Dap Chhuon to commit suicide when cornered. Frank Tatu kindly provided me with promotional material about the film.

64. U.S. Embassy Phnom Penh's 412, October 5, 1959.

65. Tran Kim Tuyen, *How to Kill a President,* 292–98. Sihanouk (*My Wars with the CIA*, 110) claimed that the package had been sent "from an American military base in South Vietnam." See Field, *Prevailing Wind,* 214, U.S. Embassy Phnom Penh's 307, September 4, 1959, and British Embassy Phnom Penh's 61, September 4, 1959.

66. On Sihanouk's views about Vietnamese Communist forces in Cambodia in 1960, see the jocular interview with Elbridge Dubrow, June 3, 1981, in Oral Histories Collection, Johnson Library, 27–29. Anne Blair kindly provided this reference. By the end of the 1950s, over two thousand political prisoners, mostly connected with these right-wing plots, were temporarily confined in a special camp on the outskirts of Phnom Penh: Martin, *Le mal cambodgien,* 75.

67. Students of Cambodian radicalism owe a large debt to Ben Kiernan's pathbreaking *How Pol Pot Came to Power* (London, 1985). Much of what follows is based on his research.

68. See Timothy Carney, *Communist Party Power in Cambodia* (Ithaca, 1977), 13, and the discussion of this issue in Kiernan and Boua, *Peasants and Politics,* 34–68. Some parts of Cambodia—several of the former Viet Minh zones in the southwest, the east, and the less developed parts of the northwest—were more susceptible to revolutionary activity than others.

69. This paragraph draws on interviews conducted between 1986 and 1990 with Thong Thel, Oeur Hun Lyy, Ith Sarin, Sok Bunthan, You Hon Chea, and S. Suon Kaset, among others.

70. U.S. Embassy Phnom Penh's 288, enclosure; Chandler, Kiernan, and Boua, *Pol Pot Plans the Future,* 235. For name "Thonn Ouk": Thonn Ouk, personal communication. On Saloth Sar at this time, You Sambo and Sok Bunthan interviews, June 1989; Sok Pirun interview, January 1990. For a time, the director of the school was Mey Mann, who had traveled to France with Saloth Sar, joined the CPF, and in the 1980s worked as a teacher in a DK refugee camp in Thailand.

See Martin, *Le mal cambodgien,* 69. On funding for Chamraon Vichea, Chhay Yat interview, February 1990.

71. Soth Polin interview, October 1988.

72. You Sambo interview, July 1989. Sok Chhan, later a minister in the Khmer Republic, has also recalled being entranced by the history of the French revolution while a student at Takeo, where he studied under Khieu Ponnary. He and several classmates in their spare time reenacted such scenes as Marat's murder and the execution of nobles by guillotine. The Cambodian word for revolution (*padevat*) was not yet in circulation, so the students used the French *révolution* instead.

73. Heder interviews (1981 typescript), 51; Becker, *When the War Was Over,* 103 ff., and Sok Chhan interview, March 1989.

74. Pol Pot speech, September 28, 1977, 22. See also Nuon Chea, "Statement of the Communist Party of Kampuchea to the Communist Workers' Party of Denmark," *Journal of Communist Studies* 3/1 (March 1987): 31: "Before 1960 there was some confusion. . . . We did not have a clear party line. We had developed bases in the countryside but the enemy had destroyed up to 90 percent of them. Moreover, we were not strong in the cities." A heroic picture also emerged from a Hou Youn speech, monitored by Lon Nol police in September 1974, which referred to the "anger" that party "successes" (*sic*) caused the government in 1959 and 1960. Untitled report, October 1, 1974 (Barnett papers, Echols Collection, Cornell University). "Summary of Annotated Party History," 11.

75. *Livre Noir,* 19. See also "Summary of Annotated Party History," undated CPK document (c. 1968) captured in 1973, 10 ff. Pol Pot speech, September 27, 1977, 22, echoes assertions in the 1973 party history, quoted by Kiernan, *HPP,* 188. See also Jeffrey Race, "An Exchange Theory of Revolution," in *Peasant Rebellion and Communist Revolution in Asia,* ed. John W. Lewis (Stanford, 1974), 169–200.

76. According to Kiernan, *HPP,* 193, Saloth Sar was Tou Samouth's secretary at this time and thus was privy to communications coming from Hanoi. On Cambodian cadre in Vietnam in the 1950s, see ibid., 178 ff. Interview with Yem Nolla, May 1988.

77. George Kahin, *Intervention* (New York, 1986), 114 ff. Gareth Porter, *Vietnam: A History in Documents,* 194–99, 202–05.

78. See Becker, *When the War Was Over,* 108–09; Kiernan, *HPP,* 190 ff. Jackson, *Cambodia 1975–1978,* 17–18. See also Keo Meas's confession, "Talking about . . . 1951 and 1960," September 30, 1976, 13–14. On antileftist campaign in August 1960, see U.S. Embassy Phnom Penh's 131, 158, 191, and 213, of August 1, 5, 17, 20, 1960.

79. See Kiernan, *HPP,* 366 ff. Intriguingly, *RC,* February 27, 1960, asserts that the "Pracheachon" had convened a "secret congress" at the end of 1959 and documents in Sihanouk's hands indicated that the party planned to "take advantage of any disorders in Cambodia." The "Annotated Party History" notes that the second congress of the party was originally planned for the end of 1959 but had to be postponed in the face of government repression. On the repression of left-wing papers, see *Seckdei srong pii sar'pot'mean ekkapeap, mittapheap, pracheachon* (Report on the newspapers *Ekkapeap, Mittapheap, Pracheachon)* (Phnom Penh, 1960). Several confessions from Tuol Sleng reveal that people trained to work in these journals in the 1950s became high-ranking cadre after 1975.

80. In 1969, Ok Sakun told friends in the CPF that the Cambodian party had been "founded in 1960"; Pierre Brocheux, interview, May 1987. See also Keo Meas's confession, "Talking about . . . 1951 and 1960," 3 ff., where Meas suggested that the name change had angered Son Ngoc Minh. Meas also noted (9) that

"ten or eleven" people were elected to the new central committee but names only four: Tou Samouth, his "assistant" (*rong*) Saloth Sar, Nuon Chea, and Ieng Sary. Kiernan, *HPP,* 190, cites a Vietnamese source that gives the full membership of the committee.

81. See *The Call,* August 28, 1978, and Stephen Heder, "Kampuchea's Armed Struggle: The Origins of an Independent Revolution," *Bulletin of Concerned Asian Scholars* (hereafter *BCAS*) 10/4 (Autumn 1978).

82. See Porter in Chandler and Kiernan, *Revolution and Its Aftermath,* 75. According to Kiernan, *HPP,* 270 ff., the decision for armed struggle was taken by the party at the end of 1967; this is confirmed in Chou Chet's confession, among others.

83. Kiernan, *HPP,* 190–93; Keo Meas, "Talking about . . . 1951 and 1960"; Becker, *When the War Was Over,* 107–08; Vickery, *Kampuchea,* 65. The congress was not mentioned by Vorn Vet in his confession, which suggests that he did not attend. See also W. B. Simons and S. White, eds., *The Party Statutes of the Communist World* (The Hague, 1984), 141.

84. Monireth memoir, 239 ff. Preschez, *La démocratie au Cambodge,* 92 ff.

85. Monireth memoir, 57. For similar arguments, see Soth Polin, "La forte personnalité de la reine," *Nokor Khmer* (Long Beach, Calif.), October 10, 1988, and U.S. Embassy Phnom Penh's 1312, April 12, 1960.

86. On royal rankings, see Jacques Nepote and Sisowath Ravivaddhana Monipong, *Etat présent de la Maison Royale du Cambodge* (Paris, 1990).

87. Monireth memoir, 239–46; Soth Polin, *Bei thngai,* October 10, 1988. At some point in the 1950s, Monireth relates, he and Sihanouk had played Monopoly in the royal villa in Kep. Sihanouk had cheated and pulled ahead. To Sihanouk's chagrin, Monireth quietly cheated his own way to a draw. Monireth memoir, 212.

88. *RC,* June 10, 1960. Six provinces reported 100 percent votes for the prince. See U.S. Embassy Phnom Penh's 1601, June 10, 1960.

89. Preschez, *La démocratie au Cambodge,* 94 ff. *RC,* July 22, 1960, gives the percentages of Sihanouk's victory. Meyer, *Derrière le sourire khmer,* 148. The constitution, as amended (article 122), allowed the assembly to "confer the powers and prerogatives of chief of state on an uncontested personality designated through the general suffrage of the nation." By running against someone condemned to death, Sihanouk was indeed uncontested, but it is inaccurate to assert that the referendum encapsulated all imaginable political alternatives.

90. Queen Kossamak died in China in April 1975. Some of those interviewed in the course of my research blamed Cambodia's troubles in the 1960s and 1970s on Sihanouk's destruction of the monarchy. By 1960, Saloth Sar was no longer in regular contact with his family (Stephen Heder and Kate Frieson interviews with Loth Suong, April 1981 and February 1990).

91. For contrasting analyses of Sihanouk's style of rule, see Monireth memoir, 240 ff., Osborne, *Power and Politics,* 70–81, and Vickery, "Looking Back at Cambodia," 67–74.

92. *RC,* January 19 and December 22, 1961. For two assessments of Sihanouk's achievements, see Martin, *Le mal cambodgien,* 76–89, and Osborne, *Politics and Power,* 84–86.

93. Sim Var interview, November 1987. See also Denis Bloodworth, *An Eye for the Dragon* (repr. Singapore, 1987), 113–25. The writers singled out by Sim Var included Jean and Simone Lacouture, J-C Pomonti, Han Suyin, and Wilfred Burchett.

94. Referring to these events after Non Suon had been arrested in 1962,

Sihanouk asserted that "many young members of the Sangkum" at the national congress had "wanted to pull out Non Suon's moustache" and that he had been given "police protection"—perhaps a way of announcing his arrest. Suon remained in prison until 1970. U.S. Embassy Phnom Penh's airgram A-224, February 27, 1962.

95. See Government of India, Ministry of External Affairs, *Ninth Interim Report of the International Commission for Supervision and Control in Cambodia,* January 1961-December 1962, 131 ff. The Pracheachon group protested (142) to the ICSC about Chou Chet's arrest, noting that it abridged his constitutional rights. Non Suon and Chou Chet were purged by the CPK in 1976 and 1978, respectively.

96. Keo Meas, "Number 10's History in the Ranks," 12, and Non Suon's confession, unnumbered, November 18, 1976, which states that the Pracheachon planned to field five candidates for the elections: Keo Meas, Non Suon himself, Maen San, Chou Chet, and Um Neng. The meeting discussing the candidacies, according to Suon, "was arranged by Keo Meas, with the approval of Tou Samouth." See also Kiernan, *HPP,* 194–95.

97. In 1970, the U.S. State Department assumed that Tou Samouth was still alive: *New York Times,* April 19, 1970. A PRK official told Serge Thion in 1981 that DK cadre in the 1970s had believed that Samouth had been betrayed to Sihanouk's police by a Communist courier. Lon Nol, as late as 1969, did not seem to have been aware that Samouth was dead, although his name did not appear in the list of "34 subversives" broadcast by Sihanouk in 1963. See "The Last Plan," in Jackson, *Cambodia 1975–1978,* 307, which states, "Sieu Heng, Say, and Ta Chea [probably Som Chea, a CPK courier] killed Tou Samouth." See Ruos Mau (Say) confession, and also W. Burchett, *The China-Cambodia-Vietnam Triangle,* 57.

98. Kiernan, *HPP,* 196, 241n135. U.S. Embassy Phnom Penh's airgram A-145, November 11, 1971, reports a rallier's testimony that Sihanouk had had Tou Samouth executed, whereas U.S. Embassy Bangkok's 2646, February 11, 1980, reports a DK defector's assertion that Pol Pot ordered the execution. Kiernan's assertion (*HPP,* 198) that DK "never explicitly denied" assassinating Tou Samouth does not constitute persuasive evidence that Saloth Sar was responsible for his death. Sihanouk (*My Wars with the CIA,* 117–18) refers to Lon Nol's "periodic witch hunts against the left, which included the summary execution of suspects at the moment of arrest"—this is possibly what happened to Tou Samouth after Lon Nol had been tipped off about his whereabouts by Sieu Heng or someone else. The implication that witch hunts were unauthorized is absurd. In 1972, Sieu Heng was asked by a U.S. embassy officer "whether Sihanouk had had Tou Samouth liquidated. He replied that 'Lon Nol knows what happened.'" U.S. Embassy Phnom Penh's airgram A-23, February 17, 1972.

99. U.S. Embassy Phnom Penh's 251, February 15, 1962, and airgram 279, April 16, 1962, and interview with Ven. Kong Chhean, October 1988. By 1969, Sihanouk was listed under *samdech euv* in the Phnom Penh telephone directory.

100. Kiernan, *HPP,* 197. On the July 20 date, see Kiernan, *HPP,* 367.

Chapter Four. Cambodia Clouds Over, 1963–1966

1. "L'état c'est lui" is the title of a eulogistic chapter about Sihanouk in S. Lacouture, *Cambodge* (Lausanne, 1963), 33–52. For a bleaker view of Cambodian society in the mid-1960s, see Soth Polin, *L'anarchiste* (Paris, 1974).

2. See Donn Noel, "Mass Media," report prepared for Alicia Patterson Foundation, April 14, 1967.

3. Sihanouk was aware of his tactics. In a speech made in November 1965 after a trip to China he reported that he had insulted the Russians less than the Chinese might have liked because "expecting to go to Russia, I tailored my pen and my mouth." BBC/ Summary of World Broadcasts (hereafter SWB) 1997/C/17.

4. An exception is Michael Vickery, who worked with newspaper files in the early 1960s and built up an invaluable archive of source material. For a scathing look at the expatriate community in Phnom Penh, see Martin, *Le mal cambodgien*, 89–91. By 1964, there were six thousand French citizens living in Cambodia, twice as many as in the early 1950s. *RC*, July 4, 1964.

5. See Serge Thion, "The Pattern of Cambodian Politics," in *The Cambodian Agony*, ed. David Ablin and Marlowe Hood (Armonk, N.Y., 1987), 149–64, and Laura Summers, "The Sources of Economic Discontent in Sihanouk's Cambodia," *Southeast Asian Journal of Social Science* 14/1 (1986): 16–33.

6. The most detailed account of the demonstrations is in the introduction to Laura Summers, ed., *Cambodia's Economy and Political Development* (Ithaca, 1979), 17, which draws on interview material. Other details from Ith Sarin interview, October 1988. See also U.S. Embassy Phnom Penh's airgram A-396, February 28, 1963, which cites "rumors reaching Phnom Penh" that more than one student had been killed, and *RC*, March 8, 1963.

7. "Elements" from *RC*, March 8, 1963. See also U.S. Embassy Phnom Penh's airgram A-592, February 22, 1963. Unknown to Sihanouk, Son Sen was already in the inner directorate of the KWP.

8. Kiernan, *HPP*, 200–01, citing a Vietnamese source, suggests that five were returned intellectuals, wrongly classifying Vorn Vet as one of these and suggesting that "Moong," Number 6, was Koy Thuon's pseudonym.

9. In 1970, Donald Lancaster, a press adviser to the prince in the 1960s, told Laura Summers that "Sihanouk opposed Lon Nol's plan for a total crackdown on 'Communists' because he wanted people in his government 'who understood how China worked'" (Summers, *Cambodia's Economy*, 18n44). The complete list is in Kiernan, *HPP*, 242n158, citing *Phnom Penh Presse*, March 8, 1963. Talking to a visiting Danish delegation in 1978, Nuon Chea boasted that in the 1960s "our enemies [i.e., Lon Nol and Sihanouk] . . . could not find out who was leading our revolution. They knew the names of a few comrades such as Khieu Samphan. They thought those comrades were the real leaders of the revolution. But they did not know the real leaders" (Laura Summers, "The Secret Vanguard of Pol Pot's Revolution," *Journal of Communist Studies* 3 [March 1987]: 3).

10. On the meeting, see U.S. Embassy Phnom Penh's airgram A-419, March 14, 1963, and Summers, *Cambodia's Economy*, 18. Two of those named in the list, Ok Sakun and Thiounn Prasith, fled to France soon afterward. The names of the two who failed to attend the meeting are unknown, although Chou Chet (confession) claimed to have fled Phnom Penh a week before the condemnations.

11. Keng Vannsak interview, May 1987, and Sok Bunthan interview, June 1989. See also Chhim Somuk confession, "Chomlaoy 010" (Answer 010), August 28, 1978, 10. S. Suon Kaset (interview, July 1989) claimed that Sary occasionally returned incognito to Phnom Penh before his wife joined him in the maquis.

12. Bu Phat confession from Becker, *When the War Was Over*, 467–70; a full text of the translation by Stephen Heder is in Becker papers, Echols Collection, Cornell University.

13. In his September 27, 1977, speech (37), Pol Pot stated, "We continued to work in the cities. In this way, we compelled the enemy to disperse his forces. . . . We attacked him simultaneously on both fronts, so as to weaken him."

14. See U.S. Embassy Phnom Penh's airgrams A-10, July 3, 1963, and A-104, August 15, 1963. On Nin Nirom, Oeur Hun Ly interview and *RC*, August 23, 1963.

15. Interviews with Dy Channa, May 1987, Tan Bun Sor, May 1988, and Hoeung Hong Kim, January 1989. See also draft notes about Khieu Samphan by Stephen Heder, 1975. On his brushes with police, *l'Observateur*, March 29, April 1, 1960. Samphan's alleged impotence was given explanatory value in John Baron and Anthony Paul, *Peace with Horror* (London, 1977), 47 ff., but see rebuttal by Vickery, *Cambodia, 1975–1982*, 173n, and Martin, *Le mal cambodgien*, 161–62. Honest officials were often attacked as being Red or sexually deviant: Ith Sarin interview, October 1988.

16. Pung Peng Cheng interview, May 1988, Ven. Kong Chhean interview, October 1988, and Hoeung Hong Kim interview, January 1989, all report terrorization of students, monks, and people suspected of Communist leanings in the 1960s.

17. Pol Pot, September 28, 1977, speech, 34–35, 37. Kiernan, *HPP*, 211 ff., 230 ff. On Saloth Sar's visit to China, see *HPP*, 221–23.

18. See Osborne, *Politics and Power*, 86–92.

19. Ibid., 87–88. See also U.S. Embassy Phnom Penh's airgram A-387, "Economic Summary—Cambodia—Fourth Quarter 1963," January 14, 1964.

20. On Scherer, personal recollections, and see *RC*, July 19, 1963. On Sprouse, personal recollections and interview with Charles Meyer, May 1987.

21. U.S. Embassy Phnom Penh's 534, December 19, 1963, lists Sihanouk's "mental state, including indications of paranoiac tendencies, compounded by a rigid diet cure" as a "major force" working on him at this time.

22. See Anthony Barnett, "Norodom Sihanouk and the Assassination of Ngo Dinh Diem," manuscript (1981), and U.S. Embassy Phnom Penh's airgram A-354, November 7, 1963. U.S. aid to Cambodia between 1954 and 1964 totalled US $367 million, of which $97 million were devoted to military aid. Field, *Prevailing Wind*, 180n.

23. U.S. Embassy Phnom Penh's airgram A-263, November 14, 1963. See Laura Summers, "The Sources of Economic Grievance," and letter from Douc Rasy to author, November 1988. After the coup in 1970, Sihanouk's minister of commerce in late 1963, Touch Kim, wrote, "Not having been consulted previously on this question, I had many difficulties in putting this measure into action" (*New Cambodge*, no. 3 [June 1970]).

24. On gold transfer, Thomas Hirschfeld (personal communication). On de Gaulle, *Souvenirs doux et amers*, 320; according to Summers, *Cambodia's Economy*, n. 8 (from a conversation with Donald Lancaster in 1970), at the end of 1963 the French freed Cambodian assets blocked in French banks since the 1950s. See also Donald Lancaster, "The Decline of Prince Sihanouk's Regime," in *Indo-China in Conflict: A Political Assessment*, ed. Joseph Zasloff and Alan Goodman (Lexington, Mass., 1972), 49, and *New York Times* (hereafter *NYT*), November 22, 1963, reporting Sihanouk's request that the French "replace" U.S. aid. U.S. Department of State, Director of Intelligence and Research, "Sihanouk Shifts Again," December 3, 1963, noted, "It has become apparent that French wilingness to offer some support does not extend to replacing the American program."

25. According to U.S. Embassy Bangkok's 881, December 6, 1963, Khmer Serei broadcasts from Thailand ceased at U.S. insistence on November 15 and resumed without U.S. approval on the twenty-second. Many paragraphs from cables dealing with the Khmer Serei have been excised before being released under FOIA, e.g., U.S. Embassy Bangkok's 882, December 6, 1963.

26. On Preap Im, Hin Sithan, *Who Are the Murderers?* 43*n.*; Sim Kin interview, November 1987. On his arrest, Michael Vickery (personal communication); on his relationship with In Tam, Soth Polin interview, October 1988. "It was at that point," Polin said, "that I began to hate Sihanouk." On events at the congress, Oeur Hun Ly interview, January 1989.

27. See also U.S. Embassy Phnom Penh's 701, January 18, 1964, in which Sihanouk, two days before the execution, accused "right-wing" critics of "working to bring down Sihanouk, throne, and Sangkum." In the same speech he referred to "Thanh's Democratic Party," telescoping disparate sources of dissent. The unsavory screenings persisted throughout the 1960s. In *My Wars with the CIA*, 122, Sihanouk claims that Khmer Serei "training manuals and operational plans" captured by NLF forces had been sent to him by the NLF in November 1963 and had assisted the prosecutors of Preap In. By the time he spoke he was militantly pro-Vietnamese.

28. Roger Hilsman, Memorandum of Conversation with the President, 11/20/63, Kennedy Library.

29. Department of State's 269 to Phnom Penh, November 26, 1963.

30. See U.S. Embassy Phnom Penh's 435, November 30, 1963, in which Sprouse noted that he was "impressed with essential political realism of Sihanouk's theatrical demand." By contrast, U.S. Embassy Saigon's 1117, December 19, 1963, from Lodge quoted a previous departmental statement rebuffing the conference with the phrase, "Nothing is further from USG mind than neutral solution for Vietnam. We intend to win." In U.S. Embassy Saigon's 1372, January 23, 1964, as hopes for the conference faded, Lodge called the proposal a "dangerous example of [the] tail wagging the dog." Anne Blair (Ph.D. diss., Monash University, forthcoming) discusses Lodge's embassy to Vietnam in detail.

31. U.S. Embassy Phnom Penh's 416, November 26, 1963. A more cautious CIA assessment, "Cambodia—Economic Effects of US Aid Withdrawal" (December 19, 1963), includes the sentence "While economic dislocation is likely to be severe, it will not be ruinous."

32. Osborne, *Politics and Power,* 90 ff.; interview with Douc Rasy, May 1988; *Souvenirs doux et amers,* 277–302.

33. Interview with Channa Samudvanija, August 1981.

34. Department of State's 305 to Phnom Penh, December 9, 1963, and U.S. Embassy Phnom Penh's 478, December 11, 1963. For the Thai reaction, see U.S. Embassy Bangkok's 907, December 11, 1963.

35. A Chinese-language newspaper in Phnom Penh monitored by the U.S. embassy also reported the essence of the communiqué, but no French translation appeared, and the communiqué was not mentioned in the French-language press.

36. See U.S. Embassy Phnom Penh's 475, December 10, and 500, December 14, 1963; the imbroglio over the broadcast soon centered on the word *barbaric.*

37. Soon afterward, however, Songsakd used some of the bank's assets to become a patron of the Khmer Serei, serving briefly in 1964 as its minister of foreign affairs. It seems likely that he and some of his depositors had attracted CIA funding before his flight and protection from the U.S. embassy in Saigon afterward. See U.S. Embassy Phnom Penh's airgram A-350, December 26, 1963. On Songsakd, see Samniet Khathachawana, "A Thought on the News," *Siam Rath,* June 30, 1970, translated by Charnwit Kasetsiri (typescript in Echols Collection, Cornell University), and Milton Osborne, *Before Kampuchea* (Sydney, 1979), 112–13. On Songsakd's politics, Michael Vickery (personal communication).

38. See U.S. Embassy Phnom Penh's 617, December 22, 1963, and *RC,* December 28, 1963.

39. Laura Summers, "Bases of Economic Discontent," and interview with Douc Rasy, May 1988.

40. *RC,* December 22, 1963.

41. In a speech given at the end of 1963, speaking of corruption in his entourage, Sihanouk said, "Many people have betrayed me. . . . I relentlessly struggle against these corrupt and negligent persons, but I am always defeated. But when struggling against foreigners, I have always emerged victorious." BBC/SWB, December 31, 1963.

42. Norodom Sihanouk, letter to the author, May 15, 1988 (my translation). Julio Jeldres kindly expedited this correspondence.

43. See BBC/SWB/FE 2004, October 28, 1965. Support for NLF forces, particularly in the form of potassium nitrate used for manufacturing munitions, was coming through Cambodia in 1963, with the knowledge of local officials, well before the rejection of American aid. See U.S. Embassy Saigon's airgram A-251, October 16, 1963, and its 2267, May 25, 1964. The 1963 airgram quotes a prisoner of war to the effect that weapons were often smuggled over the border between 1961 and 1963.

44. On percentages, Nayan Chanda, *Brother Enemy* (New York, 1986), 420, drawing on an interview in 1977 with Charles Meyer. Author's interviews with Chhon Po, November 1987, and Khut Khun, August 1987. Sihanouk's fears of South Vietnam were not unjustified. In January 1964, U.S. Ambassador Lodge met with South Vietnamese leaders to propose top secret operations, to be financed by the United States, against North Vietnam. The South Vietnamese prime minister, Mr. Tho, "said they would prefer [to] act against Cambodia than against North Vietnam." His military commander, General Minh, "agreed this preferable from military but not psychological standpoint." Lodge made no comment. Saigon's 3943, January 21, 1964, released under FOIA in July 1989. Anne Blair kindly provided this intriguing reference.

45. Kiernan, *HPP,* 214 ff., and Chhim Somuk confession.

46. On dilemmas for the left, see Kiernan, *HPP,* 210, 213 ff., and Becker, *When the War Was Over,* 115 ff.

47. On the January demonstration, see U.S. Embassy Phnom Penh's airgram A-433, February 14, 1964, and Oeur Hun Ly interview, January 1989. Copies of a pro-Communist paper that reported the event were seized by the government. Pol Pot speech, September 27, 1977, 37.

48. Interview Hin Sithan, November 1987. *RC,* March 6, 1963, claimed that U.S. officials "made faces" at the demonstrators and took their pictures. See *NYT,* March 12, 1963. On Lon Nol and demonstrators, Oeur Hun Ly interview, January 1989.

49. Vorn Vet confession, 15.

50. See Department of State's 667 to Phnom Penh, U.S. Embassy Phnom Penh's 972, March 20, 1964, and U.S. Embassy Saigon's 1792, March 20, 1964, in which Ambassador Lodge wrote that he "did not consider Cambodia any longer to be a *bona fide* neutral."

51. Thomas Hirschfeld interview, May 1986; BBC/FE/SWB 1636/; *RC,* September 18, 1964.

52. See BBC/FE/SWB 1684/C5. *Souvenirs doux et amers,* 344–45, composed after the Vietnamese invasion of Cambodia in 1979, fails to mention the presence of Vietnamese troops on Cambodian soil.

53. Interview Bernard Hamel, November 1987. See also CIA Report SC 10527/65, "Cambodia and the Viet Cong," December 22, 1965.

54. On NLF use of Cambodian territory since 1963, see Saigon MACV Message COC 3812, May 12, 1964 (Johnson Library). For Sihanouk's reactions, see BBC/SWB/FE 2161 A3/l, May 7, 1966. On the transportation of supplies, Hin Sithan interview, November 1987, and interviews with François Ponchaud, May 1988, and Ven. Kong Chhean, October 1988.

55. On Peoples' Conference, see BBC/FE/SWB 1805/A3/8-9. Cambodian delegates from South Vietnam used the meeting to complain to Sihanouk about mistreatment at the hands of Communist Vietnamese as well as the Saigon government. See BBC/FE/SWB 1829/A3/2.

56. On Delhi meetings, interview Thomas Hirschfeld, who had been Cambodian desk officer in the Department of State, May 1986.

57. On the Indochina conference, see Roger Smith, ed., *Southeast Asia: Documents on Political Development and Change* (Ithaca, 1974), 507–10. On the break in relations, see McGeorge Bundy memorandum to president, May 3, 1965 (Johnson Library), BBC/FE/SWB 1856. Interestingly, Queen Kossamak was opposed to the diplomatic break. See CIA's TDCS 314/082091-65, suggesting that her response to the *Newsweek* article had not played a major part in Sihanouk's decision.

58. *RC,* July 9, 1965.

59. Vorn Vet confession (typescript), 17. Ros Nhem's confession claims that Keo Meas attended a study session in January 1965 "inside Vietnam, near Memot." *Black Book,* 27, and Kiernan, *HPP,* 221 ff. Keo Meas, who went to North Vietnam for his health in 1967, became the front's ambassador to China in 1970 and returned to Cambodia in 1975. He was executed by the CPK in 1976. On activities in Office 100 while Pol Pot was absent, see Chhim Somuk (Pang) confession, July 1978.

60. Porter in Chandler and Kiernan, *Revolution and Its Aftermath,* 77; Kiernan, *HPP,* 220; *Black Book,* 27. On trainees, see unnumbered U.S. interrogation report, "Training Khmers in North Vietnam," March 1973, Pike Archives. The two hundred recruits may have accompanied Saloth Sar and Keo Meas to the north.

61. Serge Thion, personal communication.

62. See W. R. Smyser, *The Independent Vietnamese: Vietnamese Communism, between Russia and China, 1956–1969* (Athens, Ohio, 1980), 95-100. William Turley kindly provided this reference. Kiernan, *HPP,* 220–21. For a summary of Chinese intellectual history during the months when Saloth Sar was in China, see Paul J. Hiniker, *Revolutionary Ideology and Chinese Reality* (Beverly Hills, 1977), 207 ff. Hiniker stresses that Mao's self-aggrandizement in the first half of 1966 coincided with the destruction of the Communist Party of Indonesia (PKI) at the hands of the newly installed Suharto government.

63. Kiernan, *HPP,* 222.

64. Tim Bowden, *One Crowded Hour* (Sydney, 1988), 225.

65. Kiernan, *HPP,* 224 ff., provides details of this campaign and also of repression in early 1966. See also Sihanouk speech, February 25, 1966, BBC/FE/SWB 2106/B/10, and 2108/B/12-13. See also *Le Sangkum,* April 13, 1966, quoting a Communist text of this period: "Today's society is composed of and won over by the cult of the individual, which we must abolish at all costs."

66. *RC,* February 25 and May 6, 1966. In a speech in March 1966, Sihanouk declared that Cambodia offered "an infinitely preferable alternative" to communism than that offered by the United States. *RC,* March 25, 1966. For the decree on

Pseng Pseng, RC, May 20, 1966. Charles Meyer kindly provided copies of this journal dating from 1966–69.

67. Sihanouk's earliest films, *Double Crime on the Maginot Line* and *Tarzan among the Kuoy* (a Khmer minority), made in the 1940s, were never revived.

68. Osborne, *Before Kampuchea,* 71 ff. Philippe Devillers has recalled visiting Phnom Penh in 1946 to find the young king starved for news of the film world, in particular of Fernandel and Charlie Chaplin. See also *Souvenirs doux et amers,* 337.

69. See Vickery, "Looking Back," 106–07, Kiernan and Boua, *Peasants and Politics,* 208–09, and Kiernan, *HPP,* 231–34. See *RC,* July 7, 1966, for attacks on local Communists at the national congress. For attacks on Douc Rasy, Osborne, *Before Kampuchea,* 178; letter from Douc Rasy to author, May 1988. Ben Kiernan and Justin Corfield kindly provided statistical material on the election. Soth Polin, *Bei thngai,* October 3, 1988, speculates that the candidates vilified by Sihanouk may have become those with whom voters became the most familiar.

70. BBC/SWB/FE 2209/A3/9; *RC,* August 12, 1966. Douc Rasy, letters to author, May and November 1988.

71. Raw statistics from notes provided to me by Ben Kiernan; 1962 statistics from *RC,* June 15, 1966. The other candidates earning more than 50 percent of the vote in multicandidate electorates were Keo San, Tan Uk, Nan Ieng, Ung Mung, Pinn Yeurn, Chau Sen Cocsal, In Tam, and Hoeur Lay In. Meyer, *Derrière le sourire khmer,* 155. A collective biography of those elected to the assembly of 1966 would be rewarding.

72. On the election of 1966, interviews with Tan Bun Sor, May 1988, Ven. Kong Chhean, October 1988, and Hoeung Hong Kim, January 1989. Douc Rasy and Keuky Lim interviews, May 1988; see also Osborne, *Before Kampuchea,* 178–79, and Ben Kiernan, "The 1970 Peasant Uprisings Against Lon Nol," in Kiernan and Boua, *Peasants and Politics,* 206–24.

73. Douc Rasy letter to author, June 1988, Sim Var interview November 1987, and Vickery, "Looking Back," 106.

74. Vickery, "Looking Back," 107. Sihanouk, *L'Indochine vue de Pékin,* 82. Osborne, *Before Kampuchea,* 175 ff. See also Becker, *When the War Was Over,* 116–17. See also BBC/SWB/FE 2277/A3/8 (Sihanouk speech, 20 September 1966): "There are protests against the election results. . . . If the election were held again, there would be disputes. I am not of the opinion that the election should be held again."

75. On the formation of countergovernment, BBC/SWB/FE 2303/B/3–4. On hospitalization: BBC/SWB/FE 2288/B-15. On Lon Nol and Nhiek Tioulong, BBC/SWB/FE/2303/B5.

76. On these demonstrations, see BBC/SWB/FE 2313/B-17. Sihanouk quote from *La Nouvelle Dépêche,* November 7, 1966.

77. For Ieng Sary's analysis of the election of 1966 (made in 1971), see Sihanouk, *L'Indochine vue de Pékin,* 118 ff: "The 'free candidacies' sounded the call for Lon Nol's bayonets and the intrigues of the CIA, with the blessings of the Assembly, drawn from the far Right."

78. On Lon Nol's character, see Monireth memoir, 111 ff. Sihanouk's letter to author, May 1988, and Martin, *Le mal cambodgien,* 131.

79. Sihanouk's letter to author and Sim Var interview, November 1987. Prince Monireth was never given substantial work during Sihanouk's years in power.

80. See Osborne, *Politics and Power,* 90 ff., and *Before Kampuchea,* 175–80.

For an astute analysis, see Nayan Chanda, "The Four-Year Coup," *Far Eastern Economic Review* (hereafter *FEER*), June 25, 1970.

Chapter Five. Changing the Rules, 1967–1969

1. This paragraph is drawn from several interviews, among them those with Ung Bunheang, August 1987, and Thong Thel, March 1987.

2. See Remy Prud'homme, *L'économie du Cambodge* (Paris, 1969), 241–46.

3. Kiernan and Boua, *Peasants and Politics*, 29–86, and Carney, *Communist Party Power*, Introduction. On conditions in Svay Rieng, Thong Thel interview, March 1987. See also Meyer, *Derrière le sourire khmer,* 202–25, and Summers, "The Sources of Economic Grievance."

4. On these inspirations, Yem Nolla, Ong Thong Hoeung, and Panh Meng Heang interviews, May 1988. The latter two witnessed May 1968 as tertiary students in Paris. The influence of U.S. student activism, on the other hand, was much weaker than it was to be in Thailand in the early 1970s. On the influence of Maoism among some members of the sangha in the 1960s, Sok Chhuon interview, April 1990.

5. I owe this insight to Al Santoli, who served in U.S. Army intelligence along the Cambodian border in Vietnam in 1968. See also Report 6 029 1177 70, November 12, 1970, in Pike archives.

6. See BBC SWB/FE/ 2358. The notion that Sihanouk was a "white" Khmer occupying the middle of a tricolored spectrum was recurrent in his speeches.

7. Citations to *Phnom Penh Presse*, January 24 and March 11, 1967. While warning leftists against subversion, Sihanouk referred to Lon Nol in March 1967 as "my Suharto" (Kiernan, *HPP*, 252). Indonesia reference by CPK in Kiernan, *HPP*, 235. See also Robert Cribb, ed., *The 1955–1966 Killings in Indonesia* (Clayton, Victoria, 1991).

8. Kiernan, *HPP*, 253 ff. See also Kiernan and Boua, *Peasants and Politics*, 168 ff.

9. *Agence Khmere du Presse* (hereafter *AKP*), March 12, 1967; *Le Monde,* March 6, 1967. Bernard Hamel (interview, November 1987) has recalled a palpable rise in political tension in Phnom Penh between October 1966 and the early months of 1967. This is corroborated by a former monk, Sok Chhuon (interview, April 1990).

10. *RC,* March 10 and 17, 1967; *AKP,* March 12, 1967. Kiernan and Boua, *Peasants and Politics*, 170.

11. *RC,* March 17, 1967; BBC/SWB/FE 2414/A2 and 2414/B-21.

12. *AKP,* March 13, 1967. During the congress, two residents of Pailin who had been brought to Phnom Penh for the purpose expressed their confidence in Lon Nol's government and their anger at the demonstrations. When they got home, according to Sihanouk, they found that their houses had been burned down.

13. Sihanouk's speech at S'aang: BBC/SWB/FE/2431/A3/3; *AKP,* April 28, 1967; Meyer interview, November 1987. Wilfred Burchett has recalled that "in early 1967 . . . a leading Khmer Rouge cadre" asked him to lend his support to the "armed struggle about to be launched against Sihanouk." Burchett refused on the grounds that "it was absurd to speak of a 'revolutionary situation' in Cambodia at that time." It is possible that the "cadre" was Khieu Samphan. W. Burchett, *At the Barricades* (London, 1979), 314.

14. See Kiernan and Boua, *Peasants and Politics,* 166–205; Kiernan and Thion, *Khmers rouges!* 99–138, and Kiernan, *HPP,* 249 ff.

15. Kiernan and Boua, *Peasants and Politics,* 175 ff., Kiernan and Thion, *Khmers rouges!* 116 ff. See also Debré, *La révolution dans la forêt,* 109 ff., and Hin Sithan, *Who Are the Murderers?* 54 ff. According to Im Nath (interview, March 1987), minor members of the royal family had settled near Samlaut in the 1960s at government expense. Intriguingly, given the importance of the slogan "three tons per hectare" referring to padi production under DK, Sihanouk himself noted that in this region, long a dissident base, "a hectare can produce three or four tons [of padi]." FBIS, April 24, 1967.

16. Hin Sithan, *Who Are the Murderers?* 57. The use of the word *capitalist* indicates that these people had already absorbed some Communist phraseology or that Sithan's informant in the 1980s, having survived DK, found such a categorization easy to employ.

17. Debré, *La révolution dans la forêt,* 110 ff; interviews with Ty Sophen, January 1989, and S. Suon Kaset, February 1990.

18. Chronology of events is from Sihanouk's speech of April 3 (BBC/SWB 2434 A3/7–8), from Kiernan in Kiernan and Boua, *Peasants and Politics,* 171. See also Martin, *Le mal cambodgien,* 118. On militia, Michael Vickery (personal communication) and interviews with Im Nath, March 1987, Charles Meyer, May 1987, and François Ponchaud, May 1988.

19. Meyer interviews, November 1987, May 1988. Im Nath interview. *AKP,* April 11, 1967. On bounties, see Lancaster, "The Decline of Sihanouk," 52, and Debré, *La révolution dans la forêt,* 110.

20. BBC/SWB/FE 2247/A3/3. On executions, FBIS, April 24, 1967.

21. Sihanouk, *L'Indochine vue de Pékin,* 90. Chandler, Kiernan, and Boua, *Pol Pot Plans the Future,* 247. Vorn Vet confession, 23; *Phnom Penh Presse,* May 8, 1967. Rumors of assassination were picked up by Radio Peking. Meyer, *Derrière le sourire khmer,* 195. In *My Wars with the CIA,* 47, Sihanouk claims that "a campaign was . . . whipped up" against the representatives and that they left Phnom Penh "as a means of surviving."

22. Lon Nol's illness was serious enough to require medical attention overseas, according to Brig. Thach Ren, personal communication.

23. In Sen, a schoolteacher in Pailin in the 1960s, recalled widespread injustice toward the inhabitants of Samlaut and corruption in the officer corps. Interview, September 1987.

24. Pol Pot speech, September 27, 1977, 38. Two years earlier, Pol Pot had said that the party had requested the rebels to "postpone armed struggle in order to examine and sum up the contradictions, and the possibility of using arms." Cited in Kiernan and Boua, *Peasants and Politics,* 255.

25. On repression, see M. Leifer, "Rebellion or Subversion in Cambodia," *Current History* (February 1969): 89–93. For arguments that the 1967 rebellion was conceived by the CPK leadership, see Kiernan, *HPP,* 265–67.

26. BBC/SWB/FE 2461/A3/5–6; *AKP,* May 5, 1967.

27. In Paris, Ong Thong Hoeung was shocked to hear that many of his friends had been arrested following these demonstrations. Interview, May 1988. In July, Sihanouk claimed that "he had forbidden the Armed Forces to kill Chau Seng, Hou Youn, Khieu Samphan and Hu Nim lest they be considered martyrs." BBC/SWB/FE 2538/B/32.

28. Gareth Porter, "Vietnamese Communist Policy toward Kampuchea, 1930–1970," in Chandler and Kiernan, *Revolution and Its Aftermath,* 78. Porter draws

on interviews in 1981 with Son Sann, who told him that the Vietnamese drove a harder bargain than they were credited with in Sihanouk's public statements. See also BBC/SWB/FE 2489/A3–8, reporting Sihanouk's speech of June 8, 1967, at Snuol, and *AKP,* June 9, 1967.

29. Donald Kirk, *Wider War* (New York, 1971), 61–62. For cartoons about these agreements, see *Kambuja,* July 1967. Chinese foreign affairs were in disarray at this stage following the takeover of the ministry, in May 1967, by detachments of Red Guards.

30. BBC/SWB/FE 2489/A3/9.

31. According to Meyer, *Derrière le sourire khmer,* 192, armed forces used the end of hostilities in Battambang to mount "mopping up" operations that inflicted heavy casulaties. In 1975, the Vietnamese were unwilling to abide by the statements they had made in 1967. Stephen Heder, "Origins of the Conflict," *Indo-China Chronicle* 64 (September-October 1978).

32. Interviews with Sim Var, Douc Rasy, Soth Polin, and Lim Kim Ya. See also *RC,* July 7, 1967, *AKP,* July 19, 1967, and Kiernan, *HPP,* 260–61. Sihanouk's subsequent anger at the demonstration may have sprung from his later discovery that his and his mother's photographs had indeed been damaged or defaced. *AKP,* September 4, 1967.

33. *La Nouvelle Dépêche,* ND, June 13, 1967. For a detailed discussion of this period, see Jean-Marie Boucher, "The Relationship between Cambodia and China, 1954–1970" (Ph.D. diss., University of London [SOAS] 1978), 170–98. No Khmer-language edition of Mao's Little Red Book was ever published, but French translations abounded among high school students and younger Buddhist monks (Sok Pirun interview, January 1990). Huy Huynh (interview, February 1988), a Chinese resident of Phnom Penh, recalls teaching Mao's thought at a Chinese high school at this time.

34. See Leifer, "Rebellion or Subversion in Cambodia?" 88–93.

35. BBC/SWB/FE 2517/A3/5. On public works in Koh Thom, see *AKP,* September 1, 1967; on ralliers, *AKP,* August 16, 1967. In August also, Sihanouk resettled twenty-three Khmer Serei ralliers in Battambang. *AKP,* August 22, 1967. For the return of touring Reds, see BBC/SWB/FE 2716/A3/11.

36. See BBC/SWB/FE 2568/A3, and *AKP,* September 12 and 15, 1967. In the referendum, he proposed to have the photographs of those associated with *La Nouvelle Dépêche* and that of Mao, "whom he referred to as the Buddha," on one ballot, and his own photograph on the other.

37. BBC/SWB/FE 2571/A3. Similarly, on September 18, Sihanouk said, "Cambodia wants to be isolated. She does not want to participate in any world or regional associations." See also BBC/SWB/FE 2578/A3/2, in which Sihanouk said, "Now China is an old civilization, so is Cambodia. . . . Who will look upon whom as a child? Surely it is not China who can consider Cambodia a child. Cambodia is small, of course, but it is a small old man, ha, ha, ha."

38. See FBIS, October 7, 1967, for text of speech.

39. See U.S. Embassy Phnom Penh's airgram A-29, March 16, 1972, enclosing material from the Khmer Republic's intelligence services. Kiernan, *HPP,* 262–65, and Vorn Vet's confession, 23–24. Phouk Chhay was released from prison in 1970, joined the resistance, and was purged by the CPK in 1977. On Hu Nim, see his confession in Chandler, Kiernan, and Boua, *Pol Pot Plans the Future,* 217–317.

40. See William Shawcross, *Sideshow: Nixon, Kissinger, and the Destruction of Cambodia* (New York, 1979), 68 ff. Interview with Noel Deschamps, May 1987.

41. See Ben Kiernan, "The American Bombing of Kampuchea, 1969–1973,"

Vietnam Generation (Winter 1989): 4–41; on its relation to a proposed U.S. invasion, see *NYT,* January 17, 1971.

42. The delegation included the assistant secretary of state for far eastern affairs, Philip Habib, and Herbert Spivak, the former counsellor of the U.S. embassy in Phnom Penh. John W. Shirley, press officer from the U.S. embassy in New Delhi, submitted a report, "The Bowles Mission to Cambodia" in May 1968, released under FOIA. *NYT,* January 10, 1968. See Shawcross, *Sideshow,* 68–72. One such intelligence team, made up of four men from the U.S. 4th Infantry Division, spent a month observing Vietnamese troop movements in Cambodia in late 1969, according to Bill Gilliam (personal communication). The team was one of hundreds performing similar tasks.

43. Nine years later, Tioulong said that as far as fighting Communists went, the Cambodian army in 1968 had been "less effective than the Paris police." Shawcross, *Sideshow,* 68.

44. See "The Bowles Mission," 17, and U.S. Embassy Delhi's 2539, January 12, 1968. For arguments about Sihanouk's permission, see Shawcross, *Sideshow* (1981 ed.), appendices, 423–24, 440–41, and 451. Bernard Hamel (interview, November 1987) has recalled that Sihanouk's mood after the Bowles visit was "very satisfied," as if he had received guarantees of some sort.

45. Sihanouk's views on resuming relations with the United States are in BBC/SWB/FE 2669/A3/7.

46. See FBIS, February 28, 1968, Sihanouk speech in Takeo: "It is not Sihanouk who suffers from this civil war . . . but the social progress of the country."

47. Interviews in May 1988 with François Ponchaud, who was a missionary near Damber between early 1968 and 1970, and Kol Touch, who ran a rubber plantation within the Viet Minh zone. On northwest, see Kiernan, *HPP,* 292n113. For reports of scattered fighting, see FBIS, February 27, 1968.

48. On incidents in Battambang, see *AKP,* January 28 and February 6, 1968, and Kiernan, *HPP,* 268 ff.

49. Meyer, *Derrière le sourire khmer,* 196. See also Pomonti and Thion, *Des courtesans aux partisans,* 121, Debré, *Révolution dans la forêt,* 113, and Kate Frieson's interview with Van Team, a soldier in 1968, who remembered being sent to the northeast "to fight against the mountain people. The King wanted them to eat properly, and to wear decent clothes." Frieson kindly provided a transcription of this interview.

50. Pol Pot speech, September 29, 1977, 39. Becker, *When the War Was Over,* 124, and Kiernan, *HPP,* 268–69. See also Nuon Chea, "Statement of the CPK," 23, where Chea states that the uprising began in January 1968 in "seventeen out of nineteen provinces," following a CPK central committee meeting that decided on the move. Pol Pot's speech of September 27, 1977, 39, says that the fighting had spread to "seventeen out of nineteen provinces" in 1969.

51. Interview with Ong Thong Hoeung, February 1990, Kiernan, *HPP,* 272 ff., and *RC,* April 26, 1968.

52. Keat Chhon interview, November 1987. See also Bu Phat confession, and Kiernan's citation of Ieng Sary, *HPP,* 274; Ong Thong Hoeung interview, May 1988, and *Le Sangkum,* June 1969, 8–11. See also J. Stalin, "Dialectical and Historical Materialism," in *The Essential Stalin,* ed. B. Franklin (London, 1973), 323: "Under the primitive communal system, the means of production are socially owned. . . . Here there was no exploitation, no classes." In late 1975, at least two of Saloth Sar's bodyguards were tribal people who could not speak much Khmer (interview with Taing Kim Buon, July 1989).

53. See "Notebook Entries, August to September 1969," unnumbered document in Pike archives 9/69.

54. See Carney, "Unexpected Victory," in Jackson, ed., *Cambodia, 1975–1978,* 19, and interview with Ty Sophen, January 1989. Sophen, who knew Nuon Chea by sight, claims that local people later told him that Chea was active in the incident.

55. BBC/SWB/FE 2709/A3/14.

56. See Kiernan and Boua, *Peasants and Politics,* 186–87; BBC/SWB 2719/A3/9. Kompong Cham demonstration, BBC/SWB/FE 2715/A3/11; Kratie, BBC/SWB/FE 2716/A3/12. Also *AKP,* March 6, 1968. Sihanouk's calls for revenge did not appear in the official translations of his speeches, as published in *AKP.* See also Bernard Hamel, "Le suprénant parcours de Prince Sihanouk," *Historia* 391 (June 1979). In January 1968, Sihanouk had claimed that "various reports" indicated an alliance between the Khmer Reds and the Khmer Serei "to sink or kill the partisans of Sihanouk, and after that they will cut Cambodia in half." FBIS, January 29, 1968.

57. Kiernan, *HPP,* 274–75. Sihanouk later boasted of having ordered two hundred rebels in the northeast summarily shot. *AKP,* May 25, 1968. In August, he complained that "in Ratanakiri the Viet Minh and the Viet Cong have occupied a third of the province." BBC/SWB/FE 2860/A3/4. It seems likely that Sihanouk expected U.S. hot pursuit to alleviate pressure in this part of the country. On the September events, see BBC/SWB/FE 2932/A3/3.

58. *AKP,* March 5, 1968; Siyathay Siyarath interview, May 1987. For scattered incidents, see, e.g., *AKP,* April 9 and 18, 1967. On Lon Nol's return, *AKP,* May 3, 1968. On Sihanouk's admission about the bases, see *L'Indochine vue de Pékin,* 94–95. On the political atmosphere in Phnom Penh in early 1968, Osborne, *Politics and Power,* 103–04.

59. *NYT,* December 8, 1968. See also Kiernan, *HPP,* 283–85. Thomas Hughes, "Cambodia," *Atlantic Monthly,* February 1969, 10, states that there were "over 100" clashes between government and insurgent forces in 1968, adding that "little is known of [the Communists'] leadership, policy, or goals." See also "Capital Crisis," *FEER,* October 10, 1968, recounting the arrest in Phnom Penh in early October of "about 30 Communist Khmers."

60. This paragraph is drawn from interviews with Bernard Hamel, Charles Meyer, S. Suon Kaset, Sim Var, Soth Polin, Keng Vannsak, Douc Rasy, and several others. The arbitrary arrest of Keng Vannsak in October 1968 along with several other intellectuals whom Sihanouk called "the big bosses of the Khmer Reds" indicated his desperation and the poor quality of the intelligence he was receiving. See BBC/SWB/FE 2861/A3/1.

61. For an analysis of Cambodian agriculture in the late 1960s, see Kiernan and Boua, *Peasants and Politics,* 29–86, 134–65. On other crops, see special issue of *Europe d'outremer* (October 1968): 32–33, and Prud'homme, *L'économie du Cambodge,* 266.

62. Kol Touch (interview, May 1988) recalled that "many young Vietnamese" workers at the Tapao plantation in Kompong Cham were recruited to help with the Tet offensive in 1968.

63. Meyer, *Derrière le sourire khmer,* 215–17, and *Europe d'outremer,* 40. Interview with Bun Oulong, November 1987, and David Chandler, "Cambodia's Strategy of Survivial," *Current History* (December 1969): 344–48.

64. Kirk, *Wider War,* 87 ff. See also Terence Smith, "Shortage of Money Plagues Cambodia," *NYT,* January 17, 1969, and Prud'homme, *L'économie du Cambodge,* 104 ff.

65. Statistics from Royaume du Cambodge, Ministère du Plan, *Annuaire Statistique du Cambodge 1967,* table XI I-10. See also *RC,* December 26, 1969. Funds for this tertiary institution were provided by the French. For evidence of Phnom Penh's *jeunesse dorée,* see *Pseng Pseng,* December 1969, 41, which announces the opening of a new disco, Le Roadhouse, near Sihanouk's residence, founded because "night life in Phnom Penh is so tedious [*maussade*]." A sponsor of the club was Nhiek Tioulong's daughter, Ketty, who at one time was married to Sihanouk's son, Prince Chakrapong.

66. The reluctance of Cambodians to engage in commercial activity was a recurrent theme for many Cambodian nationalists. Sihanouk's contempt for capitalism echoed this aversion.

67. See Meyer, *Derrière le sourire khmer,* 202 ff. On economic stagnation in the 1960s, interview with Tan Bun Sor, May 1988. On Sangkum card, interviews with Yem Nolla, May 1988, and You Hon Chea, March 1989.

68. *Europe France Outremer,* 8. A copy of the issue with handwritten annotations by the prince was reprinted in Beijing in 1985. Beside this passage, Sihanouk later noted, in French, "This Cambodian miracle has been assassinated by the Blue Khmers, the Red Khmers, the Khmer-Vietminh and their foreign patrons."

69. This paragraph is drawn from several interviews. In August 1968, Nop Nem, who had appeared in several of the films, suggested that one should depict the life of Sihanouk himself—"his existence filled with self-denial, sacrifices, and continuous effort." *RC,* September 23, 1968. See also Dulong, *La dernière pagode,* 160 ff. On the drought, Kate Frieson, personal communication.

70. BBC/SWB/FE 2719/A3/9. *AKP,* October 6, 1968. Keng Vannsak, *Tragédie d'un peuple (khmer)* (Montmorency, 1976), 9. Hin Sithan MS, 84. Bernard Hamel interview, November 1987, Ven. Kong Chhean and Soth Polin interviews, October 1988, and Sok Chhoun interview, April 1990.

71. Interviews with Douc Rasy, May 1988, Pung Peng Cheng, December 1987, Thong Thel, April 1987, and Ith Sarin, October 1988. Charles Meyer interview, May 1987, likened conditions in Cambodia between 1966 and 1969 to those in Argentina in the 1970s. See Lancaster, "The Decline of Sihanouk," 53–54. On Kampot violence, see Pomonti and Thion, *Des courtesans aux partisans,* 124–25. On Cheng Heng, *RC,* October 25, 1968, and interviews with William Harben and Emory Swank, November 1987.

72. See *RC,* December 13, 1968, for a spirited discussion of pâté de foie gras, Sihanouk's favorite dish, between Sihanouk and the French journalist Jean Barré. For Sihanouk's recipe for "squab Monique," in aspic with foie gras, see *RC,* March 28, 1969. For a gloomy assessment of Cambodia at the end of 1968, see Maslyn Williams, *The Land in Between* (New York, 1970).

73. Details of bombing are in Shawcross, *Sideshow,* 20–26, 95. See also Seymour Hersh, *The Price of Power* (New York, 1983), 55–56, 200. Sihanouk knew of the bombing and may have approved of it, but no documentation corroborating this can be cited, and he was certainly in no position to call the bombing off. See BBC/SWB/FE 3090/A3/l. On Sihanouk's pledge, *RC,* April 4, 1969.

74. Meyer, *Derrière le sourire khmer,* 284. In May 1969, Nhiek Tioulong reported that the state-owned factories had run up debts (to the state) of more than 150 million riels, while the collection of taxes was running six months late. *RC,* May 9, 1969.

75. The most detailed account is in Summers, "Economic Grievances." See also *RC,* February 7, 1969, which reports daily takes of 4 to 5 million riels (approximately $100,000 at the prevailing rate of exchange).

76. Summers, "Economic Grievances," 30–31, and my memories of conversations in Phnom Penh in September 1970. See also T. D. Allman, "Casino Diced?" *FEER*, February 5, 1970. Pomonti and Thion, *Des courtesans aux partisans*, 92–94, and Osborne, *Politics and Power*, 109. In 1972, Sihanouk wrote that when he and Mao Zedong had talked about his dismissal, Mao had remarked that "opening a casino was infinitely better than accepting U.S. aid," *My Wars with the CIA*, 209.

77. See U.S. Embassy Saigon's 2529, February 7, 1969, BBC/SWB/FE 3105/A3/7, which reports a speech by Sihanouk in Svay Rieng on June 19, 1969. Meyer, *Derrière le sourire khmer*, 288–89, and Pomonti and Thion, *Des courtesans aux partisans*, 138ff.

78. Pol Pot speech, September 29, 1977, 39.

79. Notebook Entries from J-12 Section, September 1969 (unnumbered, Pike Archives).

80. On new zone, Porter in Chandler and Kiernan, *Revolution and Its Aftermath*, 81.

81. Untitled document, dated November 1969, from Pike archives. See also BBC/SWB/FE 2932/A3/3, and CIA/DP, Intelligence Information Cable IN 66718, October 16, 1969, which also refers to "friendly troops" armed with "primitive weapons." On feuding, Kiernan, *HPP*, 275. Hin Sithan, *Who Are the Murderers?* 78, and interview with Po Chhon, December 1987. In October 1969, Sihanouk complained that an estimated forty thousand "Viet Cong and Viet Minh were in the country." BBC/SWB/FE 3105/A3/6 and 3204/3/4. See also *Kambuja*, October 1969, 95–96. Interviews with François Ponchaud and Kol Touch, May 1988; Kiernan, *HPP*, 283. See also map showing "Khmer Red" activities in eastern zone, *Sangkum*, November 1969, 73.

82. See Khmer Republic, *Livre Blanc sur l'agression Vietcong et nord-vietnamienne contre la république khmere* (Phnom Penh, 1971), 23 ff., which reproduces Sihanouk's draft arrangements for the visit.

83. *RC*, August 8, 1969. See also Sihanouk, *L'Indochine vue de Pékin*, 100, where the prince claims to have left Cambodia in early 1970 so as to "allow an experiment, different from my own, to reveal itself in all its harmfulness."

84. See U.S. Embassy Bangkok's 10905, August 12, 1969. *My Wars with the CIA*, 41; Pomonti and Thion, *Des courtesans aux partisans*. By November 1969 Sihanouk's feuding with the National Assembly reached the point where he forbade the representatives "during his lifetime" to attend any ceremonies over which he presided as chief of state. See U.S. Embassy Phnom Penh's airgram A-71, November 13, 1969.

85. On Matak, interviews with S. Suon Kaset, May and November 1987, Noel Deschamps, April 1987, Olary Sisowath (Matak's daughter), February 1989, and conversations with James Gerrand, 1988–89.

86. Sihanouk's replies to the author, May 1988. Speaking to Oriana Fallaci in 1973, Sihanouk was amazed that the Americans had been able to use Lon Nol: "Besides everything else, he was a complete idiot! He never understood a damn thing, always stared at me with those ox's eyes and spent all his time praying." *NYT Magazine*, August 12, 1973.

87. Charles Meyer interview, November 1987, *RC*, September 19, 1969, and BBC/SWB/FE 3183/A3, where Sihanouk said, "Had Sihanouk not gone, the Vietnamese would have lost face." Intriguingly, Saloth Sar was also in Hanoi toward the end of 1969. For Sihanouk's account of rice crisis, Sihanouk, *My Wars with the CIA*, 40–41. Possibly Sihanouk was amused that Lon Nol had outwitted the Vietnamese. Such a reaction would be consonant with his sense of humor. In any case, although

the Lon Nol-Pham Van Dong meetings were described as cordial (SWB 31891 A3/1), the semiofficial shipments of food and medicine to the NLF were never resumed, and the money from the Chinese was not repaid. According to Hersh, *The Price of Power*, 201*n*, citing an interview in 1978 with Nguyen Cao Thach, "Lon Nol, whose grandfather was Chinese, was treated deferentially" during his visit to China in 1969 "and invited to visit the graves of his ancestors." It is more likely that Lon Nol in fact visited the graves of his second wife's ancestors. Michael Vickery, personal communication.

88. See *RC*, November 7, 1969, Meyer, *Derrière le sourire khmer*, 295. Sihanouk promised the president of Niger economic aid and advice about improving agricultural yields. See T. D. Allman, "Hearts and Minds of Princes," *FEER*, January 12, 1970. Interview with S. Suon Kaset, May 1987. See also Malcolm Caldwell and Lek Hor Tan, *Cambodia in the Southeast Asian War* (London, 1973), 236–37.

89. Meyer, *Derrière le sourire khmer*, 299–300. See also U.S. Embassy Singapore's airgram A-280, December 2, 1969, which estimated that "a sum amounting to 20% of the total money in circulation is undoubtedly in the hands of the Viet Cong." For a summary of political developments in 1969, see U.S. Embassy Phnom Penh's airgram A-82, December 11, 1969, which noted, "Externally, Cambodia [is] neutral, independent, and relatively peaceful but without a single friend."

90. *NYT Magazine*, August 12, 1973, 14.

91. On the film festival, see *RC*, November 28, 1969, *NYT*, November 30, 1969, and interviews and conversations with Claude Jacques, Charles Meyer, Serge Thion, and Keng Vannsak. Sihanouk's mildly pornographic film *Joie de vivre*, which included scenes of half-naked grappling between Nhiek Tioulong (playing a senior minister) and a nubile actress, was also screened at this time to the dismay of many in the Cambodian middle class, one of whom has remembered thinking at the time, "How could a statesman have time to make such films?" Interview with You Hon Chea, May 1987.

92. Interviews with Sim Var, November 1987, and Douc Rasy, May 1988. Meyer, *Derrière le sourire khmer*, 304–05. Pomonti and Thion, *Des courtesans aux partisans*, 142–43; *RC*, January 9, 1970. The new cabinet members included Yem Sambaur, Phlek Phoeun, and Prom Thos, all of whom had offended Sihanouk in the past. For Sihanouk's views, see Sihanouk, *L'Indochine vue de Pékin*, 103, and H. Munthe-Kaas, "Sihanouk Lashes Out," *FEER*, December 25, 1969. For a more upbeat assessment, see U.S. Embassy Phnom Penh's 287, December 31, 1969: "Sihanouk has emerged on top and in most Cambodian eyes has not been weakened, [but] his position was not strengthened. In a Western context . . . RKG confrontation would have finished him politically."

93. Meyer, *Derrière le sourire khmer*, 296–97, Shawcross, *Sideshow*, 115 ff. On Sirik Matak's proposal, Kiernan, *HPP*, 301, based on interview with Prom Thos. Hersh, *The Price of Power*, 180, suggests that in 1969–70 some elements of the U.S. government entertained the idea of assassinating the prince. In a speech on December 14, Sihanouk suggested that the Cambodian people should resist the Vietnamese "invasion" of their country, much as the "South Vietnamese people" (*sic*) were resisting the invasion of the United States. See U.S. Embassy Phnom Penh's 45, December 16, 1969.

Chapter Six. Sliding toward Chaos, 1970–1975

1. On the renewed confidence of the CPK, see the *Livre Noir*, 33–34, and Kiernan, *HPP*, 287–88.

2. *RC*, January 18, 1970. See also U.S. Embassy Phnom Penh's airgram A-45, February 12, 1970, which interprets the closing down of the office as "a weakening of Princess Monique and her gang."

3. Pierre Max, *Le Cambodge de Silence* (Paris, 1976), 114. Thach Ren, personal communication.

4. *NYT*, February 23, 1970; *RC*, February 27, 1970; Pomonti and Thion, *Des courtesans aux partisans*, 110; interview with François Ponchaud, May 1988. See also report by Samuel Jameson in the *Chicago Tribune*, July 2, 1970, that the head of the National Bank, Touch Kim, traveled to France in February to receive orders for the move from Sihanouk.

5. Interview with Sim Kin, December 1987; see also testimony of former Green Beret Robert Marasco, reported in *Le Monde*, June 4, 1970.

6. Meyer, *Derrière le sourire khmer*, 300n.

7. Interviews with Brigadier Thach Ren, May 1987, and Roy Haverkamp and Marshall Green, November 1987. See also Osborne, *Politics and Power*, 112–13, and Shawcross, *Sideshow*, 114–15, citing interviews with Frank Snepp. Defection of troops, *RC* October 24, 1969 and BBC/SWB/FE 3018/A3/3, and U.S. Embassy Phnom Penh's Airgram A-64, November 5, 1969. The story of this three-way relationship may never emerge: U.S. intelligence archives are closed, and Lon Nol, Sirik Matak, and Son Ngoc Thanh are dead.

8. See Report no. 6 029 0426 70, 4-1970, Pike archive. On Cambodian army clashes with "Viet Cong" units in January and February 1970, see BBC/SWB/FE 3331/A3/8.

9. *RC*, March 13, 1970 (i.e., before the coup); *NYT*, March 12, 1970. Meyer, *Derrière le sourire khmer*, 307–08, 313. Keuky Lim (interview, May 1988) characterized the demonstrations as "wild, but spontaneous." See also J. L. Bonniol, J. Brunel, F. Corrèze, et al., "55 témoignages sur le Cambodge en lutte" (n.d., ca. 1972 or 1973), mimeo, 23–24. Scorched American currency, set alight among other embassy papers, showed up in the Phnom Penh market for several days.

10. On Sihanouk's views from Paris, see U.S. Embassy Paris' 3010, March 14, 1970; CIA document, Shawcross, *Sideshow*, 118; on the cassette, interview with Charles Meyer, November 1987; on artillery fire, *NYT*, March 18, 1970.

11. Max, *Le Cambodge de silence*, 114. On March 11, Sihanouk lunched with the Saintenys at the Tour d'Argent and revealed nothing of his plans. Dulong, *La dernière pagode* (Paris, 1989), 230–31. See also U.S. Embassy Paris' 1129, March 14, 1970.

12. The teletyped text of the debates, translated for the BBC, is in Pike archives, "Cambodia, 3-1970." The penciled petition was premature. A man distributing anti-Sihanouk tracts to the crowd (as opposed to anti-Vietnamese ones) was beaten to the ground and "almost killed" by policemen in mufti, according to an eyewitness (Thong Thel, personal communication). Some students even carried pro-Sihanouk banners: Martin, *Le mal cambodgien*, 127.

13. On flags, Hin Sithan, *Who Are the Murderers?* 87. On the repaved road, Nayan Chanda (personal communication). On Sihanouk's "masterminding his own downfall," see speculation in *FEER*, March 26, 1970, 5. On his discouragement, *Souvenirs doux et amers*, 374–75.

14. For Podgorny, see *My Wars with the CIA*, 21; Sihanouk's draft memoir of the period, "La calice jusqu'a lie," 17, states that a telegram from his mother, delivered to him in Moscow, asked him to delay his return because his life would be endangered. The text of this telegram has never been published. According to Frank Snepp, "The CIA persuaded the Queen Mother to reassure Sihanouk that

the situation was not so serious as to require his return." Shawcross, *Sideshow*, 119, who calls this a "fatal message," also cites U.S. Embassy Phnom Penh's 289, March 20, 1970.

15. Sihanouk later claimed that he asked the Russians "to send massive military aid to the royal army, without delay, in order to assuage the discontent of Lon Nol's officers who were nostalgic for American aid." *Souvenirs doux et amers*, 405–06. In *My Wars with the CIA*, 25, he states that "the Russians agreed to supply everything we needed"; there is no corrobration for this. Shawcross, *Sideshow*, 123, cites CIA reports from the USSR that refer to Sihanouk at this time as a "blundering fool" and a "spoiled child."

16. A Cambodian diplomat who met Sihanouk at the airport in Beijing has recalled that he seemed resigned to losing office. On Irkutsk, interview with Alain Daniel, November 1987. *My Wars with the CIA*, 28; on asylum, Shawcross, *Sideshow*, 125.

17. Interviews with Col. Po Chhon, December 1987 and February 1989. Keng Vannsak claimed to have details of this confrontation from Lon Nol's brother, Lon Non. Po Chhon, then a major, overheard Sirik Matak's threat when he accompanied him and his own patron, Col. Seng Sinthay, to Lon Nol's house. Sinthay was a decorated officer of republican leanings, loyal to Sirik Matak. Keng Vannsak claimed (interview, May 1987) that Sinthay had told him about plans for a coup in late 1969. He was killed four days later under mysterious circumstances.

18. Michael Vickery, personal communication. Also interviews with Pung Peng Cheng, Charles Meyer, Po Chhon, Keng Vannsak, Thonn Ouk, and William Harbin. On Lon Nol's letters to Nixon, Frank Tatu, personal communication. See also U.S. Embassy Phnom Penh's airgram A-78, "The Anthropological Lon Nol," May 19, 1972, a mordant analysis of Lon Nol in decline.

19. Meyer, *Derrière le sourire khmer*, 319.

20. Ibid., 315 ff.; *RC*, March 28, 1970; U.S. Embassy Phnom Penh's 2057, September 26, 1970; interview with Keuky Lim, May 1988; Lim was an assemblyman at the time. One of the three voting for Sihanouk, Mme Pung Peng Cheng, told Lim about it afterward. The other two, ironically, were later killed by pro-Sihanouk mobs in Kompong Cham; Soth Polin interview, October 1988. For a defense of the coup, see Douc Rasy, *Khmer Representation at the United Nations: A Question of Law or Politics?* (London, 1974), 22 ff.

21. U.S. Embassy Phnom Penh's 310, March 23, 1970. Pro-Sihanouk demonstrations occurred only after Sihanouk's call to arms, broadcast from China on March 23. It would be unwise, in terms of the evidence available, to assert that the coup was popular among Cambodia's rural poor, but few Cambodians took up arms on Sihanouk's behalf.

22. Interview with So Bun Hor, February 1989; Shawcross, *Sideshow*, 125; Sihanouk, *L'Indochine vue de Pékin*, 109.

23. For Sihanouk's view, see "La calice," 12. On purity, interview with Alain Daniel, November 1987.

24. Sihanouk, *L'Indochine vue de Pékin*, 109, Pomonti and Thion, *Des courtesans aux partisans*, 238 ff. Saloth Sar's mission to Hanoi, like Sihanouk's conduct over March 19–22 is crucial, but available sources are contradictory. It is unclear why Saloth Sar was in Hanoi in March 1970. Scattered evidence suggests that he left Cambodia for Vietnam at the end of 1969, perhaps to attend Ho Chi Minh's funeral.

25. On Pham's promise, interviews with Keuky Lim and So Bun Hor, February

1989. Both men were friends of Nay Valentin and claimed to have heard the story from him.

26. So Bun Hor interview, February 1989. See *L'Indochine vue de Pékin,* 127–28.

27. Text printed as appendix 5 in Caldwell and Tan, *Cambodia in the Southeast Asian War,* 389–93. The phrase "social justice" is substituted for "liberty" in the French national motto, Liberty, Equality, and Fraternity.

28. False rumors that circulated at this time—e.g., that Princess Monique was half Vietnamese—cropped up in several interviews in the course of my research.

29. CPK activist from Heder interviews, pp. 53–54. The "three ghosts'" appeal appears as Appendix 6 in Caldwell and Tan, *Cambodia in the Southeast Asian War.*

30. See Ben Kiernan, "The 1970 Peasant Uprising against Lon Nol," in Kiernan and Boua, *Peasants and Politics,* 206–23, Kiernan, *HPP,* 302–03, J. Helary's account in "55 témoignages," 25–29, and *RC,* April 4, 1970, which blames Vietnamese and "Khmer Viet Minh" for instigating the peasants. See also Laura Summers, "Cambodia's Civil War," *Current History* (December 1972): 259–62. Sihanouk's estimate was tape-recorded and distributed in Kompong Cham by early May 1970; unnumbered document in Pike archives 5/70. Interviews with Kol Touch and François Ponchaud, May 1988. See In Tam, *Pii sathirnaqrot khmer mok rothabibal comruh* (From the Khmer Republic to the coalition government), *Nokor Khmer* (Salt Lake City), July 1986. On assemblymen in Prey Veng, see Earl A. Carr, "Origins of the Khmer Revolution" (Ph.D. diss., Southern Illinois University, 1977), 195.

31. See Kiernan, "The 1970 Peasant Uprising," 218–19. On postponement of republic, see Donald Kirk, *Tell It to the Dead* (New York, 1977), 133.

32. On Vietnamese expansion, see Gerald C. Hickey, "The War in Cambodia: Focus on Some of the Internal Factors Involved," RAND Report WN 7119 ARPA, October 1970, pp. 2–3 (Pike archives). See also Kuong Lumphon, "Report on Communist Party of Kampuchea," prepared April 1973 (U.S. embassy translation); Ben Kiernan kindly provided me with a copy of this document. Interview with Maj. Gen. Pok Sam An, February 1989.

33. T. D. Allman, "Honeymoon with Disaster," *FEER,* April 23, 1970. Assistant Secretary Marshall Green, visiting Cambodia for two days in July 1970, wrote, "Khmer nationalism is by far 'our' strongest asset in situation." U.S. Embassy Tokyo's 3245, July 7, 1970.

34. *FEER,* June 11, 1970, 27. In one incident, students from the Lycée Sisowath kidnapped four South Vietnamese officials and tortured them. In 1975, after the Communist victory, the remaining Vietnamese in Cambodia were repatriated to Vietnam.

35. See *NYT,* April 14 and 17, 1970. Lon Nol statement, *NYT,* April 21, 1970; communiqué, *RC,* April 24, 1970. See also J-C Pomonti, in "55 témoignages," 32–35, and W. von Marschall, *The War in Cambodia: Its Causes and Military Development* (London, 1975), 104. Shawcross, *Sideshow,* 132–33. Interview with E. C. Swank, November 1987.

36. See Shawcross, *Sideshow,* 128–60; Kiernan, *HPP,* 304–08; Tran Dinh Tao, *The Cambodian Incursion* (Washington, 1979); Douglas Pike, "Cambodia's War," *Southeast Asian Perspectives* (1971); *RC,* May 8, 1970; Central Intelligence Agency, SNIE 14. 3-1-70: "North Vietnamese Intentions in Indo-China," June 26, 1970; interview with Marshall Green, November 1987, and U.S. Embassy Tokyo's

3245, where Green comments, "Lon Nol bears striking resemblance to Suharto in appearance, manner, tone of voice, dress . . . and superstition." For Lon Nol's reactions to the incursion, see Henry Kamm, "After U.S. Withdrawal in Cambodia, Gloom" *NYT,* July 3, 1970.

37. T. D. Allman, "Is God Dead?" *FEER,* July 16, 1970. Sihanouk, "La calice," 265–66, 278–80; see also *Le Monde,* July 7, 1970, *NYT,* July 5, 1970; *RC,* July 10, 1970. See also U.S. Embassy Phnom Penh's 1697, August 18, 1970. According to Sim Kin, a Thanhist since the 1950s, Thanh was brought back as a means of keeping his Kampuchea Krom units loyal to Phnom Penh (interview, November 1987). Khmer Serei units in Thailand were also mobilized to help: interview with Lek Samoeun, February 1989.

38. Interview with W. H. Harben, November 1987; text, from *Revue de l'Armée,* no. 3 (1970), is in "55 témoignages," 44–46. See also "Guide pour soldats et cadres de l'armée," bilingual text, Phnom Penh, 1970; statement to Colby from Shawcross, *Sideshow,* 170. *NYT,* September 9, 1970. On Mam Prum Mani, *NYT,* October 28, 1970. Two years later, Mam was a captain in Lon Nol's army; he was called Friar Tuck by the Americans. *NYT,* August 13, 1972. See also U.S. Embassy Phnom Penh's airgram A-78, May 19, 1972.

39. On scarves and amulets, personal recollections, September 1970.

40. On ghost soldiers see U.S. Embassy Phnom Penh's 1939, September 12, 1970, and Shawcross, *Sideshow,* 227–28. Taing Kim Buon (interview, June 1989) claimed that high school students were often conscripted by being thrown into military trucks.

41. See T. D. Allman, "Cambodia: Where everyone loses," *FEER,* August 27, 1970. On start of Chenla 1, U.S. Embassy Phnom Penh's 1914, September 9, 1970; U.S. Embassy Phnom Penh's unn., September 10, 1970, and its 2077, September 29, 1970. "55 témoignages," 56. See also Arnold Abrams, "The Terrible Thing," *FEER,* December 5, 1970. See also Kirk, *Wider War,* 132.

42. See Becker, *When the War Was Over,* 145 ff.

43. See Sihanouk, *L'Indochine vu de Pékin,* 129 ff. By the early 1980s, Sihanouk was calling himself a rightist reactionary again. See Peter Schier and Manola Schier-Oum, *Interviews and Talks with Prince Norodom Sihanouk,* 23. David Brown, "Exporting Insurgency: The Communists in Cambodia," in *Indochina in Conflict,* ed. Joseph Zasloff and Alan Goodman (Lexington, Mass., 1972), 127.

44. The English language text appears as appendix 2 in Caldwell and Tan, *Cambodia in the Indo-China War.* Interview with Thiounn Mumm, May 1988. Mumm has claimed that the CPK (in the person of Ieng Sary) and Cambodian Communists in Hanoi (Keo Meas and Rath Samoeun) considered the manifesto "too soft."

45. *Livre noir,* 52 ff.

46. Kiernan, *HPP,* 310.

47. See Brown, "Exporting Insurgency," 130–31. On dombon 25, Heder interviews, 26. See also U.S. Embassy Phnom Penh's 5578, February 8, 1971, which reports that Khmer defectors from combined units "resented the high-handed treatment of the [Vietnamese] who would not give them good weapons and put them into exposed fighting positions."

48. Report no. 0 028 0216 71; Pike archives. Kiernan, *HPP,* 311, citing interview with Tea Sabun. See also unnumbered document (Pike archives, 5/70) which urges its readers to "organize a complete (Cambodian Communist) Party net-

work," adding that "although the Cambodian revolutionaries are enthusiastic, they are incapable. We have come to their help in time and provided them with quick assistance. . . . The Cambodian revolution is weak, and its organization loose. We have to strengthen it."

49. Pike archives, report no. 6 028 0177 71 (Cambodia, 12/70). The phrase "revolutionary organizations" (*angkar padevat*) should be read as a singular. On Pol Pot's gentle, insidious manner of speaking, see Soth Polin, "La diabolique douceur de Pol Pot," *Le Monde,* May 18, 1980; interview, October 1988, and his letter to author, December 1988.

50. See Kiernan, *HPP,* 323 ff.

51. A CIA report from Siem Reap in March 1972 also cited "fifteen moral principles"—rather than the Vietnamese twelve—as being taught by CPK cadre: Pike archives, 1/71, Document no. 01-1009–71, and Timothy Carney, ed., *Communist Party Power in Kampuchea (Cambodia): Documents and Discussion* (Ithaca, 1977), 50–51. See also Kuong Lumphon, "Report on the Communist Party of Kampuchea," 41, and CIA Report CS-311/02697–72, June 6, 1972. On tyrannization, see Andrew Walder, "Actually Existing Maoism," *Australian Journal of Chinese Affairs* 18 (July 1987): 155–66. See also François Ponchaud, "Social Change in the Vortex of Revolution," in Jackson, *Cambodia 1975–1978,* 151–78.

52. Pike archives, untitled document, 4/70. See also Central Intelligence Agency, "Communism and Cambodia," (n.d., ca. late 1971).

53. "Training Khmers in North Vietnam," in Pike archives, 3/73. See also confession of Men Tul, a.k.a. Sat, a Khmer doctor trained in North Vietnam (1978). Georges Boudarel, "La liquidation des communistes cambodgiens formés au Vietnam (*tap ket*)," *Problèmes politiques et sociaux,* no. 373 (1979): 5–7, and U.S. Embassy Phnom Penh's airgram A-5, January 10, 1972, "Khmer Rouge Rallier Keoun Kun."

54. See U.S. Embassy Phnom Penh's airgram A-179, "Conversations with Khmer Rouge Rallier Ieng Lim," November 30, 1971, and Kiernan, *HPP,* 179.

55. On military strength, Kiernan, *HPP,* 322, citing CIA analyst Sam Adams, and U.S. Embassy Phnom Penh's 6033, January 7, 1972, citing Khmer Republic assessments "which conclude that significant progress in the 'Khmerization' of enemy combat units is being realized." Some cadre from Hanoi survived under DK until 1976–77, when they were purged.

56. See, for example, Saeng Hel, *Yum min chenh tuk pnaek* (Weeping without tears) (Phnom Penh, 1971), a novel about South Vietnamese atrocities.

57. On Lon Nol's stroke, see U.S. Embassy Phnom Penh's 2996, February 8, 1971, *NYT,* February 11, 1970, CINCPAC's NODIS telegram to Phnom Penh, February 19, 1971, which diagnosed "diabetes, hypertension, and a cerebral thrombosis of the right middle cerebral artery, with complete paralysis of the left arm and partial paralysis of the left leg." Interview Brigadier Thach Ren, November 1986.

58. Interview with Brig. Gen. Theodore Mataxis, February 1989; Shawcross, *Sideshow,* 190 ff.; interview with E. C. Swank, November 1987. In his interview with Shawcross in 1977, Mataxis called Cambodia "a holding action. . . . The troika's going down the road and the wolves are closing in, and so you throw them something off and let them chew it." Shawcross, *Sideshow,* 191. See also T. A. Mataxis, "Cambodia: A New Model for Military Assistance," *Army* (January 1973): 26–30.

59. Henry Kamm, "Cambodia Is Vigilant and Restrained One Year after the

Ouster of Sihanouk," *NYT,* March 19, 1971, which quotes Douc Rasy: "Cambodia has awakened, but remains too contemplative." "55 témoignages," 67. See also U.S. Embassy Phnom Penh's 1348, March 22, 1971.

60. Shawcross, *Sideshow,* 136. Buddhist conferences in McCain's NODIS telegram of March 24, 1971, and his EXDIS cable of April 3, released by CINCPAC under FOIA. On Lon Nol's letters to McCain, U.S. Embassy Phnom Penh's 2925, June 15, and 3082, June 23, 1971. On 1955 proposal, interview with Sim Var, November 1987. Brigadier General Mataxis, interviewed in February 1989, said that Lon Nol in 1971 was "a very sick man, who got even sicker."

61. In Tam memoir, 16–20; U.S. Embassy Phnom Penh's 2120, May 3, 1971; Robert Norton, "Cambodia's Reluctant Dragons," *FEER,* May 8, 1971; Milton Osborne, "Effacing the God King," in *Indochina in Conflict,* ed. Zasloff and Goodman, 73 ff. Henry Kamm, "After the Cambodian Political Crisis," *NYT,* May 1, 1971; U.S. Embassy Phnom Penh's 3384, July 12, 1971; interview with E. C. Swank, November 1987.

62. U.S. Embassy Phnom Penh's 4448, September 7, 1971, 4854, September 27, 1971. Interview with General Mataxis, February 1989. On the campaign, see also von Marschall, *The Khmer Republic,* 108.

63. See T. D. Allman, "In Cambodia Two's Company," *FEER,* October 2, 1971; In Tam memoirs, 21–22; on "misinterpretations" of Lon Nol's statement, see SWB/FE 3820/Bl. See also U.S Embassy Phnom Penh's 5287, October 18, 1971; 5413, October 25, 1971; and 5565, November 1, 1971; *RC,* October 22, 1971; *NYT,* October 17–22, 1971; interviews with E. C. Swank and Wiliam Harben, November 1987.

64. Interview, General Mataxis, February 1989; Mataxis, "Cambodia: A New Model," 27; Department of State's 225740 to Saigon, December 15, 1971.

65. BBC/SWB/FE 3863/A3/1; Shawcross, *Sideshow,* 202–04; Kiernan, *HPP,* 330–31; *NYT,* November 24–25, 1971, December 2, 1971; Judith Coburn, "The Army Nurses Its Wounds," *FEER,* December 18, 1971. Interviews with William Harben and Marshall Green, November 1987.

66. *RC,* November 12, 1971. Ambassador Swank (interview, November 1987) referred to the "sunny emissaries"—usually military figures—sent repeatedly by the United States to encourage Lon Nol in brief, ceremonial stopovers. None of the visitors saw fit to spend the night. For a sober assessment, see Department of State's 225740 to Saigon, December 15, 1971.

67. During my research, two former Lon Nol soldiers told me that they had returned to civilian life in 1973, when they realized that they were no longer fighting Vietnamese, but Khmer. Michael Vickery and Kate Frieson encountered the same evidence in interviews. Frieson's research in progress will examine the early stages of the revolution and its impact on ordinary people.

68. Shawcross, *Sideshow,* 187.

69. Kiernan, *HPP,* 327–28; Vorn Vet confession (typescript). Chhim Somuk's confession (1978) refers to the meeting as a party congress. Keo Meas, who remained in Hanoi, was the front's ambassador to Beijing before being purged in 1976.

70. On Ieng Sary's mission, see Becker, *When the War Was Over,* 154. The declaration is printed as appendix 9 in Caldwell and Tan, *Cambodia in the Southeast Asian War.* The decision to combine September 30 (from 1960) and 1951 to

form a composite anniversary for the CPK's foundation seems to have been made in 1971.

71. See Kiernan, *HPP,* 328–29. In 1978, a Vietnamese cadre stated that the Vietnamese had considered "deposing" Saloth Sar at this time. Gareth Porter, "Vietnamese Policy and the Indochina Crisis," in *The Third Indo-China War,* ed. David W. P. Elliott (Boulder, 1981), 92*n*129.

72. Kiernan, *HPP,* 330. See CIA document 06 028 0179 72 (Pike archives).

73. Report no. 6 028 0079 72 (Pike archives, 10/71; document captured in Prey Veng). See also report number 6 029 0403 72 (Pike archives, 10/72). On purges, see Boudarel, "La liquidation des communistes cambodgiens"; Heder interviews, 33; Kiernan, *HPP,* 336 ff. At the same time, there is evidence that Vietnamese-trained cadre were still entering Cambodia in 1974, at least in the Eastern Zone (see "Briefing by [Khmer Communist] Province Committee, Prey Veng," unnumbered text, Pike archives, 4/1974).

74. In May 1972, the U.S. embassy, using Khmer Republic figures, estimated CPK armed strength at about forty thousand men. U.S. Embassy Phnom Penh's 7436, May 20, 1972. Kiernan, *HPP,* 341 ff; for "guideline document," see report 6 028 0978 71 (9/71, Pike archives). CIA report CS 311/02967–72, June 6, 1972, and report 6 028 0201 72 (Pike archives, Cambodia, 1/72).

75. Thion and Kiernan, *Khmers rouges!* 41–97. For Thion's subsequent views, see "The Cambodian Idea of Revolution," in Chandler and Kiernan, *Revolution and Its Aftermath,* 10–33, and "The Pattern of Cambodian Politics," in *The Cambodian Agony,* ed. David Ablin and Marlowe Hood (Armonk, N.Y., 1987), 149–64.

76. U.S. Embassy Phnom Penh's 2018, July 9, 1973. See Ith Sarin, *Sranoh prolung Khmer* (Regrets of the Khmer soul) (Phnom Penh, 1974), 18–20, and Kuong Lumphon, "Report on the Communist Party of Kampuchea," 13–14. Translations in Timothy Carney, *Communist Party Power in Kampuchea,* 42–60. Ith Sarin interview, October 1988.

77. Youn's remarks in Ith Sarin, *Sranoh prolung Khmer,* 35–36 (not translated in Carney). See also Kiernan, *HPP,* 344. On conditions in the Special Zone, see Heder interviews, 21–22, 26. Other figures in the zone at this time included Norodom Phurissara, Phok Chhay, Vorn Vet, Khieu Ponnary (Saloth Sar's wife), and a Sino-Khmer from Kompong Thom, Khaing Khek Iev, known as Deuch, later the supervisor of the DK's interrogation center (S-21) at Tuol Sleng. Ith Sarin recalled him as being ill-tempered, impatient, and doctrinaire.

78. Carney, *Communist Party Power in Kampuchea,* 42–52; Kuong Lumphon, "Report on the Communist Party of Kampuchea," 28–29.

79. Ith Sarin, *Sranoh prolung Khmer,* 73–74; Kuong Lumphon, "Report on the Communist Party of Kampuchea," 32. The austere ceremonies of the CPK struck many participants as being straightforward and appealing.

80. Shawcross, *Sideshow,* 251–55; and see Elizabeth Becker, "Who Are the Khmer Rouge?" *Washington Post,* March 10, 1974. Kuong Lumphon, "Report on the Communist Party of Kampuchea," 46. See also U.S. Embassy Phnom Penh's 5567, June 26, 1973. Ith Sarin interview, October 1988.

81. *NYT,* March 12, 1972; *RC,* March 17, 1972; Judith Coburn, "And Now, a King in Khaki," *FEER,* March 18, 1972.

82. T. J. S. George, "Last Round for Lon Nol," and Judith Coburn, "Magic in His Method," *FEER,* March 25, 1972; Shawcross, *Sideshow,* 229 ff.; In Tam

memoir, 26–27; von Marschall, *The Khmer Republic,* 111–12; on student disaffection with the government in early 1972, see "55 témoignages," 86–87.

83. On the constitutional referendum, see Laura Summers, "The Cambodian Civil War," *n* 9. See also Khmer Republic, *Constitution de la République Khmere,* May 10, 1972. For American views of Cambodian politics at this time, see Shawcross, *Sideshow,* 232.

84. On elections, In Tam memoir, 29–30, and Shawcross, *Sideshow,* 228–30. In Tam memoir, 85–86. Interview with E. C. Swank, November 1987, during which he commented, "Lon Nol was part of the hand I was dealt" and added, "It was impossible, all the time I was there, to carry out a sensible conversation with him." The embassy, nonetheless, reported the election as a "step forward for Cambodian democracy." See U.S. Embassy Phnom Penh's 6191, September 17, 1972.

85. *NYT,* June 6, 1972; data on elections from In Tam memoir, 29–30, and Shawcross, *Sideshow,* 232–34. Sim Var was not allowed to run, on the grounds that his wife was Japanese: *RC,* June 10, 1972. Tan Bun Sor interview, May 1987. On national movement, *NYT,* June 22, 1972, and *RC,* June 24, 1972. The election included a supposedly left-wing party by means of which Lon Nol hoped to contact the CPK. One candidate was Saloth Sar's brother, Saloth Chhay, who gained over four thousand votes in Phnom Penh. Justin Corfield kindly provided data on this election.

86. *NYT,* September 30, 1972, calls the Socio-Republican sweep "unexpected."

87. See Boris Baczynskyj, "Socio-cynicism," *FEER,* October 28, 1972.

88. On Khmer-Mon project, Harben interview, November 1987, and U.S. Embassy Phnom Penh's airgram A-78, May 15, 1972; on tailoring, Jacques Nepote, personal communication. See also Martin, *Le mal cambodgien,* 132, and the document "Neo-Khmerisme," written by Lon Nol in 1972. Harben's analysis of Cambodian phobia about Vietnamese in 1972, drawn from local papers, is in U.S. Embassy Phnom Penh's airgram A-131, August 22, 1972.

89. On governor, Harben papers. On phantom soldiers, *NYT,* November 26 and December 28, 1972, and In Tam memoir, 45–46. Lon Nol's remark, Harben interview. By mid-1972, the embassy no longer prepared reports on corruption for internal distribution. See Shawcross, *Sideshow,* 271, 314–15. In June, 1972, according to the U.S. embassy, the marshal was convinced that "the Khmer Communist Movement does not pose a serious threat to his government": U.S. Embassy Phnom Penh's 7676, June 14, 1972.

90. Kissinger visit, *NYT,* October 22 and November 6, 1972. According to Elizabeth Becker, "Three Ghosts," *FEER,* February 12, 1973, three of the four North Vietnamese infantry divisions stationed in Cambodia in 1972 had gone home by the end of the year.

91. In Tam memoir, 37–38; Harben diary, February 11, 1972; Central Intelligence Agency, Vietnam Special Studies Group, "The Situation in Cambodia, April, 1973," 23–24; *NYT,* January 28 and February 28, 1972. Shawcross, *Sideshow,* 263. See Henry Kamm, "Cambodia, Mired in War, Looks to U.S. as Only Help," *NYT,* February 16, 1973. See also Donald Kirk, "Cambodia 1973," *Asia Survey,* January 1974, 89-100.

92. In 1976, after two years spent "growing rice" and one as a helicopter instructor under Pol Pot, Pech Kim Luon defected to the West.

93. *NYT,* March 18-19, 1973; Elizabeth Becker, "A Surfeit of Pretexts," *FEER,* March 26, 1973, "The mosquito catchers," *FEER,* April 9, 1973, and Donald Kirk, "Cambodia 1973," 92.

94. *NYT,* March 18 and 24, 1973; *Washington Post,* April 25, 1973; In Tam memoir, 40–41, von Marschall, *The Khmer Republic,* 113–14; CIA/VNSSG, "Cambodia in April 1973," 24–25. Interview with Tan Bun Suor, May 1988. On Lon Non, see *Washington Post,* May 2, 1973. On In Tam, London *Times,* May 11, 1973. On cabinet, *Washington Post,* May 16, 1973.

95. CIA SNIE 57–73 (released under FOIA).

96. *NYT,* April 30, 1973. Heder interviews, 35. On Lon Nol's dependence, see R. Evans and R. Novak, "In Cambodia, A Crutch of Bombs," *Washington Post,* May 7, 1973. U.S. Embassy Phnom Penh's 6934, July 10, 1973. Shawcross, *Sideshow,* 296–99, argues that U.S. bombing halted the Communists' assault on Phnom Penh, "[stamping] out thousands and thousands" of young revolutionaries in the process. For an analysis of the effects of the bombing, see Kiernan, *HPP,* 351–57, and Becker, *When the War Was Over,* 170-171. On Lon Nol government's view, see U.S. Embassy Phnom Penh's 2565, August 13, 1973. Haig-Nixon exchange in Jerrold Schecter, *The Palace File* (New York, 1986), 203. See also Ben Kiernan, "The American Bombardment of Kampuchea, 1969-1973," *Vietnam Generation,* Winter 1989, 4–41. Military historian Earl H. Telford, Jr. (letter to author, March 1990) has pointed out that the bombing campaign in Cambodia suffered in terms of accuracy because without forward air controllers, the B-52s had to hit prearranged targets rather than troop concentrations.

97. Harben diary.

98. CIA VSSG, "Situation July 1973," estimates five thousand Vietnamese combat troops, and supporting forces "on the order of 20,000"; Samphan quotation in unnumbered document, Pike archives (7–73). On the purges, see Interrogation Report 058/74, March 21, 1974, and unnumbered report May 11, 1974, Pike archive (3–74, 5–74). See also Philip McCombs,"Hanoi Cools on Rebels," *Washington Post,* June 23, 1974: "In Cambodia, there is no known Khmer political party or force that is primarily loyal to Hanoi."

99. Shawcross, *Sideshow,* 298, drawing on an interview with General Vogt. But see Vogt's letter to Enders disputing Shawcross's claims, in Henry Kissinger, *Years of Upheaval* (New York, 1979), 1227–30. On Khieu Samphan, FBIS, January 6, 1976. See also Kiernan, "The American Bombardment," 32 ff.

100. On collectivization, Kiernan, *HPP,* 380–88, and Heder interviews, 54.

101. "Summary of Annotated Party History" (captured document, U.S. Embassy translation). See Kiernan, *HPP,* 364 ff.; Becker, *When the War War Was Over,* 157–59. See also Chandler, Kiernan, and Boua, *Pol Pot Plans the Future,* 213–26. For a comparison between this text and one circulated in 1974 by Ieng Sary, see Kiernan, *HPP,* 364–67. The latter text plays down the role played by the ICP in the early days of the party. The differences suggest that for CPK ideology 1973 was a decisive turning point.

102. Monique Sihanouk, "Voyage Historique au Cambodge en 1973," in *Bulletin mensuel de documentation* (March-April, May-June, and July-August 1987). Julio Jeldres (personal communication) has noted that the extracts represent only a fraction of the original manuscript.

103. Hu Nim, in his 1977 confession, referred to the "villa and beautiful accommodation" prepared for Sihanouk by Koy Thuon, the zone commander, already purged when Hu Nim was arrested. See Chandler, Kiernan, and Boua, *Pol Pot Plans the Future,* 265. Sok Pirun, a schoolteacher in Siem Reap, learned of the visit from friends in army intelligence soon after it occurred (interview, February 1990).

104. In the photo album of the trip, Khieu Ponnary, unlike other CPK wives (e.g., Mme Hou Youn, Mme Koy Thuon), retains her maiden name in the captions.

105. *NYT Magazine,* August 12, 1973.

106. See H. Greenway, "Men of the Forest Visit," *Washington Post,* August 8, 1973, and *RC,* February 21, 1975, where a Khmer peasant told a French newsman that "the revolution has no altars or images, and its leaders have no names."

107. Figures from *London Times,* August 18, 1973. See also CIA VSSG, "The Situation in Cambodia October 1973," 29; A Correspondent, "A Ripe Fruit, Getting Riper," *FEER,* August 13, 1973, and Fox Butterfield, "Cambodian Rebels Reported in Fight with Hanoi Force," *NYT,* August 26, 1973. On incoming refugees, see Gareth Porter and George Hildebrand, *Cambodia: Starvation and Revolution* (New York, 1976), 22–26.

108. For Swank's valedictory, see U.S. Embassy Phnom Penh's 2806, August 31, 1973. On Vietnamese refusal to reinforce Cambodian troops, see Philip McCombs, "Cambodian Victims' Rancor Recedes," *Washington Post,* February 14, 1974. Elizabeth Becker, "The Agony of Phnom Penh," *Washington Post,* January 28, 1974, and T. D. Allman, "Deeper into the Mire," *FEER,* January 7, 1974. By June 1974, the Communists had captured forty-two howitzers, and "about 20 were thought to be operational." *NYT,* June 18, 1974. Kiernan, "The American Bombardment," 36, states that CPK propaganda in rural areas in 1973 claimed that the bombers had come from Phnom Penh, intensifying antiurban feelings, as intended.

109. On governorships, interview with You Kan, November 1987. See also Soth Polin, *L'anarchiste,* 130–34. Interviews with Soth Polin, October 1988, February 1989.

110. On Dean, see Shawcross, *Sideshow,* 326 ff., and Philip McCombs, "A Man of the Middle Road," *Washington Post,* March 27, 1974.

111. On rocket and artillery attacks, see Mike Snitowsky, "Phnom Penh's Deadly Curiosity," *FEER,* March 4, 1974, and U.S Embassy Phnom Penh's 1237, March 11, 1974, which suggests that the regime should be able to use the attacks to intensify its control of the population, including "'third force' and leftist elements [who] may spawn more misguided peace initiatives." On phrase "strategic offensive," Heder interviews, 56. On Son Sann's abortive proposal, *FEER,* February 4, 1974. Son Sann's visit with Dean, interview with S. Suon Kaset, May 1987.

112. On Udong attack, see Donald Kirk, "Revolution and Political Violence in Cambodia, 1970–1974," in *Communism in Indo-China: New Perspectives,* ed. Joseph Zasloff and McAlister Brown (Lexington, Mass., 1986), 215–30, *RC,* May 11, 1974, and *Washington Post,* March 19, 1974. On CPK strategy, see Colin Smith, "Rebel Shells Get Too Close for Comfort, *Observer,* January 24, 1974. On abolition of council, *Washington Post,* March 31 and April 1, 1974.

113. "Briefing by Prey Veng Province Committee on Central Committee Instructions," unnumbered document (Pike archives, 3/74). Elsewhere in the east, Hanoi-trained cadre were "struggled" in mid-1974 by regional cadre: Kiernan, *HPP,* 386.

114. See Soth Polin, *L'anarchiste,* 130 ff. By April 1974, inflation was running at 150 percent; exit visas cost a million riels (approximately $600 at the black market rate of exchange). Sydney Schanberg, "Life Deteriorates as Cambodian Capital Struggles On," *NYT,* November 28, 1974.

115. Philip McCombs, "Murder in Cambodia," *Washington Post,* June 9, 1974, draws on eyewitness accounts. See also Mike Snitowski, "Tragedy in a

Phnom Penh School," *FEER*, June 10, 1974. Heder appears as Mike in *L'anar-chiste*, 179–80. Details in the paragraph have been verified with Heder (personal communication). The assassin was never found, and a journalist commented later that the murderers "could be the Communists, the students [or] the government." The U.S. embassy believed that Communists had killed the two men to inflame student opinion. Stephen Heder corroborated this theory in 1981, when he ran across one of the men who had been imprisoned as an accomplice. This man told him that the assassination had been carried out by a CPK "hit squad" from the Eastern Zone.

116. On Udong, see Philip McCombs, "Oudong's splendor ground to dust," *Washington Post*, August 20, 1974; on Kompong Seila, Sydney Schanberg, "A Besieged Cambodian Garrison Fights On," *NYT*, August 16, 1974; on cannibalism there, Bowden, *One Crowded Hour*, 194 ff.; on casualties, Sydney Schanberg, "War Exacts a Huge Toll on Cambodia," *NYT*, August 22, 1974. In Bucharest, Sihanouk told an interviewer that the war "was like putting a tiger and a dog in the same cage"; the tiger's devouring the dog was only a matter of time. *NYT*, August 25, 1974. The phrase "Cambodian Desk Officer" is Ambassador Swank's (interview, November 1987).

117. See H. D. Greenway, "A Child Dies in Phnom Penh," *Washington Post*, February 6, 1975; Sydney Schanberg, "Life of Phnom Penh Slowly Grinds Down," *NYT*, March 8, 1975, and Porter and Hildebrand, *Cambodia: Starvation and Revolution*, 34 ff. On river mines, Kiernan, *HPP*, 412, drawing on Frank Snepp, *Decent Interval* (Harmondsworth, 1977), 101.

118. U.S. Embassy Phnom Penh's 5612, March 29, 1975. This extraordinary document, released under FOIA in April 1990, foreshadows the U.S. "tilt" toward China and the *pro-Chinese* Red Khmers over the next decade and a half.

119. Pung Peng Cheng, Sihanouk's *chef de cabinet* in Beijing in 1975, kindly provided me with the draft text of this letter. A truncated version appears in Debré, *Révolution dans le forêt*, 208–09.

120. Interview with Julio Jeldres, November 1988. See also Shawcross, *Sideshow* (1981 edition), 360, and "additions to new edition," 409.

121. Shawcross, *Sideshow*, 362. See also Arnold Isaacs, *Without Honor* (Baltimore, 1983), 274 ff.

122. Sihanouk's physician, Armand Riche, had telephoned Matak's brother, Sisowath Essaro, in Paris urging him to tell Matak to leave Phnom Penh on the eve of the final attack. Matak refused. Interview with Olary Sisowath, February 1989. For a detailed account of the last few days of the Khmer Republic, see Justin Corfield, "The Political Machinations of the Khmer Republic, 12–18 April 1975" (B.A. Honours diss., University of Hull, 1987).

123. Shawcross, *Sideshow*, 362. Jean-Jacques Cazeau, "Witness to a Nation's Death," *Washington Post*, May 8, 1975. "Some of Last Messages from Encircled Capital," *NYT*, April 18, 1975.

Chapter Seven. Revolution in Cambodia, 1975–1979

1. Quotation from FBIS Daily Report, January 6, 1976.

2. See Serge Thion, "The Cambodian Idea of Revolution," in Chandler and Kiernan, *Revolution and Its Aftermath*, 10–33, and his "The Pattern of Cambodian Politics," in Ablin and Hood, *The Cambodian Agony*, 149–64. See also Timo-

thy Carney, "The Unexpected Victory," in *Cambodia 1975–1978,* ed. Jackson, 13–36, and Kate Frieson, "The Political Nature of Democratic Kampuchea," *Pacific Affairs* (hereafter *PA*) (Fall 1988): 405–27.

3. See, e.g., FBIS, January 20, 1976, for a reference to the "clear-sighted leadership of the organization" rather than named individuals. See also Jean Pouget, "Cambodge: La folle expérience d'un ordre nouveau," *Le Figaro,* May 31, 1976. In November 1975, Sihanouk, after returning to Cambodia, said, "The national front over which I preside is a model of monolithic unity." FBIS, November 7, 1975. There are clear continuities between the Khmer linguistics studied by Keng Vannsak in the 1950s, Lon Nol's Khmer-Monism (of which Keng Vannsak was a leading proponent), and the idea of exclusiveness claimed by Cambodian revolutionaries. On the idea of intellectuals' privileged language, see Alvin W. Gouldner, "Prologue to a Theory of Revolutionary Intellectuals," *Telos* 27:3–36.

4. See, for example, "Chaiyo kongto'p padevat reboh pak kommunist kampuchea" (Hail the revolutionary army of the CPK), *Tung Padevat* (August 1975), 24–65. See also Grant Evans, *Lao Peasants under Socialism* (New Haven, 1990), chap. 9.

5. Pol Pot speech of September 29, 1977, 26: "It was from the landlords that the peasants suffered the worst, most varied, and most direct exploitation." William Willmott, "Analytical Errors of the Kampuchean Communist Party," *PA* (Summer 1981): 209–27, Jean Delvert, *Le paysan cambodgien* (Paris, 1961), 639, and Hu Nim, "Land Tenure and Social Structure in Kampuchea," in Kiernan and Boua, *Peasants and Politics in Kampuchea,* 69–86.

6. Thiounn Mumm interview, May 1988. See Laura Summers, "Co-operatives in Democratic Kampuchea," unpublished paper, 28–29. Ian Cummins traced the Axelrod quotation for me. Khieu Samphan's speech about the DK constitution (FBIS, January 5, 1976) asserted that "total equality already exists in Cambodian society."

7. FBIS, November 4, 1975. In 1972, Ieng Sary had remarked that "political consciousness is the decisive weapon" (cited in Ponchaud, *Cambodia Year Zero,* 108). Kathleen Gough, "Roots of the Pol Pot Regime in Kampuchea," in *Themes in Ethnology and History,* ed. L. Donald (Meerut, 1987), 125–74, refers (139–41) to "the darker side of Maoism" as providing the basis for DK ideology, breaking this down into fourteen points; the seventh is "a utopian and idealist disregard of (*sic*) material and objective conditions; an apocalyptic voluntarism."

8. See "Chaiyo kongto'p," 29–30: "This event has never happened before in the history of the world. For this reason, other countries have taken our victory, and our revolutionary army, as models for the international Communist movement! a model in the world's revolutionary movement! a model for countries that have just liberated themselves!" The Shining Path guerrillas in Peru seem to be CPK's legitimate heirs. A sociological comparison of the two movements would be rewarding.

9. See Ponchaud, *Cambodia Year Zero,* chap. 7, "The *Angkar* Gave Me a Second Life," 108 ff., and Pol Pot's July 1975 address, cited by Becker, *When the War Was Over,* 175: "Never before has there been such an event in the annals of the world's revolutionary wars." *Tung Padevat* (Revolutionary flags) for September 1978 noted that the Russian Revolution was "broken by Khrushchev" and that the "Chinese Revolution is fading." Kate Frieson kindly provided this quotation.

10. On the idea that DK constituted a revival of Angkorean slave conditions, see Gough, "Roots of the Pol Pot Regime," and Anthony Barnett, "Democratic

Kampuchea: A Highly Centralized Dictatorship," in Chandler and Kiernan, *Revolution and Its Aftermath*, 212–29.

11. For examples, see Someth May, *Cambodia Witness* (London, 1986), 120 ff. Many survivors of DK say that a major legacy of the regime was that it taught them to tell lies.

12. See Mao in *Red Flag*, June 1, 1958: "China's 600 million people have two remarkable peculiarities; they are poor and . . . blank. This may seem like a bad thing, but it is really a good thing. . . . A clean sheet of paper has no blotches, and so the newest and most beautiful words can be written on it, the newest and most beautiful pictures can be painted on it." Cited by M. Meisner, "Iconoclasm and Cultural Revolution in China and Russia," in *Bolshevik Culture*, ed. A. Gleeson et al. (Bloomington, 1985), *n* 14. Elsewhere, Mao had noted that poor peasants were "semi-private owners whose point of view is comparatively easily altered." See Mao Zedong, *A Critique of Soviet Economics*, trans. Moss Roberts (New York, 1977), 46.

13. "Khmer Communist Programs in Cambodia," unnumbered U.S. Embassy document (Pike archives, 3/75). Carney, "Organization of Power," in Jackson, *Cambodia 1975–1978*, 95. See Kiernan and Boua, *Peasants and Politics*, 335. Interview Hoeung Hing Kim, January 1989. FBIS, January 20, 1976, noted, "Our brothers and sisters were looked down upon, regarded as animals. They never had enough food, never were happy, and never had the opportunity to receive an education."

14. George Steiner, "Darkness Visible," *London Review of Books*, November 24, 1988. On unnervingly gentle language, Pin Yathay, *L'Utopie meurtrière* (Paris, 1981), chap. 6, "Ils administrent le mort avec des mots aimables," 135–64, Becker, *When the War Was Over*, 186–87, and interview with François Bizot, July 1989.

15. See FBIS, January 28, 1976. "Life histories," a new genre of Cambodian literature and thinking, were also used in recruiting members of the party. See Chandler, Kiernan, and Boua, *Pol Pot Plans the Future*, 203, and François Ponchaud, "Social Change," in Jackson, *Cambodia 1975–1978*, 151–77.

16. Michael Vickery has noted resemblances between life in DK and in More's Utopia. See his *Cambodia 1975–1982*, 281: "The rigidly egalitarian communism, identical clothes and houses . . . , identical fixed working hours, mass lectures, communal farms and communal dining halls, shifting children out of families, strict rules on sexual morality, no money, and contempt for gold."

17. See Timothy Carney, "The Organization of Power," in Jackson, *Cambodia 1975–1978*, 79–106. On messengers, see Ong Thong Hoeung, "Illusions perdues," MS (Brussels, n.d.), 63, which quotes the song. The first batch of young men recuited as interrogators at S-21 (Tuol Sleng) were drawn from messengers in dombon 25.

18. A sketch of the party flag appeared on the inside rear cover of the CPK's theoretical journal, *Tung Padevat*. The flag was also on display in dombon 42 during the 1976 elections (Hing Kim Than, personal communication).

19. On Vietnamese influence, interview with Stephen Heder, November 1986. See Laura Summers and Ong Thong Hoeung, "Statutes of the Communist Party of Kampuchea," in *The Party Statutes of the Communist World*, ed. W. B. Simons and S. White, 235–59, Sheila Fitzpatrick, *The Russian Revolution* (Oxford, 1984), 129–34, and William Joseph, "A Tragedy of Good Intentions: Post Mao Views of the Great Leap Forward," *Modern China* 12/4 (October 1986): 419–51. It is not clear if Pol Pot and his colleagues knew that China's Great Leap Forward had been a

failure. See also Kenneth Quinn, "Explaining the Terror," in Jackson, ed., *Cambodia 1975–1978,* 215–40.

20. See Y Phandara, *Retour à Phnom Penh* (Paris, 1981), 154. The parallels between the ideology of the Cultural Revolution and events in Cambodia seem too close and numerous to be coincidental and may spring in part from political training courses undertaken by high-ranking members of the CPK in China in the 1960s and 1970s. See Lloyd Dittmer and Ruoxi Chen, *Ethics and Rhetoric in the Chinese Cultural Revolution* (Berkeley, 1981), esp. 109 ff.

21. In 1978, Nuon Chea noted, "Some of our cadres who have lived overseas, and who worked with foreign Communist parties, regularly request foreign documents, claiming that we neglect the study of Marxism-Leninism. But we tell them that Marxism-Leninism develops by means of the struggle of the people; *our experiences are genuine Marxist-Leninist documents"*—emphasis added. Nuon Chea, "Statement of the CPK," 26. Some DK textbooks for geography and mathematics have survived as well as copies of the CPK journals *Tung Padevat* (Revolutionary flags) and *Yuveachun yuveaneari padevat* (Revolutionary youth). In most parts of the country, schools were reserved for "base people" and cadre's children.

22. See Maurice Meisner, "Leninism and Maoism" in *Marxism, Maoism and Utopianism* (Madison, 1982), 76–117. His remarks on Russian Populist thinking (82) are perceptive: "The ambivalent attitude toward tradition, i.e. that Russia's [or Cambodia's] special socialist potential rested on the uniqueness of Russian historical traditions on the one hand, and on the other that Russia was uniquely unburdened by tradition, occurs throughout Populist thought."

23. See Lowell Dittmer, *China's Continuous Revolution: The Post-Liberation Epoch, 1949–1981* (Berkeley, 1987). On Ieng Sary and the Gang of Four, see Chanda, *Brother Enemy,* 74. Ong Thong Hoeung has recalled a DK political meeting at which a speaker noted, "the Chinese made a cultural revolution for a brief period and then stopped. We are making a cultural revolution every day." Heder interviews, 12.

24. See Porter and Hildebrand, *Starvation and Revolution,* 39 ff.; Ponchaud, *Cambodia Year Zero,* 1–22; Bernard Hamel, *De sang et des larmes* (Paris, 1977), 1–178, and J. and J. Steinbach, *Phnom Penh Libérée* (Paris, 1976), 91 ff.

25. See Kiernan, *HPP,* 415–16, and Carney, "Unexpected Victory," in Jackson, ed., *Cambodia 1975–1978,* 3: "The party could not tolerate urban centers because it did not have the sophisticated cadre needed to control the towns." Of course, hating towns, the CPK had trained none of its cadre in urban administration. See also J. Ellul, *Le Monde,* November 8, 1975: "Combining policies of evacuating and dispersing people with changing their names as well leads to a radical uprooting of these people, thereby delivering them to those in power, like a new substance onto which it is possible to print anything at all."

26. See Meisner, "Utopian Socialist Themes in Maoism: The Relationship between Town and Countryside," in *Marxism, Maoism and Utopianism,* 28–75, and Rhoades Murphey, "City and Countryside as Ideological Issues," *Comparative Studies in Society and History* (1972), 250–67. On Kratie, see Ben Kiernan, "The American Bombardment of Kampuchea, 1969–1973," 19, citing the August 1975 issue of *Tung Padevat,* and interview Huy Huynh, February 1988.

27. Charles Meyer, "Rebuilding Cambodia: A Daring Gamble," *NYT,* May 16, 1975. "From a Maoist point of view," wrote Meyer, "the Cambodian revolution is exemplary." He went on to say that the "gap" between the revolutionaries and "Lon Nol officials" had become so wide that "the victory of the new over the old, the

pure over the corrupt, had to be total." See also Jacques Decornoy, *Le Monde,* July 18, 1975: "Revolutionary happiness, it seems, has transformed the human landscape." Laura Summers, "Consolidating the Cambodian Revolution," *Current History* (December 1975): 218–22. On April 18, a Red Khmer cadre told François Ponchaud, in Phnom Penh, "The city is bad, for there is money in the city. . . . People can be reformed, but not cities." Ponchaud, *Year Zero,* 21. See also Mao Zedong, in 1969: "Now we have entered the cities. This is a good thing. If we hadn't entered the cities, Chiang Kai Shek would still be occupying them. But it is also a bad thing, because it caused our party to deteriorate." Quoted in S. Schram, *Authority Participation and Cultural Change in China* (Cambridge, 1973), 99.

28. On malaria, see Pol Pot interview, *Vietnam Courier* (1976). Soon afterward, DK purchased several million dollars' worth of DDT from abroad, but malaria remained endemic in the DK period; even the top leadership succumbed to it from time to time.

29. It would have been difficult to collectivize urban populations, and collectivization was at the heart of the CPK's economic strategy. In 1978, a party document noted, "If there were no co-operatives, true revolutionary traits would be gone. The true imperialist traits would come back. Revisionism would come back. There would be markets, there would be cities." "Confusion, Slavery," *Tung Padevat,* March 1978, in Jackson, ed., *Cambodia 1975–1978,* 297.

30. Heder interviews, 28, 60. On Hou Youn's death, Kiernan, *HPP,* 416–17. No documentary evidence of his death has come to light. In Battambang, the evacuation was "explained" by the adage "We shall turn the city into countryside, and the countryside into a city": John Barron and Anthony Paul, *Murder of a Gentle Land* (New York, 1977), 37.

31. Martin Stuart-Fox and Ung Bunheang, *Murderous Revolution* (Sydney, 1985), 3, and Boun Sokha, *La massue d'Angkar* (Paris, 1979), 14–15. See also Sydney Schanberg, "The Enigma of Khmer Rouge Purpose," *Saturday Review,* August 23, 1975, 29–30, Yin Savannary, "Diary from Darkness," *National Review,* December 10, 1976, and Cazeau, as cited in Noam Chomsky and Edward Hermann, *After the Cataclysm* (Boston, 1979), 290: "Many had probably never seen a city street or a lawn before. Their appearance was equally shocking to many of the residents of Phnom Penh."

32. These paragraphs are drawn from published accounts and interviews with You Hon Chea, May 1987, Kol Touch, May 1988, Ung Bunheang and Ung Phiny, March 1987, Seng Kan, February 1989, and Mey Komphot, June 1989.

33. See also Barron and Paul, *Murder of a Gentle Land,* 9–10, Becker, *When the War Was Over,* 36 ff., and "Témoignages sur le genocide du Cambodge," special issue of *Item,* July–August 1976.

34. Interview You Hon Chea, May 1987. Chea's wife's supervisor was a clandestine member of the CPK and became a DK official in Prey Veng. Chea and his family relocated there in 1976. Sok Pirun (interview, January 1990) told a similar story of being protected by a friend who had disappeared in the 1960s and showed up in Phnom Penh as a high-ranking CPK cadre on April 17, 1975.

35. Touch had heard that when his son presented himself to CPK officials in 1973, he had to give up his pistol, perhaps mistaken as a sign of rank. "About thirty": interview with Ong Thong Hoeung, May 1988. Dorathy was executed at Tuol Sleng in 1977.

36. Interview with Kol Touch, May 1988.

37. Interviews with Kol Touch and Ong Thong Hoeung, May 1988. For the text

of the Four-Year Plan, see Chandler, Kiernan, and Boua, *Pol Pot Plans the Future,* 119–62.

38. On Battambang massacres, see Hamel, *De sang et des larmes,* 106 ff., Ponchaud, *Cambodia Year Zero,* 40 ff. Ty Sophen interview, January 1989.

39. See David P. Chandler with Ben Kiernan and Muy Hong Lim, "Conversations with Peang Sophi," in Kiernan and Boua, *Peasants and Politics,* 318–25; *Item,* 73–80; Ty Sophen interview, January 1989. See also the comments by Dith Pran, who had worked in Phnom Penh for the *New York Times.* He described Communist cadre in his village in Siem Reap: "They didn't even look like Cambodians, they seemed to be from the jungle, or a different world." To the cadre new people like Dith Pran were inauthentic Khmer.

40. For testimonies of people who lingered without permission in Phnom Penh, see Kiernan and Boua, *Peasants and Politics,* 339, *Item,* 46, and Martin, *Le mal cambodgien,* 169 ff. Another reason for evacuating the city was to make it secure for the CPK leaders when they arrived a week later.

41. The preprinted biographical forms were headed "Exodus Reception Committee": Carney, "Unexpected Victory," 33n20. The roads out of Phnom Penh were kept open for several months, with checkpoints for travelers heading into the city: interview Seng Kan, February 1989.

42. For a discussion of these issues, see Vickery, *Cambodia 1975–1982,* 27–63; Noam Chomsky and Edward S. Herman, *After the Cataclysm,* 135–294, and William Shawcross, "Cambodia: Some Perceptions of a Disaster," in Chandler and Kiernan, *Revolution and Its Aftermath,* 230–58.

43. FBIS, February 3, 1977. In much of the country, the time favored for executions was just after sunset, the time known in French as *entre chien et loup,* but executions also occurred at night.

44. On conditions in new villages, see Barron and Paul, *Murder of a Gentle Land,* 130–32. On resentful treatment of new arrivals by base people, interview with Chan Noral, June 1989. On youthful reactions, interviews with Suong Soriya, August 1987, Ung Phinny, September 1987, and Kae Sombath, November 1987.

45. The DK constitution (chapter 9, article 14) asserts that "it is the duty of all to build and defend the country." For a discussion of new language used by the regime, see François Ponchaud, "Le Kampuchea Démocratique," *Mondes asiatiques,* June, 1976, 153–80, and Laurence Picq, "De la réforme linguistique et l'usage des mots chez les khmers rouges," *Asie du sud-est et monde insulindien* 15 (1983): 351–57. John Marston's research in progress at the University of Washington will treat the phenomenon in detail.

46. For cadre testimony, see Martin, *Le mal cambodgien,* 165 ff., and FBIS, March 16, 1976.

47. Burchett, *The China-Cambodia-Vietnam Triangle,* 145. Interview with Thach Sok, October 1987. See also Stephen Heder,"Kampuchea's Armed Struggle: The Origins of an Independent Revolution," *BCAS* 11/1 (1979): 2–24. Kiernan, *HPP,* 414–16, argues that the CPK central committee seriously considered capturing Cambodian areas of South Vietnam in April and May 1975—a charge reiterated by Vietnamese and PRK sources in 1980. On the Vietnamese recapture of Wai island, *NYT,* June 14, 1975; Chanda, *Brother Enemy,* 14. See also FBIS, January 13, 1976: "Our Combatants Defend Territorial Waters" with "rifles in one hand, looking out to sea ready to destroy enemy aggressors, and a hoe in the other hand, for increased production."

48. *Newsweek,* May 26, 1975, cover story. The event gave Americans in the White House and the Department of State an intravenous injection of prestige:

"It's good to win one, for a change," a White House aide remarked. In retrospect there is something bizarre about the photographs of President Ford and his Cabinet colleagues cheering the "victory" at night, in dinner jackets. For a full account, see Roy Rowan, *The Four Days of Mayaguez* (New York, 1975).

49. See *NYT,* May 13–22, 1975, Summers, "Consolidating the Cambodian Revolution," 222, and Chanda, *Brother Enemy,* 12–13. Thach Sok saw "many" of the American dead. President Ford, talking to Rowan, called the incident a "spark that set off a whole new sense of confidence" in the American people. Rowan, *The Four Days,* 223. According to Chou Chet's confession, Saloth Sar and Nuon Chea were both seriously ill throughout the crisis, a fact that may have slowed the government's response.

50. On informal trade developing between Thailand and Cambodia in 1975, interview with Phan Wannamethee, July 1989. Petrol, rice, and sugar were traded at the border for ivory, gemstones, and Cambodian aniquities. On pleas for forces from the party leadership in April 1975, see confession by Soeu Van Si (Doeun), April 1977. See also *Tung Padevat,* August 1975, 24–65.

51. "Conversations with Peang Sophi," in Kiernan and Boua, *Peasants and Politics,* 324.

52. On industry, see Vickery, *Cambodia 1975–1982,* 80–81, and, for the later stages of DK, M. A. Martin, "L'industrie dans le Kampuchea Démocratique (1975–1978)," *Etudes rurales* (January-September 1983): 77–110, and Charles Twining, "The Economy," in Jackson, ed.,*Cambodia 1975–1978,* 109–50.

53. Elizabeth Becker noted that the CPK leaders she met in 1978 seemed obsessed with "quiet and order" and with "purity, cleanliness, order, total loyalty and obedience, and denial of emotions that might lead to abandon." Becker, *When the War Was Over,* 186–87.

54. Interview with Denise Affonço, November 1987. Interview with Hoeung Hong Kim, January 1989: "We looked like the Sudanese look on the television now. We moved with little tiny steps." On songs, see Im Proum's analysis in *NYT,* November 14, 1976. Im Proum and Kate Frieson kindly provided me with cassette recordings of several of these songs.

55. See Someth May, *Cambodian Witness* (London, 1986), 195–97. In some districts, people were encouraged to maintain notebooks containing charges made against them by themselves and others and their projects for personal reform. These were not checked, and Sisowath Aryavady has recalled filling hers with scurrilous French proverbs (interview, July 1989).

56. See M. A. Martin, "La riziculture et la maîtrise de l'eau dans le Kampuchea Démocratique," *Etudes rurales* (July-September 1981): 7–44. On the second evacuation, see Pin Yathay, *L'Utopie meurtrière,* 121 ff., and Someth May, *Cambodian Witness,* 140 ff.

57. "Sihanouk's Return: Death of a Dream," *FEER,* October 24, 1975.

58. *NYT,* October 13, 1975, and interview Pung Peng Cheng, November 1987; Sihanouk, *Prisonnier des khmers rouges* (Paris, 1987), 16–17. See also Chanda, *Brother Enemy,* 42–43.

59. Louis Halasz, "Grey Verbiage from the Prince," *FEER,* October 24, 1975.

60. The party congress referred to here occurred in May 1975.

61. For a translation of the constitution, see Ponchaud, *Cambodia Year Zero,* 199–206. See also David P. Chandler, "The Constitution of Democratic Kampuchea: The Semantics of Revolutionary Change," *PA* (Fall 1976): 506–15. The lyrics of the national anthem were supposedly written by Pol Pot.

62. In February 1976, Khieu Samphan told Sihanouk that the "western" cus-

tom of weekly rest days was inapplicable to DK "because the workers don't want it." *Prisonnier des khmers rouges,* 58. See also Laurence Picq, *Au delà du ciel* (Paris, 1984), 143–44, in which Ieng Sary, in 1978, referred to the forty-hour week as the creation of "revisionist unions" in the West. In DK, he boasted, "we're a long way from the unemployment created by capitalism."

63. On Sihanouk's trip to the north, see *Prisonnier des khmers rouges,* 55–82, and FBIS, January 21, 1976.

64. According to Keng Vannsak (interview, November 1986), Saloth Sar had used the nickname Pol (or Paul) while a student in Paris. See also M. A. Martin, *Le mal cambodgien,* 159. Ruos Mau's 1977 confession suggests that he had also used the name Pol while working with the Pracheachon in 1955. The names of the winners were broadcast after the election, with the news that 98 percent of eligible voters had gone to the polls (FBIS, March 21, 1976).

65. See Ung Bunheang's account in Stuart-Fox and Ung Bunheang, *The Murderous Revolution,* 70, and Carney, "The Organization of Power," 90. For the central committee meeting, discussed below, see "Decisions of the Central Committee on a Variety of Questions," in Chandler, Kiernan, and Boua, *Pol Pot Plans the Future,* 1–8, esp. 2. See also *Prisonnier des khmers rouges,* 98–99, where Sihanouk suggests that there was a slate of several candidates. In Peter Schier and Manola Schier-Oum, eds., *Prince Sihanouk of Cambodia: Interviews and Talks* (Hamburg, 1985), 25, Sihanouk, forgetful of his years in power, called the election a joke because "all the candidates had been chosen by Pol Pot."

66. On the 1951–60 controversy, see Chandler, Kiernan, and Boua, *Pol Pot Plans the Future,* Preface. In August 1976 Ong Thong Hoeung was on a work team breaking up the slabs of concrete from the destroyed cathedral, looking for steel reinforcing rods to use in forging agricultural tools. See Ong Thong Hoeung, "Illusions perdues," 41–42.

67. Sihanouk knew nothing of the meeting. See also Edith Lenart, "Power behind the Throne," *FEER,* May 28, 1976. Between Zhou's death and Mao's, nine months later, China went through an ultraleftist phase. These months coincided with the heyday of the Gang of Four.

68. See *Prisonnier des khmers rouges,* 135–242, and Sihanouk's interview with *Le Matin,* January 29, 1979 (FBIS, February 8, 1979): "We were well fed each day. They gave us enough calories. Since I like cooking they gave us some beef once and on other occasions pork and duck, as well as lots of vegetables and fruit. . . . But I was virtually a prisoner."

69. Pech Kim Luon interview with Bruce Palling, April 1976. Ben Kiernan kindly provided a transcript of this text.

70. See Anthony Barnett, "Democratic Kampuchea: A Highly Centralized Dictatorship," in Chandler and Kiernan, *Revolution and Its Aftermath,* 212–29. See also the two perceptive studies Department of State, "Information on Conditions and Events in Kampuchea Before 1979" (1984) and "Addendum to Report on Conditions in Democratic Kampuchea 1975–1979" (1988). Timothy Carney kindly provided copies of these reports. Cadre privileges included packaged cigarettes (the "Liberation" brand), watches, ballpoint pens, and extra rations.

71. The most detailed assault on the STV, aside from Vickery's, is Noam Chomsky and Edward Hermann, *After the Cataclysm* (Boston, 1979), 135–294. For a discussion of the CPF's response to DK, see J-P Darde, *Le ministre de la verité* (Paris, 1983).

72. For a discussion of media distortions, see Gavan MacCormack, "The Kampuchean Revolution 1975–1978: The Problem of Knowing the Truth," *JCA* 1–2 (1980): 75 ff., Pierre Rousset, "Cambodia: Background to the Revolution," *JCA* 7/4 (1977): 513–28; Serge Thion, "Le Cambodge, la presse et ses betes noirs," in Thion and Kiernan, 305–28, and the discussion of the issue in Vickery, *Cambodia 1975–1982*, 27–63. In December 1978, Ieng Sary "objected to . . . outsiders wanting to know about the '5 to 20 percent of the Cambodians who were well off before the revolution.'" Richard Dudman, *San Francisco Examiner*, December 28, 1978. For a contrasting view, see William Shawcross, "Cambodia: Some Perceptions of a Disaster," in Chandler and Kiernan, *Revolution and Its Aftermath*, 230–58.

73. See Vickery, *Cambodia, 1975–1982*, 27–63.

74. Vickery, *Cambodia, 1975–1982*, 82–143, and Chandler and Kiernan, *Revolution and Its Aftermath*, 99–135. See also Carney, "The Organization of Power," in Jackson, ed. *Cambodia 1975–1978*, 93–94, and Honda Katuiti, *Journey to Cambodia* (Tokyo, 1982).

75. Khek Pen's confession, September 1977, includes a file called the "Geography of the Northwest," which would indicate that post-1975 dombon were anthologies of prerevolutionary srok. Inventing administrative terms (e.g., dombon) and a revolutionary vocabulary were aspects of the regime's starting from zero. See also Carney, "The Organization of Power," 105 ff.

76. Chan Narol interview, June 1987. On Stung Treng, Kate Frieson (personal communication). Stephen Heder has warned me about reifying the zones into political categories, suggesting that variations within the zones were as sharp as they were among them.

77. Heder interviews, 37. Interview with Tan Chip, December 1987. On dombon 3, Vickery, *Cambodia 1975–1982*, 110–12.

78. See Vickery, *Cambodia 1975–1982*, 114 ff., Pin Yathay, *L'Utopie meurtriere*, 195 ff., Becker, *When the War Was Over*, 250, and Hin Sithan, *Who Are the Murderers?* 102–04.

79. "Situation Report from Cambodia, 10/78": Pike archives.

80. See Chandler, Kiernan, and Boua, *Pol Pot Plans the Future*, 37, and M. A. Martin, "La politique alimentaire des Khmers rouges," *Etudes rurales*, July-December 1985, 347–65.

81. Heder interviews, 42.

82. On the September 1976 crisis, see David P. Chandler, "Revising the Past," and Chandler, Kiernan, and Boua, *Pol Pot Plans the Future*, 164–67. Cambodians who had recently returned from France and were working in a factory in Phnom Penh were told of the event when it occurred. Interview with Ong Thong Hoeung, May 1988.

83. It is possible that Pol Pot, fearing assassination, left the capital for a brief period.

84. Pol Pot's interview with Jan Myrdal, August 24, 1978. For a discussion of hostilities with Vietnam, see William J. Duiker, *Vietnam since the Fall of Saigon* (Athens, Ohio, 1985), 109 ff. Stephen Heder's research in progress examines policy differences on the Vietnam question between military leaders in the Eastern Zone on the one hand and the Pol Pot-Nuon Chea leadership on the other. See also "Pay Attention to Sweeping Out the Concealed Enemy Boring from Within," *Tung Padevat*, July 1978, 4 ff. (Heder translation).

85. The DK era still needs a detailed narrative history that draws on the ar-

chives at Tuol Sleng, DK published material, survivors' accounts, and secondary sources.

Chapter Eight. Inside the Typhoon: Testimonies

1. Two of the seven have been interviewed previously about their life under DK. Denise Affonço testified at the trials of Pol Pot and Ieng Sary in Phnom Penh in 1979, and Ong Thong Hoeung was interviewed by Stephen Heder in Thailand in 1980. I interviewed Affonço in November 1987 and Ong Thong Hoeung in May 1988 and February 1990.

2. See also Y Phandara, *Retour a Phnom Penh,* 151. On Cheng An, interview with Taing Kim Buon, June 1989.

3. DK documents captured by the Vietnamese and later translated by Vietnamese intelligence agencies indicate that a delegation of Indonesian Communists, long in exile in China, had been sent to Cambodia in 1976 to observe the revolution but encountered problems when they were unable to communicate with the Khmer. G. Lockhart, personal communication.

4. For others in Phnom Penh at this time, Pol Pot was known as Om Ti Muoy, or Uncle Number One. In the late 1980s, Pol Pot was known by the DK delegation to the UN as Om Sar. John Marston, personal communication.

5. Touch's story is corroborated for another part of the Eastern Zone by Nayan Chanda, *Brother Enemy,* 85.

6. See Kiernan, "Farm Chickens," in Chandler and Kiernan, *Revolution and Its Aftermath,* 196 ff.; Ung Bunheang and Martin Stuart-Fox, *Murderous Revolution,* 146 ff.; interview with Ung Bunheang, August 1987; Seng Kan (interview, February 1989) claimed that civilians found between Svay Rieng city and the Vietnamese border were taken off in 1978 for having failed to resist the invasion. In January 1979, while foraging on the outskirts of Phnom Penh, Kol Touch saw a Vietnamese military truck loaded with soldiers heading for the capital. They were Khmer and included some men who had been rounded up from Touch's village in 1977–78. These unarmed troops arrived after the fighting was over.

7. Burchett, *The China-Cambodia-Vietnam Triangle,* 84–91, draws on Affonço's testimony at the 1979 trials of Pol Pot and Ieng Sary in Phnom Penh.

8. The reckless disregard for hygiene and "bourgeois" medicine resembled similar experiments in China in this period, but it is unlikely that any of the young practitioners knew about Chinese *praxis,* or for that matter about hygiene.

9. See Nayan Chanda, "When the killing had to stop," FEER, October 29, 1976; Vu Can, *Kampuchea: The Nightmare is Over* (Hanoi, 1981), 87 ff., and Edward Friedman, "After Mao: Maoism and Post-Mao China," *Telos* 65 (Fall 1985): 36–37.

10. For a report by another CPT member who worked in the same village, see *Journal of Contemporary Asia* 12/4 (1982): 510–16.

11. Letter from Kasien Tejapira to author, August 27, 1987. In his interview, Kasien added that CPK cadre asked to address the CPT anniversary celebrations in December 1977 boasted about the Cambodian revolution without mentioning the CPT.

12. For corroboration of two such border raids, see *NYT,* February 13 and March 29, 1978. According to Nayan Chanda (personal communication), the Thai air force bombed at least one CPT camp inside Cambodia in 1977.

13. Prisons filled with former soldiers and civil servants existed in the southwest, north, and the east but not in the west or northwest, where executions and summary punishments of new people were widespread.

14. Interview with Ong Thong Hoeung, May 1988.

15. See Martin, *Le mal cambodgien,* 112–14, 147–55.

16. More trusted students were summoned to Tirana for briefings. Ibid., 152.

17. Ong Thong Hoeung, "Illusions perdues," 8–11. See also Picq, *Au delà du ciel,* 16–17, describing her arrival from Beijing in June 1975. For parallel accounts, see Martin, *Le mal cambodgien,* 192 ff., Becker, *When the War Was Over,* 281 ff., and Vickery, *Cambodia 1975–1982,* 161–65. Over a hundred returning students were arrested after their arrival and eventually put to death.

18. Ong Thong Hoeung, "Illusions perdues," 20, and Picq, *Au delà du ciel,* 88 ff. See also Heder interviews, 55: "People were insecure psychologically. People feared being wrong unconsciously, or being fingered so they just kept smiling but were tense inside."

19. The village had served as the CPK's headquarters in the last year of the civil war. Martin, *Le mal cambodgien,* 162, 192. In 1976–78, there were "150 intellectuals" there.

20. Interview with Yem Nolla, May 1988. In 1977, a former Cambodian school teacher told FEER correspondent Robert Wise, "*M'sieur,* Cambodia is governed by drunkards, thieves, savages, barbarians and classless illiterates"—the kinds of people whom teachers had warned their students about. Wise, "Eradicating the Old Dandruff," FEER, September 21, 1977.

21. On Tuol Sleng, see Heder interviews, 3–7, Anthony Barnett, Chanthou Boua, and Ben Kiernan, "Bureaucracy of Death," *New Statesman,* May 5, 1980, 668–76; Burchett, *The Vietnam-China-Cambodia Triangle,* 130–32, and William Shawcross, *The Quality of Mercy* (London, 1984), 39–44.

22. See Robert Conquest, *The Great Terror* (Harmondsworth, 1971), chap. 5, "The Problem of Confession," and "S-21 Interrogator's Manual," n.d. (ca. 1976–77, Hawk papers). See also Edgar H. Schein, *Coercive Persuasion* (repr. New York, 1971), which deals with Chinese Communist "brainwashing" of American civilians in the 1940s and 1950s, and Serge Thion, "Introduction" to Thion and Kiernan, *Khmers rouges!* 24–31. A former supporter of DK remarked in an interview, however, that Pol Pot and his colleagues were guilty of nothing more than "a few stupidities" (*quelques bêtises*).

23. For contrasting views, see Becker, *When the War Was Over,* 253 ff., and Ben Kiernan, "The Survival of Cambodia's Ethnic Minorities," *Cultural Survival* 14/3 (1990): 64–66.

24. The best overview of the Tuol Sleng phenomenon is still Barnett, Kiernan, and Boua, "Bureaucracy of Death." See also David Hawk, "International Human Rights Law and Democratic Kampuchea," in Ablin and Hood, *The Cambodian Agony,* 118–48, and David Hawk, "The Photographic Record," in Jackson, *Cambodia 1975–1978,* 209–14. Heder interviews, 46, suggests that some prisoners were screened before they were taken to S-21; an Eastern Zone cadre claimed to have been screened and released at the height of the purges in late 1977. At least one prisoner registered at Tuol Sleng, Hem Sambath, arrested in November 1975, was released after interrogation.

25. Statistics from Barnett, Kiernan, and Boua, "Bureaucracy of Death," 671.

26. There are valuable partial translations in Becker, *When the War Was Over,* appendices. The confessions I have consulted total perhaps two thouand pages.

Most of them were given to me by Kate Frieson, David Hawk, Stephen Heder, Ben Kiernan, Judy Ledgerwood, and Michael Vickery. I reviewed an additional hundred texts on visits to Phnom Penh in 1990 and 1991. Stephen Heder has recently completed an analysis of several important confessions. A project sponsored by Cornell University, the Social Science Research Council, and the Cambodian government aims to microfilm the archives at Tuol Sleng.

27. Notebook from S-21, 71, Hawk papers, translation by Stephen Heder. At 72, the text goes on: "Although we consider torture to be a necessary measure, we must strive to do politics to get them always and absolutely to confess to us." See also Chandler, Kiernan, and Boua, *Pol Pot Plans the Future,* 211 (document from December 1976): "Those who defend us must be truly adept. They should have practice in observing. They must observe everything, but so those who are being observed are unaware of it."

28. Chan Chakrei confession, July-October 1976; *Pravat'ruup* (autobiography), October 25, 1975; Heder interviews, 43–44. Vorn Vet's December 1978 confession (typed version), 40, claims that the Eastern Zone leader, Sao Phim (by then already dead), had informed him of Chan Chakrei's plans beforehand. See also Hu Nim's 1977 confession in Chandler, Kiernan, and Boua, *Pol Pot Plans the Future,* 299, which notes that Chakrei had been "sizzling, impetuous, proud and swaggering," as would befit someone who had pledged to "crush the Organization." The fact that nearly all the evidence against Chakrei's plot comes from S-21 should encourage us to be cautious in assessing its veracity.

29. I have not located this admission in the Chakrei confession texts. See *Kampuchea Dossier* II, 68, which misdates the incident to February 1977 but claims that "600 men of the 170th Division failed in their attempted mutiny." On balance, a genuine antigovernment plot at this time cannot be ruled out. The participation of high-ranking CPK officials like Sao Phim, however, is impossible to prove. Phim remained in place for two more years before committing suicide when charged with treason by Pol Pot. See also Duch's report to "respected elder brother" (probably Son Sen) dated June 6, 1976, while the interrogation was proceeding (Hawk papers). The report suggests collusion between "the CIA and the Vietnamese," a theme that intensified at S-21 over the next two years.

30. On the September-October events, see Chandler, Kiernan, and Boua, *Pol Pot Plans the Future,* 163–67, and Chanda, *Brother Enemy,* 82–83. See also FBIS, October 31, 1978 (Vietnam coverage), in which a former CPK cadre from the Eastern Zone reports that in October 1976 party meetings were told that it was "imperative to wipe out those of 1951." This document was written before the Vietnamese had access to the confessions at S-21.

31. Vickery, *Cambodia 1975–1982,* 148. In December 1976, Pol Pot referred to documents uncovered after October 1976 that convinced him and his colleagues to keep the identity of the CPK a secret. See Chandler, Kiernan, and Boua, *Pol Pot Plans the Future,* 330n27.

32. Chandler, Kiernan, and Boua, *Pol Pot Plans the Future,* 183. See also David P. Chandler, "A Revolution in Full Spate," in Ablin and Hood, *The Cambodian Agony,* 165–79. A similar sentiment surfaced in a Cultural Revolution document in 1967: "The enemies without guns are more hidden, cunning, sinister and vicious than the enemies with guns." Lowell Dittmer, "Thought Reform and Cultural Revolution," *American Journal of Political Science* 71 (March 1977): 75.

33. A genuine coup d'état may have been planned in the north in early 1977. See Anthony Paul, "Plot Details Filter Through," FEER, May 18, 1978, which uses

refugee testimony long before the Tuol Sleng documents became available. Intriguingly, a refugee referred to the capture by DK forces of a messenger taking news of coup plans between Kompong Thom and Kompong Cham on January 17, 1977. Koy Tuon, originally from the Northern Zone, was arrested eight days later. FBIS, October 31, 1978 (Vietnamese coverage), has a former CPK cadre speaking of a "massive crackdown on April 17, 1977." Stephen Heder points out that "plots" coincided with the anniversaries of Phnom Penh's liberation or the CPK's foundation because at these times high-ranking CPK figures from the zones would be summoned to Phnom Penh, where, bereft of armed forces, they were easy to arrest.

34. "The contemptible Ba" was Vietnam's ambassador to DK, Pham van Ba, who later claimed to have welcomed Saloth Sar into the Viet Minh maquis in 1953: Kiernan, *HPP*, 123. See also *Ompi paenkar ruom chong krooy* (On the last joint plan), July 1978, translated in Jackson, *Cambodia 1975–1978*, 299–314.

35. Hak Sieng Lay Ny confession, December 26, 1976–January 2, 1977 (typewritten). He was arrested with his wife, who had been trained as a surgeon. He was charged, according to Ieng Sary, with being a "KGB agent," "disrespectful of Angkar," and the Soviet choice to direct a pro-Soviet Communist party. Picq, *Au delà du ciel*, 100. Their eight-year-old son, Chol'na ("Movement"), committed suicide when he heard of his parents' arrest. Lay Ny's confession is the earliest evidence I have seen of DK suspicions that the Socialist Republic of Vietnam planned a military attack on Cambodia in early 1977. *Livre Noir*, 71–72, refers to "Vietnamese agents infiltrated into the ranks of the revolution, arrested in 1976," perhaps an oblique reference to this text. Chanda (*Brother Enemy*, 84) points out that in mid-December 1976 the Vietnamese Communist Party Congress had referred to "special relations between the Vietnamese people and the fraternal peoples of Laos and Kampuchea." The phrase "special relations" for the CPK suggested Vietnamese hegemony.

36. Chandler and Kiernan, *Revolution and Its Aftermath*, 171; interview with Kham Lavit, August 1987. In April 1977, a central committee directive ordered the execution of ethnic Vietnamese residents in Cambodia. See Chanda, *Brother Enemy*, 86–87.

37. See Grant Evans and Kelvin Rowley, *Red Brotherhood at War* (London, 1983), 116–17; Vickery, *Cambodia 1975–1982*, 189–96; Kiernan, "New Light on the Origins of the Kampuchea-Vietnam Conflict," BCAS 12 (1980): 61–65, and Stephen Heder, "Origins of the Conflict," *Southeast Asian Chronicle*, September-October 1978. Hun Sen fled to Vietnam in July 1977. See also captured DK document, "Decisions Concerning the Report of Eastern Region Conference 17 July 1977," translated by Stephen Heder, which urges troops to be cautious about crossing the border, but "if the enemy commits aggression against us, we must respond by stopping him and smashing him. We must cross into and stop and smash him right on his land."

38. See Chandler, Kiernan, and Boua, *Pol Pot Plans the Future*, esp. 246 ff. Heder interviews, 30, confirms that Thuon was under a cloud in 1976.

39. On Thuon and Pauk, see Heder interviews, 40. On Sihanouk visit, see Chandler, Kiernan, and Boua, *Pol Pot Plans the Future*, 266. On Thuon's behavior in the early 1970s, see "The Last Joint Plan," 301.

40. In April 1977, an uprising near Siem Reap had to be put down by troops brought in from the east. See *Sereika*, no. 28 (September 1978), Vickery, *Cambodia 1975–1982*, 126–27, and Vorn Vet confession, 43.

41. Soeu Van Si confessions, February-July 1977. On Khieu Samphan, see U.S.

Embassy Bangkok's telegram, January 1980, "Sok Sim (Lonh) on History of Khmer Rouge." Pike Archives 1/80, and Heder interviews, 78. On Doeun's wife, Roeun, see Picq, *Au delà du ciel,* 64 ff., and Men Tul confession, July 1978, 71–72.

42. Touch Kamdoeun confession, April 1977, 11. The oppressive atmosphere of B-1 in 1976–78 is conveyed by Picq, *Au delà du ciel,* and by Ngo Pen (interview, June 1989), who worked there. See also Chandler, Kiernan, and Boua, *Pol Pot Plans the Future,* 209, where a party spokesman in 1976 admitted, "Our shortcomings in the field of foreign affairs spring from the fact that we lack cadre who are attached to the movement and can at the same time perform the work of the foreign ministry. Some cadre in the ministry come from abroad and have no ties with the movement." When diplomatic relations were severed with Vietnam at the end of 1977, the Cambodian ambassador to Hanoi and his wife, summoned home for consultations, were arrested, interrogated, and put to death. Picq, *Au delà du ciel,* 117.

43. Mau Khem Noeun confession, April 16, 1977. On the ceremony for joining the CPK, see "A Short Guide for Application of Party Statutes," in Carney, *Communist Party Power in Kampuchea,* 57.

44. Mau Khem Noeun confession "About the Plan to Fight the Party," April 24, 1977, 3. Voon, the commander of the bodyguards of Office 870, the code name for the central committee, was also arrested in February 1977. See also confessions of In Van (Sovann) and Ni Muong (Yon), both personal employees of the Organization, i.e., Pol Pot.

45. Mau Khem Noeun confession, May 5, 1977. Phim's name also occurs in the list of "traitors" appended to Tiv Ol's confession in July 1977, but only as No. 83.

46. See Becker, *When the War Was Over,* 245 ff. Picq, *Au delà du ciel,* 105, asserts that officials from the northwest were brought to the Foreign Ministry (B-1) and made to believe that they would be given diplomatic posts overseas. After being taken off for "special training," they disappeared. Their former colleagues in B-1 were later told that they were traitors.

47. Chanda, *Brother Enemy,* 83, and Gareth Porter, "Vietnamese Policy and the Indo-China Crisis," in *The Third Indo-China Conflict,* ed. D. W. P. Elliott (Boulder, 1981), 95, 127. Porter has told me that his sources were U.S. government officials. A former combatant interviewed for the PBS film on Cambodia (1981) confirmed that he had heard Pol Pot in April 1977 speaking to combatants and cadre in the northwest about "purifying" the region (Stephen Heder, personal communication).

48. Khek Pen confession, typewritten précis, March 1977, and confession September 9, 1977, "Officials in the Northwest." On Pen, see also Vickery, *Cambodia 1975–1982,* 159, 167, interviews with Im Nath and In Sen, September 1987, and Ty Sophen, January 1989. At the end of 1975, Pen agreed with a Thai delegation to repay debts contracted along the border since April 1975. When the negotiations were over, Pen presented the Thai delegate with a terrified Thai farmer who had been kidnapped by CPK forces earlier in the year, as evidence of his good will. Interview Phan Wannamethee, June 1989.

49. For example, cadre who had gone to Office 100 with Saloth Sar in 1963, later purged, admitted to joining the CIA in the 1950s, falsifying devoted careers of party service. Vorn Vet, on the other hand, claimed to have joined the revolution in 1953, and to have switched to the CIA only in 1956. Vorn Vet confession (typewritten version), 5.

50. The idea of a genuine CIA-Vietnamese conspiracy seems to have been

taken seriously by the leaders of DK. See Laura Summers, "The CPK: Secret Vanguard of Pol Pot's Revolution," *Journal of Communist Studies* (March 1987): 116. By 1978, xenophobia had almost become the basis of DK ideology. People who had studied in France were accused of joining French intelligence agencies, those who had studied in Germany German ones, and so on. Similar tactics were in use in China during the Cultural Revolution, when an instruction to Red Guards asserted, "To discredit a person, the following can be used: rightist, ultra-leftist, counter-revolutionary, bad element, agents of the USSR, USA, KMT, etc." Dittmer and Chen, *Ethics and Rhetoric,* 44.

51. Interviews with Stephen Heder, November 1986, Ung Bunheang and Ung Phinny, August 1987, and Suon Samol, September 1987, who remembered that "[Sao Phim] wore ordinary clothes and loved the people." Vickery, *Cambodia 1975–1982,* 136–37. Vorn Vet confession (45) notes that communal eating was being introduced too slowly in the east: "If the Party asked about the delay, people would say they lacked dishes, pots, or food [for communal eating]." Heder's recent research, however, suggests that Phim was (in 1977 at least) more militantly anti-Vietnamese than the party center.

52. See Kiernan, "Farm Chickens," in Chandler and Kiernan, *Revolution and Its Aftermath,* 188–91, and Meas Chhon confession, June 1978. On Nhim and Phim, Ty Sophen interview, January 1989, and Ros Nhim confession, June 1978. Ros Nhim was arrested a week after Phim's suicide.

53. See Evans and Rowley, *Red Brotherhood at War,* 119; Meas Chhon confession, July 1978. Chhon, the secretary of dombon 22, attended some of the same meetings as Tal. Vorn Vet's confession (46–47) notes that troops from the Central Zone, under Ke Pauk, were more successful than Phim's troops were against the Vietnamese. Vet also suggests that Pauk had participated with Phim in some anti-DK planning, but backtracked and betrayed Phim in 1978. The use of confessions to determine where Sao Phim "really stood" yields mixed results. See also Becker, *When the War Was Over,* 320–21.

54. Chanda, *Brother Enemy,* 197 ff., and Kiernan and Thion, *Khmers rouges!* 233. See also Stuart-Fox and Bunheang Ung, *Murderous Revolution,* 147, Becker, *When the War Was Over,* 321–22, and Kiernan, *Massacre,* 95 ff. On the Vietnamese evacuation of people from Cambodia, interviews with Kol Touch, Seng Keng; Ieng Sary statement, *Peking Review,* July 7, 1978.

55. Becker, *When the War Was Over,* 417 ff.; Thiounn Mumm interview with Stephen Heder, 1981.

56. Becker, *When the War Was Over,* 332–33, citing Pol Pot's speech commemorating the eighteenth anniversary of the CPK; Y Phandara, *Retour à Phnom Penh,* 208. There is no corroboration of this event. Stephen Heder's research in progress indicates that Vet may indeed have been plotting against Pol Pot and that Malcolm Caldwell's assassination (see below) was connected with Vet's failed plot. Vorn Vet's wife and daughter were also smashed by S-21.

57. *Tung Padevat* (hereafter *TP*), July 1978, 4; see also *TP,* May-June 1978, 53: "[In 1975–76] we found ourselves to be pacifist, subjective, underestimating the enemy and overjoyed with our victories and the state power we enjoyed throughout the country" (translation by Stephen Heder).

58. See "The Last Joint Plan," in Jackson, *Cambodia 1975–1978,* 299–314. *TP* (July 1978) spoke of "concealed enemies boring from within who are CIA agents, Vietnamese running dog agents and KGB agents" (Heder translation, Hawk papers).

59. On Vietnamese policies, see G. Porter, "Vietnamese Policies and the Indo-China Crisis," in Elliott, *Third Indo-China Conflict,* 92 ff. Khieu Thirith's sister, Khieu Thirath, who was not a Communist but lived in Phnom Penh during 1975–77, died of a stroke in 1977. Khieu Thirith was convinced she had been assassinated by "plotters." Interviews with You Sambo and Ngo Pen, June 1989.

60. See, for example, FBIS Daily report, March 27, 1978: "Our guerrillas and revolutionary combatants are good at shooting. They can kill one enemy with a single shot. . . . This does not mean that [they] are from a military school, that they studied the art of shooting . . . or that [they have] a large quantity of ammunition. . . . In fact it is due to the *indignation* that our army has nurtured against the enemy" (emphasis added). By this time, Vietnamese aircraft were running as many as thirty missions a day over Cambodia, strafing and bombing Cambodian infantry positions. For a detailed argument that the CPK was not an authentically Marxist-Leninist party, see Vickery, *Cambodia 1975–1982,* 253–90, which locates the roots of the Cambodian revolution in traditions of antiurban bias in rural areas and peasant millenarianism.

61. Martin, "Les réfugiés cambodgiens," 60. Conditions varied from district to district, of course. Peasants whose communal diet was gruel were in many zones forbidden to grow supplementary vegetables or to forage for other food.

62. "Situation Report from Cambodia 10/778," in Pike archives. See also Richard Nations, "Another 40,000 CIA Traitors," FEER, August 25, 1978.

63. Evans and Rowley, *Red Brotherhood at War,* 118 ff., and Dave Hatcher, "Cambodia vs. Vietnam—a mismatch," FEER, January 13, 1978. In the event, the Vietnamese attacked north of Kompong Cham and in the southwest, outflanking DK troops, who were expecting a frontal assault. Burchett, *The China-Cambodia-Vietnam Triangle,* 202.

64. See Slavko Stanic, "Kampuchea—Socialism without a Model," *Socialist Thought and Practice* (1978): 67–84; "Kyodo Series on Cambodia," Pike archives 10/78; "Becker Series on Cambodia," cuttings in Pike archives (12/78), and Becker, *When the War Was Over,* 406–36.

65. Picq, *Au delà du ciel,* 121. Corroborated by Ngo Pen interview, June 1989.

66. Stanic, "Kampuchea—Socialism without a Model," 67, and Democratic Kampuchea, "Interview of Comrade POL POT to (*sic*) the Delegation of Yugoslav Journalists," Phnom Penh, March 1978. The Stanic quotation appears to be drawn from several points in the interview. See also Sihanouk, *Prisonnier des khmers rouges,* 299–300.

67. The Japanese delegation in October met a former monk who "smilingly said that he believed communism more than Buddhism." Kyodo series, Pike archives, 5.

68. Stanic, "Kampuchea—Socialism without a Model," 79. See also Becker, *When the War Was Over,* 323–24.

69. The secrecy surrounding party membership is corroborated by Becker, *When the War Was Over,* 421. Burchett, *The China-Vietnam-Cambodia Triangle,* 162, quotes the Yugoslavian filmmaker Vitterovich later in 1978: "What we saw was a hundred times worse than we could put on film or I could express in my commentary."

70. Nuon Chea, "Statement of the Communist Party of Kampuchea." The statement was never printed.

71. Ibid., but see "On the Last Joint Plan," in Jackson, *Cambodia 1975–1978,* 312: "As to the extent of the co-operation betweeen the Soviets, the Vietnamese and the CIA we are not yet able to grasp it for lack of evidence."

72. See *TP*, March 1978, 63: "According to our experiences of our revolution, the basic plan is secrecy. Take secrecy as the base. We can defend our forces; enemies fail to strike us. We . . . take a stand and keep secrets, but standing on secrecy is the base" (trans. Kem Sos and Timothy Carney).

73. See also *TP*, October-November 1977, "Further Raise the Quality of Party Leadership," 42–74.

74. Of course, the idea that low-ranking people would give the same responses to questions as higher-ranking ones also reflected the democratic centralism of the party.

75. *Washington Post,* December 29, 1978. The verdict on the economy is missing from Becker's book, in which she refers in a photo caption to the fact that "most of our trip we were shown Potemkin or 'model' villages that bore little resemblance to the miserable conditions most people endured." According to Khieu Khannarith (interview, October 1989), who has consulted DK confidential reports about the visit, DK officials took it for granted that Dudman and Becker were CIA agents but singled Caldwell out as a friend. One report noted that Becker had taken "bad" photographs of such unworthy subjects as "naked children."

76. Becker, *When the War Was Over,* 430 ff. The "Declaration du Gouvernement du Kampuchea Démocratique," dated January 2, 1979, however, after the Vietnamese offensive had begun, goes over the same ground, accusing Vietnam of "internationalizing" the war and blaming the USSR for the Vietnamese attacks on DK before appealing for international support.

77. Becker, *When the War Was Over,* 432–33. This account seems more believable than Sihanouk's (*Prisonnier des khmers rouges,* 303–04), which retails Wilfred Burchett's assertion that there had been a "stormy argument" between Caldwell and Pol Pot and that Pol Pot had ordered him killed. Ngo Pen served as the interpreter for the discussions and has called them friendly. He spent much of the night trying to produce an English language version. Interview, June 1989.

78. Becker, *When the War Was Over,* 433–36, 447–48; Picq, *Au delà du ciel,* 146–47, and Picq MS, 355–56. Rumors spread in DK circles that the murder had been part of a vendetta by a recently dismissed security guard against a colleague who had denounced him for sexual misdemeanors. Interview Sisowath Aryawadi, corroborated by second interview, June 1989. Stephen Heder (personal communication) leans toward a genuine plot intended to embarrass the regime.

79. Chanda, *Brother Enemy,* 341 ff., gives a detailed account. See also Burchett, *The China-Cambodia-Vietnam Triangle,* 207–08.

80. Chanda, *Brother Enemy,* 300–01; interview with Leonard Overton, May 1986.

81. See *Prisonnier des khmers rouges,* 316 ff. Sihanouk inferred from the size of the car sent to fetch him that he was back in favor. Sihanouk later told James Pringle and Nayan Chanda, on separate occasions, that he had found Pol Pot "charismatic." He told Pringle that Pol Pot talked without interruption "for three hours" (James Pringle, personal communication). Whether Sihanouk was silent for so long out of politeness, fear, or conviction is hard to say.

82. Taing Seng You (interview, July 1989) recalls going to work at the machine foundry near Pochentong where he had worked since 1976, only to find the leading cadre gone, without any warning the night before. On the train voyage, see Y Phandara, *Retour a Phnom Penh,* 184 ff. Ieng Sary reached the Thai border barefoot and exhausted on January 11 and was soon flown off to Beijing. Two days later, he was being dressed down for DK's "excesses" by Deng Xiao Peng. Chanda, *Brother Enemy,* 347–48. Deng tempered his criticisms of the CPK by suggesting

that the evacuation of Phnom Penh in 1975 had been justified, since "about half" of its population were "Vietnamese agents." He also gave Sary US $5 million to ease his cash flow problems.

83. For various accounts, see Someth May, *Cambodian Witness*, 222, Martin, *Le mal cambodgien*, 206–07, and Martin, "Les réfugiés cambodgiens," 78ff.

84. On eastern zone in 1840s, see David P. Chandler, *A History of Cambodia* (Boulder, 1983), 130–32.

85. On this congress, see Vickery, *Kampuchea* (London, 1986), 65. The Fourth Congress of the Party was held in 1981, when its name was changed to the Kampuchean People's Revolutionary Party, bringing it semantically into line with its counterpart in Laos and with the predecessor to the CPK, which had had a similar name between 1951 and 1960. The name change also had the effect of annulling the semantic "evolution" of the party between 1960 and 1966.

86. See Shawcross, *The Quality of Mercy* (New York, 1984), and Anne F. Thurston, *Enemies of the People* (Cambridge, Mass., 1988), 276–90. See also Ben Kiernan, "Kampuchea Stumbles to its Feet," in Kiernan and Boua, *Peasants and Politics*, 363–85, and Chanthou Boua, "Observations of the Heng Samrim Government," in Chandler and Kiernan, *Revolution and Its Aftermath*, 259–90.

Bibliography

Essay

My research for this book has been based largely on interviews, primary sources, and unpublished documents. What follows is a guide to book-length French and English language secondary sources.

Chapter 1. In Search of Independence, 1945–1950

There is almost nothing in English and very little in French dealing with this crucial period. See V. M. Reddi, *The History of the Cambodian Independence Movement* (Tiruipati, 1971); Norodom Sihanouk, *Souvenirs doux et amers* (Paris, 1981), which should be used with caution, and Norodom Sihanouk, *L'Indochine vue de Pékin* (Paris, 1971). Philippe Preschez, "Essai sur la démocratie au Cambodge" (Paris, 1961) provides a good narrative of Cambodia's parliamentary period. See also Ben Kiernan and Chanthou Boua, eds., *Peasants and Politics in Kampuchea, 1942–1981* (London, 1982), a valuable collection of documents, some of them translated from Khmer and not otherwise available.

Chapter 2. Political Warfare, 1950–1955

The sources cited for chapter 1 are useful for students of the early 1950s. See also Ben Kiernan, *How Pol Pot Came to Power* (London, 1985), an invaluable study which focuses on the history of radicalism; Marie-A. Martin, *Le mal cambodgien* (Paris, 1989), an overall view, and Charles Meyer, *Derrière le sourire khmer* (Paris, 1971), a disenchanted but perceptive book by a former adviser to Prince Sihanouk. Readers interested in the history of communism in France in the 1950s can consult Danielle Dessanti, *Les staliniens* (Paris, 1975), and Alain Besançon, *Une génération* (Paris, 1987), among others.

Chapter 3. Sihanouk Unopposed, 1955–1962

Michael Field, *The Prevailing Wind* (London, 1964) contains a sympathetic account of Sihanouk's rule, and so does Simone Lacouture, *Cambodge* (Lausanne, 1964). See also Roger M. Smith, *Cambodia's Foreign Policy*

(Ithaca, 1965), Charles Meyer, *Derrière le sourire khmer,* and Milton Osborne, *Power and Politics in Cambodia* (Hawthorn, Australia, 1973), which offer perceptive analyses of the Sihanouk years. The early chapters of J-C Pomonti and Serge Thion, *Des courtesans aux partisans* (Paris, 1971), which are critical of the prince, are also useful, and see Michael Vickery, "Looking Back at Cambodia," in Kiernan and Boua, eds., *Peasants and Politics,* 87–113.

Chapter 4. Cambodia Clouds Over, 1963–1966

Milton Osborne's *Before Kampuchea* (London, 1979) contains many insights from the author's time in Cambodia in 1966. Soth Polin's novel *L'anarchiste* (Paris, 1977) gives a jangled picture of Cambodia's *jeunesse dorée* at this time. Sihanouk's own memoirs, *Souvenirs doux et amers,* read well but are scarcely analytical. See also John Armstrong, *Sihanouk Speaks* (New York, 1964), a selection of interviews, and Norodom Sihanouk with Bernard Krisher, *Charisma and Leadership* (Tokyo, 1990), a selection of vignettes of other leaders. Michael Leifer, *Cambodia: The Search for Security* (New York, 1967) is a useful collection of essays on the 1960s.

Chapter 5. Changing the Rules, 1967–1969

For a bleak account of Sihanouk's last months, see Meyer, *Derrière le sourire khmer,* and also Maslyn Willams's sensitive study, based on a short visit to Cambodia in 1969, *The Land in Between* (New York, 1970). Martin, *Le mal cambodgien,* chapters 4 and 5, and Pomonti and Thion, *Des courtesans aux partisans,* part 2, are also useful. Rémy Prud'homme, *L'économie du Cambodge* (Paris, 1969) analyzes Cambodia's economy in the late 1960s. See also Khieu Samphan, *Cambodia's Economy and Industrial Development,* trans. Laura Summers (Ithaca, 1979), a translation of Samphan's Ph.D. dissertation, sometimes cited mistakenly as a blueprint for DK economic policies.

Chapter 6. Sliding toward Chaos, 1970–1975

The best study of this period is William Shawcross's mordant *Sideshow: Nixon, Kissinger and the Destruction of Cambodia* (New York, 1979). See also General Sak Sutsakhan, *The Khmer Republic at War and the Final Collapse* (Washington, D.C., 1980). Malcolm Caldwell and Lek Hor Than's *Cambodia in the Southeast Asian War* (New York, 1973) sides with the insurgents, and so does George Hildebrand and Gareth Porter, *Cambodia: Starvation and Revolution* (New York, 1976). Both contain useful data. For the politics of the insurgents, Ben Kiernan's *How Pol Pot Came to Power* is indispensable. Craig Etcheson, *The Rise and Demise of Democratic Kampuchea* (Boulder, Col.,

1985), although based on published material, contains helpful information on the Lon Nol period. See also Arnold R. Isaacs, *Without Honor: Defeat in Vietnam and Cambodia* (Baltimore, 1983).

Chapter 7, Revolution in Cambodia, 1975–1979, and Chapter 8, Inside the Typhoon: Testimonies

The revolutionary era has attracted wide attention from scholars and journalists. Several books have stood the test of time; some that have not still contain useful information. The best introduction to the ideology of DK is probably François Ponchaud's *Cambodia Year Zero* (New York, 1978). Two collections of essays dealing with the period are David P. Chandler and Ben Kiernan, eds., *Revolution and Its Aftermath in Kampuchea* (New Haven, 1983), and Karl Jackson, ed., *Cambodia 1975–1978: Rendezvous with Death* (Princeton, 1989). In the latter the chapters by Ponchaud and Timothy Carney are especially perceptive. See also David P. Chandler, Ben Kiernan, and Chantou Boua, ed. and trans., *Pol Pot Plans the Future: Confidential Leadership Documents from Democratic Kampuchea* (New Haven, 1988). A readable attempt at an overall synthesis is Elizabeth Becker's *When the War Was Over: The Voices of Cambodia's Revolution and Its People* (New York, 1986). Michael Vickery's *Cambodia, 1975–1982* (Boston, 1983), drawn from interviews with hundreds of survivors, is helpful for its analysis of regional and temporal variations. See also Kimmo Kiljunen, ed., *Kampuchea: Decade of the Genocide* (London 1984), a valuable overview; Serge Thion and Ben Kiernan, *Khmers Rouges!* (Paris, 1982), Etcheson's *The Rise and Demise of Democratic Kampuchea,* and Timothy Carney, *Communist Party Power in Cambodia* (Ithaca, 1978). Among many memoirs by survivors of the regime, perhaps the most perceptive are Pin Yathay, *L'utopie meurtrière* (Paris, 1979), Someth May, *Cambodian Witness* (London, 1986), and Molyda Szymusiak, *The Stones Cry Out* (New York, 1986). Laurence Picq, *Au delà du ciel* (Paris, 1984) is a moving memoir by a Frenchwoman who was married to a DK official who spent the years 1975–78 working in the DK Foreign Ministry.

The period since 1979, which is not dealt with in this book, is covered from various perspectives by Nayan Chanda, *Brother Enemy* (New York, 1986), Grant Evans and Kelvin Rowley, *Red Brotherhood at War* (London, 1985, rev. ed., 1990), and Michael Vickery, *Kampuchea* (London, 1984). See also William Shawcross, *The Politics of Mercy* (New York, 1984) and David A. Ablin and Marlowe Hood, eds., *The Cambodian Agony* (Armonk, N.Y., 1987), an interesting volume of essays. Martin Wright, ed., *Cambodia: A Matter of Survival* (London, 1989), and Robert J. Muscat and J. Stromseth, *Cambodia: Post-Settlement Reconstruction and Redevelopment* (New York, 1989) are clearheaded recent studies.

Unpublished Material

Collections of papers

Elizabeth Becker: Taped interviews, translations of confessions, DK documents (Echols Collection, Cornell University Library).

Justin Corfield: Biographical information on Cambodian elite; statistical data on Cambodian election (1989–90).

Philippe Devillers: Journal notes from Cambodia (1946).

Kate Frieson: Transcriptions of interviews (1986–90).

David Hawk: Material from Tuol Sleng (not confessions); documentary material from DK.

Stephen Heder: Notes on Khieu Samphan (1975); interviews on Thai–Cambodian border (1979–81); translations of DK documents; MS history of Cambodian radicalism (1978).

George Kahin: Material on Cambodia released to him under FOIA.

Ben Kiernan: Primary materials on elections of 1966.

Leonard Overton: Notes on French archival materials, Son Ngoc Thanh trial (1946–47).

Pung Peng Cheng: MS material from his time in Beijing (1973–75).

Channa Samudvanija: Son Ngoc Thanh correspondence and papers (1942–60).

Serge Thion: Typewritten material from Phnom Penh (1971–73).

Michael Vickery: Notes on Cambodian newspapers (1945–64); notes on interviews (1973–74); MS versions of chapters from his published work.

Diaries and unpublished memoirs

Douc Rasy, *La crise de conscience khmere* (1988).

William Harben, Diaries and documents (1971–73)

Hin Sithan, *No na chea khodok reastr khmaer?* (Who are the murderers of the Khmer people?) (1985)

Huy Kanthoul, untitled autobiography (1988)

Ong Thong Hoeung, *Illusions perdus* (1987–88)

Laurence Picq, draft memoir, edited and published as *Au delà du ciel* (Paris, 1984)

Eveline Porée-Maspéro, Diaries, 1944–45

Sim Kin, untitled memoir (1988)

Sisowath Monireth, selected passages of untitled memoir (1964)

Newspapers and Periodicals

Agence Khmere de Presse Daily Reports, 1967–68

Angkor (weekly newspaper, Phnom Penh), 1956–57

British Broadcasting Corporation, *Summary of World Broadcasts*, Far East, 1965–79

Cambodge (Phnom Penh), 1946–57 and 1969–70

La Démocrate (Phnom Penh), 1946–51

La Dépêche (Phnom Penh), 1959–65

Echoes de Phnom Penh, 1959–60

Etudes Cambodgiennes, 1965–68

Far Eastern Economic Review, 1960–81

Kampuchea (Phnom Penh), 1951–52

Khmer Krauk (Phnom Penh), 1952

La Liberté (Phnom Penh), 1946–57

London Times, 1973–75

Nagara Vatta (Phnom Penh), 1937–42

New York Times, 1945–80

La Nouvelle Dépêche (Phnom Penh), 1966–67

L'Observateur (Phnom Penh), 1959–60

Phnom Penh Presse, 1966–68

Realités cambodgiennes (Phnom Penh), 1956–75

United States, Foreign Broadcast Information Service, Asia and the Pacific, *Daily Reports*, 1967, 1974–79

Washington Post, 1971–75

Archival Materials

France: Archives d'outremer, Rue Oudinot, Paris: Indochine, Boxes NF 1101, 1106–08, 1117, 1213, 1219;[a] Archive d'outremer, Aix-en-Provence: Indochine, Cambodge, Boxes 135, 137–40, 144–45; Service Historique de l'Armée de Terre, Chateau de Vincennes: Indochine, Cambodge, Boxes 10 H 284, 5574, 5585, 5613–14, 5621.

United Kingdom: Public Records Office, Kew: Foreign Office records from British Legation/British Embassy Phnom Penh 1947–59, Boxes 371 F 69657, 75962–63, 92410, 101046, 101048–50, 101172, 106744, 106753–60, 106776, 102022–23, 112025,12028,12036–37, 117094, 117124–27, 117149.[b]

United States: Department of State Archives, Washington, D.C.: U.S. Legation/U.S. Embassy Phnom Penh, 1951–65, 1969–75 (released under FOIA); Central Intelligence Agency Archives, Washington, D.C.: Material related to Cambodia, 1955–75 (released under FOIA); National Archives,

[a] Records from Rue Oudinot, which I researched in 1983, were moved to Aix in 1987, after I had consulted the Aix archives.

[b] I am grateful to Anne Blair, George Kahin, and Andrew Mackay-Johnstone for supplementary notes and photocopies from the Public Records Office.

Washington, D.C.: Material related to Cambodia from U.S. Department of State, U.S. Legation/U.S. Embassy Phnom Penh, Boxes 751 H.1/11–155 and 751 H.001 9-2755, Boxes 3354–55; Lyndon B. Johnson Library, Austin Texas: Correspondence and documents dealing with Cambodia, 1963–65 (previously released under FOIA); William Joiner Center, University of Massachusetts, Amherst: Transcripts of interviews from Public Broadcasting System's Vietnam broadcasts, 1982; John F. Kennedy Library, Boston: Correspondence dealing with Cambodia, 1961–63 (previously released under FOIA), and statements by Ambassador Elbridge Dubrow and Ambassador William C. Trimble, Oral History Collection; Indo-China Archive, University of California, Berkeley (Pike Archive): Material on Cambodia collected by Prof. Douglas Pike, 1966–80.

Interviews[c]

Australia (1986–90): Noel St Clair Deschamps, Dy Channa, Hoeung Hong Kim, Hol Kong, Huy Huynh, Im Nath (2), Im Yim, Julio Jeldres (2), Kham Lavit, Khieu Kanharith, Khut Khun, Oeur Hunly, Sok Chhuon, Sok Pirun, Suon Saodi, Suong Soriya, Ven. Tep Vong, Thach Sok, Thach Tan, Thong Thel (2), Ty Sophen (2), Ung Bunheang (2), Ung Phinny (2), Yaem Chhing, You Hon Chea.

Canada (1989): Chan Noral, Khae Sopareath, Im Chanat, Mey Komphot, Pal Sim, Pen Bun, Sok Bunthan, Taing Kim Buon, Tea Guek Chou, You Sambo.

France (November 1986, May and November 1987, May 1988, June 1989, February 1990): Denise Affonço, Pierre Brocheux (2), Chhean Vam, Alain Daniel, Douc Rasy, Pierre Fuchs, Khek Gallabru (2), Bernard Hamel, Keng Vannsak (3), Keat Chhon, Keuky Lim, Kol Touch, Charles Meyer (3), Ngo Pen, Ong Thong Hoeung (2), Panh Meng Heang (2), Pung Peng Cheng (2), Seng Hin, the late Sim Var, Sisowath Arawady, Son Sann, S. Suon Kaset (3), Tan Bun Sor, Thach Ren, Thiounn Mumm (3), Thonn Ouk (2), Jacques Vergès, Yim Nolla.

Thailand (May 1988, July 1989): François Bizot, Channa Samudvanija (2), Phan Wannamethee.

United Kingdom (November 1986, May 1987): Stephen Heder (2), Siyathai Siryarath.

United States (May 1986, November 1987, October and November 1988, February 1989, February 1990): Bun Ouklong, Chhan Song, Thomas Corcoran, Marshall Green, William Harben, Heng Veasana, Hin Sithan, Thomas

---

[c] For consistency, all Cambodian names appear in the Khmer style, family name first, even though some Cambodians living abroad have now adopted a Western-style order.

Hirschfeld, Ier Kong Chea, Im Proum, Ith Sarin, Kae Sombat, Ven. Kong Chhean, Lah Tol, Lek Samoeun, Theodore Mataxis, Ngeth Sanh, Leonard Overton, Peng Samith, Phar Dollard, Po Chhon (2), Pok Saman, Seng Kan, Sieu Chheng Y, Sim Kin, Sisowath Olary, So Bun Hor, Soth Polin (2), Emory C. Swank, Kasien Tejapira, Tan Chip, Than Sun, You Kan.

Taped reply to questions: Robert S. Barrett III.

Written replies to questions: H. E. Nhiek Tioulong, HRH Norodom Sihanouk.

Index